CW01425046

The Value-at-Risk Reference

The Value-at-Risk Reference

Key Issues in the Implementation of Market Risk

Edited by Jon Danielsson

Riskbooks

Published by Risk Books, a Division of Incisive Financial Publishing Ltd

Haymarket House
28–29 Haymarket
London SW1Y 4RX
Tel: +44 (0)20 7484 9700
Fax: +44 (0)20 7484 9800
E-mail: books@incisivemedia.com
Sites: www.riskbooks.com
　　　www.incisivemedia.com

© 2007 the Editor and the named Authors, all rights fully reserved.

ISBN 978 1 904339 81 6

British Library Cataloguing in Publication Data
A catalogue record for this book is available from the British Library

Publisher: Laurie Donaldson
Editorial Assistant: Lucie Carter
Designer: Rebecca Bramwell

Typeset by Mizpah Publishing Services Private Limited, Chennai, India

Printed and bound in Spain by Espacegrafic, Pamplona, Navarra

Contents

SECTION 5: EVALUATION OF MODELS AND SYSTEMS (BACKTESTS AND STRESS TESTS)

List of Contributors

Torben Andersen is a Nathan and Mary Sharp Distinguished Professor of Finance at the Kellogg School of Management, Northwestern University and research associate at the National Bureau of Economic Research and CREATES. He holds a PhD in economics from Yale University and a masters from University of Aarhus, Denmark. Torben has published widely within financial econometrics and on return volatility modelling in particular. He has been editor of the *Journal of Business and Economic Statistics* and served on the editorial boards of the *Journal of Finance*, *Review of Financial Studies* and *Management Science*, among others. He has received *NSF* research grants, given invited lectures worldwide and consults for financial firms, central banks and policy organisations.

Philippe Artzner is professor emeritus of mathematics at Université Louis Pasteur, Strasbourg, where he was in charge (1983–1998) of the creation, development and launching of the three year actuarial programme. His recent and current research deals with multiperiod risk measurement and solvency capital requirements. In 1999 he received the NAAJ Annual Prize from SOA.

Francesco Audrino is professor of statistics at the University of St. Gallen and assistant professor for research at the Institute of Finance, University of Lugano. After graduating from the ETH Zürich, he began his research activity in financial statistics as a post-doc of the Swiss national programme NCCR FinRisk at the University of Lugano. Francesco's research focus is on the development of new models for the analysis of univariate and multivariate financial time series. Some of his recent papers have appeared in the *Journal of the Royal Statistical Society, Journal of*

Business and Economic Statistics, Journal of Applied Econometrics, Journal of Financial Econometrics, The Journal of Computational Finance and *Journal of Time Series Analysis*.

Turan Bali received his PhD from the Graduate School and University Center of the City, University of New York, in 1999, and has been a professor of finance at Baruch College since 2000. He specialises in asset pricing, risk management, fixed income securities, interest rate derivatives and dynamic asset allocation. Turan has published several articles in the *Journal of Finance, Journal of Financial Economics, Management Science, Journal of Business, Journal of Financial and Quantitative Analysis, Journal of Economic Dynamics and Control, Journal of Money, Credit, and Banking, Journal of Banking and Finance, Risk* and many others. He is an associate editor of *The Journal of Risk*.

Jeremy Berkowitz is an associate professor in the Department of Finance, College of Business, University of Houston. Prior to this position, he was an assistant professor at the University of California-Irvine and a member of the Federal Reserve Board for four years, where he worked in trading risk analysis. His research interests include financial econometrics, asset pricing theory and risk management. Jeremy has published his research in the *Journal of Finance, Rand Journal, Review of Economic Studies, Review of Economics and Statistics, Journal of Fixed Income, The Journal of Risk, Journal of Law and Economics* and *Econometric Reviews*. He has presented his work at conferences and university seminars in Canada, Europe and across the US.

Peter Blum is a research associate in the financial analysis and risk modelling group of Converium Reinsurance Ltd and a PhD student in financial and insurance mathematics at the ETH (Swiss Federal Institute of Technology) in Zurich. Both Peter's academic and industrial activities are centred around the financial valuation of reinsurance and econometric issues in insurance, reinsurance and investment, with particular emphasis on the method of dynamic financial analysis (DFA). Prior to joining Converium, Peter was a programmer, software quality engineer and project leader in the electronics industry. He holds a diploma (MA) in mathematics from ETH and a federal certificate of capacity (BSc) in software engineering.

Tim Bollerslev joined the Duke Faculty in 1998, as the first Juanita and Clifton Kreps Professor of Economics. He also holds an appointment as professor of finance at the Fuqua School of Business. Tim received his PhD from UCSD and has previously held chaired positions at the Kellogg School at Northwestern University and the University of Virginia. He is an elected fellow of the Econometric Society and has been affiliated with the National Bureau of Economic Research as a faculty research associate since 1991. An internationally recognised time series econometrician, Tim is especially well known for his expertise in financial econometrics and empirical finance. In the press release accompanying the 2003 Nobel Prize in Economics, his generalised autoregressive conditional heteroskedasticity (GARCH) model was explicitly singled out as "the model most often applied today". He has published widely in the most prominent academic journals in the area. His current research, involving the use of high-frequency financial data for better measuring volatility and understanding the impact of news, has been supported by a series of grants from the National Science Foundation. Tim routinely lectures at professional meetings and research institutions around the world and has served on editorial boards for more than 10 different academic journals and is currently serving as co-editor for the *Journal of Applied Econometrics*.

Chris Brooks is professor of finance at the ICMA Centre. He holds a PhD and a BA in economics and econometrics, both from the University of Reading. His areas of research interest include asset pricing, fund management, statistical issues in risk management and econometric analysis and modelling in finance and real estate. Chris has published widely in these areas and has over 60 articles in leading academic and practitioner journals including the *Journal of Business*, *Economic Journal*, *Financial Analysts Journal* and *Journal of Banking and Finance*. He also acts as a consultant for various banks and professional bodies in the fields of finance, real estate and econometrics.

Peter Bühlmann has been full professor of mathematics at ETH Zürich since 2004. He received his doctoral degree in mathematics (statistics) from ETH Zürich in 1993. Between 1994 and 1995 he worked as a postdoctoral fellow in the Department of Statistics at the University of California at Berkeley. Following this he spent two more years at the U.C. Berkeley as Neyman Assistant Professor. In 1997 Peter was appointed to ETH Zürich. His main research interests are in computational statistics, particularly in machine learning and methodology for high-dimensional, complex modelling. He has published widely, including papers in the *Annals of Statistics* and the *Journal of the American Statistical Association*.

Sean D. Campbell has served as economist at the Federal Reserve Board in Washington DC since 2004. Prior to joining the Federal Reserve Board staff, he was an assistant professor in the economics department at Brown University between 2002 and 2004. Sean's research focuses on applied macroeconomics and finance. His research has been published in the *Journal of Business and Economics and Statistics*, *Journal of the American Statistical Association* and *The Journal of Risk*. Sean holds a PhD in economics from the University of Pennsylvania and a BA in economics from the University of Massachusetts at Amherst.

Ali Chabaane is currently the head of risk strategies at Pioneer Investments, where he is in charge of risk budgeting and portfolio construction. He has contributed to the design, promotion and implementation of a strong risk budgeting process within Pioneer's Global Investment Team. Ali began his professional career with BNP Paribas in 1997 as a financial engineer and after three years was promoted to the position of head of the transversal financial modelling team. He also held the role of head of credit risk modelling within the risk department of BNP Paribas, where he set up methodologies and tools for regulatory and economic capital management. Ali holds a primary degree in engineering from INAPG Paris, a masters in statistical and stochastic modelling from Orsay University and a masters in finance and actuary from ENSAE.

Peter Christoffersen is associate professor of finance at McGill University, where he teaches option valuation and financial risk management for the MBA, PhD and executive programmes. He is also a research fellow at CIRANO and CIREQ. Peter's main research interests are in volatility modelling for option valuation, as well as in developing backtesting procedures for risk management systems. He has published his research in a number of leading finance and econometrics journals and is currently an associate editor of *The Journal of Risk*, *Journal of Applied Econometrics* and *Journal of Financial Econometrics*. His research has been funded by grants from SSHRC, FQRSC, VRQ and IFM2 and he has won research awards from the Q-Group, KPMG and the Montreal Exchange. Peter has given invited lectures at IFM2, CIDE, the European Central Bank, the IMF and Bank of America, among others. Before joining McGill University, he worked as an economist at the IMF in Washington, DC, where he undertook research on emerging financial markets.

Michel Dacorogna, member of the senior management of Converium, is currently heading its financial analysis and risk modelling team. His main responsibilities are the internal asset and liability model of Converium, to determine the risk-based capital and the strategic asset allocation of the investment portfolio. He also heads the Swiss Solvency Project team to comply with the new solvency regulations. Michel also conducts research in the field of insurance and reinsurance: capital allocation to risk, pricing and optimising reinsurance covers, optimal asset allocation of insurance investments, risk management of investments and forecasting models of long-term economic trends. He is the author of more than 65 scientific publications in refereed journals, covering a wide range of fields from insurance mathematics and physics to econometrics and financial theory.

Jon Danielsson has a PhD in the economics of financial markets and is currently a reader in finance at the London School of Economics. His research areas include financial risk, regulation of financial markets, market volatility, models of extreme market movements and microstructure of foreign exchange markets. Jon has published his work in a range of academic and practitioner journals and discussed his work in a number of universities, financial institutions and government agencies.

Freddy Delbaen is a full professor at the Chair of Financial Mathematics, where he directs many projects in this field. Freddy studied mathematics at the Free University of Brussels (VUB) graduating in 1971. The subject of his PhD dissertation was mathematical economics. Freddy has published many papers in journals dealing with pure and applied mathematics, as well as insurance and financial mathematics. He is a member of several editorial boards of journals including, *Insurance Mathematics and Economics* and *Finance and Stochastics*. He is co-editor of the *Journal of Mathematical Finance*.

P. J. (Riaan) de Jongh is director of the Centre for Business Mathematics and Informatics (BMI) of the North-West University at Potchefstroom, South Africa, which specialises in training students for careers in risk/reward management and analysis and focuses on research in the same field. Before joining the Centre for BMI in 1998, Riaan was employed by Deloittes Consulting and the Institute for Maritime Technology in South Africa. His research interests are mainly in the field of statistics and applications thereof. He holds a BComm from the University of Stellenbosch, an MSc from the University of South Africa and a PhD from the University of Cape Town.

Casper de Vries holds the chair of monetary economics at Erasmus School of Economics and is also vice dean of research and education at the Faculty of Economics. Casper is a fellow and board member of the Tinbergen Institute and he serves as a member of the EMU Monitor group. His graduate training was at Purdue University; he has held positions at Texas A&M University, K.U. Leuven and he has been visiting scholar at several European and American research institutes. Casper's research interests are focused on international monetary issues, such as foreign exchange rate determination and exchange rate risk, the issues surrounding the Euro, financial markets risk, risk management and systemic risk. In his research on financial risks, he has specialised in calculating the risks on extreme events by means of statistical extreme value analysis. Other research interests are applied game theory, in particular contest and auction theory which can be applied to the theory of lobbying. He has published widely in leading internationally refereed journals.

Francis Diebold is WP Carey Professor of Economics, professor of finance and statistics and Co-Director of the Wharton Financial Institutions Center at the University of Pennsylvania and its Wharton School, and faculty research associate at the National Bureau of Economic Research in Cambridge, Mass. He works in econometrics, forecasting, finance and macroeconomics, and has published extensively and has served on the editorial boards of numerous journals. Francis is an elected fellow of the Econometric Society and the American Statistical Association and the recipient of Sloan, Guggenheim and Humboldt awards. A prize-winning teacher and lecturer, he has also held visiting appointments in economics and finance at Princeton University, the University of Chicago, Cambridge University, Johns Hopkins University and New York University. Between 1986 and 1989 Francis served as an economist under Paul Volcker and Alan Greenspan at the Board of Governors of the Federal Reserve System in Washington DC. He received his BS from the Wharton School in 1981 and his PhD in 1986, also from the University of Pennsylvania.

Jean-Marc Eber founded LexiFi in 2000, after working for 10 years at Sociètè Gènèrale, where he served most recently as global head of quantitative research in the Capital Markets Division. In this capacity, he was responsible for the design and implementation of software tools and mathematical models for trading complex derivative products. Jean-Marc is a regular speaker at financial engineering conferences and has published numerous papers on financial risk management and on the application of programming language theory to financial trading and risk management. He holds an MS in econometrics and an MS in mathematics from the University of Strasbourg and a PhD in mathematical economics from the University of Bonn.

Paul Embrechts is professor of mathematics at ETH Zürich, where he specialises in actuarial mathematics and quantitative risk management. Previous academic positions include the Universities of

Leuven, Limburg and London (Imperial College). He has held visiting appointments at the University of Strasbourg, ESSEC Paris, the Scuola Normale in Pisa and the London School of Economics (Centennial Professor of Finance). Paul is an elected fellow of the Institute of Mathematical Statistics, honorary fellow of the Institute of Actuaries, corresponding member of the Italian Institute of Actuaries and is on the editorial board of numerous scientific journals. He belongs to various national and international research and academic advisory committees. He co-authored the influential books *Modelling of Extremal Events for Insurance and Finance* (1997) and *Quantitative Risk Management: Concepts, Techniques and Tools* (2005). Paul consults for a number of leading financial institutions and insurance companies and is a member of the Board of Directors of companies in insurance and finance. He recently received an honorary doctorate from the University of Waterloo.

Robert Engle, the Michael Armellino Professor of Finance at New York University Stern School of Business, was awarded the 2003 Nobel Prize in Economics for his research on the concept of autoregressive conditional heteroskedasticity (ARCH). He developed this method for statistical modelling of time-varying volatility and demonstrated that these techniques accurately capture the properties of many time series. Much of Robert's research develops time series methods for financial markets. He is the creator of common features, ACD, CAViaR, DCC and co-author of cointegration with co-prizewinner C. W. J. Granger. Before joining NYU Stern in 2000, Robert was Chancellor's Associates Professor and Economics Department Chair at the University of California, San Diego and associate professor of economics at the Massachusetts Institute of Technology. He is a fellow of the National Academy of Science, the American Academy of Arts and Sciences, the Econometric Society, the American Finance Association and American Statistical Association.

Eduardo Epperlein is managing director, head of market, model and counterparty risk analytics, and is responsible for defining market and counterparty credit risk standards, developing methodologies for calculating regulatory and economic capital, and validating all pricing and risk models. He is also the main point of contact with regulatory bodies for issues related to market risk. Eduardo joined

Citi Toronto in 1994. He holds a PhD in plasma physics from Imperial College London and spent eight years as a research scientist at the Laboratory for Laser Energetics before joining Citi.

Sílvia Gonçalves is an associate professor in the Economics Department of the Université de Montréal, where she has been since 2000, after graduating from the University of California at San Diego. Her PhD thesis was on the bootstrap for time series and financial models and her advisor was professor Halbert White. Silvia has published her work in several internationally reputed journals, including the *Journal of the American Statistical Association*, *Journal of Econometrics*, *Econometric Theory*, *Econometric Reviews*, *Journal of Business*, and *The Journal of Risk*.

Philipp Hartmann is head of the financial research division in the Directorate General Research of the European Central Bank (ECB) in Frankfurt. His previous positions include that of principal of the Economic and Financial Research Unit at the ECB and research fellow for financial regulation at the London School of Economics. Philipp is also a fellow of the Centre for Economic Policy Research (CEPR, London) and vice president of SUERF, the European Money and Finance Forum. His main research is in financial and international monetary economics, in particular banking, financial stability, financial market microstructure analysis and international currency competition. He is the author of *Currency Competition and Foreign Exchange Markets* (1998) a co-author of *Financial Regulation* (1998) and a co-editor of *The Handbook of European Financial Markets and Institutions* (forthcoming). His further research work has been published in numerous academic journals, including the *Review of Economics and Statistics, Journal of Money, Credit and Banking, Economic Policy, Journal of International Money and Finance* and *Journal of Banking and Finance*. In 2002 he was jointly awarded the first CEPR/European Summer Institute Prize for the best central bank research paper. Philipp holds a doctorat en sciences economiques from the Ecole des Hautes Etudes en Sciences Sociales in Paris, an MA in monetary and macroeconomics from the Université Catholique de Louvain in Belgium and a diploma in volkswirtschaftslehre from the Universität Mannheim in Germany.

David Heath is a specialist in applied probability. He first began working in financial applications in 1977. Many of his PhD students are employed in the financial industry. He is a co-author of the HJM framework for term structure modelling, which he teaches in the MSCF programme at CMU and continues to work on models for the fluctuations of securities prices. More recently his principal research interests have been in risk measurement, management and control, where he has, with colleagues, introduced and studied coherent measures of risk. David is a fellow of the PriceWaterhouseCoopers Risk Institute and a member of the boards of directors of Lehman Brothers Financial Products and Lehman Brothers Derivative Products. David gained a PhD from the University of Illinois in 1969.

Ronald Huisman is associate professor at the RSM/Erasmus University and is partner at the FinEdge International Group. His research focuses primarily on risks in international financial and energy markets. Ronald has published in international journals such as *Energy Economics, Journal of Banking and Finance, Journal of Business and Economics Statistics, Journal of International Finance, Journal of Portfolio Management, The Journal of Risk, Real Estate Economics,* and *Review of Financial Studies.*

John Hull is the Maple Financial Group Professor of Derivatives and Risk Management in the Joseph L. Rotman School of Management at the University of Toronto. He has written three books, *Risk Management and Financial Institutions* (first published in 2006), *Options, Futures, and Other Derivatives* (now in its sixth edition) and *Fundamentals of Futures and Options Markets* (now in its fifth edition). These books have been translated into many languages and are widely used in trading rooms throughout the world. John has won many teaching awards, including the University of Toronto's prestigious Northrop Frye award and was voted Financial Engineer of the Year in 1999 by the International Association of Financial Engineers.

Guy Kaplanski works in investment banking as a project manager and financially manages several large-scale infrastructure and development projects. He also teaches several courses in finance at the Ben-Gurion University and the Hebrew University. Previously,

Guy was a visiting assistant professor of finance at the University of Michigan-Ann Arbor. Guy's research interests are in risk management, market regulations and asset pricing. He holds a PhD (*Summa Cum Laude*) in finance from the Hebrew University, an MBA (*Summa Cum Laude*) from the Hebrew University and a BSc (*Cum Laude*) in engineering from Tel-Aviv University.

Kees G. Koedijk is currently professor of finance at RSM Erasmus University, having taken the post in 1999. He received his PhD in 1989 for his thesis on empirical studies in exchange rate economics. From 1989 to 1991 Kees was senior economist at the Dutch central bank. From 1991 to 1999 he was professor of finance and econometrics at Maastricht University and director of the Limburg Institute of Financial Economics (LIFE). Kees is a research fellow of the Centre for Economic Policy Research (CEPR) in London and holds several associate editorships of well-known journals and has published on risk management widely in international journals. He is currently also chairman of the Dutch Council of Economic Advisors to the Dutch Parliament.

Yoram Kroll is currently an associate professor of finance and head of finance studies at Ono Academic College, Israel and an emeritus associated professor at the Hebrew University in Jerusalem. He was also visiting assistant professor at Wharton School, University of Pennsylvania and a visiting associate professor at University of Florida, Virginia Tech and Baruch College, CUNY. Yoram holds PhD, graduate and undergraduate degrees from the Hebrew University. He is also serving as consultant to various industries in Israel and was a general manager of the financial organisation of the Kibbutz United Movement. He is currently the chairman of the board of Kfar Giladi Quarries. Yoram has published numerous articles in leading finance journals on VaR, stochastic dominance, experimental finance, inequality, risk preferences and optimal insurance decisions.

Paul Labys currently works as an economist with CRA International, specialising in the application of econometrics and advanced computational techniques to the areas of competition, finance and pharmaceuticals. He has published articles on volatility in

Econometrica and *Journal of the American Statistical Association* and serves as a referee for numerous academic journals. He received an AB in physics at Harvard College, an MS in electrical engineering at the University of Colorado and a PhD in economics at the University of Pennsylvania.

Jean-Paul Laurent is a professor of finance at the ISFA actuarial school within the University of Lyon and a scientific consultant to BNP Paribas, where he focuses on credit and risk management issues. Prior to this, he was a research professor at CREST, a leading academic institution in Paris. Jean-Paul has also led research groups within Paribas. He has extensively published in academic and professional journals and is known for contributions in risk assessment, mean-variance hedging and the modelling of CDOs. Jean-Paul holds a PhD from Paris-Sorbonne University and applied mathematics, economics and finance degrees from Ecole des Mines de Paris, Sciences Po and HEC.

Jose A. Lopez is a senior economist in the Financial Group of the Economic Research Department at the Federal Reserve Bank of San Francisco. He completed his doctoral dissertation in economics at the University of Pennsylvania. His current research focuses on market and credit risk measurement and management issues and using securities market information for bank supervisory purposes. Jose has published articles in the *Journal of Money, Credit and Banking, Journal of Banking and Finance, The Journal of Risk, Journal of Derivatives* and *Journal of Forecasting*.

Yannick Malevergne is an associate professor of finance at EM-Lyon Business School and a senior researcher with the Chair of Entrepreneurial Risks at ETH Zürich. An alumni of Ecole Normale Supérieure de Lyon, he holds a PhD and a "habilitation" in management science. His core research is devoted to the study of extreme risks in financial markets, to their modelling and to the development of new portfolio management methods and asset pricing models. Yannick has authored or co-authored many articles both in academic reviews and professional journals, as well as a book on the management of extreme financial risks.

Joseph Mezrich was head of US Quantitative & Derivatives Research at UBS from 2002 until mid-2005. At UBS he extended the behavioural/risk based framework for investment style forecasts, factor tilts and stock selection. From 1998 to 2002 he was head of Quantitative Strategies at Morgan Stanley and was a member of Morgan's Macro Strategy team. Whilst at Morgan he developed a factor strategy framework, integrating cash & derivatives information and centred on the impact of market risk. From 1987 to 1998 he was deputy head of the Equity Portfolio Analytics group at Salomon Brothers, where he developed new modelling approaches to volatility forecasting, risk attribution and option strategy, as well as models for asset allocation, and stock selection. Joseph received the PhD in mathematical psychology and MA in statistics from the University of Michigan, and received the EE and the SM degrees in electrical engineering from the Massachusetts Institute of Technology.

Salih Neftci teaches courses on financial economics at the graduate faculty of the University of Minnesota and is involved in several research groups at the Center for Economic Policy. He is currently at the Graduate School of City University of New York and also has teaching assignments at HEC, Lausanne University. Salih is the head of the FAME Certificate programme and is a visiting professor at the ISMA Centre, Reading University. He is a leading faculty member in courses directed towards advanced market professionals. His current research deals with numerical methods in financial asset pricing and applications of the theory of extremes to risk management. He has published *An Introduction to the Mathematics of Pricing Financial Derivates* and has also been published in several international journals such as the *Journal of Forecasting*.

Gita Persand is a lecturer for the School of Management at the University of Southampton. Currently, she is a member of the Risk Research Group within the school, which focuses on consultancy and education as well as research into risk management and promoting the group's research through the Centre for Risk Research. Gita is presently researching in the area of market timing strategies. She has published papers widely in renowned journals, such as *The*

Journal of Risk, Journal of Empirical Finance, Journal of Financial Econometrics, Journal of Risk Finance and *Journal of Forecasting*.

Andreas Pfingsten has been full professor of management, in particular in banking, at the University of Münster, Germany, since 1994. As a visitor, he spent time at the universities of Graz (Austria), Calgary (Canada) and Urbana-Champaign (Illinois, US). Andreas is a member of the Academy of Sciences of North Rhine-Westphalia and treasurer of the German Finance Association. He is co-author of a leading textbook on banking (in German) and has published papers in scholarly as well as in professional journals. Current research includes risk management, regulation and retail lending via the Internet.

Rachel A. J. Pownall graduated with a PhD in risk management from Erasmus University Rotterdam in 2001 and a first class honours degree from the University of Kent at Canterbury, UK, in 1996. She currently works as assistant professor of finance at both Maastricht University and Erasmus University, Rotterdam. Rachel has published in a number of top academic journals including the *Journal of International Money and Finance, Journal of Banking and Finance, Journal of Portfolio Management, Financial Analysts Journal,* and *The Journal of Risk.* Her recent work is forthcoming in the *Journal of Empirical Finance* and *Journal of Alternative Investments*.

Sidney Resnick received his BS from Queens College in 1966 and his MA and PhD from Purdue in 1968 and 1970. Prior to joining the faculty of the School of Operations Research and Industrial Engineering, he spent nine years at Colorado State University, six years at Stanford University and two years at the Technion, in Haifa, Israel. Sydney has also held visiting appointments at several institutions, including the Australian National University and CSIRO in Australia, the Technion in Israel, Sussex University in the UK, the University of Amsterdam and the Amsterdam Mathematics Center, Erasmus University, and Eurandom in The Netherlands, ETH Zürich in Switzerland and the University of North Carolina in the US. His research has concentrated on probability modelling, with emphasis on extreme value theory and modelling of phenomena requiring heavy tails. Recent effort has focused on the inability of standard data network models to adequately explain observed phenomena in data traces. He has written a number of articles and books.

Gennady Samorodnitsky is currently full professor, with tenure, at the School of Operations Research and Industrial Engineering at Cornell University, as well as being an associate director and director of the School. He received a BSc in computer science from the Moscow Steel and Alloys Institute in 1978, an MSc in operations research from Technion, the Israel Institute of Technology, in 1983, and a DSc in statistics from Technion in 1986. Gennady has previously been a visiting assistant professor at Boston University and an assistant professor and an associate professor, with tenure, at Cornell University. He was awarded the Chaim Weizmann Fellowship in 1986 and 1987 and the S. Yau 72 Teaching Award in 2000, as well as the Fellowship of the Institute of Mathematical Statistics in 2000. Gennady is a member of the Institute of Mathematical Statistics and the Bernoulli Society and is an associate editor of *Probability and Mathematical Statistics*, *Stochastic Models*, *Stochastic Processes and their Applications*, *Annals of Probability* and an advisory editor to the *Frontiers in Mathematics Series*, as well as having written numerous books and articles.

Didier Sornette has held the Chair of Entrepreneurial Risks at ETH Zürich since 2006. He was previously a professor of geophysics at UCLA and a research director on the theory and prediction of complex systems at the National Center for Scientific Research in France. He is also the director of research of Insight Research LLC. Didier graduated from the Ecole Normale Superieure in Paris in physical sciences in 1981, got his master thesis in 1981 at University of Nice and his PhD in physical sciences in 1985. Previously he has been the director of research with X-RS R&D in France, the scientific advisor to the technical director of Thomson-Marconi Sonar company (now THALES) in France and consultant for numerous aerospace industrial companies, banks, investment and reinsurance companies from 1991. Since the publication of his book *Why Stock Markets Crash* (2003) he has been a regular presenter to CEOs and CFOs on financial risks. Didier received the Science et Defence French National Award (1985), the 2000 Research McDonnell award on studying complex systems, the Scientific Prediction of Crises and the Risques-Les Echos prize, 2002.

He is the author and co-author of more than 350 journal research papers and more than 120 papers in books and conference proceedings. Didier is also the editor of two proceedings of two international conferences, the author of the textbook *Critical Phenomena in Natural Sciences, Chaos, Fractals, Self-organization and Disorder* (2nd edition 2004), and co-author of *Extreme Financial Risks* (2005). He has spoken and presented his work at many international conferences and universities worldwide.

Gerhard Stahl has been a statistician at the Bundesanstalt für Finanzdienstleistungs-aufsicht (BaFin) since 1995. He is currently head of the Risk Modelling Group (QRM), the unit of BaFin that is in charge of on-site inspections of risk management models and related principle work. He represents BaFin in several working groups in Basel and CEBS, the Committee of European Banking Supervisors, and co-chairs the Basel Sub-Group on liquidity. Prior to joining BaFin, Gerhard was a research fellow at the Economic Faculty of Heidelberg, and is a member of the advisory board of the CASE Institute at Humboldt and fellow of the Center for Financial Studies, Frankfurt. He also currently holds a lectureship at the Faculty of Mathematics of the Albert Einstein University, Ulm. Gerhard holds an honorary doctoral degree from the University of Bamberg. His current research interests and working fields include the stochastics of risk management, the regulation and auditing of stochastic models for market, credit, liquidity and operational risk for financial institutions. He is a regular speaker at academic and practitioner's conferences devoted to risk management or related topics.

Saygun Turkay is a senior vice president with the equity derivatives volatility analytics group at Lehman Brothers in London, where he works on quantitative modelling and research issues regarding structured and exotic equity derivatives and all volatility products. He has been with Lehman Brothers since late 2003; previously Saygun was with the risk analytics group at Citigroup in London. He holds a PhD degree on mathematical finance from the Centre for Quantitative Finance at Imperial College London and an MSc degree in engineering, also from Imperial College.

Francoise Turpin is currently in the risk department of BNP Paribas where she reviews the methodologies developed by the ALM, in order to assess overall quality and suitability. She started her professional career with BNP Paribas in 2000 as a financial engineer in a transversal team in charge of developing technical subjects in the whole group. In particular, she developed risk analysis tools to support investment decision-making, portfolio risk control and performance attribution analysis. She also participated in designing and implementing an economic capital methodology for market risks in life insurance activity.

J. H. (Hennie) Venter is currently employed at the Centre for Business Mathematics and Informatics (BMI) at the North-West University at Potchefstroom, South Africa, specialising in research and project consulting in the field of financial statistics. Before joining the Centre for BMI, he trained students at this university and published widely in statistics. Hennie holds a PhD from the University of Chicago.

Peter Wagner is currently senior associate at Westfaelisch-Lippischer Sparkassen-und Giroverband, an Association of 76 Savings Banks in the German state of Nordrhein-Westfalen, where he is responsible for mergers and acquisitions. Between 2000 and 2004 he was a research associate at the banking department of the University of Muenster, where he obtained his masters and his PhD. Peter has published several articles on turnaround management and has co-authored articles on risk measurement.

Carsten S. Wehn works as a market risk specialist at DekaBank, Frankfurt, where he currently heads the project for the implementation of a market risk model. He is also involved in the further development of the bank's economic capital model. Before joining DekaBank, Carsten worked at Deutsche Bundesbank as an auditor and audit supervisor for regulatory examinations of banks' quantitative models for risk measurement and management. He holds a PhD in mathematics and regularly gives lectures at universities. His most recent publications include a book about credit derivatives and several articles about quantitative aspects of risk modelling.

Alan White is the Peter L. Mitchelson Professor of Investment Strategy at the Rotman School of Management. He is best known for his work with colleague John Hull, with whom he did seminal work in the stochastic volatility literature, created the Hull–White Interest Rate Model and developed many numerical procedures for valuing derivatives. Alan's research has recently moved into two new areas: the analysis of credit risk and the valuation of executive stock options. He teaches in the MBA and PhD programmes and has served as the supervisor of the finance PhD programme at the Rotman School.

Carsten Wolferink is senior associate in the controlling department of Deutsche Apotheker-und Aerztebank, which is a financial specialist for the medical and pharmaceutical profession. He is responsible for the controlling sight on all IFRS questions for the bank. Prior to this, Carsten worked on the IFRS project for the WGZ Bank, the central bank of the credit cooperative banks in the western part of Germany. Before that he was PhD student and research associate at the banking department of the University of Münster, Germany. Carsten obtained a diploma and a PhD in business administration at the University of Münster. His PhD thesis was on agency theoretical analysis about the delegation of testing the creditworthiness of credit borrowers. He has also co-authored several articles on risk measurement.

Andreas Zapp is a senior analyst in the risk modelling group of the German Federal Financial Supervisory Authority (BaFin) where he started in 2003. He is involved in quantitative issues of the supervision of risk models in market, credit and operational risk. Before joining BaFin, Andreas worked for Deutsche Bundesbank. He holds a PhD in mathematics from Cologne University.

Introduction

Jon Danielsson

London School of Economics

Over the past 15 years we have observed a fundamental change in how financial institutions and non-financial firms alike manage financial risk. Previously, risk management tended to be a low-tech function of little importance, if really practiced at all.

Two parallel developments conspired to change this state of affairs. First, the emergence of quantitative methods for understanding financial risk, starting with the seminal contribution of Robert Engle in 1982, where he proposed the ARCH model for the modelling of volatility clusters. The ARCH model and subsequent developments have come to underpin most quantitative market risk models in use today. The second development spurring quantitative risk modelling comes from the banking supervisors, starting with the original Basel I Accord, and even more importantly the 1996 amendment to the Basel I Accord. This required financial institutions to set aside risk-sensitive capital to meet market risk and mandated the use of quantitative models to meet this risk. The designers of the 1996 amendment undoubtedly considered the state-of-the-art quantitative techniques at the time and concluded that those techniques were sufficiently sophisticated to underpin a critical regulatory function. A key notion in the 1996 amendment is that financial institutions measure their risk with their own internal models, meeting general guidelines set by the supervisors, but are by and large responsible themselves for developing and applying these models. This approach has subsequently become known as internal rating based (IRB).

The ARCH model and the 1996 amendment have had considerable influence on how we understand and approach the concept of market risk. They have motivated an enormous amount of research into quantitative risk models, revolutionised how financial institutions approach market risk and stimulated the market for highly trained university graduates. Consequently, there is large demand for information on all aspects of quantitative market risk modelling, ranging from technical details of how various models work to practical consequences of applying models into an existing market risk function.

In that market *Risk* magazine has been a pioneer in providing timely information about leading models and concepts to practitioners, and has published a number of seminal articles on the subject. Recognising that with the 1996 amendment there was a need for a specialised technical journal on the subject of financial risk, the publishers of *Risk* magazine launched a dedicated publication on the subject in 1998, aptly named *The Journal of Risk*. To this day it remains the only quality academic publication solely dedicated to the subject of financial risk. Just as with its sister publication, *The Journal of Risk* has published many of the key papers on the subject of financial risk. Over time, those two publications have collected papers that represent the broad spectrum of market risk and this provides the motivation for this book: a collection of some of the key papers published over the past decade in those two publications.

To provide an organised and representative selection of papers, we identify five different areas of market risk:

(1) Measures of market risk;
(2) Estimation of market risk models;
(3) Multivariate models;
(4) Extreme market movements; and
(5) Evaluation of risk models: backtesting.

The traditional measure of market risk, at least dating back to the seminal contribution of Harry Markowitz in 1952, is volatility. In what may be the first modern quantitative concept of financial risk, Markowitz proposed the mean-variance (MV) framework where investors have an explicit trade-off between risk and return. While the Markowitz MV model has had an enormous influence on how financial institutions approach risk, it is seriously deficient in that volatility is only the correct measure of risk if financial returns are normally identically and individually distributed (iid), an assumption which is known to be wrong. While for many financial applications assuming iid normality may be relatively innocuous, for financial risk it will lead to a serious underestimation of risk levels. Consequently, any reliable market risk model needs to address both the issue of iid and normality. While at a first glance one might suggest modelling the dynamic structure of financial returns, and use this distribution directly within the decision-making process, this is of course neither feasible nor desirable. Instead, we need to have a measure of risk which addresses the most serious deficiencies in volatility with the least amount of serious assumptions and practical restrictions. This risk measure is value-at-risk (VaR), proposed by JP Morgan in 1993. The key advantage of VaR is that it is not distribution dependent and therefore, at least conceptually, can be applied to every class of financial assets. Indeed, the Basel committee chose VaR as its measure of risk in the 1996 amendment.

However, it did not take long for criticism of VaR to emerge, the most serious of which was published in *Risk* magazine in 1997 by Artzner, Delbaen, Eber, and Heath. Their article, "Thinking Coherently", introduces the concept of coherent risk measures, in particular subadditivity. Their observation that VaR is not subadditive remains to this day the most severe criticism of VaR from a theoretical point of view, since it implies that it is possible that a VaR for portfolio is higher than the VaR for the individual assets, a perverse outcome that is due to deficiency of VaR, in particular its reliance on a particular quantile rather than incorporating the entire lower tail like most alternative risk measures. *The Journal of Risk* has published a number of articles on risk measures, including three chosen for this volume. Kaplanski and Kroll in a theoretical scenting compare VaR with the more traditional measures of risk and methods for making investment decisions such as stochastic dominance. By contrast, Pfingsten and Wolferink use an empirical approach to rank the various downside risk measures.

Value-at-risk is a theoretical concept which makes no assumptions about how it can be calculated. Of course, in any application VaR has to be estimated from observed financial returns and many different techniques have been proposed for that purpose. Generally, we can classify the methods for calculating VaR into two general categories: those who use returns directly to get VaR estimates, most importantly historical simulation (HS); such methods are generally known as nonparametric because they do not depend on the estimation of any parametric distribution. Alternatively, VaR can be obtained from some underlying statistical model, where we have to make assumptions about model structure and distributions. Such techniques are known as parametric, since they focus on the specification and estimation of a parametric distribution, such as ARCH. Generally, the parametric methods are much more commonly used than HS in industry, if for no other reason than they are necessary for accessing risk in portfolios containing derivative or fixed income assets.

A common parametric method for obtaining VaR is GARCH, proposed by Tim Bollerslev in 1986, and subsequent developments, most importantly exponentially weighted moving average (EWMA) proposed by JP Morgan along with a VaR in 1993. In many cases, these methods were developed with one-day volatility forecasting in mind, and may not be as attractive for VaR. Danielsson, Hartmann and de Vries, in an article in *Risk* magazine in 1998, argue that the commonly used square root of time method for scaling VaR from one-day to multi-day VaR is only accurate under very restrictive assumptions, ie, that financial returns are iid normal. A series of papers in *The Journal of Risk* have addressed the issue of estimation of VaR. In the first paper in the first issue of the journal in 1998, Hull and White propose extending the HS method to allow for the weighting of observations instead of giving them all an equal weight. Such a method has the potential to resolve the key issue in the accuracy of HS, ie, its performance around structural breaks in volatility. Andersen, Bollerslev, Diebold and Labys propose using high-frequency or intra-day returns for calculating daily volatility. Such methods have the potential to bypass the model risk issues that arise in more conventional GARCH-type estimation. Venter and de Jongh suggest an alternative route in addressing the problem of applying GARCH-type volatility forecast methods to VaR by using an innovation distribution that is more in tune with the problem of forecasting risk rather than simply forecasting volatility. Every model is wrong, and every estimation is subject to estimation risk, which is the subject of the paper by Christoffersen and Gonçalves.

Volatility models, such as GARCH, were originally designed for forecasting volatility of one asset. Financial institutions of course need to obtain the risk of portfolio of assets, where these portfolios can be very large. This necessitates the use of models for forecasting the covariance matrix of returns. As it turns out, this problem is considerably more difficult than forecasting the volatility of a single asset because there are more covariances than there are volatilities, this implies that the number of parameters in the models expands exponentially with the number of assets. A univariate GARCH model contains three model parameters, while a straightforward bivariate GARCH model contains 21 parameters. As a number of assets increase, we quickly find that the number of parameters exceed the number of observations and that estimation is no longer feasible. As a consequence, in practical applications one has to find a method for forecasting covariance matrices that is both parsimonious and captures the relevant stylised facts about covariances. At the same time, the covariance matrix need to be positive definite.

This is not a trivial task if we want capture the appropriate dynamics of volatility and covariances. For example, correlations tend to move a lot more over time than volatilities, going from being sharply negative to a highly positive in a relatively short amount of time, and correlations on the downside tend to be much higher than correlations on the upside, which relates to the concept of nonlinear dependence. Multivariate volatility methods need to allow for these sharp changes in correlations. This is the theme of the 1996 paper by Engle and Mezrich in *Risk*, while *The Journal of Risk* has published a number of papers on both estimation and evaluation of covariance matrix estimation, eg, Turkay, Epperlein and Christofides, who in 2003 studied correlation stress testing for VaR models. Malevergne and Sornette (2004) addressed the challenging issue of how to account for the extreme co-movements between individual stocks and the market.

Value-at-risk models based on conditional normality and volatility may be adequate for the forecasting of day-to-day risks focusing on 95% or 99% probability levels; however, in many applications it is necessary to consider more extreme probability levels, 99.4% or a one-year event, or even 99.94% which is a once in a decade event. Alternatively, it may be of interest to know how frequently the crash of 1987 occurs, or what is the worst market drop expected per decade. Such events are of use in both economic capital and stress testing, where the focus is on large infrequent events. For such probability events conventional VaR methods, such as GARCH (normal and fat-tailed) or historical simulation, are woefully inadequate. Indeed, in this case the only choice for obtaining accurate risk forecasts is extreme value theory (EVT). *Risk* magazine has published a number of papers on this topic, starting with Embrechts, Resnick and Samorodnisky in 1998, who introduced the concept of EVT, while Dacorogna and Blum considered extra movements in foreign exchange rates in 2003. Most recently, Hull (2007) discusses power laws for the tails of distributions, but power laws is exactly what EVT implies about details of fat-tailed distributions. In the first issue of *The Journal of Risk* in 1998, Koedijk, Huisman and Pownall discuss how one can empirically get extreme VaR forecasts. More recently in 2000, Brooks and Persand specifically addressed the issue of VaR forecasts and market crashes.

Every model is incorrect, and in implementing VaR forecasts we have to choose between degrees of inaccuracy. Unfortunately, while ideally we would want to evaluate VaR models based on actual performance, this is generally not feasible and we have to resort to evaluate VaR models using historical data, ie, backtest the models. In this case, we sequentially forecast VaR within a historical sample, and using information about the violations of VaR and the magnitude of violations of VaR as a basis for evaluating the models. The 1996 market risk amendment stipulates the use of violation ratios, ie, a simple counting of observed violations in historical sample compared to what is expected.

While this is a simple and relatively accurate approach to the issue of evaluating VaR models, it does not provide any statistical significance for the magnitude of violation ratios and does not address the issue of clustering of violations. Some proposals for addressing these problems have been made, but the relatively short backtesting sample size coupled with the low frequency of violations frustrates formal testing. In recent years, rapid developments in backtesting technology have been made. A number of papers in both *Risk* and *The Journal of Risk* have addressed these issues, eg, the *Risk* papers of Bali and Neftci (2001) and Berkowitz (2002). The regulators take a keen interest in backtesting procedures, which is the subject of two papers in *The Journal of Risk*: Lopez (1998) and Stahl, Wehn and Zapp (2005). An overview of backtesting procedures was provided by Campbell in 2006.

BIBLIOGRAPHY

Basel Committee on Banking Supervision, 1996, *Amendment to the Capital Accord to Incorporate Market Risks*, January.

Bollerslev, T., 1986, "Generalised Autoregressive Conditional Heteroskedasticity", *Journal of Econometrics* **51**, pp. 307–27.

Engle, R. F., 1982, "Autoregressive Conditional Heteroskedasticity with Estimates of the Variance of the United Kingdom Inflation", *Econometrica* **50**, pp. 987–1007.

JP Morgan, 1993, *RiskMetrics Technical Manual*.

Markowitz, H., 1952, "Portfolio Selection", *Journal of Finance* **7**, pp. 77–91.

Section 1

Measures of Market Risk

1

Thinking Coherently

Philippe Artzner; Freddy Delbaen; Jean-Marc Eber; David Heath

Université Louis Pasteur; Swiss Federal Institute of Technology; Société Générale; Cornell University

Regulatory bodies, clearing firms and many risk managers are primarily concerned with the risk associated with extreme events and the use of capital to limit this risk, rather than with consideration of risk in the choice of assets or projects. Several supervisory authorities and rating agencies advocate the value-at-risk (VaR) method of measuring extreme event risk for a position and, possibly, for taking action by requiring additional capital to be allocated or margin deposited.

With the VaR method, a probability level, say 5%, is chosen in advance, and the measure of risk of the position is the amount $q_{0.05}$ such that X, the net worth of the position at some future prescribed date T, is smaller than $q_{0.05}$ with probability 5%. The number $q_{0.05}$, the 5% quantile of X, is called the "5% VaR of X", and is denoted by $\mathrm{VaR}_{0.05}(X)$. If $q_{0.05}$ is positive, no additional capital is required (and indeed some capital may be withdrawn). If $q_{0.05}$ is negative, then $|q_{0.05}|$ would be the additional initial capital required to hold the position, assuming that capital is invested safely (see Figure 1). (An equivalent approach can also be taken in terms of loss due to change in the net worth of the position between now and date T).

In this article, we address several difficulties with this approach. We analyse them to understand better how a measure of risk should behave, given that it is being used to set the amount of extra capital to be invested "safely" at a known rate of return over the period in question. We suggest a set of properties that any "coherent" risk measure should possess, and show that coherent measures are

Figure 1 Net worth, the sign of its 5% quantile and the action taken

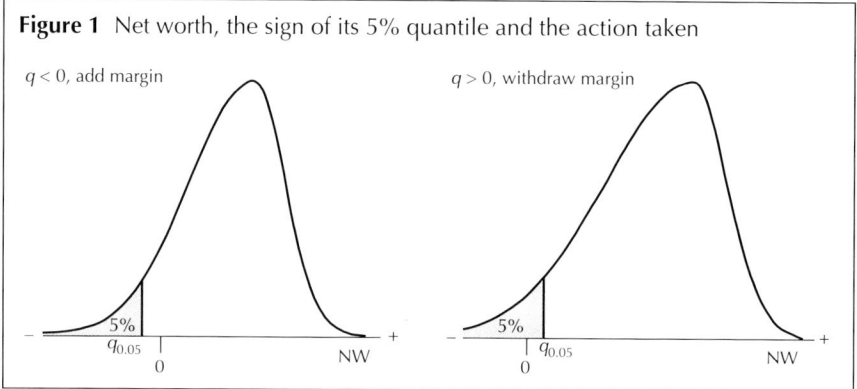

exactly those given by a worst-case approach with "generalised scenarios". Hence the choice of a coherent measure amounts to the choice of a set of generalised scenarios. A generalised scenario method is used by some organised exchanges; we do not know of any exchanges that use quantile-based risk measures. We pay little attention here to the actual calculation of risk measures: it is essential to decide what to calculate before developing calculation methods.

BASIC CRITICISMS OF VaR

VaR boils down to controlling the probability of the "bad" event, $\{X \leq \text{VaR}_{\varepsilon}(X)\}$, through the choice of the number ε, for each position of future net worth X, but not its economic consequences. It is well known, indeed, that a trader can "spike" his firm by entering into a deal that produces a comfortable gain under most circumstances and a huge loss very occasionally. Moreover, and more frighteningly, some individual traders may have chosen disjoint low-probability dangerous events by their individual choices of positions. Their firm will almost certainly then be exposed to a big loss, since there is now a large probability that at least one of these events will occur (see Figure 2).

Similarly, consider a call and a put, written by separate traders, that are both far out-of-the-money. Each individual position may lead to a loss with a probability of only 4%, and hence each position will have no risk at the 5% level. Yet the firm may now have some loss at the 5% probability level. The VaR measure therefore means

Figure 2 Individual risk under "control", global risk out of control

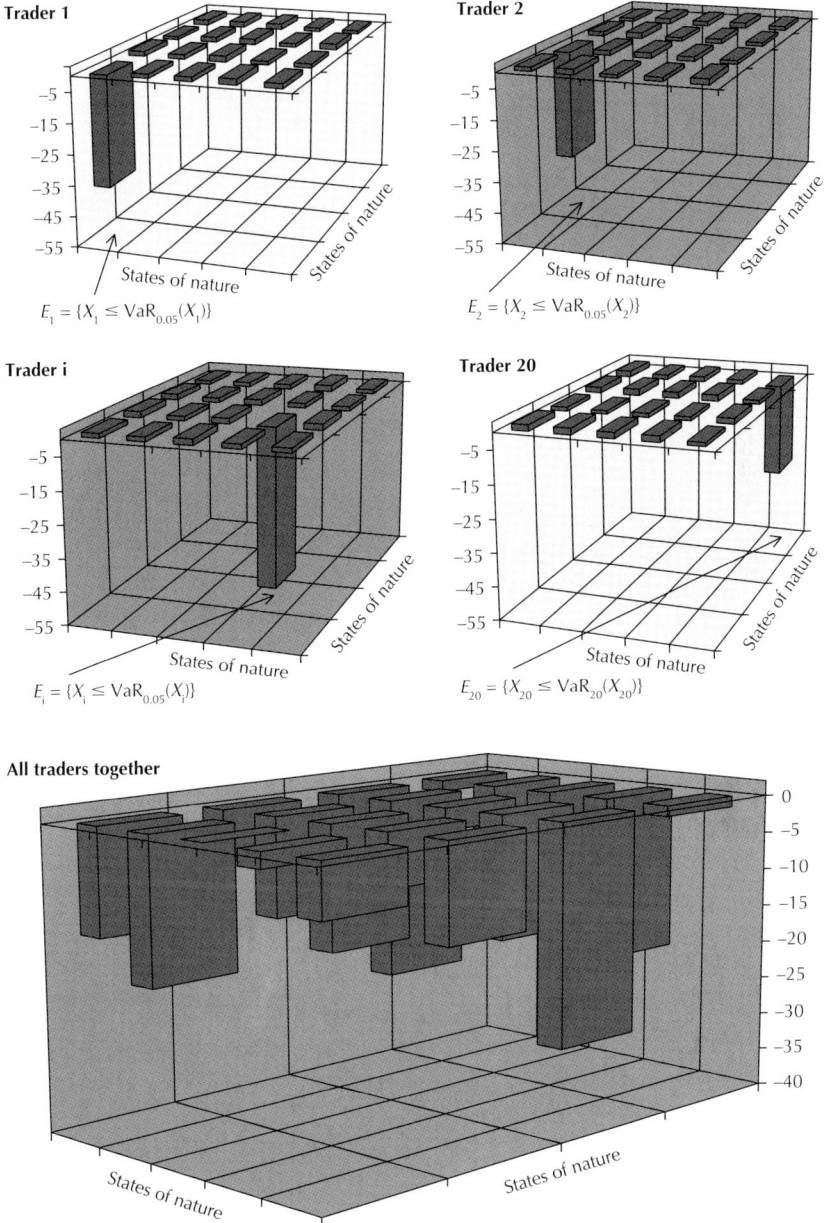

Trader 1

-5
-15
-25
-35
-45
-55

States of nature

States of nature

$E_1 = \{X_1 \leq \mathrm{VaR}_{0.05}(X_1)\}$

Trader 2

-5
-15
-25
-35
-45
-55

States of nature

States of nature

$E_2 = \{X_2 \leq \mathrm{VaR}_{0.05}(X_2)\}$

Trader i

-5
-15
-25
-35
-45
-55

States of nature

States of nature

$E_i = \{X_i \leq \mathrm{VaR}_{0.05}(X_i)\}$

Trader 20

-5
-15
-25
-35
-45
-55

States of nature

States of nature

$E_{20} = \{X_{20} \leq \mathrm{VaR}_{20}(X_{20})\}$

All traders together

0
-5
-10
-15
-20
-25
-30
-35
-40

States of nature

States of nature

that while no extra money is required to cover either (short) position independently, some additional capital is needed for the portfolio consisting of the two.

This scenario does not play out on exchanges: it would be unreasonable for an exchange to require more margin for the sum of two positions than the sum of the margins required for each individually. If it did, a customer would simply open two different accounts, one for each position. In the same vein, a financial firm would create two subsidiaries if this reduced its total equity requirement.

STANDARD DEVIATION

Measures based on standard deviation are also inappropriate to describe the risk of low-probability events. For example, suppose a free lottery ticket that pays out m dollars with probability $1/m$ is added to a portfolio. The increase in volatility introduced by the ticket may not be compensated for by the unit increase in average return that it provides, if a supervisor measures risk as three standard deviations minus the average future value. The regulator might thus end up requiring some capital to be held for holding the single (free) lottery ticket (eg, two units if $m = 2$) and also requiring more for a portfolio with the free ticket than without, although one is, under any circumstances, better off with the ticket!

COHERENT RISK MEASURES

A shortfall approach is much more promising (Embrechts, Klüppelberg and Mikosh (1997)). This consists of answering the question "how bad is bad?" by measuring (the negative of) the average future net worth X of a position, given that X is below the quantile q_ε, ie, $\rho(X) = E[-X \mid X \leq \mathrm{VaR}_\varepsilon(X)]$. This measure is therefore sensitive to spiking and, unlike VaR, can distinguish between two distributions of future net worth that have the same quantile but differ otherwise. Its nature is best illustrated by considering a simulation consisting of, say, 1,000 trials. An estimate of $\mathrm{VaR}_{0.05}(X)$ would be the *largest* of the 50 smallest realisations of the net worth X, while an estimate of the shortfall would be (the negative of) the *average* of these 50 realisations. Our general presentation below will show that the shortfall measure behaves reasonably when adding two positions.

A coherent risk measure ρ assigns a number $\rho(X)$ to each position with future net worth X, in a way that satisfies the following generalisation of the properties of the shortfall approach. For each pair of risks X and Y (dependent or not) as well as for each number n and for each positive number t, all the following relations must be satisfied:

(i) $\rho(X + Y) \leq \rho(X) + \rho(Y)$ [sub-additivity]
(ii) $\rho(t \cdot X) = t \cdot \rho(X)$ [homogeneity]
(iii) $\rho(X) \geq \rho(Y)$, if $X \leq Y$ [monotonicity]
(iv) $\rho(X + r \cdot n) = \rho(X) - n$ [risk-free condition].

Property (i) ensures that the risk measure behaves reasonably when adding two positions. It allows decentralised calculation of the risks of various positions taken within a firm, since the sum of individual measures provides a conservative estimate of the measure of aggregate risk. Properties (i) and (ii) together imply the convexity of the function ρ. Property (iv) ensures that if an initial quantity n, invested at the risk-free rate r, is added to the position under scrutiny, the additional capital requirement is diminished by n. VaR satisfies (ii), (iii) and (iv), but not (i), as shown by the put and call example, hence it is not coherent. By contrast, shortfall is an example of a coherent measure of risk, as we will show later.

We will define "acceptable positions" as those for which the number $\rho(X)$ is negative. It is possible to recover the risk measure from the relevant set of acceptable positions and there exists a characterisation of all such sets that is similar to (i) through (iv) above. Convexity is required, corresponding to risk aversion on the part of the regulator/supervisor. We also note that, for each X, we have the relation $\rho(X + r \cdot \rho(X)) = 0$. Currency invariance of the notion of acceptable positions is by no means obvious. It requests a compatibility of regulators' attitudes concerning risk, in connection with the prospect for future exchange rates. It should be noted, however, that even with invariance, there is no guarantee that the margin requirement in one currency, after conversion to another currency at the initial exchange rate, equals the requirement for the other regulatory system.

Organised exchanges' clearing houses guarantee the completion of deals entered into by their customers; they therefore have to impose some kind of security deposit without reducing the level of business too much. To our knowledge, none of them use quantile-based risk measures. More widely used is the Chicago Mercantile Exchange's Standard Portfolio Analysis (Span) methodology. Span is used for daily margin reconstitution in the interest futures market. It considers 14 scenarios where volatility can either go up or down while the futures price remains unchanged, takes one of three "up" levels or takes one of three "down" levels. Additionally, it considers two extreme up or down moves of the futures price.

The measure of risk is the maximum loss incurred using the full losses under the first 14 scenarios but only 35% of the loss under the two extreme scenarios. This is actually the maximum of the average losses under 16 probability distributions. The first 14 are traditional scenarios: that is, unit masses at 14 points of the set of securities prices. The last two distributions each have a mass of 0.65 at the point describing the initial prices and a mass of 0.35 at the chosen extreme prices point. No loss is incurred if these gener-alised scenarios choose the no-move point and only 35% of the loss incurred at the extreme-move point counts towards the average under one generalised scenario.

Standard risks are risks for which a "natural" measurement emerges upon which regulators and other participants easily agree. They provide a way of measuring other risks, namely portfolios of standard risks. An example is given by the call spread $S(H, K)$ con-sisting of a long call at strike price H and a short call at strike K, both with the same exercise date. The spread $S(H, K)$ requires no margin if $H \leq K$ and, to be very conservative, the margin $H - K$ if $H \geq K$. The US Securities and Exchange Commission (SEC) rules, as applied by the National Association of Securities Dealers (NASD), will allow a portfolio of the same number of long and short calls with the same exercise date to be margined by the smallest sum of margins on spreads (ie, the standard risks) into which the portfolio can be decomposed. This rule leads to a linear optimisation prob-lem, as pointed out long ago by Rudd and Schroeder (1982).

Now consider the options strategy known as the butterfly: two long calls at strikes $H - a$ and $H + a$, with two short calls at strike H. This can be decomposed into the sum of two call spreads $S(H - a, H)$ and $S(H + a, H)$ (see Figure 3). The first spread is margin-free, while the second requires the (conservative) margin a. We prove (Artzner, Delbaen, Eber and Heath (1997)) that this is indeed the smallest margin

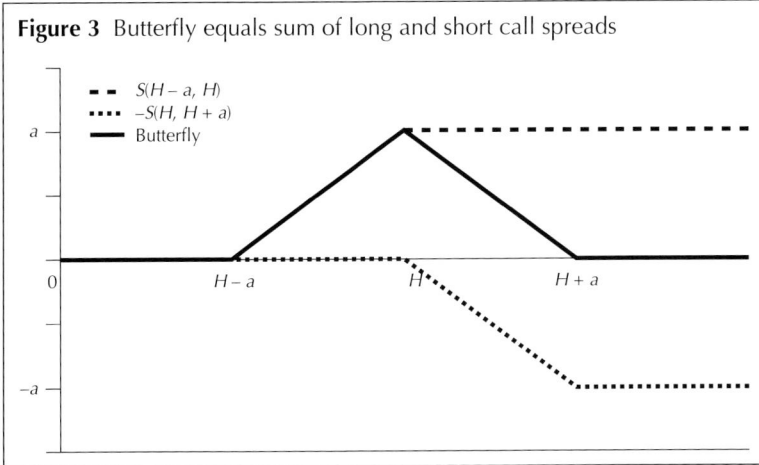

Figure 3 Butterfly equals sum of long and short call spreads

permitted, given the optimisation rule above. We conclude that this SEC rule requires the positive margin a for the butterfly, which never takes a negative value! It is intuitively obvious that this way of measuring risk cannot be extended into a coherent risk measure. Indeed, properties (ii) and (iii) together ensure that $\rho(X)$ is a negative number if the future net worth X is positive under any circumstances. We conclude that in this SEC approach, too few standard risks have been considered and that long butterflies should be added, margin-free, to the list of standard risks.

GENERALISED SCENARIOS

Generalised scenarios provide the most general form of coherent risk measure. It is easy to prove that for any set $\wp$ of probability distributions on the (finitely many) states of nature, the following procedure gives a coherent risk measure:

(i) calculate the average of the negative of the position's final net worth X, under each probability distribution belonging to $\wp$; and

(ii) calculate the largest of all the numbers found in (i) that corresponds to the formula $\rho(X) = \sup\{E_p[-X] \mid P \in \wp\}$.

Hence, for example, the use of Span provides a coherent risk measure. The shortfall risk measure associated with a reference probability distribution P is also coherent. It suffices to consider all events with probability of at least 5%, and to choose $\wp$ as the set of all conditional probabilities $P_{|A}$ where A is such an event:

$$\rho(X) = E[-X \,|\, X \le \text{VaR}_{0.05}(X)]$$
$$= \sup\{E[-X \,|\, A]; P(A) \ge 0.05\}$$

Representations of all coherent risk measures are, conversely, obtained by applying a mathematical result (Artzner, Delbaen, Eber and Heath (1997)) that ensures that for each coherent risk measure ρ there exists a set $\wp_\rho$ of generalised scenarios, such that the procedure above, acting on $\wp_\rho$, provides exactly the measure ρ. Hence there is no need to look for anything beyond a set $\wp$ of probability distributions (ie, the generalised scenarios) to obtain coherence in risk measurement.

Model risk can be dealt with by including a family of probability distributions for the future prices in the set $\wp$. This is not possible with VaR, which strongly depends on a specific distribution of probability, as does the shortfall measure. A simulation trial and a point-mass scenario should be distinguished from each other. The first is chosen randomly, according to a prescribed distribution, while the second is chosen by the investor or the supervisor.

Generalised scenarios are delicate to handle. How large the set $\wp$ should be is a crucial question. We have applied the theory of duality in linear programming to the (too) small set of standard risks in the SEC/NASD treatment of butterflies (Artzner, Delbaen, Eber and Heath (1997)). We found, of course, that this method implies too many scenarios of call price values. Some of them, in particular the optimal ones, are shown to be inconsistent with arbitrage-free markets, since they do not satisfy the condition of convexity of call prices with respect to strikes.

Using portfolios of standard risks to bound any given risk, we have found technical conditions under which an initial risk measurement of standard risks can be extended to all risks. We characterise the most conservative extension and describe its representing scenarios. Construction of the set $\wp$ of generalised scenarios, which a firm will use internally, should be made at the company level. Then, in a decentralised way, the individual business unit estimates the risk of its own position using the scenarios common to all the company. The sum of these measures is a conservative measure of the aggregate position.

As a related example, suppose that two coherent risk measures have been chosen for two kinds of risks (credit risk and market risk). We have found that scenario representation provides an algorithm to construct the most conservative coherent measure of risk for trading involving both sources of risk.

CONCLUSION

The generalised scenarios method is the universal coherent risk measurement method: it requires thinking before calculating, which can only improve risk management.

This chapter was previously published in *Risk*, November 1997.

REFERENCES

Artzner, P., F. Delbaen, J.-M. Eber, and D. Heath, 1997, "Definition of Coherent Measures of Risk", paper presented at the Symposium on Risk Management, European Finance Association, Vienna, August, pp. 27–30.

Embrechts, P., C. Klüppelberg, and T. Mikosh, 1997, *Modelling Extremal Events for Finance and Insurance*, (Berlin: Springer).

Rudd, A. and M. Schroeder, 1982, "The Calculation of Minimum Margin", *Management Science*, 28(12), December pp. 1368–79.

Standard Portfolio Analysis of Risk, Chicago Mercantile Exchange, 1995.

Value-at-Risk, Supplement to *Risk*, June 1996.

2

VaR Risk Measures vs. Traditional Risk Measures: An Analysis and Survey

Guy Kaplanski; Yoram Kroll*

Hebrew University, University of Michigan; Hebrew University

1 INTRODUCTION

In recent years, both the importance of risk measurement and the possibilities of efficient risk management have increased dramatically. This is a result of the globalisation of the financial markets, the technological revolution in trading systems and communications and, perhaps most important, the development of derivative tools and markets. The main approach to risk measurement acknowledges the fact that portfolio management relates to the entire distribution, although specific aspects of the distribution can still be quantified by a single risk measure.

The widespread adoption of value-at-risk (VaR) as a risk management tool is part of this approach.[1] Formally, VaR is primarily used for measuring market risk which is defined as a decrease in the value of a position due to changes in the financial market prices. According to the Basel Amendment (1996), financial institutions should maintain eligible capital against their market VaR in addition to the conventional capital requirements for credit risk. In addition, the Securities and Exchange Commission (SEC) allows the use of VaR in order to report market risk exposure. Recently, there has been increasing use of the VaR measure as a tool for

*The authors acknowledge the helpful comments of the editor Philippe Jorion, Allon Cohen and the anonymous referee. We thank the Kruger Center for Finance of the Hebrew University for its support and the Berliner Prize committee of Tel Aviv University for the grant awarded for the Best Analytical Research in Insurance, June 2001.

managing and regulating credit risk and as a methodology for constraining and controlling the risk exposure of a portfolio.[2]

Most chapters that have examined the validity of VaR have concentrated on its practical statistical and computational difficulties[3] and the implied perilous results (see Jorion 2000a). Other chapters have investigated VaR in the context of a portfolio.[4] Only a few pioneer chapters have investigated its theoretical merits. Artzner *et al* (1997, 1999) analyse the fundamental requirements of risk measures. They examine whether VaR is a coherent risk measure and analyse its merits and drawbacks. Basak and Shapiro (2001) address the superiority of the accumulate VaR (AVaR or mean shortfall), which is a variation of VaR, over VaR itself as a regulatory tool. Their important work was the first to examine the VaR constraints in terms of portfolio optimisation and utility maximisation.

The aim of this article is to expand the concept of VaR as a general risk measure, and to examine the validity of the various VaR measures as legitimate tools for estimating specific elements of risk for decision-making under uncertainty. In doing so, the article compares the various VaR measures and the traditional measures of risk and gives an overview of the relations between them. The article does not intend to analyse all aspects of VaR or to survey the huge high-quality literature on the subject. Instead, it attempts to provide a missing piece in the puzzle regarding the merits of VaR as a decision making measure in comparison with other risk measures.

The analysis and comparison assumes the case in which individuals are risk-averse and either maximise expected utility or lexicographic expected utility. The latter is defined as a two-step process in which "safety" is considered first (by the individuals or by the regulator) and only then is expected utility maximised.

The chapter shows that the mean–VaR criterion identifies alternatives which are inferior for all rational individuals. Similarly, the mean–AVaR criterion identifies alternatives which are inferior for all risk-averse individuals. The chapter also investigates the type of utility functions that are consistent with VaR-derived risk measures. Understanding these utility functions is important since they illustrate the behavior induced by VaR consideration. Surprisingly, the chapter shows that the use of VaR implies irrational utility functions which do not guarantee the more-over-less preference. This drawback is substantially reduced if AVaR is used in place of

VaR. These results reinforce the previous results of Artzner *et al* and Basak and Shapiro (2001) in favor of AVaR over VaR both as a risk measure and as a regulatory constraint.

The chapter is organised as follows: the following section provides preliminary background and presents some recently proposed VaR measures. The validity of these VaR measures is examined while assuming expected utility maximisation, risk aversion and decreasing absolute risk aversion (DARA). The mean–VaR criteria for specific distributions are also developed. In section 3 we review the traditional measures of risk and compare them to the VaR measures. The efficiency analysis of the various risk measures in terms of mean risk is also reviewed. Section 4 thoroughly analyses the congruence of VaR measures with expected utility. In addition, this section examines the validity of VaR under simple lexicographic utility. Section 5 concludes the chapter.

2 THE VAR MEASURES OF RISK

We denote by X a random variable with density function $f(x)$ and cumulative distribution function (cdf) $F(X)$.

We define the quantile $X(P)$ of X as the maximum value of X for which there is a probability of P to be below this value under the cdf of $F(X)$. Formally, the definition of $X(P)$ is: $\Pr(X \leq X(P)) = P$.[5]

Value-at-risk at $1 - \hat{P}$ confidence interval, $\mathrm{VaR}(\hat{P})$, can be defined as the loss below some reference target, $\eta(F(X))$, over a given period of time, where there exists a confidence interval of $1 - \hat{P}$ of incurring this loss or a smaller one.

If $\eta(F(X)) = E(X) \equiv \mu_X$, where μ_X is the expected mean of X, then the VaR is the loss below the expected mean, μ_X, and is denoted as VaR_e. If a constant reference point, such as the risk free-return or zero is selected, then it is denoted as VaR_t. For example, a weekly $\mathrm{VaR}_{t=0}$ of US\$5 million at the 99% confidence interval means that there is a probability of 1% to have a loss higher than US\$5 million below the current value within the next week.

In terms of the quantile function, $\mathrm{VaR}(\hat{P})$ can be written simply as

$$\mathrm{VaR}(\hat{P}) = \eta(F(X)) - X(\hat{P}) \qquad \text{(1)}$$

VaR calculation involves two primary steps. First, derive the forward distribution of returns.[6] Second, calculate the first $\hat{P}\%$ of this distribution. Figure 1 illustrates this process.

Figure 1 Value-at-risk

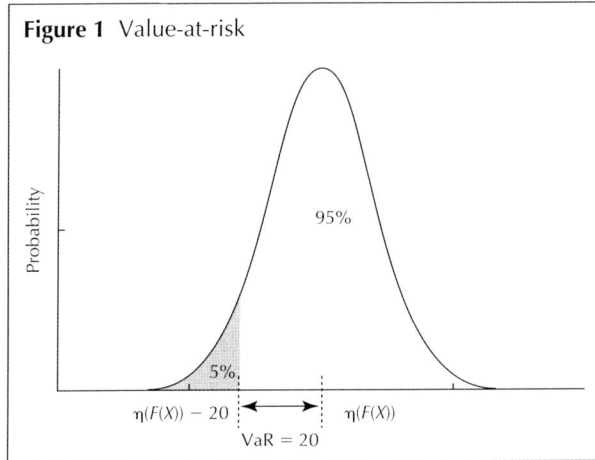

2.1 The VaR with expected mean as reference point (VaR$_e$)

Identifying a loss as being below the assumed projected mean has strong intuitive appeal. Baumol (1963, p. 174) claims that "Investment with a relatively high standard deviation will be relatively safe if its expected value is sufficiently high". Thus, he identifies the mean less k times the standard deviation as the subjective "confidence level" for the risk taken by the individual. Nevertheless, the main drawback of VaR$_e$ (as well as any other risk measure, which is based on results below the mean) is that it is unaffected by a constant shift of the whole distribution (see also Atkinson 1970, p. 253). This drawback is particularly important for regulation since it may reduce the sensitivity of this risk measure to economic turndowns and thus reduce its efficacy. This occurs because weak economic conditions may induce a decline in the returns under all states of nature such that the decrease in the quantile function is totally offset by the decrease in the expected return of the distribution (see (1)). Thus, although the absolute loss at a certain confidence interval is higher, there is no change in the magnitude of risk as measured by VaR$_e$. Therefore, it is not surprising that the official Basel Amendment (1996) recommends calculating the VaR as the potential loss below the current value, ie, VaR$_f$.

2.2 The VaR with a constant reference point (VaR$_f$)

Identifying a loss as a result below some constant reference point implies the existence of some objective standard for success and failure. This was justified by Mao (1970b) for the semi-variance measure of risk based on his finding that executives explain risk as the chance of failing to meet their target. The same argument is also valid for the VaR measures. Correspondingly, Markowitz (1959) and Mao (1970a) show that the constant reference point's semi-variance is consistent with the maximisation of expected utility using a utility function which guarantees the more-over-less preference and risk aversion assumptions. In Section 4 we show that this is also true in the case of $AVaR_t$, which is presented below, although not in the case of VaR_t.

2.3 The accumulate VaR (AVaR)

AVaR, which is also known as conditional VaR or mean shortfall, was introduced by Embrechts, Klueppelberg and Mikosch (1997), Artzner *et al* (1997, 1999), Basak and Shapiro (2001) and Longin (2001) and was further investigated by Uryasev (2000) and others. In the next section we show that a simplified version of AVaR was introduced many years ago by Domar and Musgrave (1944). This simplified version of AVaR is also a specific variation of the Fishburn (1977) $\alpha-t$ risk model.

The $1 - \hat{P}$ confidence interval $AVaR_t$ can be defined in terms of VaR as

$$AVaR_t(\hat{P}) = \int_0^{\hat{P}} VaR_t(P)dP \qquad (2)$$

where AVaR is usually normalised by the multiple $1 / \hat{P}$. AVaR averages the VaRs with a confidence interval that ranges from $1 - \hat{P}$ to 1. AVaR can be viewed as the expected loss, relative to the chosen reference point, within a constant range of probabilities 0 to $\hat{P}$.

Figure 2 presents the AVaR graphically. Analogously to VaR, the AVaR is equal to the area of probability $\hat{P}$ times the reference point $(\eta(F(X)) \times \hat{P})$, minus the expected lower results which are represented by the area to the left of the cdf $(\int_0^{\hat{P}} X(P)dP)$.[7]

Artzner *et al* show that in contrast to VaR, AVaR fulfills the four conditions of a coherent risk measure: homogeneity, monotonicity, the risk-free condition and the subadditive property which guarantees convexity. Other chapters concentrate on its advantages as a regulatory measure. Basak and Shapiro (2001) show its superiority

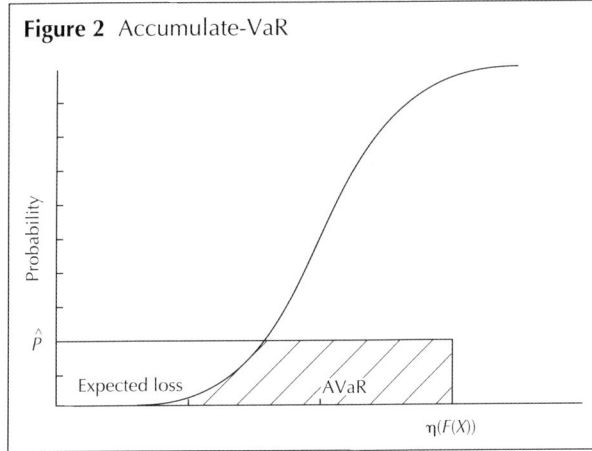

Figure 2 Accumulate-VaR

over VaR as a constraint on a portfolio in that it produces more reasonable results that are desirable for regulators. Longin (2001) takes it a step further by suggesting that AVaR be used as management and regulation tool for market risk during extraordinary market conditions. Uryasev (2000) introduces some practical advantages of AVaR, such as the ability to optimise it using linear programming and non-smooth optimisation algorithms for empirical distributions, subject to the number of scenarios being finite.

2.4 The AAVaR

In an effort to find an optimal measure of risk, AVaR can be further modified to produce the Accumulate-AVaR (AAVaR). Define $AAVaR_t$ with $1 - \hat{P}$ confidence interval as

$$AAVaR_t(\hat{P}) = \int_0^{\hat{P}} AVaR_t(P)dP \tag{3}$$

AAVaR shares the same advantages of AVaR as a regulatory measure in that it is a coherent measure of risk as well as a single value, which summarises the profile of the losses beyond VaR. Moreover, its calculation does not require any additional information beyond that required for AVaR calculation. Following Longin (2001), who suggests adopting AVaR as a tool for managing risk during extraordinary market conditions, AAVaR appears to be well-suited for this purpose. Further research in the spirit of Basak and Shapiro (2001) is required to understand the intuition behind it and to investigate its merits and the repercussions of its use as a regulatory constraint. Finally, we show below that AAVaR has additional advantages as a decision making measure.

2.5 Mean–VaR analysis

Throughout the chapter we will use a mean risk efficiency analysis in order to assess and compare the VaR measures as decision making criteria. Denote by D_{rule} the dominance relationships between two alternatives according to some given rule. For example, $XD_{mean-var}Y$ states that X dominates Y according to the mean–VaR criterion which is defined as follows:

$XD_{mean-var}Y$ if and only if

$$\mu_X \geq \mu_Y \tag{4}$$

and

$$VaR(X) \leq VaR(Y) \tag{5}$$

with at least one significant inequality.

In what follows we summarise the relations between the various mean–VaR criteria and the stochastic dominance rules. These rules are optimal criteria under specific assumptions about the individuals' utility functions (a detailed exposition of the stochastic dominance rules is given in Appendix B). The first stochastic dominance (FSD) rule is an optimal criterion for all rational individuals who maximise expected utility, where rationality is defined as a non-decreasing utility function. The second stochastic dominance (SSD) rule is an optimal criterion for all rational risk-averse individuals who maximise expected utility, where risk aversion is defined as a non-increasing marginal utility function.

It is generally assumed by economists that the higher the wealth of an individual, the lower is his Arrow–Pratt risk-aversion level. This is the decreasing absolute risk aversion (DARA). In order to fulfill the DARA property, the individual's utility function must have a positive third derivative. The third stochastic dominance

(TSD) rule is an optimal criterion for all rational risk-averse individuals with a positive third derivative of their utility function who
maximise expected utility.

Let VaR_e, VaR_t, AVaR_t and AAVaR_t be defined as in (1)–(3). Then
in the case of VaR_e:

$$XD_{\text{FSD}}Y \Rightarrow XD_{\text{mean}-\text{VaR}_e}Y \qquad (6)$$

In the case of VaR_t:

$$XD_{\text{FSD}}Y \Rightarrow XD_{\text{mean}-\text{VaR}_t}Y \qquad (7)$$

$$XD_{\text{SSD}}Y \nRightarrow XD_{\text{mean}-\text{VaR}_t}Y \qquad (8)$$

In the case of AVaR_t:

$$XD_{\text{SSD}}Y \Rightarrow XD_{\text{mean}-\text{AVaR}_t}Y \qquad (9)$$

$$XD_{\text{TSD}}Y \nRightarrow XD_{\text{mean}-\text{AVaR}_t}Y \qquad (10)$$

In the case of AAVaR_t:

$$XD_{\text{TSD}}Y \Rightarrow XD_{\text{mean}-\text{AAVaR}_t}Y \qquad (11)$$

The proofs are presented in Appendix A.

The efficient set according to the mean$-\text{VaR}_t$ rule is a subset of
the FSD-efficient set. Thus, an inferior alternative for all rational
investors is also inferior according to the mean$-\text{VaR}_t$ criterion. This
does not hold for the mean$-\text{VaR}_e$ criterion. Similarly, the efficient
set according to the mean$-\text{AVaR}_t$ rule is a subset of the SSD-
efficient set. In other words, if all risk-averse individuals prefer X over
Y, then X dominates Y according to mean AVaR_t. This important
relation does not hold for mean–VaR criteria. Note also that VaR
measures may not reflect the Rothschild and Stiglitz (1970) MPS
shift of probabilities from the center to the sides of the distribution,
which is the basic definition of an increase in risk. For example, if
the lower probability shifts from the "center" of the distribution to
any point above $\hat{P}$ then VaR is unchaged by the MPS.

Finally, if all risk-averse investors, who have a positive third derivative, prefer X over Y, then X dominates Y according to mean$-\text{AAVaR}_t$.

In order to illustrate the differences between the various mean–VaR criteria consider the folowing example. There exist two FSD-efficient alternatives, X and Y, with equal means. Assume also that $F(X)$ intersects $F(Y)$ once from below at a probability of 4%, such that $X(0.04) = Y(0.04)$. Under these assumptions, Y is inefficient according to SSD rule. However, dominance according to the mean$-$VaR$_t$ criterion depends on the selected confidence interval $1-\hat{P}$. For VaR$(\hat{P} = 0.03)$ $XD_{\text{mean}-\text{VaR}_t}Y$, for VaR$(\hat{P} = 0.05)$ $YD_{\text{mean}-\text{VaR}_t}X$ and for VaR$(\hat{P} = 0.04)$ there is no mean$-$VaR$_t$ dominance between X and Y. This example illustrates the sensitivity of VaR to the arbitrarily selected confidence interval, a drawback that was first mentioned by Artzner et al.[8] Consequently, it may rank risks incorrectly.

In contrast, AVaR$_t$ ranking remains fixed in this range. In fact, in this example X dominates Y according to SSD rule. Thus, according to (9) X dominates Y according to the mean$-$AVaR$_t$ criterion as well and hence one can conclude that for any $\hat{P}$ the AVaR$_t$ of X will be smaller than that of Y.

Note that the relations between the mean–VaR criteria and the stochastic dominance rules are analogous but not identical to Fishburn's (1977) Theorem 3, as well as Bawa's (1978) Theorem 1, regarding lower partial moments. In spite of the similarity, there is a fundamental difference in the basic assumptions of these measures and those of VaR measures. VaR measures assume that investors assess risk in a completly different process, in that the attitude toward risk is determined not only by the size of the loss but also by the probability of this loss to occur (see next section).

Also, note that the above relations coincide with Alexander and Baptista (2000) who show that the mean–VaR set is a subset of the mean standard deviation set in the case of normal and t distributions. Their article analyses the implications of using the mean–VaR criterion and the impact of the selected VaR confidence interval on the efficiency of the mean–VaR criterion.

2.6 Mean–VaR-efficiency analysis for specific distributions

One can conclude from the previous discussion that in the case of general distributions the mean–VaR criteria are superior to the mean standard deviation criterion since they provide necessary conditions for dominance among all expected utility maximising individuals. We show below that in the case of normal and lognormal distributions the VaR risk measures provide a good substitute for standard deviation in the optimal efficiency criteria.

Let X and Y be normally distributed. Then

$$XD_{SSD}Y \Leftrightarrow XD_{mean-VaR_e}Y \Leftrightarrow XD_{mean-standard\ deviation}Y \qquad (12)$$

If one prefers to use the VaR$_t$ risk measure rather than VaR$_e$,[9] then (12) can be modified as follows:

$XD_{SSD}Y$ if and only if

$$\mu_X \geq \mu_Y \qquad (13)$$

and

$$\mu_X + VaR_t(X) \leq \mu_Y + VaR_t(Y) \qquad (14)$$

The proofs are presented in Appendix A.

These relations support the use of the VaR in all cases where normality is assumed. For example, one can replace the beta in the CAPM by a new "VaR-beta" which is based on the VaR risk measure.

Note that in the general case, dominance according to the criterion in (13)–(14) implies dominance according to mean$-$VaR$_t$ criterion. The opposite does not hold true and thus in the general case the mean$-$VaR$_t$-efficient set is a subset of this criterion.

Note as well that in the normal case the AVaR measure can also be used to obtain an optimal criterion since, as Uryasev and Rockafellar (1999) show, the VaR and AVaR measures are equivalent in the case of normal distributions.

The lognormal distribution may be more appealing than the normal distribution since returns are bounded from below and it is coresponding with time-continuous trading models (see Mandelbrot 1963 and Merton 1971, 1973). Let X and Y be lognormally distributed, $X \sim \Lambda(\hat{\mu}_X, \hat{\sigma}_X)$ and $Y \sim \Lambda(\hat{\mu}_Y, \hat{\sigma}_Y)$, such that $Z_X = \log(X)$ and $Z_Y = \log(Y)$ are normally distributed with the first two moments $\hat{\mu}_X, \hat{\sigma}_X$ and $\hat{\mu}_Y, \hat{\sigma}_Y$, respectively.

Then, $XD_{SSD}Y$ if and only if

$$\mu_X \geq \mu_Y \qquad (15)$$

and

$$\ln\left(\frac{\mu_X}{t - \mathrm{VaR}_t(X)}\right) \le \ln\left(\frac{\mu_Y}{t - \mathrm{VaR}_t(Y)}\right) \tag{16}$$

where μ_X and μ_Y are the expected values of X and Y respectively, and $\hat{\mu}_X$ and $\hat{\mu}_Y$ are the expected values of the logs of X and Y, respectively.

Inequality (16) can also be written in terms of VaR_e as follows:

$$\ln\left(\frac{\mu_X}{\mu_X - \mathrm{VaR}_e(X)}\right) \le \ln\left(\frac{\mu_Y}{\mu_Y - \mathrm{VaR}_e(Y)}\right) \tag{17}$$

The proofs are presented in Appendix A.[10]

3 VAR AND TRADITIONAL RISK MEASURES

The various risk measures belong to one of two distinct groups, depending on the implied perception of risk. In the first group, risk is measured in terms of the probability-weighted dispersion of results around some reference point. These risk measures are affected by both negative and positive deviations from the target. Obviously, this attitude makes sense in the case of symmetrical distributions. However, in the general case positive deviations cannot be considered to be a source of risk.

In the second group, risk is measured only by results below some reference point. Below we review the most common measures in each group and compare them to VaR measures.

3.1 Dispersion measures
The standard deviation risk measure
The most common risk measure in the dispersion group is given by

$$\sigma_X = \sqrt{\int_{-\infty}^{\infty} f(x)(x - \mu_X)^2 \, dx} \tag{18}$$

Voluminous criticism of the standard deviation as a risk measure has been published, most of it relating to its inadequacy with regard to the expected utility theorem (see Markowitz 1959; Mao 1970a, 1970b; and many others). As previously shown, the mean standard deviation criterion is non-optimal and inferior to the mean − VaR$_t$ criterion since it is unable to screen out FSD inferior alternatives. On the other hand, in practice when the distribution has to be estimated from actual data, the standard deviation is much more robust than VaR measures since its calculation is based on the entire distribution.

The coefficient of variation risk measure
The coefficient of variation is simply the standard deviation divided by the mean. The special merit of the mean coefficient of variation criterion is its optimality in the lognormal case. However, in this case it can be replaced by an optimal criterion based on the mean and the VaR (see inequality (16)).

The expected absolute deviations risk measure
This dispersion measure is given by

$$AD = \int_{-\infty}^{\infty} f(x)\left|x - \mu_X\right| dx \tag{19}$$

Atkinson (1970) discussed this dispersion measure as a measure of inequality. More recently, Konno and Yamazaki (1991) developed a mean absolute deviation optimisation model which utilised this risk measure. The main advantage of their model over the mean standard deviation model lies in the linearity of this measure and the ability to solve the optimisation problem using a linear program. Note that the mean–AVaR criterion shares the same property, if we assume a finite number of scenarios.[11] Moreover, the mean absolute deviation criterion is inferior to the mean–VaR criteria, since it may not screen inferior alternatives according to the relevant stochastic dominance rule.

The Gini mean difference risk measure
The Gini mean difference measures the expected value of the absolute difference between every pair of realisations of the random variable and is given by

$$\Gamma = \frac{1}{2}\int_a^b \int_a^b \left|X - x\right| f(X)f(x)dXdx \tag{20}$$

As with the mean $-$ AVaR$_t$ criterion, the efficient set of the mean Gini criterion is a subset of the SSD-efficient set (see Yitzhaki 1982, 1983). However, this criterion may screen out alternatives that can be optimal for some risk-averse individuals.[12] In addition, the mathematical complexity of this measure obscured the intuition behind it and discouraged its use.

3.2 The below-a-reference-point risk measures

The risk measures in this group only consider results in the lower part of the distribution and thus they are more appealing as risk measures. In Fishburn's (1977, p. 118) own words, their attractiveness in the framework of the mean risk analysis is their ability to "recognise the desire to come out well in the long run while avoiding potentially disastrous setbacks or embarrassing failures to perform up to standard in the short run".

Fishburn's $\alpha-t$ risk measures

Most of the traditional important measures in this group are specific cases of Fishburn's $\alpha - t$ model, which is defined as

$$\int_{-\infty}^{t}(t - x)^{\alpha} f(x)\mathrm{d}x \tag{21}$$

where α describes different attitudes toward risk. The following risk measures are part of Fishburn's family:

Roy's (1952) safety-first (SF) risk measure (Fishburn's $\alpha \rightarrow 0$): Roy's SF measure is defined as the probability of being below a reference point t.

According to Fishburn (1977) and Bawa (1978), the mean–SF criterion screens out all alternatives which are inferior according to the FSD rule. However, the mean–SF criterion may not screen out alternatives which are inferior for all risk-averse individuals. In addition, the main deficiency of SF is that it measures risk only in terms of probability, while totally ignoring the size of the loss.

Domar and Musgrave's (1944) risk measure (Fishburn's $\alpha = 1$): The Domar and Musgrave (1944) risk measure (DM) is actually a simple variation of the AVaR$_t$ and is defined as:

$$DM = \int_{-\infty}^{t}(x - t)f(x)\mathrm{d}x \tag{22}$$

As in the case of AVaR$_t$, the mean–DM-efficient set is a subset of the SSD-efficient set. However, for AVaR$_t$ the integration is up to a given probability, $\hat{P}$, while the use of DM risk measure implies the comparison of two prospects over a different range of probabilities.

Markowitz's (1959) semi-variance (SV) risk measure (Fishburn's $\alpha = 2$): The Markowitz's (1959) constant reference point SV is defined as

$$SV = \int_{-\infty}^{t} f(x)(x - t)^2 \mathrm{d}x \qquad (23)$$

Mao (1970a, 1970b) shows that the mean–SV criterion is consistent with managers' perception of risk. Bawa (1975) shows that the mean–SV-efficient set is a subset of the TSD-efficient set. Bey (1979) shows that the mean–SV criterion also identifies a substantial part of the stochastic dominance-efficient set for both SSD and TSD rules.

However, according to Fishburn (1977, p. 116) "there is no compelling *a priori* reason for taking $\alpha = 2...$". Furthermore, as Bawa (1978) noted, the mean–SV criterion is not optimal for DARA utility functions.

Worst-case scenario (WCS) (Fishburn's $\alpha \to \infty$): A special case in which the VaR, AVaR, AAVaR and Fishburn's risk measures overlap is the Boudoukh, Matthew and Richardson (1995) worst-case-scenario measure, which can be written approximately as: WCS = $t - X(0)$. The main deficiency of this criterion is its tendency to screen out alternatives that can be optimal for some of the investors with finite α. In addition, it is difficult in practice to estimate this measure from actual data and it may go to infinity as the sample size increases.

Baumol's risk measure
Baumol's (1963) measure is given by the expected return minus k times the standard deviation. The parameter k is an arbitrary number which is supposed to reflect the subjective level of risk aversion. The larger k is, the higher this level is and the larger the Baumol-efficient set is.

The mean Baumol-efficient set is a subset of the mean standard deviation set. Therefore, at least in the case of the normal distribution, the smaller Baumol subset may not include optimal investments for some risk averse investors.[13]

VaR risk measures

Like other below-a-reference risk measures, VaR measures also consider risk as being below a fixed reference point. However, VaR is differentiated from Fishburn's $\alpha - t$ risk measures, which weight all the results below a fixed reference point t, in that it measures risk only in terms of the loss which has a confidence interval of $1 - \hat{P}$. Hence, VaR considers risk as one potential loss with a cumulative probability of occurrence of $\hat{P}$, while ignoring both larger and smaller potential losses.

AVaR is also differentiated from traditional below-a-reference risk measures. On the one hand, like those measures it weights large losses with a higher than $1 - \hat{P}$ confidence interval but, on the other hand, like VaR, it ignores small losses due to results below the reference point with a smaller than $1 - \hat{P}$ confidence interval. This approach may be appropriate for the regulator who wishes to insure against large losses while assuming that small losses are self-insured by the lenders.

3.3 Concluding comparison of the risk measures

Table 1 presents the mathematical expression for each measure, discusses their main properties and summarises the main differences between them.

In one way or another, none of the risk measures, including the VaR family, are necessarily consistent with the Von Neuman and Morgenstern (V&M) expected utility theory. However, the VaR family and in particular AVaR and AAVaR possess a few important advantages.

In the next section, we investigate the relationship between the VaR measures and expected utility theory in more detail.

4 VAR MEASURES, EXPECTED UTILITY AND THE LEXICOGRAPHIC EXPECTED UTILITY MODEL

In this section we analyse the congruence of VaR measures with expected utility framework. We show that while the mean$-$VaR$_t$ criterion cannot fit reasonable utility functions under the expected utility analysis, the mean$-$AVaR$_t$ analysis can be optimal for such functions. As an alternative, we show that a lexicographic utility function is consistent with the VaR constraint analysis in the case that VaR is considered to be a "top priority goal" imposed on the agent either by shareholders or the regulator.

Table 1 Summary of the most common risk measures, their main drawbacks and the relations in the general case between the mean–risk criterion using these risk measures and the stochastic dominance (SD) approach

Index	Arbitrary elements	Main drawback	SD ⇒ mean–risk*
Probability dispersion			
$SD = \sqrt{\int_{-\infty}^{\infty} f(x)(x - \mu_X)^2 dx}$		Accounts for positive dispersion	None
$Entropy = -\int_{-\infty}^{\infty} f(x)\ln(f(x))dx$			None
$Abs.dev = \int_{-\infty}^{\infty} f(x)|x - \mu_X|dx$			None
$Gini = \frac{1}{2}\int_a^b \int_a^b |X - x|f(X)f(x)dXdx$			SSD
$Co.variation = \sigma/\mu$			None

Table 1 Continued.

	Index	Arbitrary elements	Main drawback	SD ⇒ mean–risk*
Probability of dispersion below a target				
$\alpha \to 0$	$\text{Roy} = P(X \leq t)$	t	Ignores the size of loss	FSD
Fishburn = $\int_{-\infty}^{t}(t-x)^{\alpha}dF(x)$ $\alpha = 1$	$\text{D\&M} = \int_{-\infty}^{t}(x-t)f(x)dx$	t	Prospects over a changing range of probabilities	SSD
$\alpha = 2$	$\text{S-variance} = \int_{-\infty}^{t} f(x)(x-t)^2 dx$	t		TSD
$\alpha \to \infty$	$\text{WCS} = t - X(0)$	t	Ignores $0 < P \leq \hat{P}$	TSD
VaR	$\text{VaR}_t = t - X(\hat{P})$	$\hat{P}, t$	Ignores $P < \hat{P}$	FSD
	$\text{VaR}_e = \mu - X(\hat{P})$	$\hat{P}, t$		None
	$\text{AVaR} = \int_{0}^{\hat{P}} \text{VaR}(p)dp$	$\hat{P}, t$		SSD
	$\text{AAVaR} = \int_{0}^{\hat{P}} \text{AVaR}(p)dp$	$\hat{P}, t$		TSD
Baumol	$\text{Baumol} = \mu - k\sigma$	k	Ignores $X < \mu - k\sigma$	None

*The efficient set of the mean–risk criterion is a subset of the stochastic dominance (SD) criterion (note that for the SD rules the following holds: FSD ⇒ SSD ⇒ TSD).

4.1 Congruence of the VaR measures with expected utility

A congruence (or optimality) of a mean risk criterion with expected utility exists if and only if

$$XD_{\text{mean−risk}}Y \Leftrightarrow E(U(X)) > E(U(Y)) \tag{24}$$

where $E(U(X))$ and $E(U(Y))$ are the expected utilities of X and Y, respectively.

Fishburn (1977) shows that his mean $\alpha−t$ risk criterion is congruent with expected utility for the following family of utility functions:

$$U_{\alpha−t}(X) = X − \begin{cases} k(t − X)^{\alpha} & X \le t \\ 0 & \text{otherwise} \end{cases} \tag{25}$$

where $\alpha, k > 0$.[14,15]

$U_{\alpha−t}$ is linear for Xs above t. The shape of $U_{\alpha−t}$ below t differs according to the value of α. As Fishburn mentions, there is mixed support in the literature for this type of utility function. Moreover, although this utility function may exhibit some risk aversion "in the small" below t and risk aversion "in the large",[16] as Bawa (1978) noted, such a function certainly does not guarantee DARA in certain ranges.

The following theorem shows that unlike Fishburn's risk measures, the mean−VaR$_t$ criterion is congruent with expected utility theory only for utility functions that violate the basic rationality axiom of V&M expected utility theory.

THEOREM 1 *A mean−VaR$_t$ criterion is congruent with the expected utility theory for every distribution function only for the following utility function:*

$$U_{\text{mean−VaR}_t}(X) = X − k(t − X)\delta(X − X(\hat{P})) \tag{26}$$

where $k > 0$ and $\delta(\tau)$ is the impulse function which is defined as:[17]

$$\delta(\tau) = \begin{cases} \infty & \tau = 0 \\ 0 & \text{otherwise} \end{cases} \tag{27}$$

The proof is presented in Appendix A.

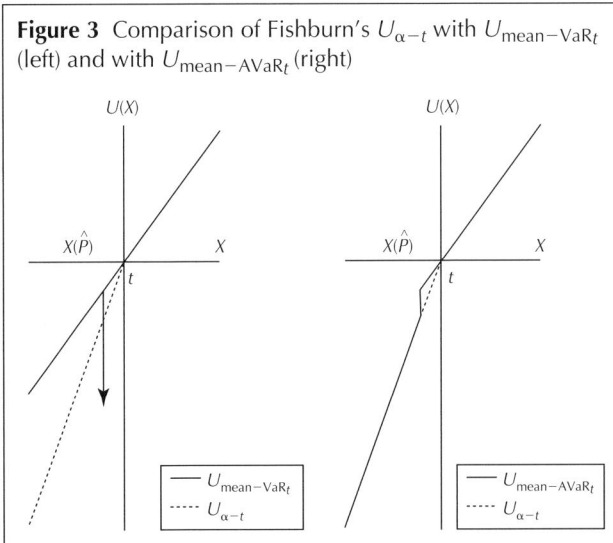

Figure 3 Comparison of Fishburn's $U_{\alpha-t}$ with $U_{mean-VaR_t}$ (left) and with $U_{mean-AVaR_t}$ (right)

The left panel of Figure 3 presents $U_{mean-VaR_t}$ as well as Fishburn's utility function, $U_{\alpha-t}$ for $k = 1$ and $\alpha = 1$. $U_{mean-VaR_t}$ is shown to be a linear function with a slope equal to 1 except for one discrete value at $X = X(\hat{P})$ at which it goes to minus infinity. Similarly to Fishburn's utility function, $U_{mean-VaR_t}$ is a risk neutral function above t. In contrast to Fishburn's utility function, $U_{mean-VaR_t}$ is also a risk-neutral function below t and more importantly has a discontinuity point at the value of $X(\hat{P})$ at which an increase in X decreases utility. This rather strange utility function represents irrational preferences, since an increase in wealth from a certain value below $X(\hat{P})$ to $X(\hat{P})$ induces an infinite utility decrease which contradicts the rationality assumption of preferring more over less.

Basak and Shapiro (2001) have already noted that using VaR for the regulation of firms may create agency costs. We see here another aspect of this agency cost since VaR minimisation is consistent with irrational expected utility maximisation. In fact, this utility function simulates the preferences of Basak and Shapiro's (2001) agent as long as the constraint has not been met since the agent must decrease the portfolio VaR to a certain point no matter what the required cost is.

The main corollary from Theorem 1 is that in the case of general distributions, except from the case of the irrational utility functions such as the one on the left panel of Figure 3, the mean$-$VaR$_t$

criterion cannot be justified on the grounds of the expected utility theory. In the following theorem we show that this problem is partially overcome by using AVaR$_t$ rather than VaR$_t$ as the risk measure.

THEOREM 2 *A mean−AVaR$_t$ criterion is congruent with the expected utility theory for the following utility function:*

$$U_{\text{mean}-\text{AVaR}_t}(X) = X - \begin{cases} k(t - X) & X \leq X(\hat{P}) \\ 0 & \text{otherwise} \end{cases} \qquad (28)$$

The proof is presented in Appendix A.

The right panel of Figure 3 depicts $U_{\text{mean}-\text{AVaR}_t}$ as well as Fishburn's utility function, $U_{\alpha-t}$ for $k = 1$ and $\alpha = 1$. It shows that $U_{\text{mean}-\text{AVaR}_t}$ is composed of two lines with a discrete "jump" in utility at $X = X(\hat{P})$. Corresponding to Fishburn's utility function, $U_{\text{mean}-\text{AVaR}_t}$ is risk-neutral in the small above the reference point and shows local risk aversion below it. Unlike Fishburn's utility function, the $U_{\text{mean}-\text{AVaR}_t}$ reference point $X(\hat{P})$ has a "jump" in utility at a value (quantile) for which there is a probability of $\hat{P}$ being below this point.[18]

The "jump" at $\hat{P}$ may be due to additional costs that are not directly reflected in X. An example of such costs is the damage to the firm's reputation, the additional cost of liquidation which is imposed by other parties, or constraints imposed by covenant terms or regulation. A legitimate way to reflect such an increase in costs is through a jump in utility at the point $X(\hat{P})$.[19] Thus, using AVaR to regulate the firm leads shareholders (managers) to act as if they possessed an artificial utility with a jump at the $X(\hat{P})$ threshold reference point. By imposing this jump, the regulator can neutralise the tendency of shareholders (managers) of a highly leveraged firm to take risks at the expense of depositors (lenders).

Another possible justification for the reduced level of utility below $X(\hat{P})$ is based on positive grounds. Accordingly, "optimistic" and even "pessimistic" investors may behave as if results with less than probability $\hat{p}$ of occurring are of less importance. These behavioral considerations should be empirically investigated.

In summary, according to Theorems 1 and 2 the use of VaR as a risk measure for decision making or as a constraint on the agent does not induce "rationality" and thus does not lead to optimal results for the investor. Using AVaR substantially improves "rationality" and thus induces better results for the investor. These conclusions reinforce the previous results of Artzner *et al* and Basak and Shapiro (2001) in favor of AVaR over VaR both as a risk measure and as a regulatory constraint.

4.2 The lexicographic utility approach

We have so far concluded that the mean-below-a-reference point risk measures can be inconsistent with the V&M expected utility theory. A possible intuitive behavioral explanation for this inconsistency could be that the below-a-reference point risk is a kind of "survival risk", but that it is not the only component of risk. The second component can be called the conventional "volatility risk", which deals with fluctuations that do not threaten survival or alternatively do not generate the extra costs that were previously discussed. The V&M expected utility theory could be extended to agree with these two components by assuming a different attitude towards these types of risk. Accordingly, there are hierarchical preferences between survival or avoiding disaster and obtaining an optimal mean risk tradeoff in the traditional manner. This hierarchical preference can be quantitatively expressed in terms of the lexicographic expected utility model which was introduced by Hausner (1954), Chipman (1960) and Fishburn (1971).[20]

On the behavioral level, the lexicographic expected utility approach is consistent with individuals' differential attitude towards various levels of loss which might be due to either differential scale of damage or any positively based behavioral pattern.[21] On the other hand, the lexicographic model suffers from the absence of substitutions between alternatives and therefore may be more relevant for modeling the behavioral pattern of a regulated firm.

In the context of a regulated firm, the imposed VaR constraints induce the shareholders (managers) to make decisions as if they possessed a "survival risk" constraint as a first priority goal in a lexicographic utility. Thus, a VaR constraint can be viewed as a survival risk constraint which lexicographically dominates the goal of maximising V&M expected utility.

5 CONCLUSIONS

The chapter compares VaR measures and traditional measures of risk in order to place these popular risk measures in the entire map of risk analysis. The main conclusion from the analysis is that the VaR family, which is currently used for risk management purposes, is at least as good as other risk measures for decision-making purposes.

In particular, it has been shown that the VaR risk measures are either a close variation or a specific case of traditional measures that consider risk in terms of results below a reference point. Some formal relationships between traditional and VaR measures have been formed and lead to conditions under which the mean–VaR analysis provides either sufficient or necessary criteria (see Appendix B).

The chapter points out that VaR measures are exposed to several deficiencies. For all non-normal distributions, the mean–VaR criterion may screen out alternatives that are considered superior by some or even all risk-averse individuals. In addition, it may not identify existing dominance for all risk-averse individuals. Moreover, in the case of VaR_e (where the mean is the reference point for calculating VaR) the VaR may not identify inferior alternatives for all rational investors and at the same time screens out efficient alternatives for rational individuals.

More seriously, unless we assume normality (or lognormality), congruence with expected utility theory is obtained only for irrational utility functions. Hence, other than in the case of normal distribution (and in the case of the lognormal distribution in which a modification of the mean–VaR criterion is required), the mean–VaR criterion cannot be justified on the grounds of expected utility theory.

Despite these conclusions, it is worth noting that most other traditional measures suffer from similar and even worse drawbacks. The mean$-VaR_t$ criterion (where a constant t is the reference point) is superior or at least as good as the well-known mean standard deviation criterion for the following reasons. First, both criteria are optimal in the normal case (and so are their variations in the lognormal case). Second, while the mean$-VaR_t$ (as opposed to mean$-VaR_e$) criterion identifies inferior alternatives according to the FSD rule, the mean standard deviation criterion cannot guarantee this property (except in particular cases, such as the quadratic utility function).

In light of the above deficiencies of VaR, the AVaR is superior both to the regular VaR as well as to most other traditional risk measures.

Apart from the practical and mathematical advantages of AVaR, we show that the mean–AVaR criterion identifies dominance when it exists for all risk-averse individuals, ie, dominance by the mean–AVaR is a necessary condition for dominance by the SSD rule. This property generates regulatory advantages and implies lower agency costs. We show as well that AVaR considers all extreme loss scenarios. AVaR is also far less sensitive than VaR to the arbitrarily selected confidence interval and has a clear economic interpretation. In addition, the mean–AVaR criterion is optimal for normal distributions when assuming any rational risk aversion utility function, or for any distribution function when assuming utility functions that have a "jump" at a critical threshold point, which reflects the extra cost incurred by being below this reference point.

Finally, the chapter presents the idea of using the VaR risk measures in a lexicographic expected utility framework. In this model, risk is divided into two components: "survival risk" and "volatility risk" where the former takes precedence over the latter. This approach may be appropriate for behavioral models as well as the case of a regulated firm in which attaining imposed constraints dominates shareholders' preferences.

APPENDIX A – PROOFS

Proof of (6)

In order to prove (6) it is sufficient to provide an example. Suppose that X takes a value of either 10 or 20, each with a probability of 0.5. Similarly, Y takes a value of either 0 or 5, each with a probability of 0.5. It can easily be seen that any rational investor would prefer alternative X over Y ($\min(X) > \max(Y) \Rightarrow XD_{FSD}Y$). However, at a 50% or higher confidence interval ($\hat{P} < 0.5$), the VaR_es of X and Y are given by: $\text{VaR}_e(X) = 5$ and $\text{VaR}_e(Y) = 2.5$, respectively. Hence, both the mean and the VaR_e of X are higher than the mean and the VaR_e of Y and, according to the mean$-\text{VaR}_e$ rule, there is no dominance between the two alternatives.

Proof of (7)

The mean condition: From the stochastic dominance necessary conditions we obtain

$$XD_{FSD}Y \Rightarrow \mu_X \geq \mu_Y$$

The VaR condition:[22]

$$XD_{FSD}Y \Rightarrow X(P) \geq Y(P); 0 \leq P \leq 1$$
$$\Rightarrow t - X(\hat{P}) \leq t - Y(\hat{P}) \Rightarrow \text{VaR}_t(X) \leq \text{VaR}_t(Y)$$

Proof of (8)

In order to prove (8) it is sufficient to provide an example. Suppose that X takes a value of either 10 or 20, each with probability of 0.25, or the value of 15 with probability of 0.5. In contrast, Y takes a value of either 10 or 20, each with a probability of 0.5. It can easily be seen that any rational risk-averse investor would prefer alternative X over Y ($XD_{SSD}Y$). However, at a 75% or higher confidence interval ($\hat{P} < 0.25$), the VaR_t of X and Y are given by: $\text{VaR}_t(X) = t - 10$ and $\text{VaR}_t(Y) = t - 10$, respectively. Hence, both the mean and the VaR_t of X are equal to those of Y and according to the mean$-\text{VaR}_t$ rule there is no dominance between the two alternatives.

Proof of (9)

The mean condition: From the stochastic dominance necessary conditions we obtain

$$XD_{SSD}Y \Rightarrow \mu_X \geq \mu_Y$$

The AVaR condition:

$$XD_{SSD}Y \Rightarrow \int_0^P X(p)dp \geq \int_0^P Y(p)dp;\ 0 \leq P \leq 1$$

$$\Rightarrow \int_0^{\hat{P}} (t - X(p))dp \leq \int_0^{\hat{P}} (t - Y(p))dp$$

$$\Rightarrow \mathrm{AVaR}_t(X) \leq \mathrm{AVaR}_t(Y)$$

Proof of (10)

In order to prove (10) it is sufficient to provide an example. Suppose that X takes a value of either 10 or 50, each with probability of 0.25, or the value of 20 with probability of 0.5. In contrast, Y takes a value of either 10 or 40, each with a probability of 0.5. It can easily be seen that any rational risk-averse investor with a positive third derivative of his utility function would prefer alternative X over Y ($XD_{TSD}Y$). However, at a 75% or higher confidence interval ($\hat{P} < 0.25$), the AVaR_t of X and Y are given by: $\mathrm{AVaR}_t(X) = t - 10 \times \hat{P}$ and $\mathrm{AVaR}_t(Y) = t - 10 \times \hat{P}$, respectively. Hence, both the mean and the AVaR_t of X are equal to those of Y and according to the mean$-\mathrm{AVaR}_t$ rule there is no dominance between the two alternatives.

Proof of (11)

The mean condition: from the stochastic dominance necessary conditions we obtain

$$XD_{TSD}Y \Rightarrow \mu_X \geq \mu_Y$$

The AAVaR condition:

$$XD_{TSD}Y \Rightarrow \int_0^P\!\!\int_0^p X(\upsilon)d\upsilon dp \geq \int_0^P\!\!\int_0^p Y(\upsilon)d\upsilon dp;\ 0 \leq P \leq 1$$

$$\Rightarrow \int_0^{\hat{P}}\!\!\int_0^p (t - X(\upsilon))d\upsilon dp \leq \int_0^{\hat{P}}\!\!\int_0^p (t - Y(\upsilon))d\upsilon dp$$

$$\Rightarrow \mathrm{AAVaR}_t(X) \leq \mathrm{AAVaR}_t(Y)$$

Proof of (12)

In the normal case:

$$XD_{SSD}Y \Leftrightarrow XD_{mean-standard\ deviation}Y \qquad \text{(A1)}$$

and

$$X(\hat{P}) = \mu + \sigma Z(\hat{P}) \qquad \text{(A2)}$$

where $Z(\hat{P})$ is the $\hat{P}$ order value (quantile) of the normal standard-ised distribution, μ is the mean and σ is the standard deviation. From (A2) and the definition of VaR we find that:

$$\sigma = \frac{X(\hat{P}) - \mu}{Z(\hat{P})} = \frac{-VaR_e}{Z(\hat{P})} \qquad \text{(A3)}$$

Substituting this into the mean standard deviation criterion produces inequality (12).

Proof of (14)

Substitute: $VaR_e = VaR_t + \mu - t$ into the mean$-VaR_e$ criterion and add the constant t to both sides in order to obtain (14).

Proof of (16)

In the lognormal case, $XD_{SSD}Y$ if and only if

$$\mu_X \geq \mu_Y \qquad \text{(A4)}$$

and

$$\hat{\sigma}_X \leq \hat{\sigma}_Y \qquad \text{(A5)}$$

where μ is the mean of the returns and $\hat{\sigma}$ is the standard deviation of the log of the returns (see Levy (1973, 1991)). Furthermore, in this case the $\hat{P}$ order value (quantile) is given by:

$$X(\hat{P}) = t - VaR_t = \exp(\hat{\mu} + \hat{\sigma}Z(\hat{P})) \qquad \text{(A6)}$$

and the mean is given by:

$$\mu = \exp\left(\hat{\mu} + \frac{1}{2}\hat{\sigma}^2\right) \qquad \text{(A7)}$$

where $Z(\hat{P})$ is the $\hat{P}$ order value (quantile) of the normal standard-ised distribution, μ and $\hat{\sigma}$ are as defined above and $\hat{\mu}$ is the mean of the logs of the returns. Substituting $\hat{\mu} = \ln(t - \text{VaR}_t) - Z(\hat{P})\hat{\sigma}$ from (A6) into (A7) yields

$$\hat{\sigma}^2 - 2Z(\hat{P})\hat{\sigma} + 2\ln\left(\frac{t - \text{VaR}_t}{\mu}\right) = 0 \qquad \text{(A8)}$$

Substituting the positive solution of (A8),

$$\hat{\sigma} = Z(\hat{P}) + \sqrt{Z^2(\hat{P}) - 2\ln\left(\frac{t - \text{VaR}_t}{\mu}\right)}$$

into (A5) with a few algebraic manipulations (subject to $\hat{P} \leq 0.5$) yields (16).

Proof of Theorem 1:
Integrating $U_{\text{mean}-\text{VaR}_t}$ from (26) yields

$$\int_{-\infty}^{\infty} U(X)f(X)dX$$

$$= \int_{-\infty}^{\infty} Xf(X)dX - k \int_{-\infty}^{\infty} (t - X)\delta(X - X(\hat{P}))dX$$

$$= \mu_X - k(t - X(\hat{P})) \qquad \text{(A9)}$$

Hence, the expected value of $U_{\text{mean}-\text{VaR}_t}$ is simply the mean minus $k\text{VaR}_t$ such that

$$XD_{\text{mean}-\text{VaR}_t}Y \Leftrightarrow \mu_X - k\text{VaR}_t(X) \geq \mu_Y - k\text{VaR}_t(Y)$$

Proof of Theorem 2:
Integrating $U_{\text{mean}-\text{AVaR}_t}$ from (28) yields

$$\int_{-\infty}^{\infty} U(X)f(X)dX$$

$$= \int_{-\infty}^{\infty} Xf(X)dX - k \int_{-\infty}^{X(\hat{P})} (t - X)dX$$

$$= \mu_X - k \int_{-\infty}^{X(\hat{P})} (t - X)dX \qquad \text{(A10)}$$

Hence:

$$XD_{\text{mean}-\text{AVaR}_t} Y \Leftrightarrow \mu_X - k\text{AVaR}_t(X) \geq \mu_Y - k\text{AVaR}_t(Y)$$

Appendix B – Stochastic dominance rules

The stochastic dominance rules (see Quirk and Saposnick (1962); Fishburn (1964); Hadar and Russell (1969); Hanoch and Levy (1969); and Whitmore (1970)) provide optimal investment criteria for several types of V&M utility functions. In the following, we present the definitions of optimal, necessary and sufficient criteria, as well as the first, the second and the third stochastic dominance rules.

Definitions

A *sufficient criterion* for dominance of X over Y is one which guarantees that all the individuals under the assumed set of utility functions prefer X over Y.

A *necessary criterion* for dominance of X over Y is one that must be fulfilled once all individuals under the assumed set of utility functions prefer X over Y.

An *optimal* criterion is a necessary and sufficient criterion for dominance.

Stochastic dominance rules

The first stochastic dominance (FSD) rule is an optimal criterion for all rational individuals who maximise expected utility where rationality is defined by a non-decreasing utility function.

According to the FSD rule, $XD_{\text{FSD}}Y$ if and only if $F \neq G$ and $F(x) \leq G(x)$ for all x, where F and G are the cdfs of X and Y.

The second stochastic dominance (SSD) rule is an optimal criterion for all rational risk-averse individuals who maximise expected utility where risk aversion is defined by a non-increasing marginal utility function.

According to the SSD rule, $XD_{\text{SSD}}Y$ if and only if $F \neq G$ and $\int_0^x F(t)dt \leq \int_0^x G(t)dt$ for all x.

The third stochastic dominance (TSD) rule is an optimal criterion for all rational risk-averse individuals with a positive third derivative of their utility function who maximise expected utility.

According to the TSD rule, $XD_{\text{TSD}}Y$ if and only if $F \neq G$, $\mu_X \geq \mu_Y$ and $\int_0^x \int_0^t F(v)dvdt \leq \int_0^x \int_0^t G(v)dvdt$ for all x.

1 An introduction and overview of VaR can be found in Linsmeier and Pearson (1996), Duffie and Pan (1997) and in the excellent books by Jorion (2000b) and Crouhy, Galai and Mark (2001).

2 For more on credit risk issues see, for example, Duffie and Pan (2000) and Crouhy, Galai, and Mark (2000). For more on the methodology used to constrain and control risk exposure see, for example, Basak and Shapiro (2001) and Jorion (2001).

3 See, for example, Beder (1995), Johansson, Seiler and Tjarnberg (1999) and others.

4 See, for example, Ho, Chen and Eng (1996) and Ahn, Boudoukh, Richardson and Whitelaw (1999).

5 Note that the requirement for the "maximum" value is relevant only in the case of discrete distributions in which there may be several values of $X(P)$ which satisfy the following condition: $\Pr(X \leq X(P)) = P$.

6 Alternatively, VaR can be defined in terms of market values by using the relevant distribution of the forward value of the position. For the relationship between the definitions of VaR in terms of returns and in terms of market values, see Hallerbach (1999).

7 The expected value of X in terms of the quantile function is given by: $E(X) = \int_0^1 X(P)\mathrm{d}P$.

8 Another aspect of the sensitivity of the selection of alternatives to the confidence interval under the mean$-\mathrm{VaR}_t$ criterion in the case of "fat-tails" can be found in Lucas and Klaassen (1998).

9 The issue of the reference point of VaR, which is negligible in the traditional use of VaR for market risk during very short periods, is becoming significant with the tendency to adopt VaR for other uses such as a decision making measure.

10 In order to compare the normal and lognormal cases, recall that $\mathrm{VaR}_t(X) = t - X(\hat{P})$ and $\mathrm{VaR}_t(Y) = t - Y(\hat{P})$ and rewrite (14) and (16) as $\mu_X - \mu_Y \leq X(\hat{P}) - Y(\hat{P})$ and $\ln(\mu_X) - \ln(\mu_Y) \leq \ln(X(\hat{P})) - \ln(Y(\hat{P}))$. The only difference between these inqualities is that the logs of the relevant parameters appear in the lognormal case. This should not be surprising since the logs of X and Y are normally distributed in the lognormal case.

11 This advantage exists only for discrete empirical distributions. Kaplanski and Kroll (2001) show that in the case of general continuous distributions a simple linear program cannot be used to obtain the analytical solution for the mean–VaR optimisation problem.

12 Except for the case of at most one intersection of the alternatives' cdfs in which this criterion is also sufficient for SSD.

13 In the context of regulation, Halpern and Kahane (1980) illustrate some basic differences between the Baumol risk measure and the "ruin constraint".

14 A previous version of this function for the mean semi-variance criterion is presented by Markowitz (1959) and further analysed by Mao (1970b). Arzac (1974) also presents a variation for the case of mean safety-first analysis.

15 According to expected utility theory, this function is determined up to a positive linear transformation. Fishburn (1977) normalises the utility function such that $U(t) = t$.

16 The expressions for risk aversion "in the small" and "in the large" are adopted from Pratt (1964).

17 The Impulse Function exhibits:

$$\int_{\tau-\epsilon}^{\tau+\epsilon} \delta(X - \tau)f(X)\mathrm{d}X = f(\tau)$$

where $f(\tau)$ is a sample of $f(X)$ at point τ.

18 Throughout the analysis we assume that $X(\hat{P}) \leq t$. Though the analysis can easily be extended to cover the opposite case $(X(\hat{P}) > t)$, it is unreasonable to assume a "loss" reference point, $X(\hat{P})$, in the high range where individuals tend to be risk-neutral.

19 The alternative approach is to add the additional cost to X. However, this will lead to an "empty" span of X below the jump point.

20 The previous use of a lexicographic safety-first rule can be found in Telser (1955), Arzac (1974) and Arzac and Bawa (1977). However, in contrast to their models, which separate the mean risk analysis into two lexicographic components, here we suggest breaking down the risk itself into separate elements. Hence, the survival element of risk lexicographically dominates all other aspects of the distribution which can still be expressed in terms of the traditional V&M expected utility theory.

21 Note that this approach is also consistent with Friedman and Savage's (1948) analysis which explains the selection of both lottery tickets and insurance by the same individual through different perceptions of risk at high and low levels of wealth. Accordingly, in the proposed lexicographic model the purchase of insurance is aimed at reducing the element of survival risk while the purchase of lottery tickets involves only the second element of wealth maximisation.

22 In the proofs of (6)–(11) we use the stochastic dominance rules in terms of the quantile functions $X(P)$ and $Y(P)$. For more details regarding this version of the stochastic dominance rules, see Levy and Kroll (1978).

This chapter was previously published in *The Journal of Risk* **4**(3), Spring 2002.

REFERENCES

Ahn, D. H., J. Boudoukh, M. Richardson, and R. F. Whitelaw, 1999, "Optimal Risk Management using Options", *Journal of Finance* **54(1)**, pp. 359–75.

Alexander, J. G. and A. M. Baptista, 2000, "Economic Implications of using a Mean-VaR Model for Portfolio Selection: A Comparison with Mean-Variance Analysis", Working Paper, University of Minnesota.

Artzner, P., F. Delbaen, J. M. Eber, and D. Heath, 1997, "Thinking Coherent", *Risk* **11**, November, pp. 68–72.

Artzner, P., F. Delbaen, J. M. Eber, and D. Heath, 1999, "Coherent Measures of Risk", *Mathematical Finance* **9**, pp. 203–28.

Arzac, E., 1974, "Utility Analysis of Chance-Constrained Portfolio Section", *Journal of Financial and Quantitative Analysis* **8**, pp. 993–1007.

Arzac, E. and V. Bawa, 1977, "Portfolio Choice and Equilibrium in Capital Markets with Safety-First Investors", *Journal of Financial Economics* **4**, pp. 277–88.

Atkinson, A. B., 1970, "On the Measurement of Inequality", *Journal of Economic Theory* **2**, pp. 244–63.

Basak, S. and A. Shapiro, 2001, "Value-at-Risk Based Risk Management: Optimal Policies and Asset Prices", *Review of Financial Studies* **14(2)**, pp. 371–405.

Basel Committee on Banking Supervision, 1996, "Amendment to the Capital Accord to Incorporate Market Risks", January.

Baumol, W. J., 1963, "An Expected Gain Confidence Limit Criterion for Portfolio Selection", *Management Science* **10**, pp. 174–82.

Bawa, V. S., 1975, "Optimal Rules for Ordering Uncertain Prospects", *Journal of Financial Economics* **2**, pp. 95–121.

Bawa, V. S., 1978, "Safety-First, Stochastic Dominance, and Optimal Portfolio Choice", *Journal of Financial and Quantitative Analysis* **13**, pp. 255–71.

Beder, T. S., 1995, "VaR: Seductive but Dangerous", *Financial Analyst Journal*, Sep–Oct, pp. 12–24.

Bey, R. P., 1979, "Estimating the Optimal Stochastic Dominance Efficient Set with Mean Semi-Variance Algorithms", *Journal of Financial and Quantitative Analysis* **14**, pp. 1059–70.

Boudoukh, J., M. Richardson, and R. Whitelaw, 1995, "Expect the Worst", *Risk*, September, pp. 100–1.

Chipman, J. S., 1960, "The Foundation of Utility", *Econometrica* **28**, April, pp. 193–224.

Crouhy, M., D. Galai, and R. Mark, 2000, "Comparative Analysis of Current Credit Risk Models", *Journal of Banking and Finance* **24**, January, pp. 59–117.

Crouhy, M., D. Galai, and R. Mark (eds), 2001, *Risk Management*, (New York: McGraw-Hill).

Domar, E. and R. A. Musgrave, 1944, "Proportional Income Taxation and Risk Taking", *Quarterly Journal of Economics* **57**, May, pp. 388–422.

Duffie, D. and J. Pan, 1997, "An Overview of Value at Risk", *Journal of Derivatives* **4**, Spring, pp. 7–49.

Duffie, D. and J. Pan, 2000, "Analytical Value-at-Risk with Jumps and Credit Risk", *Finance and Stochastics* **5**, pp. 155–80.

Embrechts, P., C. Klueppelberg, and T. Mikosch, 1997, *External Events in Finance and Insurance*, (Berlin: Springer).

Fishburn, P. C., 1964, *Decision and Value Theory*, (New York: Wiley).

Fishburn, P. C., 1971, "A Study of Lexicographic Expected Utility", *Management Science* **17**, pp. 672–8.

Fishburn, P. C., 1977, "Mean-Risk Analysis with Risk Associated with Below-Target Returns", *American Economic Review* **67**, March, pp. 116–26.

Hadar, J. and W. Russell, 1969, "Rules for Ordering Uncertain Prospects", *Amerian Economic Review* **59**, pp. 25–34.

Hallerbach, W. G., 1999, "Decomposing Portfolio Value-at-Risk: A General Analysis", Working Paper, Erasmus University Rotterdam.

Halpern, P. and Y. Kahane, 1980, "A Pedagogical Note on Baumol's Gain-Confidence Limit Criterion for Portfolio Selection and the Probability of Ruin", *Journal of banking and Finance* **4**, pp. 191–5.

Hanoch, G. and H. Levy, 1969, "The Efficiency Analysis of Choices Involving Risk", *Review of Economic Studies* **36**, pp. 335–46.

Hausner, M., 1954, "Multidimensional Utilities", in R. M. Thrall, C. H. Croombs, and R. L. Davis (eds), *Decisions Processes*, (New York: Wiley), pp. 167–80.

Ho, T. S. Y., M. Z. H. Chen, and H. T. F. Eng, 1996, "VaR Analytics: Portfolio Structure, Key Rate Convexities, and VaR Betas", *Journal of Portfolio Management* **23(1)**, Fall, pp. 89–98.

Johansson, F., M. J. Seiler, and M. Tjarnberg, 1999, "Measuring Downside Portfolio Risk", *Journal of Portfolio Management*, Fall, pp. 96–107.

Jorion, P., 2000a, "Risk Management Lessons from Long-Term Capital Management", *European Financial Management* **6**, September.

Jorion, P., 2000b, *Value at Risk: The New Benchmark for Managing Financial Risk*, (New York: McGraw-Hill).

Jorion, P., 2001, "Portfolio Optimization with Constraint on Tracking Error", Working paper, University of California at Irvine.

Konno, H. and H. Yamazaki, 1991, "Mean Absolute Deviation Portfolio Optimization Model and its Application to Tokyo Stock Market", *Management Science* **37**, pp. 519–31.

Kaplanski, G. and Y. Kroll, 2001, "Efficient VaR Portfolios", Working paper, Hebrew University.

Levy, H., 1973, "Stochastic Dominance among Log-Normal Prospects", *International Economic Review* **14**, pp. 601–14.

Levy, H., 1991, "The Mean-Coefficient of Variation Rule: The Lognormal Case", *Management Science*, June, pp. 745–7.

Levy, H. and Y. Kroll, 1978, "Ordering Uncertain Options with Borrowing and Lending", *Journal of Finance* **33(2)**, May, pp. 552–73.

Linsmeier, T. and N. Pearson, 1996, "Risk Measurement: An Introduction to Value at Risk", Working paper, University of Illinois.

Longin, M. F., 2001, "Beyond the VaR", *Journal of Derivatives*, Summer, pp. 36–48.

Lucas, A. and P. Klaassen, 1998, "Extreme Returns, Downside Risk, and Optimal Asset Allocation", *Journal of Portfolio Management*, Fall, pp. 71–9.

Mandelbrot, B., 1963, "The Variation of Certain Speculative Prices", *Journal of Business* **36**, pp. 394–419.

Mao, J. C. T., 1970a, "Models of Capital Budgeting, E-V vs E-S", *Journal of Finance and Quantitative Analysis* **4**, January, pp. 657–75.

Mao, J. C. T., 1970b, "Survey of Capital Budgeting: Theory and Practice", *Journal of Finance* **25**, May, pp. 349–60.

Markowitz, H. M., 1959, *Portfolio Selection*, (New York: John Wiley and Sons).

Merton, R. C., 1971, "Optimum Consumption and Portfolio Rules in a Continuous-Time Model", *Journal of Economic Theory* **3**, pp. 373–413.

Merton, R. C., 1973, "An Inter-Temporal Capital Asset Pricing Model", *Econometrica* **41(5)**, September, pp. 867–87.

Pratt, J. W., 1964, "Risk Aversion in the Small and in the Large", *Econometrica* **32**, pp. 122–36.

Quirk, J. P. and R. Saposnik, 1962, "Admissibility and Measurable Utility Function", *Review of Economic Studies* **29**, pp. 140–6.

Rockafellar, R. T. and S. Uryasev, 2000, "Optimization of Conditional Value-at-Risk", *The Journal of Risk* **2(3)**, pp. 21–41.

Rothschild, M. and J. E. Stiglitz, 1970, "Increasing Risk. I: A Definition", *Journal of Economic Theory* **2**, pp. 225–43.

Roy, A. D., 1952, "Safety First and the Holding of Assets", *Econometrica* **20**, July, pp. 431–49.

Tesler, L., 1955, "Safety First and Hedging", *Review of Economic Studies* **23**, pp. 1–16.

Uryasev, S., 2000, "Conditional Value-at-Risk: Optimization Algorithms and Applications", *Financial Engineering News*, February, pp. 1–5.

Whitmore, G. A., 1970, "Third Degree Stochastic Dominance", *American Economic Review* **60**, pp. 457–9.

Yitzhaki, S., 1982, "Stochastic Dominance, Mean-Variance and Gini's Mean Difference", *American Economic Review* **72**, March, pp. 178–85.

Yitzhaki, S., 1983, "On an Extension of the Gini Inequality Index", *International Economic Review* **24**, pp. 617–28.

3

An Empirical Investigation of the Rank Correlation Between Different Risk Measures

Andreas Pfingsten, Peter Wagner, Carsten Wolferink*

Institut für Kreditwesen

1 INTRODUCTION

One of the main problems in risk management is the quantification of risk. For this purpose several different risk measures have been developed. In financial analysis, for example, value-at-risk (VaR), which measures the loss that is only exceeded with a given probability (1%, say) over a certain time period (eg, one day), plays a key role in practical applications (cf. Jorion (2001)). Alas, the index has not found unanimous backing in academia. Artzner *et al* (1999) and Basak and Shapiro (2001) are among those who have contributed to a critical appraisal of VaR. These and other authors have also

*We are indebted to Paul Hagan, Robert Demon, and Jürgen W. Bauer (HSBC Trinkaus & Burkhardt, Düsseldorf) for the data and a stimulating discussion. Frank Altrock, Rolf Böve, Burkhardt Döge, Dan Gordon, Jose A. Lopez, Diderik Lund, Ulrich Müller-Funk and Dirk Thiel contributed further helpful suggestions. We also thank participants, and particularly discussants, at the European Meetings of the Econometric Society (Lausanne and Venice), the wi/if 2001 (Augsburg), the Annual Conference of the German Society of Operations Research (Duisburg), the Annual Meeting of Verband der Hochschullehrer für Betriebswirtschaft e.V. (Munich), the European Finance Association (Berlin), the German Finance Association (Cologne), the Midwestern Finance Association (St Louis) and the Eastern Finance Association (Lake Buena Vista) for helpful comments on earlier versions of the paper. The German Research Foundation (DFG) provided financial support for the latter trips. Above all, Phillippe Jorian as the editor and an anonymous referee provided most valuable suggestions. The responsibility for all shortcomings rests with us.

discussed alternative traditional risk measures which were thought to be superior for one reason or another.

It certainly is an intellectually demanding and important issue to narrow down the set of reasonable risk measures by convincing theoretical arguments. But this is not what we have in mind here. We are basically starting from the practitioner's question, although not leaving theory behind: does it really matter which index one chooses?

Apart from theoretical arguments, this calls for an empirical analysis, and that is exactly what this chapter is about. The key idea is to compare the rankings provided by different risk measures for the profit-and-loss distribution of an actual trading portfolio. If, using Spearman's rank correlation coefficient, all measures are found to be highly correlated, the choice of a particular method should not be very important. One has to admit, of course, that ranking is just one selection criterion. In some applications, such as capital allocation, the size of the risk measure is crucial. In most applications, however, the purpose of risk measures is to provide a consistent, firm-wide index that is comparable across assets and trading portfolios. Thus, ranking is central to most risk measurement systems.

Our analysis incorporates symmetric as well as pure downside risk measures. While the former evaluate the whole profit-and-loss distribution and generally consider deviations from the mean in either direction, the latter focus on a bottom part of the distribution (which need not be defined with reference to the mean). The chosen sets of indices are more or less based on Kaplanski and Kroll (2002) but are not grouped together in an identical way.

Our empirical analysis rests on the complete 1999 data for two proprietary trading books. Therefore we are justified in claiming that we are not performing an artificial analysis with self-generated data, but obviously we have to admit the limited generality of our findings to date: we are only covering one year and both books contain only interest rate-based instruments. The setup, however, is realistic for the purpose at hand. We know, for example, that there should not be any difference between the rankings given by VaR and the standard deviation if the profit-and-loss distribution is exactly normal. The distribution of interest rates, however, is highly non-normal. In addition, one portfolio contains many options that will create interesting asymmetries in the distribution.

The somewhat related analysis of Wu and Xiao (2002), who also examine and compare downside risk measures, differs from ours in a number of aspects. First, they also include stocks (S&P 500) in their data. Second, they cover a much longer time period (more than 30 years). Third, while they use this data as the basis for their own Monte Carlo simulations, we take the outcome of a bank's Monte Carlo model as our starting point. Fourth, while Wu and Xiao (2002) focus on the dynamics and appropriateness of various left-tail measures as tools for portfolio management, controlling the underlying stochastic process, we concentrate on the differences in risk rankings produced by such measures when applied to Monte Carlo data without any knowledge about the data-generating process. This latter aspect seems to be particularly interesting from a regulator's point of view.

Apart from this introduction, the chapter is divided into three sections. In Section 2 the risk measures that we examine are presented. In Section 3 we perform our empirical analysis. We describe the data, present two normality tests as well as a rank correlation analysis and investigate the robustness of our key findings. It turns out that the rankings generated by various downside risk measures, including VaR and related measures, do not in general differ much. Therefore, moving to coherent measures of risk, for example, would not have dramatic consequences. Section 4 summarises these and other main results of the chapter and concludes.

2 RISK MEASURES

In the following subsections we present two different groups of risk measures. In Subsection 2.1 we describe what we call symmetric risk measures and in Subsection 2.2 we consider downside risk measures.

Throughout the chapter we will examine situations of the following type: an actual trading book will change its value from one day to the other. There are n possible future states of nature, each yielding a change in value x_i ($i = 1, ..., n$). For simplicity, we assume that these changes are increasingly ordered $x_1 \leq x_2 \leq ... \leq x_n$. All states of nature have the same probability $1/n$, but the same change may occur in more than one state. The mean of the possible changes in value from one particular day to the next is defined as

$$\bar{x} = \frac{1}{n} \sum_{i=1}^{n} x_i \qquad (1)$$

We will analyze the data for one year, but will not distinguish the days by superscripts in order to keep the notation as simple as possible. Whenever necessary we will denote the absolute minimum by x_a, ie, x_a is the smallest of the values x_1 of all days.

2.1 Symmetric risk measures

The main feature of all symmetric risk measures is that they evaluate shortfalls (often characterised as risk in a narrow sense) as well as excess returns (normally interpreted as chance). Decision-makers in the investment context, however, may also associate risk with the failure to reach a target return. From this point of view the use of symmetric risk measures is frequently rejected.

The most famous symmetric risk measure is the *standard deviation*, σ. This measure is widely used in economic theory. But it is also often criticised in the economic literature for its shortcomings (cf. for example Markowitz (1959), Mao (1970a, b), and many others).[1] Given our notation, the standard deviation[2] is defined as

$$\sigma = \sqrt{\frac{1}{n}\sum_{i=1}^{n}(x_i - \bar{x})^2} \tag{2}$$

The second symmetric risk measure we analyse is the *Gini index*. Originally, it was suggested as a measure of the degree of inequality of an income distribution. However, there is an established literature stating that inequality measures can also be used as reasonable (symmetric) risk measures (cf. Nermuth (1993) for a survey).[3] Since the Gini index is only defined for non-negative variables whereas our daily value changes may also be negative, we decided to shift all daily distributions by the absolute minimum of the respective trading book, $-x_a$, to make the Gini index applicable. Given our notation, the Gini index can then be defined as

$$G = \frac{2\sum_{i=1}^{n} i \cdot (x_i - x_a) - (n+1)\sum_{i=1}^{n}(x_i - x_a)}{n\sum_{i=1}^{n}(x_i - x_a)} \tag{3}$$

The last measure we investigate is the *Baumol measure* (cf. Baumol (1963)). It is defined as the mean minus b times the standard deviation. The parameter b is a positive number and describes the subjective level of risk-aversion. A high level of risk-aversion means a large b and vice versa. Given our notation, the Baumol measure is defined as

$$B = \bar{x} - b \cdot \sigma \tag{4}$$

In our empirical analysis the Baumol measure is calculated with $b = 0.5$, $b = 2$, and $b = 5$, respectively. The reader should note that the Baumol measure is somewhat odd in this study because it is not purely a risk measure since it also takes the mean into account. We see it as a symmetric risk measure due to its reference to the standard deviation, whereas Kaplanski and Kroll (2002) classify it as a downside risk measure.[4] Finally, smaller (and in particular more negative) values of B mean higher risk, whereas the values of all other risk measures we apply increase with risk.

2.2 Downside risk measures

Downside risk measures take only the lower part of a distribution into account. This downside part of a distribution does not have to be identical to the outcomes below the mean. Instead, some target z will be defined which separates shortfalls from the rest. In our analysis we always assume that $z = 0$. To simplify notation, we introduce q for the number of shortfall events, ie, $q = \max\{i \,|\, x_i < z\}$. We will always assume that $x_1 < z$, which later will indeed be satisfied by our data.

2.2.1 Lower partial moments

Lower partial moments (LPM) are a special group of downside risk measures. They are specific cases of the Fishburn (1977) $\alpha - t$-model. In the discrete case and given our notation they can be written as

$$LPM_t = \frac{1}{n} \sum_{i=1}^{q} (z - x_i)^t \tag{5}$$

In our investigation we analyse LPM_0, LPM_1 and LPM_2. The LPM_0 measure, which was first used by Roy (1952), is the percentage of outcomes below the reference point z. The size of the loss is ignored (cf. Fishburn (1977) and Bawa (1978)).

Domar and Musgrave (1944) introduced the LPM_1. This measure simply averages over all differences between the target z and the outcomes below. Therefore it is similar to the expected absolute deviation risk measure and to the AVaR (see below). The LPM_2 measure is comparable to the standard deviation. For $z = \bar{x}$, the LPM_2 measure is equivalent to the semivariance (cf. Markowitz (1959)).

2.2.2 Value-at-risk

VaR measures the shortfall from the target z that is not exceeded with a given probability over a certain time period.[5] To define it formally, let α be a fixed number, called confidence level, with $0 < \alpha < 1$ ($\alpha = 0.99$ or $\alpha = 0.95$, say) and z a real number (eg, zero) as a reference point for measuring losses. For our purposes the VaR relating to α is then defined as[6]

$$VaR_z 1 - \alpha = \max\{0,\ z - x_k\} \qquad (6)$$

where k is the smallest integer greater than $(1 - \alpha) \cdot n$. As it is expressed in money units, VaR is easy to interpret and to communicate, in particular to the senior management level, and seemingly it can be compared across business units. From this point of view it should not be surprising how popular this measure is in practice. However, VaR is not subadditive, ie, the total VaR may even exceed the sum of individual VARs (cf. Artzner et al (1999), p. 216).[7] Thus the sum is not even an upper bound. From the theoretical point of view one should also note that VaR only takes one single point of the distribution function into account. This feature is very unsatisfactory and has been criticised in previous chapters.[8]

Therefore Embrechts, Klüppelberg and Mikosch (1997), Artzner et al (1999), Basak and Shapiro (2001) and others discuss the accumulated VaR (AVaR). This is also known as the conditional VaR (CVaR), or expected shortfall.[9] The AVaR averages all VARs with confidence levels from α to 1. It can therefore be viewed as the expected loss relative to the chosen reference point within a constant range of probabilities 0 to $1 - \alpha$.

With a confidence level α and a target z, AVaR can be defined as

$$AVaR1 - \alpha = \frac{1}{q}\sum_{i=1}^{q}(z - x_i) \qquad (7)$$

It is possible to modify the AVaR to obtain the accumulated AVaR. Analogous to the AVaR, the AAVaR summarises the profile of the distribution below the VaR. This measure assesses larger shortfalls more than shortfalls that are closer to the target. Define the AAVaR with confidence interval α in the discrete case as

$$AAVaR1 - \alpha = \frac{1}{q} \sum_{i=1}^{q} \frac{1}{i} \sum_{j=1}^{i} (z - x_j) \qquad (8)$$

In our analysis we calculate the VaR, the AVaR and the AAVaR with $\alpha = 0.99$ and $\alpha = 0.95$. The reference point for all measures is $z = 0$.

3 EMPIRICAL ANALYSIS

3.1 Data set

Our data were obtained from a bank which is an active participant in international investment banking. For two different trading books, referred to as the "government bond options book" and the "interest rate derivatives book", every business day of the year 1999 is covered. The data we analyse are profit-and-loss distributions for both trading books on a daily basis, generated by an internal model of the bank that is used in risk management as well as for regulatory purposes. The basis for this model is a Monte Carlo simulation.[10]

The internal model starts with 1,000 possible changes of the trading book from one business day to the next. The number of simulations is extended during the year through 1,250, 1,500 and 2,000 up to 2,500 to improve the results given by the internal model.[11] We excluded four (seven) days from further analysis for the interest rate derivatives book (government bond options book) because the bank's computations failed on these days.

Our data set is limited. It contains only the changes of the values of the trading books but not the values as such. Hence only absolute and not relative changes can be analysed. It is necessary to identify the minima over all simulations of both trading books to shift the distributions so that the Gini index can be used as a risk measure (cf. Subsection 2.1). Rounded to the next lowest integer, the minimum of the interest rate derivatives book (government bond options book), taken over all days in the sample, is $x_a^i = -1,855,364€$ ($x_a^g = -415,231€$).

A few statistical characteristics are provided in Table 1 to give a better understanding of our data. We describe the mean, $\bar{x}$, median, x_{Me}, skewness, Sk, and kurtosis, K. The values for Sk and the ranges for K give a first vague indication that the daily distributions are not normal because this would require that $Sk = 0$ and $K = 3$ (cf. Gujarati (2003), p. 148). In particular, the values for K hint at the commonly claimed fat tails of these distributions.

Table 1 Comparison of essential statistical parameters of the two trading books: lowest, x_1, and highest, x_n, simulated changes in value, mean, $\bar{x}$, median, x_{Me}, standard deviation, σ, skewness, Sk, and kurtosis, K

	<0	=0	>0	Minimum	Maximum
Interest rate derivatives book					
x_1	249	0	0	−1,855,363.20	−51,447.15
x_n	0	0	249	143,386.06	2,905,459.57
$\bar{x}$	47	0	202	−30,524.58	185,792.03
x_{Me}	45	4	200	−29,042.03	65,885.11
σ	−	−	249	48,046.43	505,443.97
Sk	66	0	183	−0.7658	2.1578
$K-3$	18	0	231	−0.4380	10.1794
Government bond options book					
x_1	246	0	0	−415,230.73	−7,759.09
x_n	0	0	246	60,630.88	2,013,522.65
$\bar{x}$	0	0	246	3,333.73	177,267.24
x_{Me}	2	0	244	−147.95	70,095.06
σ	−	−	246	7,251.79	277,857.37
Sk	0	0	246	0.1012	6.9805
$K-3$	2	0	244	−0.8687	75.2332

The table describes the distribution of profits and losses over 249 (246) trading days for the interest rate derivatives (government bond options) book. When relevant, entries are sorted by sign. For instance, the first line reports the minimum and maximum over the 249 days of the worst loss ($x_1 < 0$), where for each day between 1,000 and 2,500 simulations were run.

An important question concerning the profit-and-loss distributions is whether they are normally distributed or not. If in particular the data follow a standard normal distribution, then the standard deviation and the VaR will provide the same ordering.[12] We apply two statistical tests for normality: the Kolmogorov–Smirnov (KS) test and the Jarque–Bera (JB) test.[13] For both tests we use a significance level of $\alpha = 0.01$. Table 2 summarises the results of both tests.

Since the (non-parametric) Kolmogorov–Smirnov test is often characterised as a conservative test, it is not surprising that it recognises fewer days where the null hypothesis has to be rejected than the Jarque–Bera test. It is obvious from Table 2 that, according to both tests, more days in the interest rate derivatives book appear to have normally distributed profits and losses than in the government bond options book. A tentative explanation is that the government bond options book does indeed contain more options.

Table 2 Results of the Kolmogorov–Smirnov and Jarque–Bera tests for normality of both trading books at the 1% level of significance

Total number of days	Number of days where assumption of normal distribution had to be rejected			
	In both tests	Only in KS test	Only in JB test	In none of the tests
Interest rate derivatives book				
249	92	0	94	63
Government bond options book				
246	240	0	5	1

Their values are non-linear in the value of the underlying and, therefore, provided that they do not compensate each other, tend to yield asymmetric profit-and-loss distributions (cf. *Sk* in Table 1). We will now check whether this result has an impact on the rankings of days generated by different risk measures.

3.2 Rank correlation analysis

3.2.1 Basic results

We calculate the values of five symmetric risk measures (standard deviation, Gini index, $B_{b=0.5}$, $B_{b=2}$ and $B_{b=5}$) and of nine downside risk measures (LPM_0, LPM_1, LPM_2, $VaR1\%$, $VaR5\%$, $AVaR1\%$, $AVaR5\%$, $AAVaR1\%$ and $AAVaR5\%$) for 1999 on a day-by-day basis.

Figure 1 shows, as an example for the interest rate derivatives book, the time series of $VaR1\%$ and $VaR5\%$. It appears that both curves are somewhat parallel, indicating a fair amount of correlation. As was to be expected, $VaR1\%$ looks more volatile than $VaR5\%$ and this is confirmed by the numbers ($\sigma_{VaR1\%} = 164{,}301.84€$ and $\sigma_{VaR5\%} = 119{,}970.86€$). For the government bond options book a similar picture arises (with $\sigma_{VaR1\%} = 39{,}902.71€$ and $\sigma_{VaR5\%} = 30{,}811.26€$; cf. Figure 2).

Our calculations show that an often criticised feature of VaR – namely a reranking of days due to different confidence levels – does indeed occur for real-world data. For the interest rate derivatives book for example, according to $VaR1\%$, 29 September (215,909.61€) is less risky than 30 September (218,289.21€), which is itself indicated to be less risky than 28 September (218,717.85€). $VaR5\%$ shows a different picture, however: 28 September (143,668.29€) is the least

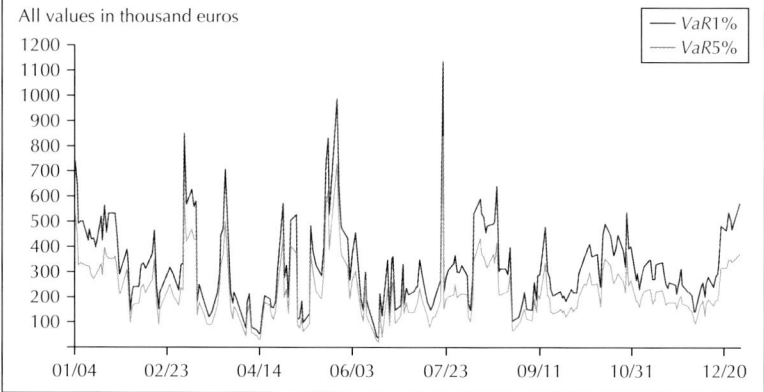

Figure 1 *VaR*1% and *VaR*5% during 1999 for the interest rate derivatives book

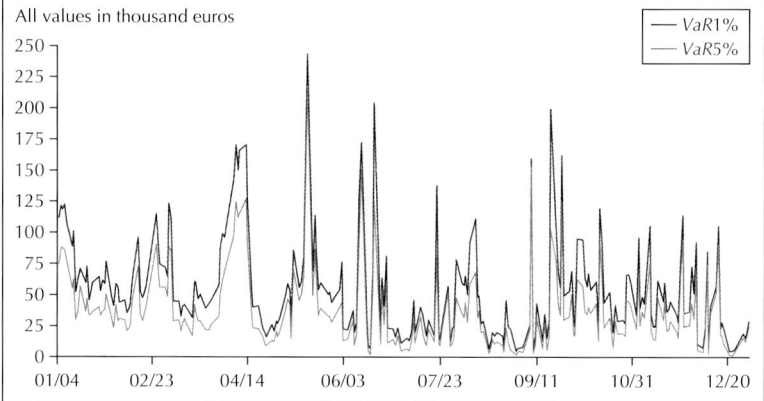

Figure 2 *VaR*1% and *VaR*5% during 1999 for the government bond options book

risky day of the three and 29 September (155,646.33€) is less risky than 30 September (156,034.31€).

On account of this interesting observation it makes sense as the next step to investigate and compare the intensity of the differences in the rankings generated by the different risk measures. We therefore sort, for each trading book, the business days of 1999 according to their risk corresponding to each risk measure. We obtain, for each trading book, a ranking of days for every risk measure, ie, the business days of 1999 are sorted according to their risk as indicated by every risk measure. We observe that each risk measure delivers a somewhat different ranking of the days according to their riskiness.

To evaluate the similarity in the risk rankings generated by the indices, we apply Spearman's rank correlation coefficient.[14] Unlike traditional correlation, it is invariant with respect to all strictly increasing transformations of the measures and not just linear transformations. Table 3 presents the rank correlation coefficients of the risk measures for the interest rate derivatives book (above the diagonal) and for the government bond options book (below the diagonal). Remember that the Baumol measure orders the days inversely because high values mean low risks.

Since most of the rank correlation coefficients in Table 3 are quite different from zero, we use a one-sided t-test to test the significance of a positive relationship between two indices. As a short cut we calculate the critical rank correlation coefficient at the 1% level, which is 0.1464 for the interest rate derivatives book and 0.1482 for the government bond options book.[15] Using this test statistic, we can reject the null hypothesis of no positive rank correlation for the interest rate derivatives book completely. There is a significant rank correlation between all indices for this trading book because every rank correlation coefficient exceeds the critical value. For the government bond options book, there are only a few exceptions. Except for one case (standard deviation and LPM_0) they involve only symmetric risk measures. The large number of high (absolute) values of pairwise rank correlation coefficients suggests that a test should be made for perfect rank correlation. Such a test, unfortunately, would be degenerate because values less than 1 imply directly that the rank correlation cannot be perfect.

The results above and below the diagonal in Table 3 seem to be fairly similar. It is clear that the differences between the distributions for the two trading books pointed out in Section 3 appear to have little impact on the rank correlation coefficients. For some qualifications to this statement and a more detailed interpretation of our results, see the following remarks.

3.2.2 Interpretation

Starting with an interpretation of the Baumol measure, we observe that the absolute value of the rank correlation[16] with the standard deviation increases as b increases from 0.5 to 5. This is exactly in

Table 3 Rank correlation coefficients of the risk measures for the interest rate derivatives book (above the diagonal) and for the government bond options book (below the diagonal)

	$B_{0.5}$	B_2	B_5	σ	G	LPM_0	LPM_1
$B_{0.5}$		0.80123	0.71440	−0.65057	−0.71487	−0.76731	−0.97030
B_2	0.06180		0.98874	−0.97036	−0.98674	−0.40992	−0.90592
B_5	−0.07101	0.98673		−0.99490	−0.99816	−0.29543	−0.84132
σ	0.13154	−0.97334	−0.99719		0.99394	0.21499	0.79090
G	0.04498	−0.98399	−0.99136	0.98678		0.28026	0.84498
LPM_0	−0.91919	−0.22006	−0.08973	0.02974	0.12158		0.65318
LPM_1	−0.79237	−0.41905	−0.30318	0.24861	0.36301	0.86869	
LPM_2	−0.72905	−0.43727	−0.32919	0.27821	0.39588	0.79477	0.98777
$VaR1\%$	−0.63278	−0.42191	−0.32618	0.28086	0.39925	0.68051	0.93743
$VaR5\%$	−0.69965	−0.44432	−0.33991	0.29063	0.40889	0.76158	0.97741
$AVaR1\%$	−0.61765	−0.39876	−0.30503	0.26078	0.37899	0.65801	0.91776
$AVaR5\%$	−0.66043	−0.42957	−0.33010	0.28323	0.40207	0.71144	0.95458
$AAVaR1\%$	−0.60606	−0.38759	−0.29537	0.25192	0.36918	0.64333	0.90329
$AAVaR5\%$	−0.63410	−0.41292	−0.31701	0.27178	0.39038	0.67828	0.93249

line with our discussion of the properties of the Baumol measure, which approaches a negative multiple of the standard deviation as b increases. The same ordering of rank correlation is obtained with the Gini index. For all of the downside risk measures, however, the absolute value of the rank correlation with the Baumol measures decreases with b. This clearly indicates a systematic difference between the Baumol measure and the downside risk measures. All these observations hold for both trading books in the same way.

Given our primary interest in downside risk measures, we note only a few specific (absolute) values of the rank correlation coefficient with the Baumol measure $B_{0.5}$. For the interest rate derivatives book, all values are above 0.93 except for LPM_0 (0.76731). For the government bond options book, the values are much smaller, ranging between 0.6 and 0.8, except for LPM_0 (0.91919). We attribute the differences between the interest rate derivatives and the government bond options books, respectively, to the symmetry of the profit-and-loss distributions. Symmetry is a worse description for the latter than for the former trading book, so it should not be surprising that the symmetric Baumol measure $B_{0.5}$ is in greater disagreement with the downside risk measures for the latter. This is also true for B_2 and B_5, for which not even LPM_0 yields an exception.

LPM_2	VaR1%	VaR5%	AVaR1%	AVaR5%	AAVaR1%	AAVaR5%
−0.95483	−0.93820	−0.94235	−0.93561	−0.94058	−0.93230	−0.93885
−0.91228	−0.87699	−0.91263	−0.86073	−0.89278	−0.84603	−0.87238
−0.85346	−0.81763	−0.85717	−0.79980	−0.83516	−0.78358	−0.81213
0.80662	0.77094	0.81262	0.75166	0.78924	0.73441	0.76445
0.85970	0.82658	0.86487	0.80827	0.84358	0.79151	0.82052
0.59509	0.55562	0.56339	0.55600	0.55607	0.55835	0.55791
0.99462	0.97421	0.98789	0.96586	0.98090	0.95782	0.97250
	0.98849	0.99758	0.98181	0.99397	0.97423	0.98725
0.97732		0.99024	0.99628	0.99763	0.99071	0.99781
0.99632	0.98426		0.98323	0.99606	0.97531	0.98876
0.96343	0.99518	0.97032		0.99423	0.99780	0.99895
0.98752	0.99727	0.99302	0.98992		0.98842	0.99737
0.95190	0.98806	0.95841	0.99776	0.98143		0.99594
0.97411	0.99789	0.98043	0.99833	0.99562	0.99421	

Standard deviation and the Gini index are the other symmetric risk measures in our study. Therefore it is not surprising that, disregarding LPM_0, the rank correlation with the downside risk measures is again higher for the interest rate derivatives book (between 0.73 and 0.87) than for the government bond options book (between 0.24 and 0.30).[17] The values are always smaller for the standard deviation than for the Gini index. The rank correlations between standard deviation and the Gini index are themselves quite high (about 0.99). Even if one had expected a high rank correlation, one would probably not have thought that it would turn out to be so high.

Turning now to lower partial moments, we first want to point out how the special role of LPM_0 as a distribution-insensitive measure affects the outcomes. Since LPM_0 basically counts only the shortfall events, no special pattern or order of magnitude is to be expected. It turns out that the rank correlation of LPM_0 with the other downside risk measures is, pairwise, higher for the government book options book (between 0.64 and 0.87) than for the interest rate derivatives book (between 0.55 and 0.66). It could be the case that the higher kurtosis in the former book allows the downside risk to be better represented by LPM_0. But this is still an open issue.

For all of the lower partial moments, and for both trading books, it is true that their rank correlation with the VaR measures is higher at the 5% level than at the 1% level. This confirms, on the one hand, what practitioners appear to feel. On the other hand, it is theoretically plausible because calculations "in the tails" are usually somewhat more volatile (cf. Figure 1). This could be due to estimation error as there are only between $1\% \times 1{,}000 = 10$ and $1\% \times 2{,}500 = 25$ observations in the left tail.

Comparing the rank correlations for the two trading books, LPM_1 and LPM_2 exhibit behaviour which is opposite to that of LPM_0 because the values of the rank correlation coefficient with the VaR measures for the interest rate derivatives book are higher (0.95782–0.98789 for LPM_1 and 0.97423–0.99758 for LPM_2) than for the government bond options book (0.90329–0.97741 for LPM_1 and 0.95190–0.99632 for LPM_2).

Comparing the lower partial moments with each other in respect of their rank correlations with the other downside risk measures, a very interesting property emerges: for both trading books, the rank correlation of the other downside risk measures with LPM_2 is always higher than with LPM_1, which in turn is higher than with LPM_0. Hence, one can argue that of all lower partial moments LPM_2 is the best representation of the other downside risk measures. Among the lower partial moments themselves, the rank correlation is greater than 0.98 between LPM_1 and LPM_2 but only between 0.59 and 0.87 between the LPM_0 and the two other lower partial moments.

Finally, we look at the rank correlations among the VaR, the AVaR and the AAVaR measures. They are all very high, the minimum of the 30 rank correlations being 0.95841 (*AAVaR1%* and *VaR5%* for the government bond options book) and 27 values being above 0.98. Pairwise comparisons between the two trading books yield, in 14 out of 15 cases, the result that the rank correlation is higher for the interest rate derivatives book, the exceptions being *AAVaR5%* and *VaR1%*.

We have mentioned above that *VaR5%* more closely resembles the rankings generated by the lower partial moments than by *VaR1%*. With respect to the AVaR and AAVaR, again for both trading books, the exact opposite is true. In all of these cases, the rank correlation with *VaR1%* is higher than with *VaR5%*.

Comparing the two AVaR measures, we obtain that for both trading books $AVaR5\%$ has a higher rank correlation with the two VaR measures than $AVaR1\%$. The opposite holds for the rank correlation with the AAVaR measures. Furthermore, for both trading books $AAVaR5\%$ has a higher rank correlation with the AVaR measures than $AAVaR1\%$.

We can draw a number of conclusions. First, the use of coherent risk measures (AVaR and AAVaR) as advocated by, for example, Artzner *et al* (1999) does not have a particularly strong effect on the ranking of the risky distributions we have examined here. Second, although $VaR5\%$ better resembles symmetric risk measures and lower partial moments than $VaR1\%$, the opposite holds for the proximity to the coherent risk measures.

With respect to the first observation, two opposite conclusions could be drawn. On the one hand, one might be happy to continue to use the now well-established VaR because a switch to some other risk measure does not seem to change much – at least, ranking-wise. On the other hand, one might feel encouraged to switch to better-founded risk measures, ie, in particular to one of the coherent risk measures AVaR or AAVaR, because one does not need to fear dramatic consequences (ranking-wise) as an unpleasant by-product of such a change. In light of the present analysis, we see no obvious justification for rejecting either of the two conclusions.

Intuitively, even high rank correlation coefficients would not be a sufficient reason to argue that the choice of index is not too important if the differences in rankings occurred mainly in the relevant range of high risk. Fortunately, Figures 3 and 4 demonstrate that relatively little reranking occurs there. The pairs of indices in these figures have been chosen because they yield the highest and lowest, respectively, rank correlation coefficients obtained within the group of LPM (excluding LPM_0), VaR, AVaR and AAVaR measures.

3.2.3 Robustness

The rank correlations observed are generally quite high. A natural question is whether or not this is an artifact of our specific data or whether it may hold in other cases too. Given our interpretations above, we exclude the less appropriate indices and limit our robustness checks to LPM_1, LPM_2 and the two VaR, AVaR and AAVaR measures. This leaves us with 28 rank correlations to be examined.

Figure 3 Risk rankings by *AAVaR5%* and *AVaR1%* for the interest rate derivatives book

Rank correlation 0.99895

· Perfect correlation

Rank according to *AVaR1%* (y-axis, 0 to 250)

Rank according to *AAVaR5%* (x-axis, 0 to 250)

Figure 4 Risk rankings by *AAVaR1%* and LPM_1 for the government bond options book

Rank correlation 0.90329

· Perfect rank correlation

Rank according to LPM_1 (y-axis, 0 to 250)

Rank according to *AAVaR1%* (x-axis, 0 to 250)

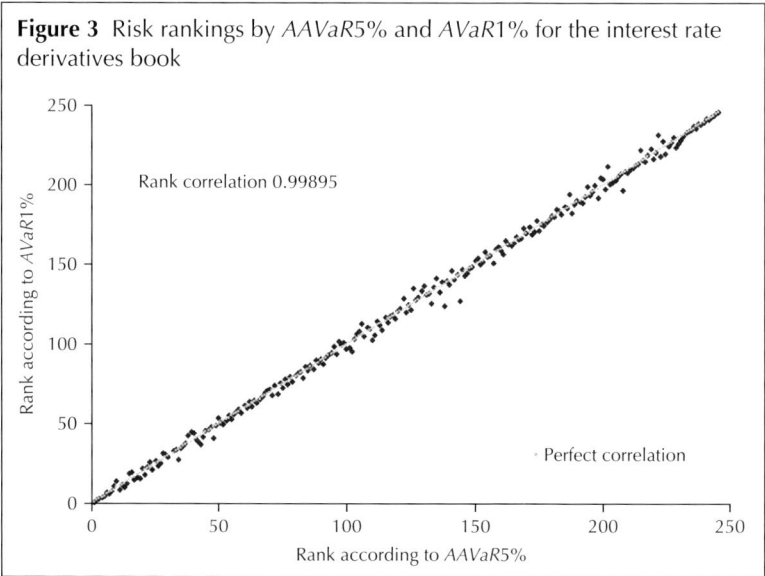

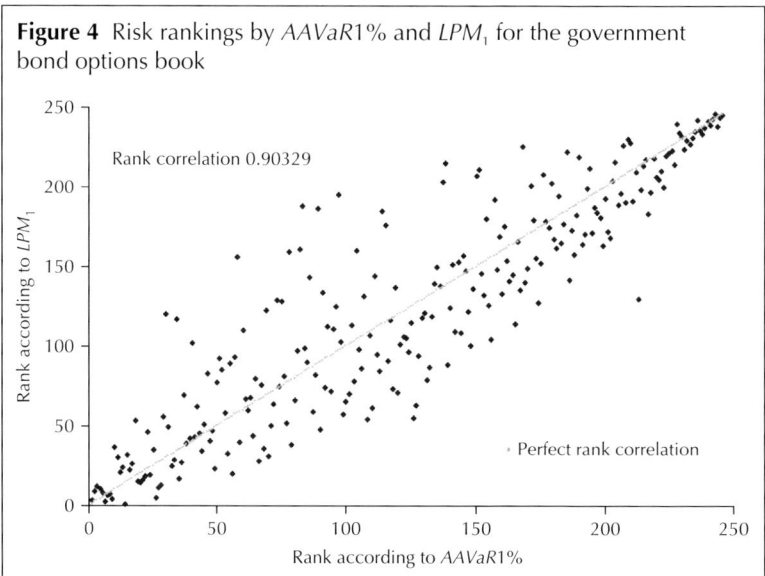

When looking at our data and results in some detail, we realised that the risk measures diagnosed pretty similar days as the most risky ones and that this also turned out to be true for the least risky days (cf. Figures 3 and 4). In order to test the robustness of the high

Table 4 Reductions in rank correlations due to eliminations of days

Days eliminated	Interest rate derivatives book	Government bond options book
Most risky	0.0000128–0.0005122	0.0000181–0.0011743
Four most risky	0.0000523–0.0020996	0.0000758–0.0047236
Least risky	0.0000128–0.0005123	0.0000205–0.0011841
Four least risky	0.0000523–0.0020990	0.0000834–0.0048616
Four most risky and four least risky	0.0001082–0.0043403	0.0001644–0.0099100

rank correlations formally, we wanted to find out how much this effect might drive the results. Therefore we eliminated up to eight days from our sample, different ones for each trading book: four days were those that appeared most frequently among the most risky days and four days that were most frequently among the least risky days when considering the LPM_1, LPM_2, and the two VaR, AVaR and AAVaR measures.

Since those days were chosen precisely because their rank was very similar for the risk measures considered, it could be expected that the rank correlation coefficients would decrease. Indeed, it turned out that eliminating the most risky day reduced all 28 rank correlations. When the second most risky day was eliminated as well, a further decrease in rank correlations was observed in all 28 cases. And the same is true for the additional elimination of the third and fourth most risky days, respectively.

Since this picture is so clear qualitatively, a few numbers may suffice to illustrate its quantitative importance (see Table 4). In a nutshell, we can say that eliminating a few days on both sides of the risk ranking reduces the rank correlations, as was expected, because the risk measures analysed basically agree on the positioning of these days. However, even when eight days are eliminated, ie, about 3%, this reduction does not exceed 0.01. Or, in absolute terms, even then the rank correlation is in all cases still greater than 0.89.

Let us now turn to a second issue. Suppose that two risk measures deliver values in €. Let these measures be such that a scaling of the distributions (and, where appropriate, the target) with some factor $\delta > 1$ increases the values of these risk measures.[18] Then the ordering of days according to their risk may be determined mainly by portfolio size, and therefore a high rank correlation would not come as a surprise. Since we do not have much information about the sizes of the daily portfolios but get the impression from Table 1 that there probably is a certain amount of variation, we have tried to come up with a check on how important such an effect may be.

We changed the scales of the original profit-and-loss distributions (leaving the target at 0) of both trading books in the following way: for each business day, t, we drew a number ϵ_t from a uniform distribution on $[0; 1]$. By means of

$$\gamma_t = 9.9 \cdot \epsilon_t + 0.1 \tag{9}$$

this was transformed into a scaling factor $\gamma_t \in [0.1; 10]$. Each entry of the profit-and-loss distribution of day t was then multiplied by γ_t, where extensions of the size of profit-and-loss distributions ($\gamma_t > 1$) are ten times as likely as compressions ($\gamma_t < 1$) because $\gamma_t = 1$ implies $\epsilon_t = 1/11$. With the modified profit-and-loss distributions we repeated our rank correlation analysis described in Subsection 3.2.1. We did the random selection for each trading book five times, though clearly not aiming at a more complete simulation study. The general picture is that in none of the cases we observe dramatic change. Therefore we report the results below jointly with two alternative manipulations of our daily profit-and-loss distributions.

Because of Equation (9), the probability of stretching the initial profit-and-loss distribution was ten times the probability for a compression of the distribution. In a second set of experiments, the draws, ϵ_t, from a uniform distribution on $[0; 1]$ were transformed into scaling factors according to

$$\eta_t = \begin{cases} \dfrac{2}{3} \cdot \epsilon_t + \dfrac{2}{3} & 0 \leq \epsilon_t \leq 0.5 \\ \epsilon_t + 0.5 & 0 \leq \epsilon_t \leq 0.5 \end{cases} \tag{10}$$

With this scaling, stretching ($\eta_t > 1$) and compression ($\eta_t < 1$) of the probability distribution are now equally likely. The interval for the scaling factor is $[2/3; 1.5]$. Again we defer a detailed interpretation because the outcome is very similar, qualitatively, to the previous case.[19]

Scaling the daily profit-and-loss distributions according to Equation (10) implies equal probabilities of stretching and compression but asymmetry in the absolute sizes of changes (with an increase of the mean). Our final variation is

$$\theta_t = \epsilon_t \tag{11}$$

This yields an expected decrease in size by 50%. With respect to the new mean, stretching and compression are equally likely and are symmetrically distributed.

We provide no tables comparable to Table 3 because for all 15 experiments (three scaling functions times five draws) and both trading books the numbers would be very similar to the original outcome when restricted to the downside risk measures LPM_1, LPM_2, VaR, AVaR and AAVaR. This is obvious from the collection of results displayed in Table 5.

Initially starting from rank correlations greater than 0.95 and 0.90 for the interest rate derivatives book and government bond options book, respectively, we see from Table 5 that the rank correlations do not change very much. Although the changes are generally a little more widespread for the government bond options book than for the interest rate derivatives book, the differences between methods (9) through (11) are not very large. In all, 0.02 is a number that represents the order of magnitude of the absolute changes.

What was surprising to us is the sign of the changes. For the interest rate derivatives book, except for a few cases with method (10) all of the 28 pairwise rank correlation coefficients increased, although already starting from high values, whereas for the government bond options book we observed cases where rank correlations decreased for all functions. The falls in value – which were, apart from method (10), smaller in absolute value than the increases – usually involved LPM_1, LPM_2, $VaR5\%$, and $AVaR5\%$.

While it is obvious that the upper limit being 1 implies that higher initial rank correlations could not increase as much, it is still not entirely clear why all the increases occur. For both trading books, the rank correlations between $AAVaR1\%$ and LPM_1 continued to be the smallest. And it is worth pointing out that exactly these cases were the ones in which, for the interest rate derivatives book (and almost for the government bond options book) the

Table 5 Changes in rank correlations due to scaling of the distributions

Scaling method	Interest rate derivatives book				Government bond options book			
	Minimal rank correlation change over index pairs		Average rank correlation change over index pairs		Minimal rank correlation change over index pairs		Average rank correlation change over index pairs	
	Min	Max	Min	Max	Min	Max	Min	Max
(9)	0.00053	0.01817	0.00061	0.02055	−0.00187	0.01419	0.00002	0.02246
(10)	−0.00212	0.00126	0.00014	0.00366	−0.02132	0.00106	−0.00832	0.00200
(11)	0.00058	0.01970	0.00064	0.02062	−0.00180	0.01107	−0.00033	0.02378

minimal and average rank correlation increased by the most for (9) and (11) but decreased by the most for (10).

4 SUMMARY AND OUTLOOK

Taking real-world data from two trading books, we have examined whether different risk measures deliver different rankings of the risk of profit-and-loss distributions. Spearman's rank correlation coefficient exhibits very high values for almost all index pairs of downside risk measures, but lower values when other measures – in particular symmetric risk measures – are involved. Generally, these observations hold for both trading books, one of which involves a large proportion of options.

Most measures agree on which days were the most, or least, risky. Eliminating these days from our sample reduced the relevant rank correlations, though not very much. The values were also not affected very much by random scaling, which was introduced to check for size effects. The scaling experiments even yielded an increase of the rank correlations in most cases.

Value-at-risk is widely applied and accepted in the financial business community but has been criticised by some academics. In light of our findings one can say that the use of some other downside risk measure would not change risk rankings much but that it may still yield differences as soon as more than just the ranking matters. Theoretically better-founded downside risk measures, on the other hand, may have better properties for other purposes.

---

1   Among other things, its use is not always compatible with expected utility maximisation. For example, one distribution may have a higher mean and a lower standard deviation than another but still have a lower expected utility.

2   Replacing the empirical standard deviation by its unbiased estimator, dividing by $(n-1)$ instead of n, would have little impact on our results.

3   Breitmeyer, Hakenes and Pfingsten (2004) develop a similar analogy between poverty measures and downside risk measures.

4   This is justified primarily if the distribution is normal. In this case losses, ie, negative changes in the portfolio value, that are only exceeded with a probability $(1-\alpha)$ can be expressed as $\bar{x}-b\cdot\sigma$ (cf. Jorion (2001), p. 112, Equation (5.8)). Coefficient b depends on the confidence level α only and will equal 1.65 (2.33) for $\alpha = 95\%$ (99%). Thus, the Baumol measure can be interpreted as a parametric VaR measure (see section 2.2), and therefore a downside risk measure, for normal distributions.

5   See Linsmeier and Pearson (1996) and Jorion (2001), p. 108. Application to credit risk management is illustrated in Crouhy, Galai and Mark (2000).

6 The measures are functions. However, to simplify the notation we refrain from repeating their arguments throughout, assuming that this will not cause ambiguities.

7 VaR is subadditive if applied to elliptical distributions.

8 Cf. Artzner *et al* (1999) and Guthoff, Pfingsten and Wolf (1997).

9 For a thorough analysis of expected shortfall and CVaR and further references see, for example, Bertsimas, Lauprete and Samarov (2001) and Rockafellar and Uryasev (2002).

10 In a true Monte Carlo analysis the parameter realisations (eg, interest rates) are drawn each day from updated distributions. The updating takes into account, for example, the actual term structure. Given the updated distributions, random draws might pick values that are biased more towards one side of a distribution on one day and more towards the other side on the next day. While the updating is done, the random draws are not quite that random (as far as the model was revealed to us) because it appears that some stability of the scenarios has been introduced to exclude odd outcomes generated by extraordinary draws. Needless to say, however, the drawn parameter realisations are eventually applied to the true positions held that day.

11 The difference in the number of daily simulations might, in principle, make sampling variability an important issue. However, for the moment we ignore this point, among others, since the empirical results presented below do not seem to suggest noticeable consequences.

12 The order would be the same because then $VaR1\% = 2.326 \cdot \sigma$ and $VaR5\% = 1.645 \cdot \sigma$. See, for example, Jorion (2001), p. 112.

13 See, for example, DeGroot and Schervish (2002), p. 568, for the former and Gujarati (2003), p. 148, for the latter.

14 For further details see Gujarati (2003), p. 406.

15 For the Baumol measures, the negatives of these values are relevant for confirmation of an inverse relationship.

16 We use the absolute value because, for the Baumol measure, unlike the other measures, smaller values mean more risk.

17 Grootveld and Hallerbach (1999) compare the variance with downside risk measures. In their empirical analysis of portfolio optimisation, they find, apart from differences in the resulting portfolio compositions, that downside risk measures are more exposed to sampling error. Only marked asymmetries in the distributions would generate visible discrepancies, however.

18 For example, LPM_2 and VaR have this property, whereas LPM_0 is scale-invariant.

19 We also tried other transformations of $\in_t$, implying $\eta_t \in [0.5; 2]$, $\eta_t \in [\frac{1}{3}; 3]$, and $\eta_t \in [0.1; 10]$. We present the results for $\eta_t \in [\frac{2}{3}; 1.5]$ because this yields the largest negative changes of the rank correlation coefficients.

This chapter was previously published in *The Journal of Risk* **6**(4), Summer 2004.

REFERENCES

Artzner, P., F. Delbaen, J.-M. Eber, and D. Heath, 1999, "Coherent Measures of Risk", *Mathematical Finance* **9**, pp. 203–28.

Basak, S. and A. Shapiro, 2001, "Value-at-risk-based Risk Management: Optimal Policies and Asset Prices", *Review of Financial Studies* **14**, pp. 371–405.

Baumol, W. J., 1963, "An Expected Gain Confidence Limit Criterion for Portfolio Selection", *Management Science* **10**, pp. 174–82.

Bawa, V. S., 1978, "Safety-first, Stochastic Dominance, and Optimal Portfolio Choice", *Journal of Financial and Quantitative Analysis* **13**, pp. 255–71.

Bertsimas, D., G. J. Lauprete, and A. Samarov, 2001, "Shortfall as a Risk Measure: Properties, Optimization and Applications", Technical Report, Massachusetts Institute of Technology, Mimeo.

Breitmeyer, C., H. Hakenes, and A. Pfingsten, 2004, "From Poverty Measurement to the Measurement of Downside Risk", *Mathematical Social Science* **47**, pp. 327–48.

Crouhy, M., D. Galai, and R. Mark, 2000, "A Comparative Analysis of Current Credit Risk Models", *Journal of Banking and Finance* **24**, pp. 59–117.

DeGroot, M. H. and M. J. Schervish, 2002, *Probability and Statistics*, Third edition. (Reading, Mass: Addison-Wesley).

Domar, E. D. and R. A. Musgrave, 1944, "Proportional Income Taxation and Risk-Taking", *Quarterly Journal of Economics* **58**, pp. 388–422.

Embrechts, P., C. Klüppelberg, and T. Mikosch, 1997, *Modelling Extremal Events for Insurance and Finance*, (Berlin: Springer).

Fishburn, P. C., 1977, "Mean-risk Analysis with Risk Associated with Below-Target Returns", *American Economic Review* **57**, pp. 116–26.

Grootveld, H. and W. Hallerbach, 1999, "Variance vs. Downside Risk; Is there Really that much Difference"? *European Journal of Operational Research* **114**, pp. 304–19.

Gujarati, D. N., 2003, *Basic Econometrics*, Fourth edition. (New York: McGraw-Hill).

Guthoff, A., A. Pfingsten, and J. Wolf, 1997, "Effects on risk taking resulting from limiting the value at risk or the lower partial moment one", in Institute of Actuaries of Australia (ed.), 7th International AFIR Colloquium Proceedings, pp. 355–78. (Sydney: Southwood Press).

Jorion, P., 2001, *Value At Risk: The New Benchmark for Managing Financial Risk*, Second edition. (New York: McGraw-Hill).

Kaplanski, G. and Y. Kroll, 2002, "VAR Risk Measures vs. Traditional Measures: An Analysis and Survey", *Journal of Risk* **4(3)**, pp. 1–27.

Linsmeier, T. J. and N. D. Pearson, 1996, "Risk Measurement: An Introduction to Value at Risk", Technical Report, Department of Accountancy and Department of Finance, University of Illinois, Urbana-Champaign.

Mao, J. C., 1970a, "Models of Capital Budgeting, E-V vs. E-S", *Journal of Financial and Quantitative Analysis* **4**, pp. 657–75.

Mao, J. C., 1970b, "Survey of Capital Budgeting: Theory and Practice", *Journal of Finance* **25**, pp. 349–60.

Markowitz, H. M., 1959, *Portfolio Selection*, (New York: JohnWiley & Sons).

Nermuth, M., 1993, "Different Economic Theories with the Same Formal Structure: Risk, Income Inequality, Information Structures, etc", in W. E. Diewert, K. Spremann and F. Stehling (eds), *Mathematical Modelling in Economics*, (Berlin: Springer), pp. 271–7.

Rockafellar, R. T. and S. Uryasev, 2002, "Conditional Value-at-Risk for General Loss Distributions"" *Journal of Banking and Finance* **26**, pp. 1443–71.

Roy, A. D., 1952, "Safety First and the Holding of Assets", *Econometrica* **20**, pp. 431–49.

Wu, G. and Z. Xiao, 2002, "An Analysis of Risk Measures", *Journal of Risk* **4(4)**, pp. 53–75.

4

Alternative Risk Measures for Alternative Investments

Ali Chabaane; Jean-Paul Laurent; Yannick Malevergne; Francoise Turpin*

ACA Consulting; IFSA Actuarial School, BNP Paribas;
IFSA Actuarial School, EM-Lyon Business School; BNP Paribas

1 INTRODUCTION

In spite of several deficiencies, the mean–variance analysis introduced by the pioneering work of Markowitz (1952) remains a popular tool in quantitative portfolio management. Many extensions of
the original setting have been proposed in order to broaden the
practical use of the method (eg, Black and Litterman (1992)) and
the main drawbacks of this approach, such as the uncertainty of the
estimation of the covariances and expected returns, have now been
assessed (Bouchaud and Potters (2000), Jorion (1985), Ledoit and
Wolf (2003)). Considering other risk measures and extending the
classical framework to take into account the skewness and kurtosis
of asset returns has also been discussed for some time (see
Kaplanski and Kroll (2002) for a survey). More recently, starting
with Artzner *et al* (1999), the theoretical properties of a series of risk
measures, such as value-at-risk (VaR), have been investigated.
Alexander and Baptista (2001) compared the use of VaR and variance as a tool for the computation of efficient frontiers. They

*A. Chabaane and F. Turpin were in the Financial Models team, ALM, at BNP Paribas
when this work was conducted. The authors acknowledge helpful discussions and
exchanges with participants at the third EIR conference in Geneva, at the workshop on
hedge funds at the University of Evry and at the 21st AFFI international conference in
Cergy-Pontoise. They thank E. Duclos for efficient computational assistance. They also
thank an anonymous referee for helpful comments. All remaining errors are theirs.

showed that, for a risk-adverse investor, the use of VaR can lead to the selection of portfolios with higher-variance returns than does mean–variance analysis. While VaR lacks the subadditivity property, some coherent alternatives, such as expected shortfall (or conditional VaR; see Pflug (2000), Acerbi, Nordio and Sirtori (2001), Acerbi and Tasche (2002a, 2002b), Rockafellar and Uryasev (2000, 2002)), the absolute deviation studied by Denneberg (2000), or the semivariance-based risk measure of Fischer (2003), have been proposed and new computational algorithms have been studied.

Here we want to evaluate the consequences of the choice of a risk measure for portfolio management, and we therefore compare mean–VaR, mean–expected shortfall and mean–semivariance efficient frontiers with a benchmark mean–variance frontier. Whenever returns are Gaussian, all mean risk efficient frontiers are equivalent. Typical investments that exhibit non-Gaussian features are hedge funds. Thus, we consider a database of such hedge funds where we might expect some significant differences regarding the chosen risk measure. We emphasise that our aim is only to compare the impact of the choice of a particular risk measure on the set of efficient portfolios. That is why, for simplicity of exposition, our analysis is conducted on an *ex post* basis. In this respect, the risk measures are computed on the basis of the sole historical series of each fund. Accordingly, the returns used for portfolio optimisation and efficient frontiers are those observed over the same time period. It is clear that it would have been desirable to analyze the joint distributions of the return series for the funds with other series from the general markets in order to provide more reliable risk and return assessments. Nevertheless, the conclusions drawn from our analysis would not have changed qualitatively.

Keeping these considerations in mind, we first investigate mean–VaR efficient frontiers and we focus on estimation techniques. VaR estimators do depend on the methodology chosen. Consigli (2002) considered several VaR estimators that take into account the asymmetry of the returns and fat-tail effects. Even under the assumption of iid returns, the estimation error for VaR is quite significant for low probability levels and realistic sample sizes. We compare different estimators of VaR, either historical or using different kernel estimators of the quantiles, and study the resulting efficient frontiers. Computational issues are not straightforward either. For instance, the set of portfolios that fulfill a VaR constraint is not necessarily convex. We thus rely on a genetic algorithm.

Some authors have recently investigated the use of alternative risk measures for portfolio management. Krokhmal, Uryasev and Zrazhevsky (2002) looked for hedge fund portfolio optimisation under different risk measures: CVaR, conditional drawdown at risk, mean absolute deviation and maximum loss. They showed that the resulting efficient frontiers are close and that combining several risk measures allows better risk management. They also considered the consequences of relaxing the constraints. Based on our hedge fund database, we compare efficient frontiers based on VaR, expected shortfall and semivariance constraints. We study how portfolio allocations depend on the structure of the risk measure. The computations of efficient frontiers under an empirical expected shortfall constraint are easier thanks to the linear programming approach of Rockafellar and Uryasev (2000). Similarly, de Athayde (2001) and Konno, Waki and Yuuki (2003) have provided optimisation algorithms under semivariance constraints that are easy to implement.

This chapter is organised as follows: in the next section we briefly describe our data set and provide its main descriptive statistics; in Section 3 we consider portfolio optimisation under VaR constraints and we investigate the use of different VaR estimators; Section 4 deals with the alternative risk constraints expected shortfall and semivariance, where we study how optimal portfolio allocations depend on the risk measure chosen; and proofs are presented in the appendix.

2 HEDGE FUND DATABASE

We consider a database of 16 hedge funds that span the most representative styles encountered in the alternative investment industry. This number is obviously unrealistically low compared to that of typical hedge fund portfolios. Indeed, funds of funds managers usually invest in a few hundred funds to reduce the impact of a single fund performing badly and to avoid the unexpected correlations that appear during market crises. However, due to the use of very lengthy optimisation algorithms and for the sake of illustration, we consider our small sample sufficient.

Focusing on the monthly returns of the funds considered over the time period January 1990–July 2001, which represents 139 data points per fund, we report their main descriptive statistics in Table 1.

Table 1 Hedge funds: summary statistics

Fund	Style	m (%)	s (%)	s	k	JB-test	p-value (%)
Axa Rosenberg	Equity market-neutral	5.61	8.01	0.82	13.65	186	0.00
Discovery MasterFund	Equity market-neutral	6.24	14.91	-0.27	0.25	0.1	93.65
Aetos Corp	Event-driven	12.52	8.13	-1.69	7.78	63	0.00
Bennet Restructuring	Event-driven	16.02	7.48	-0.74	7.37	55	0.00
Calamos Convertible	Convertible arbitrage	10.72	8.09	0.71	2.59	7	2.72
Sage Capital	Convertible arbitrage	9.81	2.45	-3.19	3	19	0.01
Genesis Emerging Markets	Emerging markets	10.54	20.03	-3.34	6.4	52	0.00
RXR Secured Note	Fixed-income arbitrage	12.29	6.45	2.33	4.84	29	0.00
Arrowsmith Fund	Fund of funds	26.91	27.08	14.51	60.7	3,895	0.00
Blue Rock Capital	Fund of funds	8.65	3.47	1.66	7.51	59	0.00
DeanWitter Cornerstone	Global macro	13.95	23.19	7.42	9.17	139	0.00
GAMut Investments	Global macro	24.73	14.43	3.38	4.61	33	0.00
Aquila International	Long short equity	9.86	16.88	-1.22	2.32	7	3.18
Bay Capital Management	Long short equity	10.12	19.31	1.94	0.7	4	11.80
Blenheim Investments LP	Managed futures	16.51	29.59	3.07	10.25	114	0.00
Red Oak Commodity	Managed futures	19.80	29.08	1.94	3.52	16	0.03

Summary statistics for the 16 hedge funds composing our data set. The two first columns identify each fund and describe its investment style. Columns three to six present the mean, standard deviation, skewness and kurtosis of the monthly returns for each fund. The two last columns give results for the Jarque–Bera normality test based on the values of skewness and kurtosis.

Table 2 Hedge fund dependence properties

Fund	Beta	*t*-statistic	Correlation (%)
Axa Rosenberg	−0.14	3.08	−28.36
Discovery MasterFund	0.01	0.17*	3.27
Aetos Corp	0.25	5.17	34.05
Bennet Restructuring	0.16	3.33	64.15
Calamos Convertible	0.37	9.22	32.75
Sage Capital	0.07	3.55	52.30
Genesis Emerging Markets	0.78	7.79	88.06
RXR Secured Note	0.21	5.21	1.14
Arrowsmith Fund	0.37	2.28	−
Blue Rock Capital	0.09	3.78	−
DeanWitter Cornerstone	−0.03	0.22*	31.62
GAMut Investments	0.06	0.67*	57.58
Aquila International	0.7	8.42	72.07
Bay Capital Management	0.24	2.1	27.85
Blenheim Investments LP	0.1	0.56*	22.77
Red Oak Commodity	0.7	4.23	21.60

This table summarises some basic properties of the dependence of the hedge funds under consideration in this chapter. The second column provides the value of the β between each fund and the S&P500 Index, while the third column gives the value of the *t*-statistic, allowing assessment of the significance of the estimated β. An asterisk against a number indicates a β not significantly different from zero at the 5% level. The fourth column gives the linear correlation coefficient between each fund and the CSFB/Tremont index that corresponds to its style.

The symbols m, σ, s and k refer, respectively, to the mean, standard deviation, skewness and kurtosis of the returns. As some of the statistics suggest, most returns exhibit significant departures from normality, an impression that is confirmed by Jarque–Bera statistics.

In Table 2 we report some basic dependence properties of the funds. The betas with respect to the S&P500 Index are given in the second column. A *t*-test (third column) shows that most of them are significant at the 5% level. More precisely, most funds have a significantly positive exposure to market risk. A noticeable exception is provided by Axa Rosenberg, which is negatively correlated with the market although it declares a market-neutral strategy. Overall, however, the betas remain relatively small, which testifies to a good diversification potential with respect to market risk.

The last column of Table 2 presents the values of the (linear) correlation coefficients between each fund and the CSFB/Tremont index that corresponds to its declared style. A wide range of correlations, spanning from −28% to 88%, is observed. Large anti-correlations are

Table 3 Correlation matrix of hedge fund monthly returns

100	14	-3	0	-20	-13	-33	-4	-15	5	7	8	-24	-7	-2	-28
14	100	-1	-13	-5	-2	-5	6	-10	28	11	-2	3	2	-5	7
-3	-1	100	35	35	21	31	12	16	11	1	-13	30	-5	0	12
0	-13	35	100	25	31	40	-3	16	-4	3	-8	31	9	-4	11
-20	-5	35	25	100	40	50	21	18	30	-15	5	49	12	1	16
-13	-2	21	31	40	100	40	8	14	7	2	1	34	-5	-2	2
-33	-5	31	40	50	40	100	15	22	10	-8	-9	64	14	16	31
-4	6	12	-3	21	8	15	100	8	25	37	41	25	10	11	31
-15	-10	16	16	18	14	22	8	100	1	-9	-1	17	7	-1	11
5	28	11	-4	30	7	10	25	1	100	8	1	21	13	-5	13
7	11	1	3	-15	2	-8	37	-9	8	100	37	-3	7	6	17
8	-2	-13	-8	5	1	-9	41	-1	1	37	100	-2	10	22	29
-24	3	30	31	49	34	64	25	17	21	-3	-2	100	14	6	24
-7	2	-5	9	12	-5	14	10	7	13	7	10	14	100	10	9
-2	-5	0	-4	1	-2	16	11	-1	-5	6	22	6	10	100	50
-28	7	12	11	16	2	31	31	11	13	17	29	24	9	50	100

Correlation matrix of the monthly returns of the 16 hedge funds. Rows (and columns) follow the same order as in Tables 1 and 2.

not a surprise. Indeed, this result is in line with the many previous studies that have underlined the existence of important disagreements between declared and actual investment styles (Dibartolomeo and Witkowski (1997) and Brown and Goetzmann (1997)). This observation can be rationalised, at least in part, by the fact that within the same class of strategies some specific strategies vary sufficiently to create the observed negative correlations. That is why it is not uncommon even to see an index component negatively correlated to the index it is part of. This remark has an important consequence: although, under normal market conditions, funds applying the same type of strategy, or arbitraging the same asset class, can be totally uncorrelated, they all become fully correlated when a crisis occurs, especially a liquidity crisis (eg, convertible arbitrage in April–May 2005).

We also present a correlation matrix of the returns (Table 3). We should emphasise that, unlike typical mutual funds, there are a large number of fairly negative correlation parameters, which again is an indication of a good potential for diversification, at least in normal times.

3 OPTIMISING UNDER VAR CONSTRAINTS
Popularised by works like that by Jorion (2000), and endorsed by the Bank for International Settlements, value-at-risk has become

one of the most prominent tools for risk management. This section discusses the impact of the way VaR is assessed on the optimal allocation of a portfolio.

3.1 Risk definitions

First we recall some useful definitions and properties concerning the higher and lower quantiles of a random variable X.

DEFINITION 1 (HIGHER AND LOWER QUANTILE) *Let* $(\Omega, \mathcal{A}, P)$ *be a probability space and* $\alpha \in]0, 1[$. *For X, being a real random variable defined on* $(\Omega, \mathcal{A}, P)$,

$$q_{\alpha}^{+}(X) = \sup \{x \in \mathbb{R}, \, P(X < x) \leq \alpha\} \tag{1}$$

is the higher quantile of order α *of X, and*

$$q_{\alpha}^{-}(X) = \inf \{x \in \mathbb{R}, \, P(X \leq x) \geq \alpha\} \tag{2}$$

is its lower quantile of order α.

We then get $Q_{\alpha}(X) = [q_{\alpha}^{-}(X), q_{\alpha}^{+}(X)]$. Let us remark that the quantiles associated with some random variable X depend only on the distribution of X (invariance in distribution). For instance, let F be the distribution function of X; then we obtain $q_{\alpha}^{-}(X) = \inf \{x \in \mathbb{R}, F(x) \geq \alpha\}$. We can thus equivalently define quantiles for real distributions. We also recall that the following relations hold:

$$q_{\alpha}^{-}(-X) = -q_{1-\alpha}^{+}(X), \quad q_{\alpha}^{+}(-X) = -q_{1-\alpha}^{-}(X) \tag{3}$$

Following Acerbi and Tasche (2002b) (see also Delbaen (2002), Pflug (2000), Acerbi, Nordio and Sirtori (2001) and Tasche (2002) for related references), we now define the value-at-risk of X.

DEFINITION 2 (VALUE-AT-RISK) *Let X be a random variable defined on a probability space* $(\Omega, \mathcal{A}, P)$ *and* $\alpha \in]0, 1[$. *We define the value-at-risk of X at the level* α, *denoted by* $VaR_{\alpha}(X)$, *as*

$$VaR_{\alpha}(X) = q_{1-\alpha}^{-}(-X) = -q_{\alpha}^{+}(X) \tag{4}$$

In the following, R, taking values in $\mathbb{R}^{p}$ with $p \in \mathbb{N}$, will represent the random vector of (monthly) asset returns defined on a probability space $(\Omega, \mathcal{A}, P)$. We will denote by $a \in \mathbb{R}^p$ the portfolio allocation. Thus, the portfolio return will be given by $a'R$, where $'$ denotes the transpose operator. The value-at-risk associated with portfolio allocation a is then given by $VaR_\alpha(a'R) = - q_\alpha^+(a'R)$. For practical applications one needs some estimator of the higher α quantile of a portfolio return distribution, $q_\alpha^+(a'R)$, to compute the VaR.

3.2 Different estimators of the historical VaR

We will now describe different non-parametric estimators of the VaR in a portfolio context. All these estimators are based on the empirical distribution of portfolio returns. They share the properties of asymptotic normality and consistency, provided that the portfolio returns are independent and identically distributed (iid).[1]

Let us denote by $r_1, \dots, r_n$ the set of historical asset returns. It can be easily checked that the higher quantile of order α associated with the empirical distribution can be written as

$$q_{n,\alpha,a}^+ = \sup\left\{ a'r_i, i = 1, \dots, n, \sum_{j=1}^{n} 1_{a'r_j < a'r_i} \leq \alpha \right\} \tag{5}$$

and corresponds to one of the historical portfolio returns associated with portfolio allocation a.

For $z \in \mathbb{R}$, we denote by $[z] = \max\{n \in \mathbb{N}, n < z\}$ the integer part of z. We denote by $(a'r)_{1:n} \leq \dots, \leq (a'r)_{n:n}$ the ordered statistics of portfolio returns. Let us remark that we may have $(a'r)_{i:n} = (a'r)_{j:n}$ for $i \neq j$ In this case, we talk of multiple scenarios and we then choose an arbitrary ordering. If there are no $j \in \{1, \dots, n\}, j \neq$, such that $(a'r)_{i:n} = (a'r)_{j:n}$, we will say that i is an isolated scenario (for portfolio allocation a). We can now state the following.

PROPOSITION 1 (EMPIRICAL HIGHER PORTFOLIO QUANTILE) *Let us consider some portfolio allocation a and risk level $\alpha \in\,]0, 1[$. The empirical higher quantile of order α can then be written as*

$$q_{n,\alpha,a}^+ = (a'r)_{[n\alpha]+1:n} \tag{6}$$

Thus, in accordance with Definition 2, the *empirical VaR* can be readily obtained from the empirical higher quantile:

DEFINITION 3 (EMPIRICAL VaR) *Let $r_1, \ldots, r_n$ be the set of historical returns, let $a \in \mathbb{R}^p$ be a portfolio allocation and let $0 < \alpha < 1$. We then define the empirical VaR as*

$$VaR_{n,\alpha,a}^{E} = -(a'r)_{[n\alpha]+1:n} \tag{7}$$

This definition provides the simplest non-parametric estimator of the value-at-risk. However, it has the drawback of not being smooth when regarded as a function of α, whereas it is sometimes convenient to deal with smooth quantile functions. That is why alternative quantile estimation techniques must be considered.

Silvapulle and Granger (2001), for instance, have used a methodology relying on work by Sheather and Marron (1990) that develops quantile estimators based on weighted averages of empirical quantiles and which are referred to in the statistical literature as L estimators or kernel quantile estimators. Let us denote by $K(x) = 1/\sqrt{2\pi}\, e^{-x^2/2}$ the Gaussian density function. We will consider the following estimator of $q_\alpha^+(a'R)$:

$$q_{n,\alpha,a}^{+} = \frac{\sum_{i=1}^{n} K\left(h^{-1} \cdot \left(\frac{i-1/2}{n} - \alpha\right)\right)(a'r)_{i:n}}{\sum_{i=1}^{n} K\left(h^{-1} \cdot \left(\frac{i-1/2}{n} - \alpha\right)\right)} \tag{8}$$

where $h = \sigma n^{-1/5}$ and $\sigma = \sqrt{(n^2-1)/12n^2}$ is the standard deviation of $1/n, \ldots, n/n$. We then define the *kernel VaR* as $VaR_{n,\alpha,a} = -q_{n,\alpha,a}^{+}$. Let us remark that this kernel VaR is a weighted average of ordered portfolio returns. So, the definition of the kernel VaR follows.

DEFINITION 4 (KERNEL VaR) *Let $r_1, \ldots, r_n$ be the set of historical returns, let $a \in \mathbb{R}^p$ be a portfolio allocation and let $0 < \alpha < 1$. We then define the kernel VaR as*

$$VaR_{n,\alpha,a}^{K} = \frac{\sum_{i=1}^{n} K\left(h^{-1} \cdot \left(\frac{i-1/2}{n} - \alpha\right)\right)(a'r)_{i:n}}{\sum_{i=1}^{n} K\left(h^{-1} \cdot \left(\frac{i-1/2}{n} - \alpha\right)\right)} \tag{9}$$

Gouriéroux, Laurent and Scaillet (2000) have proposed another kernel-based approach to the estimation of VaR in terms of quantiles of the kernel estimate of the empirical cumulative distribution function of portfolio returns. We also refer to Azzalini (1981) for a study of the asymptotic properties of such an estimator. The α-quantile estimator $q^+_{n,\alpha,a}$ is given by the unique solution of

$$\frac{1}{n}\sum_{i=1}^{n}\Phi\left(\frac{-(a'r)_{i:n} + q^+_{n,\alpha,a}}{h}\right) = \alpha \tag{10}$$

where Φ is the Gaussian cumulative distribution function. As usual, the bandwidth is chosen such that $h = (4/3)^{1/5}\sigma_{n,a}n^{-1/5}$, where

$$\sigma_{n,a} = \left(\frac{1}{n}\sum_{i=1}^{n}(a'r)^2_{i:n} - \left(\frac{1}{n}\sum_{i=1}^{n}(a'r)_{i:n}\right)^2\right)^{1/2} \tag{11}$$

is the empirical standard deviation of portfolio returns. As above, the VaR estimator is then $VaR_{n,\alpha,a} = -q^+_{n,\alpha,a}$, so that:

DEFINITION 5 (GLS VaR) *Let $r_1, \ldots, r_n$ be the set of historical returns, let $a \in \mathbb{R}^p$ be a portfolio allocation and let $0 < \alpha < 1$. We then define the GLS VaR, denoted $VaR^{GLS}_{n,\alpha,a}$, as the solution of*

$$\frac{1}{n}\sum_{i=1}^{n}\Phi\left(-\frac{(a'r)_{i:n} + VaR^{GLS}_{n,\alpha.a}}{h}\right) = \alpha \tag{12}$$

Finally, let us recall that when the returns $a'R$ are Gaussian, we have:

$$VaR_\alpha(a'R) = -E[a'R] - \Phi^{-1}(\alpha)\sigma(a'R) \tag{13}$$

where $E[a'R]$ and $\sigma(a'R)$ denote, respectively, the mean and standard deviation of portfolio returns. This leads to the following VaR estimator (which we will refer to as *Gaussian VaR*) based on the empirical counterparts of the mean and standard deviation of the portfolio returns.

DEFINITION 6 (GAUSSIAN VaR) *Let $r_1, \ldots, r_n$ be the set of historical returns, let $a \in \mathbb{R}^p$ be a portfolio allocation and let $0 < \alpha < 1$. We then define the Gaussian VaR as*

$$VaR^\Phi_{n,\alpha,a} = -\frac{1}{n}\sum_{i=1}^{n}(a'r)_{i:n}$$

$$-\Phi^{-1}(\alpha)\left(\frac{1}{n}\sum_{i=1}^{n}(a'r)^2_{i:n} - \left(\frac{1}{n}\sum_{i=1}^{n}(a'r)_{i:n}\right)^2\right)^{1/2} \qquad (14)$$

Of course, this latter VaR estimator is consistent only under the assumption of Gaussian returns – which, as noted in Section 2, is unlikely in our case.

Let us remark that the four proposed VaR estimators depend only on the ordered portfolio returns $(a'r)_{i:n}$, $i = 1, \ldots, n$. Moreover, the four VaR estimators are differentiable and positively homogeneous of degree one with respect to $(a'r)$. Thus, applying Euler's identity, we can write the following risk measure decomposition for any of the four previously defined VaR estimators:

$$VaR^{''}_{n,\alpha,a} = \sum_{i=1}^{n}\frac{\partial VaR^{''}_{n,\alpha,a}}{\partial (a'r)_{i:n}} \times (a'r)_{i:n} \qquad (15)$$

Figure 1 depicts the relative weights $((a'r)_{i:n}/VaR_{n,\alpha,a}) \times (\partial VaR_{n,\alpha,a}/\partial(a'r)_{i:n})$ associated with the different VaR estimators,[2] which sum to one (due to Equation (15)). It can be seen that the empirical and the kernel VaRs are rather similar, although of course the latter is smoother. Indeed, as expected from Definition 3, the empirical VaR puts all the weight on a single realisation – here the seventh smallest (since $[139 \times 0.05] + 1 = 7$) – while the kernel VaR involves several ordered statistics $(a'r)_{i:n}$, even if one can see that the main contribution comes from the values close to the seventh smallest observation. Let us remark that the Gaussian VaR puts an almost equal weight on any observation. It only very slightly overweights the smallest observations, and therefore it is unable to take extreme risks reliably into account. The GLS VaR stands between the Gaussian and the kernel VaR. This is due to bandwidth effects since the optimal bandwidth selection involves the standard deviation of the returns.

Figure 1 Risk decomposition of VaR constraints

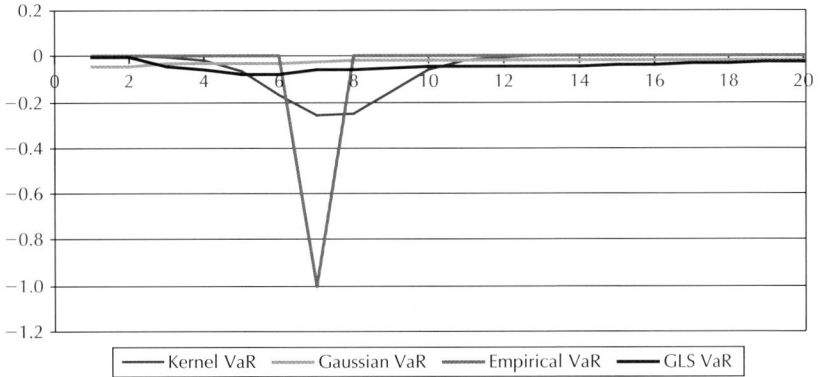

The figure presents the weights involved in the calculation of the different VaR estimators for each ordered statistic $(a'r)_{i:n}$.

3.3 Optimisation under VaR constraints

We now address the issue of computing mean–VaR efficient frontiers, that is we want to solve the following optimisation problem:

$$\max_{a \in \mathbb{R}_+^p} E[a'R] \tag{16}$$

under the constraint $VaR_\alpha(a'R) \leq v$ for different risk levels v. Optimisation is carried out over $\mathbb{R}_+^p$ since short-sells are assumed not to be allowed, which is very reasonable for a fund of hedge funds. Contrary to other risk measures such as expected shortfall (which will be discussed in the next section) or more generally coherent measures of risk, the VaR is usually non-convex, so it does not provide a very suitable objective function for an optimisation problem. Indeed, such a problem can exhibit several local minima and, hence, the usual algorithms cannot be applied since they typically fail to reach the global optimum of the problem. In the following we provide some mean–VaR efficient frontiers estimated by solving

$$\max_{a \in \mathbb{R}_+^p} \sum_{i=1}^{n} a'r_i \tag{17}$$

under the constraint $VaR_{n,\alpha,a} \leq v$ for different risk levels v. Let us remark that we need to solve different optimisation problems depending on the VaR estimator selected. These optimisation problems are no longer convex since the mapping $a \mapsto VaR_{n,\alpha,a}$ may be non-convex. Moreover, the empirical VaR and the kernel VaR are not even differentiable with respect to the portfolio allocation a, which again rules out the use of standard algorithms based on differentiation – the gradient method for instance.

3.3.1 Genetic algorithms

Two alternative approaches can be proposed: the simulated annealing algorithm or genetic algorithms. Both are able to deal with multiple local minima optimisation problems, avoiding the problem of being trapped in a local minimum, and they do not require a differentiable objective function. Thus, they appear to be well adapted to our present needs. The choice of genetic algorithms has been retained as the most relevant since this class of algorithms embeds the simulated annealing algorithms.

The idea underlying genetic algorithms is based on the mimicry of the natural selection process and genetic principles. The genetic algorithm starts with a population of trial vectors, called *genes*, which contain the parameters to optimise – namely the portfolio allocation vector a – and it proceeds as follows:

❑ The first step consists in the *replication* (or reproduction) of the initial trial vectors according to their fitness – that is, genes with the smallest VaR have the highest probability of reproducing. Thus, on average, the new population has a lower VaR than the initial one, but it also has less diversity because in the new population the fittest genes obviously appear twice or more.
❑ The second step is *crossover* (or recombination), where the different parameters from several vectors drawn from the new population are combined to mix their characteristics.
❑ The third and last step is *mutation*, where some genes undergo random changes, ie, some parameters of the vectors produced in the crossover stage are randomly modified. This step is essential to maintain the diversity of the population, which in turn ensures exploration of the whole optimisation space.

The vectors obtained after this third step are then used as an initial population and the process is repeated to obtain a new generation of genes, and so on. The convergence of this algorithm to the global minimum of the problem is ensured by the fundamental theorem of genetic algorithms, as stated by Goldberg (1989). Examples of particularly efficient genetic algorithms are the Dorsey and Mayer (1995) algorithm and the differential evolutionary genetic algorithm of Price and Storn (1997). In what follows we use the first.

3.3.2 Analysis of the mean–VaR efficient frontiers and of mean–VaR efficient portfolios

Figure 2 shows the different mean–VaR efficient frontiers obtained with the four VaR estimators defined in Section 3.2 with a probability level, α, set to 5%. It can be seen that the three non-parametric VaR-efficient frontiers (ie, those computed using the empirical, kernel and GLS VaR estimators) are rather close. For example, efficient portfolios for a 0.4% level of VaR have an expected return varying between 1.05% and 1.25%, a relative variation of 20%. As will be seen below, choices of other risk measures, such as expected shortfall or semi-variance, lead to larger differences. Not surprisingly, due to the asymmetry and the heavy tails of the returns

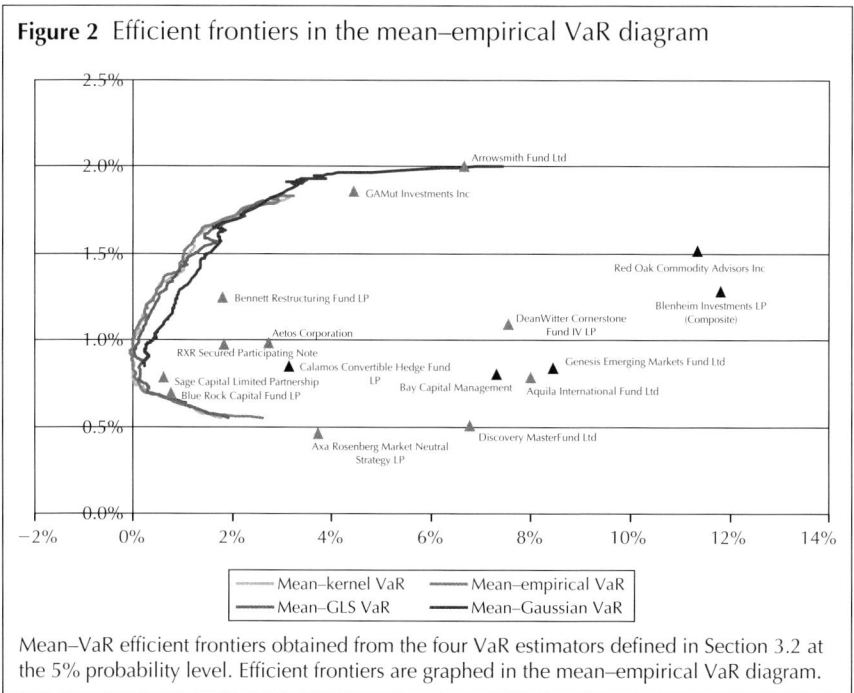

Figure 2 Efficient frontiers in the mean–empirical VaR diagram

Mean–VaR efficient frontiers obtained from the four VaR estimators defined in Section 3.2 at the 5% probability level. Efficient frontiers are graphed in the mean–empirical VaR diagram.

Figure 3 Efficient allocations

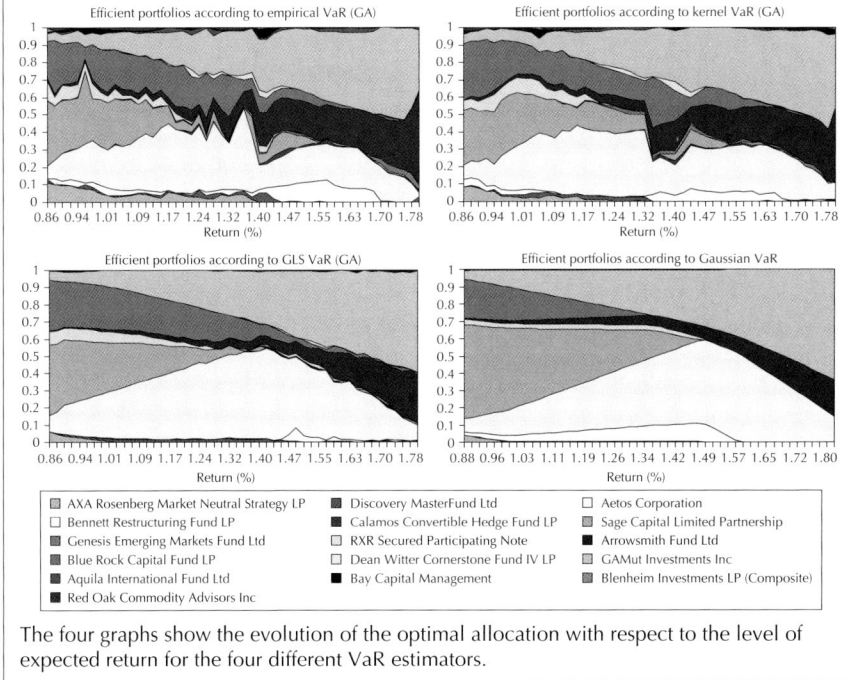

The four graphs show the evolution of the optimal allocation with respect to the level of expected return for the four different VaR estimators.

distributions, the Gaussian VaR efficient frontier[3] also differs from the non-parametric VaR efficient frontiers.

The various individual funds are also plotted in Figure 2. We clearly observe a wide scattering of the data points, showing that some funds are very far from efficiency. Among them, the five dark triangles represent those funds which do not enter into the composition of any efficient portfolio. Figure 3 and Table 4 provide a more accurate description of the evolution of the composition of efficient portfolios with respect to the VaR estimator considered.

Figure 3 shows the evolution of optimal allocations with respect to the level of expected return for the four different VaR estimators. We notice the similarity between the portfolio allocations obtained for the Gaussian and the GLS VaRs on the one hand and between the empirical and the kernel VaRs on the other. We also note that for the last two estimators portfolio allocation can change very quickly with the level of return considered. This can be related to

Table 4 Efficient portfolios for a 1.2% level of expected return

Fund	VaR(%)			
	Gaussian	**Empirical**	**GLS**	**Kernel**
Axa Rosenberg	0.00	**4**	0	0.90
Discovery Masterfund	0.50	1.10	1.70	2.20
Aetos Corp	**6.90**	0.20	0.10	0.10
Bennet Restructuring	**30.50**	**35.20**	**41.20**	**37.10**
Calamos Convertible	0.00	0.40	0.00	0.00
Sage Capital	**27.20**	**5.90**	**12.50**	**15.50**
Genesis Emerging Markets	0.00	0.50	0.00	0.70
RXR Secured Note	2.90	1.10	2.50	0.40
ArrowSmith Fund	**4.10**	**6.20**	**3.00**	**4.80**
Blue Rock Capital	**7.20**	**23.50**	**19.20**	**16.10**
DeanWitter Cornerstone	0.00	0.70	0.00	0.80
GAMut Investments	**20.10**	**19.40**	**19.60**	**19.10**
Aquila International	0.00	0.80	0.00	1.40
Bay Capital Management	0.00	0.10	0.00	0.00
Blenheim Investments LP	0.50	0.00	0.00	0.00
Red Oak Commodity	0.00	0.90	0.00	0.80

The table provides the optimal allocation according to the four VaR estimators. Figures in bold emphasise the funds whose weight is larger than 4%.

the fact that kernel and empirical VaRs actually involve a weak number of realisations of the portfolio return (see Figure 1 on VaR decomposition). Finally, we observe that the smoother the VaR estimator, the smoother are the variations of the optimal allocation.

Focusing on a given level of expected return (arbitrarily set to 1.2%), Table 4 presents the optimal allocations according to the four VaR estimators. Even if the optimal weights are significantly different, we see that the preponderant funds remain the same, namely: Bennet Restructuring, Genesis Emerging Markets, Blue Rock Capital and GAMut Investments. From Table 1 we note that all these funds have a Sharpe ratio larger than one, except for Genesis Emerging Markets, which, *a priori*, could suggest the existence of a relation between Sharpe ratio and the weights of the funds in the optimal portfolios. Reference to the rank correlations between these two quantities confirms this impression (they all range between 0.5 and 0.7). In contrast, we have found that the past average return on a fund is only significantly correlated with the proportion of invested wealth for the Gaussian and GLS VaR estimators. This means that funds that have performed poorly in

Table 5 Distance between efficient portfolios for two levels of expected return, *r*

	r = 1.75%			r = 1.15%		
	Gaussian VaR	Kernel VaR	GLS VaR	Gaussian VaR	Kernel VaR	GLS VaR
Kernel VaR	0.26			0.61		
GLS VaR	0.21	0.15		0.46	0.23	
Empirical VaR	0.28	0.08	0.12	0.57	0.08	0.24

Distance between two optimal portfolios computed under VaR constraints given by different estimators for two levels of expected return *r*.

the past are not systematically eliminated from the optimal portfolios. The optimal amount of wealth invested in a particular fund clearly depends on the diversification potential it brings to the portfolio (eg, Axa Rosenberg and the Discovery MasterFund).

Now, in order to compare the similarity of two portfolios in terms of asset allocation, we define the distance between two portfolio allocations a and b as $d(a, b) = \Sigma_{j=1}^{p} |a_j - b_j|$, where p is the number of assets (here $p = 16$), a is the p-dimensional vector of the first portfolio weights, and b is the second portfolio allocation. The distance $d(a,b)$ takes values between 0 and 2. It should be noted that $\|a'R - b'R\|_1 = E[|a'R - b'R|]$ can be small even if $d(a, b)$ is quite large due to correlation effects between assets.

Table 5 compares portfolio allocations for different efficient frontiers associated with the same level of expected return. It will be observed that the mean–variance-optimal portfolios are far from the optimal portfolios determined under non-parametric VaR constraints. Of the non-parametric approaches, kernel VaR and empirical VaR lead to very similar portfolios, while the portfolios computed under GLS VaR constraints differ slightly more. This is in line with the sensitivity analysis of the different VaR estimators with respect to the distribution of returns. One might think of using bootstrap techniques to compute confidence intervals on the distance between portfolios. However, because optimisation using genetic algorithms is slow, this was not done.

To close with an investigation of the impact of the VaR estimators on the VaR-efficient portfolios, let us try to quantify the

Figure 4 Participation ratio

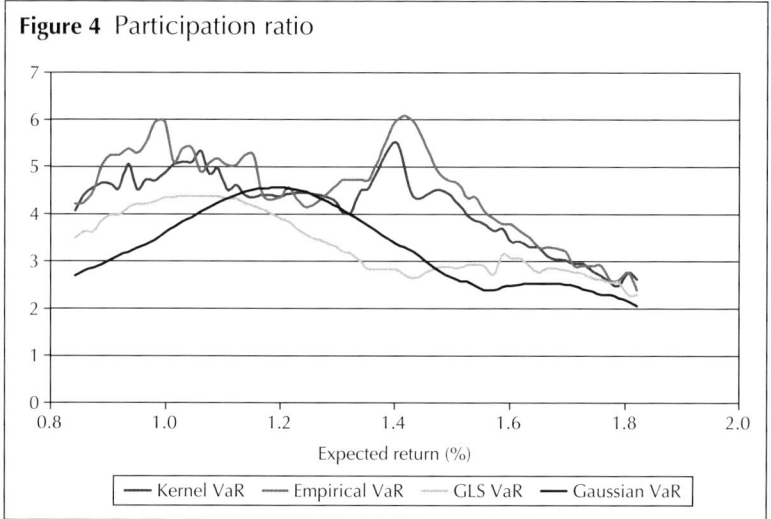

Expected return (%)

— Kernel VaR — Empirical VaR ---- GLS VaR — Gaussian VaR

diversification effects of our different VaR estimates. To this end we introduce the so-called *participation ratio* (ie, the inverse of the traditional Herfindal index), defined as $1/\Sigma_{j=1}^{p} a_j^2$, associated with a portfolio allocation $a = (a_1, ..., a_p)$. If the portfolio is based on a single asset, the value of the participation ratio is equal to 1, whereas with an equally weighted portfolio the value is p. Figure 4 shows that the level of diversification tends to be lower for higher levels of expected returns: the search for high expected returns requires investments in those funds with higher historical returns, thus reducing the participation ratio. We observe that, once again, the patterns are close for the kernel and empirical VaR constraints. Moreover, the overall degree of diversification is higher when these constraints are used than when using GLS VaR estimators or when considering mean–variance efficient frontiers. We emphasise that although empirical VaR involves only a single rank statistic, this does not preclude portfolio diversification.

Finally, it should be emphasised that introducing the S&P500 Index into a portfolio does not significantly change the shape of the efficient frontiers (see Figure 5) or the optimal allocations. It simply means that some hedge funds replicate the behavior of the market index sufficiently well. Genesis Emerging Markets, with a beta equal to 78% (see Table 2), is such an example.

Figure 5 Efficient frontiers in the mean–empirical VaR diagram with S&P500

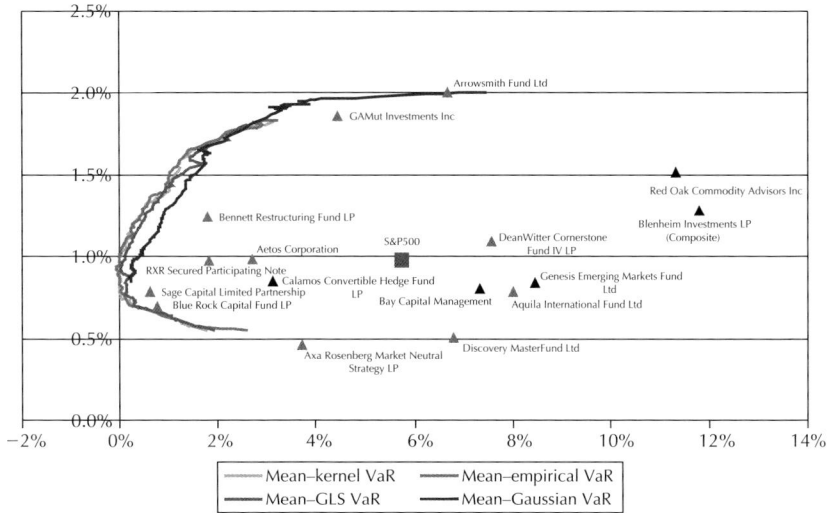

Mean–VaR efficient frontiers obtained from the four VaR estimators defined in Section 3.2 at the 5% probability level when the S&P500 Index is added to the set of hedge funds. Efficient frontiers are graphed in the mean–empirical VaR diagram.

4 OPTIMISING UNDER ALTERNATIVE RISK CONSTRAINTS

We will now deal with portfolio optimisation under alternative risk constraints, such as expected shortfall and semivariance, which enjoy coherence properties and therefore represent suitable constraints for our optimal allocation problem.

4.1 Optimisation under expected shortfall constraints

Let us first turn to another quantile-based risk measure, the *expected shortfall*.

DEFINITION 7 (EXPECTED SHORTFALL) *Let X be a random variable defined on a probability space* $(\Omega, \mathcal{A}, P)$ *with finite expectation.*[4] *Let* $\alpha \in \,]0, 1[$. *We define the expected shortfall of X at the level* α, *denoted by* $ES_\alpha(X)$, *as the solution of*

$$\inf_{\zeta \in \mathbb{R}} \frac{E^p\left[(X - \zeta)^-\right]}{\alpha} - \zeta \qquad (18)$$

In order to obtain a closed-form expression of the expected shortfall, let us now recall the following basic property shared by any quantile.

PROPOSITION 2 (QUANTILE CHARACTERISATION) *Let X be a real random variable defined on a probability space* $(\Omega, \mathcal{A}, P)$ *with finite expectation. Let* $\alpha \in]0, 1[$ *and* $\zeta \in \mathbb{R}$. *Let us consider the real function* H_α, *which takes values in* $[0, \infty[$, *defined by*

$$H_\alpha(\zeta) = \alpha E\left[(X - \zeta)^+\right] + (1 - \alpha) E\left[(X - \zeta)^-\right] \tag{19}$$

H_α *is minimal on* $Q_\alpha(X) = [q_\alpha^-(X), q_\alpha^+(X)]$.

As a consequence we get the following proposition.

PROPOSITION 3 (EXPECTED SHORTFALL CHARACTERISATION) *The criterion* $(E^P[(X - \zeta)^-]/\alpha) - \zeta$ *is minimal on the quantile set* $Q_\alpha(X)$, *so that a closed-form expression for the expected shortfall is given by*

$$ES_\alpha(X) = -\frac{1}{\alpha}\left((E^P[X1_{\{X \le q_\alpha(X)\}}] + q_\alpha(9X)((\alpha - P(X \le q_\alpha(X))))\right) \tag{20}$$

for any quantile $q_\alpha \in [q_\alpha^-(X), q_\alpha^+(X)]$.

We can also state a well-known property of the expected shortfall as follows.

COROLLARY 1 (SUBADDITIVITY OF EXPECTED SHORTFALL) *Let X, Y be two random variables with finite expectation defined on a probability space* $(\Omega, \mathcal{A}, P)$ *and* $\alpha \in]0, 1[$. *Then*

$$ES_\alpha(X + Y) \le ES_\alpha(X) + ES_\alpha(Y) \tag{21}$$

Since the expected shortfall is also invariant in law, positively homogeneous and invariant with respect to translations, it is a coherent measure of risk. It is also possible to relate expected shortfall and VaR through the following proposition, which also shows that the expected shortfall is a spectral measure of risk (see Acerbi (2002) for a study of spectral measures of risk).

PROPOSITION 4 (QUANTILE REPRESENTATION OF ES) *Let X be a random variable defined on a probability space* $(\Omega, \mathcal{A}, P)$ *with finite expectation and* $\alpha \in]0, 1[$. *We can write*

$$ES_\alpha(X) = \frac{1}{\alpha}\int_0^\alpha VaR_u(X)du \tag{22}$$

In the following, we will consider the mean–expected shortfall optimisation problem

$$\max_{a \in \mathbb{R}_+^p} E[a'R] \tag{23}$$

under the constraint $ES_\alpha(a'R) \leq v$ for different risk levels, v. We estimate the expected shortfall as in Rockafellar and Uryasev (2000), namely, as the expected shortfall corresponding to the empirical measure (we refer to Scaillet (2004) for another non-parametric approach). This is provided by the next proposition (see Rockafellar and Uryasev (2002) for a similar result).

PROPOSITION 5 (EXPECTED SHORTFALL, EMPIRICAL MEASURE) *Let us consider some portfolio allocation a and risk level $\alpha \in]0, 1[$. Then the empirical expected shortfall can be written as*

$$ES_{n,\alpha,a} = -\frac{1}{n\alpha} \left(\sum_{i=1}^{[n\alpha]} (a'r)_{i:n} + (n\alpha - [n\alpha])(a'r)_{[n\alpha]+1:n} \right) \tag{24}$$

We have implemented the algorithm proposed by Rockafellar and Uryasev (2000) for the estimation of mean–expected shortfall frontiers:

$$\max_{a \in \mathbb{R}_+^p} \sum_{i=1}^{n} a'r_i \tag{25}$$

under the constraint $ES_{n,\alpha,a} \leq v$ for different risk levels, v. This approach is based on the previous characterisations of the expected shortfall and the following proposition (see Theorems 14 and 15 in Rockafellar and Uryasev (2002)).

PROPOSITION 6 (EXPECTED SHORTFALL MINIMISATION) *Let $\alpha \in]0, 1[$ and r_i, $i = 1, \ldots, n$, be the historical returns. We then have*

$$\min_{a \in \mathbb{R}_+^p} ES_{n,\alpha,a} = \min_{(a,\zeta) \in \mathbb{R}_+^p \times \mathbb{R}} \frac{1}{n\alpha} \times \left(\sum_{i=1}^{n} (a'r_i - \zeta)^- \right) - \zeta \tag{26}$$

Moreover,

$$(a^*, \zeta^*) \in \arg\min_{(a,\zeta)} \frac{1}{n\alpha} \times \left(\sum_{i=1}^{n} (a'r_i - \zeta)^- \right) - \zeta$$

$$\Leftrightarrow \begin{cases} a^* \in \arg\min_{a} ES_{n,\alpha,a}, \\ \zeta^* \in \arg\min_{\zeta} \frac{1}{n\alpha} \times \left(\sum_{i=1}^{n} (a^{*\prime}r_i - \zeta)^- \right) - \zeta \end{cases}$$

As a consequence of this result, Rockafellar and Uryasev (2000, 2002) transformed an optimisation of the expected return under expected shortfall constraints into a linear program.

4.2 Optimisation under semivariance constraints

One-sided moments give rise to popular risk measures in portfolio management such as semivariance. Semivariance is invariant in law, subadditive and positively homogeneous of degree one. Hereafter we will use the following definition (see Fischer (2003)).

DEFINITION 8 (COHERENT RISK-MEASURE BASED ON SEMI-VARIANCE) *Let X be a square integrable random variable defined on a probability space* $(\Omega, \mathcal{A}, P)$.
We define

$$SV(X) = -E[X] + \|(X - E[X])^-\|_2 \qquad (27)$$

where $(x)^- = \max(-x, 0)$ *and* $\|X\|_2 = (E[X^2])^{1/2}$.

We note that, thanks to the expectation term, SV is translation-invariant and monotonic. Thus it is a coherent measure, but it fails to be co-monotonically additive and therefore to be a spectral or distortion risk measure, as was the expected shortfall.

As for the case of the expected shortfall, we consider the empirical counterpart of the risk measure in Definition 9.

DEFINITION 9 (COHERENT SEMIVARIANCE, EMPIRICAL MEAS-URE) *Let us consider some portfolio allocation* a *and risk level* $\alpha \in]0, 1[$. *The empirical counterpart of the coherent form of the semivariance can then be written as*

$$SV_{n,a} = -\frac{1}{n}\sum_{i=1}^{n} a'r_i + \left(\frac{1}{n}\sum_{i=1}^{n}\left(\max\left(0, a'r_i - \frac{1}{n}\sum_{j=1}^{n} a'r_j\right)\right)^2\right)^{1/2} \qquad (28)$$

The estimated mean–semivariance frontier is then provided by solving:

$$\max_{a \in \mathbb{R}_+^p} \sum_{i=1}^{n} a'r_i \qquad (29)$$

under the constraint $SV_{n,a} \leq v$ for different risk levels, v. We will use here the recursive algorithm of de Athayde (2001).

Figure 6 Risk weights

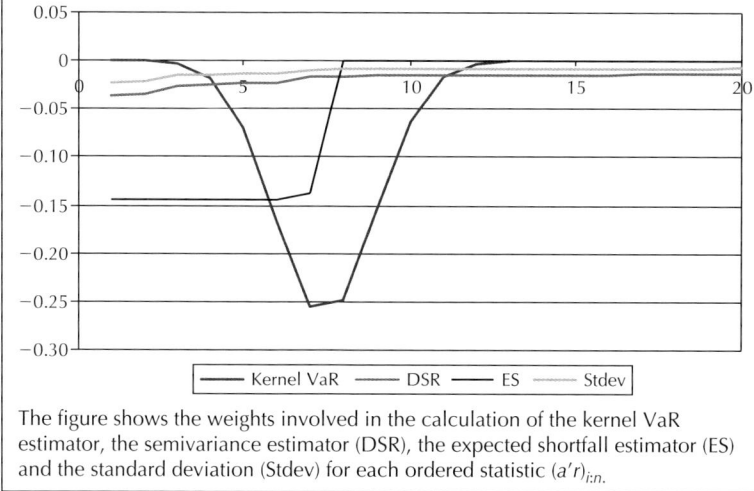

The figure shows the weights involved in the calculation of the kernel VaR estimator, the semivariance estimator (DSR), the expected shortfall estimator (ES) and the standard deviation (Stdev) for each ordered statistic $(a'r)_{i:n}$.

4.3 Analysis of individual funds

Let us first emphasise that $ES_{n,\alpha,a}$ and $SV_{n,a}$ depend only on the ordered portfolio returns $(a'r)_{i:n}$, $i = 1, ..., n$. Moreover, $ES_{n,\alpha,a}$ and $SV_{n,a}$ are differentiable and positively homogeneous of degree one with respect to portfolio values. We can therefore decompose the risk measures as in the case of VaR by use of Euler's equality. As for the VaR constraints, Figure 6 presents the weights associated with the ordered returns for the risk measures under assessment (with $\alpha = 5\%$). We clearly observe that the VaR and expected shortfall weights are concentrated on extreme rank statistics, while the weights involved in the calculation of the variance and the semi-variance exhibit a much smoother pattern.

Now, to study the relative content of each risk measure, let us assess the rank correlation between these various risk measures for the 16 hedge funds in our data set. The results are given in Table 6. We observe that the four different kinds of risk measure considered until now are very strongly correlated (the rank correlation coefficients are all larger than 90%), which simply means that, on the whole, the riskier fund according to one risk measure is also the riskier according to any of the other three risk measures. We may also note that the VaR and the expected shortfall at the 5% probability level remain very similar to the variance, involve only a small

Table 6 Rank correlation of risk measures (%)

	Kernel VaR	Expected shortfall	Semi-variance	Variance	Skewness
Expected shortfall	96				
Semivariance	95	98			
Variance	93	95	99		
Skewness	23	25	32	40	
Kurtosis	−3	6	15	15	38

Rank correlation between various risk measures and descriptive statistics for the 16 hedge funds listed in Table 1.

fraction of the information contained in the skewness, and are almost totally uncorrelated with the kurtosis. This means that at the 5% probability level the VaR and the expected shortfall are still very sensitive to the bulk of the distribution of returns (ie, the smaller risks) and almost insensitive to the far tail of the distribution (ie, the larger risks). It would therefore have been interesting to compute the VaR and the expected shortfall at the 1% probability level, but owing to the small number of historical observations at one's disposal when dealing with hedge funds, the results of this implementation appeared to be too noisy.

4.4 Efficient portfolios for alternative risk measures
We first report the efficient frontiers corresponding to VaR, expected shortfall, variance and semivariance constraints. For simplicity, we have only plotted the efficient frontiers under kernel VaR constraints. The upper panel of Figure 7 shows the four efficient frontiers in the mean–kernel VaR diagram. We see that the VaR efficient frontier is far from the others (even from the expected shortfall efficient frontier). This may be ascribed to the fact that VaR estimates involve only a few rank statistics. In addition, we do not see marked differences between the semivariance, variance and expected shortfall efficient frontiers. However, it is worth noting that in this diagram the semivariance-optimal portfolios appear to be more efficient than the expected shortfall-optimal portfolios. Indeed, for any value of the level of expected return, their VaR is lower than that of the expected shortfall-optimal portfolios at the same level of expected return. The lower panel of Figure 7 shows the same efficient frontiers

Figure 7 Efficient frontiers

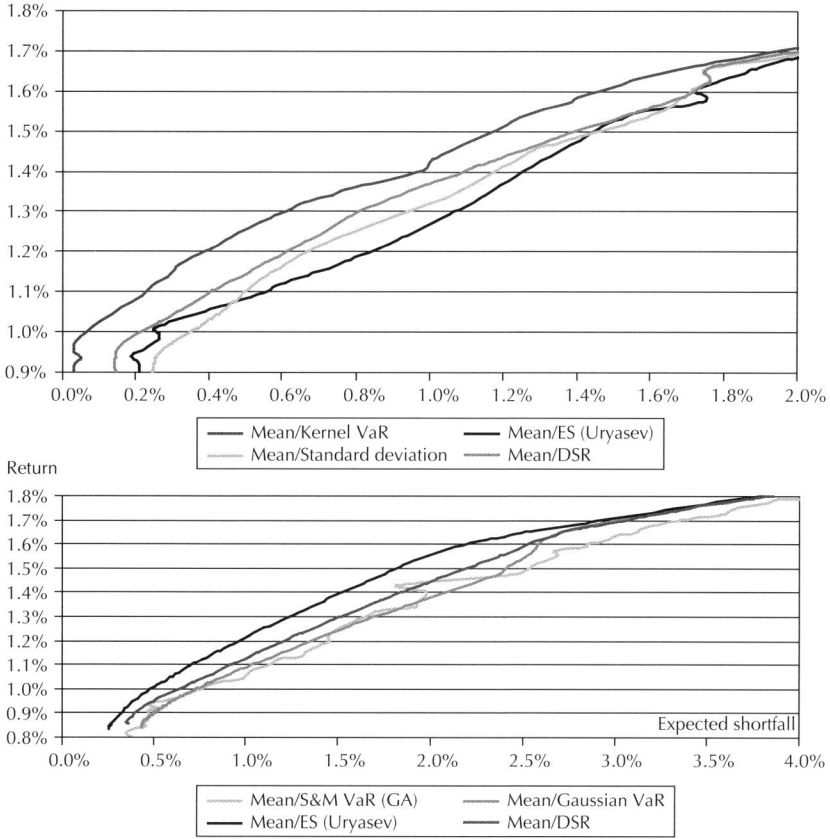

Mean–VaR efficient frontiers in the mean–empirical VaR diagram (*upper panel*) and in the mean–ES diagram (*lower panel*).

in the mean–expected shortfall diagram. We observe the same kind of behavior and, again, the semivariance-optimal portfolios appear, *ceteris paribus*, as the second most efficient.

Focusing again on a given level of expected return (which we keep equal to 1.2%), Table 7 provides the optimal allocation according to the four risk measures. As in the previous case where we considered only VaR estimators, we note that on the whole the dominant funds remain the same: Bennet Restructuring, Genesis Emerging Markets, Arrowsmith Funds, Blue Rock Capital and

Table 7 Efficient portfolios for a 1.2% level of expected return

Fund	Expected shortfall (%)	Kernel VaR (%)	Semi-variance (%)	Variance (%)
Axa Rosenberg	**6.30**	0.90	0.00	0.00
Discovery MasterFund	**4.70**	2.20	1.30	0.50
Aetos Corp	0.00	0.10	3.50	**6.90**
Bennet Restructuring	**12.00**	**37.10**	**29.90**	**30.50**
Calamos Convertible	0.00	0.00	0.00	0.00
Sage Capital	**26.00**	**15.50**	**14.00**	**27.20**
Genesis Emerging Markets	0.00	0.70	0.00	0.00
RXR Secured Note	0.00	0.40	**8.90**	2.90
Arrowsmith Fund	**8.70**	**4.80**	**4.30**	**4.10**
Blue Rock Capital	**8.00**	**16.10**	**16.50**	**7.20**
DeanWitter Cornerstone	3.00	0.80	0.00	0.00
GAMut Investments	**27.00**	**19.10**	**20.90**	**20.10**
Aquila International	0.00	1.40	0.00	0.00
Bay Capital Management	**4.30**	0.00	0.70	0.00
Blenheim Investments LP	0.00	0.00	0.10	0.50
Red Oak Commodity	0.00	0.80	0.00	0.00

The table presents optimal allocations according to the four risk measures. Figures in bold indicate those funds whose weight is greater than 4%.

GAMut Investments. Nevertheless, we have to grant that expected shortfall leads to much more diversified portfolios than the three other risk measures. Clearly the VaR, the standard deviation and the semivariance yield efficient portfolios that involve a significant contribution from only five or six funds, whereas the efficient expected shortfall portfolio consists of eight funds.

This observation is confirmed by Figures 8 and 9, which plot the composition and the participation ratio of each optimal portfolio against its level of expected return. In general, expected shortfall is the risk measure that yields the more diversified portfolios. However, for levels of expected return greater than 1.4% kernel VaR compares with it. For values of expected returns less than 1.4%, kernel VaR and semivariance give the same level of diversification and, on the whole, the variance (or Gaussian VaR) is the risk measure which yields the most concentrated portfolios.

We now compare, in Table 8, the distance between efficient portfolios associated with different risk measures and different levels of expected returns. We see that optimal portfolios tend to be closer for high levels of expected return, which simply means that the risk

Figure 8 Efficient allocations

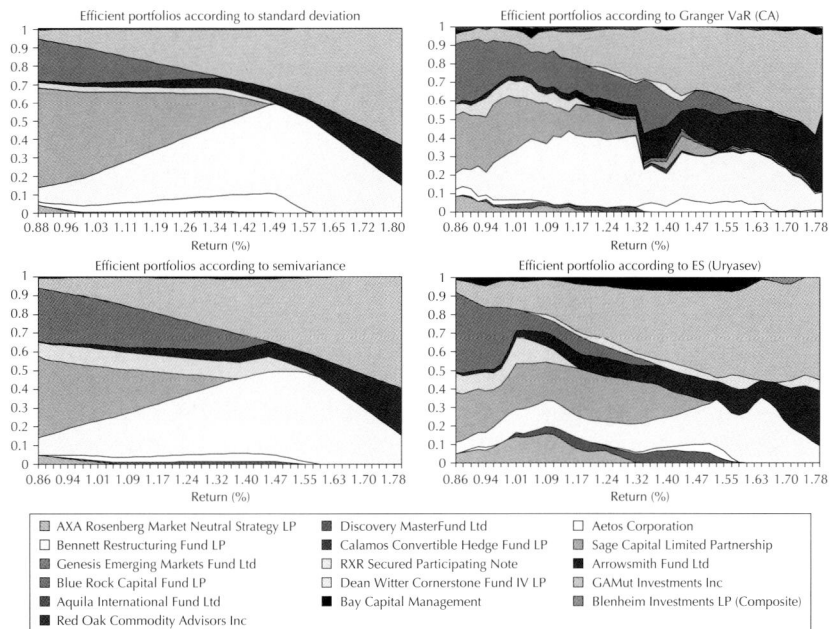

The four graphs show the evolution of the optimal allocation with respect to the level of expected return for the four different risk estimators.

Figure 9 Participation ratio

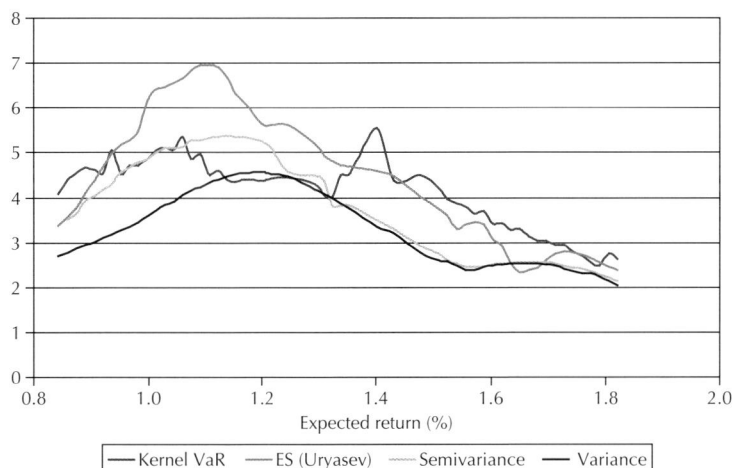

THE VALUE-AT-RISK REFERENCE

Table 8 Distance between efficient portfolios for three levels of expected return, r

	$r = 1.75\%$			$r = 1.15\%$			$r = 1.75\%$		
	VaR	ES	Stdev	VaR	ES	Stdev	VaR	ES	Stdev
ES	0.34			0.85			0.16		
Stdev	0.48	0.63		0.61	0.61		0.26	0.26	
SV	0.30	0.40	0.28	0.36	0.67	0.34	0.21	0.21	0.05

Distance between two optimal portfolios computed under different risk measures for a level of expected return r. VaR, value-at-risk; ES, expected shortfall; Stdev, standard deviation; SV, semivariance.

constraints are less binding. These tables highlight a relative proximity between VaR and semivariance on the one hand and between variance and semivariance on the other. The optimal portfolios with respect to the expected shortfall constraint stand apart, as already pointed out.

Finally, we should note that the individual risk borne by each fund does not explain its proportion in optimal portfolios. For instance, the rank correlation between the risk of individual funds and their weight in the optimal allocation is 43% according to VaR, 37% according to semivariance and only 16% according to expected shortfall. To sum up, a large amount of marginal risk is not synonymous with a low weight in the optimal allocation. Conversely, a low level of marginal individual risk does not correspond with a high weighting in optimal portfolios. This clearly highlights the importance of the dependence between risks in the tails, as has already been stressed by Geman and Kharoubi (2003) or Malevergne and Sornette (2002, 2004).

5 CONCLUSION

We have seen that the way VaR is computed is particularly important. The use of historical VaR even at a 95% level leads to portfolio allocations that change quickly with the return objectives. Under the standard choices of bandwidth, the kernel VaR of Silvapulle and Granger (2001) usually provides results that are close to those obtained under the empirical VaR constraint, while Gouriéroux, Laurent and Scaillet's (2000) kernel VaR is associated with a smoother weighting scheme of returns.

As can be seen from the risk decomposition of the risk measures, the empirical expected shortfall constraint is not so far removed from the kernel VaR constraint of Gouriéroux, Laurent and Scaillet (2000). We also point out that the variance and semivariance constraints depend to quite a large degree on extreme returns because of the squared returns in the computations. The risk decomposition of risk measures enables us to understand the structure of optimal portfolios.

Regarding implementation issues, optimising under variance, semivariance and expected shortfall constraints can be done very quickly, while optimisation under VaR constraints is an extremely lengthy process.[5] Since it is computationally easy to deal with expected shortfall constraints, one might consider relying on the Larsen, Mausser and Uryasev (2002) algorithm, which provides an approximation approach for VaR efficient frontiers based on the Rockafellar and Uryasev (2000) framework and on a fine management of confidence intervals and extreme scenarios. This results in very quick computations, unlike the use of genetic algorithms. However, there is no guarantee that the resulting portfolio is optimal and no way of checking the degree of approximation. We have implemented the algorithm to investigate the accuracy of the method. Using our hedge fund data set, we found big departures from the mean–VaR frontier.[6] This is consistent with our finding that VaR and expected shortfall-optimal portfolios are quite different in our examples.

A question that has not been dealt here with concerns the actual choice of the risk measure from the point of view of the portfolio manager. In fact (and even if this problem deserves much more attention than we have been able to give it here), our results bring some good news. We have seen that, on the whole, the composition of optimal portfolios remains dominated by the same few funds. Therefore, the choice of a particular risk measure does not seem so important. Even VaR, which lacks the property of subadditivity, does not yield very different optimal allocations. Obviously, this conclusion could turn out to be wrong if one focused on more extreme risks. Recall that our study has considered only risks of moderate size since the VaR and the expected shortfall have only be assessed at the 5% level. Such a problem is worth investigation in depth and is left for future research.

APPENDIX A: PROOFS
Proof of Proposition 1

Although the proof is quite straightforward when there are only isolated scenarios, the previous result appears to be true in the general case where multiple scenarios can occur. We note that

$$P(a'R \leq (a'r)_{i:n}) \geq \frac{i}{n}$$

for $i = 1, \ldots, n$ (strict inequality can occur when i is associated with a multiple scenario), and

$$P(a'R < (a'r)_{i:n}) \leq \frac{i-1}{n}$$

where strict inequality can occur in the case that i is associated with multiple scenarios. Let $\alpha \in [(i-1)/n, i/n[$. Then

$$P(a'R < (a'r)_{i:n}) \leq \frac{i-1}{n} \leq \alpha < \frac{i}{n} \leq P(a'R \leq (a'r)_{i:n}) \qquad \textbf{(A1)}$$

In Laurent (2003), the order-α higher quantile for discrete distributions of X taking values in $x_1, \ldots, x_n$ is characterised by $P(X < x_i) \leq \alpha < P(X \leq x_i)$. Together with Equation (A1), this shows that $(a'r)_{i:n}$ is the higher-α quantile of $a'R$. Since $\alpha \in [(i-1)/n, i/n[\Leftrightarrow i = [n\alpha] + 1$, we obtain the stated result.

Proof of Proposition 2

We denote $(X - \zeta)^+ = \max(X - \zeta, 0)$ and $(X - \zeta)^- = \max(\zeta - X, 0)$. Given X and α, we denote $Z(\zeta) = \alpha(X - \zeta)^+ + (1 - \alpha)(X - \zeta)^-$.

❑ Let $\zeta \in \mathbb{R}$ and x be an α-quantile of X. Let us first assume that $\zeta > x$.

$$Z(\zeta) - Z(x) = (1 - \alpha)(\zeta - x) \times 1_{]-\infty,x]}(X)$$
$$+ ((1 - \alpha)\zeta + \alpha x - X)1_{]x,\zeta[}(X) + \alpha(x - \zeta)1_{[\zeta,\infty[}(X)$$

On the other hand, $((1 - \alpha)\zeta + \alpha x - X)1_{]x,\zeta[}(X) \geq \alpha(x - \zeta)1_{]x,\zeta[}(X)$. Then

$$H_\alpha(\zeta) - H_\alpha(x) \geq (1 - \alpha)(\zeta - x)P(X \leq x) + \alpha(x - \zeta)P(X > x)$$

or equivalently:

$$H_\alpha(\zeta) - H_\alpha(x) \geq (\zeta - x) \times ((1 - \alpha)P(X \leq x) - \alpha P(X > x))$$

$(1 - \alpha)P(X \leq x) - \alpha P(X > x) = P(X \leq x) - \alpha \geq 0$ since x is an α-quantile. This shows that $H_\alpha(\zeta) \geq H_\alpha(x)$.

❑ Let us now assume that $\zeta < x$.

$$Z(\zeta) - Z(x) = (1 - \alpha)(\zeta - x) \times 1_{]-\infty,\zeta]}(X)$$
$$+ (X - \alpha\zeta - (1 - \alpha)x)1_{]\zeta,x[}(X) + \alpha(x - \zeta)1_{[x,\infty[}(X)$$

On the other hand, $(X - \alpha\zeta - (1 - \alpha)x)1_{]\zeta,x[}(X) \geq (1 - \alpha)(\zeta - x)$ $1_{]\zeta,x[}(X)$. Thus,

$$H_\alpha(\zeta) - H_\alpha(x) \geq (1 - \alpha)(\zeta - x)P(X < x) + \alpha(x - \zeta)P(X \geq x)$$

or, equivalently,

$$H_\alpha(\zeta) - H_\alpha(x) \geq (x - \zeta) \times (\alpha P(X \geq x) - (1 - \alpha)P(X < x))$$

$\alpha P(X \geq x) - (1 - \alpha)P(X < x) = \alpha - P(X < x) \geq 0$ since x is an α-quantile. This shows that $H_\alpha(\zeta) \geq H_\alpha(x)$.

❑ Finally, let us check that H_α is constant over $Q_\alpha(X)$. Let ζ be an interior point of $Q_\alpha(X)$. Let ζ' be another quantile with $zeta' > \zeta$. From the first point (ζ is a quantile and $\zeta' > \zeta$), $H_\alpha(\zeta') \geq H_\alpha(\zeta)$. From the second point (ζ' is a quantile and $\zeta < \zeta'$), $H_\alpha(\zeta) \geq H_\alpha(\zeta')$. Thus, $H_\alpha(\zeta) = H_\alpha(\zeta')$. We note that H_α is continuous.[7] As a consequence, H_α takes the same values on the boundary of $Q_\alpha(X)$ and on its interior.

Proof of Proposition 3

$(E^P[(X - \zeta)^-]/\alpha) - \zeta = 1/\alpha(H_\alpha(\zeta)) - E^P[X]$, where $H_\alpha(\zeta) = \alpha E^P[(X-\zeta)^+] + (1 - \alpha)E^P[(X - \zeta)^-]$. The minimum is thus attained for $\zeta \in Q_\alpha(X)$.

Now, since the criterion $(E^P[(X - \zeta)^-]/\alpha) - \zeta$ is minimal on the quantile set $Q_\alpha(X)$, we can write $1/\alpha((X - \zeta)^- - \zeta\alpha) = 1/\alpha(-X1_{\{X \leq \zeta\}} + \zeta(1_{\{X \leq \zeta\}} - \alpha))$ for any $\xi \in Q_\alpha(X)$. Thus, we can write the minimum of $(E^P[(X - \zeta)^-]/\alpha) - \zeta$ as

$$\frac{1}{\alpha}(E^P([X1_{\{X \leq q_\alpha(X)\}}] + q_\alpha(X)(\alpha - P(X \leq q_\alpha(X)))) = ES_\alpha(X),$$

$$\forall q_\alpha(X) \in Q_\alpha(X)$$

Proof of corollary 1

Let $a, b \in \mathbb{R}$. Then, $a^- + b^- \geq (a + b)^{-8}$. This yields

$$\frac{E^P[(X - a))^-]}{\alpha} - a + \frac{E^P[(Y - b)^-]}{\alpha}$$

$$-b \geq \frac{E^P[(X + Y - (a + b))^-]}{\alpha} - (a + b)$$

Since

$$\frac{E^P[(X + Y - (a + b))^-]}{\alpha} - (a + b) \geq \inf_{s \in \mathbb{R}} \frac{E^P[(X + Y - s)^-]}{\alpha} - s$$

$$= -ES_\alpha(X + Y)$$

we get $\forall a, b \in \mathbb{R}$,

$$\frac{E^P[(X - a)^-]}{\alpha} - a + \frac{E^P[(Y - b)^-]}{\alpha} - b \geq -ES_\alpha(X + Y)$$

and we can then write $-ES_\alpha(X) - ES_\alpha(Y) \geq -ES_\alpha(X + Y)$, which shows the subadditivity of the expected shortfall.

Proof of Proposition 4

We adapt the proof by Acerbi and Tasche (2002b). Since $VaR_\alpha(X) = -q_\alpha^+(X)$, we want to show that $ES_\alpha(X) = -1/\alpha \int_0^\alpha q_u^+(X)\,du$. Using:

$$ES_\alpha(X) = -\frac{1}{\alpha}(E^P[X1_{\{X \leq q_\alpha^+(X)\}}] + q_\alpha^+(X)(\alpha - P(X \leq q_\alpha^+(X))))$$

we need to show that

$$\int_0^\alpha q_u^+(X)\,du = E^P[X1_{\{X \leq q_\alpha^+(X)\}}] + q_\alpha^+(X)(\alpha - P(X \leq q_\alpha^+(X)))$$

Let U be a uniform $[0, 1]$ random variable defined on some probability space. We define $Z = q_U^+(X)$. We note that since $u \to q_u^+(X)$ is not decreasing, we have $\{U \leq \alpha\} \subset \{Z \leq q_\alpha^+(X)\}$ and $\{U > \alpha\} \cap \{Z \leq q_\alpha^+(X)\} \subset \{Z = q_\alpha^+(X)\}$. From the transfer theorem we have $\int_0^\alpha q_u^+(X)du = E[Z1_{\{U \leq \alpha\}}]$. Since $\{U \leq \alpha\} \subset \{Z \leq q_\alpha^+(X)\}$, we have

$E[Z1_{\{U\leq\alpha\}}] = E[Z1_{\{U\leq\alpha\}}1_{\{Z\leq q_\alpha^+(X)\}}]$, which we can rewrite as $E[Z1_{\{Z\leq q_\alpha^+(X)\}}] - E[Z1_{\{U>\alpha\}\cap\{Z\leq q_\alpha^+(X)\}}]$. Since $q_U^+(X)$ is distributed as X, the first expectation equals $E[X1_{\{X\leq q_\alpha^+(X)\}}]$. By using the second set relation, we write the second expectation as $q_\alpha^+(X)E[1_{\{U>\alpha\}}1_{\{Z\leq q_\alpha^+(X)\}}]$. Since where the latter equality comes from the first set relation, and since $1_{\{U>\alpha\}}1_{\{Z\leq q_\alpha^+(X)\}} = 1_{\{Z\leq q_\alpha^+(X)\}} - 1_{\{Z\leq q_\alpha^+(X)\}}1_{\{U\leq\alpha\}} = 1_{\{Z\leq q_\alpha^+(X)\}} - 1_{\{U\leq\alpha\}}$, where the latter equality comes from the first set relation, and since Z is distributed as X, we can write the second expectation as $P(X \leq q_\alpha^+(X)) - \alpha$. This proves the stated result.

Proof of Proposition 5

We start from the quantile representation of the expected shortfall, $ES_\alpha(a'R) = -1/\alpha \int_0^\alpha q_u^+(a'R)du$. By splitting the integral over $[(i-1)/n, i/n[$ intervals, we can write the expected shortfall as $ES_\alpha(a'R) = -1/\alpha\sum_{i=1}^n \int_0^1 1_{[(i-1)/n,i/n[}(u) \times q_u^+(a'R)1_{[0,\alpha]}du$ For $u\in[(i-1)/n,i/n[$, we have $q_u^+(a'R) = (a'r)_{i:n}$, which allows us to write $ES_\alpha(a'R) = -1/\alpha \sum_{i=1}^n (a'r)_{i:n} \int_0^1 1_{[(i-1)/n,i/n[}(u)1_{[0,\alpha]}du$. The different integral terms appear to be equal to $1/n$ if $i \leq [n\alpha]$, where $[z]$ is the integer part of z, $\alpha - (i-1)/n$ if $i = [n\alpha] + 1$ and 0 otherwise. We then get the stated result $ES_\alpha(a'R) = -1/\alpha (\sum_{i=1}^{[n\alpha]}(a'r)_{i:n} / n + (\alpha - [n\alpha]/n)(a'r)_{[n\alpha]+1:n})$.

Proof of Proposition 6

Let us prove the first point. We recall that $Q_\alpha(a'R = \arg\min_\zeta(E[(a'R - \zeta)^-]/\alpha) - \zeta$ and the corresponding value of the minimum equals $ES_\alpha(a'R)$. Let us consider a series (a_n,z_n) such that $(E[(a_n'R - \zeta_n)^-]/\alpha) - \zeta_n$ is converging to $\min_{(a,\zeta)}(E[(a'R - \zeta)^-]/\alpha) - \zeta$. From the stated optimisation result, we have the inequalities

$$\frac{E[(a_n'R - \zeta_n)^-]}{\alpha} - \zeta_n \geq \frac{E[(a_n'R - q_\alpha^+(a_n'R))^-]}{\alpha} - q_\alpha^+(a_n'R)$$

$$\geq \min_{(a,\zeta)}\frac{E[(a'R - \zeta)^-]}{\alpha} - \zeta$$

This shows that $\lim_{n\to\infty}E[(a_n'R - q_\alpha^+(a_n'R))^-]/\alpha - q_\alpha^+(a_n'R) = \min_{(a,\zeta)}(E[(a'R-\zeta)^-]/\alpha)-\zeta$ or, equivalently, that $\lim_{n\to\infty}ES_\alpha(a_n'R) = \min_{(a,\zeta)}(E[(a'R - \zeta)^-]/\alpha) - \zeta$ As a consequence $\min_a ES_\alpha(a'R) \leq \min_{(a,\zeta)}(E[(a'R - \zeta)^-]/\alpha) - \zeta$ On the other hand, for $a\in\mathbb{R}^p$, $ES_\alpha(a'R) = E[(a'R-q_\alpha^+(a'R))^+]/\alpha-q_\alpha^+(a'R) \geq \min_{(a,\zeta)}(E[(a'R-\zeta)^-]/\alpha)-\zeta$ shows that $\min_a ES_\alpha(a'R) \geq \min_{(a,\zeta)}(E[(a'R - \zeta)^-]/\alpha) - \zeta$. This shows that

$$\min_{a \in \mathbb{R}^p} ES_\alpha(a'R) = \min_{(a,\zeta) \in \mathbb{R}^p \times \mathbb{R}} \frac{E\left[(a'R - \zeta)^-\right]}{\alpha} - \zeta$$

This holds for any distribution of returns. By using the empirical measure, we get the stated result.

1. Such an assumption is not fulfilled for our data set. In fact, it is well known that returns on hedge funds exhibit significant serial correlation due to the illiquidity of this kind of investment vehicle (eg, Getmansky, Lo and Makarov (2004)). In the sequel, for simplicity and because of the lack of econometric literature on the accuracy of quantile estimates in the presence of time-dependence between sample realisations, we will ignore the influence of such serial correlation.
2. The weights are not constant for the GLS and Gaussian VaRs. However, the overall shape does not depend too much on the chosen portfolio. Here $\alpha = 5\%$.
3. This frontier corresponds to the mean–variance frontier.
4. We could use the weaker assumption $E[X^-] < \infty$, where $X^- = \max(0, -X)$.
5. About one week for a single efficient frontier.
6. Detailed results can be obtained from the authors on request.
7. The random variables $Z(\zeta)$ depend continuously on ζ. They can be bounded by an integrable random variable in a compact neighbourhood of ζ_0. From the dominated convergence theorem, we obtain continuity in ζ_0.
8. Indeed, $a^- \geq -a, b^- \geq -b$, thus $a^- + b^- \geq -(a + b)$. On the other hand, $a^- + b^- \geq 0$ provides $a^- + b^- \geq \max(0, -(a + b)) = (a + b)^-$.

This chapter was previously published in *The Journal of Risk* **8**(4), Summer 2006.

REFERENCES

Acerbi, C., 2002, "Spectral Measures of Risk: A Coherent Representation of Subjective Risk Aversion", *Journal of Banking and Finance* **26(7)**, pp. 1505–18.

Acerbi, C., C. Nordio, and C. Sirtori, 2001, "Expected Shortfall as a Tool for Financial Risk Management", Working paper, Derivatives Desk, Axabank.

Acerbi, C. and D. Tasche, 2002a, "Expected Shortfall: A Natural Coherent Alternative to Value at Risk", *Economic Notes* **31(2)**, pp. 379–88.

Acerbi, C. and D. Tasche, 2002b, "On the Coherence of Expected Shortfall", *Journal of Banking and Finance* **26(7)**, pp. 1487–503.

Alexander, G. and A. Baptista, 2001, "A VaR-Constrained Mean-Variance Model: Implications for Portfolio Selection and the Basle Capital Accord", Working paper, University of Minnesota.

Artzner, P., F. Delbaen, J.-M. Eber, and D. Heath, 1999, "Coherent Measures of Risk", *Mathematical Finance* **9(3)**, pp. 203–28.

Azzalini, A., 1981, "A Note on the Estimation of a Distribution Function and Quantiles by a Kernel Method", *Biometrika* **68**, pp. 326–28.

Black, F. and R. Litterman, 1992, "Global Portfolio Optimisation", *Financial Analysts Journal* **48(5)**, pp. 28–43.

Bouchaud, J.-P. and M. Potters, 2000, *Theory of Financial Risks,* (Cambridge:. Cambridge University Press).

Brown, S. and W. Goetzmann, 1997, "Mutual Fund Styles", *Journal of Financial Economics* **43**, pp. 373–99.

Chernozhukov, V. and L. Umantsev, 2002, "Conditional Value-at-Risk: Aspects of Modeling and Estimation", in *Economic Applications of Quantile Regression,* (New York: Springer).

Consigli, G., 2002, "Tail Estimation and Mean-VaR Portfolio Selection in Markets Subject to Financial Instability", *Journal of Banking and Finance* **26(7)**, pp. 1355–82.

de Athayde, G., 2001, "Building a Mean-Downside Risk Portfolio Frontier", in F. Sortino and S. Satchell (eds), *Managing Downside Risk in Financial Markets: Theory, Practice and Implementation.* Butterworth Heinemann.

Delbaen, F., 2002, "Coherent Risk Measures on General Probability Spaces", in K. Sandmann and P. J. Schonbucher (eds), *Advances in Finance and Stochastics, Essays in Honour of Dieter Sondermann,* (New York: Springer).

Denneberg, D., 1990, "Premium Calculation: Why Standard Deviation should be Replaced by Absolute Deviation", *ASTIN Bulletin* **20**, pp. 181–90.

Dibartolomeo, D. and E. Witkowski, 1997, "Mutual Funds Misclassification: Evidence Based on Style Analysis", *Financial Analysts Journal,* October, pp. 32–43.

Dorsey, R. E. and W. J. Mayer, 1995, "Genetic Algorithms for Estimation Problems with Multiple Optima, Non-Differentiability, and Other Irregular Features", *Journal of Business and Economic Statistics* **13**, pp. 53–66.

Fischer, T., 2003, "Risk Capital Allocation by Coherent Risk Measures Based on One-Sided Moments", *Insurance: Mathematics and Economics* **32**, pp. 135–46.

Gaivoronski, A. and G. Pflug, 1999, "Finding Optimal Portfolios with Constraints on Value at Risk", Working paper, University of Vienna.

Geman, H. and C. Kharoubi, 2003, "Hedge Funds Revisited: Distributional Characteristics, Dependence Structure and Diversification", *Journal of Risk* **5(4)**, pp. 55–75.

Getmansky, M., A. W. Lo, and I. Makarov, 2004, "An Econometric Model of Serial Correlation and Illiquidity in Hedge Funds Returns", *Journal of Financial Economics* **74**, pp. 529–609.

Goldberg, D. E., 1989, *Genetic Algorithms in Search, Optimisation and Learning.* Addison-Wesley.

Gouriéroux, C., J.-P. Laurent, and O. Scaillet, 2000, "Sensitivity Analysis of Values at Risk", *Journal of Empirical Finance* **7**, pp. 225–45.

Jorion, P., 1985, "International Portfolio Diversification with Estimation Risk", *Journal of Business* **58(3)**, pp. 259–78.

Jorion, P., 2000, *Value-at-Risk: the New Benchmark for Managing Financial Risk,* Second edition, (New York: McGraw-Hill).

Krokhmal, P., J. Palmquist, and S. Uryasev, 2002, "Portfolio Optimization with Conditional Value-at-Risk Objective and Constraints", *Journal of Risk* **4(2)**.

Krokhmal, P., S. Uryasev, and G. Zrazhevsky, 2002, "Risk Management for Hedge Fund Portfolios", *Journal of Alternative Investments* **5(1)**, pp. 10–29.

Konno, H., H. Waki, and A. Yuuki, 2002, "Portfolio Optimization Under Lower Partial Risk Measures", *Asia-Pacific Financial Markets* **9(2)**, pp. 127–40.

Larsen, N., H. Mausser, and S. Uryasev, 2002, "Algorithms for Optimization of Value at Risk", in P. Pardalos and V. K. Tsitsiringos (eds), *Financial Engineering, E-commerce and Supply Chain*, (Dordrecht: Kluwer Academic Press), pp. 129–57.

Laurent, J.-P., 2003, "Sensitivity Analysis of Risk Measures for Discrete Distributions", Working paper, University of Lyon – Isfa.

Ledoit, O. and M. Wolf, 2003, "Improved Estimation of the Covariance Matrix of Stock Returns with Application to Portfolio Selection", *Journal of Empirical Finance* **10(5)**, pp. 603–21.

Malevergne, Y. and D. Sornette, 2002, "Minimising Extremes", *Risk* **15(11)**, pp. 129–34.

Malevergne, Y. and D. Sornette, 2004, "How to Account for Extreme Co-Movements Between Individual Stocks and the Market", *Journal of Risk* **6(3)**, pp. 71–116.

Markowitz, H., 1952, "Portfolio Selection", *Journal of Finance* **7(1)**, pp. 77–91.

Pflug, G., 2000, "Some Remarks on the Value-at-Risk and the Conditional Value-at-Risk", in S. Uryasev (ed.), *Probabilistic Constrained Optimization: Methodology and Applications*, (Dordrechit: Kluwer Academic Press).

Price, K. and R. Storn, 1997, "Differential Evolution", *Dr. Doob's Journal*, April, pp. 18–24.

Rockafellar, R. T. and S. Uryasev, 2000, "Optimization of Conditional Value-at-Risk", *Journal of Risk* **2(3)**, pp. 21–41.

Rockafellar, R. T. and S. Uryasev, 2002, "Conditional Value-at-Risk for General Loss Distributions", *Journal of Banking and Finance* **26(7)**, pp. 1443–71.

Scaillet, O., 2004, "Nonparametric Estimation and Sensitivity Analysis of Expected Shortfall", *Mathematical Finance* **14**, pp. 115–29.

Sheather, S. J. and J. S. Marron, 1990, "Kernel Quantile Estimators", *Journal of the American Statistical Association* **85(410)**, pp. 410–16.

Silvapulle, P. and C. Granger, 2001, "Large Returns, Conditional Correlation and Portfolio Diversification: A Value-at-Risk Approach", *Quantitative Finance* **1**, pp. 542–51.

Tasche, D., 2002, "Expected Shortfall and Beyond", *Journal of Banking and Finance* **26(7)**, pp. 1519–33.

Topaloglou, N., H. Vladimirou, and S. Zenios, 2002, "CVaR Models with Selective Hedging for International Asset Allocation", *Journal of Banking and Finance* **26(7)**, pp. 1535–61.

Uryasev, S., 1995, "Derivative of Probability Functions and Some Applications", *Annals of Operations Research* **56**, pp. 287–311.

Vorst, T., 1999, "Optimal Portfolios Under a Value at Risk Constraint", Working paper, Erasmus University.

Section 2

Estimation of Risk Models

5

The Cost of Conservativism

Jon Danielsson; Phillipp Hartmann; Casper de Vries

London School of Economics, University of Iceland, Tinbergen Institute;
London School of Economics; Erasmus University Rotterdam, Tinbergen Institute

This month, the *Amendment to the Basel Capital Accord to Incorporate Market Risks* becomes effective in the G10 countries. Its main innovation compared to other market risk capital regulations, such as the European Union's Capital Adequacy Directive, is that banks will have the option of using their internal risk management models to set capital against trading book losses.

In this chapter, we will point to several important facts which we feel have been neglected in the discussion about value-at-risk (VaR) models in general, and the Basel internal models approach in particular. We argue that the current Basel requirements remain disincentives for the development of more reliable VaR models, and show that considerable improvement of current VaR models is possible by means of techniques that explicitly focus on the properties of extreme return fluctuations.

We then briefly discuss how a change in the determination of the Basel "multiplication factor" may encourage the industry to adopt improved VaR models, such as those proposed here. There are already more far-reaching reform proposals on the table, not least of which is the pre-commitment approach for market risk capital requirements (Kupiec and O'Brien (1995b, 1997)). Although it is rarely pointed out, pre-commitment actually implies an endogenous, incentive-compatible multiplication factor. These new ideas have their merits, but for the moment, the present regulatory approaches should be improved to ensure financial stability at reasonable costs for both consumers and market participants.

TRADITIONAL VAR MODELS

VaR models usually use historical data to evaluate maximum (worst case) trading losses for a given portfolio over a certain holding period and at a given confidence interval. For example, a VaR model may tell you that there is a 3% probability of a bank's daily trading loss amounting to US$1 million or more. Our first important observation is that VaR applies to the extreme lower tail of the return frequency distribution (ie, large losses), far away from the mean. This fact is recognised in the Basel market risk amendment, which specifies the use of a one-sided confidence interval of 99%.

This number clearly reflects regulators' natural leanings towards conservatism in their prudential supervision of banks. The same tendency also comes out in the Basel regulators' choice of holding period, a second important model parameter. While the industry is virtually unanimous in its use of daily VaR for internal risk control, banks are obliged under Basel to assume that they cannot liquidate their trading portfolios quicker than within 10 business days when determining their minimum regulatory capital against market risk, banks will be obliged. In order to facilitate the transition from their internal daily VaR models to the regulatory 10-day models the application of a simple scaling rule is permitted. We shall come back to this rule below, making the argument that – surprisingly – this may lead to an over-estimation of the bi-weekly VaR.

The most difficult part in VaR estimation is the derivation of the portfolio return frequency distribution. Two approaches have become widely popular: variance-covariance analysis and historical simulation.

Variance-covariance analysis relies on the assumption that financial market returns follow a multivariate normal distribution. It is easy to implement, because the VaR can be computed from a simple linear formula with variances and covariances of returns as the only inputs. Its major drawback is that financial market returns are not really normally distributed, but are rather fat-tailed, meaning that losses are much more frequent than predicted by variance-covariance analysis. It is particularly weak where a VaR model for regulatory purposes and risk control should be strong, ie, in the prediction of large losses.

Another feature of many VaR models is the exponential weighing of past returns, ie, returns closer to the present are given more

weight than those several months or even a year ago. This technique is justified by the presence of conditional heteroscedasticity
(CH) in daily financial market returns, meaning that a volatile day
is usually followed by volatile days. However, two important
observations are relevant for discussion of Basel minimum capital
requirements.

First, while daily returns exhibit strong CH effects, they can
hardly be detected in bi-weekly returns such as the regulatory 10-day
holding period. Second, CH effects largely originate from medium-
and small-range volatility periods. Extreme events, such as losses
at or beyond a 99% confidence interval, scatter rather independently over time (Danielsson and de Vries (1997b)). You don't
observe Black Mondays four or five days in a row. Nevertheless,
the many models used in the industry assume the opposite
through the exponential weighing of past events, which exacerbate
the bias in estimated bi-weekly tail probabilities because back-
wards declining weights artificially shorten the historical data window (Jackson *et al* (1997)).

Historical simulation does not suffer from the tail-bias problem,
because it does not rely on normality. By applying the full, empirical
market return distribution to all the items in the current trading portfolio, the outcome exactly reflects the historical frequency of large
losses over the specific data window. Another advantage of this
approach compared to variance-covariance analysis is that it can
incorporate non-linear positions, such as derivative positions, in a
natural way; see Kupiec and O'Brien (1995a) on this "full-valuation"
property.

The problem with historical simulation is that it is very sensitive
to the particular data window, which the Basel Committee has chosen to be at least one year of past returns. In other words, whether
October 1987 is included or not makes a huge difference for the
VaR predicted. Stated differently, the empirical return distribution
is very "dense" and smooth around the mean, so that no parametric model based on a standard distribution, such as the normal, can
beat the accuracy of the empirical distribution there. Due to the few
occurrences of extremely large price movements, however, it
becomes "discrete" in the tails. Hence, VaR predictions based on
historical simulation exhibit high variances. Moreover, at its lower
end, the empirical return distribution sharply drops to zero and

remains there, ie, the probability of more severe losses in the future than the largest one during the past year is assigned as zero, which might be considered imprudent.

Our interim conclusion is that a good VaR model to satisfy regulatory minimum capital standards should correctly represent the likelihood of extreme events by providing smooth tail estimates of the portfolio return distribution which extend beyond the historical sample (up to infinity). Exponential or other weighing schemes need not be adopted. In what follows we shall sketch a new VaR model which satisfies these requirements by combining historical simulation for the interior of the portfolio return distribution with a parametric estimator for the tails.

A NEW APPROACH: EXTREME VALUE THEORY

All heavy-tailed distributions eventually display the same tail behavior when we consider large losses or gains: they all have tail shapes which, to first order, approximate the tail shape of the Pareto distribution. Thus, if we know the distribution is heavy tailed, then the largest losses occur with the following approximate probability:

$$P\{R < -r\} = F(-r) \approx ar^{-\alpha}, \text{ as } r \to \infty \tag{1}$$

The tail probabilities depend on two parameters: a scaling constant a, and the so called tail index, α. Formula (1) says that extreme events become more likely, and the tails grow fatter, as the tail index becomes smaller. Statistical extreme value theory provides the tools for estimating the tail parameters. (See Danielsson and de Vries (1997a, 1997b) for a more detailed description of the theory and applications.)

In order to illustrate the differences between the tail estimation technique and other methods for VaR inference, we will consider a particularly volatile asset class, ie, daily returns on spot oil prices from 1986 to 1997. By applying the method of Danielsson and de Vries (1997a) we can predict from the derived tail probabilities that the maximum one-day drop expected in oil prices during a period of 15 years is 28%, and that a drop of 44% is expected once every 70 years. In a single year we expect one day where prices increase by 10%, on average.

Table 1 Performance of different VaR models (1,000 day horizon)

Confidence level	95%	99%	99.95%
Expected number of VaR violations	50	10	0.5
Average number of realised VaR violations (percentage error in parenthesis)			
Variance-Covariance	52.45	16.28	3.55
	(4%)	(63%)	(610%)
Historical simulation	43.24	7.66	0
	(−14%)	(−23%)	(−100%)
Tail estimation	43.14	8.19	0.59
	(−14%)	(−18%)	(18%)

Note: Models tested with 500 random portfolios comprising 7 US stocks for the period 1993 through 1996.

The figure illustrates a subsample of the results from 1992 to 1997. It shows the results from three different VaR estimation techniques: historical simulation, variance-covariance methods, and extreme-value analysis. The step function gives the empirically realised losses on the horizontal axis, with the frequency of losses on the vertical axis, and reflects the results one would obtain from using historical simulation. (The smaller window gives the entire empirical cumulative distribution function.) The dotted line plots the estimated tail probabilities.

The figure clearly illustrates how the tail estimator smoothes the distribution of extreme returns. Moreover, the curve extends "beyond the sample" (to the left), allowing evaluation of the frequency and magnitude of losses for a much larger time interval than we have data for. It is instructive to compare this with the losses predicted by variance-covariance analysis, which is indicated by the dashed line. This curve is located way below the other two, in the south-east corner. Clearly, the normality assumption leads to a substantial under-estimation of VaR. For example, the probability of a 6% drop in the oil price is 13 times greater under the estimated tail distribution than under the normal distribution.

Danielsson and de Vries (1997b) compare the performance of various VaR prediction methods for simulated portfolios of US stocks over a 4-year period. A subset of the results is shown in the Table 1, which compares the expected number of VaR violations for three different confidence intervals with those actually realised in the simulations.

For example, for the Basel 99% confidence interval, 10 violations are to be expected; the variance-covariance approach gave on average 16 violations, while the tail estimation predicted only 8 cases. At the 95% level, the variance-covariance method performs best with 4% error, but as the confidence level increases, the performance of this method steadily worsens, eg, at the 99% confidence level, the error is over 60%. Historical simulation has mixed performance; it provides reasonable predictions at the lower confidence levels, but worsens with higher levels and becomes uninformative at the out-of-sample 99.95% confidence level. Note that the tail estimator still provides a remarkably good estimate at that level.

THE SCALING FACTOR

As has been pointed out before (Kupiec and O'Brien (1995a)), the simple "square-root-of-time" formula used to aggregate daily VaR estimates to bi-weekly estimates can be rather imprecise when the returns of the underlying market risk factors are non-normal. This has led to concern among regulators that the simple time-aggregation rule can easily lead to an underestimation of potential losses and, therefore, to too little capital against market risk, suggesting a more stringent regulatory approach.

We come to rather the opposite conclusion, and argue that the square-root formula may lead to an *over*-estimation of VaR when returns are not normally distributed and exhibit fat tails. Assume that the observed financial market returns r have finite variance. This implies that the tail index α is larger than two in formula (1). Let t denote the length of the holding period. Increasing the holding period t increases the VaR under the normal model by a factor of $\sqrt[2]{t}$ (the "square-root-of-time rule"). If the return distribution is fat-tailed, this factor equals $\sqrt[\alpha]{t}$, and since $\alpha > 2$, $\sqrt[2]{t} > \sqrt[\alpha]{t}$.

Hence the "square-root-of-time" rule eventually results in a *higher* VaR than the value implied by a heavy-tailed distribution. This result follows from Equation (1) and is a direct implication of the linear tail additivity of fat-tailed distributed random variables, and the self-additivity of normally distributed variables (see Dacorogna *et al* (1997) for further details).

In sum, by prescribing the "square-root-of-time" rule for time-aggregation regulators have – consciously or unconsciously – introduced another element of conservatism in the internal models approach to market risk capital requirements, and one which has passed widely unnoticed.

THE BASEL MULTIPLICATION FACTOR

Basel's requirement, confirmed in December 1996, that a bank's 10-day, 99% VaR estimate should be multiplied by a factor of at least three to determine the minimum regulatory capital against market risk met with a cool reception from the industry. National bankers' associations argued that such a high factor would discourage the application of quantitative models and obstruct progress in risk management techniques (see Elderfield (1995)). As an example: even if a bank applied the tail estimation approach proposed above – which is clearly much more precise than more widely-used alternatives – it could not be granted a lower factor than three.

In addition, this factor can be increased through a variable add-on of between zero and one, depending on the performance of a bank's *one-day* model in backtesting procedures. The Basel Committee points out that the variable component provides built-in incentives to develop and use better models. However, we would argue that the fixed factor (three) is already so high that it completely dominates any potential advantages to be had from a good model which qualifies for a zero add-on.

In fact, we would propose that the fixed component should be lowered, and the range of the variable add-on potentially extended, to leave sufficient incentives for banks to use the best models. Stahl (1997) recently advanced an interesting theoretical justification for the fixed factor of three, which was previously interpreted as a somewhat arbitrary political compromise. His two arguments, one related to the tail mis-specification in variance-covariance approaches, the other to potential time-variation of portfolio return distributions over the relevant data window (in particular, unidentified increases in the variance of returns), are both based on a very general statistical result known as the Chebyshev inequality: If R is a random variable with mean μ_R and finite variance σ_R^2, then

$$P(\mu_R - k\sigma_R < R < \mu_R + k\sigma_R) \geq 1 - \frac{1}{k^2} \qquad (2)$$

Formula (2) implies, for example, that – whatever the true distribution of a random variable R – the boundaries of a 99% confidence interval ($P[\cdot] = 0.99$) are never wider than 10 standard deviations left and right from the mean (ie, $0.99 \geq 1 - 1/k^2 \Leftrightarrow |k| \leq 10$).

Note that Chebyshev's inequality is true for *any* type of distribution which has a finite variance. Applied to VaR, it says in a way: assuming that we know nothing about the structure of financial market returns, what is the extreme boundary which could cover any specification error? Of course, at this level of generality the answer must be a very conservative multiplication factor (something between 3 and 4 according to Stahl's calculations) in order to cover even the weirdest distributions. An example showing how far off this theoretical bound can be is given in de Haan *et al* (1994).

However, we know much more than "nothing" about financial market returns. As discussed above, we know that these returns have fat tails and that a single limit law determines the shape of these tails. Including this information, as in the tail estimation approach described above, is both efficient from the risk manager's perspective and prudent from the regulator's point of view. This conclusion is *not* subjective and hardly depends on any particular empirical specifications.

We conclude, therefore, that the fixed component in the Basel multiplication factor is unnecessarily conservative and should be reduced in order to give banks the opportunity to reap the benefits of better VaR models. Bad models could still be sufficiently penalised by adjusting the range of the variable add-on. This would avoid any disincentives through prudential capital requirements to future progress in banks' risk management techniques, while preserving the fundamentals of the Basel internal models approach (Goodhart *et al* (1997), Chapter 5).

To be sure, it is extremely difficult for external regulators to evaluate the extent to which they can have confidence in banks' internal risk management techniques, and some degree of conservatism is a necessary characteristic of every financial regulator confronted with the sometimes wild gyrations of financial market behavior. But it seems that in the Amendment to the Basel Capital Accord to Incorporate Market Risks this conservatism may have gone too far.

This chapter was previously published in *Risk*, January 1998.

REFERENCES

Basle Committee on Banking Supervision, 1996a, Amendment to the Capital Accord to Incorporate Market Risks, Basel: Bank for International Settlements, January.

Basle Committee on Banking Supervision, 1996b, Supervisory Framework for the Use of "Backtesting" in Conjunction with the Internal Models Approach to Market Risk Capital Requirements, Basel: Bank for International Settlements, January.

Dacorogna, M. M., U. A. Muller, O. V. Pictet, and C. G. de Vries, 1997, "The Distribution of Extremal Foreign Exchange Rate Returns in Extremely Large Data Sets", *Mimeo.*, Tinbergen Institute.

Danielsson, J. and C. G. de Vries, 1997a, "Tail Index and Quantile Estimation with Very High Frequency Data", *Journal of Empirical Finance* **4**, pp. 241–57.

Danielsson, J. C. G. de Vries, 1997b, "Value at Risk and Extreme Returns", *L.S.E. Financial Markets Group Discussion Paper*, no. 273, London School of Economics, September.

Elderfield, M., 1995, "Capital Incentives", *Risk,* September, pp. 20f.

Goodhart, C. A. E., P. Hartmann, D. T. Llewellyn, L. Rojas-Suarez, and S. R. Weisbrod, 1997, "Financial Regulation: Why, How and Where Now?", Monograph prepared for the Bank of England Central Bank Governors' Symposium, forthcoming with Routledge, Chapters 3 and 5.

de Haan, L., D. W. Jansen, K. G. Koedijk, and C. G. de Vries, 1994, "Safety First Portfolio Selection, Extreme Value Theory, and Long Run Asset Risks", in J. Galambos, J. Lechner, and E. Simmiu (eds), *Extreme Value Theory and Applications*, (Dordrecht: Kluwer Press), pp. 471–87.

Hartmann, P., 1997, "Capital Adequacy and Foreign Exchange Risk Regulation: Theoretical Considerations and Recent Developments in Industrial Countries", *Kredit und Kapital* **30**, pp. 186–218.

Jackson, P., D. J. Maude, and W. Perraudin, 1997, "Bank Capital and Value at Risk", *Journal of Derivatives* **4/3**, pp. 73–89.

Kupiec, P. H. and J. M. O'Brien, 1995a, "Internal Affairs", *Risk*, May, pp. 43–8.

Kupiec, P. H. and J. M. O'Brien, 1995b, "Model Alternative", *Risk*, June, pp. 37–41.

Kupiec, P. H. and J. M. O'Brien, 1997, "The Pre-Commitment Approach: Using Incentives to Set Market Risk Capital Requirements", *FEDS Paper*, no. 97-14, Federal Reserve Board, March.

Stahl, G., 1997, "Three Cheers", *Risk*, May, pp. 67–9.

6

Great Realisations

Torben Andersen; Tim Bollerslev; Francis Diebold; Paul Labys

Northwestern University; Duke University, NEBR;
New York University, NEBR; University of Pennsylvania

Volatility is central to many applied issues in finance and financial engineering, from asset pricing and asset allocation to risk management. Hence financial economists have been intrigued by the very high precision with which volatility can be estimated under the diffusion assumption. Precise estimation of diffusion volatility does not require a long calendar span of data. Rather, volatility can be estimated well from an arbitrarily short span of data, provided that returns are sampled sufficiently frequently. This contrasts sharply with precise estimation of the drift, which generally requires a long calendar span of data, regardless of the frequency with which returns are sampled.

Consequently, the volatility literature has steadily progressed toward the use of higher-frequency data. This is true in the parametric autoregressive conditional heteroscedasticity (Arch) and stochastic volatility literatures (see Bollerslev, Engle & Nelson (1994), for a review), as well as in the more traditional empirical finance literature. For example, Officer (1973) constructs annual volatilities from monthly returns on an equity index, whereas Merton (1980) and French, Schwert and Stambaugh (1987) use daily returns to estimate monthly volatilities. Even more recently, Schwert (1998) relies on 15-minute returns for construction of daily stock market volatilities, while Taylor and Xu (1997) and Andersen *et al* (1999a) exploit five-minute returns in the measurement of daily exchange rate volatilities.

Recent work has clarified the comparative desirability of alternative volatility estimators. This emerging theory emphasises the advantages of the so-called realised volatility estimator. Construction of realised volatility is trivial – one simply sums intra-period high-frequency squared returns (or cross products, for realised covariance), period-by-period. For example, for a 24-hour market, daily realised volatility based on five-minute underlying returns is defined as the sum of the 288 intra-day squared five-minute returns, taken day-by-day. Andersen and Bollerslev (1998) show that, under the usual diffusion assumptions, realised volatility calculated from high-frequency intra-day returns is effectively an error-free volatility measure.

As realised volatility is, in principle, error-free, it is natural to treat volatility as observable. Observable volatility creates entirely new opportunities: we can analyse it, optimise it, use it and forecast it. This article exploits this insight. We describe our recent attempts at understanding both the unconditional and conditional distributions of realised asset return volatility. Second, we describe tools for optimising the construction of realised volatility measures. In the third section, we use realised volatilities to draw inferences about the conditional distributions of asset returns. We then discuss explicit modelling and forecasting of realised volatility.

REALISED VOLATILITY AND CORRELATION

High-frequency data on Deutschmark and yen returns against the dollar are used to construct model-free estimates of daily exchange rate volatility and correlation, spanning an entire decade (Andersen *et al* (1999a)). Preliminary results indicate that the observed patterns apply more broadly to other types of assets, including the 30 individual stocks in the Dow Jones Industrial Average, as studied in Andersen *et al* (1999).

Figure 1 shows daily realised volatility for a representative asset return series of 1,000 days. (Unless otherwise noted, all of the graphs shown here are designed to be representative of daily returns.) It is clear that realised volatility changes from day-to-day, as one expects. Furthermore, its fluctuations display substantial persistence.

Although not shown here, the distribution of the realised variance is skewed, but transforming to realised standard deviation moves it toward symmetry, and transforming to log standard deviations renders it approximately Gaussian.

Figure 1 Representative realised volatility series

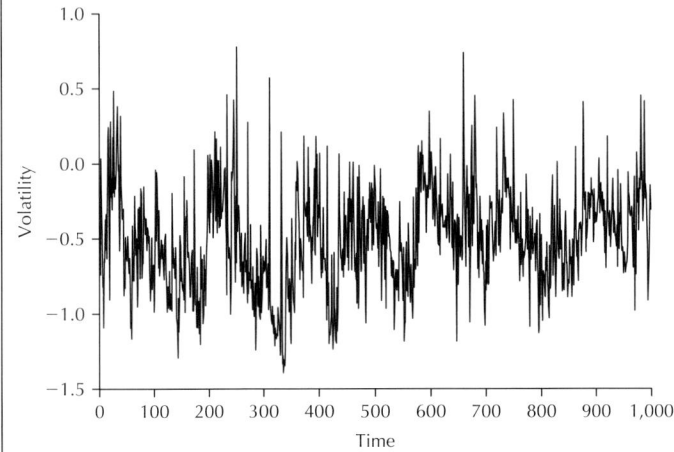

Figure 2 Representative distributions of realised covariance and correlation

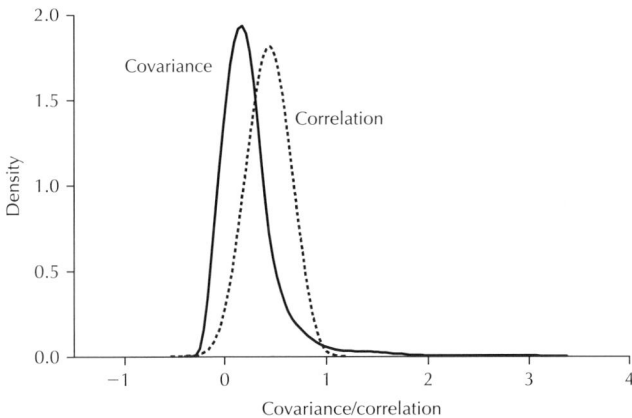

Similarly, we find that realised covariance tends to be highly skewed, but that a simple transformation to correlation delivers approximate normality (see Figure 2). Realised correlation is almost always positive, often strongly so, and it displays substantial variation. We also find that realised correlation is itself highly correlated with realised volatility, which we call the "volatility effect in correlation".

Figure 3 Distributions of realised correlation in low volatility *versus* high volatility periods

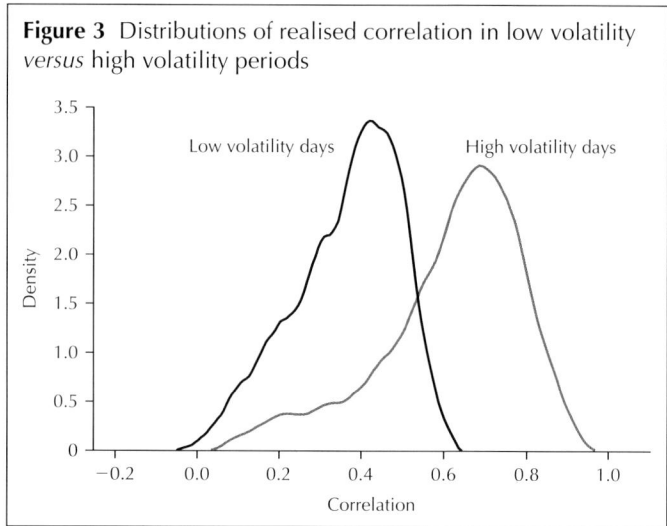

Figure 4 Sample autocorrelations of realised volatility or correlation

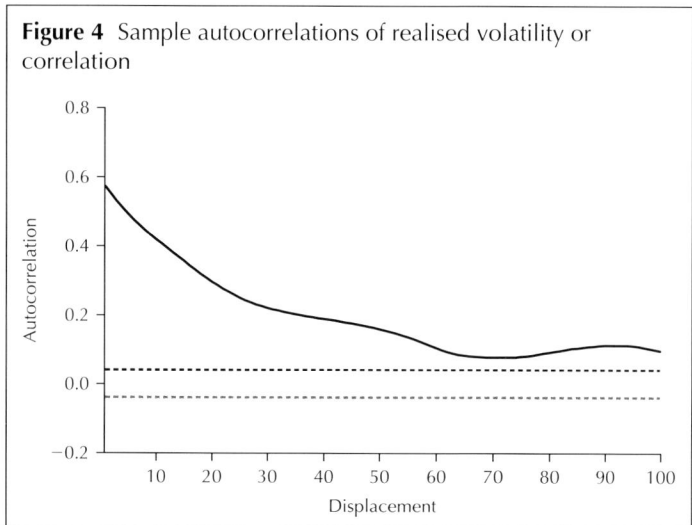

In particular, return correlations tend to rise on high-volatility days, as we illustrate in Figure 3.

We now move from unconditional to conditional aspects of the distributions of realised volatilities and correlations. Although correlograms of realised volatilities tend to exhibit a slow hyperbolic decay, as shown in Figure 4, we routinely and soundly reject the unit-root hypothesis. However, such autocorrelation behaviour is also consistent with that of fractionally integrated long-memory processes. In fact, there is strong evidence to suggest that volatility is a long-memory process, an assertion we substantiate through various analyses. First, we estimate the long-memory parameter directly. The estimates tend to be about 0.4 for various realised volatility and correlation series, and the associated standard error is very small, about 0.02. Second, we verify that the degree of fractional integration is invariant to the horizon, which is a well-known property of long-memory processes, due to their self-similarity. Finally, we verify that our realised volatility and correlation series follow scaling laws, such that the logs of the variance of partial sums of the process are proportional to the logs of the horizon, which is also a well-known characteristic of long-memory processes.

Access to the high-frequency data necessary for constructing accurate realised volatilities is increasing rapidly, but it is far from universal, and we need simple and practical ways of characterising the measurement error remaining in realised volatilities constructed from insufficiently frequently sampled data. Moreover, even when high-frequency data is available, microstructure effects such as bid/ask bounce (occurring when transactions are priced between the bid and ask prices) and asynchronous trading may distort associated realised volatilities. We now turn to a tool for identifying and mitigating such effects.

OPTIMISATION

The appeal of realised volatility calculated from high-frequency data relies at least partially on the assumption that log asset prices evolve as diffusions. This assumption becomes progressively less tolerable as transaction time is approached and market microstructure effects emerge. Hence, a tension arises: the optimal sampling frequency will probably not be the highest available, but rather some intermediate value, ideally high enough to produce a volatility estimate with negligible sampling variation, yet low enough to avoid microstructure bias. The choice of underlying return frequency is therefore critical, but the literature currently offers little guidance for making that decision.

We developed a tool designed to provide some guidance (Andersen *et al* (1999b)). A key insight is that microstructure bias, if operative, will probably manifest itself as sampling frequency

Figure 5 Representative volatility signature plots (liquid and illiquid assets)

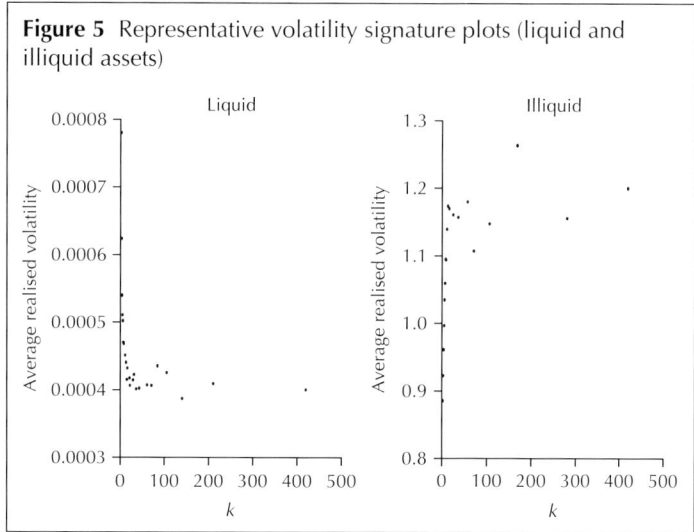

increases by distorting the average realised volatility. We construct a plot of average realised volatility against sampling frequency, which we call the "volatility signature plot". This helps to reveal the severity of microstructure bias as sampling frequency increases, and can be useful in guiding the selection of sampling frequency. We can also use the volatility signature plots to characterise different market microstructures. Interestingly, it turns out that the volatility signature has the same form as the variance-time function, which has been extensively studied in finance. However, while there is no information in the volatility signature that is not also present in high-frequency return autocorrelations, the two are complements, not substitutes, as the information relevant for construction and interpretation of realised volatilities is more directly and transparently revealed in the volatility signature plot.

In Figure 5, we show two representative volatility signature plots. The integer k represents multiples of the smallest sampling interval in the data. Thus, if we have a series for which the smallest available sampling interval is one minute, for $k = 1$ we construct average realised volatility using one-minute returns, for $k = 2$ we construct average realised volatility using two-minute returns, and so forth. The left panel of Figure 5 represents a highly liquid asset for which the largest realised volatility estimates occur at the highest sampling rates, corresponding to the smallest values of k. This can be explained by negative serial correlation in the returns, most likely induced by bid-ask bounce. At the smallest sampling intervals, the volatility measures are very high, but as returns are aggregated across larger and larger sampling intervals the oscillating swings in the returns series tend to cancel, and overall volatility is lower. The volatility signature plot stabilises at roughly $k = 20$ (in this case corresponding to a 20-minute return sampling interval). Although high-frequency microstructural effects will also be small for sampling intervals larger than $k = 20$, realised volatility estimates constructed from larger return intervals will begin to suffer from a higher sampling error. Thus, for this particular example, we would recommend the use of a sampling interval of $k = 20$. which represents a reasonable trade-off between minimising microstructural bias and minimising sampling error.

The right panel of Figure 5 represents a less liquid asset, whose volatility signature is quite different from that of the asset in the top panel. In this case, microstructural factors cause a positive serial correlation at high frequencies, resulting in a smaller estimate of realised volatility, which does not stabilise until the sampling interval reaches $k = 15$, or 15 minutes. In this case, the microstructure bias is probably induced by inactive trading.

Again, much remains to be done. For example, the standard microstructural biases due to bid-ask bounce remain relevant in the multivariate case – and hence for estimation of correlation. Moreover, new complications arise due, for example, to asynchronous trading (see Epps (1979)). Nevertheless, we feel confident that high-quality realised volatilities and correlations can be constructed in liquid markets, and we are optimistic regarding the potential for using volatility and correlation signature plots to assist in the choice of underlying sampling frequency. We are also interested in assessing various volatility estimators' robustness to microstructural effects, particularly those based on the range, as in Alizadeh, Brandt and Diebold (1999).

USE

Andersen *et al* (1999c) characterise the distribution and temporal dependence of $\varepsilon_t = r_t/\sigma_t$, which we call the σ-standardised return. (σ denotes the realised standard deviation.)

Figure 6 Representative QQ plots (standardised and unstandardised returns)

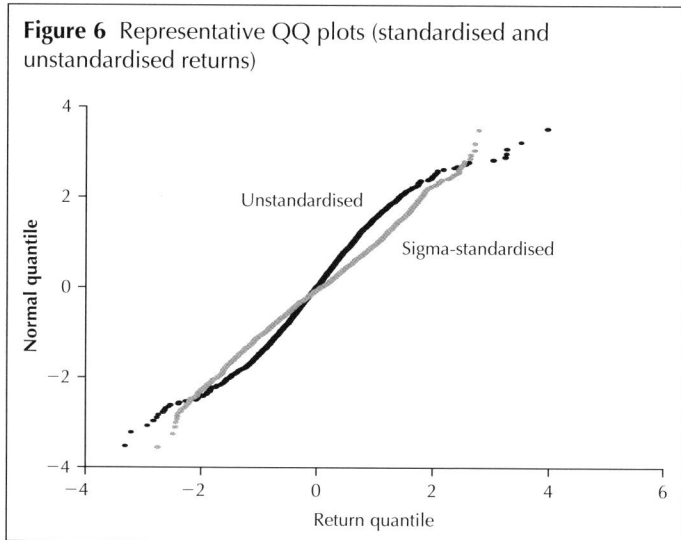

There is a long tradition in the econometrics literature of needing and allowing for a fat-tailed conditional distribution of ε_t, as in Bollerslev (1987). But that literature typically works with returns standardised by volatilities obtained from discrete-time Arch or stochastic volatility models, in which day-t volatility depends only on information at day $t - 1$ and earlier. The situation is different with realised volatility. Day-t realised volatility is based on information within day t, and the theoretical predictions for distributions of returns standardised by realised volatility are unambiguous: under the diffusion assumption they should be Gaussian.

This is, in fact, what we tend to find. The red points on Figure 6 displays a representative QQ plot for unstandardised returns. Because the points do not fall into a straight line, we conclude that the returns are not distributed normally. The blue points on Figure 6 displays a representative QQ plot for σ-standardised returns. It is close to linear, indicating that the σ-standardised returns are approximately Gaussian.

Much work remains to be done. It is, for example, of practical importance to examine the distribution of returns standardised by forecasts of realised volatility, based on prior information only. On the theoretical side, it will be interesting to develop more formal tests for the presence of jumps from the distribution of the returns standardised by the realised volatility.

FORECASTING

Our construction, optimisation and use of realised volatilities has helped us reach two general conclusions: realised variances tend to be lognormally distributed, and asset returns standardised by realised standard deviations tend to be normally distributed. In turn, this suggests that a lognormal-normal mixture may be a good model for asset returns, an idea that inspires a simple modelling and forecasting strategy. This section briefly outlines an operational procedure for the univariate case, but extensions to the multivariate setting, exploiting realised covariances as well as volatilities, are straightforward.

In essence, forecasting return volatility is equivalent to forecasting realised volatility (as long as high-quality intra-day return data are available). Because realised volatility is effectively observed, it is amenable to direct analysis via standard time-series methods. It is natural to assume that the log-volatility process falls within the usual Gaussian autoregressive moving average (Arma) class of models. However, we have already noted the long-memory characteristics of the realised volatility series. Consequently, it is desirable to allow for fractional integration in the specification, leading to a so-called autoregressive fractionally integrated moving average (Arfima) model.

First, one determines the degree of fractional integration, d, in the realised log-volatility series. As noted above, the typical estimates suggest a value of d around 0.4. Next, one obtains the fractionally differenced series, say, $y_t = (1-L)^d \log \sigma_t$. This involves calculating a long (in theory infinite, in practice long, but truncated) distributed lag of the underlying log-volatility series. This transformation ideally removes the long-run dependence in the series. For illustration, we display such a fractionally differenced log-volatility series in Figure 7 and the associated correlogram in Figure 8. They provide remarkable contrasts to Figures 1 and 4; any indication of long memory has been annihilated. The final step of the modelling procedure is to obtain a parsimonious Gaussian Arma representation for this fractionally differenced (residual) series.

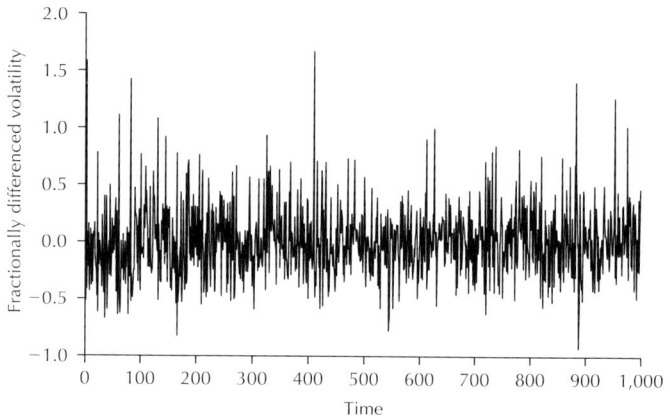

Figure 7 Representative fractionally differenced realised volatility series

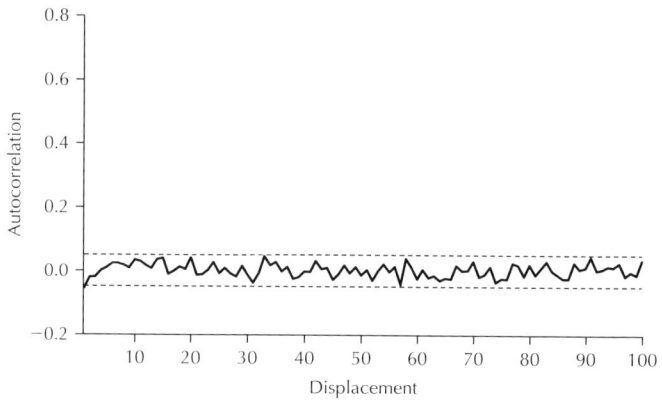

Figure 8 Sample autocorrelations of fractionally differenced realised volatility or correlation

Standard Arfima procedures may now be applied to generate predictions of future realised log-volatility. The result is a sequence of volatility forecasts with associated prediction errors that are (approximately) log-normally distributed. Moreover, because returns are normally distributed conditional on realised volatility, one may readily calculate the fractiles of the conditional return distribution in closed form from the standard log-normal-normal mixture distribution.

The striking feature of this approach is that it builds directly on observed time series and utilises only standard linear Gaussian modelling and forecasting techniques. Hence, it is simple to assess in-sample performance and evaluate model forecasts through well-established out-of-sample procedures. It will be interesting in future work to investigate the actual performance of such an approach relative to popular frameworks such as Arch, stochastic volatility and RiskMetrics. Because our approach exploits an arguably superior volatility measure along with more sound distributional assumptions, it may outperform the standard procedures currently in use.

CONCLUSION

Our findings have potentially wide-ranging implications for applied finance. The results on the unconditional and conditional distributions of asset return volatility are relevant for pricing derivatives. In fact, with the advent of volatility and covariance swaps, realised volatility itself is now the underlying. Such swaps are useful for, among others, holders of options who wish to vega-hedge their holdings. Proper pricing of derivatives on volatility depends critically on how volatility itself varies over time ("the volatility of volatility"). Our methodology allows for a direct approach to this issue through the construction and analysis of historical realised volatility series.

Improved volatility and correlation forecasts will also be useful for portfolio allocation and management. Concrete indications that more traditional volatility forecasts can be of value in guiding portfolio allocation decisions are provided by Fleming, Kirby and Ostdiek (1999). To the extent that our procedures are able to improve on the volatility forecast performance, the implied economic benefits could be high.

Finally, our forecasting procedures for realised volatility and correlation lead directly to a characterisation of the conditional return distribution (ignoring significant short-term variation in the conditional mean). The evaluation of fractiles of the conditional return distribution is, of course, a critical input into any active financial risk management programme. Hence, extensions of our methodology to a richer multi-asset setting should provide potentially valuable inputs for practical risk management.

This chapter was previously published in *Risk*, March 2000.

REFERENCES

Alizadeh, S., M. Brandt, and F. Diebold, 1999, "Range-based Estimation of Stochastic Volatility Models, or: Exchange Rate Dynamics are More Interesting than You Think", Manuscript, available at http://www.ssc.upenn.edu/~diebold.

Andersen, T. and T. Bollerslev, 1998, "Answering the Skeptics: Yes, Standard Volatility Models do Provide Accurate Forecasts", *International Economic Review* **39**, pp. 885–905.

Andersen, T., T. Bollerslev, F. Diebold, and H. Ebens, 1999, "The Distribution of US Stock Return Volatility", Manuscript, available at http://www.ssc.upenn.edu/~diebold.

Andersen, T., T. Bollerslev, F. Diebold, and P. Labys, 1999a, "The Distribution of Exchange Rate Volatility", Wharton Financial Institutions Center working paper 99-08 and NBER working paper 6961, available at http://www.ssc.upenn.edu/~diebold.

Andersen, T., T. Bollerslev, F. Diebold, and P. Labys, 1999b, "Microstructure Bias and Volatility Signatures", Manuscript in progress.

Andersen, T., T. Bollerslev, F. Diebold, and P. Labys, 1999c, "Exchange Rate Returns Standardized by Realized Volatility are (nearly) Gaussian", Manuscript, available at http://www.ssc.upenn.edu/~diebold.

Bollerslev, T., 1987, "A Conditional Heteroskedastic Time Series Model for Speculative Prices and Rates of Return", *Review of Economics and Statistics* **69**, pp. 542–7.

Bollerslev, T., R. Engle, and D. Nelson, 1994, "ARCH Models", in R. Engle and D. McFadden, editors. Handbook of Econometrics, Volume IV, 2959–3038, Amsterdam: North-Holland

Epps, T., 1979, "Comovements in Stock Prices in the Very Short Run", *Journal of the American Statistical Association* **74**, pp. 291–98.

Fleming, J., C. Kirby, and B. Ostdiek, 1999, "The Economic Value of Volatility Timing", Manuscript, *Department of Finance*, Rice University.

French, K., G. Schwert, and R. Stambaugh, 1987, "Expected Stock Returns and Volatility", *Journal of Financial Economics* **19**, pp. 3–29.

Merton, R., 1980, "On Estimating the Expected Return on the Market: An Exploratory Investigation", *Journal of Financial Economics* **8**, pp. 323–61.

Officer, R., 1973, "The Variability of the Market Factor of the NYSE", *Journal of Business* **46**, pp. 434–53.

Schwert, G., 1998, "Stock Market Volatility: Ten Years after the Crash", Brookings-Wharton Papers on Financial Services, Washington DC, Brookings Institution.

Taylor, S. and X. Xu, 1997, "The Incremental Volatility Information in One Million Foreign Exchange Quotations", *Journal of Empirical Finance* **4**, pp. 317–40.

7

Selecting an Innovation Distribution for GARCH Models to Improve Efficiency of Risk and Volatility Estimation

Johannes H. Venter, Peter J. de Jongh*

North-West University

1 INTRODUCTION

Time series of financial variables generally exhibit volatility cluster-ing. GARCH models have become important tools to describe, esti-mate and forecast risks implied by financial variables taking into account such time-dependent volatility. For example, in banking profit and loss modelling and value-at-risk (VaR) estimation for the purpose of determining market risk capital requirements, Berkowitz and O'Brien (2002) find that using GARCH models per-mits comparable risk coverage while requiring less regulatory capi-tal than when using structural bank VaR models. The GARCH approach to volatility modelling works with the simplifying assumption that current volatility is at most a function of past data. This makes it relatively easy to write down the likelihood function when fitting GARCH models to observed time series so that the standard inference tools of maximum likelihood estimation become available. However, the underlying innovation density must be specified to make this possible, and it has recently become clear that there is no universally acceptable choice of this innovation density. This chapter focuses on the issue of choosing this density.

*We want to thank the referee and Editor-in-Chief for raising several issues that led to an improved paper. This material is based on work supported by the National Research Foundation under Grant number 2053331.

More formally, let $Y_1, Y_2, ..., Y_T$ denote a time series and suppose that we propose to describe it in terms of a GARCH model of the form

$$Y_t = \mu_t + \sqrt{h_t} Z_t \quad \text{for } t = 1, 2, ..., T \tag{1}$$

where μ_t represents an expected (or structural) component, $\sqrt{h_t}$ is the volatility and Z_t is the innovation at time t. It is assumed that μ_t and h_t are at most functions of the past observations $Y_1, Y_2, ..., Y_{t-1}$ and these functions may involve a number of parameters. Further, $Z_1, Z_2, ..., Z_T$ are assumed to be independent random variables with common density function (the "innovation density") g, which, to facilitate interpretation of μ_t and h_t, is a *unit density* in the sense that its expectation is zero and its variance is one. This density may possibly also depend on a number of further parameters, and we represent all the parameters needed in the model by a vector θ.

The log of the likelihood function may then be written as

$$l_g(\theta) = \sum_{t=1}^{T} \left[\log \left\{ g(Y_t - \mu_t / \sqrt{h_t}) \right\} - \frac{1}{2} \log(h_t) \right] \tag{2}$$

and the maximum likelihood estimate of θ is found by maximising (2) over θ. To do this we must make an explicit choice for the innovation density g. In much of the GARCH literature the unit normal density $g = \varphi$ is chosen, but there is now abundant empirical evidence that this assumption of normality is often violated in practical financial contexts, especially when dealing with high-frequency (eg, daily) series. Unless we are sure that the true innovation density is normal, estimating the parameters of a GARCH model by maximising $l_\varphi(\theta)$ cannot be described as true maximum likelihood and is referred to as "pseudo" maximum likelihood estimation (PMLE). Below it will be more convenient to refer to this as normal MLE. We consider other choices of g as well and then speak of "g MLE".

Engle and Gonzalez-Rivera (1991) studied the loss of estimation efficiency inherent in normal MLE and found that it may be severe if the true innovation density is heavy-tailed and especially so if it is skewed. They also proposed a non-parametric alternative to get around the problem, but this requires large samples to be effective. Bollerslev and Wooldridge (1992) and Gouriéroux (1997) provide conditions under which normal MLE yields consistent and asymptotically normally distributed estimates; they also give expressions for asymptotic variances and covariances of these estimates, valid even if the true innovation density is not normal. These results make the use of normal MLE practical, but the issue of the efficiency of the estimators remains open.

An approach to dealing with this issue is to use classes of distributions that allow for more general shapes than the normal distribution. An example is provided by the T-distribution with low degrees of freedom, ie, we take g to be the T-density with ν (>2) degrees of freedom but scale-adjusted to have a variance of one. The T-distribution is symmetric, which may be too restrictive in applications. Recently, Fernandez and Steel (1998), introduced a skewed form of the T-distribution and Lambert and Laurent (2001) explored its use in GARCH modelling. More details on this approach are given in Section 2 below.

Another family to consider are the normal inverse Gaussian (NIG) distributions, which have already been used in financial contexts with considerable success by a number of authors. For example, Forsberg and Bollerslev (2002) provide convincing empirical support for the NIG choice via the notion of realised volatility. Other pertinent studies include Barndorff-Nielsen and Prause (2001), Lillestol (2001) and Venter and de Jongh (2002). We are not aware of any systematic study that compares the efficiencies of estimates of GARCH parameters, risk measures and volatility based on normal, T, skewed-T or NIG maximum likelihood, and this is our primary objective here. In addition, we reconsidered the non-parametric approach of Engle and Gonzalez-Rivera (1991) and supplemented it with a non-parametric approach based on the popular kernel density estimation methodology that is currently available.

Our main finding is that the NIG-based approach is competitive with the other methods in most of the cases considered, and this is our method of choice.

The chapter is organised as follows. In Section 2 we provide some details of the distributions relevant for our purposes. Of particular importance is the effect of scale standardisation on the tail-heaviness of the distributions, an issue that tends to be overlooked in the literature. We also approximate and compare the families of distributions in terms of each other in order to gain some understanding of their respective potential in the GARCH context. In Section 3 we give details of the design of an extensive Monte Carlo study aimed at a systematic comparison of the relative efficiencies of the various estimation methods. The results of this study are discussed in Section 4. In Section 5 we illustrate the results with an example and close with some remarks in the last section.

2 DETAILS OF DISTRIBUTIONS

2.1 T-distributions

The unit T-distribution is obtained from the ordinary $T(\nu)$-distribution by scaling to make the variance one. We then refer to it as the $UT(\nu)$-distribution with ν (>2) denoting the degrees of freedom. Its cumulative distribution function (CDF) is given by

$$G_{UT(\nu)}(z) = G_{T(\nu)}\left(z\sqrt{\nu/(\nu - 2)}\right) \tag{3}$$

with $G_{T(\nu)}$ denoting the ordinary $T(\nu)$-CDF. It is well known that the tails of the $T(\nu)$-distribution become heavier as the degrees of freedom, ν, decrease, and it may be thought that this property carries over to the $UT(\nu)$-distribution, but such is *not* the case.[1]

Fernandez and Steel (1998) introduced a skewed form of the T-distribution. We shall denote the unit form of this distribution by $SUT(\nu, \gamma)$. Following Lambert and Laurent (2001), its density is given by

$$g_{SUT(\nu,\gamma)}(z) = \begin{cases} \dfrac{2s}{\gamma + \dfrac{1}{\gamma}}\, g_{UT(\nu)}(\gamma\{sz + m\}) & \text{if } z < -m/s \\[4mm] \dfrac{2s}{\gamma + \dfrac{1}{\gamma}}\, g_{UT(\nu)}(\{sz + m\}/\gamma) & \text{if } z \geq -m/s \end{cases} \tag{4}$$

with

$$m = \frac{\Gamma((\nu - 1)/2)\sqrt{\nu - 2}}{\sqrt{\pi}\,\Gamma(\nu/2)}\left(\gamma - \frac{1}{\gamma}\right) \quad \text{and} \quad s = \sqrt{\gamma^2 + \gamma^{-2} - 1 - m^2}$$

$$\text{where } \nu > 2, \gamma > 0$$

Here $\gamma > 0$ determines the skewness, with $0 < \gamma < 1$ yielding negative skewness, $\gamma = 1$ symmetry (in fact $SUT(\nu, 1) \equiv UT(\nu)$), and $\gamma > 1$ yielding positive skewness. Other skewed T-distributions were defined by Hansen (1994) and, more recently, by Jones and

Faddy (2003), where further references can be found. We argue below that these alternative families of T-distributions can be well approximated in terms of each other so that it is sufficient for the purposes of this article to focus on only one of them, and we have elected to use the Fernandez and Steel (1998) family.

2.2 NIG distributions

The NIG distribution can be parameterised in many ways. The most common specification is the $(\alpha, \beta, \mu, \delta)$ parameters subject to the restrictions

$$0 < |\beta| < \alpha, \quad -\infty < \mu < \infty, \quad \delta > 0 \tag{6}$$

In terms of $\xi = \delta\sqrt{\alpha^2 - \beta^2}$ and the function $q(x) = \sqrt{1 + x^2}$ the NIG density is

$$g_{NIG(\alpha,\beta,\mu,\delta)}(z) = \frac{\alpha \exp(\zeta + \beta(z - \mu))K_1(\alpha\delta q((z - \mu)/\delta))}{\pi q((z - \mu)/\delta)} \tag{7}$$

where K_1 is the modified Bessel function of the third order and index one. Here μ and δ are location and scale parameters, respectively, while α and β are parameters specifying the shape of the distribution. In particular, $\beta = 0$ corresponds to a symmetric distribution (see Lillestol (2000), or the cited references for more details). Barndorff-Nielsen et al (1985) also introduced the tail-heaviness (or peakedness) and asymmetry parameters ξ and χ given by

$$\xi = \left(1 + \delta\sqrt{\alpha^2 - \beta^2}\right)^{-1/2} = (1 + \zeta)^{-1/2} \quad \text{and} \quad \chi = \beta\xi/\alpha = \rho\xi \tag{8}$$

The parameters ξ and χ are scale- and translation-invariant and they may be used as shape parameters instead of α and β. Their domain is the so-called NIG shape triangle

$$0 \leq |\chi| < \xi < 1 \tag{9}$$

For $\chi < 0$ we get negatively skewed distributions, for $\chi = 0$ symmetric and for $\chi > 0$ positively skewed distributions. The parameter ξ controls the tail thickness of the distributions, with ξ close to 0 yielding normal like tails and ξ close to 1 yielding heavier tails depending on what we do with the other parameters. To serve as the innovation distribution in GARCH models, we want the mean to be 0 and the variance to be 1. In general the mean and variance of the NIG distribution are given by

$$\kappa_1 = \mu + \delta\rho / \sqrt{1 - \rho^2} \quad \text{and} \quad \kappa_2 = \delta^2 / \varsigma(1 - \rho^2) \quad \text{with } \rho = \beta / \alpha$$

(10)

These equations together with (8) may be solved to express $(\alpha, \beta, \mu, \delta)$ in terms of $(\xi, \chi, \kappa_1, \kappa_2)$ so that we may parameterise the NIG distribution in terms of $(\xi, \chi, \kappa_1, \kappa_2)$ rather than the original $(\alpha, \beta, \mu, \delta)$. In this new parameter set we now take $\kappa_1 = 0$ and $\kappa_2 = 1$ to obtain the unit form of the NIG distribution, which depends only on the shape parameters (ξ, χ) and is skew when $\chi \neq 0$. We will denote it by SUNIG(ξ, χ). When $\chi = 0$ we get the symmetric form, which we denote by UNIG(ξ) = SUNIG($\xi, 0$). Using the characteristic function for which explicit expressions are available (see Barndorff-Nielsen and Prause (2001)), it can be shown that the SUNIG(ξ, χ) distribution tends to the N(0, 1) distribution when $\xi \to 0$ and to the degenerate distribution concentrated on 0 when $\xi \to 1$. That the degenerate distribution is found both for the UT(ν) and the SUNIG (ξ, χ) families when the tail-heaviness parameter approaches its limit is a special case of a wider phenomenon.[2]

2.3 Contaminated normal distributions

In a large part of the Monte Carlo study reported in Section 3 we assume that the true innovation distribution is from the SUT or SUNIG families and then evaluate efficiencies of estimates based on the SUT or SUNIG MLE methods. Of course, SUT (SUNIG) MLE tends to do best when the true innovation density is from the SUT (SUNIG) family ("home-ground" cases). To see what happens outside the home-ground cases we also need an innovation density outside these families, and the contaminated normal distribution is used for this purpose. The unit contaminated normal distribution is denoted by UCN(q, c) and is obtained by scaling to one the variance of the distribution, which is N(0, 1) with probability q and N(0, c^2) with probability $1 - q$. Its CDF is given by

$$G_{UCN(q,c)}(z) = (1 - q)\Phi(z\sigma_c) + q\Phi(z\sigma_c / c) \quad \text{where } \sigma_c^2 = 1 - q + qc^2$$

(11)

Since $\sigma_c \to \infty$ and $\sigma_c/c \to \sqrt{q}$ when $c \to \infty$, it follows that the limiting distribution of $UCN(q, c)$ is a mixed distribution, which is 0 with probability $1 - q$ and $N(0, 1/q)$-distributed with probability q.

2.4 Approximating distributions by relative entropy

Relative entropy helps one to understand the behavior of maximum likelihood estimation in the case of misspecified innovation densities (see, eg, Soofi and Retzer (2002)). For example, to calculate the choice of $(\hat{\nu}, \hat{\gamma})$ for a $SUT(\nu, \gamma)$ distribution that best approximates a distribution with a given density, g, we solve the minimisation problem

$$\min_{\nu, \gamma} \int_{-\infty}^{\infty} \log\left(\frac{g(z)}{g_{SUT(\nu, \gamma)}(z)}\right) g(z)dz \qquad (12)$$

$(\hat{\nu}, \hat{\gamma})$ may be interpreted as the maximum likelihood estimate of (ν, γ) that would be obtained if we fitted a $SUT(\nu, \gamma)$-distribution to an infinite sample of observations from g. In a GARCH context we may argue that $(\hat{\nu}, \hat{\gamma})$ is what SUT MLE is trying to estimate if the true innovation density is actually g. If $g_{SUT(\hat{\nu}, \hat{\gamma})}$ approximates g very accurately, then SUT MLE virtually amounts to true MLE. In particular, numerical studies showed that if g happens to be one of the Hansen (1994) or Jones and Faddy (2003) forms of skewed T-distributions, it is well approximated by a $g_{SUT(\hat{\nu}, \hat{\gamma})}$ density, so that no efficiency would be lost by using SUT MLE. For this reason we only report results here in terms of the SUT choice among the alternative T-distributions.

The Monte Carlo results below can be interpreted to some extent by studying the accuracy with which members of one family (eg, the T) can be approximated by members of another family (eg, the NIG). We did such a study and concluded that the NIG distributions are particularly successful in approximating the other distributions, except for extreme cases. Some illustrative examples follow.

First consider the symmetric case. UNIG fits to the UT(3) and UT(6) distributions are shown in Figure 1(b) and (d). Here (and further on) we use log-density plots in order to show more detail in the tails of the distributions. We also fitted UT distributions to the

Figure 1 Comparison of symmetric UT and UNIG fits

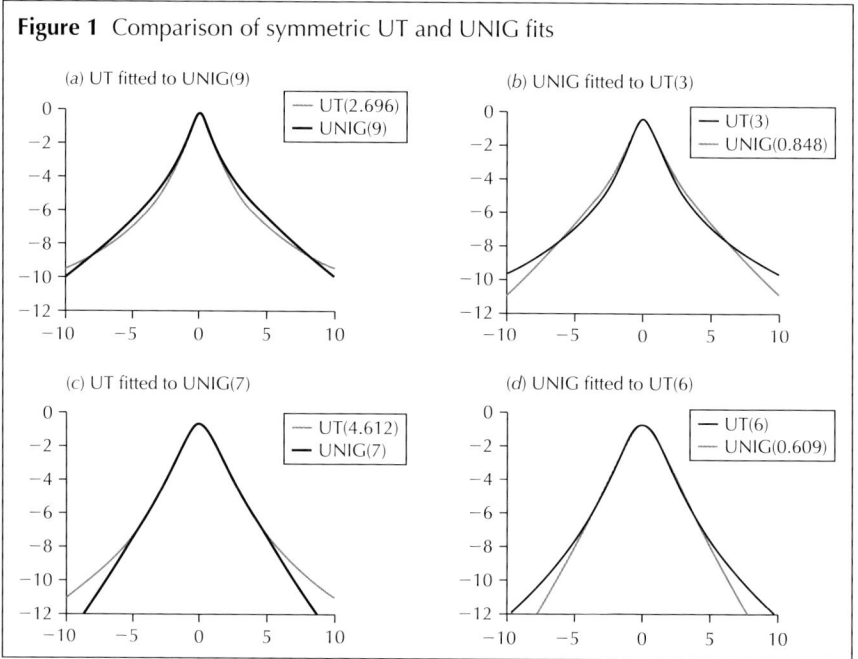

(a) UT fitted to UNIG(9)

(b) UNIG fitted to UT(3)

(c) UT fitted to UNIG(7)

(d) UNIG fitted to UT(6)

UNIG(0.9) and the UNIG(0.7) distributions. The quality of the resulting fits is depicted in Figure 1(a) and (c). It is clear that the fits for the "mild" cases (Figure 1(c) and (d)) are almost perfect in the range $(-5, 5)$, which carries more than 0.998 of the probability under either distribution. However, in the more extreme cases (Figures 1(a) and 2(b)) more serious discrepancies in the fits are visible.

The fits of the UT and UNIG distributions to the UCN(0.1, 3) and UCN(0.1, 10) distributions are depicted in Figure 2(a) and (b). As expected, in both cases discrepancies in the fits are visible, especially so in the latter case. In the first case the two fits do about equally well, but in the second case it seems that the UNIG does better than the UT when the tail of the contaminated distribution in the range $(2, 5)$ is considered. Clearly, the UCN(0.1, 10) distribution has very heavy tails, which are not matched well by either the UT or UNIG distributions.

Figure 2 Comparison of UT and UNIG fits to UCN densities

(a) UNIG and UT fitted to UCN(0.1, 3)   (b) UNIG and UT fitted to UCN(0.1, 10)

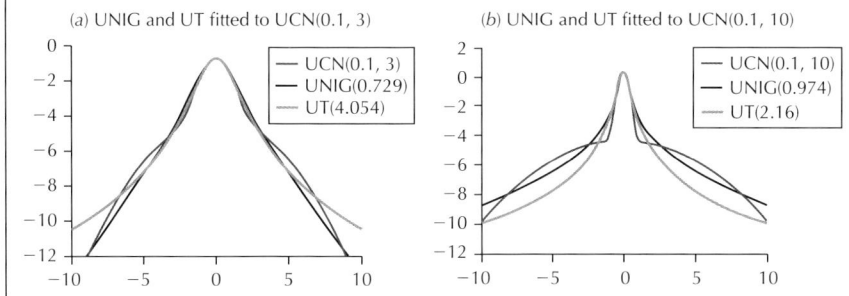

3 DESIGN OF MONTE CARLO STUDY

3.1 Model

We consider only the popular AR(1)–GARCH(1, 1) model, which has the form of (1) with

$$\mu_t = \phi Y_{t-1} \quad \text{and} \quad h_t = \alpha_0 + (\alpha_1 Z_{t-1}^2 + \beta)h_{t-1} \tag{13}$$

Here ϕ is the AR parameter, α_0 and α_1 are the two ARCH parameters and β is the GARCH parameter. Various choices of values for these parameters were studied, but here we report only results for the choice $\phi = 0.1$, $\alpha_0 = 0.1$, $\alpha_1 = 0.1$ and $\beta = 0.8$. We found that the conclusions arrived at with these values remain largely true for other choices.

The following innovation distributions with varying degrees of skewness and kurtosis were used.

❑ N(0, 1).
❑ SUNIG(ξ, χ) with the following choices of parameter sets:
   (0.5, 0), (0.5, 0.3), (0.5, −0.3),
   (0.7, 0), (0.7, 0.6), (0.7, 0.3), (0.7, −0.3), (0.7, −0.6),
   (0.9, 0), (0.9, 0.6), (0.9, 0.3), (0.9, −0.3), (0.9, −0.6)
For the first row of these the SUNIG distribution is still fairly close to N(0, 1), but for the others the tails increase in heaviness while the skewness varies from extremely positive to extremely negative.

❏ UCN(q, c) with choices of parameter sets (0.1, 3), (0.2, 3) and (0.2, 10).
❏ SUT(v, γ) with v = 3, 6 and 9 and γ = 1.5, 1.2, 1, 0.8 and 0.5.

We considered sample sizes of 250, 500 and 1,000. For each run we first generated 100 values according to the model to allow the process to settle and then generated the series of observations that were actually used.

3.2 Methods

Seven MLE-based methods are compared. The normal approach fits the AR(1)–GARCH(1, 1) model by maximum likelihood using a standard normal density for the innovations. Similarly the UT, SUT and SUNIG methods fit the same model by maximum likelihood estimation but using, respectively, the UT(v), SUT(v, γ), UNIG(ξ) or SUNIG(ξ, χ) densities for the innovations. Each of these methods can also be implemented in a two-step way: in the first step a normal fit is done to get estimates of the AR, ARCH and GARCH parameters as well as the estimated innovation residuals; in the second step we then fit a UT(v), SUT(v, γ), UNIG(ξ) or SUNIG(ξ, χ) density by maximum likelihood to these residuals, pretending that they are iid from the relevant distribution, thus obtaining estimates for the relevant parameters. We may also obtain risk estimates (VaR and ESF) by applying extreme value theory to the estimated innovation residuals obtained in the first step (see McNeil and Frey (2000)). However, we have found that these two-step methods generally do not outperform the full MLE-based methods, so for the sake of brevity we will not report the results here.

A further approach based on MLE but using a non-parametric kernel density estimate for the innovations is included. To describe this method, consider given values (ϕ, α_0, α_1, β) of the model parameters. Corresponding residuals $\hat{Z}_1$, $\hat{Z}_2$, ..., $\hat{Z}_t$ may be calculated. Let

$$\bar{Z} = \sum_{t=1}^{T} \hat{Z}_t$$

and

$$s_Z^2 = \sum_{t=1}^{T} \left[\hat{Z}_t - \bar{Z} \right]^2 \Big/ T$$

Let $k(x)$ be a density function symmetric around 0 and with variance

$$\sigma_k^2 = \int_{-\infty}^{\infty} x^2 k(x) dx$$

and put

$$h = s_Z \left[\int_{-\infty}^{\infty} k(x)^2 dx \Big/ T\sigma_k^2 \int_{-\infty}^{\infty} \varphi''(x)^2 dx \right]^{\frac{1}{5}}$$

Then the corresponding kernel estimate is given by

$$\hat{f}(z) = \sum_{t=1}^{T} k\left(\left\{z - \hat{Z}_t\right\}\Big/h\right)\Big/Th$$

(see Silverman (1990), or Wand and Jones (1995)). Now $\hat{f}$ has mean $\bar{Z}$ and variance $\hat{\sigma}_{\hat{f}}^2 = s_z^2 + h^2\sigma_k^2$, which need not be 0 and 1, respectively, as is required for an innovation density. To correct for this requirement, we take $\hat{g}(z) = \hat{f}(\bar{Z} + z\sigma_{\hat{f}})\sigma_{\hat{f}}$ as the estimated innovation density corresponding to the parameter values (ϕ, α_0, α_1, β). Then $\hat{g}$ replaces g in (2), and this must be maximised to obtain the estimates of the model parameters (ϕ, α_0, α_1, β). We used the bi-weight kernel since this has finite support, making numerical evaluation faster. We refer to this as the "Kern" method. It also has a simpler two-step variation. In the first step the residuals are calculated from a normal fit and an innovation density estimate, $\hat{g}(z)$, is calculated exactly as above from these normal residuals. This $\hat{g}$ is then kept fixed, used to replace g in (1.2), and the resulting function is maximised over (ϕ, α_0, α_1, β) in the second step. We refer to this as the "2sKern" method. This method is akin to the non-parametric method of Engle and Gonzalez-Rivera (1991) but uses kernel estimates rather than the discrete maximum penalised likelihood estimation technique of Tapia and Thomson (1978). We also worked with the Engle and Gonzalez-Rivera (1991) approach but experienced more numerical difficulties with the maximisation steps than we did with the kernel approach. Moreover, it does seem more satisfactory to use continuous density estimates since we are actually dealing with a continuous context here.

3.3 Parameters

We are interested in the efficiency with which the methods are able to estimate the model parameters (ϕ, α_0, α_1, β). Each method produces an estimate of the innovation density from which estimates of innovation risk measures follow and the efficiencies of the resulting innovation risk are compared. We looked at innovation VaR and ESF (expected shortfall). If the true innovation density is g with distribution function G, then the true VaR at probability level τ is given by $\text{VaR}_\tau = G^{-1}(\tau)$ and the corresponding expected shortfall by

$$EsF_\tau = \tau^{-1} \int_{-\infty}^{\text{VaR}_\tau} xg(x)dx$$

The corresponding estimates are given by the same expressions with g and G replaced by their estimates $\hat{g}$ and $\hat{G}$. Probability levels $\tau = 0.005, 0.01, 0.025$ and 0.05 were used here.

Efficiencies of volatility estimates were also studied in this context. In each Monte Carlo run the squared volatilities, $\{h_t\}$, must be generated along with the observations $\{Y_t\}$ and are therefore actually known. Each method produces estimated squared volatilities, $\{\hat{h}_t\}$, based on the observations $\{Y_t\}$ as part of the fitting procedure and these estimates may then be compared with the known values $\{h_t\}$ to judge their accuracy and efficiencies. More details on how this is done follow below.

3.4 Estimated efficiencies

If method m (varying over the methods indicated above) produces an estimate $\hat{\theta}_m$ for a real parameter θ, then we may use the root mean-squared error (RMSE) defined by $RMSE_m = \{E[\hat{\theta}_m - \theta]^2\}^{1/2}$ as the relevant measure of estimation risk. If m^* is the method with the lowest RMSE, we define the efficiency of method m as $100 \times RMSE_{m^*}/RMSE_m$. Such efficiencies are calculated for all methods and for the model parameters as well as for the innovation risk measures.

When it comes to volatility estimation we are dealing with a whole sequence of parameters and suitable summary measures must be defined. If method m produces the estimate $\sqrt{\hat{h}_{t,m}}$ of the true volatility $\sqrt{h_t}$ at time t, the relative error is

$$\sqrt{\hat{h}_{t,m}/h_t} - 1$$

with squared error loss

$$\left[\sqrt{\hat{h}_{t,m}/h_t} - 1\right]^2$$

Averaging this over time, taking expectation and square roots, we get the root mean average squared relative error (RMASRE) of method m, which is given by

$$\text{RMASRE}_m = \left\{E\sum_{t=1}^{T}\left[\sqrt{\hat{h}_{t,m}}/\sqrt{h_t} - 1\right]^2 \Big/ T\right\}^{\frac{1}{2}}$$

The efficiency of method m can then be computed by reference to the method with the smallest RMASRE as above. Volatilities over all times enter into this measure, but high volatilities are of special interest and various weighting schemes may be used to focus more on these. We report only on the root mean maximum squared relative error (RMMSRE) given by

$$\text{RMMSRE}_m = \left\{E\left[\sqrt{\max_t \hat{h}_{t,m}}/\sqrt{\max_t h_t} - 1\right]^2\right\}^{\frac{1}{2}}$$

for method m. The efficiency of method m can again be computed by reference to the method with the smallest RMMSRE. Our main conclusions were similar when we used other measures of volatility estimation risk.

All the results reported in the next section are based on $N = 1,000$ Monte Carlo runs and the expectations in the expressions for the efficiency measures are estimated by the average over runs of the realised losses in the usual way. Because the tables are already quite extensive, we do not show the standard errors of the quantities displayed, but we have checked the stability of the conclusions by doing additional runs for selected cases.

4 MONTE CARLO RESULTS
We discuss the results of the Monte Carlo study under three headings, namely the efficiency of the model parameter estimates, the efficiency of the risk estimates (VaR and ESF) and the efficiency of the volatility estimates. We only present the results for a sample size of 500 since the efficiencies obtained for the other sample sizes

largely lead to similar conclusions. Where necessary, we make some remarks concerning our findings for the larger (1,000) and smaller (250) sample sizes.

4.1 Comparing efficiencies of GARCH model parameter estimates

The results for the *symmetric* innovation distributions were largely as expected and are in line with the results reported by Engle and Gonzalez-Rivera (1991). Details are not included here, but they can be summarised as follows. The more heavy-tailed the innovation distribution, the less the efficiency of the normal method and the more efficient the UT and UNIG methods. The UNIG method performs exceptionally well, since it compares well with the UT on its home ground, while the UT does not do that well on the UNIG's home ground (eg, at UNIG(0.9)). We present the estimated efficiencies only for the negatively *skewed* innovation distributions in Table 1 as the conclusions for the positively skewed innovation distributions are similar.

In the case of the extreme heavy-tailed and asymmetric innovation distributions the efficiency of the normal method is poor (eg, when the true innovation distribution is SUNIG(0.9, -0.6) or SUT(3, 0.5)). The MLE methods based on the asymmetric innovation distributions (SUNIG and SUT) and the MLE methods based on the non-parametric kernel densities outperform the other methods in this case. SUNIG again performs surprisingly well and closely matches the performance of SUT on its home ground, while SUT sometimes breaks down when SUNIG is on its home ground (eg, when the true innovation distribution is SUNIG(0.9, -0.6)) and especially with respect to the two ARCH parameters.

Overall, the SUNIG MLE method is the preferred choice, but the two kernel-based methods do well in all cases and are good alternatives, especially in larger samples.

4.2 Comparing efficiencies of risk estimates (VaR and ESF)

We present the efficiencies with which VaR is estimated in Table 2 (symmetric innovation distributions) and Table 4 (negatively skewed innovation distributions) below. Similarly, we present the efficiencies with which ESF is estimated in Table 3 (symmetric innovation distributions) and Table 5 (negatively skewed innovation

Table 1 Efficiencies (%) of parameter estimation for negatively skewed innovation distributions

Innovation distribution	MLE method	ϕ	α_0	α_1	β	Innovation distribution	MLE method	ϕ	α_0	α_1	β
	Normal	88	63	65	63		Normal	86	68	65	66
	UT	96	73	92	72		UT	91	79	88	76
	UNIG	95	74	91	72		UNIG	90	81	87	78
SUT(6, 0.8)	SUT	100	71	93	71	**SUNIG(0.5, −0.3)**	SUT	99	94	100	94
	SUNIG	100	73	94	73		SUNIG	100	92	100	93
	2sKern	95	100	100	100		2sKern	96	100	95	100
	Kern	75	86	93	88		Kern	75	86	86	88
	Normal	56	57	33	55		Normal	76	53	62	54
	UT	93	84	86	81		UT	92	72	88	72
	UNIG	91	99	97	84		UNIG	92	74	92	71
SUT(3, 0.8)	SUT	100	84	86	91	**SUNIG(0.7, −0.3)**	SUT	98	74	90	81
	SUNIG	99	100	100	88		SUNIG	100	82	99	83
	2sKern	87	94	71	93		2sKern	95	100	100	100
	Kern	77	98	92	100		Kern	74	87	91	86
	Normal	70	49	51	52		Normal	45	54	42	57
	UT	74	56	75	58		UT	92	35	53	90
	UNIG	73	62	74	64		UNIG	91	100	100	94
SUT(9, 0.5)	SUT	100	100	100	100	**SUNIG(0.9, −0.3)**	SUT	98	23	46	95
	SUNIG	97	95	92	100		SUNIG	100	67	98	99
	2sKern	86	71	81	78		2sKern	82	58	79	89
	Kern	78	97	86	95		Kern	79	85	86	100
	Normal	65	43	41	46		Normal	47	24	29	26
	UT	72	64	78	64		UT	52	48	63	44
	UNIG	71	64	75	63		UNIG	49	50	62	43

Table 1 Continued.

Innovation distribution	MLE method	ϕ	α_0	α_1	β
SUT(6, 0.5)	SUT	100	97	100	99
	SUNIG	97	91	95	97
	2sKern	85	94	83	95
	Kern	77	100	88	100
	Normal	36	27	19	31
	UT	59	68	74	55
	UNIG	56	70	70	54
SUT(3, 0.5)	SUT	100	74	86	100
	SUNIG	97	100	100	96
	2sKern	75	63	60	63
	Kern	81	82	81	82

Innovation distribution	MLE method	ϕ	α_0	α_1	β
SUNIG(0.7, −0.6)	SUT	95	65	71	94
	SUNIG	100	100	100	100
	2sKern	81	70	81	72
	Kern	81	85	84	84
	Normal	32	36	28	37
	UT	56	54	60	68
	UNIG	51	100	82	68
SUNIG(0.9, −0.6)	SUT	94	18	42	84
	SUNIG	100	54	100	94
	2sKern	82	82	90	95
	Kern	81	100	90	100

Table 2 Efficiencies (%) of VaR estimation methods at different quantiles for symmetric innovation distributions at probability levels 0.005, 0.01, 0.025 and 0.05

Innovation distribution	MLE method	0.005	0.01	0.025	0.05
N(0, 1)	Normal	*	*	*	*
	UT	70	76	100	36
	UNIG	100	100	97	100
	SUT	48	37	16	8
	SUNIG	43	34	16	9
	2sKern	30	25	12	5
	Kern	28	23	11	5
CN(0.1, 3)	Normal	43	34	100	42
	UT	100	75	88	94
	UNIG	98	100	42	57
	SUT	93	66	65	85
	SUNIG	91	80	38	55
	2sKern	89	47	44	100
	Kern	86	46	44	99
CN(0.2, 3)	Normal	23	34	41	49
	UT	78	55	25	69
	UNIG	100	100	100	100
	SUT	69	53	25	65
	SUNIG	81	88	70	91
	2sKern	63	84	39	78
	Kern	60	81	39	78
UT(6)	Normal	28	25	24	48
	UT	99	100	100	100
	UNIG	100	82	25	92
	SUT	68	50	14	58
	SUNIG	64	43	11	55
	2sKern	35	27	8	37
	Kern	34	26	8	36
UT(3)	Normal	11	29	87	37
	UT	100	100	100	100
	UNIG	48	36	46	58
	SUT	49	62	86	95
	SUNIG	34	32	44	57
	2sKern	13	22	49	68
	Kern	13	20	49	68
UNIG(0.5)	Normal	39	37	37	50
	UT	97	100	87	41
	UNIG	100	93	100	100
	SUT	70	58	30	20
	SUNIG	66	52	28	23
	2sKern	44	37	19	14
	Kern	43	35	18	13

Table 2 Continued.

Innovation distribution	MLE method	0.005	0.01	0.025	0.05
CN(0.1, 10)	Normal	29	37	100	12
	UT	24	24	7	100
	UNIG	97	70	31	28
	SUT	23	23	7	81
	SUNIG	92	68	29	28
	2sKern	100	99	17	68
	Kern	98	100	17	70
UT(9)	Normal	40	38	28	51
	UT	98	100	100	84
	UNIG	100	91	46	100
	SUT	69	55	16	34
	SUNIG	64	49	14	34
	2sKern	41	34	10	22
	Kern	39	32	9	20

Innovation distribution	MLE method	0.005	0.01	0.025	0.05
UNIG(0.7)	Normal	18	19	14	33
	UT	100	82	15	21
	UNIG	92	100	100	100
	SUT	64	53	13	19
	SUNIG	57	51	19	38
	2sKern	32	29	10	20
	Kern	31	28	10	19
UNIG(0.9)	Normal	9	7	23	22
	UT	13	6	3	11
	UNIG	100	100	100	100
	SUT	13	6	3	11
	SUNIG	55	36	30	82
	2sKern	18	12	10	35
	Kern	18	12	10	35

Table 3 Efficiencies (%) of ESF estimation methods at different quantiles for symmetric innovation distributions at probability levels 0.005, 0.01, 0.025 and 0.05

Innovation distribution	MLE method	0.005	0.01	0.025	0.05	Innovation distribution	MLE method	0.005	0.01	0.025	0.05
N(0, 1)	Normal	*	*	*	*	UT(6)	Normal	14	9	3	19
	UT	100	100	100	100		UT	100	100	100	100
	UNIG	83	64	24	40		UNIG	43	32	10	67
	SUT	68	49	16	21		SUT	69	50	14	58
	SUNIG	61	45	16	24		SUNIG	65	43	11	55
	2sKern	43	33	12	15		2sKern	36	27	8	37
	Kern	41	31	11	14		Kern	34	26	8	36
CN(0.1, 3)	Normal	28	18	14	19	UT(3)	Normal	15	13	12	39
	UT	100	95	100	44		UT	100	100	100	100
	UNIG	71	47	47	100		UNIG	48	57	64	52
	SUT	93	83	75	40		SUT	81	68	47	62
	SUNIG	91	100	44	26		SUNIG	44	46	37	41
	2sKern	89	60	51	47		2sKern	28	25	21	35
	Kern	86	57	50	46		Kern	28	24	20	34
CN(0.2, 3)	Normal	14	15	15	19	UNIG(0.5)	Normal	39	39	39	37
	UT	65	41	36	54		UT	76	84	96	100
	UNIG	100	100	69	100		UNIG	100	100	100	95
	SUT	57	39	35	51		SUT	65	67	63	49
	SUNIG	67	64	100	72		SUNIG	74	70	60	45
	2sKern	52	61	56	62		2sKern	51	55	54	43
	Kern	50	59	56	61		Kern	50	54	54	43

Table 3 Continued.

Innovation distribution	MLE method	0.005	0.01	0.025	0.05
	Normal	11	12	19	26
	UT	12	13	25	100
	UNIG	100	100	60	93
CN(0.1, 10)	SUT	12	13	24	81
	SUNIG	48	37	100	28
	2sKern	52	55	57	68
	Kern	51	55	57	70
	Normal	39	39	39	38
	UT	88	91	97	100
	UNIG	100	100	100	95
UT(9)	SUT	75	72	63	47
	SUNIG	76	70	59	43
	2sKern	50	52	51	40
	Kern	49	51	50	39

Innovation distribution	MLE method	0.005	0.01	0.025	0.05
	Normal	21	20	19	18
	UT	47	65	100	89
	UNIG	100	100	96	100
UNIG(0.7)	SUT	43	53	59	44
	SUNIG	71	66	54	41
	2sKern	39	43	41	33
	Kern	37	42	40	33
	Normal	11	10	8	5
	UT	83	32	11	3
	UNIG	100	100	100	100
UNIG(0.9)	SUT	65	30	11	3
	SUNIG	69	63	46	20
	2sKern	27	27	22	10
	Kern	27	27	22	10

Table 4 Efficiencies (%) of VaR estimation at different quantiles for negatively skewed innovation distributions at probability levels 0.005, 0.01, 0.025 and 0.05

Innovation distribution	MLE method	0.005	0.01	0.025	0.05	Innovation distribution	MLE method	0.005	0.01	0.025	0.05
SUT(6, 0.8)	Normal	23	21	21	53	SUNIG(0.5, −0.3)	Normal	18	16	13	12
	UT	43	34	24	29		UT	27	22	15	9
	UNIG	42	36	28	38		UNIG	26	22	16	10
	SUT	99	100	100	100		SUT	80	79	73	56
	SUNIG	100	83	63	86		SUNIG	100	100	100	100
	2sKern	51	49	41	45		2sKern	48	54	44	24
	Kern	49	47	40	43		Kern	47	51	42	23
SUT(3, 0.8)	Normal	11	17	10	45	SUNIG(0.7, −0.3)	Normal	15	14	12	21
	UT	24	28	5	55		UT	26	20	13	11
	UNIG	28	50	100	100		UNIG	26	22	16	15
	SUT	100	100	9	59		SUT	95	67	33	23
	SUNIG	53	36	4	32		SUNIG	100	100	100	100
	2sKern	22	27	4	37		2sKern	44	45	36	26
	Kern	21	26	4	37		Kern	43	44	33	25
SUT(9, 0.5)	Normal	20	16	9	8	SUNIG(0.9, −0.3)	Normal	10	9	15	75
	UT	27	20	9	7		UT	12	8	7	12
	UNIG	26	20	10	7		UNIG	24	19	20	51
	SUT	100	100	100	100		SUT	16	10	7	12
	SUNIG	99	78	49	76		SUNIG	100	100	100	100
	2sKern	57	52	31	21		2sKern	28	24	22	37
	Kern	55	50	30	20		Kern	55	23	22	37

Table 4 Continued.

Innovation distribution	MLE method	0.005	0.01	0.025	0.05	Innovation distribution	MLE method	0.005	0.01	0.025	0.05
	Normal	14	13	6	17		Normal	8	7	4	8
	UT	20	17	7	13		UT	12	9	4	5
	UNIG	19	17	7	15		UNIG	11	10	4	6
SUT(6, 0.5)	SUT	82	100	100	100	**SUNIG(0.7, −0.6)**	SUT	100	31	7	7
	SUNIG	100	80	32	69		SUNIG	94	100	100	100
	2sKern	40	42	20	33		2sKern	29	30	14	15
	Kern	38	41	20	32		Kern	29	29	14	14
	Normal	7	11	44	37		Normal	6	4	9	100
	UT	10	15	39	24		UT	8	4	6	8
	UNIG	10	17	66	100		UNIG	11	7	11	27
SUT(3, 0.5)	SUT	100	100	100	22	**SUNIG(0.9, −0.6)**	SUT	9	5	6	7
	SUNIG	51	31	35	10		SUNIG	100	100	100	53
	2sKern	16	21	40	11		2sKern	21	14	17	18
	Kern	15	21	40	12		Kern	21	13	17	18

Table 5 Efficiencies (%) of ESF estimation at different quantiles for negatively skewed innovation distributions at probability levels 0.005, 0.01, 0.025 and 0.05

Innovation distribution	MLE method	0.005	0.01	0.025	0.05
	Normal	13	11	8	9
	UT	43	34	24	29
	UNIG	24	19	13	14
SUT(6, 0.8)	SUT	99	100	100	100
	SUNIG	100	83	63	86
	2sKern	51	49	41	45
	Kern	49	47	40	43
	Normal	15	13	12	19
	UT	36	29	23	28
	UNIG	26	25	25	41
SUT(3, 0.8)	SUT	100	100	100	100
	SUNIG	56	71	66	49
	2sKern	36	37	43	57
	Kern	36	37	42	56
	Normal	17	18	18	14
	UT	27	26	24	17
	UNIG	24	24	23	17
SUT(9, 0.5)	SUT	66	78	99	100
	SUNIG	100	100	100	83
	2sKern	45	59	81	81
	Kern	45	59	81	82

Innovation distribution	MLE method	0.005	0.01	0.025	0.05
	Normal	19	18	17	15
	UT	35	31	24	20
	UNIG	31	28	24	20
SUNIG(0.5, −0.3)	SUT	71	76	80	82
	SUNIG	100	100	100	100
	2sKern	50	58	71	81
	Kern	49	58	71	81
	Normal	16	15	14	13
	UT	42	34	24	18
	UNIG	31	28	24	20
SUNIG(0.7, −0.3)	SUT	55	77	95	73
	SUNIG	100	100	100	100
	2sKern	45	54	66	74
	Kern	45	54	67	74
	Normal	12	11	10	9
	UT	32	20	12	8
	UNIG	30	27	21	17
SUNIG(0.9, −0.3)	SUT	66	31	15	9
	SUNIG	100	100	100	100
	2sKern	35	41	47	45
	Kern	36	42	47	45

Table 5 Continued.

Innovation distribution	MLE method	0.005	0.01	0.025	0.05
	Normal	8	7	3	5
	UT	20	17	7	13
	UNIG	12	10	4	6
SUT(6, 0.5)	SUT	82	100	100	100
	SUNIG	100	80	32	69
	2sKern	40	42	20	33
	Kern	38	41	20	32
	Normal	11	9	7	11
	UT	18	14	10	14
	UNIG	15	12	10	16
SUT(3, 0.5)	SUT	100	100	100	100
	SUNIG	41	51	63	41
	2sKern	33	34	38	52
	Kern	33	35	38	51

Innovation distribution	MLE method	0.005	0.01	0.025	0.05
	Normal	10	9	6	6
	UT	20	16	9	7
	UNIG	15	13	9	8
SUNIG(0.7, −0.6)	SUT	29	52	100	30
	SUNIG	100	100	85	100
	2sKern	35	42	46	59
	Kern	35	43	47	61
	Normal	8	7	5	4
	UT	17	12	6	3
	UNIG	15	13	9	5
SUNIG(0.9, −0.6)	SUT	36	18	8	4
	SUNIG	100	100	100	100
	2sKern	32	38	42	27
	Kern	32	38	42	27

Figure 3 Comparison of VaRs of a target distribution and its approximations

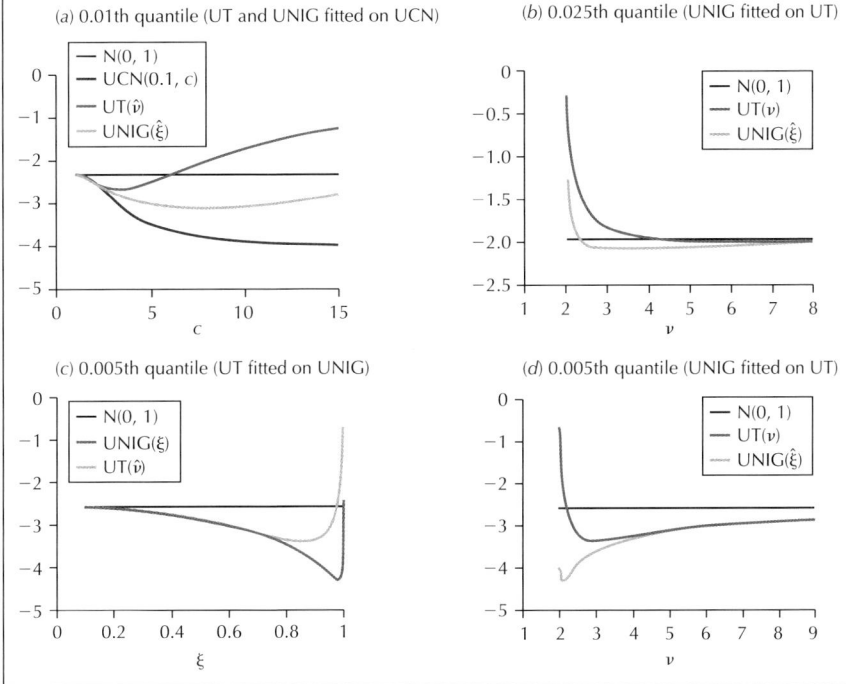

(a) 0.01th quantile (UT and UNIG fitted on UCN)

(b) 0.025th quantile (UNIG fitted on UT)

(c) 0.005th quantile (UT fitted on UNIG)

(d) 0.005th quantile (UNIG fitted on UT)

distributions) below. The conclusions for the positively skewed innovation distributions are similar to those for negatively skewed ones and are not included here.

We will first discuss the results obtained for VaR and for the *symmetric* innovation distributions (Table 2) and we will explain them using the relative entropy approximations discussed earlier. In Figure 3(a) the UT and UNIG distributions are fitted to the UCN(0.1, c) distribution and their 0.01th quantiles are compared for a range of values of c. When c is small (between 0 and 2.5) the quantiles agree well; however, when c gets large the agreement becomes poor. Clearly UT and UNIG approximation struggle to describe the UCN(0.1, c) 0.01th quantiles when c is large and we would expect this to show up in the results of the simulation study, which indeed happens. For example, consider the VaR(0.01) efficiencies of the MLE methods when the innovation distribution is UCN(0.1, 10). The results in Table 2 show that, of the parametric methods, UNIG does

Figure 4 Comparison of ESFs of a target distribution and its approximations

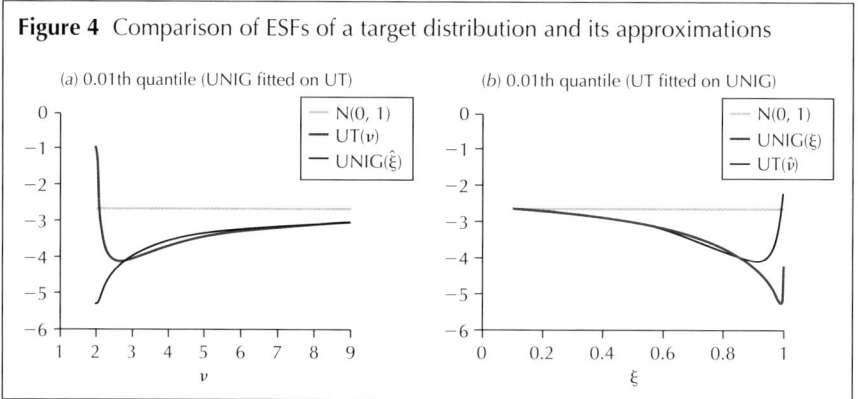

(a) 0.01th quantile (UNIG fitted on UT)

(b) 0.01th quantile (UT fitted on UNIG)

best (70%), normal second best (37%) and UT third best (24%). Figure 3(a) suggests that bias is the main contributing factor to MSE, which is in line with the results of Table 2. By studying the remaining graphs in Figure 3, the reader will find that the conclusions suggested by comparing the true and approximating quantiles match those of the simulation study. The same is true for ESF when the graphs in Figure 4 are compared with the results in Table 3.

As far as the results in Tables 2 and 3 are concerned, for innovation distributions that are moderately heavy-tailed the UT and UNIG methods clearly outperform the other methods for VaR and ESF (see N(0, 1), UCN(0.1, 3) and UNIG(0.5)). As expected, the UT method also outperforms the other methods in terms of both risk measures when it is on home ground (see UT(9), UT(6) and UT(3)). For UCN(0.2, 3) the UNIG method performs well for both risk measures and over the range of probability levels considered.

Most methods struggle to estimate VaR and ESF when the innovation distribution is UCN(0.1, 10), but the UNIG seems to do reasonably well, especially for ESF. As expected UNIG performs best for both risk measures when the innovation distribution is a heavy-tailed UNIG. The asymmetric methods SUNIG and SUT lose some efficiency with respect to their symmetric counterparts UNIG and UT when the true innovation density is indeed symmetric, as one would expect. Some methods do very well at particular quantiles – but not at all quantiles. This is due to the fact that the particular quantile happens to cross close to the true quantile at that point (the *quantile crossing* effect).

Figure 5 Comparison of VaRs of a target distribution and its approximations

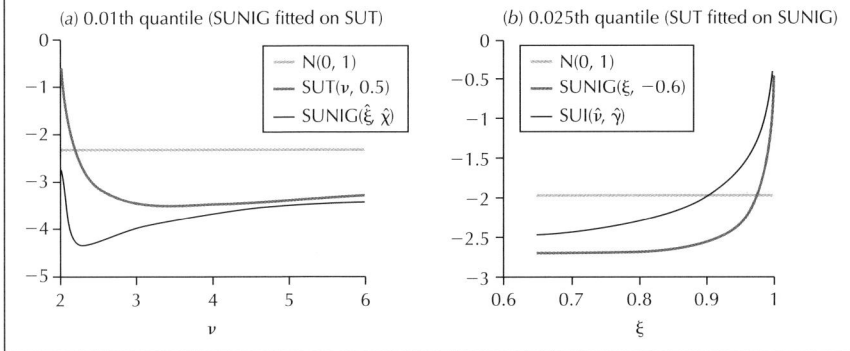

(a) 0.01th quantile (SUNIG fitted on SUT)

(b) 0.025th quantile (SUT fitted on SUNIG)

Coming now to the negatively *skewed* innovation distributions, we again interpret the Monte Carlo results by comparing quantiles. In Figure 5 two examples are given. On the left-hand side, a SUNIG(ξ, χ) distribution is fitted to a SUT(v, 0.5) distribution and the 0.01th quantiles are compared. At $v = 6$ the quantiles agree well, and much better so than the normal quantile. At $v = 3$, the agreement is poorer, but slightly better than the normal quantile. The efficiencies in Table 4 are again in line with the suggested biases from these findings.

In the right-hand plot of Figure 5 a SUT(v, γ) distribution is fitted to a SUNIG(ξ, -0.6) distribution and the 0.025th quantiles are compared. At $\xi = 0.9$ the SUT(v, γ) quantile compares poorly with the SUNIG(ξ, -0.6) quantile and is slightly worse than the normal quantile. At $\xi = 0.7$, the SUT(v, γ) quantile compares better with that of SUNIG(ξ, -0.6) and is clearly better than the normal quantile. Again the simulation results of Table 4 are in line with this comparison. Graphs for ESF may be used to explain the results in Table 5. An example is given in Figure 6. The results obtained for the negatively skewed innovation distributions (Tables 4 and 5) are now summarised. As expected, when both risk measures are considered a method operating on home ground is generally the best performer. This holds over all sample sizes and for most quantiles.

The extent of the outperformance is more severe the larger the sample size and the more extreme the innovation distribution. It is interesting to note, however, that the SUNIG method is usually the second choice method when SUT is on home ground. Specifically,

Figure 6 Comparison of ESFs of a target distribution and its approximations

(a) 0.01th quantile (SUNIG fitted on SUT) (b) 0.01th quantile (SUT fitted on SUNIG)

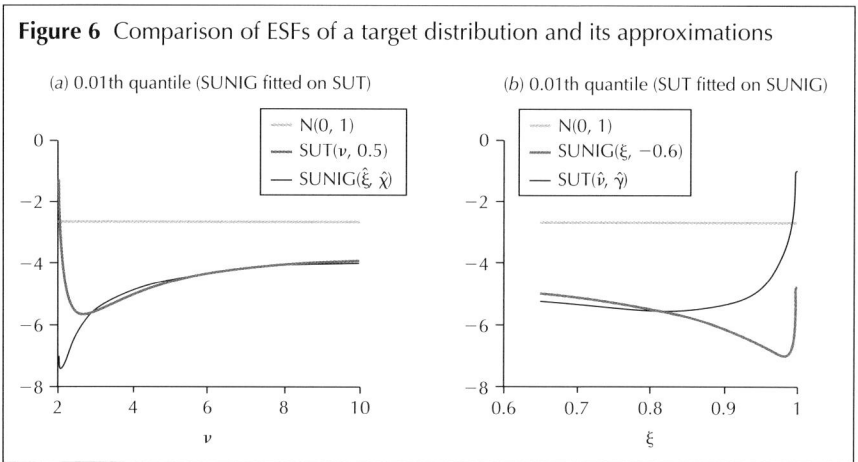

for the moderately heavy-tailed innovation distributions and at the smaller sample sizes (250 and 500), SUNIG closely matches SUT on home ground. The same cannot be said about SUT, which is often outperformed by Kern and 2sKern when the innovation distribution is SUNIG.

4.3 Comparing efficiencies of volatility estimates

The results for efficiency of volatility estimation appear in Table 6 (symmetric innovation distributions) and Table 7 (negatively skewed innovation distributions). Rather surprisingly, SUNIG is the preferred method when all performance measures and innovation distributions are considered. It is seldom outperformed by the other methods, and, if so, SUNIG's efficiency is mostly higher than 93%, with the exception that at the UCN(0.1, 10) innovation distribution it drops to 86%. In the latter rather extreme case, Kern is the best-performing method.

SUT performs reasonably well when the innovation distribution is SUT and when the innovation distribution (SUNIG or UCN) is not very heavy-tailed. In the very heavy-tailed cases SUT breaks down and performs poorly. The 2sKern and Kern methods compare favorably with the SUNIG method in most of the cases considered, with the latter the best when innovation distributions are very heavy-tailed.

Table 6 Efficiencies (%) of volatility estimation for symmetric innovation distributions

Innovation distribution	MLE method	MSE	Max	Innovation distribution	MLE method	MSE	Max
	Normal	95	94		Normal	90	79
	UT	91	92		UT	98	96
	UNIG	95	94		UNIG	100	97
N(0, 1)	SUT	94	93	**UT(6)**	SUT	97	96
	SUNIG	95	93		SUNIG	99	96
	2sKern	100	100		2sKern	97	100
	Kern	86	77		Kern	96	94
	Normal	81	67		Normal	79	52
	UT	91	94		UT	90	93
	UNIG	100	99		UNIG	100	100
CN(0.1, 3)	SUT	89	95	**UT(3)**	SUT	89	88
	SUNIG	100	99		SUNIG	100	99
	2sKern	97	100		2sKern	96	83
	Kern	96	99		Kern	95	94
	Normal	86	74		Normal	97	92
	UT	58	70		UT	98	95
	UNIG	98	97		UNIG	100	96
CN(0.2, 3)	SUT	58	71	**UNIG(0.5)**	SUT	98	95
	SUNIG	98	96		SUNIG	100	95
	2sKern	99	100		2sKern	100	100
	Kern	100	97		Kern	93	87
	Normal	73	47		Normal	90	79
	UT	40	66		UT	84	89
	UNIG	86	92		UNIG	99	93
CN(0.1, 10)	SUT	33	54	**UNIG(0.7)**	SUT	84	89
	SUNIG	86	94		SUNIG	98	93
	2sKern	87	86		2sKern	100	100
	Kern	100	100		Kern	94	87
	Normal	96	90		Normal	80	62
	UT	99	98		UT	27	53
	UNIG	100	98		UNIG	100	100
UT(9)	SUT	99	97	**UNIG(0.9)**	SUT	26	54
	SUNIG	100	97		SUNIG	100	100
	2sKern	99	100		2sKern	68	85
	Kern	93	85		Kern	85	94

Often one needs to combine volatility with innovation risk to express effective risk by $\sqrt{h_t}\mathrm{VaR}_\tau$ or $\sqrt{h_t}ESF_\tau$ (see Jorion (2002)). Then it is particularly important that both volatility and innovation risk are estimated efficiently. That SUNIG MLE performs well on both accounts speaks loudly in its favor.

Table 7 Efficiencies (%) of volatility estimation for negatively skewed innovation distributions

Innovation distribution	MLE method	MSE	Max	Innovation distribution	MLE method	MSE	Max
	Normal	83	72		Normal	79	68
	UT	95	96		UT	90	88
	UNIG	97	96		UNIG	90	87
SUT(6, 0.8)	SUT	97	99	SUNIG(0.5, −0.3)	SUT	99	100
	SUNIG	100	99		SUNIG	100	100
	2sKern	92	100		2sKern	88	92
	Kern	91	97		Kern	85	83
	Normal	63	46		Normal	78	69
	UT	91	89		UT	84	90
	UNIG	91	95		UNIG	93	94
SUT(3, 0.8)	SUT	89	91	SUNIG(0.7, −0.3)	SUT	81	92
	SUNIG	100	100		SUNIG	100	100
	2sKern	89	80		2sKern	93	99
	Kern	81	95		Kern	87	89
	Normal	71	55		Normal	73	54
	UT	83	77		UT	32	53
	UNIG	83	75		UNIG	100	97
SUT(9, 0.5)	SUT	100	100	SUNIG(0.9, −0.3)	SUT	25	51
	SUNIG	98	94		SUNIG	100	100
	2sKern	85	81		2sKern	73	85
	Kern	86	85		Kern	80	91
	Normal	63	47		Normal	51	38
	UT	81	78		UT	64	70
	UNIG	81	75		UNIG	65	68
SUT(6, 0.5)	SUT	93	100	SUNIG(0.7, −0.6)	SUT	76	73
	SUNIG	100	96		SUNIG	100	100
	2sKern	82	81		2sKern	71	83
	Kern	81	86		Kern	75	87
	Normal	53	31		Normal	47	36
	UT	70	75		UT	47	66
	UNIG	69	72		UNIG	70	80
SUT(3, 0.5)	SUT	94	96	SUNIG(0.9, −0.6)	SUT	23	48
	SUNIG	100	100		SUNIG	100	100
	2sKern	81	71		2sKern	78	85
	Kern	77	88		Kern	68	88

4.4 Using skewness–kurtosis boundaries

The referee pointed out the notion of the skewness–kurtosis (SK) boundary introduced by Jondeau and Rockinger (2003) and

Figure 7 SK boundaries and locations of some SK pairs used in the Monte Carlo study

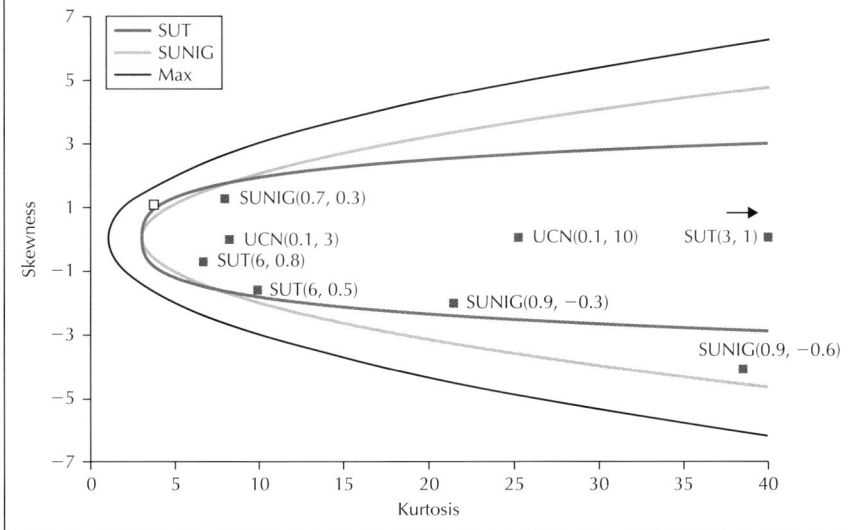

suggested that it may be useful in the interpretation of efficiency results. All the innovation densities considered here have zero means and unit variances but may differ in their levels of skewness (μ_3) and kurtosis (μ_4). Jondeau and Rockinger (2003) show that $\mu_4 > 1 + \mu_3^2$, so that the curve $\mu_4 = 1 + \mu_3^2$ in SK space defines a universal boundary within which all SK pairs of families of innovation distributions must necessarily be located. They also computed the boundary corresponding to the skewed-T distribution of Hansen (1994). As a further point of comparison we consider the SK boundaries of the SUT and SUNIG densities. The relation

$$\mu_3 = \sqrt{3}\rho\sqrt{\mu_4 - 3}\Big/\sqrt{1 + 4\rho^2}$$

can be established for the SUNIG family with ρ given by (8) and $-1 < \rho < 1$. It follows that its SK boundary is defined by $\mu_4 = 3 + 5\mu_3^2/3$. This is shown in Figure 7. A simple expression for the SK boundary of the SUT distributions is not available, but it can be computed numerically and the result is also shown in Figure 7. The SK boundary of the SUT family is largely included in that of the SUNIG family except for the small region in the vicinity of the point indicated by an unfilled block on the SUT boundary. This point corresponds to the limiting case $v = \infty$, $\gamma = \infty$, yielding a half-normal distribution with no left tail and the light right tail of a normal distribution. This density and others close to it do not appear to be interesting candidates for innovation densities, so this region does not seem to be of much concern. We conclude that the SUNIG and SUT families cover similar SK values in the smaller kurtosis region, while the SUNIG family enables modelling of a larger range of SK values than allowed by the SUT family in the larger kurtosis region. Figure 7 also shows the SK locations of some of the distributions used in our Monte Carlo study. It may be thought that the location of the SK values of a distribution largely determines its estimation efficiencies, but this is at most only partially true. As a first example, consider SUNIG(0.9, −0.6). Since it is outside the SUT boundary, we expect it would be inefficient to use the SUT density if the actual density is SUNIG(0.9, −0.6), and, indeed, inspection of the SUT and SUNIG entries in the SUNIG(0.9, −0.6) blocks of Tables 1, 4, 5 and 7 shows that this is the case.

On the other hand, SUNIG(0.9, −0.3) is located within both boundaries, which suggests that the two densities should yield similar efficiencies, but inspection of Tables 1, 4, 5 and 7 shows that in many instances SUT is substantially worse than SUNIG. This also applies to SUNIG(0.7, 0.3). Again, for SUT(6, 0.8) and SUT(6, 0.5) we would expect similar performance going by their SK locations only, and here this is fairly correct. Finally, for UCN(0.1, 3), UCN(0.1, 10) and SUT(3, 0.5) (located at infinite kurtosis) we would expect similar performance from use of the relevant innovation densities, but this is not the case. In summary, while the SK locations of innovation densities add an interesting perspective, they provide only partial explanations of the efficiency performance of the corresponding estimators.

5 EXAMPLE

In this section we illustrate the results in terms of the daily South African rand/US dollar exchange rate. We use the rand/dollar spot rate data as given by the Federal Reserve Board[3] over the period 3 January, 2000 to 1 December, 2003. This series is shown on the left of Figure 8 and the corresponding returns are on the right. A regime change in the development of the series is apparent in the middle of the period, and we analyse the two halves separately.

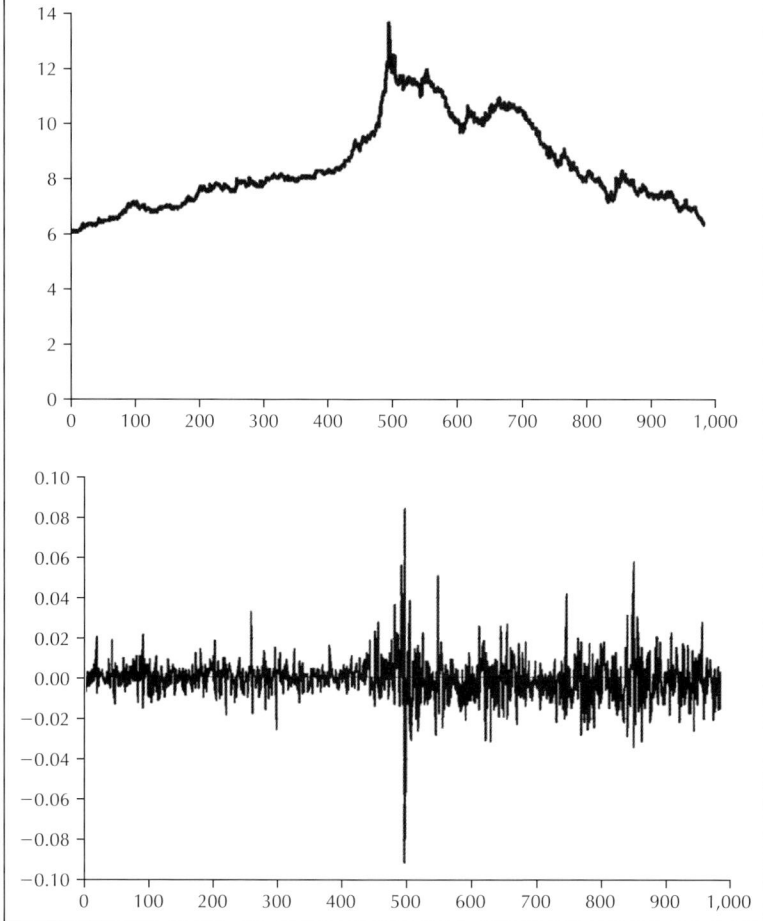

Figure 8 Rand/US dollar spot rate (top) and returns (bottom) from January 3, 2000, to December 1, 2003

We model the returns at time t by

$$Y_t = \varsigma + \phi(Y_{t-1} - \varsigma) + \sqrt{h_t}\,Z_t$$

where the squared volatility is given by

$$h_t = \alpha_0 + (\alpha_1 Z_{t-1}^2 + \beta)h_{t-1}$$

Here ζ is the mean, ϕ is the AR-parameter, α_0 and α_1 are the ARCH parameters and β is the GARCH parameter. For the first half of the series the SUNIG MLE estimate for the skewness parameter turned out to be $\hat{\chi} = 0.1199$ with a standard error of 0.0335 based on standard large-sample MLE methodology. This confirms the requirement of a positively skewed innovation density. For the second half of the series the SUNIG MLE estimate for the skewness parameter was $\hat{\chi} = 0.1001$ with a standard error of 0.0433, again confirming the requirement of a positively skewed innovation density. We then focused our analysis on the second half of the series; we carried out the three MLE methods that cater for skewed cases together with the normal method for comparison purposes and obtained the parameter estimates shown in Table 8. With $\hat{\xi}$ about 0.5 and $\hat{\chi}$ about 0.1 the example differs mildly from the normal case. It is to be expected that the parameter estimates would not differ much in such a case, and Table 8 reflects this.

The estimate of the SUT skewness parameter $\hat{\gamma}$ agrees with the positively skewed suggestion, while tail heaviness is confirmed by the estimates of both ξ and ν. The estimated innovation log-densities are shown in Figure 9. The SUT and SUNIG estimates are close together as expected. However, the fits differ markedly from normal, especially in the right-hand tail. The Kern method is substantially different from the others and exhibits unstable behavior. This is probably due to the fewer large estimated innovations, making it more difficult for the non-parametric estimate to be accurate in this region. The logs of the volatility estimates based on the different methods are shown in Figure 10. All methods seem to yield very similar volatility estimates.

6 CONCLUDING REMARKS

In this study we investigated the behavior of several maximum likelihood-based methods for estimating the GARCH model parameters and for estimating volatility and risk measures (VaR and expected shortfall). We considered innovation distributions derived from NIG, skewed-T, T and non-parametric kernel densities for this purpose and compared the efficiency of the resulting estimates with those based on the normal distribution. We found the NIG-based approach to be very competitive with the other methods on all criteria, and in most of the cases considered

Table 8 Parameter estimates for second half of rand/US dollar return series

Method	$\hat{s}$	$\hat{\phi}$	$\hat{\alpha}_0$	$\hat{\alpha}_1$	$\hat{\beta}$	$\hat{\xi}$	$\hat{\chi}$	$\hat{\nu}$	$\hat{\gamma}$
Normal	−0.00159	−0.04241	0.00001	0.09153	0.83678				
SUNIG	−0.00156	−0.09101	0.00001	0.06893	0.85934	0.50488	0.10009		
SUT	−0.00168	−0.08971	0.00001	0.06956	0.85994			7.57001	1.08834
Kern	−0.00156	−0.02391	0.00001	0.07765	0.85262				

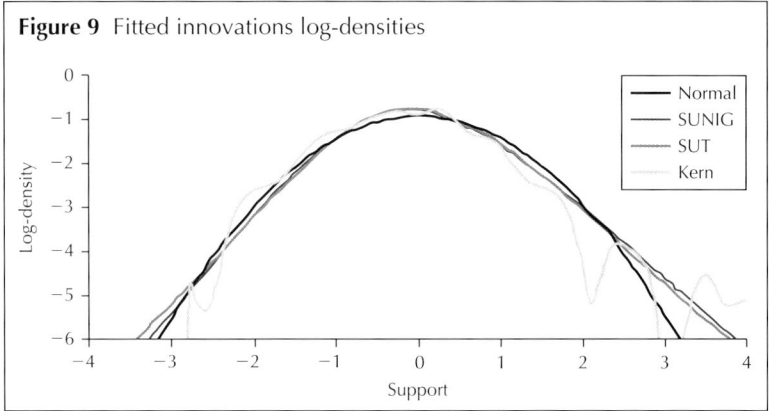

Figure 9 Fitted innovations log-densities

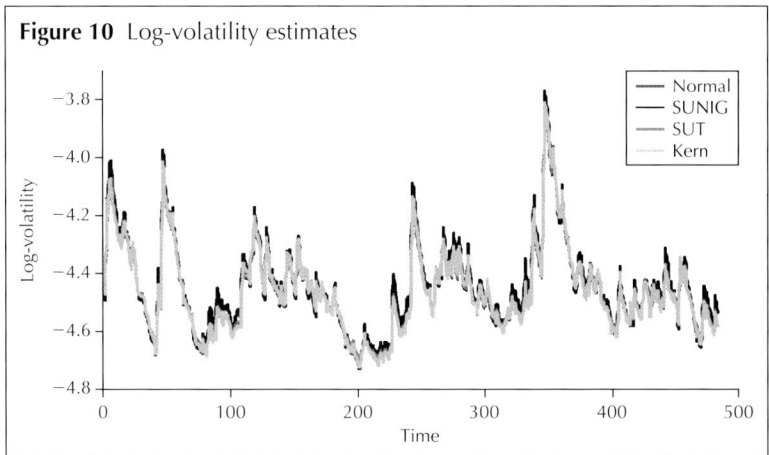

Figure 10 Log-volatility estimates

this is the method we recommend for routine application in practice.

1 In fact it follows from (3) that $G_{UT(v)}(z) \to 0$ for $z < 0$ and $G_{UT(v)}(z) \to 1$ for $z > 0$ as $v \downarrow 2$. This means that the UT(v)-distribution tends to the degenerate distribution with all probability mass at 0 when $v \downarrow 2$ and, in particular, both tails eventually become lighter when $v \downarrow 2$.

2 In general, suppose that $F(z; \delta)$ is a family of CDFs with variance s_δ^2 with the property that $s_\delta^2 \to \infty$ as $\delta \to \delta_0$. Then the corresponding unit variance family of CDFs are $F(s_\delta z; \delta)$ and it is readily shown that they tend to the degenerate distribution with all mass at 0 as $\delta \to \delta_0$ under mild regularity conditions.

3 At http://www.federalreserve.gov/releases/h10/Hist/.

This chapter was previously published in *The Journal of Risk* **6**(3), Spring 2004.

REFERENCES

Barndorff-Nielsen, O. E. and K. Prause, 2001, "Apparent Scaling", *Finance and Stochastics* **5**, pp. 103–13.

Barndorff-Nielsen, O. E., P. Blaesid, J. L. Jensen, and M. Sorensen, 1985, "The Fascination of Sand", in A. C. Atkinson and S. E. Feinberg (eds), *A Celebration of Statistics*, pp. 57–87. (New York: Springer-Verlag).

Barndorff-Nielsen, O. E. and N. Shephard, 2001, "Normal Modified Stable Processes", Unpublished manuscript available from the Centre for Mathematical Physics and Stochastics, University of Aarhus, Denmark.

Bollerslev, T. and J. M. Wooldridge, 1992, "Quasi-Maximum Likelihood Estimation of Dynamic Models with Time Varying Covariances", *Econometric Reviews* **11**, pp. 143–72.

Berkowitz, J. and J. O'Brien, 2002, "How Accurate are Value-at-Risk Models at Commercial Banks?", *Journal of Finance* **LVII**, pp. 1093–111.

Engle, R. F. and G. Gonzalez-Rivera, 1991, "Semi-Parametric ARCH Models", *Journal of Business and Economic Statistics* **9**, pp. 345–59.

Fernandez, C. and M. Steel, 1998, "On Bayesian Modeling of Fat Tails and Skewness", *Journal of the American Statistical Association* **93**, pp. 359–71.

Forsberg, L. and T. Bollerslev, 2002, "Bridging the Gap Between the Distribution of Realized (ecu) Volatility and ARCH Modelling (of the Euro): The GARCH-NIG Model", *Journal of Applied Econometrics* **17**, pp. 535–48.

Gouriéroux, C., 1997, *ARCH Models and Financial Applications*. (New York: Springer).

Hansen, B. E., 1994, "Autoregressive Conditional Density Estimation", *International Economic Review* **35(3)**, pp. 705–30.

Jondeau, E. and M. Rockinger, 2003, "Conditional Volatility, Skewness and Kurtosis: Existence, Persistence, and Comovements", *Journal of Economic Dynamics and Control* **27**, pp. 1699–737.

Jones, M. C. and M. J. Faddy, 2003, "A Skew Extension of the *t*-Distribution, with Applications", *Journal of the Royal Statistical Society, Series B* **65**, Part 1, pp. 159–74.

Jorion, P., 2002, "Fallacies about the Effects of Market Risk Management Systems", *Journal of Risk* **5(1)**, pp. 75–96.

Lambert, P. and S. Laurent, 2001, "Modelling Financial Time Series Using GARCH-Type Models with a Skewed Student Density", Mimeo, Université de Liège.

Lillestol, J., 2000, "Risk Analysis and the NIG-Distribution", *Journal of Risk* **2(4)**, pp. 41–56.

McNeil, A. and R. Frey, 2000, "Estimation of Tail-Related Risk Measures for Heteroscedastic Financial Time Series: An Extreme Value Approach", *Journal of Empirical Finance* **7**, pp. 271–300.

Silverman, B. W., 1990, *Density Estimation for Statistics and Data Analysis*. (New York: Chapman and Hall).

Soofi, E. S. and J. J. Retzer, 2002, "Information Indices: Unification and Applications", *Journal of Econometrics* **107**, pp. 17–40.

Tapia, R. A. and J. R. Thomson, 1978, *Nonparametric Probability Density Estimation*. (Baltimore: John Hopkins University Press).

Venter, J. H. and P. J. de Jongh, 2002, "Risk Estimation Using the Normal Inverse Gaussian Distribution", *Journal of Risk* **4(2)**, pp. 1–23.

Wand, M. P. and M. C. Jones, 1995, *Kernel Smoothing*. (New York: Chapman and Hall).

Widder, D. V., 1946, *The Laplace Transform*. (Princeton, NJ: Princeton University Press).

8

Incorporating Volatility Updating into the Historical Simulation Method for Value-at-Risk

John Hull, Alan White*

University of Toronto

1 INTRODUCTION

In recent years value-at-risk (VaR) has become a very popular measure of market risk. It is widely used by financial institutions, fund managers, and nonfinancial corporations to control the market risk in a portfolio of financial instruments. As discussed by Jorion (1997), it has been adopted by central bank regulators as the major determinant of the capital banks are required to keep to cover potential losses arising from the market risks they are bearing.

The VaR of a portfolio is a function of two parameters, a time period and a confidence level. It equals the dollar loss on the portfolio that will not be exceeded by the end of the time period with the specified confidence level. If $X\%$ is the confidence level and N days is the time period, the calculation of VaR is based on the probability distribution of changes in the portfolio value over N days. Specifically VaR is set equal to the loss on the portfolio at the $100 - X$ percentile point of the distribution. Bank regulators have chosen N equal to 10 days and X equal to 99%. They set the capital required for market risk equal to three times the value of VaR calculated using these parameters.

In practice the VaR for N days is almost invariably assumed to be $\sqrt{N}$ times the VaR for one day. A key task for risk managers has

---

*We are grateful to the editor, Philippe Jorion, for many suggestions that improved this chapter.

therefore been the development of accurate and robust procedures for calculating a one-day VaR.

One common approach to calculating VaR involves assuming that daily percentage changes in the underlying market variables are conditionally multivariate normal with the mean percentage change in each market variable being zero. This is often referred to as the "model building" approach. If the daily change in the portfolio value is linearly dependent on daily changes in market variables that are normally distributed, its probability distribution is also normal. The variance of the probability distribution, and hence the percentile of the distribution corresponding to VaR, can be calculated in a straightforward way from the variance–covariance matrix for the market variables. In circumstances where the linear assumption is inappropriate, the change in the portfolio value is often approximated as a quadratic function of percentage changes in the market variables. This allows the first few moments of the probability distribution of the change in the portfolio value to be calculated analytically so that the required percentile of the distribution can be estimated.[1] An alternative approach to handling nonlinearity is to use Monte Carlo simulation. On each simulation trial daily changes in the market variables are sampled from their multivariate distribution and the portfolio is revalued. This enables a complete probability distribution for the daily change in the portfolio value to be determined.[2]

Many market variables have distributions with fatter tails than the normal distribution. This has led some risk managers to use "historical simulation" rather than the model building approach. Historical simulation involves creating a database consisting of the daily movements in all market variables over a period of time. The first simulation trial assumes that the percentage changes in the market variables are the same as on the first day covered by the database; the second simulation trial assumes that they are the same as on the second day; and so on. The change in the portfolio value is calculated for each simulation trial and the required percentile of the probability distribution of this change is estimated.[3] As an example, suppose that 1,000 days of data are used and the 1 percentile of the distribution is required. This would be estimated as the tenth worst change in the portfolio value.

The advantage of the model building approach is that the underlying variance–covariance matrix can be updated using an exponentially weighted moving average (EWMA) or GARCH model.[4] The disadvantage is that the market variables are assumed to be conditionally multivariate normal. The model building approach takes no account of skewness or kurtosis in the distributions of market variables and no account of nonlinear correlations between market variables. Historical simulation, by contrast, has the advantage that it accurately reflects the historical multivariate probability distribution for the market variables. Its main disadvantage is that it incorporates no volatility updating.

Hull and White (1998) show how the assumption of multivariate normality in the model building approach can be relaxed. Their approach allows any probability distribution to be assumed for the daily changes in a market variable. A transformation is used to convert the assumed distribution to a standard normal distribution. This transformation is defined so that the X-percentile point of the assumed distribution is transformed to the X-percentile of a standard normal distribution. The transformed market variables are assumed to be multivariate normal. The approach was tested using nine years of data on 12 different currencies and found to perform well.

The assumed distribution for each market variable in Hull and White (1998) can be chosen in a variety of ways. One possibility is to select an appropriate standard distribution (eg, a mixture of normals) and use maximum likelihood methods to find the best fit parameters. Another possibility is to use the historical distribution. A third possibility is to smooth the historical distribution; for example, by using a kernel estimator.[5] The Hull and White approach provides one way of bridging the gap between the model building and historical simulation approaches. It shows how the model building approach can be modified to incorporate some of the attractive features of the historical simulation approach. In this chapter we propose an alternative approach that allows volatility updating to be incorporated into historical simulation.

2 INCORPORATING VOLATILITY UPDATING SCHEMES INTO A HISTORICAL SIMULATION

The probability distribution of a market variable, when scaled by an estimate of its volatility, is often found to be approximately stationary. This suggests that historical simulation can be improved by taking account of the volatility changes experienced during the period covered by the historical data. If the current volatility of a market variable is 1.5% per day and two months ago the volatility was only 1% per day, the data observed two months ago understates the changes we expect to see now. On the other hand, if the volatility was 2% per day two months ago the reverse is true.

We consider a portfolio dependent on a number of market variables and assume that the variance of each market variable during the period covered by the historical data is monitored using either a GARCH or EWMA model. We are interested in estimating VaR for the portfolio at the end of day $N - 1$ (ie, for day N).

Define:

h_{tj}: the historical percentage change in variable j on day t of the period covered by the historical sample ($t < N$); and

σ_{tj}^2: the historical GARCH/EWMA estimate of the daily variance of the percentage change in variable j made for day t at the end of day $t - 1$.

The most recent GARCH/EWMA estimate of the daily variance is σ_{Nj}^2. This is the estimate, made at the end of day $N - 1$, of the variance of the percentage change in variable j during day N. We assume that the probability distribution of h_{tj} / σ_{tj} is stationary. We therefore replace each h_{tj} by h_{tj}^*, where

$$h_{tj}^* = \sigma_{Nj} \frac{h_{tj}}{\sigma_{tj}} \tag{1}$$

and set the tth sample percentage change for variable j to h_{tj}^* instead of h_{tj}.

This approach (which will be referred to as HW) is a straightforward extension of traditional historical simulation (which will be referred to as HS). Instead of using the actual historical percentage changes in market variables for the purposes of calculating VaR, we use historical changes that have been adjusted to reflect the ratio of the current daily volatility to the daily volatility at the time of the observation. Suppose that 20 days ago the observed percentage change in a market variable was 1.6% and the daily volatility was estimated to be 1%. If the daily volatility is now estimated to be 1.5%, the sample percentage change corresponding to the observation 20 days ago is 2.4%.

3 THE BRW APPROACH

One of the ways in which risk managers attempt to allow for stochastic volatility is by sampling more frequently from recent observations than from observations generated in the distant past. Boudoukh, Richardson and Whitelaw (1998) proposed one version of this approach (which will be referred to as BRW). The weight given to the observation $n + 1$ days ago is λ times the weight given to the observation n days ago, where $0 < \lambda < 1$.[6] To determine a particular percentile of the probability distribution in BRW, it is necessary to order the observations over the last N days and then, starting from the lowest one, accumulate weights until the percentile is reached.[7]

We define a "5% tail event" as the occurrence of an observation that lies in the 5% tail of the historical distribution and a "1% tail event" as the occurrence of an observation that lies in the 1% tail of the historical distribution. Boudoukh, Richardson and Whitelaw (1998) indicate that, when regular historical simulation is used, 5% tail events do happen approximately 5% of the time and 1% tail events do happen approximately 1% of the time. However, there is significant "bunching"; that is, tail events tend to happen in close succession rather than occurring randomly throughout the days covered by the data. An attractive feature of the BRW approach is that it greatly reduces bunching.

BRW can be criticised on the grounds that it is an indirect and somewhat inefficient way of allowing for stochastic volatility. In BRW (and all schemes that involve sampling more frequently from recent observations) a short run sequence of abnormally large positive (or negative) returns will markedly skew the predicted distribution to the right (or the left). In BRW, when $\lambda = 0.98$, the most recent observation is assigned a probability of about 2% so that a single large outcome is enough to generate this sort of skew. BRW and similar schemes shorten the effective sampling period to capture the behavior of stochastic volatility. Unfortunately, in doing so, they capture the stochastic behavior of all other sample moments of the distribution.

4 COMPARISON OF APPROACHES

We tested the three schemes (HS, BRW and HW) using daily data on 12 different exchange rates between 4 January, 1988 and 15 August,

1997 and five different stock indices between 11 July, 1988 and 10 February, 1998. The currencies were the Australian dollar (AUD), Belgian franc (BEF), Swiss franc (CHF), Deutschmark (DEM), Danish krone (DKK), Spanish peseta (ESP), French franc (FRF), British pound (GBP), Italian lira (ITL), Japanese yen (JPY), Dutch guilder (NLG) and Swedish krona (SEK). The stock indices were the S&P 500, CAC-40, FT-SE 100, Nikkei 225, and Toronto Stock Exchange 300. For each market variable, we had over 2,400 daily observations. For BRW we used $\lambda = 0.98$.[8] In HW, the daily variance was updated using the EWMA model

$$\sigma_{tj}^2 = \alpha \sigma_{t-1,j} + (1 - \alpha) h_{t-1,j} \qquad (2)$$

with $\alpha = 0.94$.[9]

For all three approaches and all market variables, a probability distribution of the daily percentage change was estimated each day from the most recent 500 days of data. The 5 and 1 percentiles of the distribution were noted. For each market variable, we define indicator functions $I(t)$ and $J(t)$ for day t. We set $I(t) = 1$ if the observation on day t is a 5% tail event, and zero otherwise; and we set $J(t) = 1$ if the observation on day t is a 1% tail event, and zero otherwise.

One issue in historical simulation is whether historical data should be adjusted to bring the mean percentage change to zero. Consider, for example, the S&P 500. During the 500 days ending 10 February, 1998 the mean change was 0.09% per day. If we make no adjustment to the historical data, we are implicitly assuming that this is the expected change on 11 February, 1998. We tested each of the three approaches with and without a mean adjustment. In the case of regular historical simulation, mean adjustment involved subtracting the mean daily percentage change from each of the 500 observations prior to estimating the 5% and 1% tails of the distribution. In the case of BRW, it involved calculating a weighted mean percentage change and subtracting it from each observation. In the case of HW, it involved calculating the mean of the normalised observations, h_{tj} / σ_{tj}, and subtracting this mean from each normalised observation before multiplying by the estimate of the current volatility σ_{Nj}.

Table 1 shows the percentage of days when tail events happen for exchange rates. Table 4 reports similar results for stock indices. If the tails of the estimated distributions were unbiased, 5% of tail

Table 1 Percentage of time that change in exchange rate is within 5% and 1% tails of estimated distribution using different approaches (based on 1923 observations). Asterisk indicates that the hypothesis of unbiasedness can be rejected with 95% confidence

HS: Distribution estimated by giving equal weights to 500 most recent observations.

BRW: Distribution estimated by giving weights that decline exponentially to 500 most recent observations.

HW: Distribution estimated by giving equal weights to 500 most recent observations after they have been adjusted for volatility changes.

	HS No Mean Adj	HS Mean Adj	BRW No Mean Adj	BRW Mean Adj	HW No Mean Adj	HW Mean Adj
5% Tail						
AUD	4.05	4.21	4.94	4.89	4.78	4.68
BEF	4.73	4.57	4.89	4.57	5.09	4.99
CHF	4.68	4.57	5.25	4.89	5.09	4.78
DEM	4.57	4.57	5.04	4.73	4.78	4.73
DKK	4.68	4.37	4.99	4.52	4.89	4.57
ESP	4.78	4.83	4.99	4.78	5.25	5.20
FRF	4.73	4.47	5.20	5.09	4.78	4.68
GBP	4.83	4.68	5.04	4.78	4.68	4.68
ITL	4.78	4.78	5.15	5.15	5.20	4.89
JPY	4.73	4.47	5.20	4.73	5.30	4.83
NLG	4.68	4.68	5.20	4.94	5.09	4.94
SEK	5.41	5.25	5.35	5.15	5.09	4.83
AVE	4.72	4.62*	5.10	4.85	5.00	4.82
1% Tail						
AUD	0.78	0.78	1.40	1.40	1.04	0.99
BEF	0.99	0.94	1.56*	1.35	0.94	0.88
CHF	1.04	0.94	1.35	1.30	0.88	0.94
DEM	0.94	0.83	1.51*	1.25	1.09	1.09
DKK	0.78	0.78	1.40	1.40	1.04	0.99
ESP	0.94	0.94	1.72*	1.72*	0.94	0.94
FRF	0.99	0.94	1.35	1.14	1.09	0.99
GBP	0.94	0.94	1.30	1.14	1.14	1.14
ITL	0.99	0.99	1.40	1.25	0.88	0.88
JPY	0.83	0.83	1.72*	1.46*	0.83	0.78
NLG	0.88	0.88	1.35	1.20	1.04	1.04
SEK	1.14	1.09	1.51*	1.40	1.04	0.94
AVE	0.94	0.91	1.46*	1.33*	1.00	0.97

Table 2 Mean absolute error in percentage of 5% and 1% tail events for exchange rates in 100 consecutive days. (Results based on a total of 1,823 100-day windows)

HS: Distribution estimated by giving equal weights to 500 most recent observations.

BRW: Distribution estimated by giving weights that decline exponentially to 500 most recent observations.

HW: Distribution estimated by giving equal weights to 500 most recent observations after they have been adjusted for volatility changes.

	HS No Mean Adj	HS Mean Adj	BRW No Mean Adj	BRW Mean Adj	HW No Mean Adj	HW Mean Adj
5% Tail						
AUD	2.42	2.56	1.50	1.65	1.53	1.69
BEF	3.15	3.12	1.52	1.76	1.54	1.47
CHF	3.07	3.06	1.75	1.78	1.55	1.42
DEM	3.47	3.47	1.58	1.63	1.50	1.40
DKK	3.48	3.17	1.88	1.90	1.65	1.59
ESP	3.21	3.21	2.10	2.21	1.69	1.62
FRF	3.20	3.14	1.87	1.88	1.54	1.54
GBP	3.02	2.98	1.66	1.45	1.59	1.59
ITL	3.50	3.50	2.02	1.96	1.72	1.82
JPY	2.90	3.02	1.86	1.62	1.54	1.56
NLG	3.56	3.49	1.74	1.69	1.73	1.59
SEK	3.79	3.71	1.69	1.68	1.82	1.71
AVE	3.23	3.20	1.76	1.77	1.62	1.58
1% Tail						
AUD	0.73	0.73	0.77	0.77	0.72	0.73
BEF	1.09	1.09	0.98	0.72	0.48	0.53
CHF	1.36	1.28	0.90	0.99	0.55	0.51
DEM	1.24	1.15	0.91	0.77	0.69	0.69
DKK	0.95	0.95	0.91	0.90	0.79	0.73
ESP	0.91	0.91	1.04	1.05	0.55	0.55
FRF	1.01	0.96	0.78	0.63	0.69	0.69
GBP	0.91	0.91	0.89	0.75	0.70	0.70
ITL	1.22	1.22	0.77	0.71	0.65	0.65
JPY	1.10	1.10	0.98	0.73	0.72	0.72
NLG	1.19	1.19	0.95	0.90	0.68	0.68
SEK	0.99	1.05	0.77	0.76	0.80	0.73
AVE	1.06	1.05	0.89	0.81	0.67	0.66

Table 3 Ljung–Box statistic for autocorrelations between tail events in exchange rates. Results based on autocorrelations with lags of between 1 and 15 days for indicator function which equals 1 if tail event happens and 0 otherwise. Zero autocorrelation cannot be rejected with 95% confidence when statistic is less than 25

HS: Distribution estimated by giving equal weights to 500 most recent observations.

BRW: Distribution estimated by giving weights that decline exponentially to 500 most recent observations.

HW: Distribution estimated by giving equal weights to 500 most recent observations after they have been adjusted for volatility changes.

	HS No Mean Adj	HS Mean Adj	BRW No Mean Adj	BRW Mean Adj	HW No Mean Adj	HW Mean Adj
5% Tail						
AUD	33.5	32.5	20.5	18.5	27.2	25.3
BEF	85.6	88.2	39.2	41.6	21.8	25.6
CHF	52.5	47.6	13.0	19.6	21.2	24.0
DEM	104.5	104.5	24.9	21.3	13.3	16.2
DKK	112.3	77.9	41.9	36.1	26.6	21.0
ESP	89.5	85.7	22.6	25.9	13.1	17.4
FRF	108.6	88.2	22.5	25.6	20.8	17.1
GBP	86.5	87.7	23.6	22.9	19.5	19.5
ITL	119.6	120.5	20.7	21.0	21.3	21.1
JPY	43.9	46.5	13.1	10.3	14.4	10.4
NLG	87.0	71.3	19.2	22.6	13.2	19.5
SEK	78.8	73.8	26.6	27.2	10.8	7.9
AVE	83.5	77.0	24.0	24.4	18.6	18.7
1% Tail						
AUD	8.5	8.5	7.9	7.9	6.1	6.3
BEF	53.1	60.4	21.7	22.4	6.6	7.1
CHF	153.4	147.8	26.3	37.3	7.4	6.9
DEM	79.2	56.7	18.3	15.6	42.4	42.4
DKK	21.8	21.8	33.5	39.7	14.7	9.7
ESP	67.3	67.3	28.4	27.6	6.6	6.6
FRF	16.5	14.6	13.8	18.0	10.8	9.7
GBP	50.8	50.8	46.6	52.6	7.9	7.9
ITL	134.4	134.4	20.1	17.1	12.6	12.6
JPY	59.1	59.1	10.1	9.4	8.1	9.0
NLG	73.3	73.3	29.1	20.2	11.8	11.8
SEK	83.0	92.5	8.6	10.5	9.0	10.6
AVE	66.7	65.6	22.0	23.2	12.0	11.7

Table 4 Percentage of time that change in stock index is within 5% and 1% tails of estimated distribution using different approaches (based on 1,923 observations). Asterisk indicates that the hypothesis of unbiasedness can be rejected with 95% confidence

HS: Distribution estimated by giving equal weights to 500 most recent observations.

BRW: Distribution estimated by giving weights that decline exponentially to 500 most recent observations.

HW: Distribution estimated by giving equal weights to 500 most recent observations after they have been adjusted for volatility changes.

	HS No Mean Adj	HS Mean Adj	BRW No Mean Adj	BRW Mean Adj	HW No Mean Adj	HW Mean Adj
5% Tail						
S&P	5.67	5.09	5.30	4.63	5.04	4.57
CAC	5.61	5.41	5.51	5.25	5.15	5.15
FTSE	5.61	5.25	5.61	5.09	5.09	4.42
NIKKEI	5.51	5.77	5.41	5.93	5.09	5.30
TSE	5.51	4.94	5.77	4.94	4.78	4.31
AVE	5.58*	5.29	5.52*	5.17	5.03	4.75
1% Tail						
S&P	1.40	1.20	1.46*	1.35	0.83	0.83
CAC	1.51*	1.30	1.51*	1.56*	1.09	1.09
FTSE	1.20	1.04	1.40	1.30	1.04	1.04
NIKKEI	1.25	1.30	1.35	1.66*	0.73	0.78
TSE	1.14	1.04	1.20	0.99	0.88	0.78
AVE	1.30*	1.17	1.38*	1.37*	0.91	0.90

events would happen on 5% of the days and 1% of tail events would happen on 1% of the days. Each result in Tables 1 and 4 is calculated from 1923 observations.[10] The samples generating the empirical distributions are overlapping, but $I(t)$ and $J(t)$ are each independent and identically distributed under the null hypothesis that the tail of the distribution is unbiased. The standard deviation of the percentage of days when tail events happen is therefore

$$\sqrt{\frac{p(1-p)}{n}}$$

where p is the probability of a tail event and n is the sample size. Asterisks in Tables 1 and 4 indicate situations where the hypothesis

Table 5 Mean absolute error in percentage of 5% and 1% tail events for stock indices in 100 consecutive days. (Results based on a total of 1,823 100-day windows)

HS: Distribution estimated by giving equal weights to 500 most recent observations.

BRW: Distribution estimated by giving weights that decline exponentially to 500 most recent observations.

HW: Distribution estimated by giving equal weights to 500 most recent observations after they have been adjusted for volatility changes.

	HS No Mean Adj	HS Mean Adj	BRW No Mean Adj	BRW Mean Adj	HW No Mean Adj	HW Mean Adj
5% Tail						
S&P	2.68	2.57	1.62	1.48	1.52	1.47
CAC	2.99	2.88	1.61	1.53	1.66	1.69
FTSE	3.23	3.29	1.88	1.67	1.83	1.49
NIKKEI	3.80	3.83	2.19	2.81	2.22	2.29
TSE	2.71	2.33	1.86	1.49	1.58	1.60
AVE	3.08	2.98	1.83	1.79	1.76	1.71
1% Tail						
S&P	1.15	0.98	0.72	0.61	0.63	0.63
CAC	1.14	0.99	0.79	0.77	0.69	0.69
FTSE	0.99	0.83	0.70	0.67	0.58	0.58
NIKKEI	1.21	1.22	0.85	1.20	0.67	0.61
TSE	0.89	0.87	0.72	0.59	0.49	0.42
AVE	1.08	0.98	0.75	0.77	0.61	0.59

that the tail of the distribution is unbiased can be rejected with 95% confidence. The tables show that the BRW method has a marked tendency to understate 1% tail events. The results reported by Boudoukh, Richardson and Whitelaw (1998) show a similar phenomenon.

Boudoukh, Richardson and Whitelaw (1998) propose a mean absolute percentage error measure (MAPE) for measuring bunching. This is calculated as follows: for each period of 100 consecutive days for which estimates are made, the absolute difference between the actual number of tail events and the expected number of tail events is calculated. (For 5% tail events the expected number of tail events is 5; for 1% tail events the expected number of tail events is 1.) The measure is set equal to the mean of these absolute differences.

Table 6 Ljung–Box statistic for autocorrelations between tail events in stock indices. Results based on autocorrelations with lags of between 1 and 15 days for indicator function which equals 1 if tail event happens and 0 otherwise. Zero autocorrelation cannot be rejected with 95% confidence when statistic is less than 25

HS: Distribution estimated by giving equal weights to 500 most recent observations.

BRW: Distribution estimated by giving weights that decline exponentially to 500 most recent observations.

HW: Distribution estimated by giving equal weights to 500 most recent observations after they have been adjusted for volatility changes.

	HS No Mean Adj	HS Mean Adj	BRW No Mean Adj	BRW Mean Adj	HW No Mean Adj	HW Mean Adj
5% Tail						
S&P	36.5	42.2	22.9	14.0	12.7	10.7
CAC	137.9	132.3	36.3	55.9	48.5	50.0
FTSE	100.1	104.0	15.2	26.0	37.1	17.3
NIKKEI	319.6	293.7	60.2	81.9	57.4	48.2
TSE	104.6	98.0	21.7	17.8	16.6	17.6
AVE	139.7	134.0	31.3	39.1	34.4	28.8
1% Tail						
S&P	24.6	21.8	30.4	29.2	7.7	7.7
CAC	254.4	206.8	24.2	22.2	29.8	29.8
FTSE	26.8	33.2	7.3	7.4	3.2	3.2
NIKKEI	124.4	112.0	12.4	37.2	17.4	15.1
TSE	52.7	43.0	11.0	13.1	7.1	1.8
AVE	96.6	83.3	17.1	21.8	13.0	11.5

MAPE is a combined measure of both bias and bunching. The impact of a bias in the measurement of tail events is clear. If the procedure for measuring tail events is biased so that in every 100-day period we observe two 1% tail events then MAPE = 1. To see how the bunching component of the measure works, consider the following example.

Suppose that there are 599 observations numbered 1 to 599. This allows us to compute 500 overlapping 100-day samples. If every 100th observation (observations 100, 200, 300, 400 and 500) are 1% tail events then every 100-day sample will contain exactly one 1% tail event and MAPE will be zero. Now suppose that the 1% tail events are bunched together so that observations 100, 101, 300, 301 and 500 are tail events. Calculations shows that there are 198 samples with no tail events (absolute error = 1), 104 with 1 tail event (absolute error = 0), and 198 with 2 tail events (absolute error = 1). In this case, MAPE = 396/500 or 0.792.

The MAPE measure is similar to a standard deviation measure. If it were based on the difference between the observed number of tail events and the sample mean number of tail events, it would be even closer to a standard deviation measure. The definition used here was chosen to maintain consistency with BRW. The measure is shown in Tables 2 and 5. For each market variable, the results are based on 1,823 different 100-day windows. Since the windows are overlapping, standard tests of statistical significance cannot be used.

As an alternative measure of bunching, we calculated the Ljung–Box statistic using the first 15 autocorrelations of the indicator functions $I(t)$ and $J(t)$. In the case of 5% tail events, the autocorrelations were between the $I(t)$; in the case of 1% tail events, they were between the $J(t)$.[11] The results are reported in Tables 3 and 6. A value of the statistic less than 25 indicates that zero autocorrelation cannot be rejected at the 95% level. The numbers for each market variable are based on 1,923 observations of the indicator functions.

Tables 2, 3, 5 and 6 show that BRW and HW both produce big improvements over HS as far as bunching is concerned. On average, HW performs better than BRW. Tables 3 and 6 show that, for 5% tails, the hypothesis of zero autocorrelation cannot be rejected for 12 out of the 17 market variables considered when both HW (no mean adjustment) is used and BRW (no mean adjustment) is used. For 1% tails, the hypothesis of zero autocorrelation cannot be rejected for 15 of the market variables in the case of HW (no mean adjustment) and for 11 of the market variables in the case of BRW (no mean adjustment).

Overall, the results with mean adjustment are similar to those without mean adjustment. Most of the rest of the chapter will focus on the results obtained without mean adjustment.

5 CAPITAL UTILISATION
Define P as the 1 percentile of daily changes in a market variable. The regulatory risk capital for an investment of US$1 in a long position in the market variable is three times the 10-day 99% VaR, or $-3\sqrt{10}P$.

Figure 1 Capital required under three methods for an investment of US$1 in DEM

HS: Distribution estimated by giving equal weights to 500 most recent observations.

BRW: Distribution estimated by giving weights that decline exponentially to 500 most recent observations.

HW: Distribution estimated by giving equal weights to 500 most recent observations after they have been adjusted for volatility changes.

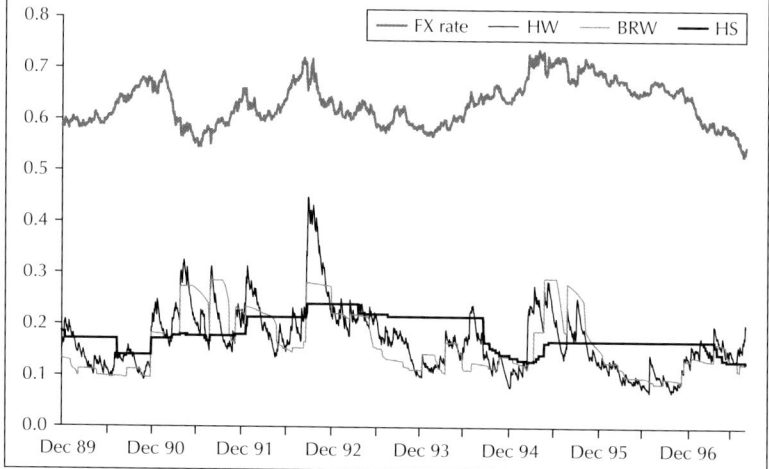

Figure 1 illustrates the three approaches for calculating P by showing the regulatory capital that would be required for an investment of US$1 in DEM. The DEM exchange rate is also shown. As illustrated by the figure, the capital is significantly more variable under BRW and HW than under HS.

In the HS method, the risk capital is unchanged for long periods of time due to the length of the window. The risk capital is affected by large observations that appear in, and drop off from, the window. An interesting aspect of BRW, illustrated in Figure 1, is that the capital tends to increase to a new level for a period of time and then drop off sharply. To understand the reason for this, consider a day (day d) where there is a sharp decrease in the value of a portfolio, worse than anything seen on the previous 500 days. Assuming no worse observation occurs subsequently, when $\lambda = 0.98$ this increases the capital for exactly 35 subsequent days. The reason is as follows. On day $d + 1$ the observation for day d is given a weight of about 0.02, so that the 1 percentile of the distribution of daily returns equals the day d observation. Between day 1 and day 35, the weight given to day d remains above 1%, so that the 1 percentile continues to equal the day d observation. On day 36, the weight given to the observation is just below 1% and the next worst observation starts to influence the 1 percentile point. BRW can be contrasted with HW where capital requirements are determined by the most recent estimate of volatility and are therefore much more responsive to recent observations.

For long positions in a single foreign currency, we found that the capital required under BRW is on average 11.0% less than under HS and that the capital required under HW is on average 7.8% less than under HS. For long positions in a stock index, we found that the capital required under BRW is on average 0.2% higher than under HS and the capital required under HW is on average 6.7% higher than under HS. Clearly BRW scores high marks if the objective is to minimise capital. However, this is hardly surprising. Tables 1 and 4 show that BRW's 1% tail are not extreme enough. A consistent result from our data is that there is a greater than 1% chance of an observation being in BRW's 1% tail.

Of course, the objective should not be to choose the method that minimises capital requirements. We contend that the best method is the one that, for a given average investment of capital, maximises the protection against losses. Define:

A: average capital required under regular historical simulation;
C_{ave}: average capital required under an alternative scheme;
C_t: capital required on day t under the alternative scheme; and
L_{tn}:   losses incurred on the n days following day t.

The ratio L_{tn}/C_t is the proportion of the capital required to cover the losses (if any) during the n days following day t under the alternative scheme. The extreme values of this expression measure the chances of financial difficulties being experienced when the alternative scheme is used. However, it does not take account of the average amount of capital used by the alternative scheme. We propose that the measure

$$\frac{L_{t_n}}{C_t} \cdot \frac{C_{ave}}{A} \tag{3}$$

Table 7 Percentiles of the capital utilisation ratio for investments in currencies. The capital utilisation ratio measures the proportion of the capital used to cover losses during the specified time period. Results are the averages of those obtained from investments in each of 12 different currencies

Time period (days)	Percentile	HS No Mean Adj	HS Mean Adj	BRW No Mean Adj	BRW Mean Adj	HW No Mean Adj	HW Mean Adj
1	99.5	12.54	12.44	12.08	11.93	11.71	11.66
1	99.0	10.35	10.33	10.50	10.29	9.87	9.79
10	99.5	38.49	38.25	38.12	37.50	38.05	37.61
10	99.0	32.38	32.16	32.33	32.48	32.12	31.88

Table 8 Percentiles of the capital utilisation ratio for investments in stock indices. The capital utilisation ratio measures the proportion of the capital used to cover losses during the specified time period. Results are the averages of those obtained from investments in each of 5 different stock indices

Time period (days)	Percentile	HS No Mean Adj	HS Mean Adj	BRW No Mean Adj	BRW Mean Adj	HW No Mean Adj	HW Mean Adj
1	99.5	13.68	13.52	14.36	14.56	13.24	13.30
1	99.0	11.26	11.31	11.92	11.97	11.17	11.06
10	99.5	41.14	40.56	43.28	43.18	43.40	43.00
10	99.0	33.61	33.26	36.17	35.95	36.16	35.93

be used for choosing between schemes. This is the proportion of capital that would be required on day t to cover losses in the subsequent n days under the alternative scheme if a constant multiplier is applied to the capital each day so that it is the same on average as the capital used under regular historical simulation. We will refer to this as the "capital utilisation ratio". The extreme values of the capital utilisation ratio provide a measure of capital adequacy.

We calculated the 99.5 percentile and 99 percentile of the probability distribution of the capital utilisation ratio for investments in each of the currencies and each of the stock indices for $n = 1$ and $n = 10$. The average of the results for each currency are shown in Table 7 and the average of the results for each stock index are shown in Table 8. The results indicate that for currencies HW and BRW provide better capital utilisation than HS. HW performs better than BRW and the mean adjustment appears to improve the performance of HW slightly. For stock indices the results are less clear. HW performs slightly better than HS for a one-day time horizon, but worse for a 10-day time horizon. BRW performs worse than either HS or HW for a one-day time horizon, and about the same as HW for a 10-day time horizon.

6 SUMMARY

This chapter shows how a volatility updating scheme such as GARCH can be used in conjunction with historical simulation for calculating VaR. Risk managers sometimes attempt to allow for stochastic volatility by sampling from recent observations more frequently than from those generated in the distant past. One such approach, BRW, involves applying weights that decline exponentially to the observations. The approach we propose is more direct. It involves adjusting observations to reflect the difference between the volatility at the time of the observation and the current volatility.

We compare our approach with BRW. We use approximately nine years of daily data on 12 different exchange rates and five different stock indices. Our approach provides better 1-percentile estimates of daily returns and is as good, if not better, at eliminating the bunching of tail events.

We have proposed a new way of assessing the effectiveness of a scheme for calculating VaR. It is designed to test the proportion of the capital likely to be used in extreme situations. We find that our method performs better than BRW. It is superior to regular historical simulation for investments in currencies. For investments in stock indices the results are mixed.

---

1 When only two moments are calculated the distribution of the change in the portfolio value is assumed to be normal. When three or more moments are calculated, the Cornish–Fisher expansion can be used to estimate the required percentile.

2 Revaluing the complete portfolio on each simulation trial is usually not feasible because of the computation time involved. One approach to speeding up calculations is to assume that the change in the portfolio value is a quadratic function of the change in the market variables.

3 As in the case of Monte Carlo simulation, the quadratic approximation can be used as an alternative to a full portfolio revaluation on each simulation trial.

4 For a discussion of these models, see J. P. Morgan (1995) or Engle and Mezrich (1995).

5 An approach involving the use of historical simulation in conjunction with a kernel estimator is suggested by Butler and Schachter (1998).

6 Note that BRW use an EWMA approach to define the weights given to observations, but this is quite different from the EWMA model for updating volatilities.

7 Note that percentiles can be computed in a variety of ways. Suppose that a data set consists of the numbers 1, 2, 3 and 4. The definition we use throughout this chapter implies 1, 2, 3 and 4 are 25, 50, 75 and 100 percentiles, respectively, and the values for intermediate percentiles are calculated using linear interpolation. An alternative definition (used by Microsoft's Excel) implies that 1, 2, 3 and 4 are the 0, 33.33, 66.67 and 100 percentiles, respectively, and the values for intermediate percentiles are calculated using linear interpolation.

8 Boudoukh, Richardson and Whitelaw (1998) tested $\lambda = 0.99$ and $\lambda = 0.97$.

9 This is the model used by J. P. Morgan in their RiskMetrics database (see J. P. Morgan 1995).

10 In the case of each currency, the indicator functions can only be calculated from day 500 onward. This explains why, although we started with over 2,400 observation per market variable, Tables 1 and 4 are based on 1923 observations per market variable.

11 The Ljung–Box statistic is $m\sum_{k=1}^{15} w_k \eta_k^2$, where m is the number of observations, η_k is the autocorrelation with a time lag of k days, and $w_k = (m - 2)/(m - k)$.

This chapter was previously published in *The Journal of Risk* **1**(1), Fall 1998.

REFERENCES

Boudoukh, J., M. Richardson, and R. Whitelaw, 1998, "The Best of Both Worlds", *Risk*, May, pp. 64–7.

Butler, J. S. and B. Schachter, 1998, "Estimating Value-at-Risk With a Precision Measure by Combining Kernel Estimation With Historical Simulation", *Review of Derivatives Research* **1**, pp. 371–90.

Engle, R. F. and J. Mezrich, 1995, "Grappling With GARCH" *Risk*, September, pp. 112–7.

Hull, J. and A. White, 1998, "Value-at-Risk When Daily Changes in Market Variables are not Normally Distributed", *Journal of Derivatives* **5**(3), pp. 9–19.

Jorion, P., 1997, *Value at Risk: The New Benchmark for Controlling Market Risk*, (Chicago: Irwin Professional Publishing).

J. P. Morgan, 1995, *RiskMetrics Technical Manual*, (New York: J. P. Morgan Bank).

9

Estimation Risk in Financial Risk Management

Peter Christoffersen; Sílvia Gonçalves*

McGill University; Université de Montréal

1 MOTIVATION

Value-at-risk (VaR) is increasingly used in portfolio risk measurement, risk capital allocation and performance attribution, and financial risk managers are rightfully concerned with the precision of typical VaR techniques. VaR is defined as the conditional quantile of the portfolio loss distribution for a given horizon (typically a day or a week) and for a given coverage rate (typically 1% or 5%), and the expected shortfall (ES) is defined as the expected loss beyond the VaR. The VaR and ES measures are, thus, statements about the left tail of the return distribution, and in realistic sample sizes (500 or 1,000 daily observations) such statements are likely to be made with considerable error.

The purpose of this chapter is twofold: first, we want to assess the potential loss of accuracy from estimation error when calculating VaR and ES. Second, we want to assess our ability to quantify *ex ante* the magnitude of this error through the construction of confidence intervals around the VaR and ES measures. This issue of the estimation risk for VaR has been considered previously in the iid return case by, for example, Jorion (1996) and Pritsker (1997). But a key challenge in constructing proper VaR and ES confidence intervals arises from

*We are grateful for comments, particularly from the Editor-in-Chief, Philippe Jorion, as well as from Sean Campbell, Valentina, Corradi, Frank Diebold, Jin Duan, René Garcia, Éric Jacquier, Simone Manganelli, Stefan Mittnik, Nour Meddahi, Matt Pritsker, Éric Renault and Enrique Sentana. FQRSC, IFM2 and SSHRC provided financial support. The usual disclaimer applies.

the conditional variance dynamics that are typically found in speculative returns. We quantify these dynamics using the celebrated GARCH model of Engle (1982) and Bollerslev (1986). Due to its ability to capture salient features of the return dynamics in very parsimonious and easily estimated specifications, GARCH has become the workhorse model in financial risk management. Nevertheless, and surprisingly, very little is known about the uncertainty in the GARCH VaR and ES forecasts that arises from parameter estimation error.[1]

Our chapter extends the resampling technique of Pascual, Romo and Ruiz (2001), which takes into account parameter estimation error in dynamic models of portfolio variance, to the case of VaR and ES forecasts. To our knowledge no asymptotic theory has been established for calculating confidence intervals for risk measures in this context. The resampling technique we propose can be relatively easily extended to longer horizons, to multivariate risk models and to allowing for model specification error.

Our Monte Carlo evidence suggests that, when returns are assumed to be independent, the bootstrap intervals work well for the commonly used historical simulation VaR model. However, when allowing for realistic GARCH effects the historical simulation VaR implies nominal 90% confidence intervals for the one-day, 1% VaR that are much too narrow. Historical simulation essentially ignores the time-varying risk from GARCH, and the finding of poor confidence intervals is therefore not surprising in this case. Methods that properly take conditional variance dynamics into account – such as filtered historical simulation (FHS), as suggested by Hull and White (1998) and Barone-Adesi, Giannopoulos and Vosper (1998, 1999) – imply 90% VaR confidence intervals that contain close to 90% of the true VaRs.

In our benchmark GARCH case, the average width of the VaR interval for the best model is 27–38% of the true VaR depending on the estimation sample size. The average width of the ES confidence interval is 22–42% of the true ES value (again, depending on the sample size) for the best model. Estimation risk is thus found to be substantial even in tightly parameterised models. Importantly, we find that it is in general more difficult to construct accurate confidence intervals for the ES measure. Typically, the confidence intervals from risk models we consider tend to contain the true ES less frequently than the 90% they should.

Accurate confidence intervals reported along with the VaR point estimate will facilitate the use of VaR in active portfolio management as the following example illustrates. Consider a portfolio manager who is allowed to take on portfolios with a VaR of up to 15% of the current capital. If the risk manager calculates the actual point-estimate VaR to be 13% with a confidence interval of 10–16%, then the cautious portfolio manager should rebalance the portfolio to reduce risk because the 16% confidence interval upper limit is above the VaR limit. Relying instead only on the point estimate of 13% would not signal any need to rebalance.

The chapter is organised as follows: Section 2 presents our conditionally nonnormal GARCH portfolio return-generating process and defines five risk models which we will consider in the subsequent analysis; Section 3 presents the resampling methods used to generate the VaR and ES confidence intervals; Section 4 presents the Monte Carlo setup and discusses the results we obtained; finally, Section 5 concludes and suggests avenues for future research.

2 MODEL AND RISK MEASURES

In this chapter we model the dynamics of the daily losses (the negative of returns) on a given financial asset or portfolio according to the model

$$L_t = \sigma_t \varepsilon_t \quad t = 1, \dots, T \tag{1}$$

where ε_t are iid with mean zero, variance one and distribution function G. In particular, we focus on the case in which G is a standardised Student's t-distribution with d degrees of freedom,[2] ie,

$$\sqrt{d/(d-2)}\varepsilon_t \sim t(d)$$

To model the volatility dynamics we use a symmetric GARCH(1, 1) model for σ_t^2:

$$\sigma_t^2 = \omega + \alpha L_{t-1}^2 + \beta \sigma_{t-1}^2$$

where $\alpha + \beta < 1$. The GARCH(1, 1) model with standardised Student's t innovations has been very successful in capturing the volatility clustering and non-normality found in daily asset return data (see, Bollerslev (1987) and Baillie and Bollerslev (1989)). Although we focus on this particular model of returns, our approach applies to more complex models of σ_t^2 and/or to other distributions for ε_t.

At a given point in time, we are interested in describing the risk in the tails of the conditional distribution of losses over a given horizon, say one day, using all the information available at that time. We consider two popular risk measures. One is the *value-at-risk* (VaR), which is simply a conditional quantile of the loss distribution. The other is the *expected shortfall* (ES), which measures the expected losses over the next day given that losses exceed the VaR.

The VaR measure for time $T + 1$ with coverage probability p, based on information at time T, is defined as the (positive) value VaR_{T+1}^p such that

$$\Pr\left(L_{T+1} > VaR_{T+1}^p \middle| \mathcal{F}^T\right) = p \tag{2}$$

where $\mathcal{F}^T$ denotes the information available at time T. Typically, p is a small number, eg, $p = 0.01$ or $p = 0.05$.

Similarly, we define the ES measure for time $T + 1$ with coverage probability p, given information at time T, as the (positive) value ES_{T+1}^p such that

$$ES_{T+1}^p = E\left(L_{T+1} \middle| L_{T+1} > VaR_{T+1}^p, \mathcal{F}^T\right) \tag{3}$$

Given model (1), we can obtain simplified expressions for VaR_{T+1}^p and ES_{T+1}^p. More specifically, we can show that

$$VaR_{T+1}^p = \sigma_{T+1} G_{1-p}^{-1} \equiv \sigma_{T+1} c_{1,p} \tag{4}$$

where G_{1-p}^{-1} denotes the $(1 - p)$th quantile of G, the distribution of standardised losses $\varepsilon_t = L_t / \sigma_t$, and σ_{T+1} is the conditional volatility for time $T + 1$. For instance, if G is the standard normal distribution Φ and $p = 0.05$, we have that $G_{1-p}^{-1} = \Phi_{0.95}^{-1} = 1.645$, and thus $VaR_{T+1}^p = 1.645\sigma_{T+1}$. In the general case where $\varepsilon \sim G$, Equation (4) shows that we can express VaR_{T+1}^p as the product of σ_{T+1} with a constant $c_{1,p} \equiv G_{1-p}^{-1}$, whose value depends on G and on p.

Similarly, under model (1) we can show that

$$ES_{T+1}^p = \sigma_{T+1} E(\varepsilon | \varepsilon > G_{1-p}^{-1}) \equiv \sigma_{T+1} c_{2,p} \tag{5}$$

where ε is an iid random variable with mean zero, variance one and distribution G. If $\varepsilon \sim N(0, 1)$, we can show that $E(\varepsilon \,|\, \varepsilon > a) = \phi(a)/(1 - \Phi(a))$ for any constant a, where ϕ and Φ denote the density and the distribution functions of a standard normal random variable. Thus, in this particular case,

$$ES^p_{T+1} = \sigma_{T+1}\frac{\phi(\Phi^{-1}_{1-p})}{p} \quad \text{and} \quad c_{2,p} \equiv \frac{\phi(\Phi^{-1}_{1-p})}{p}$$

When ε has a standardised Student distribution with d degrees of freedom, $c_{2,p}$ is given by a different formula. To describe this formula, let t_d be a random variable following a Student's t-distribution with d degrees of freedom. Andreev and Kanto (2005) show that, for any a,

$$E(t_d \,|\, t_d > a) = \left(1 + \frac{a^2}{d}\right)\frac{d}{d-1}\frac{f(a)}{1 - F(a)}$$

where f and F denote the probability density and the cumulative density functions of t_d. Using this result, we can show that in this case,

$$c_{2,p} \equiv E(\varepsilon \,|\, \varepsilon > G^{-1}_{1-p}) = \left(1 + \frac{\left(\sqrt{\frac{d}{d-2}}G^{-1}_{1-p}\right)^2}{d}\right)$$

$$\frac{d}{d-1}\frac{f\left(\sqrt{\frac{d}{d-2}}G^{-1}_{1-p}\right)}{p}\sqrt{\frac{d}{d-2}}$$

where G^{-1}_{1-p} is the $(1 - p)$th quantile of the distribution of ε. In particular,

$$G^{-1}_{1-p} = \sqrt{\frac{d-2}{d}}t^{-1}_{d,1-p}$$

where $t^{-1}_{d,1-p}$ is the $(1 - p)$th quantile of the distribution of t_d.

In practice, we cannot compute the true values of VaR^p_{T+1} and ES^p_{T+1}, since they depend on the characteristics of the data-generating process (ie, they depend on G and on the conditional variance model, σ_{T+1}^2). Thus, we need to estimate these measures, which introduces estimation risk. Our ultimate goal in this chapter is to quantify the estimation risk by constructing a confidence – or prediction – interval for the true but unknown risk measures.

We will consider six different estimation methods, divided into three groups.

2.1 Historical simulation
The first and most commonly used method is referred to as *historical simulation* (HS). It calculates VaR and ES using the empirical distribution of past losses. In particular, the HS estimate of VaR_{T+1}^p is given by

$$HS\text{-}VaR_{T+1}^p = Q_{1-p}(\{L_t\})$$

where $Q_{1-p}(\{L_t\})$ denotes the $(1-p)$th empirical quantile of the loss data $\{L_t\}_{t=1}^T$. In the simulations below we compute the empirical quantiles by linear interpolation between adjacent ordered sample values. The HS estimate of ES_{T+1}^p is given by

$$HS\text{-}ES_{T+1}^p = \frac{1}{\#(L_t > HS\text{-}VaR_{T+1}^p)}\left(\sum_{L_t > HS\text{-}VaR_{T+1}^p} L_t\right)$$

where $\#(L_t > HS\text{-}VaR_{T+1}^p)$ denotes the number of observations of $\{L_t\}_{t=1}^T$ that are above the HS estimate of the VaR.

The HS method is completely non-parametric and does not depend on any distributional assumption, thus capturing the non-normality in the data. It nevertheless ignores the potentially useful information in the volatility dynamics.

The estimation methods that we consider next take into account the volatility dynamics by explicitly relying on the GARCH(1, 1) model for predicting σ_{T+1}. In particular, given (4) and (5), estimates of VaR_{T+1}^p and ES_{T+1}^p can be obtained in three steps:

Step 1 Estimate the GARCH(1, 1) parameters through Gaussian QMLE, maximising

$$\ln L \propto -\frac{1}{2}\sum_{t=1}^T \ln(\sigma_t^2) + \left(\frac{L_t}{\sigma_t}\right)^2$$

Given the QML estimates $(\hat{\omega}, \hat{\alpha}, \hat{\beta})$, we can compute the variance sequence $\hat{\sigma}_t^2$ and the implied residuals $\hat{\varepsilon}_t = L_t / \hat{\sigma}_t$ from the past observed squared losses and the past estimated variance using the recursion

$$\hat{\sigma}_{t+1}^2 = \hat{\omega} + \hat{\alpha} L_t^2 + \hat{\beta} \hat{\sigma}_t^2$$

where $\hat{\sigma}_1^2 = \hat{\omega} / (1 - \hat{\alpha} - \hat{\beta})$, the unconditional variance of L_t. A prediction of σ_{T+1} is given by $\hat{\sigma}_{T+1}$, where

$$\hat{\sigma}_{T+1}^2 = \hat{\omega} + \hat{\alpha} L_T^2 + \hat{\beta} \hat{\sigma}_T^2$$

Step 2 Choose values for the constants $c_{1,p}$ and $c_{2,p}$. Call these $\hat{c}_{1,p}$ and $\hat{c}_{2,p}$, respectively.

Step 3 Compute the estimates of VaR_{T+1}^p and ES_{T+1}^p as

$$\widehat{VaR}_{T+1}^p = \hat{\sigma}_{T+1} \hat{c}_{1,p},$$
$$\widehat{ES}_{T+1}^p = \hat{\sigma}_{T+1} \hat{c}_{2,p}$$

We can distinguish between two groups of methods according to the rule that is used to choose the constants $c_{1,p}$ and $c_{2,p}$ in step 2: the normal model and non-parametric methods.

2.2 Normal conditional distribution
Erroneously imposing the normal distribution on the innovation term ε_t gives the following estimates of VaR_{T+1}^p and ES_{T+1}^p:

$$N\text{-}VaR_{T+1}^p = \hat{\sigma}_{T+1} \hat{c}_{1,p}^N,$$
$$N\text{-}ES_{T+1}^p = \hat{\sigma}_{T+1} \hat{c}_{2,p}^N$$

where

$$\hat{c}_{1,p}^N = \Phi_{1-p}^{-1},$$
$$\hat{c}_{2,p}^N = \frac{\phi(\Phi_{1-p}^{-1})}{p}$$

with Φ_{1-p}^{-1} the $(1 - p)$th quantile of a standard normal distribution. We will call this the "normal" method. This method imposes conditional normality, which does not hold for real data, and it is included only for comparison purposes.

2.3 Non-parametric methods

These methods estimate $c_{1,p}$ and $c_{2,p}$ using the implied GARCH(1, 1) residuals $\hat{\varepsilon}_t = L_t / \hat{\sigma}_t$. They differ in the way they use the residuals to compute $\hat{c}_{1,p}$ and $\hat{c}_{2,p}$.

2.3.1 Extreme value theory

The *extreme value theory* (EVT) approach estimates $c_{1,p}$ and $c_{2,p}$ under the assumption that the tail of the conditional distribution of the GARCH innovation is well approximated by a heavy-tailed distribution. This approach was proposed by McNeil and Frey (2000), who derived estimates of $c_{1,p}$ and $c_{2,p}$ based on the maximum likelihood estimator of the parameters of a generalised Pareto distribution (GPD).

Here we suppose that the tail of the conditional distribution of ε_t is well approximated by the distribution function

$$F(z) = 1 - L(z)z^{-1/\xi} \approx 1 - cz^{-1/\xi}$$

whenever $\varepsilon_t > u$, where $L(z)$ is a slowly varying function that we approximate with a constant c, and ξ is a positive parameter. u is a threshold value such that all observations above u will be used in the estimation of ξ. We let T_u denote the number of observations that exceed u. The Hill estimator (Hill 1975) $\hat{\xi}$ corresponds to the MLE estimator of ξ under the assumption that the standardised residuals $\hat{\varepsilon}_t$ are approximately iid It is defined as

$$\hat{\xi} = \frac{1}{T_u} \sum_{t=1}^{T_u} \ln(\hat{\varepsilon}_{(T-T_u+t)}) - \ln(u)$$

where $\hat{\varepsilon}_{(t)}$ denote the tth-order statistic of $\hat{\varepsilon}_t$ (ie, $\hat{\varepsilon}_{(t)} \geq \hat{\varepsilon}_{(t-1)}$ for $t = 2, \dots, T$). The important choice of T_u will be discussed at the beginning of the Monte Carlo results section below.

Given $\hat{\xi}$, an estimate of the tail distribution, F, is obtained by choosing $c = (T_u / T)u^{1/\hat{\xi}}$, which derives from imposing the condition $1 - F(u) = T_u / T$. We thus obtain the following estimate of F:

$$\hat{F}(z) = 1 - \frac{T_u}{T}\left(\frac{z}{u}\right)^{-1/\hat{\xi}}$$

The EVT approach relies on $\hat{F}(z)$ to estimate the constants $c_{1,p}$ and $c_{2,p}$. In particular, the estimate of $c_{1,p}$ is equal to $\hat{F}_{1-p}^{-1}$, the $(1-p)$th quantile of the tail distribution $\hat{F}$. We can show that

$$\hat{c}_{1,p}^{\text{Hill}} = u\left(p\frac{T}{T_u}\right)^{-\hat{\xi}}$$

Similarly, to compute an estimate of $c_{2,p}$ we use $\hat{F}(z)$ to compute $E(\varepsilon | \varepsilon > \hat{F}_{1-p}^{-1})$, where $\varepsilon \sim$ iid $\hat{F}$. We can show that the following closed-form expression holds true:

$$E\left(\varepsilon | \varepsilon > \hat{F}_{1-p}^{-1}\right) = \frac{\hat{F}_{1-p}^{-1}}{1-\hat{\xi}}$$

This implies the following Hill's estimate of $c_{2,p}$:

$$\hat{c}_{2,p}^{\text{Hill}} = \frac{\hat{c}_{1,p}^{\text{Hill}}}{1-\hat{\xi}}$$

The Hill's estimates of VaR_{T+1}^p and ES_{T+1}^p are given by

$$Hill\text{-}VaR_{T+1}^p = \hat{\sigma}_{T+1}\hat{c}_{1,p}^{\text{Hill}},$$
$$Hill\text{-}ES_{T+1}^p = \hat{\sigma}_{T+1}\hat{c}_{2,p}^{\text{Hill}}$$

respectively.

2.3.2 Gram–Charlier and Cornish–Fisher expansions
This method relies on the Cornish–Fisher and Gram–Charlier expansions to approximate the conditional density of the standard-ised losses, ε_t. For a standardised random variable, a Gram–Charlier expansion produces an approximate density function that can be viewed as an expansion of the standard normal density augmented by terms that capture the effects of skewness and excess kurtosis. Thus, Gram–Charlier expansions are a convenient tool with which to take into account departures from conditional normality.[3]

The Cornish–Fisher expansion approximates the inverse cumulative density function directly. The approximation to $c_{1,p}$ is thus:

$$CF_{1-p}^{-1} = \Phi_{1-p}^{-1} + \frac{\gamma_1}{6}\left[(\Phi_{1-p}^{-1})^2 - 1\right] + \frac{\gamma_2}{24}\left[(\Phi_{1-p}^{-1})^3 - 3\Phi_{1-p}^{-1}\right]$$
$$- \frac{\gamma_1^2}{36}\left[2(\Phi_{1-p}^{-1})^3 - 5\Phi_{1-p}^{-1}\right]$$

where

$$\gamma_1 = E(\varepsilon^3),$$
$$\gamma_2 = E(\varepsilon^4) - 3$$

with $\varepsilon \sim G(0, 1)$. We will refer to the expansion methods generically as GC (for Gram–Charlier). Thus, we have

$$\hat{c}_{1,p}^{GC} = \widehat{CF}_{1-p}^{-1}$$

where $\widehat{CF}_{1-p}^{-1}$ is the sample analogue of CF_{1-p}^{-1}, ie, it replaces γ_1 and γ_2 with their sample analogues evaluated on the standardised residuals $\hat{\varepsilon}_t = L_t / \hat{\sigma}_t$:

$$\hat{\gamma}_1 = \frac{1}{T}\sum_{t=1}^{T}\hat{\varepsilon}_t^3,$$
$$\hat{\gamma}_2 = \frac{1}{T}\sum_{t=1}^{T}\hat{\varepsilon}_t^4 - 3$$

Thus, we obtain the following estimate of VaR_{T+1}^p:

$$GC\text{-}VaR_{T+1}^p = \hat{\sigma}_{T+1}\hat{c}_{1,p}^{GC}$$

Similarly, we can define an approximation to $c_{2,p}$ that relies on the Gram–Charlier and Cornish–Fisher expansions. In particular, we can show that

$$c_{2,p}^{GC} = E(\varepsilon|\varepsilon > CF_{1-p}^{-1}) = \frac{\phi(CF_{1-p}^{-1})}{p}$$
$$\left(1 + \frac{\gamma_1}{6}\left[(CF_{1-p}^{-1})^2 - 1\right] + \frac{\gamma_2}{24}CF_{1-p}^{-1}\left[(CF_{1-p}^{-1})^2 - 3\right]\right)$$

The Gram–Charlier estimate of ES_{T+1}^p is given by

$$GC\text{-}ES_{T+1}^p = \hat{\sigma}_{T+1}\hat{c}_{2,p}^{GC}$$

where $\hat{c}_{2,p}^{GC}$ is obtained from $c_{2,p}^{GC}$ by replacing CF_{1-p}^{-1}, γ_1 and γ_2 with their sample analogues.

When G is the standard normal distribution, the Gram–Charlier estimates of VaR and ES coincide with those obtained with the "normal" method.

2.3.3 Filtered historical simulation

The *filtered historical simulation* (FHS) method estimates $c_{1,p}$ and $c_{2,p}$ from the empirical distribution of the (centred) residuals. Thus it combines a model-based variance with a data-based conditional quantile. Several authors, including Hull and White (1998), Barone-Adesi, Giannopoulos and Vosper (1999) and Pritsker (2001), have found the FHS method to perform well.

The FHS estimates of $c_{1,p}$ and $c_{2,p}$ are given by

$$\hat{c}_{1,p}^{FHS} = Q_{1-p}\left(\left\{\hat{\varepsilon}_t - \bar{\hat{\varepsilon}}\right\}_{t=1}^T\right)$$

and

$$\hat{c}_{2,p}^{FHS} = \frac{1}{\#(\hat{\varepsilon}_t - \bar{\hat{\varepsilon}} > \hat{c}_{1,p}^{FHS})}\left(\sum_{\hat{\varepsilon}_t > \hat{c}_{1,p}^{FHS}} (\hat{\varepsilon}_t - \bar{\hat{\varepsilon}})\right)$$

where $\bar{\hat{\varepsilon}} = T^{-1}\sum_{t=1}^T \hat{\varepsilon}_t$. Centred residuals are considered because their sample average is zero by construction, thus better mimicking the true mean zero expectation of the standardised errors ε_t. If a constant is included in the loss model, $\sum_{t=1}^T \hat{\varepsilon}_t = 0$ and centring of the residuals becomes irrelevant.

This implies the following FHS estimates of VaR_{T+1}^p and ES_{T+1}^p:

$$FHS\text{-}VaR_{T+1|T}^p = \hat{\sigma}_{T+1}\hat{c}_{1,p}^{FHS}$$
$$ES\text{-}VaR_{T+1}^p = \hat{\sigma}_{T+1}\hat{c}_{2,p}^{FHS}$$

3 RESAMPLING METHODS FOR ESTIMATION RISK

In this section we describe the bootstrap methods we use to assess the estimation risk in the risk estimates presented above.

Our first bootstrap method applies to historical simulation. This bootstrap method ignores any volatility dynamics and simply treats losses as being iid This "naive" bootstrap method generates pseudo-losses by resampling with replacement from the set of original losses, according to the following algorithm.

3.1 Bootstrap algorithm for historical-simulation risk measures

Step 1 Generate a sample of T bootstrapped losses $\{L_t^* : t = 1, \ldots, T\}$ by resampling with replacement from the original data set $\{L_t\}$.

Step 2 Compute the HS estimates of VaR and ES on the bootstrap sample:

$$HS\text{-}VaR_{T+1}^{*p} = Q_p(\{L_t^*\}_{t=1}^T),$$

$$HS\text{-}ES_{T+1}^{*p} = \frac{1}{\#(L_t^* > HS\text{-}VaR_{T+1}^{*p})} \left(\sum_{L_t^* > HS\text{-}VaR_{T+1}^p} L_t^* \right)$$

Step 3 Repeat Steps 1 and 2 a large number of times, say B, and obtain a sequence of bootstrap HS risk measures. For instance, $\{HS\text{-}VaR_{T+1}^{*p(i)} : i = 1, \ldots, B\}$ denotes a sequence of bootstrap VaR measures. We set $B = 999$ in our Monte Carlo simulations below.

Step 4 The $100(1 - \alpha)$ bootstrap prediction interval for VaR_{T+1}^p is given by

$$\left[Q_{\alpha/2}\left(\{HS\text{-}VaR_{T+1}^{*p(i)}\}_{i=1}^B \right), Q_{1-\alpha/2}\left(\{HS\text{-}VaR_{T+1}^{*p(i)}\}_{i=1}^B \right) \right]$$

where $Q_\alpha(\cdot)$ is the α-quantile of the empirical distribution of $\{HS\text{-}VaR_{T+1}^{*p(i)}\}$. A similar bootstrap interval can be computed for ES_{T+1}^p.

Following the historical simulation approach, this naive bootstrap method is completely non-parametric, avoiding any distributional assumptions on the data. However, by implicitly assuming that returns are i.i.d., this method fails to capture the dependence in returns when it exists. In particular, as our simulations will show, this method of computing confidence intervals for risk measures is not appropriate when returns follow a GARCH model.

The validity of the bootstrap for financial data depends crucially on its ability to correctly mimic the dependence properties of returns. A natural and often used bootstrap method for GARCH models consists of resampling with replacement the standardised residuals, the idea being that the standardised errors are iid in the population. The bootstrap returns are then recursively generated using the GARCH volatility dynamic equation and the resampled standardised residuals. The bootstrap methods that we describe next are based on this general idea.

As described in the previous section, under model (1) the VaR and ES have the following simplified expressions:

$$VaR_{T+1}^{p} = \sigma_{T+1} c_{1,p} \qquad (6)$$

and

$$ES_{T+1}^{p} = \sigma_{T+1} c_{2,p} \qquad (7)$$

where $c_{1,p}$ and $c_{2,p}$ are a function of G and p, and σ_{T+1} is given by the square root of

$$\sigma_{T+1}^{2} = \omega + \alpha L_{T}^{2} + \beta \sigma_{T}^{2} \qquad (8)$$

Given (6) and (7), there are two sources[4] of risk associated with predicting VaR_{T+1}^{p} and ES_{T+1}^{p} using information available at T. One is the uncertainty in computing $c_{1,p}$ and $c_{2,p}$. If the risk model correctly specifies G, this source of risk is not present. The other source of risk relates to predicting the volatility σ_{T+1} using day T's information. For our GARCH(1, 1) model, it is easy to see that σ_{T+1}^{2} depends on information available at day T and on the unknown parameters ω, α and β. In particular, using the GARCH Equation (8), we can write σ_{T}^{2} as a function of past losses:

$$\sigma_{T}^{2} = \frac{\omega}{1 - \alpha - \beta} + \alpha \sum_{j=0}^{\infty} \beta^{j} \left(L_{T-j-1}^{2} - \frac{\omega}{1 - \alpha - \beta} \right)$$

Replacing ω, α and β with their MLE estimates yields

$$\hat{\sigma}_T^2 = \frac{\hat{\omega}}{1 - \hat{\alpha} - \hat{\beta}} + \hat{\alpha}\sum_{j=0}^{T-2} \hat{\beta}^j \left(L_{T-j-1}^2 - \frac{\hat{\omega}}{1 - \alpha - \beta} \right) \qquad (9)$$

which delivers a point estimate $\hat{\sigma}_{T+1}^2 = \hat{\omega} + \hat{\alpha}L_T^2 + \hat{\beta}\hat{\sigma}_T^2$. The need to estimate the GARCH parameters introduces the second source of estimation risk.

The presence of estimation risk in computing VaR_{T+1}^p and ES_{T+1}^p is our main motivation for using the bootstrap to obtain prediction intervals for these risk measures. The bootstrap methods we use are based on Pascual, Romo and Ruiz (2001), who proposed a bootstrap method for building prediction intervals for return volatility, σ_t, based on the GARCH(1, 1) model. In particular, for the non-parametric methods, we extend the Pascual, Romo and Ruiz (2001) resampling scheme to the case of VaR_{T+1}^p and ES_{T+1}^p by using the bootstrap to account for estimation error not only in σ_{T+1} but also in the constants $c_{1,p}$ and $c_{2,p}$ that multiply σ_{T+1}.

3.2 Bootstrap alogrithm for GARCH-based measures of risk

Step 1 Estimate the GARCH model by MLE and compute the centred residuals $\hat{\varepsilon}_t - \bar{\hat{\varepsilon}}$, where $\hat{\varepsilon}_t = L_t / \hat{\sigma}_t$, $t = 1, \ldots, T$. Let $\hat{G}_T$ denote the empirical distribution function of $\hat{\varepsilon}_t$.

Step 2 Generate a bootstrap pseudo-series of portfolio losses $\{L_t^* : t = 1, \ldots, T$ using the recursions

$$\hat{\sigma}_t^{*2} = \hat{\omega} + \hat{\alpha}L_{t-1}^{*2} + \hat{\beta}\hat{\sigma}_{t-1}^{*2},$$
$$L_t^* = \hat{\sigma}_t^* \varepsilon_t^* \text{ for } t = 1, \ldots, T$$

where $\varepsilon_t^* \sim$ iid $\hat{G}_T$ and where $\hat{\sigma}_1^{*2} = \hat{\sigma}_1^2 = (\hat{\omega} / 1 - \hat{\alpha} - \hat{\beta})$. With the bootstrap pseudo-data $\{L_t^*\}$, compute the bootstrap MLE's $\hat{\omega}^*, \hat{\alpha}^*$ and $\hat{\beta}^*$.

Step 3 Obtain a bootstrap prediction of volatility $\hat{\sigma}_{T+1}^*$ according to

$$\hat{\sigma}_{T+1}^{*2} = \hat{\omega}^* + \hat{\alpha}^* L_T^{*2} + \hat{\beta}^* \hat{\sigma}_T^{*2}$$

given the initial values

$$L_T^* = L_T,$$

$$\hat{\alpha}_T^{*2} = \frac{\hat{\omega}^*}{1 - \hat{\alpha}^* - \hat{\beta}^*} + \hat{\alpha}^* \sum_{j=0}^{T-2} \hat{\beta}^{*j} \left(L_{T-j-1}^2 - \frac{\hat{\omega}^*}{1 - \hat{\alpha}^* - \hat{\beta}^*} \right) \tag{10}$$

Step 4 Compute $\hat{c}_{1,p}^*$ and $\hat{c}_{2,p}^*$, the bootstrap estimates of $c_{1,p}$ and $c_{2,p}$. These bootstrap estimates are computed in exactly the same fashion as $\hat{c}_{1,p}$ and $\hat{c}_{2,p}$, with the difference that they are evaluated on the bootstrap data instead of the real data. In particular, for the "normal" model we simply set

$$\hat{c}_{1,p}^* = \hat{c}_{1,p}^N \quad \text{and} \quad \hat{c}_{2,p}^* = \hat{c}_{2,p}^N$$

where $\hat{c}_{1,p}^i$ and $\hat{c}_{2,p}^i$ are as described before. In contrast, for the non-parametric methods, we first compute the bootstrap residuals

$$\hat{\varepsilon}_t^* = \frac{L_t^*}{\hat{\sigma}_t^*}$$

with $\hat{\sigma}_t^{*2} = \hat{\omega}^* + \hat{\alpha} R_{t-1}^{*2} + \hat{\beta}^* \hat{\sigma}_{t-1}^{*2}$ and $\hat{\sigma}_1^{*2} = \hat{\sigma}_1^2$. Next, we evaluate the estimates of $c_{1,p}$ and $c_{2,p}$ on the data set $\{\hat{\varepsilon}_t^*\}_{t=1}^T$. For instance,

$$\hat{c}_{1,p}^{*FHS} = Q_{1-p} \left(\left\{ \hat{\varepsilon}_t^* - \bar{\varepsilon}^* \right\}_{t=1}^T \right)$$

Step 5 For each estimation method, compute the bootstrap estimates of VaR_{T+1}^p and ES_{T+1}^p using $\hat{\sigma}_{T+1}^*$ and $\hat{c}_{1,p}^*$ and $\hat{c}_{2,p}^*$.

Step 6 Identical to steps 3 and 4 in the naive bootstrap.

Step 3 takes the estimation risk into account in computing $\hat{\sigma}_{T+1}$ by replacing the estimates $\hat{\omega}, \hat{\alpha}$ and $\hat{\beta}$ by their bootstrap analogues $\hat{\omega}^*, \hat{\alpha}^*$ and $\hat{\beta}^*$ when computing $\hat{\sigma}_{T+1}^*$. In particular, (10) replicates the way in which $\hat{\sigma}_T^2$ is computed in (9). Note, however, that $\hat{\sigma}_T^{*2}$ is conditional on the observed past observations on the losses $\{L_t : t = 1, \ldots, T\}$, not on the bootstrap losses generated in step 2, implying that it is small when the (true) losses are small at the end of the sample and large when they are large.

For the FHS method, bootstrap residuals are centred before computing the empirical quantile as a way to enforce the mean zero property on the estimated bootstrap residuals (centring of the residuals is not needed if a constant is included in the returns model since in that case the residuals have mean zero by construction).

We conclude this section by noting that it may be possible to apply asymptotic approximations such as the delta method to calculate prediction intervals for the GARCH variance forecast.[5] However, it is not at all obvious how prediction intervals for VaR and ES can be calculated using the delta method in the non-parametric risk models we consider. Furthermore, even in parametric cases, the approximate delta method is likely to perform worse than the resampling techniques considered here. In the following we therefore restrict attention to prediction intervals calculated with our resampling technique.

4 MONTE CARLO RESULTS

As indicated in the introduction, the purpose of our chapter is twofold: first, we want to assess the potential loss of accuracy from estimation error when calculating VaR and ES. Second, we want to assess our ability to quantify *ex ante* the magnitude of this error through the construction of confidence intervals around the risk measures. This section provides quantitative evidence on these two issues using a Monte Carlo study. The main focus of our analysis will be the realistic situation of time-varying portfolio risk, driven in our case by a GARCH model. However, before venturing into the more complicated GARCH case, it is sensible to apply our analysis to the case of simple, independent losses.

4.1 Independent losses

In Table 1 we simulate independent daily loss data from a Student distribution with mean zero and variance $20^2/252$, implying a volatility of 20% per year, and calculate VaR (top panel) and ES (bottom panel) risk measures by historical simulation.[6] Each row in the table corresponds to one of four experiments with degrees of freedom equal to 8 or 500, and estimation sample sizes equal to 500 or 1,000 days, respectively. The table reports the properties of the point estimates (left panel) of VaR and ES as well as the properties of the corresponding bootstrap intervals (right panel).

Table 1 90% prediction intervals for 1% VaR and ES: historical simulation method when losses are i.i.d.

DGP: $L_t \sim$ i.i.d. $t(d)$ with $E(L_t) = 0$ and $VaR(L_t) = (20)^2 / 252$							
d	**T**	**VaR properties**			**VaR bootstrap interval properties**			
		Average	Bias	RMSE	Coverage rate	Lower limit	Upper limit	Width % VaR
8	500	3.200	0.040	0.339	89.44	2.70	3.87	37.18
	1,000	3.165	0.004	0.229	88.58	2.81	3.56	23.75
500	500	2.950	0.016	0.221	88.52	2.60	3.35	25.27
	1,000	2.929	−0.006	0.152	88.46	2.69	3.18	16.86

d	**T**	**ES properties**			**ES bootstrap interval properties**			
		Average	Bias	RMSE	Coverage rate	Lower limit	Upper limit	Width % ESL
8	500	3.823	−0.095	0.496	71.74	3.08	4.42	34.06
	1,000	3.859	−0.058	0.353	79.44	3.30	4.35	26.73
500	500	3.304	−0.053	0.267	75.74	2.86	3.61	22.39
	1,000	3.324	−0.033	0.190	81.38	3.00	3.58	17.08

We simulate T independent daily Student's $t(d)$ losses and calculate VaR (top panel) and ES (bottom panel) risk measures by historical simulation. The four experiments correspond to degrees of freedom equal to 8 and 500 and estimation sample sizes equal to 500 and 1,000 days. The table reports the properties of the point estimates (left panel) of VaR and ES as well as the properties of the corresponding bootstrap intervals (right panel). The true VaR values are 3.160 (for $d = 8$) and 2.934 (for $d = 500$). The true ES values are 3.918 (for $d = 8$) and 3.357 (for $d = 500$).

The top left panel shows that the HS-VaRs have little bias, but the root mean squared errors (RMSEs) indicate that the VaRs are somewhat imprecisely estimated. The RMSE is around 10% of the true VaR value when the degree of freedom equals 8. The top right panel shows that the VaR confidence intervals from the bootstrap have nominal coverage rates close to the promised 90%. The average width of the bootstrap intervals is between 17 and 37% of the true VaR value depending on the sample size and on the degrees of freedom. In the most realistic case where $d = 8$ and $T = 500$, the average 90% interval width is a substantial 37% of the true VaR value.

The bottom left panel shows that the bias of the ES point estimates is small but, again, that the RMSEs are substantial in the leading case where $d = 8$ and $T = 500$. Furthermore, the bottom right panel shows that the coverage rates of the 90% confidence intervals are substantially less than 90%. The confidence intervals can therefore not be trusted for the ES risk measures. This finding is often repeated in the GARCH analysis below.

4.2 GARCH losses

We will now consider four versions of the GARCH-$t(d)$ data-generating process (DGP) below. In each version we set $\alpha = 0.10$ and $\omega = (20^2/252) \times (1 - \alpha - \beta)$. The unconditional volatility is thus 20% per year. Our four chosen parameterisations are:

❏ benchmark: $\beta = 0.80$, $d = 8$;
❏ high persistence: $\beta = 0.89$, $d = 8$;
❏ low persistence: $\beta = 0.40$, $d = 8$;
❏ normal distribution: $\beta = 0.80$, $d = 500$.

Recall that, before applying the Hill estimator for the extreme value distribution, we need to choose a cut-off point, T_u, which defines the sub-sample of extremes from which the tail index parameter will be estimated. In order to pick this important parameter we perform an initial Monte Carlo experiment in which we simulate data from the four DGPs above, estimate the tail index on a grid of cut-off values, and finally compute the resulting bias and root mean squared error measures (RMSEs) from the one-day VaR and ES forecasts. Figures 1 and 2 show the results for the case of 500 and 1,000 total estimation sample points, respectively. In each case, we choose a grid of truncation points that correspond to including the 0.5%–10% largest losses in the sub-sample of extremes. The horizontal axis in each figure denotes the number of included extreme observations (out of 500 and 1,000, respectively), and the vertical axis shows the bias and RMSEs. From the viewpoint of minimising RMSE subject to achieving a bias that is close to zero, and looking broadly across the four DGPs, it appears that a percentage cut-off of 2% is reasonable for both VaR and ES. Notice that we do not want to choose the truncation point on a case-by-case basis as that would potentially bias the overall results in favor of the Hill-based risk model.

Tables 2–5 contain the Monte Carlo results corresponding to the four DGPs above. The top half of each table contains the VaR results and the bottom half the ES results. The left half of each table contains the accuracy properties of the point estimates of the

Figure 1 RMSE and bias of Hill estimator for various samples of extremes (total sample = 500 daily loss observations)

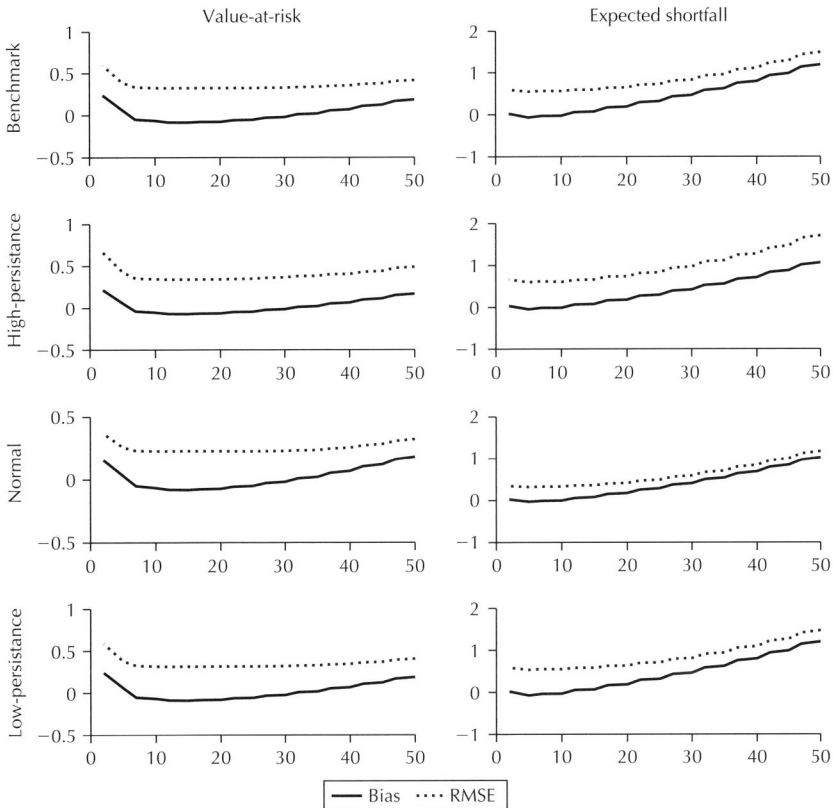

We perform a Monte Carlo study of the choice of sample size of extremes in EVT parameter estimation. The figure shows the root mean squared error (dashed) and bias (solid) of the VaR (left panel) and ES (right panel) estimates against the extremes estimation sample size.

relevant risk measure and the right half contains the 90% bootstrap interval properties. For both the VaR and ES forecasts we consider two estimation sample sizes, $T = \{500, 1000\}$.

In all the experiments we calculate the properties of the point estimates from 100,000 Monte Carlo replications. For the properties of the bootstrap prediction intervals, we consider only 5,000 Monte Carlo replications, each with 999 bootstrap replications. Any Monte Carlo study of the bootstrap is computationally demanding, and this is particularly so in our study due to the non-linear optimisation that is involved in estimating GARCH.

Figure 2 RMSE and bias of Hill estimator for various samples of extremes (total sample = 1,000 daily loss observations)

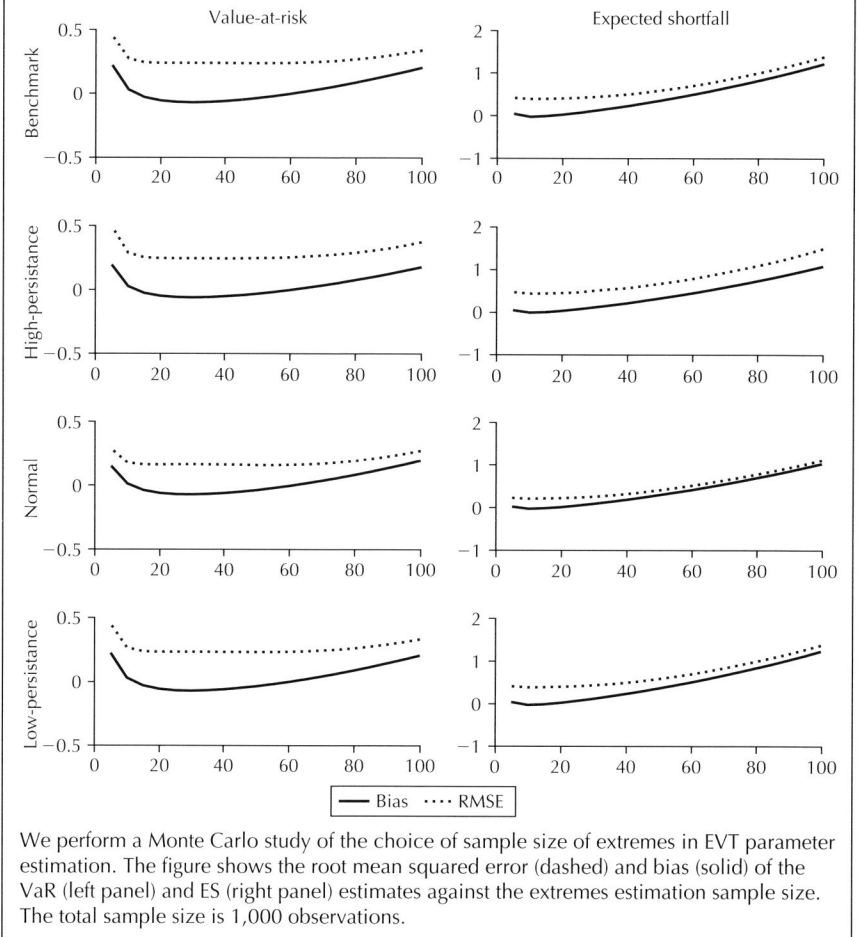

We perform a Monte Carlo study of the choice of sample size of extremes in EVT parameter estimation. The figure shows the root mean squared error (dashed) and bias (solid) of the VaR (left panel) and ES (right panel) estimates against the extremes estimation sample size. The total sample size is 1,000 observations.

4.3 Point predictions of VaR and ES

Although the main focus of our chapter is on constructing finite sample prediction intervals of the VaR and ES measures, we first consider the various models' ability to accurately point-forecast the risk measures. The point prediction results on VaR and ES are reported in terms of bias and root mean squared error, which are reported in the left half of each table.

Table 2 90% prediction intervals for 1% VaR and ES: benchmark GARCH case

		DGP: GARCH-$t(d)$ with $\alpha = 0.10$, $\beta = 0.80$ and $d = 8$						
T	Method	VaR properties			VaR bootstrap interval properties			
		Average	Bias	RMSE	Coverage rate	Lower limit	Upper limit	Width % VaR
500	HS	3.282	0.175	0.748	61.00	2.73	4.02	41.65
	Normal	2.866	−0.240	0.331	60.18	2.53	3.18	20.99
	Hill	3.043	−0.064	0.327	84.88	2.55	3.50	30.79
	GC	3.194	0.088	0.493	85.20	2.60	3.66	34.13
	FHS	3.138	0.032	0.383	91.32	2.57	3.76	38.40
1,000	HS	3.240	0.134	0.671	47.64	2.85	3.69	27.07
	Normal	2.872	−0.234	0.289	41.22	2.63	3.09	14.86
	Hill	3.051	−0.055	0.238	84.94	2.69	3.38	22.09
	GC	3.245	0.139	0.435	87.46	2.77	3.62	27.39
	FHS	3.106	0.000	0.268	90.58	2.70	3.52	26.65
T	Method	ES properties			ES bootstrap interval properties			
		Average	Bias	RMSE	Coverage rate	Lower limit	Upper limit	Width %ESL
500	HS	3.966	0.115	0.978	60.86	3.15	4.60	37.76
	Normal	3.283	−0.568	0.631	19.10	2.90	3.64	19.39
	Hill	3.806	−0.046	0.561	81.60	2.99	4.60	41.73
	GC	2.609	−1.242	1.435	41.58	1.98	3.79	47.02
	FHS	3.728	−0.123	0.539	74.62	2.95	4.35	36.50
1,000	HS	4.020	0.169	0.893	53.34	3.40	4.56	30.28
	Normal	3.289	−0.561	0.601	6.22	3.01	3.54	13.73
	Hill	3.865	0.014	0.411	87.18	2.69	3.38	22.09
	GC	2.490	−1.360	1.484	12.94	1.99	3.33	34.64
	FHS	3.771	−0.079	0.394	79.30	3.18	4.27	28.23

We simulate T daily GARCH(1, 1) losses with Student's $t(d)$ innovations (benchmark parameter configuration) and calculate VaR (top panel) and ES (bottom panel) risk measures by various methods. The two experiments correspond to estimation sample sizes equal to 500 and 1,000 days. The table reports the properties of the point estimates (left panel) of VaR and ES as well as the properties of the corresponding bootstrap intervals (right panel).

4.3.1 The benchmark case

The top panel of *Table 2* contains the VaR results for our bench-mark DGP when the sample size is T 5 500. Considering first the bias of the VaR estimates, the main thing to note is the upward bias of the HS and the downward bias of the normal. The latter is, of course, to be expected as the normal imposes a distribution tail

Table 3 90% prediction intervals 1% VaR and ES: high persistence

		DGP: GARCH-$t(d)$ with $\alpha = 0.10$, $\beta = 0.89$ and $d = 8$						
T	Method	VaR properties			VaR bootstrap interval properties			
		Average	Bias	RMSE	Coverage rate	Lower limit	Upper limit	Width % VaR
500	HS	3.242	0.537	1.958	32.98	2.61	4.04	53.03
	Normal	2.471	−0.235	0.341	61.30	2.11	2.81	25.91
	Hill	2.654	−0.051	0.345	84.56	2.14	3.10	35.42
	GC	2.771	0.066	0.556	86.34	2.18	3.30	41.63
	FHS	2.738	0.033	0.418	90.82	2.17	3.32	43.03
1,000	HS	3.330	0.619	2.064	20.68	2.84	3.91	40.34
	Normal	2.485	−0.226	0.299	45.86	2.22	2.65	16.35
	Hill	2.663	−0.048	0.247	85.14	2.27	2.89	23.41
	GC	2.821	0.110	0.549	87.76	2.35	3.15	30.01
	FHS	2.711	0.001	0.280	91.02	2.28	3.02	27.79
T	Method	ES properties			ES bootstrap interval properties			
		Average	Bias	RMSE	Coverage rate	Lower limit	Upper limit	Width %ESL
500	HS	3.968	0.614	2.444	32.40	3.08	4.62	46.04
	Normal	2.830	−0.524	0.650	32.24	2.42	3.22	23.93
	Hill	3.328	−0.026	0.603	83.50	2.53	4.10	47.07
	GC	2.222	−1.132	1.571	43.54	1.60	3.30	50.81
	FHS	3.260	−0.094	0.576	77.18	2.49	3.88	41.59
1,000	HS	4.286	0.926	2.751	22.92	3.52	4.95	43.49
	Normal	2.846	−0.514	0.617	12.76	2.54	3.03	15.10
	Hill	3.380	0.020	0.446	87.04	2.75	3.84	33.29
	GC	2.135	−1.225	1.592	13.28	1.64	2.82	36.09
	FHS	3.298	−0.062	0.417	80.54	2.70	3.68	29.84

We simulate T daily GARCH(1, 1) losses with Student's $t(d)$ innovations (high-persistence parameter configuration) and calculate VaR (top panel) and ES (bottom panel) risk measures by various methods. The two experiments correspond to estimation sample sizes equal to 500 and 1,000 days. The table reports the properties of the point estimates (left panel) of VaR and ES as well as the properties of the corresponding bootstrap intervals (right panel).

which is too thin for the 1% coverage rate. The other models appear to show only minor biases, with the FHS model displaying the smallest bias overall.

In terms of the root mean squared error of the VaR estimates, we see that the HS has by far the highest RMSE, followed by the GC model. The Hill model in particular, but also the FHS model, are

Table 4 90% prediction intervals 1% VaR and ES: low persistence

		DGP: GARCH-$t(d)$ with $\alpha = 0.10$, $\beta = 0.4$ and $d = 8$						
T	Method	VaR properties			VaR bootstrap interval properties			
		Average	Bias	RMSE	Coverage rate	Lower limit	Upper limit	Width %VaR
500	HS	3.226	0.078	0.464	82.14	2.71	3.93	38.84
	Normal	2.910	−0.238	0.321	52.02	2.63	3.19	18.08
	Hill	3.083	−0.065	0.318	84.24	2.63	3.53	28.73
	GC	3.245	0.096	0.497	84.92	2.69	3.71	32.55
	FHS	3.180	0.031	0.374	91.28	2.65	3.80	36.80
1,000	HS	3.186	0.039	0.382	75.10	2.83	3.60	24.61
	Normal	2.914	−0.233	0.284	36.22	2.70	3.13	13.65
	Hill	3.091	−0.056	0.234	85.56	2.76	3.43	21.31
	GC	3.291	0.144	0.437	86.98	2.84	3.70	27.20
	FHS	3.147	0.000	0.263	90.46	2.76	3.58	25.97
T	Method	properties			bootstrap interval properties			
		Average	Bias	RMSE	Coverage rate	Lower limit	Upper limit	Width %ESL
500	HS	3.867	−0.036	0.638	73.14	3.11	4.50	35.77
	Normal	3.333	−0.570	0.622	12.70	3.01	3.66	16.70
	Hill	3.857	−0.047	0.552	81.70	3.08	4.67	40.97
	GC	2.648	−1.255	1.425	40.54	2.01	3.83	46.85
	FHS	3.778	−0.125	0.533	73.52	3.03	4.41	35.33
1,000	HS	3.901	−0.001	0.524	75.56	3.33	4.42	27.80
	Normal	3.337	−0.564	0.595	5.68	3.09	3.59	12.61
	Hill	3.915	0.014	0.406	86.74	3.32	4.55	31.53
	GC	2.528	−1.373	1.473	12.18	2.01	3.36	34.67
	FHS	3.820	−0.081	0.389	79.50	3.25	4.34	27.90

We simulate T daily GARCH(1, 1) losses with Student's $t(d)$ innovations (low-persistence parameter configuration) and calculate VaR (top panel) and ES (bottom panel) risk measures by various methods. The two experiments correspond to estimation sample sizes equal to 500 and 1,000 days. The table reports the properties of the point estimates (left panel) of VaR and ES as well as the properties of the corresponding bootstrap intervals (right panel).

much lower. The RMSE of the normal is also low but, as mentioned before, it displays considerable bias.

Increasing the sample size to 1,000 in the second panel of Table 2 implies smaller biases in general. The HS is still biased upwards and the normal downwards. In terms of RMSE, the Hill and FHS methods perform very well.

Table 5 90% prediction intervals 1% VaR and ES: approximately normal distribution

DGP: GARCH-$t(d)$ with $\alpha = 0.10$, $\beta = 0.80$ and $d = 500$							
T	Method	VaR properties			VaR bootstrap interval properties			
		Average	Bias	RMSE	Coverage rate	Lower limit	Upper limit	Width % VaR
500	HS	3.023	0.123	0.545	55.96	2.63	3.50	29.95
	Normal	2.889	−0.011	0.172	88.76	2.61	3.13	17.96
	Hill	2.835	−0.065	0.227	83.62	2.48	3.14	23.13
	GC	2.874	−0.026	0.209	87.06	2.54	3.16	21.68
	FHS	2.903	0.003	0.255	91.30	2.49	3.30	27.95
1,000	HS	2.999	0.097	0.502	39.96	2.72	3.30	19.77
	Normal	2.895	−0.008	0.124	89.54	2.70	3.07	12.72
	Hill	2.845	−0.057	0.166	84.32	2.59	3.07	16.52
	GC	2.889	−0.014	0.150	87.92	2.65	3.11	15.65
	FHS	2.888	−0.014	0.180	90.36	2.60	3.17	19.54

T	Method	ES properties			ES bootstrap interval properties			
		Average	Bias	RMSE	Coverage rate	Lower limit	Upper limit	Width %ESL
500	HS	3.447	0.129	0.647	54.48	2.92	3.83	27.26
	Normal	3.309	−0.009	0.196	88.82	2.99	3.59	17.98
	Hill	3.302	−0.016	0.318	85.56	2.79	3.74	28.82
	GC	3.416	0.098	0.489	87.92	2.79	4.31	45.91
	FHS	3.347	−0.070	0.308	80.00	2.76	3.62	26.25
1,000	HS	3.480	0.160	0.608	41.90	3.09	3.80	21.25
	Normal	3.315	−0.005	0.141	89.76	3.10	3.52	12.73
	Hill	3.343	0.023	0.232	89.20	2.97	3.62	21.42
	GC	3.365	0.045	0.340	89.82	2.91	3.97	32.12
	FHS	3.274	−0.046	0.220	83.58	2.92	3.57	19.60

We simulate T daily GARCH(1, 1) losses with approximately normal innovations and calculate VaR (top panel) and ES (bottom panel) risk measures by various methods. The two experiments correspond to estimation sample sizes equal to 500 and 1,000 days. The table reports the properties of the point estimates (left panel) of VaR and ES as well as the properties of the corresponding bootstrap intervals (right panel).

We next examine the quality of the point predictions of ES by the various models. We now find a very large downward bias for the GC and again for the normal model. In comparison with the VaR results, the various estimated ES models have RMSEs that are considerably larger. The increase in RMSE is due partly to increases in the bias. The results for the GC model indicate that the way we have implemented it here it is not useful for ES calculations. Note that in the ES case the GC model is an aggregate of two approximations: first, the Cornish–Fisher approximation to the VaR, and second the Gram–Charlier approximation to the cumulative density. Unfortunately, the two approximation errors appear to compound each other for the purpose of ES calculation.

4.3.2 The high-persistence case

The top half of Table 3 reports the VaR findings for a DGP of high volatility persistence, and therefore also high kurtosis. We see that the biases and RMSEs are comparable to the benchmark DGP in Table 2 for the conditional models but not for the HS model. The HS model is now even more biased and has a RMSE of more than 50% of the average true VaR, which is approximately 2.71. The Hill and FHS models again perform very well. The bottom half of Table 3 reports results for ES using the high volatility persistence DGP. We find that the results are very close to those given in the bottom half of Table 2 for the conditional models but not for HS. This finding matches the results for VaR reported in the top halves of Tables 2 and 3, respectively. As before, the bias and RMSEs of the HS model are very large, and for the ES the GC model again performs poorly.

4.3.3 The low-persistence case

In the top half of Table 4 we consider the VaR case of low volatility persistence. Not surprisingly, the HS model now performs much better. Interestingly, the Hill and FHS models perform very well here also. The bottom half of the table shows the results for ES forecasting in the low-persistence process. As in the VaR case, we see that the HS model now performs relatively well.

4.3.4 The conditional normal case

The top half of Table 5 contains VaR results for the conditionally normal GARCH DGP. Comparing with Table 2, we see that the bias and RMSEs are considerably smaller now. It is still the case that the HS model performs much worse than the conditional models. The normal model, of course, performs very well now as it is the true model. Interestingly, the Hill and FHS models, which do not directly nest the normal model, still perform decently. This is important as the risk manager never knows exactly the degree of conditional non-normality in the return distribution. The bottom half of Table 5 considers the ES risk measure. Comparing this with the bottom of Table 2, we see that the biases and RMSEs are generally much smaller under conditional normality. The biases and RMSEs for ES are very much in line with those from VaR in the top half of Table 5. This is sensible from the perspective that under conditional normality the ES does not contribute information over and beyond the VaR.

4.4 Bootstrap prediction intervals for VaR and ES

The above discussion was concerned with the precision of the VaR and ES point forecasts. We now turn our attention to the results for the bootstrap prediction intervals from the different VaR and ES models. That is, we want to assess the ability of the bootstrap to reliably predict *ex ante* the accuracy of each method in predicting the one-day-ahead 1% VaR and ES. The prediction interval results are reported on the right-hand side of each table. We show the true coverage rate of nominal 90% intervals as well as the average limits of the confidence intervals and the average width of the confidence interval as a percentage of the true VaR point forecast.

4.4.1 The benchmark case

Turning back to Table 2 and looking at the top panel, we remark that the historical simulation VaR (HS) intervals (calculated from the iid bootstrap) have a very low effective coverage for a promised nominal coverage of 90%. Furthermore, the confidence intervals are, on average, very wide. The HS method ignores the dynamics in the DGP, which is costly in terms of both coverage and width.[7]

The VaR with the conditional normal distribution ("normal") imposed has a coverage that is as bad as the HS model but which has a much smaller average width. The small width does not, of course, offer much comfort here as the nominal coverage is much too small. The GC model has larger coverage than the Hill but has wider intervals. Finally, the FHS model has slight over-coverage, which arguably is to be preferred to under-coverage, but it also has a fairly wide average coverage intervals.

In the second panel of Table 2 we increase the risk manager's sample size to 1,000 past-return observations in each simulation. Comparing with the top panel of Table 2, the results are as follows:

the HS model coverage actually gets worse with sample size. In the short (500 observations) sample the HS model is able to pick up some of the dynamics in the return process, but it is less able to do so as the sample size increases. The average width is smaller as the sample size increases due to the higher precision in estimating the (unconditional) VaR. The normal model also has worse coverage and better width. This may seem puzzling, but note that there is no reason to believe that a larger sample size will improve the coverage of a misspecified model. The Hill and GC models now both have better coverages and widths. Finally, notice that the FHS model also benefits from the larger estimation samples and shows better coverages and lower widths.

The bottom half of Table 2 reports results for the bootstrap prediction intervals from the different ES models. We notice the following: the historical simulation ES intervals (calculated from the iid bootstrap) have a low effective coverage for a promised nominal coverage of 90%. Furthermore the confidence intervals on average are quite wide. The HS results for ES are roughly comparable with those for VaR in Table 2. The ES with the conditional normal distribution ("normal") imposed has a surprisingly low coverage. Thus, while the normal distribution is bad for VaR prediction intervals, it is much worse for ES prediction intervals. The Hill model has the best coverage but is quite wide. The GC model has very low coverage and quite wide intervals. Finally, the FHS model has considerable under-coverage. This is in contrast with the VaR intervals in the top half of the table.

Looking more broadly at the results in Table 2, we see that the Hill model has the best coverage, followed by the FHS model. The HS, normal and GC models have poor coverage. Comparing with the top half of the table, it thus appears that although the FHS performs well for VaR prediction interval calculation, it is less useful for ES prediction intervals. The Hill estimator appears to be preferable here. Generally, the coverage rates are considerably worse for ES than for VaR.

4.4.2 The high-persistence case
The top right-hand side of Table 3 reports VaR interval results from a return-generating process with relatively high persistence. Comparing panel for panel with the benchmark process in Table 2,

we notice that the HS model has worse coverage and worse width, whereas the normal model has better coverage. The GC model has similar coverage but wider intervals. The FHS has good coverage under high persistence but the intervals are wider here as well. Thus, the higher persistence associated with higher kurtosis leads to wider prediction intervals overall.

The bottom right-hand side of Table 3 reports ES results. Comparing the VaR and ES results in Table 3, we see that the coverage rates are typically much worse for ES than for VaR.

A comparison of the results for ES against the benchmark process in Table 2 reveals that the HS model has worse coverage and worse width. The normal model still has very poor coverage. The Hill model generally has better coverage but wider intervals. The GC model still has very poor coverage. Finally, the FHS has roughly the same coverage under high persistence but the widths are worse here as well. The higher persistence again leads to wider prediction intervals overall.

4.4.3 The low-persistence case

The top right hand side of Table 4 reports VaR results from returns with low variance persistence. Not surprisingly the results are reversed from those in Table 3, which contained high persistence variances. We now find that the HS model has much better coverage and slightly better widths. The low-persistence process is closer to i.i.d., the only assumption under which the HS model is truly justified. The normal model has worse coverages, but it has better widths. The Hill and GC models have similar coverages and better widths than before. Finally, the FHS model has worse coverages, but the widths are slightly better.

The bottom right-hand side of Table 4 reports ES results from returns with low variance persistence. We now find that the HS performs much better as we are closer to the iid case, but otherwise the results are similar to the benchmarks in Table 2.

4.4.4 The conditional normal case

In Table 5 we generate returns that are close to conditionally normally distributed. Comparing the VaR panels in Table 5 with the corresponding panels in Table 2 – where the conditional returns were $t(8)$ – we see the following: the HS model now has worse coverage but also lower width than before. The normal model has better coverage and better width. This is not surprising as the normal model is now closer to the truth. The Hill and GC models have similar coverage and better width than before. The FHS model also has roughly the same coverage under conditional normality but better width than under the conditional $t(8)$. Not surprisingly, the models generally perform better under conditional normality. It is perhaps surprising that the Hill model performs well under conditional normality as the tail index parameter may be biased in this case.

In the bottom half of Table 5 we report the ES results. As expected, the models generally perform better under conditional normality in terms of coverage. The HS model is again notably worse than the other models, and the FHS is also worse than the others. The normal model, and the GC model that nests the normal models, naturally have very good coverages.

4.5 Summary of results

Based on the results in Tables 2–5, we reach the conclusion that the HS model not only gives bad point estimates of VaR and ES estimates (see also Pritsker (2001)) but it also implies very poor confidence intervals. This is true even when the degree of volatility persistence is relatively modest. The normal model of course works reasonably well when the normality assumption is close to true in the data, but otherwise it does not. The Hill and FHS models perform quite well, even for the conditionally normal distribution. We noticed also that the GC model has serious problems when calculating ES point estimates and intervals for conditionally non-normal returns. Finally, the FHS model works particularly well for VaR calculations.

In general, we found that the RMSEs were much higher (relative to the true value) when calculating ES compared to VaR measures. Thus, though in theory the ES measure conveys more information about the loss distribution tail, it is also harder to estimate precisely. This point is important to consider when arguing over the relative merits of the two risk measures.

Unfortunately, it is also much harder to reliably assess *ex ante* the accuracy of ES measures compared with the VaR measures. While the Hill, GC and particularly the FHS model give quite reliable coverage rates for the 90% confidence intervals around the VaR point forecast, the corresponding coverage rates for the ES measure are typically much lower than 90% and are thus unreliable. We suspect that the higher bias of the ES forecasts is responsible for the under-coverage in this case. Note that, from a conservative risk management perspective, over-coverage would be preferred to under-coverage.

Finally, while the FHS model appears to be preferable for calculating VaR forecasts and forecast intervals, the Hill model performs well in the ES case. The distribution-free FHS model is useful for quantile forecasting, but, when the mean beyond the quantile must be forecast, the functional form estimation implicit in the Hill method adds value.

5 CONCLUSIONS

Risk managers and portfolio managers often haggle over the precision of a VaR estimate. A trader faced with a point estimate VaR that exceeds the agreed VaR limit may be forced to rebalance the portfolio at an inopportune time. Quantifying the uncertainty of the VaR point estimate is important because it allows risk managers to make more informed decisions when dictating a portfolio rebalance.

Consequently, we suggest a bootstrap method for calculating confidence intervals around the VaR point estimate. The procedure is valid even under conditional heteroskedasticity and non-normality, which are important features of speculative asset returns. We find that the FHS VaR models yield confidence intervals that have correct coverage but which are also quite wide. In our benchmark case, the average width of the VaR interval for the FHS model is 27–38% of the true VaR depending on the sample size. VaR models based on the normal distribution are much narrower – but also often too narrow, causing under-coverage of the intervals. We also find that the accuracy of ES forecasts is typically much lower than that of VaR forecasts. Furthermore, the accuracy of the ES forecasts is harder to quantify *ex ante*. In our benchmark case, the average width of the ES confidence interval is 22–42% of the true ES value (again depending on the sample size) for the best model. We believe that this quantification of the level of estimation risk in common risk models has important implications for the choice of risk model and risk measure.[8]

We have studied the effects of estimation risk at the portfolio level only (see Benson and Zangari (1997), Engle and Manganelli (2004) and Zangari (1997)). Many banks rely instead on multivariate risk factor models, such as those considered by Glasserman, Heidelberger and Shahabuddin (2000, 2002). The issue of estimation risk is, of course, equally important but is even more complicated in the case of multiple risk factors. We leave this issue for future work.

1   Baillie and Bollerslev (1992) construct approximate prediction intervals for GARCH variance forecasts at multiple horizons but ignore estimation error. Furthermore, risk management surveys and textbooks such as those by Christoffersen (2003), Duffie and Pan (1997) and Jorion (2000) pay little or no attention to the estimation error issue.
2   The model can be generalised to allow for skewness following Theodossiou (1998). See also Tsay (2002), Chapter 7.
3   For an application of Gram–Charlier expansions in finance, see Backus, Foresi, Li and Wu (1997).
4   In general, model risk is a third source of uncertainty when forecasting VaR_{T+1}^p and ES_{T+1}^p. Here, we abstract from this source of uncertainty since we take the GARCH model of returns as being correctly specified.
5   This approach is taken, for example, in Duan (1994).
6   We only analyse the historical simulation risk model here as the GARCH-based risk models are not identified when returns are independent.
7   We also calculated GARCH-bootstrap confidence intervals for the HS model. These performed better than the iid bootstrap intervals reported in the tables, but they were still very inaccurate and were therefore not included in the tables. The iid bootstrap is shown here because it is arguably most in line with the model-free spirit of the HS model.
8   Note that one of the industry benchmarks, RiskMetrics, relies on calibrated rather than estimated parameters and does not allow for the calculation of estimation risk. The issue of VaR uncertainty is nevertheless crucial in those models as well, but it is not easily quantified.

This chapter was previously published in *The Journal of Risk* **7**(3), Spring 2005.

REFERENCES

Andreev, A. and A. Kanto, 2005, "Conditional Value-at-Risk Estimation Using Non-integer Degrees of Freedom in Student's *t*-Distribution", *Journal of Risk* **7(2)**, pp. 55–61.

Backus, D., S. Foresi, K. Li, and L. Wu, 1997, "Accounting for Biases in Black–Scholes", Manuscript, The Stern School at New York University.

Baillie, R. and T. Bollerslev, 1989, "The Message in Daily Exchange Rates: A Conditional Variance Tale", *Journal of Business and Economic Statistics* **7**, pp. 297–309.

Baillie, R. and T. Bollerslev, 1992, "Prediction in Dynamic Models with Time Dependent Conditional Variances", *Journal of Econometrics* **52**, pp. 91–113.

Barone-Adesi, G., K. Giannopoulos, and L. Vosper, 1998, "Don't Look Back", *Risk* **11(8)**, pp. 100–4.

Barone-Adesi, G., K. Giannopoulos, and L. Vosper, 1999, "VaR Without Correlations for Non-linear Portfolios", *Journal of Futures Markets* **19**, pp. 583–602.

Benson, P. and P. Zangari, 1997, "A General Approach to Calculating VaR Without Volatilities and Correlations", *RiskMetrics Monitor,* JP Morgan–Reuters, Second Quarter, pp. 19–23.

Bollerslev, T., 1986, "Generalized Autoregressive Conditional Heteroskedasticity", *Journal of Econometrics* **31**, pp. 307–27.

Bollerslev, T., 1987, "A Conditionally Heteroskedastic Time Series Model for Speculative Prices and Rates of Return", *Review of Economics and Statistics* **69**, pp. 542–7.

Christoffersen, P., 2003, *Elements of Financial Risk Management.* (San Diego: Academic Press).

Duan, J.-C., 1994, "Maximum Likelihood Estimation Using Price Data of the Derivative Contract", *Mathematical Finance* **4**, pp. 155–67.

Duffie, D. and J. Pan, 1997, "An Overview of Value at Risk", *Journal of Derivatives* **4**, pp. 7–49.

Engle, R., 1982, "Autoregressive Conditional Heteroskedasticity with Estimates of the Variance of United Kingdom Inflation", *Econometrica* **50**, pp. 987–1007.

Engle, R. and S. Manganelli, 2004, "CAViaR: Conditional Autoregressive Value at Risk by Regression Quantiles", *Journal of Business and Economic Statistics* **22**, pp. 367–81.

Glasserman, P., P. Heidelberger, and P. Shahabuddin, 2000, "Variance Reduction Techniques for Estimating Value-at-Risk", *Management Science* **46**, pp. 1349–64.

Glasserman, P., P. Heidelberger, and P. Shahabuddin, 2002, "Portfolio Value-at-Risk with Heavy-Tailed Risk Factors", *Mathematical Finance* **12**, pp. 239–70.

Hill, B., 1975, "A Simple General Approach to Inference about the Tail of a Distribution", *Annals of Statistics* **3**, 1163–74.

Hull, J. and A. White, 1998, "Incorporating Volatility Updating into the Historical Simulation Method for VAR", *Journal of Risk* **1**, pp. 5–19.

Jorion, P., 1996, "Risk^2: Measuring the Risk in Value-at-Risk", *Financial Analysts Journal* **52**, pp. 47–56.

Jorion, P., 2000, *Value at Risk: The New Benchmark for Managing Financial Risk,* Second edition. (New York: McGraw-Hill).

McNeil, A. and R. Frey, 2000, "Estimation of Tail-Related Risk Measures for Heteroskedastic Financial Time Series: An Extreme Value Approach", *Journal of Empirical Finance* **7**, pp. 271–300.

Pascual, L., J. Romo, and E. Ruiz, 2001, "Forecasting Returns and Volatilities in GARCH Processes Using the Bootstrap", Manuscript, Departamento de Estadistica y Econometria, Universidad Carlos III de Madrid.

Pritsker, M., 1997, "Towards Assessing the Magnitude of Value-at-Risk Errors Due to Errors in the Correlation Matrix", *Financial Engineering News,* October/November, pp. 14–16.

Pritsker, M., 2001, "The Hidden Dangers of Historical Simulation", Working paper 2001–27, Federal Reserve Board, Washington, DC.

Theodossiou, P., 1998, "Financial Data and the Skewed Generalized *t* Distribution", *Management Science* **44**, pp. 1650–61.

Tsay, R., 2002, *Analysis of Financial Time Series*. (New York: Wiley).

Zangari, P., 1997, "Streamlining the Market Risk Measurement Process", *RiskMetrics Monitor*, JP Morgan–Reuters, First Quarter, pp. 29–36.

Multivariate Models, Correlations and Copulas

10

GARCH for Groups

Robert Engle; Joseph Mezrich

University of California; Salomon Brothers

Correlations are fundamental parameters in most portfolio allocation models, hedging strategies, value-at-risk calculations and pricing formulas for multivariate options.[1]

However, just as it is now well known that variances cannot be
taken to be constant over time, it is becoming increasingly clear
that correlations also vary over time. Correlation can be viewed as
a stochastic process, which evolves over time and can be analysed
statistically. Thus there is an incentive to find the best methods to
measure and forecast correlations.

Many of the techniques used for volatility (variance) analysis
can be generalised immediately to look at covariances and, hence,
correlations also. In this chapter we will discuss some of the most
promising techniques for measuring, forecasting and hedging correlation. This chapter extends the analysis in Engle and Mezrich
(1995) to multivariate generalised autoregressive conditional heteroscedasticity (GARCH) systems.

Because of the wealth of traded derivatives on single assets,
there is often a choice between using a volatility derived from
options prices or volatilities forecast from historical data. Under
certain circumstances, these are alternative estimates of the same
future volatility. Because there are relatively few exchange-traded
multivariate options, however, there is rarely an implied correlation that can be used to calibrate a correlation model. The exception
is the few markets in which spread options are traded, an important example being currencies where options are traded on cross

Figure 1 Implied correlation of dollar/yen and dollar/Deutschmark

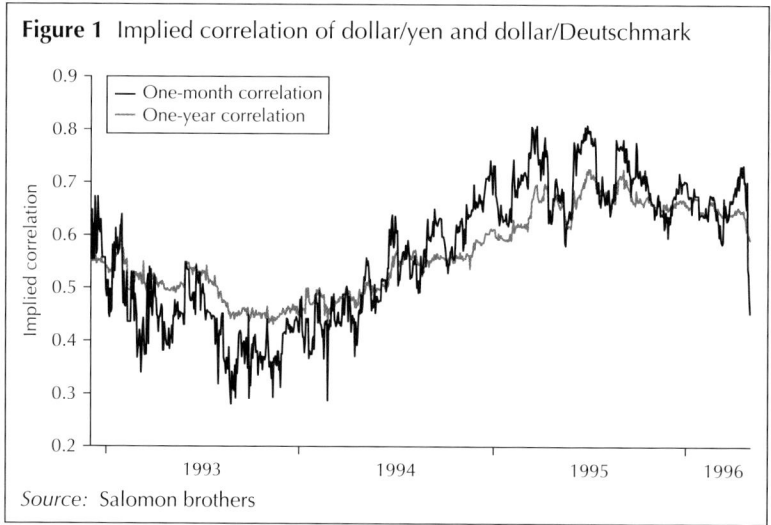

Source: Salomon brothers

rates as well as dollar-denominated rates. Since the cross rate volatility is equal to:

$$\sqrt{\sigma_{1,t}^2 + \sigma_{2,t}^2 - 2\rho_{1,2,t}\sigma_{1,t}\sigma_{2,t}}$$

the implied correlation can easily be computed from the three observed volatilities.

Figure 1 presents the implied correlations between the dollar/Deutschmark exchange rate and the dollar/yen exchange rate, derived from one-month and one-year over-the-counter option prices. The picture shows clearly that implied correlations have changed substantially over the past three years, from a minimum monthly correlation of 0.3 in late 1993, when the annual correlation was 0.45, to a maximum monthly correlation of 0.8 in early 1995, when the annual correlation was 0.65. Thus the term structure of implied correlations was upward sloping in mid-1993 and downward sloping in mid-1995. There is much more variability in short-term correlations than long-term correlations, which is consistent with mean reversion in correlations.

Similar evidence on the variability of correlations is available from the underlying assets themselves. As discussed by many authors since Engle (1982), autocorrelation in squared returns (r_k^2) is evidence of time-varying volatility. This is easily calculated and assessed using the Ljung–Box (1978) statistic:

$$\text{Ljung–Box}(K) = T \sum_{k=1}^{K} w_k \gamma_k^2 \tag{1}$$

which converges to a chi squared random variable with K degrees of freedom if there is no serial correlation. If K is set to 15, a value of the statistic bigger than 25 would only occur 5% of the time if there truly is no autocorrelation. Here $w_k = (T + 2)/(T - k)$ and:

$$\gamma_k = \frac{\sum (r_t^2 - \sigma^2)(r_{t+k}^2 - \sigma^2)}{\sum (r_t^2 - \sigma^2)^2} \tag{2}$$

For example, using 1983–1995 daily data on the dollar/ Deutschmark rate (known hereafter as the "Deutschmark" rate for simplicity) and the dollar/sterling rate (known hereafter as the "sterling" rate), the Ljung–Box (15) statistic for the Deutschmark rate is 262 while for sterling it is 390. In both cases these statistics dramatically exceed the 5% value of 25, indicating the importance of time-varying volatility.

A similar statistic can be calculated using the product of Deutschmark and sterling as the series rather than squared returns. In this case, the Ljung–Box (15) statistic is 2,020, indicating that the covariances are also time-varying. Finally, cross correlations between squared Deutschmark and sterling can be inserted in the Ljung–Box statistic in place of the autocorrelations. In this case, the test for Deutschmark squares predicting sterling volatility is 127 while the test for sterling squares predicting Deutschmark volatility is 195. This is evidence that volatility in one asset can predict volatility in the other, which is called "causality in variance". Another version of the test can detect predictability of volatility based on the direction of returns.

These test statistics can also be used to determine whether a model has adequately described the variances and covariances of a system. This diagnostic role is achieved by transforming the data using the hypothesised variances and covariances and then checking to see if the Ljung–Box tests are satisfied.

For example, a single series can be divided by its hypothesised standard deviation to construct standardised residuals. These standardised residuals should have no autocorrelation in squares if the standard deviations are accurately estimated. In a multivariate context, the whole set of returns can be transformed to construct standardised residuals which are supposed to be independent and identically distributed and which should therefore pass all forms of Ljung–Box tests. If the variances and covariances are incorporated in a matrix Σ, the transformation is simply:

$$\tilde{r}_t = \Sigma_t^{-1/2} r_t \tag{3}$$

These standardised residuals can be tested for autocorrelation in squares, for asymmetry, for predictability from one series to another and for autocorrelation in covariances. These diagnostic tests are powerful tools for determining the adequacy of a model.

Multivariate or vector GARCH models are a general class of models designed to measure and forecast the entire variance/ covariance matrix of a set of assets based upon historical data. Periods of high correlation (or volatility) may be temporary or permanent; statistical procedures are used to determine how long such episodes lasted in the past and thereby forecast the future pattern of correlations.

It is well-known that a true correlation coefficient must be less than or equal to one and greater than or equal to minus one. It is also true that one portfolio of assets must have a correlation with another portfolio of assets which lies between plus and minus one. A mathematical property which ensures this for all possible portfolios of assets is that the covariance matrix of the assets must be positive definite. A good estimator of correlations in a multivariate system would also have this property, as do many, but not all, of the methods discussed below.

NON-GARCH HISTORICAL ESTIMATES
Rolling correlation is a method of estimation where the covariances are defined as:

$$\sigma_{i,j,t} = \frac{1}{L} \sum_{i=1}^{L} r_{i,t-1}\, r_{j,t-1} \tag{4}$$

where r_i is the excess return to asset i. The correlation then becomes:

$$\rho_{i,j,t} = \sigma_{i,j,t} / \sqrt{\sigma_{i,i,t}\sigma_{j,j,t}} \qquad (5)$$

It is important to note the assumptions made here:

❑ All observations within the last L periods are given equal weight and all observations older than L periods are given zero weight. This is clearly extreme and gives rise to "shadows" – spikes in the correlation estimate – L periods after a major event.
❑ There is no historical guidance about how to choose L meaning that the choice of window depends upon calibration against other information sets (such as option prices, when these are available).
❑ The correlation is predicted to be the same in the future as it is today, reflecting the inability of the model to separate permanent and transitory effects; it does not mean-revert toward normal levels of correlation with longer forecasts.

A somewhat more sophisticated model is the exponential smoother, an intrinsic component of JP Morgan's RiskMetrics. It is defined by the following equation:

$$\sigma_{i,j,t} = (1 - \pi)\sigma_{i,j,t-1} + \pi r_{i,t-1} r_{j,t-1} \qquad (6)$$

This model avoids the sharp cut-off which produces the shadows, but does not give any guidance on the choice of the parameter π. Forecasts from this model can be examined by rewriting equation (6) as:

$$\Delta\sigma_{i,j,t} = \pi(r_{i,t-1} r_{j,t-1} - \sigma_{i,j,t-1}) \qquad (7)$$

which shows that covariances increase whenever both assets move strongly in the same direction.

By writing the same equation for periods $t + k$, where $k > 1$, it is clear that no further changes in covariance can be predicted, since the expected value of Equation (7) is zero. Thus today's forecast for variances and covariances will persist for all future periods; the exponential smoother does not exhibit mean reversion in volatilities or correlations.

GARCH MODELS

We now turn to a partial list of multivariate GARCH models. These vary widely in terms of their parameterisation and flexibility. Most have been used for applications, some of which will be illustrated below. In each case, it is necessary to formulate an equation defining how each variance and covariance depends upon information previously available. Each equation is therefore a forecasting equation for the covariance one period ahead. Taken together, these provide forecast equations for all the covariances.

An attractive feature of these models is the ability to predict volatilities and correlations. The term structure of volatility is the picture of the expected volatility of an asset over various time horizons; such plots are familiar from data on implied volatilities. Similarly, we can define the term structure of correlation as a plot of the correlation which can be expected between two series over some future horizon.

All these models can be used to forecast volatilities and correlations multiple time steps ahead by simple analytical recursive formulas. To predict variances and covariances k steps into the future, one simply takes the expected value of the chosen equation at time $t + k$. Note that for all i, j and k:

$$E_t(r_{i,t+k} r_{j,t+k}) = E_t(\sigma_{i,j,t+k}) \tag{8}$$

so successive substitution into Equation (8) of the relevant equations from the model gives an expression for the variance/covariance matrix on date $t + k$, using only information known at time t. For first order GARCH models, such as scalar GARCH (discussed below) or a univariate GARCH (1,1):

$$\begin{aligned} E_t(\sigma_{i,j,t+k}) &= \omega_{i,j} + (\alpha + \beta) E_t(\sigma_{i,j,t+k-1}) \\ &= \bar{\sigma}_{i,j} + (\alpha + \beta)^{k-1}(\sigma_{i,j,t+1} - \bar{\sigma}_{i,j}) \end{aligned} \tag{9}$$

so the deviation from the one-step covariance forecast and the long-run forecast is expected to decay exponentially, with a decay parameter $\alpha + \beta$.

These formulas can be used to calculate the forward correlations. To calculate the correlations between average returns for two assets, the covariances and variances must be cumulated. Assuming the returns are serially uncorrelated, the expected value of the square of the sum is the sum of the expected value of the squares. Thus the term structure of correlation can be computed in terms of the forward variances and covariances:

$$\rho_{i,j,t}^{(k)} = \frac{\sum_{l=1}^{k} \sigma_{i,j,t+l/t}}{\sqrt{\left(\sum_{l=1}^{k} \sigma_{i,t+l/t} \right) \left(\sum_{l=1}^{k} \sigma_{j,t+l/t} \right)}} \tag{10}$$

Although we will not discuss optimisation methods for multivariate GARCH models in this chapter, a key feature of all models is the ability to estimate the parameters solely based on the data on past returns. The method used is maximum likelihood, in which the values of the parameters are computed which make estimates of past volatilities and correlations as close as possible to their real values. The procedure maximises a nonlinear objective function; the smaller the number of parameters, the easier it is to find an optimum. However, the more parameters there are, the better the optimum which can potentially be computed.

Scalar GARCH

The simplest multivariate GARCH model is called scalar GARCH and generalises the exponential smoother in an important fashion. The variances and covariances are assumed to follow a process defined by:

$$\sigma_{i,j,t} = \omega_{i,j} + \alpha r_{i,t-1} r_{j,t-1} + \beta \sigma_{i,j,t-1} \tag{11}$$

where the parameters α and β are assumed to be the same for all variances and covariances, while the intercepts $\omega_{i,j}$ determine the long-run covariance matrix. This model is attractive because it has only two more parameters than a conventional static covariance matrix and because it is guaranteed to give a positive definite covariance matrix whenever the covariance of $\omega_{i,j}$ is positive definite.

The scalar GARCH model itself has several parameters when the ωs are estimated, since there are $n(n + 1)/2$ unique ω elements. To simplify this estimation problem while ensuring that the long-run volatility forecasts are reasonable, exponentially smoothed estimates of ω can be used as a separate input, or a device called "variance targeting" can be used.

Variance targeting can be used with all GARCH models so it is useful to define it here. Let the observed sample covariance matrix be:

$$\bar{\sigma}_{i,j} = \frac{1}{T}\sum_{t=1}^{T} r_{i,t}r_{j,t} \tag{12}$$

where T is the sample size. Then write each term as deviations from the long-run covariance matrix:

$$\sigma_{i,j,t} = \bar{\sigma}_{i,j} + \alpha(r_{i,t-1}r_{j,t-1} - \bar{\sigma}_{i,j}) +$$
$$\beta(\sigma_{i,j,t-1} - \bar{\sigma}_{i,j})$$
$$= \bar{\sigma}_{i,j}(1 - \alpha - \beta) + \alpha(r_{i,t-1}r_{j,t-1}) + \beta\sigma_{i,j,t-1} \tag{13}$$

The model now only has two parameters which need to be estimated from a nonlinear optimiser, yet it has dynamic estimates of variances and covariances which mean-revert to the observed sample values which constitute the "target covariance matrix".

This model, with or without variance targeting, can be criticised as being too simple in various ways:

❏ all variances and covariances have the same dynamics;
❏ there is no distinction between permanent and transitory volatilities;
❏ there is no asymmetry in the response to return; and
❏ there is no feedback from volatility of one asset to another.

The rest of this article will seek to remedy most of these points by proposing various models and tests. We will then turn to examples where the models are used successfully.

Vector GARCH

This is a very general model which encompasses all the models discussed below:

$$\sigma_{i,j,t} = \omega_{i,j} + \sum_{i\geq j,k\geq m,l=1}^{L} \{\alpha_{i,j,k,m,l}(r_{k,t-1}r_{m,t-1})$$
$$+ \beta_{i,j,k,m,l}\sigma_{k,m,t-1} + \gamma_{i,j,k,m,l}(r_{k,t-1}r_{m,t-1})\delta_{k,m,t-1}\} \tag{14}$$

where the covariance of returns is modelled as depending upon all the variances and covariances of the data at time steps one through

L, as well as the past conditional variances and covariances. The dummy variable $\delta_{i,j,k,m,l}$ takes the value of zero or one, depending upon whether returns with the subscripts k and m take on particular values at time $t-1$. This model clearly has a vast number of parameters and will only possess the positive definite property needed to analyse correlations if we are lucky.

The diagonal vector GARCH model (Bollerslev, Engle and Wooldridge (1988)) is given by:

$$\sigma_{i,j,t} = \omega_{i,j} + \beta_{i,j}\sigma_{i,j,t-1} + \alpha_{i,j}(r_{i,t-1}r_{j,t-1})$$ (15)

It is more flexible than scalar GARCH but does not impose positive definiteness unless restrictions are imposed across the equations (Ding and Engle (1995)).

BEKK representation
This model (Engle and Kroner (1995)) is a positive definite representation which can best be written in matrix notation:

$$\Sigma_t = \Omega + A'r_{t-1}r'_{t-1}A + B'\Sigma_{t-1}B$$ (16)

where Σ is the variance/covariance matrix, r is the vector of returns and A, B and Ω are matrices. In this case Σ is positive definite because it is the sum of terms which are positive semi-definite. Clearly, more terms can be added which have other lags or particular parameterisations. In simple cases, A and B have few elements: if A and B are diagonal, then this reduces to a restricted diagonal vector GARCH.

Constant conditional correlation
In this model (Bollerslev (1990)):

$$\sigma_{i,j,t} = \rho_{i,j}\sigma_{i,t}\sigma_{j,t}$$ (17)

where $\sigma_{i,t}$ and $\sigma_{j,t}$ are univariate GARCH processes. This is easy to estimate for large systems but *assumes* that the correlations are constant.

Multivariate component model
Engle and Lee (1993a, 1993b) proposed a component model and a multivariate generalisation. Here, we consider the particularly useful specification:

$$\Sigma_t = Q_t + A'(r_{t-1}r'_{t-1} - Q_{t-1})A + B'(\Sigma_{t-1} - Q_{t-1})B$$
$$Q_t = \Omega + R'(Q_{t-1} - \Omega)R + F'(r_{t-1}r'_{t-1} - \Sigma_{t-1})F \qquad (18)$$

This model has the property that if all eigenvalues of A and B are substantially less than one, $\Sigma_t - Q_t$ will be a transitory covariance matrix and will be forecast to rapidly approach zero. If R has eigenvalues close to one, Q will be the permanent component of volatility which will gradually approach Ω as the forecast horizon increases. Thus the forward correlations will approach those of Ω as the horizon increases, although the dynamics may be complex. Variance targeting can be used directly with the second equation to constrain the matrix Ω.

As an example of this model-building strategy, consider the Deutschmark-sterling correlation discussed above. We first build[2] a simple model, then check the diagnostics to see if it has adequate properties. In this case, the first model is the scalar GARCH with variance targeting. The estimates are:

$$\sigma_{i,j,t} = \omega_{i,j} + 0.083r_{i,t-1}r_{j,t-1} + 0.888\sigma_{i,j,t-1}$$

with the intercept constrained by variance targeting and with t-statistics of the two coefficients of 29 and 204 respectively. The Ljung–Box tests for this model are presented in Table 1, the Akaike information criterion, Schwarz information criterion and log likelihood are given in the endnote. Good models should minimise the first two and maximise the last.

The first four columns and the ninth and tenth measure whether the volatilities and correlations are time-varying in the data. The others measure whether there is still time variation after taking out the GARCH effects. There are two black numbers in the standardised residual section of the table which are bigger than 25 which indicate that the model is not good. These are 46 and 33, which reveal, respectively, that there is information in both past sterling returns and past Deutschmark returns which could improve predictions of sterling volatility.

As a result, more generous models were parameterised and estimated, arriving at the following multivariate component model:

Table 1 Diagnostics for (a) scalar and (b) multivariate component GARCH models

	Ljung–Box correlation tests (rows predict columns, 5% critical value is 25)								Ljung–Box autocorrelation test of cross products			
	Squared residuals				Squared standardised residuals				Residuals		standardised residuals	
	DM		£		DM		£		DM		DM	
DM	262	**262**	127	**127**	15	**23**	10	**11**				
£	195	**195**	390	**390**	33	**25**	46	**18**	2,020	*2,020*	18	*15*

Note: Figures for (b) are in; (a) AIC = 10,266, SIC = 10,278, L = −5,130; (b) AIC = 10,160, SIC = 10,197, L = −5,074

$$\Sigma_t = Q_t + A'(r_{t-1}r'_{t-1} - Q_{t-1})A$$
$$+ B'(\Sigma_{t-1} - Q_{t-1})B$$
$$Q_t = \Omega + R'(Q_{t-1} - \Omega)R + F'(r_{t-1}r'_{t-1} - \Sigma_{t-1})F$$
$$A = \begin{bmatrix} 0 & -0.176 \\ 0 & 0.324 \end{bmatrix}, B = \begin{bmatrix} 0 & 0 \\ 0 & 0.738 \end{bmatrix},$$
$$R = \begin{bmatrix} 0.987 & 0 \\ 0 & 0.994 \end{bmatrix}, F = \begin{bmatrix} 0.241 & 0 \\ 0 & 0.241 \end{bmatrix}$$

which has four more parameters than the scalar model above. It not only passes the diagnostic tests but has better AIC and SIC measures and a log likelihood which is more than 50 points better than the original model (see bold figures in Table 1).

Using this model, the correlations between the Deutschmark and sterling rates are computed for each of the 21 trading days over a one-month sample period. These are plotted against the implied correlations for the period in which these are available (see Figure 2). Very similar correlations are obtained from recursive estimates of the model where the model is re-estimated every day, using only past data, and this model is then used to forecast 21 trading days into the future.

It can be seen that the match is generally quite close, although there are periods where the correlation estimates differ. In particular, the GARCH correlations dropped more than the options-based correlations immediately after the exchange rate mechanism crisis of

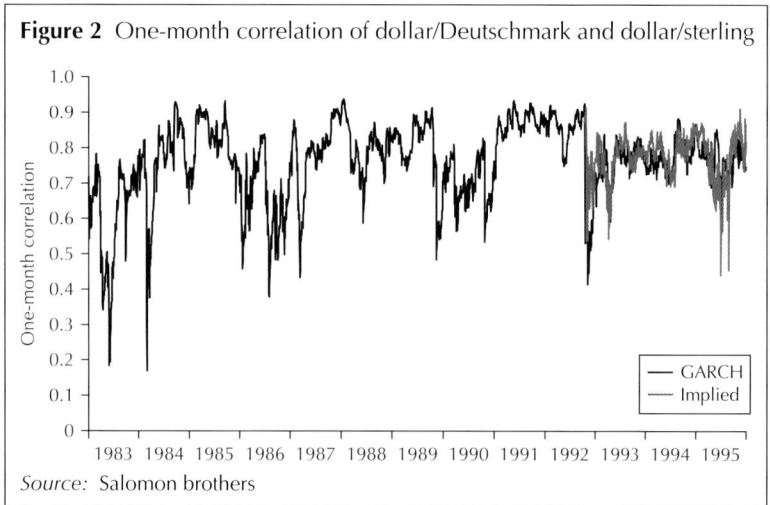

Figure 2 One-month correlation of dollar/Deutschmark and dollar/sterling

Source: Salomon brothers

September 1992, when the UK dropped out of the European monetary system. In this rather striking environment, it is hard to know which is the more appealing answer. It is also interesting to note that this is not the most dramatic drop in correlations over the sample period. Several other events had a similar impact on short-run correlations.

A similar multivariate component GARCH model,[3] with the addition of leverage effects, was used to estimate correlations between the S&P 500 and US Treasury bond futures over 30-day, six-month and one-year horizons. Figure 3 shows the estimates since 1982. All the correlations average about 0.42 but the shorter maturities are more volatile, with a maximum of 0.60 and a minimum of 0.11, while the annual correlations have a maximum of 0.48 and a minimum of 0.18. Other than the sharp drops in October 1987 and 1989, the correlations were high in the late 1980s. They were low in the early 1990s and then rose in 1994 when every whisper about the Fed moved both markets.

Although the models discussed thus far can, in principle, be used for large numbers of assets, the estimation may become unwieldy. A natural class of models designed for large systems are factor ARCH models introduced in Engle, Ng and Rothschild (1990).

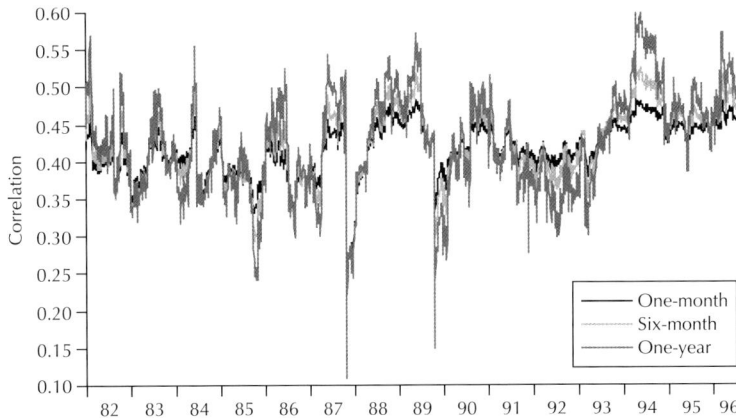

Figure 3 GARCH correlations between US Treasuries and the S&P 500

Source: Salomon brothers

These assume that there are one or more factors which drive the entire variance/covariance matrix of returns. These factors are very closely related to those in the familiar arbitrage pricing theory models. In many cases, estimation of a factor ARCH model only requires univariate GARCH models.

Factor ARCH

In the one-factor case:

$$\sigma_{i,j,t} = \lambda_{if}\lambda_{jf}\sigma^2_{f,t} + \omega_{ij} \tag{19}$$

where σ^2_f is the variance of the factor, λ is the factor loading and $\omega_{i,j}$ is the covariance between the idiosyncratic errors of asset i and j. These are often taken to be zero in arbitrage pricing theory models, but this is unnecessary.

For a K-factor model, the covariances are given in terms of the variances and covariances of the factors as well as the factor loadings and the idiosyncrasies:

$$\sigma_{i,j,t} = \omega_{i,j} + \sum_{f=1}^{K}\sum_{f'=1}^{K}\lambda_{if}\lambda_{jf'}\sigma^{FACTOR}_{f,f',t} \tag{20}$$

Again, all the covariances, variances and correlations depend on the factor variances and covariances. In this way, the correlations between hundreds or even thousands of assets can be allowed to vary over time with the covariances of a small number of factors.

The important modelling issue is the specification of the factor(s). These series determine the movement of all variances and covariances, so this is a highly parsimonious structure and one which is quite familiar from an economic standpoint. When modelling the returns on individual stocks, it is natural to take at least a market factor as a determinant of individual volatilities. Other factors could be interest rates, exchange rates or commodity prices. Similarly, when modelling global equities, there is likely to be a global factor as well as possibly regional or industrial factors.

Consider the task of modelling the volatility of an individual stock. In a one-factor model the return is naturally decomposed into systematic and idiosyncratic returns. For stock i with market returns given by r^m, the beta of the stock is given by λ and the idiosyncrasy by ε, as in the following equation:

$$r_{i,t} = \lambda_i r_t^m + \varepsilon_{i,t} \tag{21}$$

The variance of the return is then given by the square of the market beta multiplied by the market volatility plus the variance of the idiosyncratic error. If we let the idiosyncratic error itself be a univariate GARCH process or a process which depends upon market volatility directly, estimation and forecasting are simple tasks. The model is called a double beta model because there is a beta in the mean and another beta in the idiosyncratic variance. It is estimated by univariate GARCH with the market volatility as an input.

For IBM and Ford, the double beta model and parameters are given in Table 2, where the S&P 500 is taken as the market. The 60-day volatilities of Ford and IBM calculated from this model are plotted in Figure 4 along with the same maturity volatility from S&P. These curves are roughly parallel, representing the fact that the betas are close to one and the idiosyncratic volatility of Ford is generally higher than IBM. However, in 1993, IBM idiosyncratic volatility rose sufficiently to give it volatilities exceeding Ford temporarily.

Correlation between Ford and IBM can be computed from the factor model once an assumption has been made about the idiosyncratic covariance. Since these firms are in different industries, a

Table 2 Double beta model for IBM and Ford

$$r_{i,t} = \mu + \lambda_i r_t^{S\&P} + \varepsilon_{i,t}, V_{t-1}(\varepsilon_{i,t}) = \sigma_t^2$$
$$= q_t + \alpha(\varepsilon_{t-1}^2 - q_{t-1}) + \beta(\sigma_{t-1}^2 - q_{t-1}) + \gamma(d_{t-1}\varepsilon_{t-1}^2 - 0.5q_{t-1}) + \delta V_{t-1}(r_t^{S\&P})$$
$$q_t = \omega + \rho q_{t-1} + \phi(\varepsilon_{t-1}^2 - \sigma_{t-1}^2)$$

Likelihood based on student-t distribution with v degrees of freedom

Parameter	μ	λ	α	β	γ	δ	ρ	ϕ	v
IBM	−0.03	1.01	0.09	0.46	0.03	0.09	0.996	0.02	6.2
Ford	−0.02	1.22	0.07	0.37	0.00	0.25	0.999	0.01	7.9

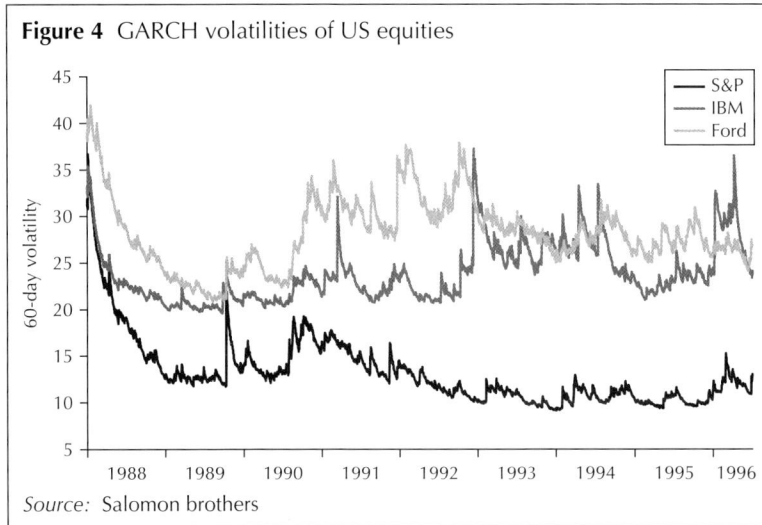

Figure 4 GARCH volatilities of US equities

Source: Salomon brothers

reasonable assumption is that this covariance is zero. From Equation (19) the correlation is given by:

$$\rho_{IBM,Ford,t} = \frac{\lambda_{IBM}\lambda_{Ford}S\&Pvol^2}{IBMvol * Fordvol}$$

where vol represents the annualised volatilities plotted in the previous figure. The correlation is plotted in Figure 5.

After the October 1987 stock market crash, the correlation falls until it hits a low of 0.1 in 1993, after which it rises slightly. Most of

Figure 5 Ford and IBM factor model correlation

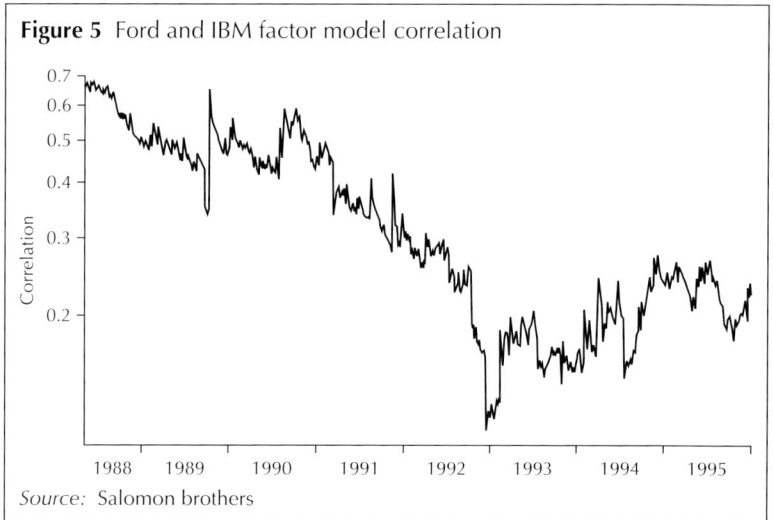

Source: Salomon brothers

the movement in these correlations is due to changes in market volatility, which generally declines from the crash into the mid-1990s. However, the details of the pattern are influenced in important ways by the idiosyncratic volatility. A similar picture can be computed between any pair of stocks; in fact, we have estimated the double beta model for all S&P stocks, as well as many of the smaller capitalisation stocks.

1   A multivariate option is an option whose payout depends on more than one underlying variable. Examples are spread options, "best of" options, quantos, rainbows, options to exchange, knock-out and knock-in options where the payout is based upon a different variable from the barrier, and many others.

2   All estimates were calculated using routines creatively and effectively developed by Patrick Burns for Salomon Brothers.

3   The model is defined by [18] where there are two R and two F terms and there is a leverage term with coefficient matrix G.

$$r = \begin{bmatrix} r_{\text{SPX}} \\ r_{\text{BOND}} \end{bmatrix}, A = \begin{bmatrix} 0.0 & 0.14 \\ 0.19 & 0.0 \end{bmatrix}, B = \begin{bmatrix} 0.67 & 0.0 \\ -0.35 & 0.0 \end{bmatrix},$$

$$R1 = \begin{bmatrix} 0.9966 & 0.0 \\ 0.0 & 0.9966 \end{bmatrix}, R2 = \begin{bmatrix} 0.0 & 0.0 \\ 0.087 & 0.0 \end{bmatrix}, G = \begin{bmatrix} 0.53 & 0.0 \\ -0.35 & 0.0 \end{bmatrix},$$

$$F1 = \begin{bmatrix} 0.14 & 0.0 \\ 0.0 & 0.14 \end{bmatrix}, F2 = \begin{bmatrix} -0.11 & 0.0 \\ 0.11 & 0.11 \end{bmatrix}$$

This chapter was previously published in *Risk*, August 1996.

REFERENCES

Bollerslev, T., 1990, "Modeling the Coherence in Short-run Nominal Exchange Rates: A Multivariate Generalized Arch Model", *Review of Economics and Statistics* **74**, pp. 498–505.

Bollerslev, T., R. Engle, and J. M. Wooldridge, 1988, "A Capital Asset Pricing Model with Time-varying Covariance", *Journal of Political Economy* **96**, pp. 116–31.

Ding, Z. and R. Engle, 1995, "Large-scale Conditional Covariance Matrix Modeling, Estimation and Testing", manuscript.

Engle, R., 1982, "Autoregressive Conditional Heteroscedasticity with Estimates of the Variance of UK Inflation", *Econometrica* **50**, pp. 987–1008.

Engle, R. and K. Kroner, 1995, "Multivariate Simultaneous Generalized Arch", *Econometric Theory* **11**, pp. 122–50.

Engle, R. and G. Lee, 1993a, "A Permanent and Transitory Component Model of Stock Return Volatility", UCSD discussion paper 92-44R.

Engle, R. and G. Lee, 1993b, "Long Run Volatility Forecasting for Individual Stocks in a One Factor Model", UCSD discussion paper 93-30.

Engle, R. and J. Mezrich, 1995, "Grapp.ling with Garch", *Risk*, September, pp. 112–7.

Engle, R., V. Ng, and M. Rothschild, 1990, "Asset Pricing with a Factor Arch Covariance Structure: Empirical Estimates for Treasury Bills", *Journal of Econometrics* **45**, pp. 213–37.

Ljung, G. and G. Box, 1978, "On a Measure of Lack of Fit in Time Series Models", *Biometrika* **66**, pp. 67–72.

11

Correlation Stress Testing for Value-at-Risk

Saygun Turkay; Eduardo Epperlein;*
Nicos Christofides

Citigroup Market Risk Analytics; Citigroup, Imperial College

1 INTRODUCTION

It is a well known fact that under extreme market conditions financial institutions can be rendered helpless by the inadequacy of the models that they use. As a safety cushion against these cases *stress testing* is an important tool for financial institutions. Under normal market conditions, *value-at-risk* (VaR) is the widely used risk measure to calculate a bank's exposure. The covariance matrix of asset returns is very often used in order to model the portfolio return distribution.

Value-at-risk gives a good estimate of market risk provided that the same market conditions prevail but fails in the face of events which are not reflected in the past data. Stress testing is a complementary tool to the VaR calculation, and is discussed in this context by Kupiec (1998). The underlying concept is based on finding the covariance matrix conditioned on the assets which are deterministically moved under a given scenario.

Scenarios can also be used to stress the volatility of an asset or the correlations between a group of assets. The covariance matrix Σ can be decomposed as $\Sigma = \Lambda \Omega \Lambda^T$ where Λ is a diagonal matrix with positive entries representing volatilities, and Ω is the correlation

*The analysis and conclusions set forth are those of the authors. Citigroup is not responsible for any statement or conclusion herein, and opinions or theories presented herein do not necessarily reflect the position of the institution.

matrix. It is quite straightforward to stress the volatilities by stressing the diagonal terms of Λ. However, care must be taken in modifying the correlation matrix to ensure that it remains positive definite. This ensures that the portfolio variance is always positive.

The focus of this chapter is the problem of modifying a correlation matrix Ω *locally* to a desired target matrix while ensuring that the irrelevant correlations not included in the scenario remain intact, and that the new matrix $\hat{\Omega}$ remains positive definite. Once the correlation matrix is modified, one can compare the change in VaR using the original matrix Ω and the stressed matrix $\hat{\Omega}$. Original contributions of the chapter are as follows.

An analytical solution for the bounds of a single correlation term of a positive definite correlation matrix is given. The methodology is based on the re-ordering of the assets that define the matrix and application of *Cholesky* decomposition to *localise* the stress. An iterative application of the single stress methodology in order to stress a number of correlation terms on a correlation matrix (while keeping the remaining correlations intact) is presented. An efficient one-step (local eigenvalue modification) methodology to modify the correlations of a *submatrix* of a positive definite correlation matrix is developed. The idea of matrix re-ordering also plays a crucial part in this methodology. In summary, our work mainly focuses on applying a *local stress* to the correlation matrix, unlike the work presented in literature which does not consider local scenarios.

There are a number of studies in the literature (either in financial or matrix algebra) that address the topic of correlation bounds and stressing, although none seems to address the issue of applying *local correlation stress* while keeping the rest of the matrix intact. Stress testing in the context of VaR is given in Kupiec (1998), where an iterative method is proposed for stressing the correlation matrix. In a more mathematical rather than financial setting, the matrix bounds given in Sun (1991) are not tight and the inequalities presented can be improved. Edelman and Mascarenhas (1995) and Drmac *et al* (1994) map the perturbation on the matrix to a perturbation of its Cholesky decomposition, but assume that the stressed matrix remains positive definite. Gill *et al* (1974), Schnabel and Eskow (1993), Cheng and Higham (1998), and Higham (1988) (described in detail in Section 3.2.1) propose algorithms which convert a non-positive definite matrix into a positive definite one but changes affect the whole matrix. Higham (1988) proves that the spectral decomposition approach gives the optimum positive semidefinite solution in the Frobenius sense. The spectral decomposition method is also presented by Rebonato and Jäckel (2000) and Jäckel (2002).

A recent interesting approach by Rebonato and Jäckel (2000) and Jäckel (2002) is the *hypersphere decomposition* method, which views row vectors of the decomposition matrix as coordinates lying on a hypersphere. This decomposition implicitly makes use of the interpretation of correlation coefficient as the cosine of the angle between two vectors; see Rodgers and Nicewander (1988). Rebonato and Jäckel (2000) propose to use an optimisation scheme to minimise the error between the constructed matrix and the target matrix. Since, for a matrix of size $n \times n$, there are $n \times (n - 1)/2$ unknown variables (θ_{ij}, $i = 2, ..., n, j = 1, ..., (i - 1)$), the number of unknowns (optimization variables) is large even for matrices of moderate sizes, eg, 1,225 unknown variables for a matrix of size 50×50. Furthermore, the methodology affects all elements of the correlation matrix, ie, does not address the issue of *local correlation stress*. The reduced form of the hypersphere decomposition is also used by Bhansali and Wise (2001).

Section 2 of the chapter presents the analytic bounds to apply a single correlation stress. Section 3 presents new methodologies to apply local correlation stress. Section 4 presents an example on which all presented methodologies are applied. Section 5 summarises.

2 SINGLE STRESS METHODOLOGY
2.1 Re-ordering of the correlation matrix
Let us denote the correlation matrix with $\Omega = (\Delta\rho_{ij}) \in \mathbb{R}^{n\times n}$, which is positive definite. Changing the order of assets which specify the correlation matrix does not affect the positive definiteness. Call this re-ordered matrix $\tilde{\Omega} = (\Delta\tilde{\rho}_{ij})$.

Let L be the lower triangular Cholesky decomposition matrix of $\tilde{\Omega}$ such that $\tilde{\Omega} = LL^T$ and let l_i be the columns of L such that $L = (l_1, ..., l_n)$. Note that due to the lower triangular structure of L, the first $i - 1$ entries of l_i are zeros. The Cholesky decomposition can also be expressed by

$$\tilde{\Omega} = \sum_{i=1}^{n} l_i l_i^T \tag{1}$$

243

Since the first $i-1$ entries of l_i are zeros, the first $i-1$ rows and columns of $l_i l_i^T$ are zeros, eg, $l_1 l_1^T$ is a full nonzero $n \times n$ matrix, $l_2 l_2^T$ is an $n \times n$ matrix with first row and first column equal to zero, and so on. Obviously $l_n l_n^T$ is an $n \times n$ matrix with all entries equal to zero except the lower-right-most entry. This structure implies that a perturbation applied to the nonzero entries of l_i affect only the $(n-i+1) \times (n-i+1)$ lower-right sub matrix of $\tilde{\Omega}$. That is, a perturbation applied to the single nonzero entry of l_n affects only the lower-right-most entry of $\tilde{\Omega}$. A perturbation applied to the 2 nonzero entries of l_{n-1} affects the lower 2×2 sub-matrix of $\tilde{\Omega}$, and so on.

2.2 Application to the single stress case

Let us be more specific and assume that we want to apply a stress to a single correlation term in a matrix; namely to the correlation ρ_{ij} of assets S_i and S_j. The original ordering of assets is $(S_1, ..., S_i, ..., S_j, ... S_n)$. Now, let us do a re-ordering of assets to obtain

$$(S_1, ..., S_{i-1}, S_{i+1} ..., S_{j-1}, S_{j+1} ... S_n, S_i, S_j)$$

Let the corresponding correlation matrix be $\tilde{\Omega}$. Let $L = (l_1, ..., l_n)$ be the corresponding lower triangular Cholesky matrix. If a stress is applied to the nonzero elements of l_{n-1} and l_n, they will affect the lower-right-most 2×2 sub-matrix of $\tilde{\Omega}$. Because of our re-ordering, this exactly corresponds to a stress on the correlations of the assets i and j and the diagonal terms of this matrix. Note that, having put the desired stress to the correlation of the assets S_i and S_j by a stress on the Cholesky decomposition, we have preserved the triangular structure and positive definiteness. Now we can reconstruct the matrix and re-order the assets to bring them back to their original locations.

To be more specific, let us denote the column vectors l_{n-1} and l_n as

$$l_{n-1} = (0, 0, ..., 0, a, b)^T, \quad l_n = (0, 0, ..., 0, 0, c)^T \tag{2}$$

Let δ_a, δ_b, and δ_c be perturbations on terms a, b, and c respectively. After these perturbations, we get

$$\hat{l}_{n-1} = (0, 0, ..., 0, a + \delta_a, b + \delta_b)^T, \quad \hat{l}_n = (0, 0, ..., 0, 0, c + \delta_c)^T$$

Let the corresponding Cholesky matrix be $\hat{L}$ and the corresponding correlation matrix be $\hat{\Omega}$. Therefore, we have

$$L = (l_1, \ldots, \hat{l}_{n-1}, \hat{l}_n) \tag{3}$$

and

$$\hat{\Omega} = \hat{L}\hat{L}^T = \hat{l}_{n-1}\hat{l}_{n-1}^T + \hat{l}_n\hat{l}_n^T + \sum_{i=1}^{n-2} \hat{l}_i\hat{l}_i^T$$

$$= \begin{pmatrix} 0 & \cdots & & & 0 \\ \vdots & & & & \vdots \\ \vdots & \ddots & 0 & & 0 \\ 0 & 0 & (a + \delta_a)^2 & (a + \delta_a)(b + \delta_b) \\ 0 & 0 & (a + \delta_a)(b + \delta_b) & (b + \delta_b)^2(c + \delta_c)^2 \end{pmatrix} + \sum_{i=1}^{n-2} l_i l_i^T$$

Let us denote the lower right 2×2 sub-matrix of the first term as

$$A + \Delta A = \begin{pmatrix} (a + \delta_a)^2 & (a + \delta_a)(b + \delta_b) \\ (a + \delta_a)(b + \delta_b) & (b + \delta_b)^2(c + \delta_c)^2 \end{pmatrix} \tag{4}$$

where

$$A = \begin{pmatrix} a^2 & ab \\ ab & b^2 + c^2 \end{pmatrix},$$

$$\Delta A = \begin{pmatrix} \delta_a^2 + 2a\delta_a & a\delta_b + b\delta_a + \delta_a\delta_b \\ a\delta_a + b\delta_a + \delta_a\delta_b & \delta_b^2 + 2b\delta_b + \delta_c^2 + 2c\delta_c \end{pmatrix} \tag{5}$$

The term ΔA is obviously the stress applied to the re-ordered correlation matrix. The diagonal terms of ΔA have to be zero, because the diagonal terms of the correlation matrix must be equal to 1. The off diagonal terms are the perturbations to the correlation of S_i and S_j.

2.3 The minimisation problem
Since the diagonal terms of $\hat{\Omega}$ must be preserved to be 1, the diagonal terms of ΔA must be zero. Assume that the desired stress to the

correlation of S_i and S_j is given by $\Delta\rho_{ij}$. We now have a constrained minimisation problem:

$$\min_{\delta_a, \delta_b, \delta_c} (a\delta_b + b\delta_a + \delta_a\delta_b - \Delta\rho_{ij})^2 \qquad (6)$$

$$\delta_a^2 + 2a\delta_a = 0, \qquad \delta_b^2 + 2b\delta_b + \delta_c^2 + 2c\delta_c = 0 \qquad (7)$$

Remember that a, b, c are obtained from the Cholesky decomposition and $\Delta\rho_{ij}$ is the desired stress. The solution is investigated for two cases. First, the existence of an exact solution (which minimises the cost function to zero) is investigated. The allowed range of $\Delta\rho_{ij}$ for a given set of (a, b, c) is then specified. Secondly, the solution is given when no exact solution exists.

2.3.1 Exact solution

Instead of the objective function given by (6), we can substitute the equality

$$a\delta_b + b\delta_a + \delta_a\delta_b - \Delta\rho_{ij} = 0 \qquad (8)$$

Equation (7) immediately gives two solutions for δ_a: $\delta_a = 0$ and $\delta_a = -2a$.

LEMMA 2.1 *Let a, b, c and δ_a, δ_b, δ_c be defined as above. If the desired stress $\Delta\rho_{ij}$ lies in the interval*

$$\Delta\rho_{ij} \in \left[\min\left(-ab\left(1 \pm \sqrt{1 + \frac{c^2}{b^2}} \right) \right), \quad \max\left(-ab\left(1 \pm \sqrt{1 + \frac{c^2}{b^2}} \right) \right) \right]$$

then for $\delta_a = 0$ and $\delta_a = -2a$, we can find real δ_b and δ_c which satisfy the exact solution given by Equations (7) and (8).

Proof
CASE (A) EXACT SOLUTION FOR $\delta_a = 0$: It is obvious that $\delta_a = 0$ satisfies (7). Replacing $\delta_a = 0$ in (8) yields

$$a\delta_b - \Delta\rho_{ij} = 0 \qquad (9)$$

We can express δ_b as

$$\delta_b = -b \pm \sqrt{-\delta_c^2 - 2c\delta_c + b^2} \qquad (10)$$

In order to have real roots for δ_b, we need $-\delta_c^2 - 2c\delta_c + b^2 \geq 0$. The roots of the last inequality are $\delta_c = -c \pm \sqrt{b^2 + c^2}$, which are obviously real. The solution set is clearly the interval between the roots, ie,

$$\delta_c \in \left[-c - \sqrt{b^2 + c^2}, -c + \sqrt{b^2 + c^2} \right] \tag{11}$$

In this case, both δ_b and δ_c are real and satisfy (7). Now, if we substitute $\delta_b = \Delta\rho_{ij}/a$ from (9) into (7) we get

$$a^2\delta_c^2 + 2a^2c\delta_c^2 + (\Delta\rho_{ij}^2 + 2ab\Delta\rho_{ij}) = 0 \tag{12}$$

The roots of (12) are

$$\delta_c = -c \pm \sqrt{c^2 - \frac{1}{a^2}(\Delta\rho_{ij}^2 + 2ab\Delta\rho_{ij})}$$

These roots must be real and must also lie in the interval given by (11). Therefore, the following conditions must hold

$$c^2 - \frac{1}{a^2}(\Delta\rho_{ij}^2 + 2ab\Delta\rho_{ij}) \geq 0 \tag{13}$$

$$b^2 \geq -\frac{1}{a^2}(\Delta\rho_{ij}^2 + 2ab\Delta\rho_{ij}) \tag{14}$$

By simple algebraic manipulation, (13) becomes $\Delta\rho_{ij}^2 + 2ab\Delta\rho_{ij} - a^2c^2 \leq 0$. The roots of this inequality are given by

$$\Delta\rho_{ij} = -ab\left(1 \pm \sqrt{1 + c^2/b^2}\right)$$

Obviously the roots are always real. For the inequality to hold, $\Delta\rho_{ij}$ must lie between its roots, ie,

$$\Delta\rho_{ij} \in \left[\min\left(-ab\left(1 \pm \sqrt{1 + \frac{c^2}{b^2}}\right)\right), \max\left(-ab\left(1 \pm \sqrt{1 + \frac{c^2}{b^2}}\right)\right) \right] \tag{15}$$

must hold. Similarly from (14) we get

$$b^2 \geq -\frac{1}{a^2}(\Delta\rho_{ij}^2 + 2ab\Delta\rho_{ij}) \Rightarrow a^2b^2 \geq -\Delta\rho_{ij}^2 - 2ab\Delta\rho_{ij}$$

$$\Rightarrow \Delta\rho_{ij}^2 + 2ab\Delta\rho_{ij} + a^2b^2 \geq 0 \Rightarrow (\Delta\rho_{ij} - ab)^2 \geq 0$$

This is true for all values of $\Delta\rho_{ij}$, a and b. This shows that if $\Delta\rho_{ij}$ is in the interval defined in (15) then there are real δ_b and δ_c which satisfy (7).

Note that the above proof also inherently gives the solution set for $(\delta_a, \delta_b, \delta_c)$. If the desired stress $\Delta\rho_{ij}$ is in the interval specified in (15) then pick $\delta_a = 0$, $\delta_b = \Delta\rho_{ij}/a$ and δ_c to be any of the roots of (7). This gives the desired stress to the off diagonal terms (correlation of S_i and S_j) and does not alter the diagonal terms.

CASE (B) EXACT SOLUTION FOR $\delta_a = -2a$: It is obvious that $\delta_a = -2a$ satisfies (7). Replacing $\delta_a = -2a$ in (8) yields:

$$a\delta_b + 2ab + \Delta\rho_{ij} = 0, \qquad \delta_b = -(\Delta\rho_{ij}/a) - 2b$$

Direct substitution of $\Delta\rho_{ij}$ into (7) yields (12). This suffices to state that the same solution interval (15) is valid for $\Delta\rho_{ij}$, and for this interval, we can find real δ_b and δ_c which give the exact solution following the same reasoning as in the proof of Case (a) above.

2.3.2 Optimal solution when no exact solution exists

We do not have an exact solution to the minimisation problem specified by (6), and (7) when $\Delta\rho_{ij}$ lies outside the interval specified by (15). Two cases of concern arise again. Equation (7) immediately gives us $\delta_a = 0$ and $\delta_a = -2a$. Let us express $\delta_b = -b \pm \sqrt{\Psi}$ where $\Psi = -\delta_c^2 - 2c\delta_c + b^2$. For $\delta_a = 0$ we have the following minimisation problem:

$$\min_{\delta_c}(a\delta_b - \Delta\rho_{ij})^2, \qquad \text{subject to } \Psi \geq 0 \tag{16}$$

By substituting $\delta_b = -ab \pm \sqrt{\Psi}$ into (16) and after some tedious but straightforward algebra we get

$$\min_{\delta_c} f(\delta_c) = \left(-a^2\delta_c^2 - 2a^2c\delta_c \mp 2a(ab - \Delta\rho_{ij})\sqrt{\Psi}\right) \tag{17}$$

The extrema of this function are given by the solution to

$$\left(\frac{a(ab - \Delta\rho_{ij})}{\sqrt{\Psi}} - 2a^2 \right) = 0, \qquad \delta_c + c = 0$$

The first equation yields $a^2\delta_c^2 + 2a^2c\delta_c + (\Delta\rho_{ij}^2 + 2ab\Delta\rho_{ij}) = 0$, which is exactly Equation (12). We have shown in Section 2.3.1 that this requires $\Delta\rho_{ij}$ to be in the interval shown in (15). This is a contradiction to our starting point. We proceed to the other equation, namely $\delta_c = -c$, which can easily be shown to lead to a minimum.

Now we have the solution set for $(\delta_a, \delta_b, \delta_c)$. If the desired stress $\Delta\rho_{ij}$ is not in the interval specified in (15) then pick $\delta_a = 0$, $\delta_c = -c$ and δ_b as that one of the two roots of (10), which makes the cost function in (16) minimal. This gives a stress to the off diagonal term that is closest to the desired stress without altering the diagonal terms.

LEMMA 2.2 *If the desired stress* $\Delta\rho_{ij}$ *is not in the interval shown in (15), then the actual stress* $\Delta\tilde{\rho}_{ij}$ *obtained by the method described above is one of the boundary points of the interval specified in (15) for the exact solution.*

Proof

$\Delta\tilde{\rho}_{ij}$ satisfies (15), because δ_c satisfies (11). Then there is an exact solution to this problem that satisfies (12), which is reproduced below:

$$a^2\delta_c^2 + 2a^2c\delta_c^2 + (\Delta\tilde{\rho}_{ij}^2 + 2ab\Delta\tilde{\rho}_{ij}) = 0$$

Simple substitution of $\delta_c = -c$ yields $\Delta\tilde{\rho}_{ij}^2 + 2ab\Delta\tilde{\rho}_{ij} - a^2c^2 = 0$, whose roots are exactly the boundary points of interval (15). This completes the proof.

In practice $\delta_c = -c$ poses a problem because the last column $\hat{l}_n$ of the stressed Cholesky matrix $\hat{L}$ becomes zero. Consequently, the stressed correlation matrix $\hat{\Omega}$ becomes singular. Therefore the boundary points of the interval specified in (15) should not be used. Practically, one can pick $\delta_c = -c + \varepsilon$ where $\varepsilon \in \mathbb{R}$ of arbitrarily small magnitude such that $\Delta\rho_{ij}$ lies inside the interval (15). The value of δ_b shifts slightly as well. This preserves positive definiteness. Collecting together the previous results we have:

THEOREM 2.1 *Let* $\Omega = (\rho_{ij}) \in \mathbb{R}^{n\times n}$ *be a correlation matrix. Assume that a single stress* $\Delta\rho_{ij}$ *is to be applied to the correlation term* ρ_{ij} *(and* *obviously to its symmetric counterpart ρ_{ij}). Let $\tilde{\Omega}$ be the re-ordered corre-lation matrix such that correlation of S_i and S_j are placed in the lower right 2×2 sub-matrix of $\tilde{\Omega}$. Let $L = (l_1, \ldots, l_{n-1}, l_n)$ be a lower triangular $n \times n$ matrix such that $\tilde{\Omega} = LL^T$. Let (a, b, c) be defined as in equation (2). If the stress $\Delta\rho_{ij}$ is in the interval below*

$$\Gamma = \left[\min\left(-ab\left(1 \pm \sqrt{1 + \frac{c^2}{b^2}} \right) \right), \quad \max\left(-ab\left(1 \pm \sqrt{1 + \frac{c^2}{b^2}} \right) \right) \right]$$

then applying the stress directly on Ω does not disturb positive definiteness. If $\Delta\rho_{ij}$ is not in the interval above, then the nearest boundary point is the optimal solution.

The proof is a direct consequence of lemmas 2.1 and 2.2. Theorem 2.1 basically states that all that is required is to check the stress against the interval Γ. If it is inside Γ, one only needs to replace $\Delta\rho_{ij}$ with $\rho_{ij} + \Delta\rho_{ij}$ in the original correlation matrix Ω. It also states that this result is best possible if all remaining terms of Ω are to remain at their original values. In the case that $\Delta\rho_{ij}$ lies outside Γ, the best solution is to pick $\Delta\rho_{ij}$ just inside the nearest boundary point of Γ.

3 MULTIPLE CORRELATION STRESS

In this section we present methodologies for stressing a number of terms of a correlation matrix simultaneously. As in Section 2, the aim is to find the best solution while keeping the matrix positive definite.

3.1 Iterative application of the single stress method

Assume that a scenario involves modifying correlations of a set of assets, rather than only the correlation between two assets. In this case it is possible to apply the single stress method in an *ad hoc* way, by stressing each correlation term within the scenario individually and sequentially. Once the single stress method is applied sequentially, the matrix has changed and the stress bounds of each term are different.

However, the solution found by the *sequential application* of the method is not optimal. The bounds of the new correlation terms are still not as tight as possible after the application of a stress sequence

once, since each single stress of a sequence is optimal for one correlation stress but not for the whole set of scenario correlations. The
method can now be applied again onto the new matrix, using the
same or another sequence, for the same target matrix. This *iterative
procedure* is then repeated until a certain convergence criterion is
satisfied.

3.2 Local eigenvalue modification

This section introduces a method to stress the correlations of a
group of assets simultaneously (as opposed to sequentially, as in
the iterative single stress method) within the correlation matrix.
The local eigenvalue modification method is based on the *spectral
decomposition* method presented by Higham (1988), Rebonato and
Jäckel (2000) and Jäckel (2002). Below we give a brief account
of that method before we describe the new methodology that we
propose.

3.2.1 Spectral decomposition method

Take an arbitrary matrix $A \in \mathbb{R}^{n \times n}$. Assume that A is not positive
semidefinite. The closest positive semidefinite matrix to A with
respect to the Frobenius norm of the error is given by Higham
(1988). Frobenius norm is one of the most frequently used matrix
norms in numerical algebra. Let $D = (d_{ij})_{n \times n}$ be the difference
matrix between a target matrix and achieved matrix. The Frobenius
norm of D is defined as follows:

$$\|D\|_F = \sqrt{\sum_{i=1}^{n} \sum_{j=1}^{n} |d_{ij}|^2}$$

See Golub and Van Loan (1996) for more details on Frobenius
norm. The result of Higham (1988) is valid for symmetric A since
the space of symmetric matrices is a subspace of arbitrary matrices
of the same size. Let us work on symmetric A. Higham's result
(1988) can be summarised as follows.

The non-positive definite A can be decomposed as $A = Q\Lambda Q^T$,
where $Q \in \mathbb{R}^{n \times n}$ is an orthogonal matrix, ie, $QQ^T = Q^TQ = I$, and Λ
is a diagonal matrix of the eigenvalues Λ_{ii}, $i = 1, \dots, n$ of A. Define
$\tilde{\Lambda}$ to be a diagonal matrix equal to Λ except that the negative diagonal terms are replaced by zeros. If we reconstruct the matrix $\tilde{A}$

using $\tilde{\Lambda}$ and the same set of eigenvectors which are represented by Q such that $\tilde{A} = Q\tilde{\Lambda}Q^T$ then $\tilde{A}$ is the closest positive semidefinite matrix to A with respect to the Frobenius norm. One property of this method is that it changes all the terms on a matrix. If the matrix is to be stressed using only a subset of correlations then this method is not convenient. Another problem is that the diagonal terms are no longer equal to one after the reconstruction, which requires further normalisation of the reconstructed matrix. This action would disturb the optimality of the solution but the effect is generally small.

3.2.2 Application to local stress

The new proposed method employs the same re-ordering principle described in Section 2.1. Again, the correlation stress is applied to the Cholesky decomposition rather than the matrix itself. It is easy to visualise this by a simple example. Assume that we want to modify correlations between three assets in a correlation matrix of size 5×5. Let $\tilde{\Omega} = (\tilde{\rho}_{ij})$ be the reordered correlation matrix such that the 3×3 lower-right submatrix constitutes the scenario matrix. Let $\tilde{\Omega} = (\tilde{\rho}_{ij}) = LL^T$ where L is the lower triangular Cholesky decomposition matrix of $\tilde{\Omega}$. Let us now express L as $L = L_u + L_s$ where L_s denotes that part of cholesky matrix that corresponds to the scenario matrix with all other terms equal to zero, as follows (nonzero terms are marked by "×"):

$$L_u = \begin{pmatrix} \times & 0 & 0 & 0 & 0 \\ \times & \times & 0 & 0 & 0 \\ \times & \times & 0 & 0 & 0 \\ \times & \times & 0 & 0 & 0 \\ \times & \times & 0 & 0 & 0 \end{pmatrix}, \quad L_s = \begin{pmatrix} 0 & 0 & 0 & 0 & 0 \\ 0 & 0 & 0 & 0 & 0 \\ 0 & 0 & \times & 0 & 0 \\ 0 & 0 & \times & \times & 0 \\ 0 & 0 & \times & \times & \times \end{pmatrix} \quad (18)$$

Note that L_u and L_s are orthogonal to each other, and hence $\tilde{\Omega} = LL^T = L_u L_u^T + L_s L_s^T$ where $\Omega_u = L_u L_u^T$ is a full 5×5 nonzero matrix whereas $\Omega_s = L_s L_s^T$ is a 5×5 matrix with the first 2 rows and columns equal to zero. Both Ω_u and Ω_s are positive semidefinite. Similar to Section 2.2, a stress applied to L_s is confined to correlations of the 3×3 scenario matrix.

Generalise the idea above by defining n to be the matrix size ($n = 5$ above), n_s the size of the scenario matrix ($n_s = 3$ above) and n_u is defined such that $n = n_s + n_u$.

Assume that an *arbitrary stress* is applied directly onto $\tilde{\Omega}$, ie, the stress is not applied via the Cholesky matrix. Call the resulting stressed matrix $\hat{\Omega}$, and assume that $\hat{\Omega}$ is non-positive definite. Because of the re-ordering, $\hat{\Omega}$ is equal to $\tilde{\Omega}$ in the first n_u rows and columns. Call the lower right $n_s \times n_s$ submatrix of $\hat{\Omega}$ as $\Delta\hat{\Omega}$. We then have

$$\hat{\Omega} - \Omega_u = \begin{pmatrix} 0_{(n_u \times n_u)} & 0_{(n_u \times n_s)} \\ 0_{(n_s \times n_u)} & \Delta\hat{\Omega}_{(n_s \times n_s)} \end{pmatrix}_{n \times n}$$

Since $\hat{\Omega}$ is non-positive definite and Ω_u is positive semidefinite, $\Delta\hat{\Omega}$ is non-positive definite. Now we can apply the result of Higham (1988). We can find the closest positive semidefinite approximant to $\Delta\hat{\Omega}$ by taking its eigenvalue decomposition and setting negative eigenvalues to zero. This gives the closest approximant with respect to the Frobenius norm. Let us call this approximant $\Delta\hat{\Omega}'$. Now, if we add this $\Delta\hat{\Omega}'$ to the lower right $n_s \times n_s$ submatrix of Ω_u, ie,

$$\Omega_u + \begin{pmatrix} 0_{(n_u \times n_u)} & 0_{(n_u \times n_s)} \\ 0_{(n_s \times n_u)} & \Delta\hat{\Omega}'_{(n_s \times n_s)} \end{pmatrix}_{n \times n} \tag{19}$$

we get a positive semidefinite matrix since both terms are positive semidefinite.

One problem with Higham's result in the context of the correlation matrix is that the diagonal terms of the approximant are not normalised. It is possible to eliminate this problem by subsequent normalisation. However, particular care must be taken in this case because the diagonal terms of the resulting matrix – after the addition as in (19) – must be one. In other words, $\Delta\hat{\Omega}' = (\hat{\rho}'(ij))$ must be rescaled such that when added to the lower right submatrix of Ω_u the diagonal is equal to one. This is done as follows.

Let us denote the lower right $n_s \times n_s$ submatrix of Ω_u by $\Omega_u^s = (\rho_u^s(ij))$. Obviously $\rho_u^s(ii) < 1$. Call the rescaled submatrix $\Delta\hat{\Omega}'' = (\hat{\rho}''(ij))$. Then $\hat{\rho}''(ii) = 1 - \rho_u^s(ii)$ must be satisfied. Hence the following scaling suffices:

$$\Delta\hat{\Omega}'' = Q(\Delta\hat{\Omega}')Q^T \tag{20}$$

where the scaling matrix $Q = (q(ij))$ is given by:

$$q(ij) = \begin{cases} 0 & \text{if } i \neq j \\ \dfrac{\sqrt{1 - p_u^s(ii)}}{\sqrt{\hat{p}'(ii)}} & \text{if } i = j \end{cases}$$

With the scaling shown above the following matrix

$$\Omega_u + \begin{pmatrix} 0_{(n_u \times n_u)} & 0_{(n_u \times n_s)} \\ 0_{(n_s \times n_u)} & \Delta\hat{\Omega}''_{(n_s \times n_s)} \end{pmatrix}_{n \times n} \tag{21}$$

is a positive semidefinite approximant to $\hat{\Omega}$ which is the same in the first n_u rows and columns.

Note that by construction, (19) gives the closest positive semidefinite approximant to the non-positive definite stressed correlation matrix with the constraint that the correlation terms outside the scenario matrix (represented by the first n_u rows and columns of the re-ordered matrix) remain unaltered. However, since we have the additional constraint that diagonal terms of the correlation matrix must equal one, we have to perform the normalisation shown in (19). Although the non-normalised stress matrix in (19) is the closest positive semi-definite approximant to $\hat{\Omega}$ in the Frobenius sense, we expect that the normalised stress matrix shown in (21) is near optimal.

4 EXAMPLE

Assume we have the following correlation matrix that corresponds to market variables S_i, $i = 1, \ldots, 4$.

$$\Omega = \begin{pmatrix} 1 & -0.55 & -0.15 & -0.10 \\ -0.55 & 1 & 0.40 & 0.30 \\ -0.15 & 0.40 & 1 & 0.50 \\ -0.10 & 0.30 & 0.50 & 1 \end{pmatrix}$$

We have selected S_1 to be negatively correlated with the other 3 variables. For example S_1 can represent an index's returns, and S_2, S_3, S_4 can represent implied volatilities (at different strikes and maturities) associated with this index.[1] The correlation matrix $\tilde{\Omega}$ is positive definite. Let the scenario be such that the general volatility in the market rises, increasing the correlations between the implied volatilities. The scenario includes only S_2, S_3, and S_4, ie, $\tilde{\Omega}$ is already the reordered correlation matrix. Assume that the target correlation matrix in this scenario is

$$
\hat{\Omega} = \begin{pmatrix}
1 & -0.55 & -0.15 & -0.10 \\
-0.55 & 1 & 0.90 & 0.90 \\
-0.15 & 0.90 & 1 & 0.90 \\
-0.10 & 0.90 & 0.90 & 1
\end{pmatrix}
$$

The target matrix is not positive definite. In the following let ρ_{ij} denote the correlation between daily returns or daily differences of S_i and S_j.

4.1 Sequential application of single stress

Assume that we first want to stress $\rho_{23} = 0.40$. By reordering, performing the Cholesky decomposition, finding (a, b, c), and applying Theorem 2.1 we find the allowed stress range for ρ_{23} as follows:

$$
\tilde{\Omega} = \begin{pmatrix}
1 & -0.10 & -0.55 & -0.15 \\
-0.10 & 1 & 0.30 & 0.50 \\
-0.55 & 0.30 & 1 & 0.40 \\
-0.15 & 0.50 & 0.40 & 1
\end{pmatrix}
$$

$$
\Rightarrow L = \begin{pmatrix}
1 & 0 & 0 & 0 \\
-0.10 & 0.9950 & 0 & 0 \\
-0.55 & 0.2462 & 0.7980 & 0 \\
-0.15 & 0.4874 & 0.2474 & 0.8238
\end{pmatrix}
$$

$$
\Rightarrow (a, b, c) = (0.7980, 0.2474, 0.8238)
$$
$$
\Rightarrow \Delta\rho_{23} \in (-0.8839, 0.4890) \Rightarrow (\rho_{23}\Delta\rho_{23}) \in (0.4839, 0.8890)
$$

We choose a point just inside the allowed range and replace 0.40 with 0.8890. Proceeding with the resulting matrix using the same steps to modify ρ_{24} and ρ_{34}, the resulting matrix is Ω_1 below. If, instead of the sequence $(\rho_{23}, \rho_{24}, \rho_{25})$ we (arbitrarily) choose another sequence, say $(\rho_{34}, \rho_{23}, \rho_{24})$, the resulting matrix would be Ω_2 as shown below.

$$
\Omega_1 = \begin{pmatrix} 1 & -0.55 & -0.15 & -0.10 \\ -0.55 & 1 & 0.8890 & 0.6103 \\ -0.15 & 0.8890 & 1 & 0.8141 \\ -0.10 & 0.6103 & 0.8141 & 1 \end{pmatrix},
$$

$$
\Omega_2 = \begin{pmatrix} 1 & -0.55 & -0.15 & -0.10 \\ -0.55 & 1 & 0.6460 & 0.8304 \\ -0.15 & 0.6460 & 1 & 0.8141 \\ -0.10 & 0.8304 & 0.9000 & 1 \end{pmatrix}
$$

4.2 Iterative-sequential application of single stress

Let us now take the two output matrices Ω_1 and Ω_2, and apply the same sequences of single stresses respectively. Then we continue recursively, ie, apply the same sequences to each output respectively until each correlation term on the matrix has converged. We choose the convergence criterion such that $\left| \rho_{ij}^k - \rho_{ij}^{k-1} \right| < 10^{-12}$ where k denotes the iteration number. The resulting matrix, using either of the sequences, is the same (up to the specified tolerance), and is given by

$$
\Omega_3 = \begin{pmatrix} 1 & -0.55 & -0.15 & -0.10 \\ -0.55 & 1 & 0.9000 & 0.8462 \\ -0.15 & 0.9000 & 1 & 0.9000 \\ -0.10 & 0.8462 & 0.9000 & 1 \end{pmatrix}
$$

It takes 3 and 4 iterations using the first and second sequences, respectively, to reach this outcome. Interestingly, both for this example and in every other matrix that we have tried, the iterative application of the single stress leads to the same final matrix, independent of the chosen sequence. Interestingly, ρ_{23} and ρ_{34} reach the target correlations (within machine precision) for this example, but this situation does not necessarily arise for other examples.

4.3 Local eigenvalue modification

We now proceed as follows:

$$
L = \begin{pmatrix}
1 & 0 & 0 & 0 \\
-0.55 & 0.8352 & 0 & 0 \\
-0.15 & 0.3802 & 0.9127 & 0 \\
-0.10 & 0.2934 & 0.4092 & 0.8582
\end{pmatrix}
$$

$$
L_u = \begin{pmatrix}
1 & 0 & 0 & 0 \\
-0.55 & 0 & 0 & 0 \\
-0.15 & 0 & 0 & 0 \\
-0.10 & 0 & 0 & 0
\end{pmatrix}, L_s = \begin{pmatrix}
0 & 0 & 0 & 0 \\
0 & 0.8352 & 0 & 0 \\
0 & 0.3802 & 0.9127 & 0 \\
0 & 0.2934 & 0.4092 & 0.8582
\end{pmatrix},
$$

$$
\hat{\Omega} - \Omega_u = \begin{pmatrix}
0 & 0 & 0 & 0 \\
0 & 0.6975 & 0.8175 & 0.8450 \\
0 & 0.8175 & 0.9445 & 0.8850 \\
0 & 0.8450 & 0.8850 & 0.9900
\end{pmatrix},
$$

$$
\Delta\hat{\Omega} = \begin{pmatrix}
0.6975 & 0.8175 & 0.8450 \\
0.8175 & 0.9775 & 0.8850 \\
0.8450 & 0.8850 & 0.9900
\end{pmatrix}
$$

By replacing the negative eigenvalue of $\Delta\hat{\Omega}$. with zeros, we obtain $\Delta\hat{\Omega}''$, With proper scaling as shown by (20), we find $\Delta\hat{\Omega}'$, and subsequently the solution Ω_4 as

$$
\Delta\hat{\Omega}' = \begin{pmatrix}
0.7201 & 0.8095 & 0.8332 \\
0.8095 & 0.9803 & 0.8892 \\
0.8332 & 0.8892 & 0.9962
\end{pmatrix}
$$

$$
\Rightarrow \Delta\hat{\Omega}'' = \begin{pmatrix}
0.6975 & 0.7956 & 0.8175 \\
0.7956 & 0.9775 & 0.8851 \\
0.8175 & 0.8851 & 0.9900
\end{pmatrix}
$$

$$
\Omega_4 = \Omega_u + \begin{pmatrix} 0 & 0_{1\times3} \\ 0_{3\times1} & \Delta\hat{\Omega}' \end{pmatrix} = \begin{pmatrix}
1 & -0.55 & -0.15 & -0.10 \\
-0.55 & 1 & 0.8781 & 0.8725 \\
-0.15 & 0.8781 & 1 & 0.9001 \\
-0.10 & 0.8725 & 0.9001 & 1
\end{pmatrix}
$$

It is not straightforward to compare Ω_3 to Ω_4. The latter loses optimality slightly due to the normalisation in $\Delta\hat{\Omega}''$. The former includes a non-optimal sequential single stress application at each iteration until convergence is achieved. Both results are good for all practical purposes.

5 SUMMARY

We have presented computationally efficient methodologies that enable local stressing of a correlation matrix. A risk manager can use these methodologies to obtain sensitivity of VaR computations to changes in correlation matrices.

1 It is generally the case that the implied volatility movements are negatively correlated with underlying stock returns.

This chapter was previously published in *The Journal of Risk* **5**(4), Summer 2003.

REFERENCES

Bhansali, V. and B. Wise, 2001, "Forecasting Portfolio Risk in Normal and Stressed Markets", *Journal of Risk* **4(1)**.

Cheng, S. H. and N. J. Higham, 1998, "A Modified Cholesky Algorithm Based on a Symmetric Indefinite Factorization", *SIAM Journal of Matrix Analysis and Applications* **19(4)**, pp. 1097–110.

Drmac, Z., M. Omladic, and K. Veselic, 1994, "On the Perturbation of the Cholesky Factorization", *SIAM Journal of Matrix Analysis and Applications* **15(4)**, pp. 1319–32.

Edelman, A. and W. F. Mascarenhas, 1995, "On Parlett's Matrix Norm Inequality for the Cholesky Decomposition", *Numerical Linear Algebra with Applications* **2(3)**, pp. 243–50.

Gill, P. E., W. Murray, and M. H. Wright, 1974, "Newton-type Methods for Unconstrained and Linearly Constrained Optimization", *Math. Programming* **28**, pp. 311–50.

Golub, G. H. and C. F. Van Loan, 1996, *Matrix Computations.* (Maryland: Johns Hopkins University), third edition.

Higham, N. J., 1988, "Computing a Nearest Symmetric Positive Semidefinite Matrix", *Linear Algebra and its Applications,* **103**, pp. 103–18.

Jäckel, P., 2002, *Monte Carlo Methods in Finance.* (New York: John Wiley and Sons Ltd).

Kupiec, P. H., 1998, "Stress Testing in a Value-at-Risk Framework", *The Journal of Derivatives* **6(1)**, pp. 7–24.

Rebonato, R. and P. Jäckel, 2000, "The Most General Methodology for Creating a Valid Correlation Matrix for Risk Management and Option Pricing Purposes", *Journal of Risk* **2(2)**, pp. 17–27.

Rodgers, J. L. and W. A. Nicewander, 1988, "Thirteen Ways to Look at the Correlation Coefficient", *The American Statistician* **42(1)**, pp. 59–66.

Schnabel, R. B. and E. Eskow, 1990, "A New Modified Cholesky Factorization", *SIAM J. Sci. Statist. Computing* **11**, pp. 1136–58.

Sun, J.-G., 1991, "Perturbation Bounds for the Cholesky and QR Factorizations", *BIT* **31(2)**, pp. 341–52.

12

Synchronising Multivariate Financial Time Series

Francesco Audrino; Peter Bühlmann*

Università della Svizzera Italiana; ETH Zürich

1 INTRODUCTION

The time of measurement of daily financial data – typically at the close of trading – varies because markets around the world have different trading hours. For example, markets in the US and Japan have no opening hours in common, and there is only partial overlap between those in the US and Europe. As a consequence, correlations across assets are often rather small[1] when such asynchronous data are used. Therefore, the value of real global portfolios constructed using daily data from different markets is never known at a fixed point in time, and attempts to calculate risk measures such as the value-at-risk (VaR, quantile of the profit-and-loss distribution of a given portfolio over a prescribed holding period) and the conditional VaR or expected shortfall (the expected loss given that the loss exceeds VaR) may lead to inaccurate and misleading results.

We propose here a method for the synchronisation of daily data in real global portfolios. Proceeding as in Burns, Engle and Mezrich (1998), our general approach recognises that even when a market is closed, the asset values may change before the market reopens. Synchronising the data involves estimating asset values at a specified (synchronisation) time point every day.[2] The estimated asset values at the same synchronisation time across markets are then referred to as

*We thank Michel Dacorogna for some interesting remarks. The data were provided by Olsen & Associates, Zürich, We also thank an anonymous referee and the Editor-in-Chief, Philippe Jorion, for constructive comments.

"synchronised". Unlike Burns, Engle and Mezrich (1998), who did not test the forecasting power of the synchronised data they obtained, we propose the use of any reasonable multivariate model for the constructed synchronised data and testing of their out-of-sample predictive performance for applications in risk management. In particular, to model the dynamics of the synchronised data, we consider the CCC-GARCH(1,1) model introduced by Bollerslev (1990), allowing for time-varying conditional variances and covariances but imposing constant conditional correlations. The CCC-GARCH(1,1) model for synchronised data represents a new and different model in terms of the original asynchronous data. This new model is referred to as "synchronous CCC-GARCH(1,1)" and allows an estimation of synchronisation and model parameters in a simultaneous way.

In our empirical investigations we compare the performance results obtained using synchronised and asynchronous data for a real global portfolio with daily log-returns of seven equity indices around the world. When synchronised data are used the resulting gains are sometimes considerable, depending on how we measure performance. Thus, this finding supports the usefulness of the synchronisation of the data in a first step. Our model for synchronised returns also yields some improvements over the synchronisation method of Burns, Engle and Mezrich (1998).

Moreover, our multivariate modelling approach, taking into account the synchronisation of the data, is superior to univariate models for a portfolio index that are exposed to a loss of information through the averaging of previous individual prices.[3] Moreover, we show that no gain over a simple univariate GARCH(1,1) model for the portfolio returns can be achieved using a multivariate GARCH model without synchronisation, confirming the recent results of Berkowitz and O'Brien (2002). We also find that univariate modelling yields risk estimates that are too conservative (validated by using backtests). For example, the capital needed to cover possible portfolio losses is usually overestimated by univariate modelling.

The plan of this chapter is as follows. Section 2 presents our synchronisation model and the corresponding estimation procedure. The empirical goodness-of-fit results for a real global portfolio of seven equity indices around the world are summarised in Section 3. Results are computed using our model in comparison with other standard approaches for synchronised and asynchronous data. In

Section 4 we discuss the impact of synchronisation on the calculation of risk measures such as the VaR and expected shortfall for the same seven-dimensional real data example. Section 5 includes a summary and presents our conclusions.

2 THE SYNCHRONOUS CCC-GARCH(1,1) MODEL

2.1 Synchronisation of the data

Our synchronisation technique follows very closely that proposed by Burns, Engle and Mezrich (1998). As an illustrative example, consider a global portfolio that includes stocks traded in London and New York. When New York closes, the value of the portfolio should be measured with an estimate of the value of the London stocks at the New York closing time. For example, to take the closing prices of the London stocks on a day when the US market falls by 1% after London has closed is inappropriate for pricing of the portfolio at the New York closing time.[4] We associate with synchronisation some estimates of the prices of shares traded in London at the New York closing time.[5]

We denote by $S_{t,j}, j = 1, \ldots M$, the continuous-time price of an asset j. The time t is here always measured as New York local time (in units of days), and $t \in \mathbb{N}$ corresponds to 4.00pm New York local time on day t. For example, $S_{1,1}$ denotes the price of an asset on the NYSE at 4.00pm New York local time on the first day. Since 4.00pm corresponds to 9.00pm in London, and since London closes four hours before New York at 5.00pm, the observed closing price of asset 2 in London on the first day would be denoted by $S_{0.83,2}$. This is illustrated in Figure 1, which is taken from Burns, Engle and Mezrich (1998).

Generally, the observed data are taken at the closing times of different markets. They have the structure

$$S_{t_j,j} (j = 1, \cdots, M), \quad \text{where} \quad t_j = t_1 - c_j \ (0 \le c_j < 1), j = 1, \ldots, M$$

We always synchronise to the closing time, t_1, in New York of asset $j = 1$, where $t_1 \in \{1, 2, \ldots, T\}$. The goal is to construct synchronised prices $S_{t,j}^s$, with $t \in \{1, 2, \ldots, T\}$, for all j. These prices, or the returns thereof, are more appropriate for many multivariate discrete time series models than their asynchronous counterparts.

Let us define the synchronised prices $S_{t,j}^s$ by

$$\log(S_{t,j}^s) = \mathbb{E}\left[\log(S_{t,j}) \mid \mathcal{F}_t\right], \quad \text{where} \quad \mathcal{F}_t = \{S_{t_j,j}; t_j \le t, j = 1, \ldots, M\}$$

$$(1)$$

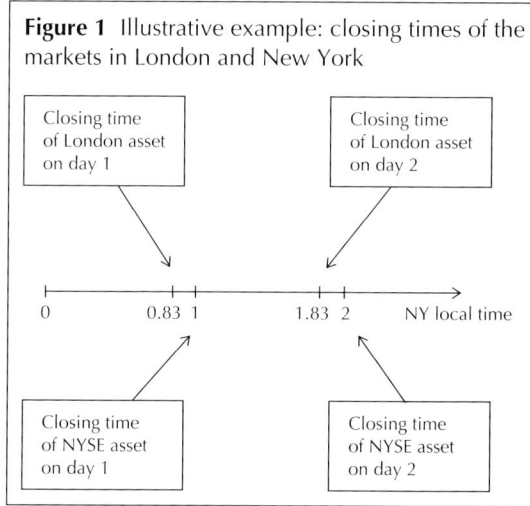

Figure 1 Illustrative example: closing times of the markets in London and New York

where logarithms are used to be consistent with continuously compounded returns. Hence, the synchronised log-prices are defined as the best predicted log-prices at t given the complete information, $\mathcal{F}_t$, of all *recorded* prices up to time t. Note that $\mathcal{F}_t$ contains only the prices $S_{t_{j,j}}$ with closing times $t_j \leq t$, and often with a strict relation $t_j < t$ if the trading place for equity j has a closing time other than that for the first equity in New York.

Clearly, if the closing price S is observed at time $t \in \mathbb{N}$, then its conditional expectation given $\mathcal{F}_t$ is the observed price. This is the case for the stocks from New York. If a market closes before t, then its past prices and those in all the other markets are potentially useful for predicting S at time t.

As a simplifying but reasonable approximation we assume that, given the information $\mathcal{F}_t$, the best predicted log-prices at t and at the nearest succeeding closing time $t_j + 1$ remain the same, saying that future changes from predictions at time t to predicted prices at $t_j + 1$ are unpredictable:

$$\log(S^s_{t,j}) = \mathbb{E}\left[\log(S_{t,j})\big|\mathcal{F}_t\right]$$
$$= \mathbb{E}\left[\log(S_{t_j+1,j})\big|\mathcal{F}_t\right], \quad t_j \leq t < t_j + 1 \ (t \in \mathbb{N}) \qquad (2)$$

The first equality holds by the definition in (1). As we will see, the approximation (2) allows us to derive the main synchronisation formula (7).

We denote the vector of negative log-returns (expressed as a percentage),[6] in different markets and at various time points on day t, by $\mathbf{X_t}$:

$$\mathbf{X_t} = -100 \cdot \begin{pmatrix} \log\left(\dfrac{S_{t_1,1}}{S_{t_1-1,1}}\right) \\ \vdots \\ \log\left(\dfrac{S_{t_M,M}}{S_{t_M-1,M}}\right) \end{pmatrix} = -100 \cdot (\log(\mathbf{S_t}) - \log(\mathbf{S_{t-1}})) \tag{3}$$

where $\mathbf{t} = (t_1, t_2, \ldots, t_M)$ is a multi-index.

We define the *synchronised returns* as the change in the logarithm of the synchronised prices:

$$\mathbf{X_t^s} = -100 \cdot \begin{pmatrix} \log\left(\dfrac{S_{t,1}^s}{S_{t-1,1}^s}\right) \\ \vdots \\ \log\left(\dfrac{S_{t,M}^s}{S_{t-1,M}^s}\right) \end{pmatrix} = -100 \cdot (\log(\mathbf{S_t^s}) - \log(\mathbf{S_{t-1}^s})), \quad t \in \mathbb{N} \tag{4}$$

The synchronised returns depend on unknown conditional expectations and have to be modelled (and estimated). We assume a simple "auxiliary" multivariate AR(1) model for the synchronisation, given by

$$\mathbf{X_t} = A \cdot \mathbf{X_{t-1}} + \epsilon_t \tag{5}$$

with errors ϵ_t such that $\mathbb{E}[\epsilon_t | \mathcal{F}_{t-1}] \equiv 0$, and A an $M \times M$ matrix. Contrary to the approach of Burns, Engle and Mezrich (1998), which employs a first-order vector moving average, we choose a first-order vector autoregressive synchronisation that considerably simplifies the analysis, since $\mathbb{E}[\mathbf{X_t} | \mathcal{F}_{t-1}]$ in (5) depends only on the previous $\mathbf{X_{t-1}}$ (due to the Markovian structure of an autoregressive model). As we will show in (7), the synchronised returns obtained with (5) are then functions of X_t and X_{t-1} only, and not of unobservable innovations ϵ_t or infinitely many lagged variables X_{t-1}, X_{t-2}, ... as in Burns, Engle and Mezrich (1998). Moreover, we will also provide empirical evidence that our synchronisation model incorporating (5) is better in terms of predictive performance than when a first-order vector moving average is used.

Substituting (2) into (4) yields the synchronised returns

$$X_t^s = -100 \cdot (\log(S_t^s) - \log(S_{t-1}^s))$$
$$= -100 \cdot (\mathbb{E}[\log(S_{t+1})|\mathcal{F}_t]) - \mathbb{E}[\log(S_t)|\mathcal{F}_{t-1}] \quad (6)$$

Now, we want the synchronised returns to be written only in terms of asynchronous returns. For this purpose, we add and subtract on the right-hand side of (6) the terms $\mathbb{E}[\log(S_t)|\mathcal{F}_t] = \log(S_t)$ for t and $t-1$. Substituting (3) and (5) into (6) then yields

$$X_t^s = -100 \cdot \left(\mathbb{E}\left[\log(S_{t+1}) - \log(S_t)|\mathcal{F}_t\right] \right.$$
$$\left. - \mathbb{E}\left[\log(S_t) - \log(S_{t-1})|\mathcal{F}_{t-1}\right] + \log\left(\frac{S_t}{S_{t-1}}\right) \right)$$
$$= \mathbb{E}\left[X_{t+1}|\mathcal{F}_t\right] - \mathbb{E}\left[X_t|\mathcal{F}_{t-1}\right] + X_t = X_t + A \cdot X_t - A \cdot X_t.$$

and thus

$$X_t^s = X_t + A \cdot (X_t - X_{t-1}) \quad (7)$$

The synchronised returns equal the asynchronous returns plus a correction, which consists of linear combinations of increments from time point $t-1$ to t, representing some aspects of the dynamics of the multivariate return process. Clearly, if A is the zero matrix, $X_t^s = X_t$ and the data are already synchronised. Since the New York market data are already synchronised, the row of A corresponding to the New York stocks is a zero row.

Computing synchronised returns from (7) boils down to estimating A in model (5) or a more specific version. An estimation procedure for A is described in Section 2.3.

2.2 The model

For the synchronised returns, we consider the standard CCC-GARCH(1,1) model introduced by Bollerslev (1990), allowing for time-varying conditional variances and covariances but imposing constant conditional correlations:

$$\mathbf{X}_t^s = \mathbf{\mu}_t^s + \mathbf{\epsilon}_t^s = \mathbf{\mu}_t^s + \sum_t{}^s \mathbf{Z}_t \quad (t \in \mathbb{Z})$$

$$\mathbf{X}_t^s = \mathbf{X}_t + A(\mathbf{X}_t - \mathbf{X}_{t-1}) = (I_M + A)\mathbf{X}_t - A\mathbf{X}_{t-1} \tag{8}$$

where we make the following assumptions:

(A1) $(\mathbf{Z}_t)_{t \in \mathbb{Z}}$ is a sequence of iid. multivariate innovation variables with spherical distribution (eg, the multivariate normal or the multivariate t distribution) with zero mean, covariance matrix cov $(\mathbf{Z}_t) = I_M$ and $\mathbf{Z}_t$ independent from $\{\mathbf{X}_k^s, \ k < t\}$;

(A2) (CCC construction) $\Sigma_t^s(\Sigma_t^s)' = H_t^s$ is almost surely positive definite for all t, where the typical element of H_t^s is $h_{ij,t}^s = \rho_{ij}^s(h_{ii,t}^s \, h_{jj,t}^s)^{1/2}$, for $i, j = 1, \ldots, M$;

(A3) (GARCH(1,1) part) $h_{ii,t}^s = (\sigma_{t,i}^s)^2 = \alpha_0^{(i)} + \alpha_1^{(i)}(X_{t-1,i}^s)^2 + \beta^{(i)}(\sigma_{t-1,i}^s)^2$, with $\alpha_0^{(i)}, \alpha_1^{(i)}, \beta^{(i)} > 0, \alpha_1^{(i)} + \beta^{(i)} < 1$ for $i = 1, \ldots, M$; and

(A5) $\mathbf{\mu}_t^s = \mathbb{E}[\mathbf{X}_t^s | \mathcal{F}_{t-1}] = (I_M + A)\mathbb{E}[\mathbf{X}_t | \mathcal{F}_{t-1}] - A\mathbf{X}_{t-1}, \mathbb{E}[\mathbf{X}_t | \mathcal{F}_{t-1}] = A\mathbf{X}_{t-1}$ (as in (5)).

We call this model "synchronous CCC-GARCH(1,1)". Note that ρ_{ij}^s in (A2) equals the constant conditional correlation corr $(X_{t,i}^s, X_{t,j}^s | \mathcal{F}_{t-1})$.

PROPOSITION 1 *Assume that the matrix $(I_M + A)$ is invertible. The synchronous CCC-GARCH(1,1) model (8) can be then represented with asynchronous returns $\mathbf{X}_t$ as*

$$\mathbf{X}_t = A \cdot \mathbf{X}_{t-1} + (I_M + A)^{-1}\Sigma_t^s \mathbf{Z}_t \tag{9}$$

where the matrix Σ_t^s has the same CCC-GARCH(1,1) structure already defined in (8).

Proposition 1 implies that the synchronous CCC-GARCH(1,1) model is still a constant conditional correlation model in terms of asynchronous data. Moreover, we should view it as a super-model of the classical CCC-GARCH(1,1) type: setting $A = 0$ yields the classical sub-model. Generally, A is a sparse parameter matrix whose structure will be estimated from data (see Section 2.3).

PROOF OF PROPOSITION 1 Using (7), the fact that $\mathbf{X}_{t-1} \in \mathcal{F}_{t-1}$ and (5), we calculate the conditional mean of the synchronised returns as

$$
\begin{aligned}
\mu_t^s &= \mathbb{E}\left[\mathbf{X}_s^t \,\big|\, \mathcal{F}_{t-1}\right] = \mathbb{E}\left[(I_M + A) \cdot \mathbf{X}_t \,\big|\, \mathcal{F}_{t-1}\right] - \mathbb{E}\left[A \cdot \mathbf{X}_{t-1} \,\big|\, \mathcal{F}_{t-1}\right] \\
&= (I_M + A) \cdot \mathbb{E}\left[\mathbf{X}_t \,\big|\, \mathcal{F}_{t-1}\right] - A \cdot \mathbf{X}_{t-1} \\
&= (I_M + A) \cdot A \cdot \mathbf{X}_{t-1} - A \cdot \mathbf{X}_{t-1} = A^2 \cdot \mathbf{X}_{t-1}
\end{aligned}
$$

It follows that (8) is equivalent to

$$
\mathbf{X}_t^s = A^2 \cdot \mathbf{X}_{t-1} + \Sigma_t^s \mathbf{Z}_t
$$

Using (7), we obtain the assertion

$$
\begin{aligned}
\mathbf{X}_t^s &= (I_M + A) \cdot \mathbf{X}_t - A \cdot \mathbf{X}_{t-1} = A^2 \cdot \mathbf{X}_{t-1} + \Sigma_t^s \mathbf{Z}_t \\
&\Leftrightarrow \mathbf{X}_t = (I_M + A)^{-1}(A + A^2) \cdot \mathbf{X}_{t-1} + (I_M + A)^{-1} \Sigma_t^s \mathbf{Z}_t \\
&\Leftrightarrow \mathbf{X}_t = A \cdot \mathbf{X}_{t-1} + (I_M + A)^{-1} \Sigma_t^s \mathbf{Z}_t
\end{aligned}
$$

2.3 Estimating the model

2.3.1 Model structure

The synchronous CCC-GARCH(1,1) model involves the matrix A: we insist on sparseness by setting the matrix elements to zero if they are found to be statistically insignificant. This is important to reduce the number of parameters in the case of high-dimensional portfolios with hundreds of assets. We proceed with a computationally fast and feasible procedure for estimating the structure (the nonzero elements) of the matrix A; the actual values of A will then be estimated by maximum likelihood in the model (8).

Step 1 Find the estimates for the M^2 parameters of the matrix A and for the matrix Σ using the Yule–Walker estimator.[7] The Yule–Walker covariance relations for a multivariate AR(1) model are given by

$$
\begin{aligned}
R(0) &= R(-1) \cdot A' + \Sigma = R(1)' \cdot A' + \Sigma \\
R(1) &= R(0) \cdot A', \quad \text{where } R(k) = \mathbb{E}[\mathbf{X}_{t-k} \cdot \mathbf{X}_t']
\end{aligned}
$$

Calculate some model-based standard errors of the estimated elements of A using a bootstrap strategy as follows. Compute residuals

$$
\hat{\mathbf{Z}}_t = (\hat{\Sigma}_t^s)^{-1}(\hat{\mathbf{X}}_t^s - \hat{\mu}_t^s)
$$

where $\hat{\mathbf{X}}_t^s$ and $\hat{\mu}_t^s$ involve the Yule–Walker estimate $\hat{A}$, and $\hat{\Sigma}_t^s$ involves the estimates $\hat{\alpha}_0^{(i)}$, $\hat{\alpha}_1^{(i)}$, $\hat{\beta}^{(i)}(i = 1, \ldots, M)$ and $\hat{\rho}_{ij} (i, j = 1, \ldots, M)$. Now do an iid. resampling from the empirical distribution of the residuals $\hat{\mathbf{Z}}_t$ to obtain

$$\mathbf{Z}_1^*, \ \mathbf{Z}_2^*, \ldots \mathbf{Z}_n^*$$

and generate recursively the bootstrap sample

$$\mathbf{X}_t^* = (I_M + \hat{A})^{-1}(X_t^{s*} + \hat{A}\mathbf{X}_{t-1}^*);$$
$$\mathbf{X}_t^{s*} = \hat{\mu}_t^{s*} + \Sigma_t^{s*}\mathbf{Z}_t^*;$$

$\hat{\Sigma}_t^{s*}$ satisfies (A2) and (A3) from Section 2.2 with estimated parameters and the lagged $X_{t-1,i}^{s*}$ and $\sigma_{t-1,i}$:

$\hat{\mu}_t^{s*}$ satisfies (A4) from Section 2.2 with estimated $\hat{A}$ and lagged X_{t-1}^*. This is a semi-parametric model-based bootstrap that is related to an early idea in Freedman (1984). Now, calculate standard errors:

$$\text{s.e.}(\hat{A}_{ij}) = \sqrt{\widehat{\text{var}(\hat{A}_{ij})}} = \sqrt{\frac{1}{B-1}\sum_{b=1}^{B}\left(\hat{A}_{ij(b)}^* - \overline{\hat{A}}_{ij}^*\right)^2}$$

where $\overline{\hat{A}}_{ij}^* = 1/B\sum_{b=1}^{B}\hat{A}_{ij(b)}^*$, $\hat{A}_{ij(b)}^*$ is the estimate of the ijth element of the matrix A in the bth bootstrap iteration and B is the number of bootstrap iterations.

Step 2 Set $A_{ij} = 0$ if the t-statistics

$$t_{ij} = \left|\frac{\hat{A}_{ij}}{\text{s.e.}(\hat{A}_{ij})}\right| \le 1.96 \quad (5\% \text{ significance level})$$

and $A_{ij} = 0$ for all j, with i corresponding to the New York stocks (in our case $i = 1$).

2.3.2 Parameter estimation
The parameters $A, \alpha_0^{(j)}, \alpha_1^{(j)}, \beta^{(j)}, \rho_{ij}^s (j = 1, \ldots, M)$ in the synchronous CCC-GARCH(1,1) model (9) can be estimated with the maximum likelihood method. We assume the innovations $\mathbf{Z}_t$ to be multivariate t_ν-distributed with zero mean and covariance matrix $\text{cov}(\mathbf{Z}_t) = I_M$,

where the number of degrees of freedom, ν, also has to be estimated, ie, $\mathbf{Z}_t \sim t_\nu(0, I_M)$. The negative log-likelihood is then given by

$$
-l\left(\theta; X_2^n\right) = \frac{TM}{2} \log(\pi \nu) - T \log \left(\frac{\Gamma\left(\dfrac{M + \nu}{2}\right)}{\Gamma\left(\dfrac{\nu}{2}\right)} \right) + \frac{T}{2} \log |R^s|
$$

$$
+ \sum_{t=1}^{T} \left(\log \left| \sqrt{(\nu - 2) / \nu} \; D_t^s \right| \right)
$$

$$
+ \frac{M + \nu}{2} \sum_{t=2}^{T} \left(\log \left(1 + \frac{(\epsilon_t^s)'(R^s)^{-1}\epsilon_t^s}{\nu} \right) \right) - T \log \left(\left\| (I_M + A) \right\| \right)
$$

(10)

where, from the CCC-construction, $H_t^s = D_t^s R^s D_t^s$, with D_t^s a diagonal $M \times M$ matrix with diagonal elements $\sigma_{t,1}^s, \ldots, \sigma_{t,M}^s$, $R^s = [\rho_{ij}^s]_{1 \le i, j \le M}$ and

$$
\epsilon_t^s = \left(\sqrt{(\nu - 2) / \nu} \; D_t^s \right)^{-1} (\mathbf{X}_t^s - \mathbf{\mu}_t^s)
$$

θ denotes the vector of all parameters involved and $\mathbf{X}_t^s = \mathbf{X_t} + A(\mathbf{X_t} - \mathbf{X_{t-1}})$ as before. Also, we use the sparse structure of the matrix A as described above.

For a preliminary correlation matrix estimate $\hat{R}^s = I_M$, we estimate the remaining parameters of the matrix A and the parameters $\alpha_0^{(j)}, \alpha_1^{(j)}, \beta^{(j)} (j = 1, \ldots, M)$ by minimising the negative log-likelihood in (10). This yields estimates $\hat{\mu}_t^s = (\hat{\mu}_{t,1}^s, \ldots, \hat{\mu}_{t,M}^s)$ and $\hat{\sigma}_{t,j}^s, j = 1, \ldots, M$. We then construct the estimate for the correlation matrix R^s as follows. We build the residuals

$$
\hat{\epsilon}_{t,j} = (\hat{X}_{t,j}^s - \hat{\mu}_{t,j}^s) / \hat{\sigma}_{t,j}^s, \quad t = 1, \ldots, T
$$

and define

$$
\hat{R}^s = T^{-1} \sum_{t=1}^{T} \hat{\epsilon}_t \hat{\epsilon}_t^T, \quad \hat{\epsilon}_t = (\hat{\epsilon}_{t,1}, \ldots, \hat{\epsilon}_{t,M})^T
$$

(11)

We can then iterate (once) by minimising the negative log-likelihood in (10) using $\hat{R}^s$ from (11).

3 NUMERICAL RESULTS

We consider a global portfolio of seven equity indices: the US Dow Jones Industrial Average (DJIA), the French CAC40 Index, the German Deutsche Aktien (DAX), the Italian BCI General Index, the Dutch CBS All-Share, the UK FTSE-A All-Share Index (FTAS) and the Japanese NIKKEI 225 Average (NIK). The daily data are taken from the time period between January 17, 1990 and June 22, 1994, corresponding to 1,000 days without holidays in the different countries (ie, a holiday in one country led to that day being omitted in all the components of the whole multivariate series). The closing times for the seven market indices are given in Table 1.

We use here (negative) relative difference returns (in percentages):

$$X_{t_j,j} = -100 \cdot \frac{S_{t_j,j} - S_{t_j-1,j}}{S_{t_j-1,j}}$$

where $St_{j,j}$ denotes the price of the asset j at the local closing time, t_j, on day t because they are close approximations of the log-returns and because they allow for much simpler portfolio and risk computations as used in Section 3.3. Nevertheless, we still synchronise such relative difference returns as in (7).

The aim of this section is to provide empirical support for the effect of synchronisation. We compare our synchronous CCC-GARCH(1,1) model in (9) with the asynchronous classical CCC-GARCH(1,1) model and the synchronous approach of Burns, Engle

Table 1 Closing times for a seven-dimensional real data example consisting of (negative) equity index return series of developed capital markets around the world

Index	Closing time	
	Local time	**NY time**
NIKKEI	3.00pm	2.00am
CBS	5.30pm	11.30am
BCI	5.30pm	11.30am
CAC40	5.30pm	11.30am
FTAS	5.00pm	12.00pm
DAX	8.00pm	2.00pm
DJIA	4.00pm	4.00pm

and Mezrich (1998). Note that all goodness-of-fit measures and out-of-sample tests in this section are computed for the usual asynchronous returns. This allows us to compare our results with those obtained with other approaches. For the numerical optimisation of log-likelihoods we use a quasi-Newton method.

3.1 Estimate of A and synchronisation

We first examine the effect of synchronisation from a descriptive point of view. The parsimoniously estimated matrix A is obtained using the procedure for structure determination described in Section 2.3 and from maximum likelihood in (10):

$$\hat{A} = \begin{pmatrix} 0 & 0 & 0 & 0 & 0 & 0 & 0 \\ 0.2223 & 0 & 0.0189 & 0.0212 & 0 & 0 & -0.0663 \\ 0.3012 & 0.0873 & -0.0086 & 0 & 0 & 0 & -0.0916 \\ 0.2883 & 0 & 0 & 0 & -0.0107 & 0.0970 & -0.0164 \\ 0.2493 & 0 & -0.0033 & 0 & 0 & 0 & -0.0401 \\ 0.1749 & 0 & 0 & 0.0073 & 0 & 0.0412 & -0.0507 \\ 0.3168 & 0.0510 & 0 & 0 & 0 & 0 & 0 \end{pmatrix} \quad (12)$$

where the variables are ordered as DJIA, CAC40, DAX, BCI, CBS, FTAS, NIK. The column with the highest coefficients (in terms of magnitude) corresponds to the DJIA: there is substantial predictability of all other markets from the DJIA the day before. Besides the US market being a major determining factor in the financial world, the observed pattern is natural since the exchange in New York is the last to close. There also seems to be predictability of all other markets from the Japanese returns (NIK), although in this case the coefficients are small and negative. The negative sign, acting as a kind of correction impulse for the European indices, could be explained by some joint effect from the DJIA and the NIK index and could be a consequence of the large impact of the US market on the Japanese market. In addition, the German DAX and the British FTAS seem to be autocorrelated. The coefficients for the three markets that close simultaneously (French, Italian and Dutch) are all equal to zero, except for two which are still close to zero but have t-statistics below 2.3. All the other coefficients have t-statistics greater than 3 except the three coefficients in Germany and the -0.0164 and -0.0401 in Japan.

Using $\hat{A}$ from (12) and the synchronisation formula (7), we obtain the synchronised returns $\hat{X}_t^s$. The effect of synchronisation in terms of empirical correlations is described in Table 2: synchronised data often exhibit larger instantaneous correlations between different returns from indices from the same day.

The empirical correlations are typically too small for highly asynchronous markets. This is the case, for example, for the US and the Japanese markets: the empirical correlation between the DJIA and the NIK is much bigger with synchronisation (0.328 vs. ~0.189). Of course, there is no reason to believe that synchronisation would always yield higher correlations. This result is consistent with and similar to the analysis in Burns, Engle and Mezrich (1998).

However, it is important to remark here that empirical (unconditional) correlations have no direct relation to empirical conditional quantities such as volatility or risk measures, eg, the VaR defined in Section 4. In the following sections we will demonstrate empirically that our synchronous CCC-GARCH(1,1) model has lower mean volatility when averaged over time and multivariate components, and that it leads to lower, less conservative risk estimates than the asynchronous CCC-GARCH(1,1) model.

3.2 Estimates for the synchronous CCC-GARCH(1,1) model and its performance

The parameters are estimated by maximum likelihood as in Section 2.3. To quantify the goodness-of-fit of the models, we consider the following statistics:

AIC statistic:

$$-2 \log \text{-likelihood} + 2(\text{number of parameters})$$

Outsample – Log-likelihood:

$$-\log \text{-likelihood} \, (\tilde{X}_1^T; \hat{A}, \hat{V}, \hat{R}^s, \{\hat{\alpha}_0^{(j)}, \hat{\alpha}_1^{(j)}, \hat{\beta}^{(j)}; j = 1, \ldots, M\})$$

where $\tilde{X}_1^T = \tilde{X}_1, \ldots, \tilde{X}_T$ are new test data, and the parameter estimates, equipped with hats, are from the training sample $X_1^n = X_1, \ldots, X_n$. The likelihood itself is given in (10). The two statistics are measures for out-of-sample performance. A low value for the statistics indicates that the model is better. In our analysis, we

Table 2 *Top*: instantaneous empirical correlations between components of usual asynchronous returns, $\mathbf{X}_t$, for a seven-dimensional series of (negative) equity index returns. *Bottom*: instantaneous empirical correlations between components of estimated synchronised returns, $\hat{\mathbf{X}}_t^s$, using the synchronous CCC-GARCH(1,1) model

	DJIA	CAC40	DAX	BCI	CBS	FTAS	NIK
Raw empirical correlations							
DJIA	1	0.26569	0.23928	0.11794	0.13863	0.21754	0.18972
CAC40	0.26569	1	0.75794	0.51368	0.76965	0.70239	0.31629
DAX	0.23928	0.75794	1	0.55304	0.76055	0.59974	0.32281
BCI	0.11794	0.51368	0.55304	1	0.56079	0.47805	0.25427
CBS	0.13863	0.76965	0.76055	0.56079	1	0.73521	0.29812
FTAS	0.21754	0.70239	0.59974	0.47805	0.73521	1	0.30296
NIK	0.18972	0.31629	0.32281	0.25427	0.29812	0.30296	1
Synchronous empirical correlations							
DJIA	1	0.36616	0.38101	0.27009	0.29308	0.31922	0.32770
CAC40	0.36616	1	0.80167	0.56694	0.78070	0.70587	0.31191
DAX	0.38101	0.80167	1	0.57977	0.77477	0.62009	0.28068
BCI	0.27009	0.56694	0.57977	1	0.58814	0.53707	0.28324
CBS	0.29308	0.78070	0.77477	0.58814	1	0.73965	0.28781
FTAS	0.31922	0.70587	0.62009	0.53707	0.73965	1	0.28548
NIK	0.32770	0.31191	0.28068	0.28324	0.28781	0.28548	1

take $n = 1{,}000$ and the test-set values $\tilde{\mathbf{X}}_1^T = \mathbf{X}_{n+1}^{n+500}$ are the next 500 consecutive observations (days between June 23, 1994 and September 9, 1996). We take $T = 500$ (a little more than two years) because it seems a reasonable period over which the multivariate return series of the seven equity indices are believed to be stationary (at least approximately).

The resulting values for the AIC statistic and the out-of-sample negative log-likelihood (OS-neg.LL) statistic are:

Synchronous CCC-GARCH(1,1): 19058.3 (AIC), 4235.9 (OS-neg.LL)
Classical CCC-GARCH(1,1): 19137.9 (AIC), 4285.9 (OS-neg.LL)

The synchronous CCC-GARCH(1,1) model is better than the asynchronous CCC-GARCH(1,1) model with respect to both statistics, although the difference is small (in the order of 1%). Moreover, the synchronous CCC-GARCH(1,1) model also yields some improvement over the model for synchronised returns proposed by Burns, Engle and Mezrich (1998), for which the respective statistics are 19064.9 (AIC) and 4247.2 (OS-neg.LL).

We also report here the mean of absolute empirical correlations between actual outsample values $\tilde{X}_{t,i}\tilde{X}_{t,j}, t = 1, \ldots, T$, and one-step-ahead predicted values of the conditional covariance, $\text{cov}(\tilde{X}_{t,i}, \tilde{X}_{t,j} \mid \tilde{\mathbf{X}}_{t-1}, \tilde{\mathbf{X}}_{t-2}, \ldots), t = 1, \ldots, T$, averaged over all possible components $1 \leq i \leq j \leq M$:

Synchronous CCC-GARCH(1,1): 0.1325
Synchronous model of Burns, Engle and Mezrich (1998): 0.1233
Classical CCC-GARCH(1,1): 0.1139

As before, the differences between the models seem to be small, although our methodology shows some improvement. Such small differences could be obscured by the low signal-to-noise ratio the unobservable conditional covariances are replaced by their corresponding actual return values, which are noisy estimates. It is often useful to consider differences of performance terms and to use the concept of hypothesis testing, rather than quantify differences in terms of percentages. Testing our synchronisation method on the seven-dimensional asynchronous equity index returns against both the asynchronous CCC-GARCH(1,1) model and the synchronisation method of Burns, Engle and Mezrich (1998), we find evidence of statistical significance, implying that our synchronous model is to be preferred over both alternatives. The exact construction of the tests, as well as a description of the results, is deferred to Appendix A.

3.3 Estimating performance at the portfolio level

We now examine the effect of synchronisation for the estimation of volatility in a portfolio. Let P_t denote the price of a portfolio on day t:

$$P_t = \sum_{j=1}^{7} \alpha_j S_{t,j}, \quad t = 1, \dots, m \tag{13}$$

This portfolio employs a constant division of assets. For illustrative purposes, we use the data $S_{t,i}$ from before and choose $\alpha_1 = 0.4$, $\alpha_2 = \dots = \alpha_6 = 0.08$ and $\alpha_7 = 0.2$, corresponding roughly to the market capitalisation of the different stock exchanges. We also translate all prices to US dollars, using daily currency exchange rates. It is known that the (negative) portfolio returns Δ_t on day t then become a linear combination of the individual (negative) asset returns X_t:

$$\Delta_t = -100 \cdot \left(\frac{P_t - P_{t-1}}{P_{t-1}} \right) = -100 \cdot \frac{\sum_{j=1}^{7} \alpha_j (S_{t,j} - S_{t-1,j})}{P_{t-1}}$$

$$= \sum_{j=1}^{7} \left(\frac{\alpha_j S_{t-1,j}}{P_{t-1}} \left(-100 \cdot \frac{S_{t,j} - S_{t-1,j}}{S_{t-1,j}} \right) \right) = \beta'_{t-1} X_t$$

where

$$\beta_{t-1,j} = \alpha_j \frac{S_{t-1,j}}{P_{t-1}}, \quad t = 1, \dots, 7 \tag{14}$$

Our general model for Δ_t is

$$\Delta_t = \mu_{t,P} + \epsilon_t = \mu_{t,P} + \sigma_{t,P} Z_t$$

where $\mu_{t,P} \in R$ and $\sigma_{t,P} \in R^+$ are measurable functions of $\mathcal{F}_{t-1}$ (see (1)).

We compare portfolio volatility estimates from the following four models: the multivariate synchronous CCC-GARCH(1,1) model (9), the synchronous model introduced by Burns, Engle and

Mezrich (1998), the asynchronous CCC-GARCH(1,1) model and a classical GARCH(1,1) univariate analysis (and extensions thereof) for the portfolio returns Δ_t. Clearly, the different approaches give rise to different $\mu_{t,P}$ and $\sigma_{t,P}$. Note that, in the more realistic case, the weights $\alpha_i = \alpha_{t,i}$ depend on t. As a consequence, the univariate analysis of the returns Δ_t will be inappropriate because the returns of portfolio prices would typically be far from stationarity.

For univariate analysis based on returns Δ_t, we always assume the model

$$\Delta_t = \mu_{t,P} + \epsilon_t = \phi\Delta_{t-1} + \phi_{t,P}Z_t \qquad (15)$$

where $\sigma_{t,P}$ is a measurable function of previous returns $\Delta_{t-1}, \Delta_{t-2}, \cdots$, and iid. innovations $Z_t \sim \sqrt{(v-2)/v}t_v$. The scaling factor $\sqrt{(v-2)/v}$ is used so that var $(Z_t) = 1$. The univariate GARCH(1,1) specification is

$$\sigma_{t,P}^2 = \alpha_0 + \alpha_1\epsilon_{t-1}^2 + \beta\sigma_{t-1,P}^2, \qquad \epsilon_{t-1} = \Delta_{t-1} - \phi\Delta_t$$

where $\alpha_0, \alpha_1, \beta > 0$. The negative log-likelihood, conditioned on the first observation Δ_1 and some starting value $\sigma_{1,P}$ (eg, the square root of the sample variance), is then

$$- l(\alpha_0, \alpha_1, \beta, \phi, v; \Delta_2^n) = - \sum_{t=2}^{n} \log\left(c(v)^{-1}\sigma_{t,P}^{-1}f_{t_v}\left(\frac{\Delta_t - \phi\Delta_{t-1}}{c(v)\sigma_{t,P}}\right)\right),$$

$$c(v) = ((v-2)/v)^{1/2} \qquad (16)$$

where f_{t_v} denotes the density of the univariate t_v distribution. Minimising the negative log-likelihood yields estimates $\hat{\mu}_{t,P} = \hat{\phi}\Delta_{t-1}$ and $\hat{\sigma}_{t,P}^2 = \hat{\alpha}_0 + \hat{\alpha}_1\epsilon_{t-1}^2 + \hat{\beta}\sigma_{t-1,P}^2$. In particular, we find the parameter estimates $\hat{\alpha}_0 = 0.020, \hat{\alpha}_1 = 0.049, \hat{\beta} = 0.917, \hat{\phi} = 0.154$ and $\hat{v} = 5.659$.

When using the multivariate synchronous CCC-GARCH(1,1) model, we calculate estimates of the portfolio conditional means $\hat{\mu}_{t,P}$ and variances $\hat{\sigma}_{t,P}^2, t = 1, \ldots, n$ as follows. We always take the innovations $\mathbf{Z}_t$ of the model (9) to be multivariate t_v-distributed (v unknown) with zero mean and covariance matrix cov$(\mathbf{Z}) = I_M$. Using the representation in Proposition 1, assuming that $(I_M + A)^{-1}$

exists, it follows that the asynchronous returns $\mathbf{X}_t$ given the information up to time $t-1$ are multivariate t_ν-distributed:

$$\mathbf{X}_t\big|\mathcal{F}_{t-1} \sim t_\nu\left(A\mathbf{X}_{t-1},(I_M + A)^{-1}\Sigma_t^s((I_M + A)^{-1}\Sigma_t^s)'\right)$$

Exploiting a nice property of elliptical distributions,[8] we see that the portfolio return Δ_t given the information up to time $t-1$ is univariate t_ν-distributed with the following mean and variance:

$$\Delta_t\big|\mathcal{F}_{t-1} \sim t_\nu(\beta'_{t-1}A\mathbf{X}_{t-1},\beta'_{t-1}(I_M + A)^{-1}\Sigma_t^s(\beta'_{t-1}(I_M + A)^{-1}\Sigma_t^s)')$$

where the vector of coefficients β_{t-1} is given in (14). Thus, we compute

$$\hat{\mu}_{t,P} = \beta'_{t-1}\hat{A}\mathbf{X}_{t-1}$$

and

$$\hat{\sigma}_{t,P}^2 = \beta'_{t-1}(I_M + \hat{A})^{-1}\hat{\Sigma}_t^s(\beta'_{t-1}(I_M + A)^{-1}\hat{\Sigma}_t^s)'$$

where $\hat{A}$ and $\hat{\Sigma}_t^s$ are the maximum likelihood estimates in the model (9). The estimates from the classical asynchronous CCC-GARCH(1,1) model are of the same form but with $\hat{A} = 0$ and $\hat{\Sigma}_t^{\text{asynch}}$.

The predicted portfolio conditional variances using the synchronous CCC-GARCH(1,1) model, the asynchronous CCC-GARCH(1,1) model and a univariate GARCH(1,1) model for the portfolio returns are plotted in Figure 2.

The predicted (squared) volatilities are generally larger when the univariate approach is used. This seems to be due to the fact that univariate approaches are exposed to an information loss through the averaging of individual prices. It may cause a bias that results in higher risk estimates for the data set considered here (see Section 4). In contrast, multivariate methods do not estimate the portfolio dynamics directly but are based on a multivariate analysis of all individual return series before the portfolio volatility predictions are constructed. The differences between the two multivariate methods are (visibly) much smaller.

Now we test the goodness of the residuals

Figure 2 Predicted portfolio conditional variances, $\hat{\sigma}^2_{t,P}$, for the backtesting period between June 23, 1994 and September 9, 1996 (500 trading days). Predictions are constructed using a standard univariate Garch(1,1) model on the (negative) port folio returns (*solid line*), and both the synchronous CCC-GARCH(1,1) model (*dotted line*) and the standard CCC-GARCH(1,1) model without synchronisation (*dashed line*) on the seven-dimensional series of (negative) equity index returns

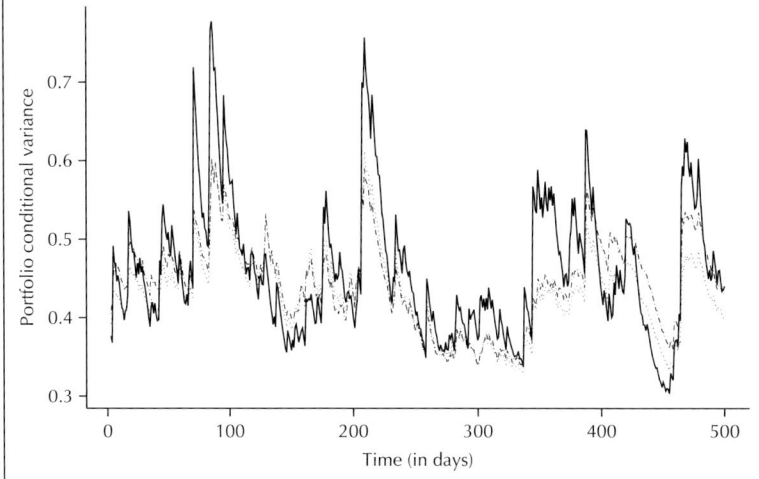

$$\hat{Z}_t = \frac{\tilde{\Delta}_t - \hat{\mu}_{t,P}}{\hat{\sigma}_{t,P}}, \quad t = 1, \ldots, T \tag{17}$$

in the different approaches. Here $\tilde{\Delta}_t$ is from new test-set data $\Delta_{n+1}, \ldots, \Delta_{n+500}$ over the next 500 days; and $\hat{\mu}_{t;P}$ and $\hat{\sigma}_{t;P}$ are from the different models, estimated with the training data $\Delta_1, \ldots, \Delta_n$, and naturally evaluated using the immediate lagged values in the test set.

We are particularly interested in the null hypothesis that the dynamics of the (negative) portfolio returns follow model (15). Under the null hypothesis and assuming Gaussian innovations, the statistic $\sqrt{T}\bar{Z}$ is approximately standard normally distributed. The observed values, including the corresponding P-values in parentheses, of the test for the synchronous CCC-GARCH(1,1), the asynchronous CCC-GARCH(1,1) and the univariate model are -1.570 (0.058), -1.898 (0.029) and -1.527 (0.063), respectively. Thus, only the asynchronous CCC-GARCH(1,1) model appears to be incompatible with the data.

Table 3 Values of different portfolio out-of-sample goodness-of-fit statistics. Results are computed using the synchronous CCC-GARCH(1,1) model, the synchronous BEM model of Burns, Engle and Mezrich (1998), and the CCC-GARCH(1,1) model without synchronisation on the seven-dimensional series of (negative) equity index returns, and a standard AR(1)–GARCH(1,1) model on the univariate series of (negative) portfolio returns

	Synchronous CCC-GARCH (1,1)	Synchronous BEM model	CCC-GARCH (1,1) without synchronisation	Univariate approach
OS-PL$_1$	210.0009	211.6876	218.7766	216.5164
OS-PL$_2$	227.6059	230.9892	241.4637	234.3302
Port. out. log-lik.	459.5995	461.8611	469.9058	464.3049

To quantify the goodness-of-fit of the models, we consider again the out-of-sample log-likelihood performance:

$$-\text{log-likelihood}\left(\tilde{\Delta}_1^T; \hat{\mu}_{t;P}, \hat{\sigma}_{t,P}, \hat{\nu}\right)$$

where, as in (17), $\tilde{\Delta}_1^T = \Delta_{n+1}^{n+500}$ are new test data and $\hat{\mu}_{t,P}, \hat{\sigma}_{t,P}$ are estimated from the training data. The exact form of the log-likelihood is given in (16). In addition, we consider the following out-of-sample prediction loss statistics:

$$\text{OS-PL}_i = \sum_{t=1}^{T}\left|\hat{\sigma}_{t,P}^2 - (\tilde{\Delta}_t - \hat{\mu}_{t,P})^2\right|^i, \quad i = 1, 2$$

The OS-PL statistics and the portfolio out-of-sample log-likelihood are, as before, measures of predictive performance. A low value for the statistics indicates that the model is better.

The values of these statistics are summarised in Table 3. Results are computed using the multivariate synchronous CCC-GARCH(1,1) model, the synchronous model of Burns, Engle and Mezrich (1998) (denoted BEM), the asynchronous CCC-GARCH(1,1) model and a standard univariate GARCH(1,1) analysis of the negative portfolio returns.

As with the results reported in Section 3.2, we again find that the synchronous CCC-GARCH(1,1) model performs better at the portfolio level than the asynchronous CCC-GARCH(1,1) model or the univariate approach with respect to all goodness-of-fit measures. Table 3 also shows that, in this case, the improvements are more relevant than at the multivariate level. In particular, with respect to the OS-PL performances the values decrease by 3–6%. The synchronous CCC-GARCH(1,1) model also yields some improvements over the synchronous BEM model. In contrast, the univariate GARCH(1,1) analysis exhibits slight advantages over multivariate modelling without the use of synchronisation.

As already mentioned in Section 3.2, more impressive gains may be masked by a low signal-to-noise ratio. The t- and sign-type tests described in Appendix A can be used to better compare the accuracy of the estimates from the different approaches, also at the portfolio level. The results are summarised in Table 4.

The t-type tests yield significant differences only in the comparison between the synchronous CCC-GARCH(1,1) model and the univariate approach, preferring the former over the latter. This may be just a fact of low power due to non-Gaussian observations. In contrast, the sign-type tests, which are robust against deviations from Gaussianity, yield significant results in most cases. The synchronous CCC-GARCH(1,1) model is better than both alternatives, whereas the univariate approach is about as good as (maybe slightly better than) the asynchronous CCC-GARCH(1,1) model. It seems that classical multivariate modelling without synchronisation does not yield any particular gain over a simple univariate analysis of the portfolio returns, confirming the results found recently by Berkowitz and O'Brien (2002).[9]

4 ESTIMATING RISK MEASURES

We will now test the effect of synchronisation on the computation of conditional (dynamical) risk measures for negative portfolio returns Δ_t following (14)–(15) given the information $\mathcal{F}_{t-1}$ from previous prices. The most popular risk measure, which has also been adopted for regulatory purposes,[10] is VaR. A one-day VaR is given by

$$\delta_q^1 = \inf\{\delta \in \mathbb{R} : F_{\Delta_t|\mathcal{F}_{t-1}}(\delta) \geq q\}, \quad 0 < q < 1$$

where $F_{\Delta_t|\mathcal{F}_{t-1}}(\cdot)$ denotes the cumulative distribution function of Δ_t given $\mathcal{F}_{t-1}$ and q is the confidence level at which we want to compute

Table 4 Testing differences of performance terms between Model 1 and Model 2 at the portfolio level. We consider three different models: the synchronous CCC-GARCH(1,1) model and the classical CCC-GARCH(1,1) model without synchronisation on the seven-dimensional series of (negative) equity index returns, and a standard AR(1)-GARCH(1,1) model on the univariate series of (negative) portfolio returns. The values of t-type and sign-type test statistics adapted to the case of dependent observations are summarised. The corresponding P-values are given in parentheses

		Performance measure	
Model 1	Model 2	Portfolio out. log-likelihood	OS-PL$_2$
t-type tests			
Synchronous CCC-GARCH(1,1)	Asynchronous CCC-GARCH(1,1)	−1.3944 (0.082)	−1.3738 (0.085)
Synchronous CCC-GARCH(1,1)	Univariate approach	−1.7781 (0.038)	−2.1519 (0.016)
Asynchronous CCC-GARCH(1,1)	Univariate approach	0.6822 (0.248)	0.7238 (0.235)
Sign-type tests			
Synchronous CCC-GARCH(1,1)	Asynchronous CCC-GARCH(1,1)	2.0393 (0.021)	2.1820 (0.015)
Synchronous CCC-GARCH(1,1)	Univariate approach	−0.5808 (0.281)	1.7631 (0.039)
Asynchronous CCC-GARCH(1,1)	Univariate approach	−1.7456 (0.040)	0.0486 (0.481)

the VaR. This is the quantile of the predictive distribution of the negative portfolio return over the next day.

A second, widely used risk measure is the so-called "expected shortfall" or "conditional VaR", which is defined as the expected loss on condition that the loss has exceeded the VaR. Thus, a one-day expected shortfall is

$$S_q^t = E\left[\Delta_t \,\middle|\, \Delta_t > \delta_q^t, \mathcal{F}_{t-1}\right], \quad 0 < q < 1$$

where, as before, q is the confidence level. We typically choose $q \in \{0.90, 0.95, 0.99\}$ (note that we consider negative returns). The expected shortfall is a coherent measure of risk.[11] The empirical investigations of the next sections are performed for the same real global portfolio consisting of the seven equity indices listed in Section 3.3.

4.1 The estimates

We assume that the dynamics of the negative asynchronous portfolio returns, $\Delta_t (t \in \mathbb{Z})$, are given by (15). Since

$$F_{\Delta_t | \mathcal{F}_{t-1}}(\delta) = P\left[\mu_{t,P} + \sigma_{t,P} Z_t \leq \delta \,\middle|\, \mathcal{F}_{t-1}\right] = F_Z\left(\frac{\delta - \mu_{t,P}}{\sigma_{t,P}}\right)$$

the risk measures can be written as

$$\delta_q^t = \mu_{t,P} + \sigma_{t,P} z_q, \quad 0 < q < 1$$

and

$$S_q^t = \mu_{t,P} + \sigma_{t,P} E[Z \,|\, Z > z_q], \quad 0 < q < 1$$

where z_q is the qth quantile of $F_Z(\cdot)$, which by assumption does not depend on time, t.

Estimates of the VaR and of the expected shortfall are constructed using the assumption of scaled t_ν-distributed innovations Z_t in (15), ie, $Z_t \sim \sqrt{(\nu - 2)/\nu}\, t_\nu$. Thus, an estimate for the VaR is given by

$$\hat{\delta}_q^t = \hat{\mu}_{t,P} + \hat{\sigma}_{t,P} \sqrt{\frac{\hat{\nu} - 2}{\hat{\nu}}} \tilde{z}q$$

Figure 3 Expected shortfall estimates, $\hat{S}_t^q$, for the (negative) portfolio returns $\tilde{\Delta}_t$ during the backtesting period beginning June 23, 1994 and ending September 9, 1996 (for a total of 500 trading days). The estimates $\hat{S}_t^q$ for $q = 0.95$ (*top*) and $q = 0.99$ (*bottom*) are obtained using a standard univariate GARCH(1,1) model on the (negative) portfolio returns (*solid line*), and both the synchronous CCC-GARCH(1,1) model (*dotted line*) and the standard CCC-GARCH(1,1) model without synchronisation (*dashed line*) on the seven-dimensional series of (negative) equity index returns

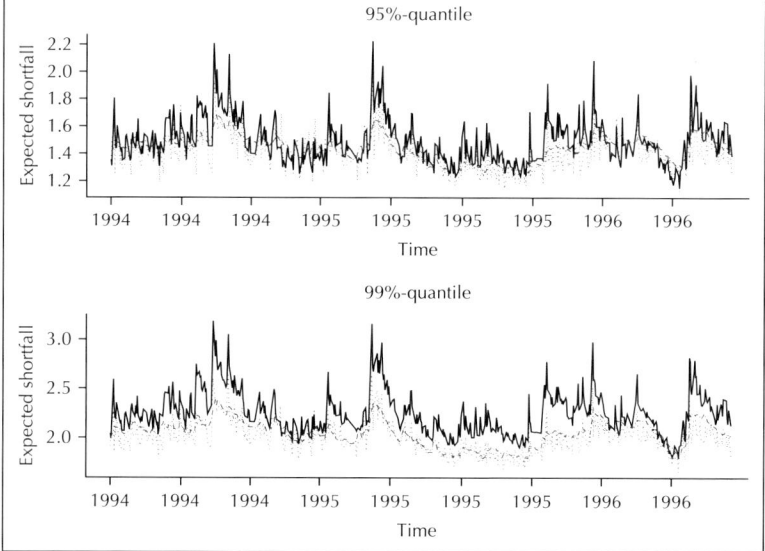

and an estimate for the expected shortfall is given by

$$\hat{S}_q^t = \hat{\mu}_{t,P} + \hat{\sigma}_{t,P}\sqrt{\frac{\hat{\nu}-2}{\hat{\nu}}}\left(\frac{1}{1-q}\,c\,\frac{\hat{\nu}}{\hat{\nu}-1}\left(1+\frac{(\tilde{z}_q)^2}{\hat{\nu}}\right)^{\frac{1-\hat{\nu}}{2}}\right)$$

where the constant c equals $\Gamma(\frac{1}{2}(\hat{\nu}+1))/\Gamma(\frac{\hat{\nu}}{2})(\hat{\nu}\pi)^{1/2}$, $\tilde{z}_q$ is the qth quantile of a standard t_ν-distributed random variable and $\hat{\nu}$ is the maximum likelihood estimate from the multivariate or univariate models, as before. Clearly, the t_ν assumption made for the distribution of the innovations is not restrictive. Alternatively, we can use, for example, extreme value theory and the peaks-over-threshold method[12] to model the tails of $F_Z(\cdot)$.

For illustrative purposes, in Figure 3 we show estimates of the conditional expected shortfall. The estimates are constructed using the multivariate synchronous CCC-GARCH(1,1) model and the asynchronous CCC-GARCH(1,1) model on the seven-dimensional series of negative equity index returns, and a standard univariate GARCH(1,1) model on the portfolio negative returns.

Figure 2 shows that expected shortfall estimates constructed using multivariate models are in general lower and change more slowly than those from a univariate approach. Moreover, estimates from the synchronous CCC-GARCH(1,1) model wiggle more than those from the asynchronous CCC-GARCH(1,1) model and exhibit small-scale fluctuations. Performance results from Section 3 suggest that these small-scale movements are a good feature.

4.2 Backtesting

Backtesting expected shortfall estimates can be very difficult because a tail phenomenon is estimated. As a descriptive tool (rather than a formal test), in Figure 4 we show boxplots of residuals

$$\hat{R}_t = \frac{\Delta_t - \hat{S}_q^t}{\hat{\sigma}_{t,P}} I_{\left\{\Delta_t > \delta_q^t\right\}} \tag{18}$$

Under model assumptions (15) and ignoring estimation effects, we can easily show that the theoretical residuals R_t are an iid. sequence with expected value zero. Figure 3 yields additional evidence that expected shortfall estimates from a classical univariate GARCH (1,1) analysis of the negative portfolio returns are too conservative (values of residuals too low). However, standard tests for unconditional coverage examining whether losses exceed VaR estimates at the $q \cdot 100\%$ confidence level more frequently than $q\%$ of the time never rejected the null hypothesis of unconditional unbiasedness of VaR estimates.[13] Therefore, all the models seem to be compatible with the data.

5 CONCLUSIONS

The need to synchronise multivariate financial time series is strongly motivated by the fact that information continues to flow for closed markets while others are still open. Apart from the neat interpretative structure of synchronisation, we found empirically that it improved the predictive performance of the CCC-GARCH(1,1)

Figure 4 Boxplots of residuals, $\hat{R}t$, from the expected shortfall estimates computed during the backtesting period beginning June 23, 1994 and ending September 9, 1996 (for a total of 500 trading days). Expected shortfall estimates are constructed at the 95% (*top*) and at the 90% (*bottom*) confidence levels using the synchronous CCC-GARCH(1,1) model (*left*) and the standard CCC-GARCH(1,1) model without synchronisation (*center*) on the seven-dimensional series of (negative) equity index returns, and a standard univariate GARCH(1,1) model (*right*) on the (negative) portfolio returns. The number of violations is given between parentheses. If the model is correct, the expected numbers of violations are 25 (*top*) and 50 (*bottom*), respectively. The horizontal lines indicate the expected value of the residuals equalling zero if the model is correct

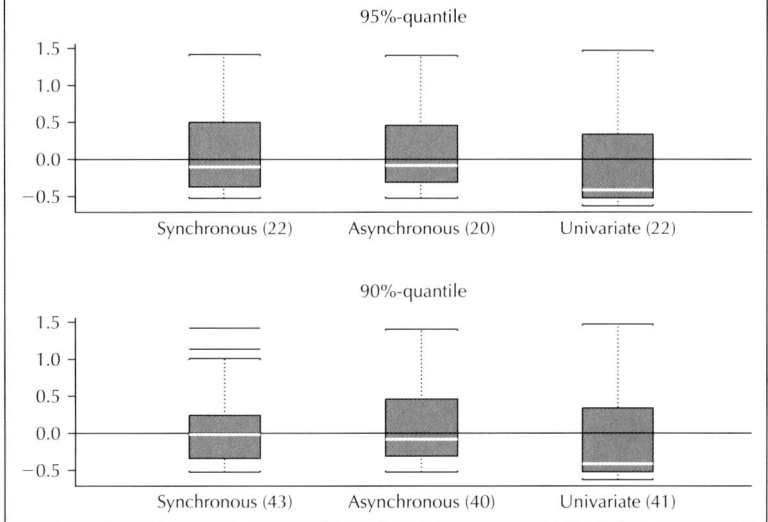

model for a seven-dimensional time series of daily equity index returns. The predictive gain with synchronisation often seems to be greater than when trying to extend the CCC-GARCH(1,1) model to a more complex model for approximating more general volatility functions and allowing for leverage effects (Audrino (2002), Section 3.5). The question whether more sophisticated volatility models are able to outperform the simple GARCH(1,1) model has also been investigated recently by Hansen and Lunde (2002) at the univariate level. In their empirical analysis they found that it is very difficult to beat the simple GARCH(1,1) model. Our empirical comparisons confirm that, in our particular example, synchronisation yields more prominent improvements than extending the multivariate GARCH to a more complex model.

Backtesting VaR and expected shortfall estimates computed using our synchronous CCC-GARCH(1,1) model on a real global portfolio consisting of seven equity indices around the world, we provide empirical evidence of the power of our synchronisation methodology. Backtest results support the evidence that synchronisation leads to better risk estimates than those from a classical CCC-GARCH(1,1) model without synchronisation and from a direct univariate GARCH(1,1) analysis of the portfolio returns. Risk estimates from our model change more slowly and exhibit more small-scale fluctuations than those obtained from alternative approaches. We also found that the univariate analysis of the portfolio returns seems to be biased for the calculation of risk measures, and it turned out to be too conservative. In contrast, we showed that no improvement (in terms of predictive performance and measurement of risk) over a simple univariate GARCH(1,1) model for the portfolio returns could be achieved using a multivariate GARCH model without synchronisation. This also emphasises the importance of synchronisation in multivariate approaches.

APPENDIX A

A1 *t*-type and sign-type tests

Consider differences $\hat{D}_t, t = 1, \ldots, T$, of performance terms

$$\hat{D}_t = \tilde{U}_{t;\text{model}_1} - \tilde{U}_{t;\text{model}_2}, \quad t = 1, \ldots, T$$

where the sum, $\Sigma_{t=1}^T \tilde{U}_{t;\text{model}}$ equals the total out-of-sample performance of a model.[14] We now test the null hypothesis that the differences $\hat{D}_t$ have mean zero against the alternative of mean less than zero, ie, the estimates from model 1 are better than those from model 2. For this purpose, we use versions of the *t*-test and sign-test adapted to the case of dependent observations.

The *t*-type test statistic is

$$\sqrt{T} \, \frac{\bar{D}}{\hat{\sigma}_{D;\infty}}, \quad \text{where } \bar{D} = \frac{1}{T} \sum_{t=1}^T \hat{D}_t \tag{A1}$$

In (A1), $\hat{\sigma}_{D;\infty}^2 = (2\pi)\hat{f}_{\hat{D}}(0)$, where $\hat{f}_{\hat{D}}(0)$ is smoothed periodogram estimate at frequency zero, based on $\hat{D}_1, \ldots, \hat{D}_T$; see for example Brockwell and Davis (1991). The motivation for this estimate is based on the assumption that $\{\hat{D}_t\}_t$ is stationary (conditional on the training data) and satisfies suitable dependence conditions, eg, mixing. Then, conditional on the training data,

$$\sqrt{T} \left(\bar{D} - E[\hat{D}_t] \right) \Rightarrow \mathcal{N}(0, \sigma_{D;\infty}^2) \quad (T \to \infty)$$

$$\sigma_{D;\infty}^2 = \sum_{k=-\infty}^{+\infty} \text{cov}\left[\hat{D}_0, \hat{D}_k \right] = (2\pi)f_{\hat{D}}(0) \tag{A2}$$

where $f_{\hat{D}}(0)$ is the spectral density at zero of $\{\hat{D}_t\}_t$.

Thus, using (A2) for the test statistic in (A1), and conditional on the training data,

$$\sqrt{T} \, \frac{\bar{D}}{\hat{\sigma}_{D;\infty}} \Rightarrow \mathcal{N}(0, 1) \quad (T \to \infty) \tag{A3}$$

under the null hypothesis.

Analogously, the version of the sign test in the case of dependent observations is based on the number of negative differences

$$\hat{W}_t = I_{\{\hat{D}_t \leq 0\}}, \qquad t = 1, \dots, T$$

for the null hypothesis that the negative differences $\hat{W}_t$ have mean $\frac{1}{2}$ against the alternative of mean larger than $\frac{1}{2}$. The test statistic is given by

$$\sqrt{T} = \frac{\bar{W} - \frac{1}{2}}{\hat{\sigma}_{W;\infty}}, \qquad \text{where } \bar{W} = \frac{1}{T} \sum_{t=1}^{T} \hat{W}_t \qquad (A4)$$

and $\hat{\sigma}_{W;\infty}^2$ as in (A1) but based on $\hat{W}_1, \dots, \hat{W}_T$. As in the derivation of the t-type test above, we have, conditional on the training data,

$$\sqrt{T} = \frac{\bar{W} - \frac{1}{2}}{\hat{\sigma}_{W;\infty}} \Rightarrow \mathcal{N}(0,1) \qquad (T \to \infty) \qquad (A5)$$

under the null hypothesis.

A2 Multivariate negative out-of-sample log-likelihood results

We report here the results of the t-type and sign-type tests for the multivariate negative out-of-sample log-likelihood statistic introduced in Section 3.2. The observed values for the t-type test statistic (A1) are -1.7822 and -1.6923 with corresponding P-values of 0.037 and 0.045 when our synchronisation method is tested against the asynchronous CCC-GARCH(1,1) model and the synchronisation method of Burns, Engle and Mezrich (1998), respectively. These results imply that our synchronised model is significantly better than both alternative approaches. Analogously, we find 308 and 254 negative differences (among a total of $T = 500$), and the observed values of the sign-type test statistic (A4) are 1.708 and 0.186 with corresponding P-values of 0.044 and 0.426, respectively. Therefore, these tests also lead to rejection of the null hypothesis (ie, equal performance of the models) at the 5% significance level, implying a preference of our synchronous CCC-GARCH(1,1) model over the asynchronous CCC-GARCH(1,1) model.

1 See, for example, Burns, Engle and Mezrich (1998).

2 For instance, we always use the closing time of the New York Stock Exchange, ie, 4.00pm local New York time, as the synchronisation time point.

3 Moreover, note that in the more realistic case where the portfolio weight changes over time, stationarity of all individual prices does not imply stationarity of the portfolio prices, which makes the direct univariate portfolio modelling difficult.

4 It follows that when US shares in the portfolio decline on any day, London's will decline the following day, mainly due to the asynchronous trade in different places.

5 Clearly, from the viewpoint of a British investor, the data could also be synchronised at the London closing time. The choice of the synchronisation time point is arbitrary.

6 Like McNeil and Frey (2000) we use the negative returns, ie, the losses, because they are of major interest in risk analysis.

7 For more details on the Yule–Walker estimator, see Brockwell and Davis (1991) or Reinsel (1991).

8 See, for example, Fang, Kotz and Ng (1990).

9 We also analysed whether the improvements obtained with the synchronous CCC-GARCH(1,1) model could be achieved or even surpassed by more sophisticated models for volatilities or conditional means. Of course, the synchronous CCC-GARCH(1,1) model is also a more complex model for asynchronous data than the classical CCC-GARCH(1,1) (see Proposition 1), but in respect of synchronisation is motivated with a simple linear transform. We analysed different extensions of the asynchronous classical GARCH(1,1) model (eg, including a conditional mean term and more complex, potentially high-dimensional parameterisations for approximating more general volatility functions). Considering the same goodness-of-fit measures as used above, we found that more sophisticated models (not of the synchronisation type) did not show worthwhile improvements. Hence, synchronisation seems to have a more substantial effect than attempts to improve the model dynamics. This finding confirms the results of Hansen and Lunde (2002) for univariate series.

10 More specifically, the 1996 Market Risk Amendment to the Basel Accord stipulates that the minimum capital requirement for market risk should be based on a 10-day VaR at a 99% confidence level. The amendment allows 10-day VaR to be measured as a multiple of one-day VaR.

11 See Artzner *et al* (1999) and Rockafellar and Uryasev (2002) for more details.

12 See Embrechts, Klüppelberg and Mikosch (1997) or McNeil and Frey (2000) for a detailed description of the method.

13 Note that this can be due to the very low power of such tests in detecting errors in VaR estimates; see, for example, Kupiec (1995).

14 In case of the negative log-likelihood loss, $\hat{D}_t$ is the difference between out-of-sample deviance residuals, up to a change of signs; see McCullagh and Nelder (1989).

This chapter was previously published in *The Journal of Risk* **6**(2), Winter 2003/04.

REFERENCES

Artzner, P., F. Delbaen, J.-M. Eber, and D. Heath, 1999, "Coherent Measures of Risk", *Mathematical Finance* **3**, pp. 203–28.

Audrino, F., 2002, "Statistical Methods for High-multivariate Financial Time Series", Dissertation no. 14565, ETH Zürich.

Berkowitz, J. and J. O'Brien, 2002, "How Accurate are Value-at-Risk Models at Commercial Banks", *Journal of Finance* **57(3)**, pp. 1093–111.

Bollerslev, T., 1990, "Modelling the Coherence in Short-run Nominal Exchange Rates: A Multivariate Generalized ARCH Model", *Review of Economics and Statistics* **72**, pp. 498–505.

Brockwell, P. J. and R. A. Davis, 1991, *Time Series: Theory and Methods.* (New York: Springer).

Burns, P., R. F. Engle, and J. Mezrich, 1998, "Correlations and Volatilities of Asynchronous Data", *Journal of Derivatives* (Summer), pp. 1–12.

Embrechts, P., C. Klüppelberg, and T. Mikosch, 1997, *Modelling Extremal Events for Insurance and Finance.* (Berlin: Springer).

Fang, K. T., S. Kotz, and K. W. Ng, 1990, *Symmetric Multivariate and Related Distributions.* (London: Chapman & Hall).

Freedman, D., 1984, "On Bootstrapping Two-stage Least-squares Estimates in Stationary Linear Models", *Annals of Statistics* **12**, pp. 827–42.

Hansen, P. R. and A. Lunde, 2002, "A Forecast Comparison of Volatility Models: Does Anything Beat a GARCH(1, 1)?" Manuscript, Brown University.

Kupiec, P., 1995, "Techniques for Verifying the Accuracy of Risk Measurement Models", *Journal of Derivatives* **3** (Winter), pp. 73–84.

McCullagh, P. and J. A. Nelder, 1989, *Generalized Linear Models.* Chapman & Hall, London.

McNeil, A. J. and R. Frey, 2000, "Estimation of Tail-related Risk Measures for Heteroscedastic Financial Time Series: An Extreme Value Approach", *Journal of Empirical Finance* **7**, pp. 271–300.

Reinsel, G. C., 1991, *Elements of Multivariate Time Series Analysis.* (New York: Springer).

Rockafellar, R. T. and S. Uryasev, 2002, "Conditional Value-at-Risk for General Loss Distributions", *Journal of Banking and Finance* **26**, pp. 1443–71.

13

How to Account for Extreme Co-movements between Individual Stocks and the Market

Yannick Malevergne; Didier Sornette*

Université Claude Bernard Lyon I; University of California,
Université de Nice-Sophia Antipolis

1 INTRODUCTION

Consider a portfolio made of 50% of Standard & Poor's 500 (S&P 500) and 50% of one stock such as Boeing Co. or Chevron Corp. Let us estimate the probability P_r that this portfolio incurs a loss larger than n times its standard deviation for ($n = 2, ..., 5$). For the same portfolio, let us also estimate the probability P_g that it incurs the same loss (ie, n times its standard deviation) when the dependence between the index and the stock is reduced to that described by the Gaussian copula ("Gaussian dependence") while the marginals remain the same. Table 1 gives P_r and P_g for 20 such portfolios corresponding to 20 major stocks of the NYSE as well as their mean ratio P_r/P_g (average value of P_r/P_g over the 20 portfolios). For two- and three-standard deviation shocks, the value of P_r/P_g close to 1 indicates that the dependence structure is correctly captured by a Gaussian copula. However, for larger and larger shocks, they become more and more probable compared with the prediction of the Gaussian dependence, notwithstanding the use of marginals with heavy tails. This simple exercise illustrates the non-Gaussian nature of the dependence between financial assets, which becomes all the more important the

*We acknowledge helpful discussions and exchanges with C. W. G. Granger, J.-P. Laurent, V. Pisarenko, R. Valkanov and D. Zajdenweber. This work was partially supported by the James S.McDonnell Foundation 21st century scientist award/studying complex system.

Table 1 Probabilities of joint losses

	$100 \times P_r\,(R < -n \cdot \sigma)$							
	$n = 2$		$n = 3$		$n = 4$		$n = 5$	
	P_r	P_g	P_r	P_g	P_r	P_g	P_r	P_g
Abbott Labs	2.07	2.06	0.58	0.51	0.21	0.15	0.09	0.07
American Home Products Corp.	1.98	2.07	0.51	0.56	0.30	0.24	0.17	0.13
Boeing Co.	2.03	1.96	0.53	0.51	0.21	0.18	0.13	0.09
Bristol-Myers Squibb Co.	1.56	1.81	0.55	0.48	0.26	0.22	0.11	0.10
Chevron Corp.	1.94	1.99	0.40	0.42	0.13	0.15	0.08	0.07
Du Pont (E.I.) de Nemours & Co.	2.13	2.02	0.51	0.47	0.21	0.19	0.09	0.07
Disney (Walt) Co.	1.83	1.87	0.47	0.53	0.24	0.22	0.15	0.12
General Motors Corp.	1.73	1.95	0.45	0.42	0.21	0.13	0.08	0.06
Hewlett-Packard Co.	1.77	2.08	0.53	0.51	0.21	0.19	0.08	0.09
Coca-Cola Co.	1.60	1.83	0.45	0.50	0.19	0.18	0.09	0.07
Minnesota Mining & MFG Co.	1.85	2.01	0.57	0.49	0.19	0.19	0.08	0.09
Philip Morris Cos Inc.	2.00	2.07	0.45	0.50	0.21	0.19	0.13	0.12
Pepsico Inc.	1.92	2.08	0.51	0.49	0.15	0.18	0.15	0.07
Procter & Gamble Co.	1.51	1.67	0.45	0.48	0.24	0.21	0.13	0.09
Pharmacia Corp.	1.81	1.94	0.53	0.54	0.23	0.25	0.11	0.12
Schering-Plough Corp.	1.85	1.94	0.49	0.44	0.11	0.14	0.08	0.06
Texaco Inc.	1.90	1.94	0.55	0.55	0.28	0.23	0.11	0.11
Texas Instruments Inc.	1.87	2.02	0.49	0.50	0.21	0.15	0.06	0.07
United Technologies Corp.	2.17	2.10	0.47	0.45	0.17	0.14	0.11	0.06
Walgreen Co.	1.81	1.96	0.47	0.41	0.23	0.14	0.09	0.08
Mean ratio P_r/P_g		0.95		1.02		1.15		1.24

A portfolio made of 50% of S&P 500 and 50% of one stock (whose name is indicated in the first column) is considered. We estimate the probability P_r that this portfolio incurs a loss, R, larger than n times its standard deviation ($n = 2, ..., 5$). For the same portfolio, we estimate the probability P_g that it incurs the same loss (ie, n times its standard deviation) when the dependence between the index and the stock is given by a Gaussian copula. The mean ratio P_r/P_g gives the average value of P_r/P_g over the 20 portfolios.

more extreme the amplitude of the shock. Consequently, predictions of very large shocks in portfolios, based on standard Gaussian measures of dependences, become less and less reliable, even when using marginals with heavy tails. We thus need, and develop here, novel concepts and tools to address this question.

Our approach is based on the concept of extreme or "tail dependence," which probes the reaction of a variable to the realisation of another variable when this realisation is of extreme amplitude (much larger than the five-standard deviations of the above example) and very low probability. The dependence, and especially the extreme dependence, between two assets or between an asset and any other exogenous economic variable is an issue of major importance both for practitioners and for academics. The determination of extreme dependences is crucial for financial institutions. It is also fundamental for the establishment of a rational investment policy striving for the best diversification of the various sources of risk. In all these situations, the objective is to prevent or at least minimise the simultaneous occurrence of large losses across the different positions held in the portfolio.

From an academic perspective, taking into account the extreme dependence properties provides useful yardsticks and important constraints for the construction of models, which should not underestimate or overestimate risks. From the point of view of univariate statistics, extreme values theory provides the mathematical framework for the classification and quantification of very large risks. This has been made possible by the existence of a "universal" behavior summarised by the Gnedenko–Pickands–Balkema–de Haan theorem, which gives a natural limit law for peak-over-threshold values in the form of the generalised Pareto distribution (see Embrechts, Klüppelberg, and Mikosh 1997). Moreover, most of these univariate extreme values results are robust with respect to the time dependences observed in financial time series (see, for instance, de Haan *et al* (1989), or Starica (1999)). In contrast, no such result is yet available in the multivariate case. In the absence of such theoretical guidelines, the alternative is therefore to impose some dependence structure in a rather *ad hoc* and arbitrary way. This was the stance taken, for instance, by Longin and Solnik (2001) in their study of the phenomenon of contagion across international equity markets.

This approach, where the dependence structure is not determined from empirical facts or from an economic model, is not fully satisfying. As a remedy, we propose a new approach, which does not rely directly on multivariate extreme values theory but rather derives the extreme dependence structure from the characteristics of a financial model of assets. Specifically, we use the general class of factor models, which is probably one of the most versatile and relevant and whose introduction in finance can be traced back at least to Ross (1976). The factor models are now widely used in many branches of finance, including stock return models, interest rate models (Vasicek (1977), Brennan and Schwarz (1978), Cox, Ingersoll, and Ross (1985)), credit risks models (Carey (1998), Gordy (2000), Lucas *et al* (2001)), and so on, and are found at the core of many theories and equilibrium models.

Here, following the examples in Table 1, we shall first focus on the characterisation of the extreme dependence between stock returns and the market return and then on the extreme dependence between two stocks that share a common explaining factor. The role of the market return as a factor explaining the evolution of individual stock returns is both assumed by theoretical models such as the capital asset pricing model (CAPM) (Sharpe (1964), Lintner (1965), Mossin (1966)) or the arbitrage pricing theory (APT) (Ross (1976)) and supported by empirical studies (Fama and McBeth (1973), Kandel and Staumbaugh (1987) – among many others). It has even been shown in Roll (1988) that in certain dramatic circumstances, such as the October 1987 stock-market crash, the (global) market was the sole relevant factor needed to explain the stock market movements and the propagation of the crash across countries. Thus, the choice of factor models is a very natural starting point for studying extreme dependences from a general point of view. The main gain is that, without imposing any *a priori ad hoc* dependences other than the definition of the factor model, we shall be able to derive the general properties of extreme dependence between an asset and one of its factors and to determine these properties empirically by a simple estimation of the factor model parameters.

Our results are directly relevant to a portfolio manager using any of the factor models such as the CAPM or the APT to estimate the impact on their extreme risks upon the addition or removal of an asset in their portfolio. In this framework, our results stated for single assets can easily be extended to an entire portfolio, and some examples will be given. This problem is particularly acute in funds of funds. From a more global perspective, our analysis of the tail dependence of two assets is the appropriate setting for analysing the strategic asset allocation facing a portfolio manager striving to diversify between a portfolio of stocks and a portfolio of bonds, or between portfolios constituted of domestic and of international assets.

Our main addition to the literature is to provide a completely general analytical formula for the extreme dependence between any two assets, which holds for any distribution of returns of these two assets and of their common factor and which thus embodies their intrinsic dependence. Our second innovation is to provide a novel

and robust method of estimating empirically the extreme dependence, which we test on 20 majors stocks of the NYSE. By comparing
it with historical co-movements in the last 40 years, we check that
our prediction is validated out-of-sample and thus provide an *ex
ante* method to quantify future stressful periods, so that our results
can be directly used to construct a portfolio that aims to minimise
the impact of extreme events. We are also able to detect an anomalous co-monotonicity associated with the October 1987 crash.

The plan of our chapter is as follows. Section 2 defines the concepts needed for the characterisation and quantification of extreme
dependences. In particular, we recall the definition of the coefficient of tail dependence, which captures in a single number the
properties of extreme dependence between two random variables:
the tail dependence is defined as the probability for a given random variable to be large, assuming that another random variable is
large, at the same probability level. We shall also need some basic
notions on dependences between random variables using the
mathematical concept of copulas. In order to provide some perspective on the following results, this section also contains the
expression of some classical examples of tail-dependence coefficients for specific multivariate distributions.

Section 3 states our main result in the form of a general theorem
allowing the calculation of the coefficient of tail dependence for
any factor model with arbitrary distribution functions of the factors
and of the idiosyncratic noise. We find that the factor must have
sufficiently "wild" fluctuations (to be made precise below) in order
for the tail dependence not to vanish. For normal distributions of
the factor, the tail dependence is identically zero, while for regularly varying distributions (power laws), the tail dependence is in
general nonzero. We also show that the most interesting coefficients of tail dependence are those between each individual stock
and their common factor, since the tail dependence between any
pair of assets is shown to be nothing but the minimum of the tail
dependence between each asset and their common factor.

Section 4 is devoted to the empirical estimation of the coefficients of tail dependence between individual stock returns and the
market return. The tests are performed for daily stock returns. The
estimated coefficients of tail dependence are found to be in good
agreement with the fraction of historically realised extreme events

that occur simultaneously with any of the 10 largest losses of the market factor (these 10 largest losses were not used to calibrate the tail dependence coefficient). We also find some evidence for co-monotonicity in the crash of October 1987, suggesting that this event is an "outlier," providing additional support to a previous analysis of large and extreme drawdowns (Johansen and Sornette (2002)).

We summarise our results and conclude in Section 5.

2 INTRINSIC MEASURE OF CASUAL AND OF EXTREME DEPENDENCES

This section provides a brief informal summary of the mathematical concepts used in this chapter to characterise the normal and extreme dependences between asset returns.

2.1 How is the full dependence between two random variables uniquely characterised?

The answer to this question is provided by the mathematical notion of "copulas," first introduced by Sklar (1959),[1] which allows one to study the dependence of random variables independently of the behavior of their marginal distributions. Our presentation focuses on two variables but is easily extended to the case of N random variables, whatever N may be. Sklar's theorem states that, given the joint distribution function $F(\cdot, \cdot)$ of two random variables X and Y with marginal distribution $F_X(\cdot)$ and $F_Y(\cdot)$ respectively, there exists a function $C(\cdot, \cdot)$ with range in $[0,1] \times [0,1]$ such that

$$F(x, y) = C(F_X(x), F_Y(y)) \tag{1}$$

for all (x, y). This function C is the *copula* of the two random variables X and Y, and is unique if the random variables have continuous marginal distributions. Moreover, the following result shows that copulas are intrinsic measures of dependence. If $g_1(X)$, $g_2(Y)$ are strictly increasing on the ranges of X, Y, the random variables $\tilde{X} = g_1(X), \tilde{Y} = g_2(Y)$ have exactly the same copula C (see Lindskog (2000)). The copula is thus invariant under strictly increasing transformation of the variables. This provides a powerful way of studying scale-invariant measures of associations. It is also a natural starting-point for construction of multivariate distributions. We refer to Scaillet (2003) for a non-parametric method to estimate copulas, to Malevergne and Sornette (2003) for empirical tests and to Geman and Kharoubi (2003) for tests of diversification provided by hedge funds using copulas.

2.2 Tail dependence between two random variables

A standard measure of dependence between two random variables is provided by the correlation coefficient. However, this suffers from at least three deficiencies. First, as stressed by Embrechts, McNeil and Straumann (1999), the correlation coefficient is an adequate measure of dependence only for elliptical distributions and for events of moderate sizes. Second, the correlation coefficient measures only the degree of linear dependence and does not account for any other nonlinear functional dependence between the random variables. Third, it aggregates both the marginal behavior of each random variable and its dependence. For instance, a simple change in the marginals generally implies a change in the correlation coefficient, while the copula, and therefore the dependence, remains unchanged. Mathematically speaking, the correlation coefficient is said to lack the property of invariance under increasing changes of variables.

Since the copula is the unique and intrinsic measure of dependence, it is desirable to define measures of dependences that depend only on the copula. Such measures have in fact been known for a long time. Examples are provided by the concordance measures, among which the most famous are Kendall's tau and Spearman's rho (see Nelsen (1998), for a detailed exposition). In particular, Spearman's rho quantifies the degree of functional dependence between two random variables: it equals one (minus one) when and only when the first variable is an increasing (decreasing) function of the second variable. However, as for the correlation coefficient, these concordance measures do not provide a useful measure of the dependence for extreme events, since they are constructed over the whole distributions.

Another natural idea, widely used in the contagion literature, is to work with the conditional correlation coefficient, conditioned only on the largest events. But, as stressed by Boyer, Gibson and Lauretan (1997), such conditional correlation coefficient suffers from a bias: even for a constant *unconditional* correlation coefficient, the *conditional* correlation coefficient changes with the conditioning set. Therefore, changes in the conditional correlation do not provide a characteristic signature of a change in the true correlations. The conditional concordance measures suffer from the same problem. To circumvent this, Ang and Chen (2001) have advocated the use of asymmetric correlations. In doing so, they account for the bias reported by Boyer, Gibson and Lauretan (1997). However, this measure of dependence does not emphasise the extreme dependence between the assets as it is mostly sensitive to their moderate moves. To make this point clear, consider two assets whose dependence structure is Gaussian with asymmetric marginal distributions. It is clear that the asymmetric correlation of Ang and Chen (2001) will be different from the symmetric correlation as a result of the asymmetry of the marginal distributions. The asymmetric correlation may even be quite large. However, the copula between these two assets is symmetric, since it is Gaussian, independently of the shape of the marginals by construction of the copula. Therefore, the tail dependence will remain identically zero. Thus, the asymmetric correlation does not give any information on the dependence between extremes.

In view of these deficiencies, it is natural to come back to a fundamental definition of dependence through the use of probabilities. We thus study the conditional probability that the first variable is large conditioned on the second variable being large too: $\bar{F}(x|y) = \Pr\{X > x | Y > y\}$, when x and y goes to infinity. Since the convergence of $\bar{F}(x|y)$ may depend on the manner with which x and y go to infinity (the convergence is not uniform), we need to specify the path taken by the variables to reach infinity. Recalling that it would be preferable to have a measure which is independent of the marginal distributions of X and Y, it is natural to reason in the quantile space. This leads us to choose $x = F_X^{-1}(u)$ and $y = F_Y^{-1}(u)$ and replace the conditions $x, y \to \infty$ by $u \to 1$. In doing so, we define the so-called coefficient of upper tail dependence (see Coles, Heffernan and Tawn (1999), Lindskog (2000), or Embrechts, McNeil and Straumann (2001)):

$$\lambda_+ = \lim_{u \to 1^-} \Pr\left\{X > F_X^{-1}(u) \middle| Y > F_Y^{-1}(u)\right\} \qquad (2)$$

As required, this measure of dependence is independent of the marginals, since it can be expressed in terms of the copula of X and Y as

$$\lambda_+ = \lim_{u \to 1^-} \frac{1 - 2u + C(u, u)}{1 - u} \qquad (3)$$

This representation shows that λ_+ is symmetric in X and Y, as it should for a reasonable measure of dependence.

In a similar way, we define the coefficient of lower tail dependence as the probability that X incurs a large loss, assuming that Y incurs a large loss at the same probability level:

$$\lambda_- = \lim_{u \to 0^+} \Pr\left\{X < F_X^{-1}(u) \middle| Y < F_Y^{-1}(u)\right\} = \lim_{u \to 0^+} \frac{C(u, u)}{u} \qquad (4)$$

This last expression has a simple interpretation in terms of value-at-risk (VaR). Indeed, the quantiles $F_X^{-1}(u)$ and $F_Y^{-1}(u)$ are nothing but the VaR of assets (or portfolios) X and Y at the confidence level $1 - u$. Thus, the coefficient λ_- simply provides the probability that X exceeds the VaR at level $1 - u$, assuming that Y has exceeded the VaR at the same level confidence level $1 - u$, when this level goes to one. As a consequence, the probability that both X and Y exceed their VaR at the level $1 - u$ is asymptotically given by $\lambda_- \cdot u$ as $u \to 0$. As an example, consider a daily VaR calculated at the 99% confidence level. Then, the probability that both X and Y undergo a loss larger than their VaR at the 99% level is approximately given by $\lambda_-/100$. Thus, when λ_- is about 0.1, the typical recurrence time between such concomitant large losses is about four years, while for $\lambda_- \approx 0.5$ it is less than 10 months.

The values of the coefficients of tail dependence are known explicitly for a large number of different copulas. For instance, the Gaussian copula, which is the copula derived from the Gaussian multivariate distribution, has a zero coefficient of tail dependence. In contrast, Gumbel's copula, used by Longin and Solnik (2001) in the study of the contagion between international equity markets, which is defined by

$$C_\theta(u, v) = \exp\left(-\left[(-\ln u)^\theta + (-\ln v)^\theta\right]^{\frac{1}{\theta}}\right), \qquad \theta \in [0, 1] \qquad (5)$$

has an upper tail coefficient $\lambda_+ = 2 - 2^\theta$. For all as smaller than one, λ_+ is positive and the Gumbel's copula is said to present tail dependence, while for $\theta = 1$, the Gumbel's copula is said to be asymptotically independent. One should, however, use this terminology carefully, as "tail independence" (quantified by $\lambda_+ = 0$ or $\lambda_- = 0$) does not necessarily imply that large events occur independently (see Coles, Heffernan and Tawn (1999), for a precise discussion of this point).

3 TAIL DEPENDENCE OF FACTOR MODELS

3.1 Tail dependence between an asset and one of its explaining factors

Now we state the first part of our main theoretical result. Let us consider two random variables X and Y of cumulative distribution functions $F_X(X)$ and $F_Y(Y)$, where X represents the return of a single stock and Y is the market return for instance. Let us also introduce an idiosyncratic noise ε, which is assumed independent of the market return Y. The factor model is defined by the following relationship between the individual stock return X, the market return Y and the idiosyncratic noise ε:

$$X = \beta \cdot Y + \epsilon \qquad (6)$$

β is the usual coefficient introduced by the CAPM (Sharpe (1964)). Let us stress that ε may embody other factors Y', Y'', ..., as long as they remain independent of Y. Under such conditions and a few other technical assumptions detailed in the theorem established in Appendix A.1, the coefficient of (upper) tail dependence between X and Y defined in (2) is obtained as

$$\lambda_+ = \int_{\max\left\{1,\frac{l}{\beta}\right\}}^{\infty} dx f(x) \qquad (7)$$

where l denotes the limit, when $u \to 1$, of the ratio of the quantiles of X and Y,

$$l = \lim_{u \to 1} \frac{F_X^{-1}(u)}{F_Y^{-1}(u)} \qquad (8)$$

and $f(x)$ is the limit, when $t \to +\infty$, of $t \cdot P_Y(tx) / \bar{F}_Y(t)$:

$$f(x) = \lim_{t \to +\infty} t \frac{P_Y(tx)}{\bar{F}_Y(t)} \qquad (9)$$

P_Y is the distribution density of Y and $\bar{F}_Y = 1 - F_Y$ is the complementary cumulative distribution function of Y. A similar expression obviously holds, *mutatis mutandis*, for the coefficient of lower tail dependence.

The measure of tail dependence given by Equation (7) depends on two limits defined in (8) and (9) and thus seems likely to be difficult to estimate. As it turns out, we will show that this is not the case in the empirical section below. Indeed, the first limit (8) is nothing but a ratio of quantiles, while the second limit (9) can be easily calculated for almost all distributions of the factor. For instance, let us consider the Pareto distribution $\bar{F}_Y(y) = 1/(y/y_0)^\mu$ defined for $y \geq y_0$, whose density is equal to $P_Y(y) = (\mu/y_0) / (y/y_0)^{1+\mu}$; the limit (9) gives $f(x) = \mu/x^{1+\mu}$. In contrast, for the Poisson law $\bar{F}_Y(y) = e^{-ry}$ defined for $y \geq 0$ with density $P_Y(y) = re^{-ry}$, the limit (9) gives $f(x) = \lim_{t \to \infty} rte^{-rt(x-1)} = 0$ for $x > 1$. Thus an estimation of the tail of the factor distribution is sufficient to infer the limit function $f(x)$. Moreover, equation (7) has a rather simple interpretation since it shows that a non-vanishing coefficient of tail dependence results from the combination of two phenomena. First, the limit function $f(x)$, which only depends on the behavior of the factor distribution, must be nonzero. Second, the constant l must remain finite to ensure that the integral in (7) does not vanish. Thus, the value of the coefficient of tail dependence is controlled by $f(x)$ solely function of the factor and a second variable l quantifying the competition of the tails of the distribution of the factor Y and of the idiosyncratic noise ε.

The fundamental result (7) should be of vivid interest to financial economists because it provides a general, rigorous and simple method for estimating one of the key variables embodying the occurrence of, and risks associated with, extremes in joint distributions. From a theoretical view point, it also anchors the derivation and quantification of a key variable on extremes in the general class of financial factor models, thus extending their use and relevance also to this rather novel domain of extreme dependence, extreme risks and extreme losses.

Up to now, we have assumed that the factor Y and the idiosyncratic noise ε were independent. In fact, it is important to stress for the sake of generality that the result (7) holds even when they are dependent, provided that this dependence is not too strong, as explained and made specific at the end of Appendix A.1.

We now derive two direct consequences of this result (7) (see Corollaries 1 and 2 in Appendix B), concerning rapidly varying and regularly varying factors,[2] which clearly illustrate the role of the factor itself and the impact of the trade-off between the factor and the idiosyncratic noise.

3.2 Absence of tail dependence for rapidly varying factors

Let us assume that the factor Y and the idiosyncratic noise ε are normally distributed (the second assumption is made for simplicity and will be relaxed below). As a consequence, the joint distribution of (X, Y) is the bivariate Gaussian distribution. Referring to the results stated in Section 2.1.2, we conclude that the copula of (X, Y) is the Gaussian copula whose coefficient of tail dependence is zero. In fact, it is easy to show that $\lambda = 0$ for any non-degenerated distribution of ε.

More generally, let us assume that the distribution of the factor Y is rapidly varying, which describes the Gaussian, exponential and any other distribution decaying faster than any power law. Then, the coefficient of tail dependence is identically zero. This result holds for any arbitrary distribution of the idiosyncratic noise (see Corollary 1 in Appendix B). It also holds for mixtures of normals or other distributions fatter than Gaussians, some of which are thought to be reasonable approximations to empirical stock return distributions.

These statements are somewhat counter-intuitive since one could expect *a priori* that the coefficient of tail dependence does not vanish as soon as the tail of the distribution of factor returns is fatter than the tail of the distribution of noise returns. In other words, when the standard deviation of the idiosyncratic noise ε is small (but not zero), then the idiosyncratic noise component is small and X and Y are practically identical, and it seems strange that their tail dependence can be equal to zero. This non-intuitive result stems from the fact that the tail dependence is quantifying not just a dependence but a specific dependence for extreme co-movements. Thus, in order to get a non-vanishing tail dependence, the fluctuations of the factor must be "wild" enough, which is not realised with rapidly varying distributions, irrespective of the relative values of the standard deviations of the factor and the idiosyncratic noise.

3.3 Coefficient of tail dependence for regularly varying factors

3.3.1 Example of the factor model with student distribution

In order to account for the power-law tail behavior observed for the distributions of assets returns it is logical to consider that the factor and the idiosyncratic noise also have power-law tailed distributions. As an illustration, we will assume that Y and ε are distributed according to a Student's distribution with the same number of degrees of freedom v (and thus same tail exponent v). Let us denote by σ the scale factor of the distribution of ε while the scale factor of the distribution of Y is chosen equal to one.[3] Applying the theorem previously established, we find that $f(x) = v/x^{v+1}$ and $l = \beta[1 + (\sigma/\beta)^v]^{1/v}$, so that the coefficient of tail dependence is

$$\lambda_\pm = \frac{1}{1 + \left(\dfrac{\sigma}{\beta}\right)^v}, \quad \text{and } \beta > 0 \tag{10}$$

As expected, the tail dependence increases as β increases and as σ decreases. Since the idiosyncratic volatility of the asset increases when the scale factor σ increases, this results simply means that the tail dependence decreases when the idiosyncratic volatility of a stock increases relative to the market volatility. The dependence with respect to v is less intuitive. In particular, let v go to infinity. Then, $\lambda \to 0$ if $\sigma > \beta$ and $\lambda \to 1$ if $\sigma < \beta$. This is surprising, as one could argue that, as $v \to \infty$, the Student distribution tends to the Gaussian law. As a consequence, one would expect the same coefficient of dependence $\lambda_+ = 0$ as for rapidly varying functions. The reason for the non-certain convergence of λ_+ to zero as $v \to \infty$ is rooted in a subtle non-commutativity (and non-uniform convergence) of the two limits $v \to \infty$ and $u \to 1$. Indeed, when taking first the limit $u \to 1$, the result $\lambda \to 1$ for $\beta > \sigma$ indicates that a sufficiently strong factor coefficient β always ensures the validity of the power-law regime, whatever the value of v. Correlatively, in this regime $\beta > \sigma$, $\lambda_\pm$ is an increasing function of v.

The result (10) is of interest for financial economics purpose because it provides a simple parametric illustration and interpretation of how the risk of large co-movements is affected by the three key parameters entering in the definition of the factor model. It allows one to weight the ingredients of the factor model with regard to how they impact on the large risks captured by $\lambda_\pm$ and thus links the financial basis underlying the factor model to the extreme multivariate risks.

3.3.2 General result

We now provide the general result valid for any regularly varying distribution. Let factor Y follow a regularly varying distribution with tail index α: in other words, the complementary cumulative distribution of Y is such that $\bar{F}_Y(y) = L(y) \cdot y^{-\alpha}$, where $L(y)$ is a slowly varying function, ie:

$$\lim_{t\to\infty} \frac{L(ty)}{L(t)} = 1, \quad \forall y > 0 \tag{11}$$

Corollary 2 in Appendix B shows that

$$\lambda = \frac{1}{\left[\max\left\{1, \dfrac{l}{\beta}\right\}\right]^\alpha} \tag{12}$$

where l denotes the limit, when $u \to 1$, of the ratio $F_X^{-1}(u) / F_Y^{-1}(u)$. In the case of particular interest when the distribution of ε is also regularly varying with tail index α and if, in addition, we have $\bar{F}_Y(y) \sim C_y \cdot y^{-\alpha}$ and $\bar{F}_\varepsilon(\varepsilon) \sim C_\varepsilon \cdot \varepsilon^{-\alpha}$ for large y and ε, then the coefficient of tail dependence is a simple function of the ratio C_ε/C_y of the scale factors:

$$\lambda = \frac{1}{1 + \beta^{-\alpha} \cdot \dfrac{C_\varepsilon}{C_y}} \tag{13}$$

When the tail indexes α_Y and α_ε of the distribution of the factor and the residue are different, then $\lambda = 0$ for $\alpha_Y < \alpha_\varepsilon$ and $\lambda = 1$ for $\alpha_Y > \alpha_\varepsilon$.

The results in (12) and (13) are very important both for a financial and an economic perspective because they express in the most general and straightforward way the risk of extreme co-movements quantified by the tail dependence parameter λ within the important class of factor models. That λ increases with the β factor is intuitively clear. Less obvious is the dependence of λ on the structure of the marginal distributions of the factor and of the idiosyncratic noise, which is found to be captured uniquely in terms of the ratio of their scale factors C_ε and C_y. The scale factors C_ε and C_y together with the factor β thus replace the variance and covariance in their role as the sole quantifiers of the extreme risks occurring in co-movements.

Until now, we have only considered a single asset X. Let us now consider a portfolio of assets X_i, where each of the assets follows exactly the *one* factor model (6)

$$X_i = \beta_i \cdot Y + \varepsilon_i \tag{14}$$

with independent noises ε_i, whose scale factors are C_{ε_i}. The portfolio $X = \Sigma w_i X_i$, with weights w_i, also follows the factor model with a parameter $\beta = \Sigma w_i \beta_i$ and noise ε, whose scale factor is $C_\varepsilon = \Sigma |w_i|^\alpha \cdot C_{\varepsilon i}$.[4]

Thus, Equation (13) shows that the tail dependence between the portfolio and the factor is

$$\lambda = \left[1 + \frac{\sum |w_i|^\alpha \cdot C_{\varepsilon_i}}{\left(\sum w_i \beta_i \right)^\alpha \cdot C_Y} \right]^{-1} \tag{15}$$

When unlimited short sells are allowed, one can follow a "market neutral" strategy yielding $\beta = 0$ and thus $\lambda = 0$. But in the more realistic case where only limited short sells are authorised, one cannot reach $\beta = 0$, and the best portfolio, which is the less "correlated" with the large market moves, has to minimise the tail dependence (15).

This simple example clearly shows that minimising the extreme co-movements, according to (15), is very different from minimising the (linear) correlation ρ between the portfolio and the market factor given by

$$\rho = \left[1 + \frac{\sum w_i^2 \cdot \mathrm{var}(\varepsilon_i)}{\left(\sum w_i \beta_i \right)^2 \mathrm{var}(Y)} \right]^{-\frac{1}{2}} \tag{16}$$

Since the minimum of ρ may be very different from the minimum of λ, minimising ρ almost surely leads to the acceptance of a level of extreme risks that is not optimal. Recall that ρ is much more sensitive to the small upward or downward moves of assets than to extreme moves. The objective function (15) is thus much more relevant than (16) for portfolio allocations striving to minimise extreme co-movements with the market. Accounting for the asymmetric correlations (introduced by Ang and Chen 2001) provides some improvements over the usual symmetric correlation but is still lacking in that it focuses mostly on the small fluctuations of the assets. A simple example illustrating the pre-eminence of the tail dependence as a very efficient objective function in order to build portfolios that are immune from the largest moves of the market can be found in Malevergne and Sornette (2002).

3.4 Tail dependence between two assets related by a factor model

We now present the second part of our theoretical result. Let X_1 and X_2 be two random variables (two assets) of cumulative distributions functions F_1, F_2 with a common factor Y. Let ε_1 and ε_2 be the idiosyncratic noises associated with these two assets X_1 and X_2. We allow the idiosyncratic noises to be dependent random variables, as occurs for instance if they embody the effect of other factors $Y', Y'', \dots$ that are independent of Y. Our essential assumption is that the distribution of the factor Y must have a tail not thinner than the tail of the distributions of the other factors $Y', Y'', \dots$ This hypothesis is crucial in order to detect the existence of tail dependence. This means that, for the purposes of characterising tail dependences in factor models, our model can always be re-stated as a single-factor model, where the single factor is the factor with the thickest tail. This makes our results quite general. Then, the model can be written as

$$X_1 = \beta_1 \cdot Y + \varepsilon_1 \tag{17}$$
$$X_2 = \beta_2 \cdot Y + \varepsilon_2 \tag{18}$$

We prove in Appendix A.2, that the coefficient of (upper) tail dependence $\lambda_+ = \lim_{u \to 1} \Pr\{X_1 > F_1^{-1}(u) | X_2 > F_2^{-1}(u)\}$, between the assets X_1 and X_2, is given by the expression

$$\lambda_+ = \int\limits_{\max\left\{\frac{l_1}{\beta_1}, \frac{l_2}{\beta_2}\right\}}^{\infty} \mathrm{d}x f(x) \tag{19}$$

which is very similar to that found for the tail dependence between an asset and one of its explaining factors (see Equation (7)). As previously, $l_{1,2}$ denotes the limit, when $u \to 1$, of the ratio $F_{1,2}^{-1}(u) / F_Y^{-1}(u)$, and $f(x)$ is the limit, when $t \to +\infty$, of $t \cdot P_Y(tx) / \bar{F}_Y(t)$.

The result (19) can be cast in a different illuminating way. Let $\lambda(X_1,Y)$ (resp. $\lambda(X_2,Y)$) denote the coefficient of tail dependence between the asset X_1 (resp. X_2) and their common factor Y. Let $\lambda(X_1, X_2)$ denote the tail dependence between the two assets. Equation (19) allows us to assert that

$$\lambda(X_1, X_2) = \min\{\lambda(X_1, Y), \lambda(X_2, Y)\} \qquad (20)$$

The tail dependence between the two assets X_1 and X_2 is nothing but the smallest tail dependence between each asset and the common factor. Therefore, a decrease of the tail dependence between the assets and the market will also lead automatically to a decrease of the tail dependence between the two assets. This result also shows that it is sufficient to study the tail dependence between the assets and their common factor to obtain the tail dependence between any pair of assets.

As asserted above, the result (20) is also useful in the context of portfolio analysis. Not only does it provide a tool for assessing the probability of large losses of a portfolio composed of assets driven by a common factor, it also allows us to define novel strategies of portfolio optimisation based on the selection and weighting of stocks chosen so as to balance the risks associated with extreme co-movements. Such an approach has been tested in Malevergne and Sornette (2002) with encouraging results.

4 EMPIRICAL STUDY

We now apply our theoretical results to the daily returns of a set of stocks traded on the New York Stock Exchange. In order to estimate the parameters of the factor model (6), the S&P 500 index is chosen to represent the common "market factor." It has been preferred over the Dow Jones Industrial Averages Index, for instance, because it is more diversified and represents about 80% of the total market capitalisation.

We describe the set of selected stocks in the next sub-section. Next, we estimate the parameter β in (6) and check the independence of the market returns and the residues. Then, applying the commonly used hypothesis according to which the tail of the distribution of assets return is a power law, or at least regularly varying (see Longin (1996), Lux (1996), Pagan (1996), or Gopikrishnan *et al* (1998)), we estimate the tail index and the scale factor of these distributions, which allows us to calculate the coefficients of tail dependence between each asset return and the market return. Finally, we perform an analysis of the historical data to check the compatibility of our prediction on the fraction of realised large losses of the assets that occur simultaneously with the large losses of the market.

The results of our analysis are reported below in terms of the returns rather than in terms of the excess returns above the risk-free interest rate, in apparent contradiction with the prescription of the CAPM. However, for daily returns, the difference between returns and excess returns is negligible. Indeed, we checked that neglecting the difference between the returns and the excess returns does not affect our results by re-running all of the study described below in terms of the excess returns and found that the tail dependence did not change by more than 0.1%.

4.1 Description of the data

We study a set of 20 assets traded on the New York Stock Exchange. The criteria presiding over the selection of the assets (see column 1 of Table 2) are, first, that they should be among the stocks with the largest capitalisations, and second, that each of them should have a weight smaller than 1% in the S&P 500 index, so that the dependence studied here does not stem trivially from their overlap with the market factor (taken as the S&P 500 index).

The time interval we have considered ranges from July 3, 1962 to December 29, 2000, which corresponds to 9,694 data points and represents the largest set of daily data available from the Center for Research in Security Prices (CRSP). This large time interval is important for letting us collect as many large fluctuations of the returns as is possible in order to sample the extreme tail dependence. Moreover, to allow for non-stationarity over the four decades of the study, to check the stability of our results, and to test the stationarity of the tail dependence over the time, we split this set into two subsets. The first one ranges from July 1962 to December 1979, a period with few very large return amplitudes, while the second one ranges from January

Table 2 Statistical properties of the data

	July 1962–December 1979				January 1980–December 2000				July 1962–December 2000			
	Mean	Std	Skew.	Kurt.	Mean	Std	Skew.	Kurt.	Mean	Std	Skew.	Kurt.
Abbott Labs	0.6677	0.0154	0.2235	2.192	0.9217	0.0174	−0.0434	2.248	0.8066	0.0165	0.0570	2.300
American Home Products Corp.	0.4755	0.0136	0.2985	3.632	0.8486	0.0166	0.1007	8.519	0.6803	0.0154	0.1717	7.557
Boeing Co.	0.8460	0.0228	0.6753	4.629	0.7752	0.0193	0.1311	4.785	0.8068	0.0209	0.4495	4.901
Bristol-Myers Squibb Co.	0.5342	0.0152	−0.0811	2.808	0.9353	0.0175	−0.3437	16.733	0.7546	0.0165	−0.2485	12.573
Chevron Corp.	0.4916	0.0134	0.2144	2.442	0.6693	0.0169	0.0491	4.355	0.5885	0.0154	0.1033	4.209
Du Pont (E.I.) de Nemours & Co.	0.2193	0.0126	0.3493	2.754	0.6792	0.0172	−0.1021	4.731	0.4715	0.0153	0.0231	4.937
Disney (Walt) Co.	0.9272	0.0215	0.2420	2.762	0.8759	0.0195	−0.6661	17.655	0.8997	0.0204	−0.1181	9.568
General Motors Corp.	0.3547	0.0126	0.4138	4.302	0.5338	0.0183	−0.0128	5.373	0.4538	0.0160	0.0872	6.164
Hewlett-Packard Co.	0.7823	0.0199	0.0212	3.063	0.8913	0.0238	0.0254	4.921	0.8420	0.0221	0.0256	4.624
Coca-Cola Co.	0.4829	0.0138	0.0342	5.436	0.9674	0.0170	−0.1012	14.377	0.7483	0.0157	−0.0513	12.611
Minnesota Mining & MFG Co.	0.3459	0.0139	0.3016	2.997	0.6885	0.0150	−0.7861	20.609	0.5333	0.0145	−0.3550	14.066
Philip Morris Cos Inc.	0.7930	0.0153	0.2751	2.799	0.9664	0.0180	−0.2602	10.954	0.8863	0.0169	−0.0784	8.790
Pepsico Inc.	0.4982	0.0147	0.2380	2.867	0.9443	0.0180	0.1372	4.594	0.7431	0.0166	0.1786	4.413
Procter & Gamble Co.	0.3569	0.0115	0.3911	4.343	0.7916	0.0164	−1.6610	46.916	0.5947	0.0144	−1.2408	44.363
Pharmacia Corp.	0.3801	0.0145	0.2699	3.508	0.9027	0.0191	−0.6133	13.587	0.6666	0.0172	−0.3773	12.378

Table 2 Continued.

	July 1962–December 1979				January 1980–December 2000				July 1962–December 2000			
	Mean	Std	Skew.	Kurt.	Mean	Std	Skew.	Kurt.	Mean	Std	Skew.	Kurt.
Schering-Plough Corp.	0.6328	0.0163	0.2619	3.112	1.0663	0.0192	0.1781	7.9979	0.8703	0.0179	0.2139	6.757
Texaco Inc.	0.3416	0.0134	0.2656	2.596	0.6644	0.0166	0.1192	6.477	0.5197	0.0152	0.1725	5.829
Texas Instruments Inc.	0.6839	0.0198	0.2076	3.174	1.0299	0.0268	0.1595	7.848	0.8726	0.0239	0.1831	7.737
United Technologies Corp.	0.5801	0.0185	0.3397	2.826	0.7752	0.0170	0.0396	3.190	0.6876	0.0177	0.1933	3.034
Walgreen Co.	0.5851	0.0165	0.3530	3.030	1.1996	0.0185	0.1412	3.316	0.9217	0.0176	0.2260	3.295
S&P 500	0.1783	0.0075	0.2554	3.131	0.5237	0.0101	-1.6974	36.657	0.3674	0.0090	-1.2236	32.406

This table gives the main statistical features of the three samples we have considered. The columns Mean, Std, Skew. and Kurt., respectively, give the average return multiplied by one thousand, the standard deviation, the skewness and the excess kurtosis of each asset over the time intervals from July 1962 to December 1979, January 1980 to December 2000 and July 1962 to December 2000. The excess kurtosis is given as indicative of the relative weight of large return amplitudes, and can always be calculated over a finite time series even if it may not be asymptotically defined for power tails with exponents less than 4.

1980 to December 2000, a period that witnessed several very large price changes (see Table 2, which shows the good stability of the standard deviation between the two sub-periods while the higher cumulants, such as the excess kurtosis, often increased dramatically in the second sub-period for most assets). Table 2 presents the main statistical properties of our set of stocks during the three time intervals. All assets exhibit an excess kurtosis significantly different from zero over the three time intervals, which is inconsistent with the assumption of Gaussianly distributed returns. While the standard deviations remain stable over time, the excess kurtosis increases significantly from the first to the second period. This is in resonance with the financial community's belief that stock price volatility has increased over time, a still controversial result (Jones and Wilson (1989), Campbell *et al* (2001), or Xu and Malkiel (2003)).

4.2 Calibration of the factor model

The determination of the parameters β and of the residues ε entering in the definition of the factor model (6) is performed for each asset by regressing the stocks returns on the market return. The coefficient β is thus given by the ordinary leastsquares estimator, which is consistent as long as the residues are weak white noise and with zero mean and finite variance. The idiosyncratic noise ε is obtained by subtracting β times the market return to the stock return. Table 3 presents the results for the three periods under consideration. For each period, we give the value of the estimated coefficient β (first column of Table 3 for each of the three time intervals). We then check the hypothesis of independence of the factor and the estimated residuals. To this aim, we estimate the Kendall's tau values between the factor and the residuals and the correlation coefficient between the square of the factor and the square of the error-terms. In Table 3, their values are given in the second and third columns presented for each of the three time periods. Some of the Kendall's tau values are found significantly different from zero, at the 95% confidence level, indicating the existence of significant dependence between the factor and the residuals. In addition, a Fisher's test shows that, at the 95% confidence level, all the correlation coefficients between the square of the factor and the square of the residuals are significantly different from zero. This result is not surprising and shows the existence of small but significant correlations

Table 3 Betas and dependences

	July 1962–December 1979			January 1979–December 2000			July 1962–December 2000		
	β	$\tau(Y, \varepsilon)$	$\rho_{y^2, \varepsilon^2}$	β	$\tau(Y, \varepsilon)$	$\rho_{y^2, \varepsilon^2}$	β	$\tau(Y, \varepsilon)$	$\rho_{y^2, \varepsilon^2}$
Abbott Labs	0.8994	−0.0168*	0.0879	0.9122	0.0439	0.1879	0.9081	0.0187	0.1597
American Home Products Corp.	0.9855	−0.0465	0.1253	0.8102	0.0031*	0.0587	0.8652	−0.0108*	0.0736
Boeing Co.	1.4416	−0.0089*	0.1196	0.9036	−0.0007*	0.0928	1.0715	0.0028*	0.1279
Bristol-Myers Squibb Co.	1.0832	−0.0171*	0.1056	1.0435	−0.0233	0.0457	1.0559	−0.0203	0.0481
Chevron Corp.	1.0062	−0.0304	0.1191	0.8333	0.0117*	0.0776	0.8873	0.0034*	0.0906
Du Pont (E.I.) de Nemours & Co.	1.0818	−0.0164*	0.0960	0.9451	0.0232	0.0433	0.9880	0.0158	0.0595
Disney (Walt) Co.	1.5530	−0.0175*	0.0960	1.0016	−0.0313	0.1304	1.1736	−0.0188	0.0641
General Motors Corp.	1.0945	−0.0070*	0.1531	1.0112	0.0044*	0.0400	1.0371	0.0048*	0.0563
Hewlett-Packard Co.	1.3910	−0.0202	0.1023	1.3074	0.0201	0.0739	1.3332	0.0059*	0.0832
Coca-Cola Co.	1.0347	−0.0557	0.2146	0.9833	−0.0057*	0.1254	0.9995	−0.0235	0.1238
Minnesota Mining & MFG Co.	1.1339	−0.0231	0.1203	0.8756	−0.0270	0.2605	0.9564	−0.0166	0.1706
Philip Morris Cos Inc.	1.0894	−0.0303	0.0723	0.8598	0.0213	0.0340	0.9314	0.0072*	0.0545
Pepsico Inc.	0.9587	−0.0369	0.1233	0.9004	0.0167*	0.3294	0.9187	−0.0020*	0.3169
Procter & Gamble Co.	0.8293	−0.0426	0.1873	0.8938	−0.0202	0.1188	0.8738	−0.0308	0.1287
Pharmacia Corp.	1.0750	−0.0241	0.0783	0.8824	−0.0111*	0.0373	0.9429	−0.0086*	0.0357
Schering-Plough Corp.	1.1244	−0.0338	0.1284	1.0480	−0.0126*	0.0494	1.0720	−0.0191	0.0540
Texaco Inc.	0.9414	−0.0141*	0.1354	0.6600	−0.0020*	0.0823	0.7481	0.0048*	0.1053
Texas Instruments Inc.	1.4578	−0.0038*	0.1410	1.3811	−0.0084*	0.0674	1.4049	−0.0049*	0.0766
United Technologies Corp.	1.1336	−0.0102*	0.1243	0.9049	0.0145*	0.1175	0.9763	0.0067*	0.1098
Walgreen Co.	0.6354	−0.0204	0.1052	0.8554	−0.0076*	0.1087	0.7869	−0.0171	0.0798

This table presents the estimated coefficient β for the factor model (6), the Kendall's tau $\tau(Y, \varepsilon)$ between the factor and the residuals, and the correlation coefficient $\rho_{y^2, \varepsilon^2}$ between the square of the factor and the square of the estimated idiosyncratic noise, for the different time intervals we have considered. An asterisk after the figures in the column giving the estimated Kendall's tau denotes a value significantly different from zero, at the 95% confidence level. A Fisher's test shows that the correlation coefficients $\rho_{y^2, \varepsilon^2}$ are all significantly different from zero, at the 95% confidence level.

between the market volatility and the idiosyncratic volatility. However, this will not invalidate the empirical tests of our theoretical results, since they hold even in the presence of weakly dependent factor and noise.

The coefficients β that we obtain by regressing each of the asset returns on the S&P 500 returns are very close, within their uncertainties, to the βs given by the CRSP database, which are estimated by regressing the assets returns on the valueweighted market portfolio. Thus, the choice of the S&P 500 index to represent the whole market portfolio is reasonable.

4.3 Estimation of the tail indexes

Assuming that the distributions of stocks and market returns are asymptotically power-law distributions (Longin (1996), Lux (1996), Pagan (1996), or Gopikrishnan et al (1998)), we now estimate the tail index of the distribution of each stock and its corresponding residue by the factor model, both for the positive and negative tails. Each tail index α is given by Hill's estimator:

$$\hat{\alpha} = \left[\frac{1}{k} \sum_{j=1}^{k} \log x_{j,N} - \log x_{k,N} \right]^{-1} \tag{21}$$

where $x_{1,N} \geq x_{2,N} \geq \ldots \geq x_{N,N}$ denotes the ordered statistics of the sample containing N independent and identically distributed realisations of the variable X.

Hill's estimator is asymptotically normally distributed with mean α and variance α^2/k. But, for finite k, it is known that the estimator is biased. As the range k increases, the variance of the estimator decreases while its bias increases. The competition between these two effects implies that there is an optimal choice for $k = k^*$, which minimises the mean squared error of the estimator. To select this value k^*, one can apply Danielsson and de Vries's (1997) algorithm, which is an improvement over Hall's (1990) subsample bootstrap procedure. One can also prefer the more recent algorithm of Danielsson et al (2001) for the sake of parsimony. We have tested all three algorithms to determine the optimal k^*. It emerges that Danielsson et al's (2001) algorithm, developed for high-frequency data, is not well adapted to samples containing less than 100,000 data points, as is the case here. Thus, we have focused on the other two algorithms. An accurate determination of k^* is rather difficult with any of them, but in every case, we found that the relevant range for the tail index estimation was between the 1% and 5% quantiles. Tables 4 and 5 give the estimated tail index for each asset and residues at the 1%, 2.5% and 5% quantiles, for both the positive and the negative tails, for the two time sub-intervals. The second time interval from January 1980 to December 2000 is characterised by values of the tail indexes that are homogeneous over the various quantiles and range between three and four for the negative tails and between three and five for the positive tails. There is slightly more dispersion in the first time interval from July 1962 to December 1979.

For each asset and their residue of the regression on the market factor, we tested whether the hypothesis, according to which the tail index measured for each asset and each residue is the same as the tail index of the S&P 500 index, can be rejected at the 95% confidence level for a given quantile. Before proceeding with the presentation of our tests, two caveats have to be accounted for. First, owing to the phenomenon of volatility clustering in financial time series, extremes are more likely to occur together. In this situation, Hill's estimator is no more normally distributed with variance α^2/k. In fact, for weakly dependent time series, it can only be asserted that the estimator remains consistent (see Rootzén and de Haan (1998)). Moreover, as shown by Kearns and Pagan (1997) for heteroskedastic time series, the variance of the estimated tail index can be seven times larger than the variance given by the asymptotic normality assumption. Second, the idiosyncratic noise is estimated by subtracting β times the factor from the asset return. Thus, even when the factor and the error-term are independent, the empirically estimated residues depend on the realisations of the factor. As a consequence, the tail index estimators for the factor and for the idiosyncratic noise are correlated. This correlation obviously depends on the exact form of the distributions of the factor and the idiosyncratic noise. Even without the knowledge of the true test statistics, for both problematic points, we can assert that the fluctuations of the estimators are larger than those given by the asymptotically normal statistics for iid realisations. Thus, performing the test under the asymptotic normality assumption is more constraining than under the true (but unknown) test statistics, so that the non-rejection of the equality hypothesis under the assumption of

Table 4 Tail indexes (1962–79)

	Negative tail						Positive tail					
	$q = 1\%$		$q = 2.5\%$		$q = 5\%$		$q = 1\%$		$q = 2.5\%$		$q = 5\%$	
	Asset	ε	Asset	ε	Asset	ε	Asset	ε	Asset	ε	Asset	ε
Abbott Labs	5.54	5.31	3.94	4.02	3.27	3.31	5.10	4.50	4.09	3.71	3.53*	3.14
American Home Products Corp.	4.58	5.11	3.89	3.81	3.02*	3.21*	3.64	4.66	3.60	3.81	3.11	3.15
Boeing Co.	6.07	4.90	4.57	3.74	3.32	3.49	4.04	4.27	3.95	4.19	3.35*	2.93
Bristol-Myers Squibb Co.	4.32	4.27	3.31	3.95	2.99*	3.16*	5.96*	5.19	3.94	4.82*	3.62*	4.03*
Chevron Corp.	5.24	4.78	3.75	3.29	2.91	3.12*	5.21	5.15	3.90	4.26	3.25*	3.07
Du Pont (E.I.) de Nemours & Co.	5.26	4.36	3.69	3.76	3.17*	3.23*	5.35	5.15	4.00	3.37	3.13	3.04
Disney (Walt) Co.	3.59	4.23	3.59	3.84	3.08*	3.22*	4.90	4.34	4.26	3.73	3.33*	3.29*
General Motors Corp.	4.82	3.50	3.72	3.66	2.94*	3.36	3.91	4.78	3.64	3.86	2.94	3.07
Hewlett-Packard Co.	3.76	3.89	3.12*	3.05*	2.81*	3.00*	4.64	5.08	4.08	4.20	3.41*	3.42
Coca-Cola Co.	3.45	3.45	3.05*	3.71	2.75*	3.17*	3.91	4.26	3.16	3.61	2.81	3.16
Minnesota Mining & MFG Co.	5.16	4.86	4.06	4.35	3.43	3.71	4.35	4.47	3.96	3.31	3.14	3.06
Philip Morris Cos Inc.	4.63	3.79	3.82	3.90	3.38	3.48	4.10	4.64	3.59	3.85	3.03	3.06
Pepsico Inc.	4.89	5.35	3.93	4.49	3.02*	3.27	4.07	4.67	3.49	3.86	3.15	3.21*
Procter & Gamble Co.	4.42	3.77	3.77	3.74	3.13*	3.42	4.14	5.39	3.59	3.73	2.97	3.40*
Pharmacia Corp.	4.73	4.24	4.05	3.45	2.88*	3.34	4.46	3.72	3.95	3.90	3.14	2.99
Schering-Plough Corp.	4.59	4.70	4.20	3.87	3.37	3.33	4.60	5.88*	3.50	3.91	3.07	3.22*
Texaco Inc.	5.34	4.59	3.99	3.84	3.07*	3.19*	3.83	4.10	3.94	3.67	3.14	2.98
Texas Instruments Inc.	4.08	4.54	3.36	3.13*	3.22*	2.87*	4.52	4.20	3.67	3.79	3.16	3.07
United Technologies Corp.	4.00	4.49	3.52	3.92	3.27	3.46	4.78	4.97	3.73	3.98	3.26*	3.49*
Walgreen Co.	4.63	6.50	3.85	4.26	2.94*	3.18*	5.16	4.56	3.47	3.30	3.15	2.82
S&P 500	5.17	–	4.16	–	3.91	–	3.74	–	3.34	–	2.64	–

This table gives the estimated value of the tail index for the 20 considered assets, the S&P 500 index and the residues ε obtained by regressing each asset on the S&P 500 index, for both the negative and the positive tails, during the time interval from July 1962 to December 1979. The tail indexes are estimated by Hill's estimator at the quantile 1%, 2.5% and 5%, which are the optimal quantiles given by the Hall (1990) and Danielson and de Vries (1997) algorithms. The values with asterisks represent the tail indexes which cannot be considered equal to the S&P 500 index's tail index at the 95% confidence level.

317

Table 5 Tail indexes (1980–2000)

	Negative tail						Positive tail					
	$q = 1\%$		$q = 2.5\%$		$q = 5\%$		$q = 1\%$		$q = 2.5\%$		$q = 5\%$	
	Asset	ε	Asset	ε	Asset	ε	Asset	ε	Asset	ε	Asset	ε
Abbott Labs	3.59	3.60	3.35	3.62	3.22	3.39	5.14	4.60	4.16	3.76	3.77	3.07
American Home Products Corp.	3.03	3.07	3.11	2.78	2.73	2.49*	4.01	3.47	3.28	3.02	2.87	2.79
Boeing Co.	3.39	3.97	3.23	3.53	3.02	3.21	4.86	3.65	3.45	3.16	3.13	3.23
Bristol-Myers Squibb Co.	3.21	3.15	2.90	3.41	2.80	3.16	2.98	3.74	3.35	3.12	3.20	2.75
Chevron Corp.	4.13	4.48	3.99	3.91	3.30	3.45	5.16	4.53	3.88	3.81	3.01	3.06
Du Pont (E.I.) de Nemours & Co.	3.99	3.49	3.76	3.23	3.02	3.04	5.36	4.33	4.31	3.35	3.44	2.76
Disney (Walt) Co.	2.83	3.24	2.76	2.97	2.85	2.83	3.97	3.70	3.68	3.33	3.15	2.87
General Motors Corp.	4.44	4.79	3.88	4.27*	3.44	3.56	5.76	5.32	4.45	3.86	3.43	3.22
Hewlett-Packard Co.	3.73	3.45	3.52	3.12	3.00	2.73	4.31	3.40	3.47	3.29	3.24	2.99
Coca-Cola Co.	3.01	3.76	3.14	3.48	2.99	2.86	4.06	3.47	3.45	3.16	3.37	2.87
Minnesota Mining & MFG Co.	3.52	3.38	3.21	3.39	2.88	3.04	3.76	3.46	3.95	3.22	3.10	2.76
Philip Morris Cos Inc.	3.58	3.34	3.33	3.12	2.68	2.53*	3.42	3.16	3.70	3.07	2.85	2.81
Pepsico Inc.	4.14	4.46	3.39	3.60	2.99	3.27	4.00	3.87	3.61	3.34	3.44	3.31
Procter & Gamble Co.	2.65	2.46	3.29	3.19	3.19	2.87	4.35	3.90	3.48	3.20	3.14	2.91
Pharmacia Corp.	2.96	3.20	3.09	2.79	2.80	2.70	4.12	4.70	3.44	3.50	3.31	2.89
Schering-Plough Corp.	4.22	5.20*	3.29	3.68	3.11	3.05	3.23	3.51	3.45	3.08	3.06	2.87
Texaco Inc.	3.09	3.20	3.10	3.15	2.88	2.84	3.65	3.36	3.20	3.04	2.86	2.70
Texas Instruments Inc.	3.49	3.53	3.35	3.31	2.89	2.99	4.00	3.42	3.36	3.30	2.97	3.06
United Technologies Corp.	4.21	3.98	3.82	3.46	3.34	3.18	5.39	4.50	4.00	3.80	3.51	3.26
Walgreen Co.	4.06	4.35	3.81	4.04	3.20	3.40	4.60	5.12	3.79	3.54	3.20	3.07
S&P 500	3.16	–	3.17	–	3.16	–	4.00	–	3.65	–	3.19	–

This table gives the estimated value of the tail index for the 20 considered assets, the S&P 500 index, and the residues ε obtained by regressing each asset on the S&P 500 index, for both the negative and the positive tails, during the time interval from January 1980 to December 2000. The tail indexes are estimated by Hill's estimator at the quantile 1%, 2.5% and 5%, which are the optimal quantiles given by Hall (1990) and Danielson and de Vries (1997) also.

a normally distributed estimator ensures that we would not be able to reject this hypothesis under the real statistics of the estimator.

The values which reject the equality hypothesis are indicated by an asterisk in Tables 4 and 5. During the second time interval, from January 1980 to December 2000, only four residues have a tail index significantly different from that of the S&P 500, and only in the negative tail. The situation is not as good during the first time interval, especially for the negative tail, for which no fewer than 13 assets and 10 residues out of 20 have a tail index significantly different from the S&P 500 ones, for the 5% quantile. Recall that the equality tests have been performed under the assumption of a normally distributed estimator with variance α^2/k, which, as explained above, is too strong a hypothesis. As a consequence, a rejection under the normality hypothesis does not imply necessarily that the equality hypothesis would have been rejected under the true statistics. While providing a note of caution, this statement is nevertheless not very useful from a practical point of view. More importantly, we stress that the equality of the tail indexes of the distribution of the factor and of the idiosyncratic noise is not crucial. Indeed, we shall propose below two different estimators for the coefficient of tail dependence. One of them does not rely on the equality of these two tail indexes and thus remains operational even when they are different and in particular when the tail index of the idiosyncratic noise appears larger than the tail of the factor.

To summarise, our tests confirm that the tail indexes of most stock return distributions range between three and four, even though no better precision can be given with good significance. Moreover, in most cases, we can assume that the asset, the factor, and the residue have the same tail index. We can also add that, as asserted by Loretan and Phillips (1994) or Longin (1996), we cannot reject the hypothesis that the tail index remains the same over time. Nevertheless, it seems that the tail indexes were slightly larger during the first period from July 1962 to December 1979 than during the second period from January 1980 to December 2000.

4.4 An alternative one-step estimation procedure of the parameters of the factor model

The two-step estimation procedure presented in the two previous sections may not be the most efficient one. For instance, using the ordinary least-squares estimator is not the most efficient way to estimate the coefficient β when the residuals are fat-tailed. A generally more efficient approach is to jointly estimate β and α. The adaptive least-squares estimation procedure proposed by McDonald and Newey (1988) provides a versatile framework in which to perform this task. We have chosen a slightly simpler approach, which consists of performing a maximum likelihood estimation of the parameters (α, β) under the assumption that the residuals follow Student's *t*-distribution with α degree of freedom. The results of this estimation for the parameter β are reported in Table 6. The values obtained are not significantly different from those obtained by the OLS method.

The correlation between the square of the factor and the square of the residuals is found to be still significantly different from zero, while the Kendall's tau values are all (but one) not significant at the 95%, showing that the one-step estimation provides slightly better estimates of the βs than the two-step procedure based on the OLS insofar as the factor and the residuals exhibit weaker dependence.

As far as the estimates of the tail index α are concerned, we obtained values very close to those given in Tables 4 and 5, obtained using the Hill estimator. We therefore do not report these values.

4.5 Determination of the coefficient of tail dependence

Using the just-established empirical fact that we cannot reject the hypothesis that the assets, the market, and the residues have the same tail index, we can use the theorem of Appendix A and its second corollary stated in Section 3. This allows us to conclude that one cannot reject the hypothesis of a non-vanishing tail dependence between the assets and the market.

In addition, the coefficient of tail dependence is given by Equations (12) and (13). These equations provide two ways of estimating the coefficient of tail dependence: non-parametric with (12) and parametric with (13). The first one is more general since it only requires the hypothesis of a regular variation, while the second one explicitly assumes that the factor and the residues have distributions with power-law tails.

To estimate the tail dependence according to Equation (12), we need only to determine the constant *l* defined in (8). Consider *N*

Table 6 Betas and dependences

	July 1962–December 1979			January 1979–December 2000			July 1962–December 2000		
	β	$\tau(Y, \varepsilon)$	ρ_{y^2, e^2}	β	$\tau(Y, \varepsilon)$	ρ_{y^2, e^2}	β	$\tau(Y, \varepsilon)$	ρ_{y^2, e^2}
Abbott Labs	0.8407	0.0038	0.0846	0.9768	0.0164	0.2445	0.9308	0.0098	0.1756
American Home Products Corp.	0.8865	-0.0053	0.1304	0.796 2	0.0098	0.0574	0.8251	0.0073	0.0676
Boeing Co.	1.3495	0.0143	0.1145	0.8848	0.0064	0.0851	1.0311	0.0154*	0.1113
Bristol-Myers Squibb Co.	1.0318	0.0013	0.1048	1.0101	-0.0075	0.0518	1.0140	-0.0025	0.0546
Chevron Corp.	0.9379	-0.0008	0.1184	0.8431	0.0076	0.0786	0.8821	0.0056	0.0896
Du Pont (E.I.) de Nemours & Co.	1.0229	0.0134	0.0935	0.9897	0.0031	0.0525	1.0076	0.0065	0.0644
Disney (Walt) Co.	1.5177	-0.0078	0.0969	0.9600	-0.0145	0.1512	1.1248	-0.0022	0.0764
General Motors Corp.	1.0598	0.0100	0.1509	1.0092	0.0052	0.0400	1.0282	0.0087	0.0556
Hewlett-Packard Co.	1.3067	0.0050	0.1038	1.3359	0.0106	0.0835	1.3276	0.0076	0.0815
Coca-Cola Co.	0.9128	-0.0052	0.2329	0.9908	-0.0092	0.1219	0.9645	-0.0080	0.1387
Minnesota Mining & MFG Co.	1.0867	-0.0027	0.1231	0.8313	-0.0038	0.3063	0.9226	-0.0004	0.1945
Philip Morris Cos Inc.	1.0330	-0.0093	0.0767	0.8970	0.0051	0.0417	0.9433	0.0023	0.0575
Pepsico Inc.	0.8722	-0.0040	0.1275	0.9502	-0.0032	0.3716	0.9245	-0.0043	0.3213
Procter & Gamble Co.	0.7525	-0.0051	0.1968	0.8760	-0.0113	0.1246	0.8313	-0.0099	0.1432
Pharmacia Corp.	1.0330	-0.0072	0.0778	0.8711	-0.0066	0.0391	0.9318	-0.0041	0.0368
Schering-Plough Corp.	1.0487	-0.0082	0.1342	1.0392	-0.0091	0.0507	1.0419	-0.0080	0.0575
Texaco Inc.	0.8940	0.0060	0.1339	0.6519	0.0015	0.0813	0.7497	0.0041	0.1057
Texas Instruments Inc.	1.4111	0.0107	0.1376	1.3231	0.0086	0.0641	1.3478	0.0122	0.0726
United Technologies Corp	1.0577	0.0124	0.1177	0.9348	0.0015	0.1307	0.9717	0.0084	0.1080
Walgreen Co.	0.5572	0.0035	0.1005	0.8367	-0.0006	0.1020	0.7428	-0.0019	0.0735

This table presents the estimated coefficient β for the factor model (6), the Kendall's tau $\tau(Y, \varepsilon)$ between the factor and the residuals, and the correlation coefficient ρ_{y^2, e^2} between the square of the factor and the square of the estimated idiosyncratic noise, for the different time intervals we have considered. The joined estimation procedure of (α, β) has been used. An asterisk after the figures in the column giving the estimated Kendall's tau denotes a value significantly different from zero, at the 95% confidence level. A Fisher's test shows that the correlation coefficients ρ_{y^2, e^2} are all significantly different from zero, at the 95% confidence level.

sorted realisations of X and Y denoted by $x_{1,N} \geq x_{2,N} \geq \ldots \geq x_{N,N}$ and $y_{1,N} \geq y_{2,N} \geq \ldots \geq y_{N,N}$. The quantiles of $F_X^{-1}(u)$ and of $F_Y^{-1}(u)$ are estimated by

$$\hat{F}_X^{-1}(u) = x_{[(1-u) \cdot N],N} \quad \text{and} \quad \hat{F}_Y^{-1}(u) = y_{[(1-u) \cdot N]}, \tag{22}$$

where $[\cdot]$ denotes the integer part. Thus, the constant l is non-parametrically estimated by

$$\hat{l}_k = \frac{x_{k,N}}{y_{k,N}} \quad \text{as} \quad k \to 0 \text{ or } N \tag{23}$$

As u goes to zero or one (or k goes to zero or N), the number of observations decreases dramatically. However, we observe a large interval of small or large ks such that the ratio of the empirical quantiles remains remarkably stable and thus allows for an accurate estimation of l. A more precise estimation could be performed with a kernel-based quantile estimator (see Shealter and Marron (1990), or Pagan and Ullah (1999), for instance). A non-parametric estimator for λ is then obtained by replacing l by its estimated value in Equation (12)

$$\hat{\lambda}_{NP} = \frac{1}{\max\left\{1, \left(\dfrac{\hat{l}}{\hat{\beta}}\right)^\alpha\right\}} = \frac{1}{\max\left\{1, \left(\dfrac{x_{k,N}}{\hat{\beta} \cdot y_{k,N}}\right)^\alpha\right\}} \tag{24}$$

It can also be advantageous to follow a parametric approach, which generally allows for a more accurate estimation of (the ratio of) the quantiles, provided that the assumed parametric form of the distributions is not too far from the true one. For this purpose, we will use formula (13), which requires the estimation of the scale factors for the different assets. To get the scale factors, we proceed as follows. Consider a variable X which asymptotically follows a power-law distribution $\Pr\{X > x\} \sim C \cdot x^{-\alpha}$. Given a rank-ordered sample $x_{1,N} \geq x_{2,N} \geq \ldots \geq x_{N,N}$, the scale factor C can be consistently estimated from the k largest realisations by

$$\hat{C} = \frac{k}{N} \cdot (x_{k,N})^\alpha \tag{25}$$

The estimated value of the scale factor must not depend on the rank k for k large enough, in order for the parameterisation of the distribution in terms of a power-law to hold true. Thus, denoting by $\hat{C}_Y$ and $\hat{C}_\varepsilon$ the estimated scale factors of the factor Y and of the noise ε defined in Equation (6), the estimator of the coefficient of tail dependence is

$$\hat{\lambda} = \frac{1}{1+\hat{\beta}^{-\alpha}\cdot\dfrac{\hat{C}_Y}{\hat{C}_\varepsilon}} = \frac{1}{1+\left(\dfrac{\varepsilon_{k,N}}{\hat{\beta}\cdot y_{k,N}}\right)^{\alpha}} \tag{26}$$

where $\hat{\beta}$ denotes the estimated coefficient β. Since the estimators $\hat{C}_Y, \hat{C}_\varepsilon$ and $\hat{\beta}$ are consistent and using the continuous mapping theorem, we can assert that the estimator $\hat{\lambda}$ is also consistent.

Since the tail indexes α are impossible to determine with sufficient accuracy other than saying that the αs probably fall in the interval 3–4, as we have seen above, our strategy is to determine the coefficient of tail dependence using (24) and (26) for three different common values, $\alpha = 3, 3.5$ and 4. This procedure allows us to test for the sensitivity of the scale factor and therefore of the tail coefficient with respect to the uncertain value of the tail index.

The coefficients of tail dependence have been assessed using both the one-step and the two-step estimation procedure for the coefficient β described above. These two approaches do not yield significantly different results, so that it is enough to show the results obtained by only one of them, which we take to be the two-step procedure for the sake of simplicity of implementation. Tables 7 and 8 give the values of the coefficients of lower tail dependence over the whole time interval from July 1962 to December 2000, under the assumption that the tail index α equals 3, for the non-parametric estimator (Table 7) and the parametric one (Table 8). For each table, the coefficient of tail dependence is estimated over the first centile, the first quintile and the first decile to also test for any possible sensitivity on the tail asymptotics. For each of these quantiles, the mean values, their standard deviations and their minimum and maximum values are given. First, we remark that the standard deviation of the tail dependence coefficient remains small compared with its average value and that the minimum and maximum

Table 7 Tail dependence: non-parametric method (24)

	First centile				First quintile				First decile			
	Mean	Std	Min.	Max.	Mean	Std	Min.	Max.	Mean	Std	Min.	Max.
Abbott Labs	0.1264	0.0106	0.1039	0.1745	0.1232	0.0058	0.1039	0.1745	0.1185	0.0069	0.1039	0.1745
American Home Products Corp.	0.1181	0.0091	0.0796	0.1288	0.1349	0.0111	0.0796	0.1494	0.1401	0.0096	0.0796	0.1505
Boeing Co.	0.1116	0.0128	0.0954	0.1653	0.1090	0.0074	0.0954	0.1653	0.1066	0.0066	0.0954	0.1653
Bristol-Myers Squibb Co.	0.1927	0.0171	0.1407	0.2175	0.2220	0.0220	0.1407	0.2474	0.2180	0.0180	0.1407	0.2474
Chevron Corp.	0.1566	0.0194	0.1334	0.2368	0.1407	0.0121	0.1265	0.2368	0.1365	0.0101	0.1257	0.2368
Du Pont (E.I.) de Nemours & Co.	0.2089	0.0142	0.1785	0.2424	0.2067	0.0105	0.1785	0.2424	0.2021	0.0106	0.1785	0.2424
Disney (Walt) Co.	0.1317	0.0160	0.0930	0.1613	0.1587	0.0161	0.0930	0.1754	0.1566	0.0123	0.0930	0.1754
General Motors Corp.	0.2210	0.0149	0.2045	0.2996	0.2109	0.0096	0.1947	0.2996	0.2020	0.0120	0.1808	0.2996
Hewlett-Packard Co.	0.1455	0.0103	0.1188	0.1769	0.1615	0.0116	0.1188	0.1776	0.1603	0.0095	0.1188	0.1776
Coca-Cola Co.	0.1870	0.0259	0.1199	0.2522	0.2159	0.0204	0.1199	0.2522	0.2160	0.0164	0.1199	0.2522
Minnesota Mining & MFG Co.	0.2311	0.0254	0.1851	0.3268	0.2262	0.0126	0.1851	0.3268	0.2218	0.0115	0.1851	0.3268
Philip Morris Cos Inc.	0.1251	0.0078	0.1050	0.1526	0.1334	0.0089	0.1050	0.1526	0.1340	0.0070	0.1050	0.1526
Pepsico Inc.	0.1263	0.0111	0.1014	0.1706	0.1242	0.0071	0.1014	0.1706	0.1239	0.0057	0.1014	0.1706
Procter & Gamble Co.	0.1980	0.0325	0.1131	0.2351	0.2017	0.0153	0.1131	0.2351	0.1972	0.0131	0.1131	0.2351
Pharmacia Corp.	0.1180	0.0172	0.0596	0.1378	0.1291	0.0109	0.0596	0.1432	0.1337	0.0091	0.0596	0.1434
Schering-Plough Corp.	0.1759	0.0143	0.1320	0.2403	0.1733	0.0078	0.1320	0.2403	0.1663	0.0102	0.1320	0.2403
Texaco Inc.	0.0214	0.0017	0.0170	0.0269	0.0246	0.0023	0.0170	0.0278	0.0248	0.0018	0.0170	0.0278
Texas Instruments Inc.	0.5657	0.0687	0.3897	0.6572	0.6162	0.0438	0.3897	0.6623	0.6168	0.0368	0.3897	0.6761
United Technologies Corp.	0.1300	0.0123	0.0990	0.1872	0.1254	0.0073	0.0990	0.1872	0.1192	0.0086	0.0990	0.1872
Walgreen Co.	0.0739	0.0109	0.0664	0.1185	0.0682	0.0058	0.0629	0.1185	0.0674	0.0044	0.0629	0.1185

This table gives the average (Mean), the standard deviation (Std), the minimum (Min.) and the maximum (Max.) values of the coefficient of lower tail dependence estimated over the first centile, quintile and decile during the entire time interval from July 1962 to December 2000, under the assumption that the tail of the distributions of the assets and the market are regularly varying with an index equal to three and applying the non-parametric estimator $\hat{\lambda}_{NP}$ given by Equation (24).

Table 8 Tail dependence: parametric method (26)

	First centile				First quintile				First decile			
	Mean	Std	Min.	Max.	Mean	Std	Min.	Max.	Mean	Std	Min.	Max.
Abbott Labs	0.1670	0.0127	0.1442	0.2137	0.1633	0.0071	0.1442	0.2137	0.1540	0.0120	0.1331	0.2137
American Home Products Corp.	0.1423	0.0207	0.0910	0.1720	0.1728	0.0205	0.091	0.1963	0.1823	0.0175	0.0910	0.2020
Boeing Co.	0.1372	0.0127	0.1101	0.1804	0.1349	0.0064	0.1101	0.1804	0.1289	0.0078	0.1101	0.1804
Bristol-Myers Squibb Co.	0.2720	0.0231	0.1878	0.3052	0.2751	0.0115	0.1878	0.3052	0.2696	0.0110	0.1878	0.3052
Chevron Corp.	0.1853	0.0188	0.1656	0.2564	0.1790	0.0105	0.1634	0.2564	0.1748	0.0096	0.1606	0.2564
Du Pont (E.I.) de Nemours & Co.	0.2547	0.0148	0.2127	0.2871	0.2695	0.0117	0.2127	0.2876	0.2685	0.0103	0.2127	0.2876
Disney (Walt) Co.	0.1772	0.0149	0.1368	0.1957	0.1938	0.0123	0.1368	0.2094	0.1900	0.0109	0.1368	0.2094
General Motors Corp.	0.2641	0.0259	0.2393	0.3652	0.2565	0.0138	0.2349	0.3652	0.2545	0.0108	0.2349	0.3652
Hewlett-Packard Co.	0.1701	0.0096	0.1389	0.1914	0.2018	0.0230	0.1389	0.2303	0.2039	0.0176	0.1389	0.2303
Coca-Cola Co.	0.2343	0.0223	0.1686	0.2719	0.2576	0.0163	0.1686	0.2731	0.2579	0.0123	0.1686	0.2731
Minnesota Mining & MFG Co.	0.2844	0.0196	0.2399	0.3407	0.2873	0.0099	0.2399	0.3407	0.2802	0.0117	0.2399	0.3407
Philip Morris Cos Inc.	0.1369	0.0168	0.0983	0.1673	0.1700	0.0206	0.0983	0.1919	0.1729	0.0155	0.0983	0.1919
Pepsico Inc.	0.1634	0.0132	0.1483	0.2106	0.1535	0.0083	0.1448	0.2106	0.1512	0.0067	0.1434	0.2106
Procter & Gamble Co.	0.2284	0.0292	0.1434	0.2673	0.2461	0.0169	0.1434	0.2673	0.2413	0.0141	0.1434	0.2673
Pharmacia Corp.	0.1279	0.0104	0.0863	0.1432	0.1588	0.0192	0.0863	0.1822	0.1643	0.0149	0.0863	0.1822
Schering-Plough Corp.	0.2195	0.0190	0.1920	0.2863	0.2179	0.0103	0.1920	0.2863	0.2107	0.0123	0.1877	0.2863
Texaco Inc.	0.0327	0.0027	0.0243	0.0369	0.0369	0.0033	0.0243	0.0414	0.0371	0.0027	0.0243	0.0414
Texas Instruments Inc.	0.4355	0.0195	0.3389	0.4906	0.4500	0.0142	0.3389	0.4906	0.4515	0.011	0.3389	0.4906
United Technologies Corp.	0.1570	0.0153	0.1298	0.2182	0.1562	0.0075	0.1298	0.2182	0.1511	0.0084	0.1298	0.2182
Walgreen Co.	0.0937	0.0112	0.0808	0.1384	0.0837	0.0071	0.0776	0.1384	0.0786	0.0078	0.0669	0.1384

This table gives the average (Mean), the standard deviation (Std), the minimum (Min.) and the maximum (Max.) values of the coefficient of lower tail dependence estimated over the first centile, quintile and decile during the entire time interval from July 1962 to December 2000, under the assumption that the tail of the distributions of the assets and the market are power laws with an exponent equal to three and applying the parametric estimator λ given by Equation (26).

values cluster closely around its mean value. This shows that the coefficient of tail dependence is well-estimated by its mean over a given quantile. Secondly, we find that these estimated coefficients of tail dependence exhibit a good stability over the various quantiles. These two observations enable us to conclude that the average coefficient of tail dependence over the first centile is sufficient to provide a good estimate of the true coefficient of tail dependence.

Note that the two estimators yield essentially equivalent results, even if the coefficients of tail dependence given by the non-parametric estimator exhibit a systematic tendency to be slightly smaller than the estimates provided by the parametric estimator. Since the results given by these two estimators are very close to each other, we choose to present below only those given by the parametric one. This choice has also been guided by the lower sensibility of this last estimator to small changes of the tail exponent α. Indeed, since the evaluation of the scale factors $\hat{C}_Y$ and $\hat{C}_\varepsilon$ by formula (25) involves the tail exponent α, the small deviations from its true value are compensated by the estimated scale factors. This explains the observation that the parametric estimator appears more robust than the non-parametric one with respect to small changes in α. For this reason, it appears that the parametric estimator provides more reliable estimates than the non-parametric estimator and thus should be preferred for practical purpose.

Tables 9, 10 and 11 summarise the different values of the coefficient of tail dependence for both the positive and the negative tails, under the assumptions that the tail index α equals 3, 3.5 and 4 respectively, over the three considered time intervals. Overall, we find that the coefficients of tail dependence are almost equal for both the negative and the positive tails and that they are not very sensitive to the value of the tail index in the interval considered. More precisely, during the first time interval from July 1962 to December 1979 (Table 9), the tail dependence is symmetric in both the upper and the lower tail. During the second time interval from January 1980 to December 2000 and over the whole time interval (Tables 10 and 11), the coefficient of lower tail dependence is slightly but systematically larger than the upper one. Moreover, since these coefficients of tail dependence are all less than 1/2, they decrease when the tail index α increases, and the smaller the coefficient of tail dependence, the larger the decay.

Table 9 Tail dependence: 1962–79

	Negative tail			Positive tail		
	$\alpha = 3$	$\alpha = 3.5$	$\alpha = 4$	$\alpha = 3$	$\alpha = 3.5$	$\alpha = 4$
Abbott Labs	0.12	0.09	0.06	0.11	0.08	0.06
American Home Products Corp.	0.22	0.18	0.15	0.25	0.22	0.19
Boeing Co.	0.16	0.13	0.10	0.13	0.10	0.07
Bristol-Myers Squibb Co.	0.22	0.19	0.16	0.28	0.25	0.23
Chevron Corp.	0.21	0.17	0.14	0.26	0.23	0.20
Du Pont (E.I.) de Nemours & Co.	0.38	0.37	0.35	0.37	0.35	0.33
Disney (Walt) Co.	0.24	0.20	0.17	0.23	0.19	0.16
General Motors Corp.	0.39	0.37	0.35	0.48	0.47	0.47
Hewlett-Packard Co.	0.15	0.12	0.09	0.23	0.20	0.17
Coca-Cola Co.	0.26	0.22	0.19	0.26	0.23	0.20
Minnesota Mining & MFG Co.	0.35	0.32	0.30	0.35	0.33	0.31
Philip Morris Cos Inc.	0.25	0.22	0.19	0.20	0.17	0.14
Pepsico Inc.	0.15	0.12	0.09	0.17	0.14	0.11
Procter & Gamble Co.	0.23	0.19	0.16	0.24	0.21	0.18
Pharmacia Corp.	0.23	0.19	0.16	0.26	0.23	0.20
Schering-Plough Corp.	0.21	0.18	0.15	0.20	0.17	0.14
Texaco Inc.	0.06	0.04	0.03	0.07	0.05	0.03
Texas Instruments Inc.	0.47	0.46	0.46	0.49	0.49	0.49
United Technologies Corp.	0.13	0.10	0.07	0.13	0.10	0.07
Walgreen Co.	0.03	0.02	0.01	0.02	0.01	0.01

This table summarises the mean values over the first centile of the distribution of the coefficients of (upper or lower) tail dependence for the positive and negative tails during the time interval from July 1962 to December 1979, for three values of the tail index $\alpha = 3, 3.5, 4$.

During the first time interval, most of the coefficients of tail dependence range between 0.15 and 0.35 in both tails, while during the second time interval, almost all range between 0.10 and 0.25 in the lower tail and between 0.10 and 0.20 in the upper one. Thus, the tail dependence is smaller during the last period than during the first one. This result is interesting because it is in agreement with, and confirms the recent studies by, Campbell *et al* (2001) and Xu and Malkiel (2003), which show that the idiosyncratic volatility of each stocks have increased relative to the market volatility. And, as already discussed, the coefficient of tail dependence given by Equation (10) must decrease when the idiosyncratic volatility of the stocks increases relative to the market volatility.

The strong similarity of the tail dependences in the upper and lower tails is an interesting empirical finding which suggests that

Table 10 Tail dependence: 1980–2000

	Negative tail			Positive tail		
	$\alpha = 3$	$\alpha = 3.5$	$\alpha = 4$	$\alpha = 3$	$\alpha = 3.5$	$\alpha = 4$
Abbott Labs	0.20	0.17	0.14	0.16	0.13	0.10
American Home Products Corp.	0.12	0.09	0.06	0.10	0.08	0.05
Boeing Co.	0.14	0.11	0.08	0.10	0.07	0.05
Bristol-Myers Squibb Co.	0.32	0.29	0.26	0.25	0.21	0.19
Chevron Corp.	0.18	0.14	0.11	0.13	0.09	0.07
Du Pont (E.I.) de Nemours & Co.	0.23	0.20	0.17	0.16	0.13	0.10
Disney (Walt) Co.	0.16	0.13	0.10	0.15	0.12	0.09
General Motors Corp.	0.26	0.22	0.19	0.20	0.16	0.13
Hewlett-Packard Co.	0.19	0.15	0.13	0.21	0.18	0.15
Coca-Cola Co.	0.24	0.20	0.18	0.20	0.17	0.14
Minnesota Mining & MFG Co.	0.26	0.23	0.20	0.20	0.17	0.14
Philip Morris Cos Inc.	0.11	0.08	0.06	0.11	0.08	0.06
Pepsico Inc.	0.17	0.14	0.11	0.14	0.11	0.09
Procter & Gamble Co.	0.24	0.21	0.18	0.20	0.16	0.13
Pharmacia Corp.	0.10	0.08	0.05	0.10	0.07	0.05
Schering-Plough Corp.	0.23	0.20	0.17	0.16	0.13	0.10
Texaco Inc.	0.02	0.01	0.01	0.02	0.01	0.01
Texas Instruments Inc.	0.43	0.42	0.41	0.31	0.28	0.26
United Technologies Corp.	0.20	0.16	0.14	0.18	0.14	0.11
Walgreen Co.	0.15	0.12	0.09	0.09	0.07	0.05

This table summarises the mean values over the first centile of the distribution of the coefficients of (upper or lower) tail dependence for the positive and negative tails during the time interval from January 1980 to December 2000, for three values of the tail index $\alpha = 3, 3.5, 4$.

extreme co-movements reflect behaviors of agents that are more sensitive to large amplitudes than to a specific direction (loss or gain). Pictorially, the specific mechanism triggering co-movements of extreme amplitudes may well be different for losses compared to gains, such as fear for the former and greed for the latter, but the resulting large co-movements have similar frequencies of occurrence.

The observed lack of stationarity of the coefficient of tail dependence in the two time sub-intervals suggests that it could be necessary to have a model where the tail-dependence index is not constant but varies as a function of past shocks (just as the volatility varies with time in a GARCH model) in order to investigate whether large recent common shocks lead to higher future tail dependence. This point is beyond the scope of the present study,

Table 11 Tail dependence: 1962–2000

	Negative tail			Positive tail		
	$\alpha = 3$	$\alpha = 3.5$	$\alpha = 4$	$\alpha = 3$	$\alpha = 3.5$	$\alpha = 4$
Abbott Labs	0.17	0.13	0.11	0.15	0.12	0.09
American Home Products Corp.	0.14	0.11	0.08	0.15	0.11	0.09
Boeing Co.	0.14	0.10	0.08	0.10	0.07	0.05
Bristol-Myers Squibb Co.	0.27	0.24	0.21	0.27	0.24	0.21
Chevron Corp.	0.19	0.15	0.12	0.17	0.13	0.10
Du Pont (E.I.) de Nemours & Co.	0.25	0.22	0.19	0.23	0.19	0.16
Disney (Walt) Co.	0.18	0.14	0.11	0.17	0.13	0.11
General Motors Corp.	0.26	0.23	0.20	0.24	0.21	0.18
Hewlett-Packard Co.	0.17	0.14	0.11	0.23	0.19	0.16
Coca-Cola Co.	0.23	0.20	0.17	0.23	0.20	0.17
Minnesota Mining & MFG Co.	0.28	0.25	0.23	0.25	0.22	0.19
Philip Morris Cos Inc.	0.14	0.10	0.08	0.14	0.11	0.08
Pepsico Inc.	0.16	0.13	0.10	0.16	0.12	0.10
Procter & Gamble Co.	0.23	0.20	0.17	0.22	0.18	0.15
Pharmacia Corp.	0.13	0.10	0.07	0.14	0.10	0.08
Schering-Plough Corp.	0.22	0.19	0.16	0.19	0.15	0.12
Texaco Inc.	0.03	0.02	0.01	0.03	0.02	0.01
Texas Instruments Inc.	0.44	0.42	0.41	0.37	0.35	0.33
United Technologies Corp.	0.16	0.12	0.10	0.15	0.12	0.09
Walgreen Co.	0.09	0.07	0.05	0.06	0.04	0.03

This table summarises the mean values over the first centile of the distribution of the coefficients of (upper or lower) tail dependence for the positive and negative tails during the time interval from July 1962 to December 2000, for three values of the tail index $\alpha = 3, 3.5, 4$.

but in our concluding remarks we will provide some ways to account explicitly for this lack of stationarity.

4.6 Comparison with the historical extremes

Our determination of the coefficients of tail dependence provides predictions on the probability that future large moves of stocks may be simultaneous to large moves of the market. This begs for a check over the available historical period to determine whether our estimated coefficients of tail dependence are compatible with the realised historical extremes.

For this, we consider the 10 largest losses of the S&P 500 index during the two time sub-intervals.[5] Since λ_- is by definition equal to the probability that a given asset incurs a large loss (say, one of its 10 largest losses) conditional on the occurrence of one of the

10 largest losses of the S&P 500 index, the probability, for this asset, to undergo n of its 10 largest losses simultaneously with any of the 10 largest losses of the S&P 500 index is given by the binomial law with parameter λ_-:

$$P_{\lambda_-}(n) = \binom{10}{n} \lambda_-^n (1 - \lambda_-)^{(10-n)} \tag{27}$$

We stress that our consideration of only the 10 largest drops ensures that the present test is not embodied in the determination of the tail dependence coefficient, which has been determined on a robust procedure over the 1%, 5% and 10% quantiles. We checked that the removal of these largest drops does not modify the determination of λ_-. Our present test can thus be considered as "out-of-sample" in this sense.

Table 12 presents, for the two time sub-intervals, the number of extreme losses among the 10 largest losses incurred by a given asset which occurred simultaneously with one of the 10 largest losses of the S&P 500 index. For each asset, we give the probability of occurrence of such a realisation, according to (27). We notice that during the first time interval, only two assets are incompatible, at the 95% confidence level, with the value of λ_- previously determined: Du Pont (E.I.) de Nemours & Co. and Texaco Inc. In contrast, during the second time interval, four assets reject the value of λ_-: Coca-Cola Corp., Pepsico Inc., Pharmacia Corp. and Texas Instruments Inc.

These results are very encouraging. However, there is a noticeable systematic bias. Indeed, during the first time interval, 17 out of the 20 assets have a realised number of large losses lower than their expected number (according to the estimated λ_-), while during the second time interval, 19 out of the 20 assets have a realised number of large losses larger than their expected one. Thus, it seems that during the first time interval the number of large losses is overestimated by λ_-, while it is underestimated during the second time interval.

We propose to explain the underestimation of the number of large losses between January 1980 and December 2000 by a possible co-monotonicity that occurred during the October 1987 crash. Indeed, on October 19, 1987 12 out of the 20 considered assets incurred their most severe loss, which strongly suggests a co-monotonic effect. Table 13 shows the same results as Table 12, but

Table 12 Binomial tests

	Jul 1962–Dec 1979			Jan 1980–Dec 2000		
	Extremes	λ_-	p-value	Extremes	λ_-	p-value
Abbott Labs	0	0.12	0.2937	4	0.20	0.0904
American Home Products Corp.	1	0.22	0.2432	2	0.12	0.2247
Boeing Co.	0	0.16	0.1667	3	0.14	0.1176
Bristol-Myers Squibb Co.	2	0.22	0.2987	4	0.32	0.2144
Chevron Corp.	3	0.21	0.2112	4	0.18	0.0644
Du Pont (E.I.) de Nemours & Co.	0	0.38	0.0078	4	0.23	0.1224
Disney (Walt) Co.	2	0.24	0.2901	2	0.16	0.2873
General Motors Corp.	2	0.39	0.1345	4	0.26	0.1522
Hewlett-Packard Co.	0	0.15	0.1909	2	0.19	0.3007
Coca-Cola Co.	2	0.26	0.2765	5	0.24	0.0494
Minnesota Mining & MFG Co.	2	0.35	0.1784	4	0.26	0.1571
Philip Morris Cos Inc.	1	0.25	0.1841	2	0.11	0.2142
Pepsico Inc.	2	0.15	0.2795	5	0.17	0.0141
Procter & Gamble Co.	1	0.23	0.2245	3	0.24	0.2447
Pharmacia Corp.	2	0.23	0.2956	4	0.10	0.0128
Schering-Plough Corp.	0	0.21	0.0946	4	0.23	0.1224
Texaco Inc.	0	0.06	0.5222	2	0.02	0.0212
Texas Instruments Inc.	1	0.47	0.0161	3	0.43	0.1862
United Technologies Corp.	1	0.13	0.3728	4	0.20	0.0870
Walgreen Co.	1	0.03	0.2303	3	0.15	0.1373

This table gives, for the time intervals from July 1962 to December 1979 and from January 1980 to December 2000, the number of losses within the ten largest losses incurred by an asset, which have occurred together with one of the ten largest losses of the S&P 500 index during the same time interval. The probability of occurrence of such a realisation is given by the p-value derived from the binomial law (27) with parameter λ_-.

corrected by subtracting this co-monotonic effect to the number of large losses. The compatibility between the number of large losses and the estimated λ_- becomes significantly better, since only Pepsico Inc. and Pharmacia Corp. are still rejected, and only 16 assets out of 20 are underestimated, representing a slight decrease in the bias.

Previous studies have shown that, in periods of crashes, the market conditions change, and herding effects may become more important and almost dominant, so that the market enters an unusual regime, which can be characterised by outliers present in the distribution of drawdowns (Johansen and Sornette (2002)). Our detection of an anomalous co-monotonicity can thus be considered

Table 13 Modified binomial tests

	Jul 1962–Dec 1979			Jan 1980–Dec 2000		
	Extremes	λ_-	*p*-value	Extremes	λ_-	*p*-value
Abbott Labs	0	0.12	0.2937	4	0.20	0.0904
American Home Products Corp.	1	0.22	0.2432	1	0.12	0.3828
Boeing Co.	0	0.16	0.1667	3	0.14	0.1176
Bristol-Myers Squibb Co.	2	0.22	0.2987	3	0.32	0.2653
Chevron Corp.	3	0.21	0.2112	3	0.18	0.1708
Du Pont (E.I.) de Nemours & Co.	0	0.38	0.0078	3	0.23	0.2342
Disney (Walt) Co.	2	0.24	0.2901	1	0.16	0.3300
General Motors Corp.	2	0.39	0.1345	3	0.26	0.2536
Hewlett-Packard Co.	0	0.15	0.1909	1	0.19	0.2880
Coca-Cola Co.	1	0.26	0.1782	4	0.24	0.1318
Minnesota Mining & MFG Co.	2	0.35	0.1784	3	0.26	0.2561
Philip Morris Cos Inc.	1	0.25	0.1841	2	0.11	0.2142
Pepsico Inc.	2	0.15	0.2795	5	0.17	0.0141
Procter & Gamble Co.	1	0.23	0.2245	3	0.24	0.2447
Pharmacia Corp.	2	0.23	0.2956	4	0.10	0.0128
Schering-Plough Corp.	0	0.21	0.0946	3	0.23	0.2342
Texaco Inc.	0	0.06	0.5222	1	0.02	0.1922
Texas Instruments Inc.	1	0.47	0.0161	3	0.43	0.1862
United Technologies Corp.	1	0.13	0.3728	3	0.20	0.2001
Walgreen Co.	1	0.03	0.2303	3	0.15	0.1373

This table gives, for the time intervals from July 1962 to December 1979 and from January 1980 to December 2000, the number of losses within the ten largest losses incurred by an asset which have occurred together with one of the ten largest losses of the S&P 500 index during the same time interval, provided that the losses are not both the largest of each series. The probability of occurrence of such a realisation is given by the *p*-value derived from the binomial law (27) with parameter λ_-.

as an independent confirmation of the existence of this abnormal situation.

Another explanation for this slight discrepancy may be ascribed to a limitation of the CAPM. Indeed, the CAPM is known to explain the relation between the expected return on an asset and its amount of systematic risk. But, it is questionable whether extreme systematic risks as those measured by the coefficient of tail dependence are really accounted for by the economic agents and then effectively priced.

As far as the overestimation of the number of large losses during the first time interval is concerned, it can obviously not be ascribed to the co-monotonicity of very large events, which in fact only occurred once for the Coca-Cola Corp. This overestimation is probably linked with the low "volatility" of the market during this period, which can have two effects. The first one is to lead to a less accurate estimation of the scale factor of the power-law distribution of the assets. The second one is that a market with smaller volatility produces fewer large losses. As a consequence, the asymptotic regime for which the relation $\Pr\{X < F_X^{-1}(u) \mid Y < F_Y^{-1}(u)\} \approx \lambda_-$ holds may not be reached in the sample, and the number of recorded large losses remains lower than that asymptotically expected.

5 CONCLUDING REMARKS

We have used the framework offered by factor models to derive a general theoretical expression for the coefficient of tail dependence between an asset and any of its explanatory factor or between any two assets. The coefficient of tail dependence represents the probability that a given asset incurs a large loss (say), assuming that the market (or another asset) has also undergone a large loss. We find that factors characterised by rapidly varying distributions, such as normal or exponential distributions, always lead to a vanishing coefficient of tail dependence with other stocks. In contrast, factors with regularly varying distributions, such as power-law distributions, can exhibit tail dependence with other stocks, provided that the idiosyncratic noise distributions of the corresponding stocks are not fatter-tailed than the factor.

Applying this general result to individual daily stock returns, we have been able to estimate the coefficient of tail dependence between the returns of each stock and those of the market. This determination of the tail dependence relies only on the simple estimation of the parameters of the underlying factor model and on the tail parameters of the distribution of the factor and of the idiosyncratic noise of each stock. As a consequence, the two strong advantages of our approach are the following:

❏ The coefficients of tail dependence are estimated non-parametrically. Indeed, we never specify any explicit expression of the dependence structure, contrary to most previous studies (see Longin and Solnik (2001), Malevergne and Sornette (2003), or Patton (2001), for instance); and

❑ Our theoretical result enables us to estimate an extreme parameter, not accessible by a direct statistical inference. This is
achieved by the measurement of parameters whose estimation
involves a significant part of the data with sufficient statistics.

Having performed this estimation, we have checked the compatibility of these estimated coefficients of tail dependence with the
historically realised extreme losses observed in the empirical time
series. A good agreement is found, not-withstanding a slight bias
which leads to an overestimate of the occurrence of large events
during the period from July 1962 to December 1979 and to an
underestimate during the time interval from January 1980 to
December 2000.

This bias can be explained by the low volatility of the market
during the first period and by a co-monotonicity effect, due to the
October 1987 crash, during the second period. Indeed, from July
1962 to December 1979, the volatility was so low that the distributions of returns have probably not sampled their tails sufficiently
for the probability of large conditional losses to be represented by
its asymptotic expression given by the coefficient of tail dependence. The situation is very different for the period from January
1980 to December 2000. On October 19, 1987 many assets incurred
their largest loss ever. This is presumably the manifestation of an
"abnormal" regime, probably due to herding effects and irrational
behaviors, and has been previously characterised as yielding signatures in the form of outliers in the distribution of drawdowns.

Finally, the observed lack of stationarity exhibited by the coefficient of tail dependence across the two time sub-intervals suggests
the importance of going beyond a stationary view of tail dependence and of studying its dynamics. This question, which could be
of great interest in the context of the contagion problem, could be
easily treated with the new conditional quantile dynamics proposed by Engle and Manganelli (1999). Moreover, it should be
interesting to account fo the change of the βs with incoming bad or
good news, as shown by Cho and Engle (2000), for instance. These
points are left for a future study.

From a practical point of view, we stress that the coefficient λ
studied here can be seen as a generalisation or a complementary
tool to the CAPM's β. These two coefficients have in common that

they probe the dependence between a given stock and the market. However, the coefficient β quantifies only the correlations between moderate movements of both an asset and the market. In contrast, the coefficient λ offers a measure of *extreme* co-movements, which is particularly useful in periods of high market volatility. In such periods, a prudent fund manager should overweight its portfolio with assets whose λ is very small, such as Texas Instruments or Walgreen.

Moreover, the observed decrease of the tail dependence during the last year, concomitant with the increase of the idiosyncratic volatility, suggests that the main source of risk in such a period does not consist in the dependence between assets but rather in their intrinsic fluctuations measured by the idiosyncratic volatility.

Our study has focused on the dependence between different risks. In fact, our theorem can obviously be applied to extreme temporal dependences, when the variable follows an autoregressive process. This should provide an estimate of the probability that a large loss (resp. gain) is followed by another large loss (resp. gain) in the following period. Such information is very interesting in investment and hedging strategies.

APPENDIX A – PROOF OF THE THEOREM
A.1 Tail dependence between an asset and the factor
A.1.1 Statement
We consider two random variables X and Y, related by the relation

$$X = \beta \cdot Y + \varepsilon \tag{A1}$$

where ε is a random variable independent of Y and β a non-random positive coefficient.

Let P_Y and F_Y denote respectively the density with respect to the Lebesgue measure and the distribution function of the variable Y. Let F_X denote the distribution function of X and F_ε the distribution function of ε. We state the following theorem:

THEOREM 1 *Assuming that*
H0: The variables Y and ϵ have distribution functions with infinite support, H1: For all $x \in [1, \infty)$,

$$\lim_{t \to \infty} \frac{t P_Y(tx)}{\bar{F}_Y(t)} = f(x) \tag{A2}$$

H2: There are real numbers $t_0 > 0$, $\delta > 0$ and $A > 0$, such that for all $t \geq t_0$ and all $x \geq 1$

$$\frac{\bar{F}_Y(tx)}{\bar{F}_Y(t)} \leq \frac{A}{x^\delta} \tag{A3}$$

H3: There is a constant $l \in \mathbb{R}_+$, such that

$$\lim_{u \to 1} \frac{F_X^{-1}(u)}{F_Y^{-1}(u)} = l \tag{A4}$$

then, the coefficient of (upper) tail dependence of (X, Y) is given by

$$\lambda = \int_{\max\left\{1, \frac{l}{\beta}\right\}}^{\infty} dx f(x) \tag{A5}$$

A.1.2 Proof
We first give a general expression for the probability for X to be larger than $F_X^{-1}(u)$, knowing that Y is larger than $F_Y^{-1}(u)$:

LEMMA 1 The probability that X is larger than $F_X^{-1}(u)$, knowing that Y is larger than $F_Y^{-1}(u)$ is given by

$$\Pr\left[X > F_X^{-1}(u)\big|Y > F_Y^{-1}(u)\right]$$

$$= \frac{\bar{F}_Y^{-1}(u)}{1-u} \int_1^\infty dx P_Y\left(F_Y^{-1}(u)x\right) \cdot \bar{F}_\varepsilon\left[F_X^{-1}(u) - \beta F_Y^{-1}(u)x\right] \quad \text{(A6)}$$

Proof:

$$\Pr\left\{X > F_X^{-1}(u), Y > F_Y^{-1}(u)\right\} = \mathrm{E}\left[1_{\left\{X > F_X^{-1}(u)\right\}} \cdot 1_{\left\{Y > F_Y^{-1}(u)\right\}}\right] \quad \text{(A7)}$$

$$= \mathrm{E}\left[\mathrm{E}\left[1_{\left\{X > F_X^{-1}(u)\right\}} \cdot 1_{\left\{Y > F_Y^{-1}(u)\right\}}\big|Y\right]\right] \quad \text{(A8)}$$

$$= \mathrm{E}\left[1_{\left\{Y > F_Y^{-1}(u)\right\}} \cdot \mathrm{E}\left[1_{\left\{X > F_X^{-1}(u)\right\}}\big|Y\right]\right] \quad \text{(A9)}$$

$$= \mathrm{E}\left[1_{\left\{Y > F_Y^{-1}(u)\right\}} \cdot \mathrm{E}\left[1_{\left\{\varepsilon > F_X^{-1}(u) - \beta Y\right\}}\right]\right] \quad \text{(A10)}$$

$$= \mathrm{E}\left[1_{\left\{Y > F_Y^{-1}(u)\right\}} \cdot \bar{F}_\varepsilon(F_X^{-1}(u) - \beta Y)\right] \quad \text{(A11)}$$

Assuming that the variable Y admits a density P_Y with respect to the Lebesgue measure, this yields

$$\Pr\left\{X > F_X^{-1}(u), Y > F_Y^{-1}(u)\right\} = \int_{F_Y^{-1}(u)}^\infty dy P_Y(y) \cdot \bar{F}_\varepsilon\left[F_X^{-1}(u) - \beta y\right] \quad \text{(A12)}$$

Performing the change of variable $y = F_Y^{-1}(u) \cdot x$, in the equation above, we obtain

$$\Pr\left\{X > F_X^{-1}(u), Y > F_Y^{-1}(u)\right\}$$

$$= F_Y^{-1}(u)\int_1^\infty dx P_Y\left(F_Y^{-1}(u)x\right) \cdot \bar{F}_\varepsilon\left[F_X^{-1}(u) - \beta F_Y^{-1}(u)x\right] \quad \text{(A13)}$$

and, dividing by $\bar{F}_Y\left(F_Y^{-1}(u)\right) = 1 - u$, this concludes the proof.

Let us now define the function

$$f_u(x) = \frac{F_Y^{-1}(u)}{1-u} P_Y\left(F_Y^{-1}(u)x\right) \cdot \bar{F}_\varepsilon\left[F_X^{-1}(u) - \beta F_Y^{-1}(u)x\right] \quad \text{(A14)}$$

We can state the following result

LEMMA 2 *Under Assumptions H1 and H3, for all $x \in [1, \infty)$,*

$$f_u(x) \to 1_{\left\{x > \frac{l}{\beta}\right\}} \cdot f(x) \quad \text{(A15)}$$

almost everywhere, as u goes to 1.

Proof: Let us apply Assumption H1. We have

$$\lim_{u \to 1} \frac{F_Y^{-1}(u)}{1-u} P_Y\left(F_Y^{-1}(u)x\right) = \lim_{t \to \infty} \frac{t P_Y(tx)}{\bar{F}_Y(t)} \quad \text{(A16)}$$

$$= f(x) \quad \text{(A17)}$$

Applying now Assumption H3, we have

$$\lim_{u \to 1} F_X^{-1}(u) - \beta F_Y^{-1}(u)x = \lim_{u \to 1} \beta F_Y^{-1}(u)\left(\frac{F_X^{-1}(u)}{\beta F_Y^{-1}(u)} - x\right) \quad \text{(A18)}$$

$$= \begin{cases} -\infty & \text{if } x > \frac{l}{\beta} \quad \text{(A19)} \\ \infty & \text{if } x < \frac{l}{\beta} \quad \text{(A20)} \end{cases}$$

which gives

$$\lim_{u \to 1} \bar{F}_\varepsilon\left[F_X^{-1}(u) - \beta F_Y^{-1}(u)x\right] = 1_{\left\{x > \frac{l}{\beta}\right\}} \quad \text{(A21)}$$

and finally

$$\lim_{u \to 1} f_u(x) = \lim_{u \to 1} \frac{F_Y^{-1}(u)}{1-u} P_Y\left(F_Y^{-1}(u)x\right) \cdot \lim_{u \to 1} \bar{F}_\varepsilon\left[F_X^{-1}(u) - \beta F_Y^{-1}(u)x\right] \quad \text{(A22)}$$

$$= 1_{\left\{x > \frac{l}{\beta}\right\}} \cdot f(x) \quad \text{(A23)}$$

which concludes the proof.

Let us now prove that there exists an integrable function $g(x)$ such that, for all $t \geq t_0$ and all $x \geq 1$, we have $f_t(x) \leq g(x)$. Indeed, let us write

$$\frac{t P_Y(tx)}{\bar{F}_Y(t)} = \frac{t P_Y(tx)}{\bar{F}_Y(tx)} \cdot \frac{\bar{F}_Y(tx)}{\bar{F}_Y(t)} \tag{A24}$$

For the leftmost factor in the right-hand-side of equation (A24), we easily obtain

$$\forall t, \forall x \geq 1, \quad \frac{t P_Y(tx)}{\bar{F}_Y(tx)} \leq \frac{x^* P_Y(x^*)}{\bar{F}_Y(x^*)} \cdot \frac{1}{x} \tag{A25}$$

where x^* denotes the point where the function $x P_Y(x) / \bar{F}_Y(x)$ reaches its maximum. The rightmost factor in the right-hand-side of (A24) is smaller than A / x^δ by Assumption H2, so that

$$\forall t \geq t_0, \forall x \geq 1, \quad \frac{t P_Y(tx)}{\bar{F}_Y(t)} \leq \frac{x^* P_Y(x^*)}{\bar{F}_Y(x^*)} \cdot \frac{A}{x^{1+\delta}} \tag{A26}$$

Posing

$$g(x) = \frac{x^* P_Y(x^*)}{\bar{F}_Y(x^*)} \cdot \frac{A}{x^{1+\delta}} \tag{A27}$$

and recalling that, for all $\varepsilon \in \mathbb{R}, \bar{F}_\varepsilon(\varepsilon) \leq 1$, we have found an integrable function such that for some $u_0 \geq 0$, we have

$$\forall u \in [u_0, 1), \forall x \geq 1, \quad f_u(x) \leq g(x) \tag{A28}$$

Thus, applying Lebesgue's theorem of dominated convergence, we can assert that

$$\lim_{u \to 1} \int_1^\infty dx f_u(x) = \int_1^\infty dx 1_{\left\{x > \frac{l}{\beta}\right\}} \cdot f(x) \tag{A29}$$

Since

$$\lim_{u \to 1} \int_1^\infty dx f_u(x) = \lim_{u \to 1} \Pr\left[X > F_X^{-1}(u) \middle| Y > F_Y^{-1}(u)\right] \tag{A30}$$

$$= \lambda \tag{A31}$$

the proof of Theorem 1 is concluded.

Remark: This result still holds in the presence of dependence between the factor and the idiosyncratic noise. Indeed, denoting by $\bar{F}_{\varepsilon|Y}$ the survival distribution of ε conditional on Y, Lemma 1 can easily be generalised:

$$\Pr\left[X > F_X^{-1}(u) \middle| Y > F_Y^{-1}(u) \right]$$

$$= \frac{F_Y^{-1}(u)}{1-u} \int_1^\infty dx P_Y \left(F_Y^{-1}(u)x \right) \cdot \bar{F}_{\varepsilon|Y=F_Y^{-1}(u)x} \left[F_Y^{-1}(u) - \beta F_Y^{-1}(u)x \right] \quad \textbf{(A32)}$$

where the only change in (A32) compared to (A6) is to replace $\bar{F}_\varepsilon(\cdot)$ by $\bar{F}_{\varepsilon|Y=F_Y^{-1}(u)x}(\cdot)$. Let us now assume that the function $\bar{F}_{\varepsilon|Y=y}(x)$ admits a uniform limit when x and y tend to $\pm\infty$. Then, Equation (A21) still holds and Lemma 2 remains true.

As an example, let F denote any one-dimensional distribution function. Then, one can easily check that, for any conditional distribution whose form is

$$\bar{F}_{\varepsilon|Y=y}(x) = \bar{F}\left(\frac{y^2}{y_0^2 + y^2} x \right) \quad \textbf{(A33)}$$

the uniform limit condition is satisfied and Theorem 1 and Lemma 2 still hold. In contrast, conditional distributions of the form

$$\bar{F}_{\varepsilon|Y=y}(x) = \bar{F}(x - \rho y) \quad \textbf{(A34)}$$

do not fulfill the uniform limit condition, so that the result given by Theorem 1 does not hold.

The full understanding of the impact of more general dependences between the factor and the idiosyncratic noise on the coefficient of tail dependence requires a full-fledged investigation that we defer to a future study. Our goal here has been to show that one can reasonably expect our results to survive in the presence of weak dependence.

A.2 Tail dependence between two assets

A.2.1 Statement

We consider three random variables X_1, X_2 and Y, related by the relations

$$X_1 = \beta_1 \cdot Y + \varepsilon_1 \tag{A35}$$

$$X_2 = \beta_2 \cdot Y + \varepsilon_2 \tag{A36}$$

where ε_1 and ε_2 are two random variables independent of Y and β_1, β_2 two non-random positive coefficients.

Let P_Y and F_Y denote respectively the density with respect to the Lebesgue measure and the distribution function of the variable Y. Let F_1, (resp. F_2) denote the distribution function of X_1 (resp. X_2) and F_{ε_1} (resp. F_{ε_2}) the marginal distribution function of ε_1 (resp. ε_2). Let $F_{\varepsilon_1,\varepsilon_2}$ denote the joined distribution of $(\varepsilon_1, \varepsilon_2)$. We state the following theorem:

THEOREM 2 *Assuming that*

H0: The variables Y, ε_1 and ε_2 have distribution functions with infinite support, H1: For all $x \in [1, \infty)$,

$$\lim_{t \to \infty} \frac{t P_Y(tx)}{\bar{F}_Y(t)} = f(x) \tag{A37}$$

H2: There are real numbers $t_0 > 0$, $\delta > 0$ and $A > 0$, such that for all $t \geq t_0$ and all $x \geq 1$

$$\frac{\bar{F}_Y(tx)}{\bar{F}_Y(t)} \leq \frac{A}{x^\delta} \tag{A38}$$

H3: There are two constants $(l_1, l_2) \in \mathbb{R}_+ \times \mathbb{R}_+$, such that

$$\lim_{u \to 1} \frac{F_1^{-1}(u)}{F_Y^{-1}(u)} = l_1, \quad \text{and} \quad \lim_{u \to 1} \frac{F_2^{-1}(u)}{F_Y^{-1}(u)} = l_2 \tag{A39}$$

then, the coefficient of (upper) tail dependence of (X, Y) is given by

$$\lambda = \int_{\max\left\{\frac{l_1}{\beta_1}, \frac{l_2}{\beta_2}\right\}}^{\infty} dx f(x) \tag{A40}$$

A.2.2 Proof

We first give a general expression for the probability for X to be larger than $F_X^{-1}(u)$, knowing that Y is larger than $F_Y^{-1}(u)$:

LEMMA 3 The probability that X is larger than $F_X^{-1}(u)$, knowing that Y is larger than $F_Y^{-1}(u)$ is given by:

$$\Pr\left[X > F_X^{-1}(u) \middle| Y > F_Y^{-1}(u)\right] = \frac{F_Y^{-1}(u)}{1-u}\int dx P_Y(F_Y^{-1}(u)x)$$

$$\times \bar{F}_{\varepsilon_1,\varepsilon_2}\left[F_1^{-1}(u) - \beta_1 F_1^{-1}(u)x, F_2^{-1}(u) - \beta_1 F_Y^{-1}(u)x\right] \quad \textbf{(A41)}$$

Proof: The proof is the same for Lemma 1.

Let us now define the function

$$f_u(x) = \frac{F_Y^{-1}(u)}{1-u}P_Y(F_Y^{-1}(u)x)$$

$$\times \bar{F}_{\varepsilon_1,\varepsilon_2}\left[F_1^{-1}(u) - \beta_1 F_Y^{-1}(u)x, F_2^{-1}(u) - \beta_2 F_Y^{-1}(u)x\right] \quad \textbf{(A42)}$$

We can state the following result

LEMMA 4 *Under Assumptions H1 and H3, for all $x \in [1, \infty)$,*

$$f_u(x) \to 1_{\left\{x > \max\left\{\frac{l_1}{\beta_1}, \frac{l_2}{\beta_2}\right\}\right\}} \cdot f(x) \quad \textbf{(A43)}$$

almost everywhere, as u goes to 1.

Proof: Applying Assumption H3, we have

$$\lim_{u \to 1} F_1^{-1}(u) - \beta_1 F_Y^{-1}(u)x = \lim_{u \to 1} \beta_1 F_Y^{-1}(u)\left(\frac{F_1^{-1}(u)}{\beta_1 F_Y^{-1}(u)} - x\right) \quad \textbf{(A44)}$$

$$= \begin{cases} -\infty & \text{if } x > \frac{l_1}{\beta_1} \quad \textbf{(A45)} \\ \infty & \text{if } x < \frac{l_1}{\beta_1} \quad \textbf{(A46)} \end{cases}$$

and

$$\lim_{u \to 1} F_2^{-1}(u) - \beta_2 F_Y^{-1}(u)x = \lim_{u \to 1} \beta_2 F_Y^{-1}(u)\left(\frac{F_2^{-1}(u)}{\beta_2 F_Y^{-1}(u)} - x\right) \quad \textbf{(A47)}$$

$$= \begin{cases} -\infty & \text{if } x > \frac{l_2}{\beta_2} \\ \infty & \text{if } x < \frac{l_2}{\beta_2} \end{cases} \qquad \begin{array}{l} \text{(A48)} \\ \\ \text{(A49)} \end{array}$$

which give

$$\lim_{u \to 1} \bar{F}_{\varepsilon_1,\varepsilon_2} \left[F_1^{-1}(u) - \beta_1 F_Y^{-1}(u)x, F_2^{-1}(u) - \beta_2 F_Y^{-1}(u)x \right] = 1_{\left\{ x > \max\left\{ \frac{l_1}{\beta_1}, \frac{l_2}{\beta_2} \right\} \right\}}$$

(A50)

and following the same calculations as in part A.1, it concludes the proof.

We can now apply Lebesgue's theorem of dominated convergence (see part A.1 for the justification), which allows us to assert that

$$\lim_{u \to 1} \int dx f_u(x) = \int dx 1_{\left\{ x > \max\left\{ \frac{l_1}{\beta_2}, \frac{l_2}{\beta_2} \right\} \right\}} \cdot f(x) \qquad \text{(A51)}$$

Since

$$\lim_{u \to 1} \int dx f_u(x) = \lim_{u \to 1} \Pr\left[X_1 > F_1^{-1}(u) \middle| X_2 > F_2^{-1}(u) \right] \qquad \text{(A52)}$$

$$= \lambda \qquad \text{(A53)}$$

the proof of Theorem 2 is concluded.

APPENDIX B – PROOFS OF THE COROLLARIES
B.1 First corollary
COROLLARY 1 *If the random variable Y has a rapidly varying distribution function, then* $\lambda = 0$.

Proof: Let us write

$$\frac{tP_Y(tx)}{\bar{F}_Y(t)} = \frac{tP_Y(tx)}{\bar{F}_Y(tx)} \cdot \frac{\bar{F}_Y(tx)}{\bar{F}_Y(t)} \qquad \text{(B1)}$$

For a rapidly varying function $\bar{F}_Y$, we have

$$\forall x > 1, \quad \lim_{t \to \infty} \frac{\bar{F}_Y(tx)}{\bar{F}_Y(t)} = 0 \qquad \text{(B2)}$$

while the leftmost factor of the right-hand side of Equation (B1) remains bounded as t goes to infinity, so that

$$\lim_{t \to \infty} \frac{t P_Y(tx)}{\overline{F}_Y(tx)} \cdot \frac{\overline{F}_Y(tx)}{\overline{F}_Y(t)} = f(x) = 0 \tag{B3}$$

Since $f(x) = 0$, we can apply Lemma 2 without Hypothesis H3, which concludes the proof.

B.2 Second corollary

COROLLARY 2 *Let Y be regularly varying with index $(-\alpha)$, and assume that Hypothesis H3 is satisfied. Then, the coefficient of (upper) tail dependence is*

$$\lambda = \frac{1}{\left[\max\left\{ 1, \dfrac{l}{\beta} \right\} \right]^{\alpha}} \tag{B4}$$

where l denotes the limit, when $u \to 1$, of the ratio $F_X^{-1}(u) / F_Y^{-1}(u)$.

Proof: Karamata's theorem (see Embrechts, Klüppelberg and Mikosh (1997), p 567) ensures that H1 is satisfied with $f(x) = \alpha / x^{\alpha+1}$, which is sufficient to prove the corollary. To go one step further, let us define

$$\overline{F}_y(y) = y^{-\alpha} \cdot L_1(y) \tag{B5}$$

$$\overline{F}_\varepsilon(\varepsilon) = \varepsilon^{-\alpha} \cdot L_2(\varepsilon) \tag{B6}$$

where $L_1(\cdot)$ and $L_2(\cdot)$ are slowly varying functions.

Using the proposition stated in Feller (1971, p 278), we obtain, for the distribution of the variable X

$$\overline{F}_X(x) \sim x^{-\alpha} \left(\beta^\alpha \cdot L_1\left(\frac{x}{\beta} \right) + L_2(x) \right) \tag{B7}$$

for large x.

Assuming now, for simplicity, that L_1 (resp. L_2) goes to a constant C_1 (resp. C_2), this implies that H3 is satisfied, since

$$l = \lim_{u \to 1} \frac{F_X^{-1}(u)}{F_Y^{-1}(u)} = \beta \left[1 + \frac{C_2}{\beta^\alpha C_1} \right]^{\frac{1}{\alpha}} \tag{B8}$$

This allows us to obtain the Equations (10) and (13).

1   The reader is refered to Joe (1997), Frees and Valdez (1998), or Nelsen (1998) for a detailed survey of the notion of copulas and a mathematically rigorous description of their properties.
2   See Bigham, Goldie and Teugel (1987) or Embrechts, Klüppelberg and Mikosh (1997) for a survey of the properties of rapidly and regularly varying functions.
3   Such a choice is always possible via a rescaling of the coefficient β.
4   In the more realistic case where the ε_is are not independent but still embody one or several common factors Y', Y'', …, the resulting scale factor C_ε can be calculated with the method described in Bouchaud et al (1998).
5   We do not consider the whole time interval since the 10 largest losses over the whole period coincide with the 10 largest ones over the second time subinterval, which would bias the statistics towards the second time interval.

This chapter was previously published in *The Journal of Risk* **6**(3), Spring 2004.

REFERENCES

Ang, A. and J. Chen, 2002, "Asymmetric Correlations of Equity Portfolios", *Journal of Financial Economics* **63**, pp. 443–94.

Bigham, N. H., C. M. Goldie, and J. L. Teugel, 1987, *Regular Variation*. (Cambridge: Cambridge University Press).

Bouchaud, J. P., D. Sornette, C. Walter, and J. P. Aguilar, 1998, "Taming Large Events: Optimal Portfolio Theory for Strongly Fluctuating Assets", *International Journal of Theoretical and Applied Finance* **1**, pp. 25–41.

Boyer, B. H., M. S. Gibson, and M. Lauretan, 1997, "Pitfalls in Tests for Changes in Correlations", Working paper, International Finance Discussion Paper 597, Board of the Governors of the Federal Reserve System.

Brennan, M. J. and E. J. Schwarz, 1978, "A Continuous Time Approach to the Pricing of Bonds", *Journal of Banking and Finance* **3**, pp. 133–55.

Campbell, J. Y., M. Lettau, B. G. Malkiel, and Y. Xu, 2001, "Have Individual Stocks Become More Volatile? An Empirical Exploration of Idiosyncratic Risk", *Journal of Finance* **56**, pp. 1–43.

Carey, M., 1998, "Credit Risk in Private Debt Portfolio", *Journal of Finance* **53**, pp. 56–61.

Cho, Y.-H. and R. F. Engle, 2000, "Time-varying Betas and Asymmetric Effects of News: Empirical Analysis of Blue Chip Stocks", Working paper, University of California, San Diego.

Coles, S., J. Heffernan, and J. Tawn, 1999, "Dependence Measures for Extreme Value Analyses", *Extremes* **2**, pp. 339–65.

Cox, J. C., J. E. Ingersoll, and S. A. Ross, 1985, "A Theory of the Term Structure of Interest Rates", *Econometrica* **51**, pp. 385–408.

Danielsson, J., L. de Haan, L. Peng, and C. G. de Vries, 2001, "Using a Bootstrap Method to Choose the Optimal Sample Fraction in Tail Index Estimation", *Journal of Multivariate Analysis* **76**, pp. 226–48.

Danielsson, J. and C. G. de Vries, 1997, "Tail Index and Quantile Estimation with Very High Frequency Data", *Journal of Empirical Finance* **4**, pp. 241–57.

de Haan, L., S. I. Resnick, H. Rootzen, and C. G. de Vries, 1989, "Extremal Behaviour of Solutions to a Stochastic Difference Equation with Application to ARCH Processes", *Stochastic Processes and their Applications* **32**, pp. 213–24.

Embrechts, P., C. P. Klüppelberg, and T. Mikosh, 1997, *Modelling Extremal Events.* (Berlin: Springer-Verlag).

Embrechts, P., A. J. McNeil, and D. Straumann, 1999, *Correlation: Pitfalls and Alternatives. Risk* **12(5)**, pp. 69–71.

Embrechts, P., A. J. McNeil, and D. Straumann, 2001, "Correlation and Dependency in Risk Management: Properties and Pitfalls", in M. Dempster, ed, *Value at Risk and Beyond.* Cambridge University Press, pp. 176–223.

Engle, R. F. and S. Manganelli, 1999, "CAViaR: Conditional Autoregressive Value-at-Risk by Regression Quantiles", Working paper, University of California, San Diego.

Fama, E. and J. McBeth, 1973, "Risk, Return and Equilibrium: Empirical tests", *Journal of Political Economy* **81**, pp. 607–36.

Feller, W., 1971, *An Introduction to Probability Theory and Its Applications II.* (New York: Wiley).

Fermanian, J.-D. and O. Scaillet, 2003, "Nonparametric Estimation of Copulas for Time Series", *Journal of Risk* **5(4)**, pp. 25–54.

Frees, E. and E. Valdez, 1998, "Understanding Relationships Using Copulas", *North American Actuarial Journal* **2**, pp. 1–25.

Geman, H. and C. Kharoubi, 2003, "Hedge Funds Revisited: Distributional Characteristics, Dependence Structure and Diversification", *Journal of Risk* **5(4)**, pp. 55–75.

Gopikrishnan, P., M. Meyer, L. A. N. Amaral, and H. E. Stanley, 1998, "Inverse Cubic Law for the Distribution of Stock Price Variations", *European Physical Journal* **B3**, pp. 139–40.

Gordy, M. B., 2000, "A Comparative Anatomy of Credit Risk Models", *Journal of Banking and Finance* **24**, pp. 119–49.

Hall, P., 1990, "Using the Bootstrap Method to Estimate Mean Squared Error and Select Smoothing Parameter in Non Parametric Problems", *Journal of Multivariate Analysis* **32**, pp. 177–203.

Joe, H., 1997, *Multivariate Models and Dependence Concepts.* (London: Chapman & Hall).

Johansen, A. and D. Sornette, 2002, "Large Stock Market Price Drawdowns are Outliers", *Journal of Risk* **4**, pp. 69–110.

Jones, C. P. and J. W. Wilson, 1989, "Is Stock Price Volatility Increasing?" *Financial Analysts Journal* **45**, pp. 20–6.

Kandel, S. and R. Staumbaugh, 1987, "On Correlations and the Sensitivity of Inference about Mean-variance Efficiency", *Journal of Financial Economics* **18**, pp. 61–90.

Kearns, P. and A. R. Pagan, 1997, "Estimating the Density Tail Index for Financial Time Series", *Review of Economics and Statistics* **79**, pp. 171–5.

Lindskog, F., 2000, "Modelling Dependence with Copulas", Working Paper, RiskLab", http://www.firisklab.ich/Papers.html#MTLindskog.

Lintner, J., 1965, "The Valuation of Risk Assets and the Selection of Risky Investments in Stock Portfolios and the Capital Budgets", *Review of Economics and Statistics* **41**, pp. 13–37.

Longin, F. M., 1996, "The Asymptotic Distribution of Extreme Stock Market Returns", *Journal of Business* **96**, pp. 383–408.

Longin, F. M. and B. Solnik, 2001, "Extreme Correlation of International Equity Markets", *Journal of Finance* **56**, pp. 649–76.

Loretan, M. and P. C. B. Phillips, 1994, "Testing the Covariance Stationarity of Heavy-tailed Times Series", *Journal of Empirical Finance* **1**, pp. 211–48.

Lucas, A., P. Klaassen, P. Spreij, and S. Straetmans, 2001, "An Analytic Approach to Credit Risk of Large Corporate Bond and Loan portfolios", *Journal of Banking and Finance* **25**, pp. 1635–64.

Lux, T., 1996, "The Stable Paretian Hypothesis and the Frequency of Large Returns: An Examination of Major German Stocks", *Applied Financial Economics* **6**, pp. 463–75.

Malevergne, Y. and D. Sornette, 2002, "Minimising Extremes", *Risk* **15(11)**, pp. 129–34.

Malevergne, Y. and D. Sornette, 2003, "Testing the Gaussian Copula Hypothesis for Financial Assets Dependences", *Quantitative Finance* **3**, pp. 231–50.

McDonald, J. B. and W. K. Newey, 1988, "Partially Adaptive Estimation of Regression Models via the Generalised *t*-Distribution", *Econometric Theory* **4**, pp. 428–57.

Mossin, J., 1966, "Equilibrium in Capital Asset Market", *Econometrica* **35**, pp. 768–83.

Nelsen, R. B., 1998, *An Introduction to Copulas.* (New York: Springer-Verlag).

Pagan, A., 1996, "The Econometrics of Financial Markets", *Journal of Empirical Finance* **3**, pp. 15–102.

Pagan, A. and A. Ullah, 1999, *Non-parametrics Econometrics.* (Cambridge: Cambridge University Press).

Patton, J. A., 2001, "Estimation of Copula Models for Time Series of Possibly Different Lengths", Working paper, University of California, *Econ. Disc. Paper* No. 2001-17.

Roll, R., 1988, "The International Crash of October 1987", *Financial Analysts Journal* **44(5)**, pp. 19–35.

Rootzén, H., M. R. Leadbetter, and L. de Haan, 1998, "On the Distribution Tail Array Sums for Strongly Mixing Stationary Sequences", *Annals of Applied Probability* **8**, pp. 868–85.

Ross, S. A., 1976, "The Arbitrage Theory of Capital Asset Pricing", *Journal of Economic Theory* **17**, pp. 254–86.

Sharpe, W., 1964, "Capital Assets Prices: A Theory of Market Equilibrium Under Conditions of Risk", *Journal of Finance* **19**, pp. 425–42.

Shealter, S. J. and J. S. Marron, 1990, "Kernel Quantile Estimators", *Journal of the American Statistical Association* **85**, pp. 410–5.

Sklar, A., 1959, "Fonction de Répartition à *n* Dimensions et Leurs Marges", *Publ. Inst. Statist. Univ. Paris* **8**, pp. 229–31.

Starica, C., 1999, "Multivariate Extremes for Models with Constant Conditional Correlations", *Journal of Empirical Finance* **6**, pp. 515–53.

Vasicek, O., 1977, "An Equilibrium Characterisation of the Term Structure of Interest Rates", *Journal of Financial Economics* **5**, pp. 177–88.

Xu, Y. and B. G. Malkiel, 2003, "Idiosyncratic Volatility", *Journal of Business* **76**, pp. 613–45.

347

Section 4

Large Events, Crisis and Fat tails

14

Living on the Edge

Paul Embrechts, Sidney Resnick,* Gennady Samorodnitsky

Cornell University

Few of the conceptual discussions that have shaped modern risk management have been more heated than the one on value-at-risk. As is now widely known, conventional VaR models fail to account for the fact that rates and returns are not normally distributed in real life. This, in turn, means they are least effective where it is most important: at the edges – extreme movements – which occur more frequently than predicted by the normal model.

For the purposes of this chapter, some of the problems related to VaR are best captured in Boudoukh, Richardson and Whitelaw (1995). They stress that, from a risk management perspective, managers care more about the size of losses than how often they occur, something which conventional VaR discusses only in terms of a specified lower bound. They continue by offering a worst-case scenario (WCS) approach, which they claim "is a concept most often associated with the analysis of rare or extreme events. WCS is concerned with the nature of an event which by definition is bound to happen."

They continue by stressing that, since VaR incorporates a signifi-cant probability of financial ruin, be it 5% or 1%, there is a need for additional prudence, via a larger capital requirement. The approach commonly used in the context of the VaR measure, and embraced by regulators such as the Basel Committee on Banking Supervision,

*Sidney Resnick and Gennady Samorodnitsky were partially supported by NSF Grant DMS-9400535 at Cornell University. Paul Embrechts gratefully acknowledges the hospitality of the School of Operations Research and Industrial Engineering, Cornell University during Fall 1996.

is to use the VaR number as an indication and then simply to multiply this measure by some "hysteria factor". (See page 96 of Jorion (1997) for the reasoning behind the use of this factor and page 101 of this issue for a critique based on extreme value theory.)

The hysteria factor also alleviates a second criticism often made of conventional VaR models: that they do not not cater for the fat tails that commonly appear in the data. More fundamentally, Artzner *et al* (1997) show how to define "coherent" risk measures in finance and that VaR is not such a measure. Let us summarise the main points of this discussion:

❏ risk management is interested in estimating tail probabilities and quantiles of profit/loss (P&L) distributions, and indeed, of general financial data;
❏ extremes matter;
❏ we want to have methods for estimating conditional probabilities concerning tail-events, ie, given that we incur a loss beyond VaR, how far do we expect the excess to go?; and
❏ financial data show fat tails.

These are all dealt with by extreme value theory (EVT). We believe EVT has a very important role to play in technical discussions of risk management. However, nobody can claim to have a definitive answer concerning VaR and related risk measures. What one can say with more confidence, however, is that EVT will be an important part of the working methodology.

In the next section we summarise some of the main results of EVT and indicate where they can be used in the overall risk management context. Clearly, we are not able to give all details here and the interested reader is referred to pages 98 and 101 of this issue, as well as to Resnick (1987), Leadbetter, Lindgren and Rootzén (1983) and Embrechts, Klüppelberg and Mikosch (1997) for comprehensive overviews. The latter, in particular, gives emphasis to applications to finance and insurance. See also Zangari (1997) for a treatment of event risk.

Finally, this chapter can also be seen as a reaction to the remark made by Alan Greenspan, chairman of the Federal Reserve Board of Governors, at a Research Conference on Risk Management and Systemic Risk in Washington DC on November 16, 1996: "Work that characterises the statistical distribution of extreme events would be useful, as well." EVT offers precisely the methodology underlying such a characterisation.

PROBABILITIES AND LOSSES

To state the main results from EVT in their easiest form, we concentrate on a sample $X_1, X_2, ..., X_n$ of independent, identically distributed random variables with common distribution function (DF) F. It is very important to note that the independent, identically distributed assumption can be relaxed. EVT has also been worked out for processes in both discrete and continuous time, with or without independence and/or stationarity assumptions. It is fair to say that relevant EVT tools are available for most models encountered in finance – see Embrechts, Klüppelberg and Mikosch (1997) and the references therein for more details.

For the purposes of this chapter, we can define X_i as the loss (gain) of transaction (portfolio) i, the ith absolute log-return of an underlying financial instrument or the ith claim relating to an insurance loss. The latter example is particularly important, as such events can be contingent for catastrophe bonds. Indeed, EVT has proved to be particularly useful in modelling catastrophic claims in reinsurance; see McNeil (1997) and Resnick (1997). A final application involves the definition of X_i as credit losses. Here, EVT will undoubtedly become useful to estimate the unexpected loss and the stress loss. The latter nomenclature is taken from Swiss Bank Corporation's Actuarial Credit Risk Accounting (Acra) and is also to be found in JP Morgan's CreditMetrics. Within Acra, the stress loss is defined as a possible – although improbable – extreme scenario that the bank must be able to survive.

The classical probability theory that underlies most of the stochastic methods used in finance concerns the sums S_n of the individual X_i for $i = 1$ to n. The relevant theorems relating to $\{S_n\}$ are:

❑ the law of large numbers, which dictates that the sample averages S_n/n approximate the mathematical expectation $\mu = E(X)$; and
❑ the central limit theorem (CLT), which says that S_n, centred and scaled to have mean 0 and variance 1, has an approximately normal distribution.

Indeed, it is the CLT that underlies the lognormality assumption in the Black–Scholes model, yields Brownian motion as the cornerstone of most analytic models and leads to analytic VaR estimates based on normal quantiles.

To show how EVT offers tools and techniques with potential uses in finance, we summarise below some of its main ideas, in the case where independent, identically distributed loss data $X_1, \ldots, X_n$ with common, but unknown, F are available. In practice, of course, VaR is calculated directly from a data-driven model (the Black–Scholes log-normal model, say) and not from a specific sample of losses, but the above framework may be more relevant at the backtesting and cali-bration level. Also, for ease of exposition and to highlight the main EVT procedures, we will stick to a somewhat idealised, sample-based VaR calculation. The reader should have no problem in translating our findings to other areas of insurance and finance. For the moment, it is the key ideas that matter; refinements can be built in later.

Whereas S_n/n would correspond to an "average loss", the most extreme case within the range of the data concerns the largest loss $M_n = \max\{X_1, \ldots, X_n\}$. More generally, if we order the data:

$$\min\{X_1, \ldots, X_n\} = X_{n,n} \leq X_{n-1,n} \leq \ldots \leq X_{2,n} \leq X_{1,n} = M_n$$

we might be interested in the behaviour of the k largest losses $X_{1,n}$, $X_{2,n}, \ldots, X_{k,n}$. Based on the P&L data $X_1, \ldots, X_n$ and given a confi-dence level α, an empirical VaR estimate would produce the kth largest observation $X_{k,n}$ where k is approximately αn. By producing that estimate (or, indeed, any more sophisticated VaR measure), we would give management the dollar value that, based on our data, will typically only be surpassed in $\alpha \cdot 100\%$ of cases. We often have insufficient data (especially when α is small, eg, $\alpha = 0.001$ and $n = 100$, say) so we have to extrapolate beyond the range of the data. So here is our first fundamental problem concerning tail esti-mation for P&L distributions. For given (small) α, calculate the level (the α-quantile) u_α such that:

$$P(X > u_\alpha) = 1 - F(u_\alpha) = \alpha$$

Remember F is not known. If X stands for monthly (log-) returns for a particular portfolio, u_α would (in the language of insurance) correspond to a so-called $1/\alpha$-month return period. If, for instance, $\alpha = 0.05$, then u_α is the 20-month return period, ie, that value which, on average, is only surpassed once in 20 months.

Second, once the above level u_α is fixed, one would want to estimate the size of potential losses beyond that level. We therefore need to be able to estimate the conditional probability DF:

$$P(X - u_\alpha \leq x | X > u_\alpha)$$

ie, the conditional probability that, given that there is a loss beyond u_α, the excess loss $X - u_\alpha$ is no bigger than some level x. An estimate of this conditional probability will (in the case of sufficient data) involve the losses $X_{l,n}, X_{l-1,n}, \ldots, X_{1,n}$ above some (large) loss $X_{l+1,n}$. If insufficient data are available, we have to find a suitable model or approximation for the above conditional probability. Though this conditional DF has long been used as a standard measure in fields such as insurance (excess-loss) and reliability/medical statistics (residual-life), its importance in finance is only now becoming clear. Names such as "shortfall", "beyond-VaR", and so on are now used for the quantity:

$$e(u_\alpha) = E(X - u_\alpha | X > u_\alpha)$$

the (conditional) mean excess loss, given that a loss above u_α has occurred. Within the actuarial literature, much is known about $e(u_\alpha)$; see Embrechts, Klüppelberg and Mikosch (1997). The function $e(u_\alpha)$ is very useful in distinguishing between short-tailed and fat-tailed DFs. In the former case, it typically decreases (in the normal case, even to zero), whereas for fat-tailed DFs $e(u_\alpha)$ increases for α tending to 0 (ie, for u_α tending to infinity).

One can easily show (*ibid*, p 161), that for normally distributed data $e(u_\alpha) \approx u_\alpha^{-1}$ and $E(X | X > u_\alpha) = e(u_\alpha) + u_\alpha \approx u_\alpha$. Hence, if $u_\alpha = \text{VaR}$, then $E(X) | X > \text{VaR}) \approx \text{VaR}$.

However, in the fat-tailed Pareto case with tail-parameter $\beta > 1$, ie, $1 - F(x) = (1 + x)^{-\beta}$, $x \geq 0$, say, one can easily show that $e(u_\alpha) = (1 + u_\alpha)/(\beta - 1)$ and consequently:

$$E(X | X > u_\alpha) \approx \frac{\beta}{\beta - 1} u_\alpha$$

If $u_\alpha = \text{VaR}$, then:

$$E(X | X > \text{VaR}) \approx \frac{\beta}{\beta - 1} \text{VaR}$$

Empirical studies have found that typically $1 < \beta < 2$ within insurance, whereas in finance a range $1.5 < \beta < 5$ is standard. The consequence of this for applications of the VaR methodology are obvious! For further discussions and examples, see Artzner *et al* (1997) and Longin (1997).

DISTRIBUTION FUNCTIONS

EVT offers empirical finance in general, and risk management in particular, methods for estimating the quantities above under flexible model assumptions. Such models include time dependent-parameter models (ie, non-stationarity) and models involving exogenous variables. Note also that EVT-based solutions allow a wide variety of shapes of the underlying DFs (whether a P&L distribution, return DF, credit-loss DF, insurance claims DF, etc).

Without going into exhaustive detail on how EVT works, we will sketch the main ingredients in the solution of the above problems. We begin by observing that under widely applicable conditions, the DF of the largest observation M_n of an independent, identically distributed sample $X_1, \ldots, X_n$ can be approximated by a member of the following class of extreme value distributions:

$$H_{\xi,\mu,\psi}(x) = \exp\left\{ -\left(1 + \xi\frac{x - \mu}{\psi}\right)_+^{-1/\xi} \right\}$$

Here $y_+ = \max(y, 0)$. This three-parameter family of distributions has a location parameter $\mu \in \Re$, scale parameter $\psi > 0$ and, most importantly, a shape parameter $\xi \in \Re$. The case $\xi = 0$ is interpreted as:

$$H_{\xi,\mu,\psi}(x) = \exp\left\{ -\exp\left(-\frac{x - \mu}{\psi}\right)\right\}, \quad x \in \Re$$

and is referred to as the double exponential, or Gumbel, distribution. For $\xi > 0$, $H_{\xi,\mu,\psi}$ is called the Fréchet distribution, which has unbounded support to the right; for $\xi < 0$, the Weibull, which has unbounded support to the left. Figure 1 contains the density functions for the standard cases $H_{\xi,0,1}$ for $\xi = 0, \xi = \frac{2}{3}$ and $\xi = -\frac{2}{3}$.

From Figure 1, we see the typical skew behaviour of extreme value distributions. Moreover, in the case $\xi > 0$, which is most important

Figure 1 Extreme value distributions

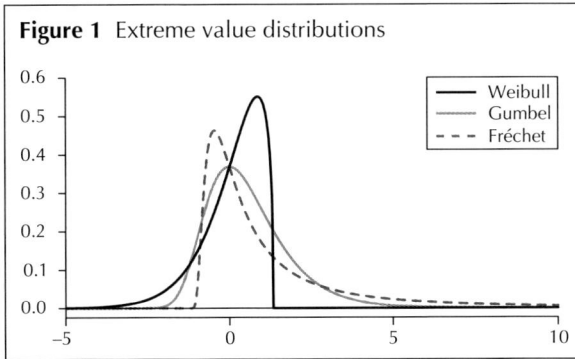

for finance, the tail $1 - H_{\xi,0,1}(x)$ behaves like $x^{-1/\xi}$, ie, is fat-tailed. To be clear about the significance of the extreme value DFs and their link to the normal DF, observe that for independent, identically distributed and normally distributed $X_{1,l}, \ldots, X_n$ with $M_n = \max(X_{1,l}, \ldots, X_n)$:

$$P(M_n > x) \approx \Lambda\left(\frac{x - b_n}{a_n}\right) = H_{0,0,1}\left(\frac{x - b_n}{a_n}\right)$$

for suitable sequences a_n and b_n, which can be calculated explicitly as functions of n, μ and σ. Hence the two-sided, skew Gumbel DF Λ approximates the law governing the largest observation in a normal sample. A similar result, with different a_n and b_n, holds, for instance, for exponential and lognormal data. In the case of fat-tailed data, with $1 - F(x) \approx x^{-\alpha}$, say, the right-hand side in (2.5) has to be replaced by the Fréchet DF $H_{1/\alpha,0,1}$. For details on these approximations, see Embrechts, Klüppelberg and Mikosch (1997).

Returning to the crucial question of estimating beyond VaR (or short-fall), under reasonable conditions on F, there exists a canonical class of DFs approximating the conditional DF above for large u_α, ie, small α. This is crucial for finance and insurance applications. These *generalised Pareto distributions* (GPD) are defined as:

$$G_{\xi,v,\beta}(x) = 1 - \left(1 + \xi\frac{x - v}{\beta}\right)_+^{-1/\xi}$$

where ξ is the shape parameter corresponding to the extreme value distribution, and υ and β are again location and scale parameters. In the case $\xi > 0$ (the most important case for finance), the GPD takes the form of a heavy-tailed Pareto distribution. We have therefore reached the conclusion that these DFs are natural approximations to the excess DF (conditional VaR DF). The conditions needed to decide on the GPD fit depend on the approximation coming out of the definition of $H_{\xi,\mu,\psi}(x)$ above.

We have sketched some of the main problems EVT can solve. It remains to flesh out the theory in such a way that an end-user can safely apply the methodology. There is now a substantial body of work on EVT, whose main tools and techniques have been worked out for a large variety of data and models; standardised software is available.[1]

To illustrate some of the above techniques, we briefly discuss an example based on daily return data for BMW equity over the period January 2, 1973–July 23, 1996. We concentrate on the left tail (ie, negative daily return values). For consistency with the positive sign for losses used in the previous section, we take absolute values and denote the DF of these values by F. The resulting series has $n = 2{,}770$ observations. In Figure 2, we have plotted the empirical estimate $e_n(u)$, $u \geq 0$, of the mean excess function $e(u)$ in (2.4). This means that:

$$e_n(u) = \frac{1}{N_u} \sum_{i=1}^{n} (X_i - u)_+$$

where N_u is the number of "exceedances" of u, ie:

$$N_u = \text{number} \quad \text{of } \{l = 1, \ldots, n \,|\, X_i > u\}$$

Note the increasing behaviour from about $u = 0.02$ onwards, clearly indicating fat (even Pareto type) tails. In Figure 3, we have fitted the generalised Pareto distribution to the excess DF. All the data above the threshold $u = 0.02$ were used for this plot; the crucial shape parameter ξ has the value 0.223, which corresponds to a Pareto tail with value $1/\xi = 4.484$. From this plot, one can read off the conditional probability of high excesses, given that we have an exceedance of $u = 0.02$. Of course, we can change the latter value as

Figure 2 Sample mean excess plot

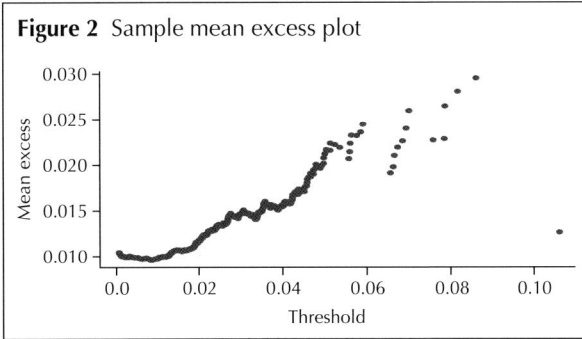

Figure 3 Generalised Pareto distribution for BMW equity

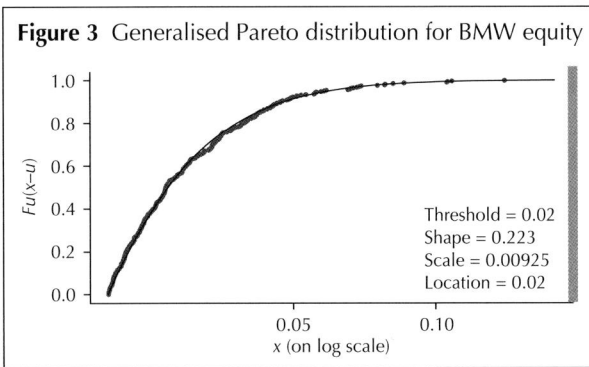

Threshold = 0.02
Shape = 0.223
Scale = 0.00925
Location = 0.02

desired: for each u, a new model has to be fitted. On the other hand, one might be interested in the tail probabilities $1-F(x)$, or high quantiles. A plot of this is given in Figure 4. Note that we use a log scale for both axes, in order to magnify the tail of F. An exact Pareto tail would be linear on this scale. In Figure 4, we have also plotted some quantiles u_α together with 95% confidence intervals. These intervals are the sections cut off by the two parabolas of the horizontal line through 95. The resulting values are:

$$\alpha = 0.01 \quad u_\alpha = 0.040 \quad CI(95\%) = (0.038, 0.043)$$
$$\alpha = 0.001 \quad u_\alpha = 0.081 \quad CI(95\%) = (0.070, 0.101)$$

Hence a 95% confidence interval for a 0.1% event in these daily return data is (7.0%, 10.1%). There is a lot more we could examine at this point: dependency in the data, sensitivity of estimates to the

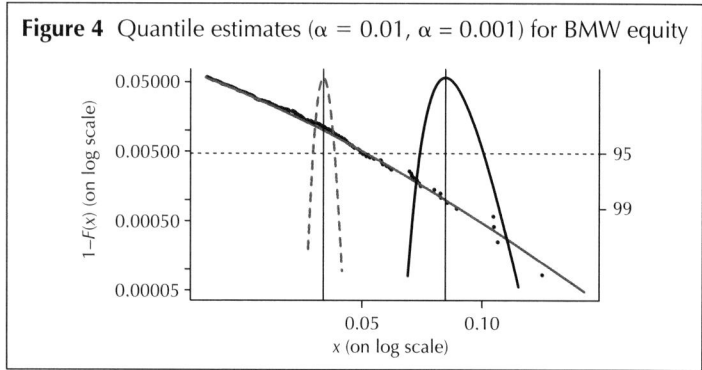

Figure 4 Quantile estimates ($\alpha = 0.01$, $\alpha = 0.001$) for BMW equity

threshold $u = 0.02$, more details on the statistical tools used, etc. All these, and indeed many more points, can be addressed through careful use of EVT.

The above discussion has only scratched the surface of what EVT offers. We believe its applicability to finance will be examined in much greater detail in the near future. The fact that the method already has proven important in fields like reliability, reinsurance, hydrology and environmental science enhances our belief that relevant applications in the realm of finance in general and risk management in particular will be found.

There is no alternative: if risk managers want to look at the edge, the proper tools must be used, which implies reliance on classical EVT and its numerous extensions to dependent and multivariate data, as well as to stochastic processes (including some of the standard stochastic volatility models).

1   A sample of S-plus routines can be downloaded from www.math.ethz.ch/mcneil/software.html

This chapter was previously published in *Risk*, January 1998.

REFERENCES

Artzner, P., F. Delbaen, J.-M. Eber, and D. Heath, 1997, "Thinking Coherently", *Risk*, November, pp. 68–71.

Boudoukh, J., M. Richardson, and R. Whitelaw, 1995, "Expect the Worst", *Risk*, September, pp. 100–1.

Embrechts, P., C. Klüppelberg, and T. Mikosch, 1997, "Modelling Extremal Events for Insurance and Finance", (Berlin: Springer-Verlag).

Jorion, P., 1997, "Value at Risk", (Chicago: Irwin)

Leadbetter, M., G. Lindgren, and H. Rootzén, 1983, "Extremes and Related Properties of Random Sequences and Processes", (New York: Springer-Verlag).

Longin, F., 1997, "Beyond the VAR", Preprint, ESSEC, Paris.

McNeil, A., 1997, "Estimating the Tails of Loss Severity Distributions using Extreme Value Theory", ASTIN Bulletin 27, pp. 117–37.

Resnick, S., 1987, "Extreme Values, Regular Variation and Point Processes", (New York: Springer-Verlag).

Resnick, S., 1997, "Discussion of the Danish Data on Large Fire Insurance Losses", ASTIN Bulletin 27, pp. 139–51.

Zangari, P., 1997, "Catering for an Event", *Risk*, July, pp. 34–6.

15

Extreme Forex Moves

Peter Blum, Michel Dacorogna

ETH Zürich

Since risk management has been established on a quantitative basis in financial institutions, the prevailing model has been Gaussian (JP Morgan (1996)). In particular, the model is widely used to determine the value-at-risk of assets or, more generally, of portfolios of assets or in pricing options with the Black–Scholes model (Black and Scholes (1973)). By using a model, it is possible to determine the probability of a movement of a certain size occurring. The Gaussian model, however, implies that extreme movements are very improbable. Unfortunately, we have learned the hard way that extreme movements in financial markets are more the rule than the exception (Koedijk, Schafgans and De Vries (1990), and Longin (1996)). This fact means more sophisticated ways of assessing the risk of extreme events are needed. Extreme value theory[1] gives us a way of going beyond the normal assumptions and quantifying the risk of extreme events in financial markets more accurately.

In this chapter, we present empirical studies of daily log returns (later called returns) of foreign exchange rates that demonstrate the existence of extreme events in this market and quantify the failure of the Gaussian model. Then we show how it is possible to estimate the probability distribution of extreme movements using a simple method derived from extreme value theory. We compare the results obtained with historical data and make predictions for longer periods than those already observed. We also propose a way of calculating the limits that a risk manager can set to open positions in order to avoid the occurrence of large losses.

LARGE MOVEMENTS

To examine extreme movements in the forex market, we use a set of daily observations of four major forex rates, namely the Swiss franc/dollar, the euro/dollar, the sterling/dollar and the yen/dollar.[2] For all rates except the euro/dollar, we cover the time interval from January 2, 1980 to December 31, 2001, resulting in some 5,600 daily observations per rate. For the euro/dollar rate, we cover the period from December 29, 1988 to December 31, 2001, resulting in 3,358 daily observations. For the time before January 1, 1999, we use a synthetic euro rate calculated from a portfolio of the constituent currencies.[3] Based on this data, we construct the logarithmic returns:

$$r_i = \ln\left(\frac{P_i}{P_{i-1}}\right) \tag{1}$$

where P_i indicates the closing price on day i. This transformation allows us to work with a stationary time series (see Dacorogna *et al* (2001)), and is the usual quantity considered in statistical studies of financial data.

For the rest of this chapter, we shall assume that the daily logarithmic returns r_i are independent and identically distributed. In addition, it is fairly popular among practitioners to assume that each r_i follows a Gaussian distribution, that is, the probability density function of r_i is given by:

$$f(x) = \frac{1}{\sigma\sqrt{2\pi}} e^{-\frac{1}{2\sigma^2}(x-\mu)^2} \equiv N(\mu, \sigma) \tag{2}$$

This model is fully determined by two parameters, namely the average μ and the variance σ^2. Empirical estimates $\hat{\mu}$ and $\hat{\sigma}$ to calibrate the model to the characteristics of a specific exchange rate can be easily obtained from the historical data. Then, given a specific return r_i, it is possible to calculate its probability according to the Gaussian model by using Equation (2).

In Table 1, we report estimates of both μ and σ for the four forex rates as well as the largest negative and positive returns observed in our samples. These values are compared with their probability

Table 1 Empirical estimates of the averages ($\hat{\mu}$) and the standard deviations ($\hat{\sigma}$) of log returns of major forex rates

Forex rate	$\hat{\mu}$ (%)	$\hat{\sigma}$ (%)	Max. (%)	One event over no. of years	Min. (%)	One event over no. of years
€/US$	−0.0089	0.83	5.05	10,838,489	−3.86	1,243
¥/US$	0.0105	0.69	3.98	1,519,105	−7.20	$>10^{12}$
£/US$	−0.0077	0.65	4.05	24,533,626	−4.70	3,269,448,288
Sfr/US$	−0.0009	0.75	3.76	21,157	−4.51	1,543,769

We show the largest (Max.) and the smallest (Min.) returns in the sample with their probabilities of occurrence according to the Gaussian model parameterised with the estimated empirical averages and standard deviations.

of occurrence in the Gaussian model. To aid understanding, we present the Gaussian probability as the one event in a certain number of years. It is easily seen from the numbers that the Gaussian model gives completely unrealistic probabilities given that our sample, and the extremes observed in it, cover an observation period of only 22 years (or 13 for the euro/dollar cross).

To complete the picture, we calculate Value-at-risk (VaR) as it is given by our historical data. VaR has become a standard way of measuring the extreme risk of a portfolio (Jorion (1997)). Given a certain model, the VaR is equivalent to the quantile corresponding to a certain risk threshold. One usual threshold is the 1% event. In the Gaussian model, VaR is determined by the average μ and the standard deviation σ. Once we have the VaR, we can calculate the expected number of exceedances to this threshold according to the Gaussian model. Theoretically, given the quantiles of 1% (left tail) or of 99% (right tail), this number is a function of the amount of data. If one looks at the data, only 1% of the losses should be beyond the VaR. Our study counts the number of returns that were beyond the given thresholds. In Table 2, we present the results of the study. It is clear that the number of values that lie beyond the VaR is much larger than expected by the Gaussian model. It is one more clear sign that the Gaussian model is not appropriate to represent the risk of extreme movements in the forex market.

Extreme events do indeed occur much more often than is foreseen by the Gaussian model. Hence, to get a better understanding

Table 2 Theoretical and observed numbers of exceedances of a VaR at 99% (or 1%) calculated according to the Gaussian model

Forex rate	Expected positive	Observed positive	Expected negative	Observed negative
€/US$	34	48	34	57
¥/US$	56	119	56	71
£/US$	56	88	56	102
Sfr/US$	56	106	56	80

of the dangers posed by extreme fluctuations in forex rates, we have to go for alternative models that assign more realistic – that is, higher – probabilities to these extreme events.

TAIL ANALYSIS

As long as we are interested only in extreme events, we do not need to consider models that cover the full range of possible outcomes. Indeed, we can restrict our attention to dedicated methods for analysing extreme events, that is, the analysis of the tails of the probability distribution. Powerful methods for this tail analysis come from the realm of extreme value theory, which has become popular in various areas of quantitative risk management in the past few years (Embrechts, Resnick and Samorodnitzky (1998)).

Essentially, extreme value theory aims to estimate tail events, and by definition does not consider fitting the centre of the distribution. Depending on the distributional properties of the underlying model, various statistical techniques are available. See, for example, Embrechts, Klüppelberg and Mikosch (1997) for a survey and pointers to the rich literature on this topic. In our case, we look at so-called heavy-tailed models (also referred to as the Fréchet class) for which:

$$1 - F(x) = x^{-\alpha}L(x) \tag{3}$$

In this equation, the crucial parameter determining the tail properties is $\alpha > 0$. The unknown function $L(x)$ is defined in such a way that it will typically not appear in statistical estimates for models satisfying Equation (3). It does, however, play an important role when it comes to statistical properties of these estimates (see Embrechts,

Klüppelberg and Mikosch (1997), for technical details). Hence, the problem becomes how to estimate the tail index α from the data. There are many ways of doing this, and we concentrate here on the Hill estimator (Hill (1975)), which is a consistent estimator of $\gamma = 1/\alpha$. Given a sequence of n observations, $X_1, X_2, \ldots, X_n$, drawn from an independent and identically distributed process whose probability distribution F is unknown, we order the observations in descending order statistics $X_{(1)} \geq X_{(2)} \geq \ldots \geq = X_{(n)}$. We can then define the Hill estimator $\hat{\gamma}_{n,m}^H$ by:

$$\hat{\gamma}_{n,m}^H = \frac{1}{m-1} \sum_{i=1}^{m-1} \ln X_{(i)} - \ln X_{(m)} \tag{4}$$

where the number of order statistics m is an additional parameter to be determined. In fact, the Hill estimator is the maximum likelihood estimator of γ and $\alpha = 1/\gamma$ holds for the tail index. For finite samples, however, the expected value of the Hill estimator is biased. There are many ways of trying to reduce this bias, from graphical techniques (Resnick (1987)) to sophisticated bootstrap procedures (Danielsson *et al* (1997), and Pictet, Dacorogna and Müller (1998)). In practice, however, we find that taking a value of $m = \sqrt{n}$, where n is the number of observations in the sample, leads to reasonable results.

Here, we do not aim to assess in detail the significance or the bias of the estimator[4] but rather to design a simple recipe to quantify the probability of extreme movements from a given data set. The results might vary slightly from one method to the other but the order of magnitude stays the same and, as we shall see, the improvement compared with the Gaussian model is such that a certain imprecision in the estimation is a price worth paying. However, if one puts the model into practical use, it is nevertheless important to obtain an idea of the accuracy of the estimated parameters. To this end, the jackknife method is simple and powerful. It consists of modifying the data sample in 10 different ways, each time removing one-tenth of the total sample. The tail index is separately calculated for each of the 10 modified samples, and the analysis of the deviations between the 10 results yields an estimate of the standard error. With the asymptotic properties of the Hill estimator, this allows us to calculate, for example, a 95% confidence interval, as shown for our estimates in Table 3. More detailed information can be found in Pictet,

Table 3 Results of the estimations of the tail index with the 95% jackknife confidence interval

Forex rate	Number of observations (n)	Number of order statistics (m)	Tail index $\hat{\alpha} = 1/\hat{\gamma}_{n,m}^H$
(A) Tall index $\hat{\alpha}$ on full sample			
€/US$	3,357	58	3.86 ± 0.80
¥/US$	5,642	75	3.96 ± 0.85
£/US$	5,634	75	3.76 ± 0.83
Sfr/US$	5,641	75	4.67 ± 1.07

Forex rate	On sub-sample years 1980–1990	On sub-sample years 1991–2001
(B) Tail index $\hat{\alpha}$ calculated on sub-samples		
¥/US$	4.11 ± 0.88	3.04 ± 0.86
£/US$	3.85 ± 1.10	3.67 ± 0.80
Sfr/US$	4.83 ± 1.15	4.28 ± 1.11

(A) shows the estimates obtained from the full sample (years 1980–2001), whereas (B) shows estimates of the tail index on two disjoint sub-samples of the data (years 1980–1990 and years 1991–2001).

Dacorogna and Müller (1998) and more examples and background information in Dacorogna et al (2001).

Using Equation (4) with $m = \sqrt{n}$ and the jackknife method, we estimate the tail indexes and the 95% confidence bounds for the four forex rates chosen for this analysis. The results are reported in panel A of Table 3. The results are relatively stable and remarkably similar across rates, except for the Swiss franc/dollar rate. They differ slightly from the results obtained in Dacorogna et al (2001), but are still clearly within the error bounds given therein. The confidence intervals reported here are not negligible, but much narrower than those given in Dacorogna et al (2001). Differences may be due to the considerably longer data samples and to the simplified estimation procedure in this study. In any case, the differences are not material and do not affect the rest of our study. To get an idea about the stability of the Hill estimates, and to do some additional backtesting, we also estimated the tail indexes on two disjointed sub-samples of the full data sets[5] (covering 1980–1990 and 1991–2001, respectively). We notice that the yen/dollar tail index for the second sub-sample (1991–2001) is significantly different from the respective tail indexes for the full sample and for the first sub-sample, which can probably be explained by the related economic history in the 1990s and which suggests that there may be limitations to the predictive power of the method suggested here in case of significant regime switches. For the other two rates, the tail indexes of the two sub-samples are clearly related to each other (indicating some degree of historical stability in the underlying data series) and to the tail index of the full sample (indicating stability of the estimator itself). It should be noticed that tail index estimates for considerably shorter sub-samples (eg, five years) are not usable any more due to lack of precision. Indeed, the Hill estimator requires relatively large amounts of data to be acceptably accurate. For a detailed account on this and other caveats around the Hill estimator, see Embrechts, Klüppelberg and Mikosch (1997).

EXTREME RISKS AND LIMIT SETTING

From the practitioner's point of view, one of the most interesting questions that tail studies can answer is: what are the extreme movements that can be expected in financial markets? Have we already seen the largest ones or will we experience even larger movements? Are there theoretical processes that can model the type of fat tails that come out of the empirical analysis? The answers to such questions are essential for good risk management of financial exposures. It turns out that we can partially answer them here. Once we know the tail index, we can apply extreme value theory outside our sample to consider possible extreme movements that have not yet been observed historically.

This can be achieved by calculating the extreme quantiles in the daily returns, as proposed in section 5.4.3 of Dacorogna *et al* (2001). In this work, the derivation of the following quantile estimator is presented for a given probability p:

$$\hat{x}_p = X_{(m)} \left(\frac{m}{np} \right)^{\frac{1}{\hat{\alpha}}} \tag{5}$$

where all the quantities on the right-hand side are now known. Dacorogna *et al* (2001) also gives a way to estimate the error of this quantile calculation, but here we concentrate on the calculation of

Table 4 Extreme daily returns over periods of 5–40 years (%)

Forex rate	Method of calculation	Worst daily movement within...				
		5 years	10 years	20 years	30 years	40 years
€/US$	Observed	3.79	3.84	–	–	–
	Hill	4.30	5.17	6.22	6.93	7.49
	Gaussian	2.68	2.85	3.01	3.10	3.17
¥/US$	Observed	3.53	4.85	6.09	–	–
	Hill	3.97	4.74	5.67	6.30	6.80
	Gaussian	2.24	2.38	2.51	2.59	2.64
£/US$	Observed	3.21	3.88	4.54	–	–
	Hill	3.38	4.08	4.93	5.51	5.96
	Gaussian	2.09	2.22	2.34	2.41	2.46
Sfr/US$	Observed	3.22	3.61	4.11	–	–
	Hill	3.54	4.12	4.80	5.24	5.58
	Gaussian	2.41	2.56	2.71	2.79	2.84

The values are calculated by three different methods: historically observed in our sample, using the Hill estimator and using the Gaussian model.

quantiles using the numbers obtained in Table 3. Since we have a sample covering 22 years, we choose the probabilities of occurrence at which to calculate the quantiles so that we obtain at least two numbers that we can compare with our historic data and two that represent an out-of-sample prediction: one over five years (probability of 0.0008)[6], one over 10 years (0.0004), one over 20 years (0.0002), one over 30 years (0.000133) and one over 40 years (0.0001), which are low probabilities sitting far out in the tails.

In Table 4, we report the results for three different methods of calculation: first the observed quantile (at least for the probabilities still covered by the samples), the quantile computed with the Hill estimator (Equation (5)) and then the quantile calculated using the Gaussian model as introduced and calibrated above. The results are striking: as long as we can compare the predicted quantiles with empirically observed ones, we can clearly see that the estimates from the Hill estimator are much closer to the observable reality than the ones from the normal model. The Gaussian values are clearly underestimating the extremes we saw above. One can also observe that the increase of the large movement size with respect to the decrease of its probability is more accentuated than in

Table 5 Quantile estimates according to Equation (5) (%)

Forex rate		Worst daily movement within . . .				
		5 years	10 years	20 years	30 years	40 years
€/US$	at upper	3.67	4.25	4.94	5.38	5.73
	at lower	5.20	6.53	8.19	9.36	10.28
¥/US$	at upper	3.43	3.96	4.57	4.97	5.28
	at lower	4.73	5.91	7.39	8.42	9.24
£/US$	at upper	2.90	3.38	3.93	4.29	4.57
	at lower	4.20	5.22	6.22	7.60	8.39
Sfr/US$	at upper	3.11	3.51	3.96	4.25	4.47
	at lower	4.17	5.05	6.13	6.86	7.43

Evaluated at the upper and lower bounds of the 95% confidence interval for as shown in Table 3.

the Gaussian case and better reproduces the observed increase in the sample.

Given the non-negligible width of the confidence intervals stated in Table 3, it is worthwhile exploring the variability of the quantile estimates shown in Table 4. We can do this by evaluating Equation (5) at the upper and lower bounds of the 95% confidence intervals for $\hat{\alpha}$ given in Table 3. We show the respective values in Table 5. Comparing these bounds with the values given in Table 4, we notice that the observed values – where available – are close to or below the lower bound for the Hill estimates, suggesting that the latter are rather conservative estimates for the potential extreme movements. However, the Hill estimates are still much more closely related to the observable reality than the estimates from the Gaussian model. From this, we can conclude that our model is better suited than the Gaussian one to explain the historical tail behaviour of the data.

The numbers given in Table 4 can also be considered as an in-sample backtest of the Gaussian and the Hill methods. "In-sample" means that we use estimates calculated from the full sample to predict (or rather explain) the extremes of the sample itself. For risk management purposes, however, it is more interesting to know whether the estimators are also able to predict future extreme values that have not been used for the estimation of the tail index. This

Table 6 Predictions made for extreme daily returns over periods of five and 10 years (%)

Forex rate	Gaussian prediction		Hill prediction		Observed 1991–2001	
	5y-event	10y-event	5y-event	10y-event	5y-event	10y-event
¥/US$	2.09	2.22	3.67	4.34	4.75	6.53
£/US$	2.22	2.36	3.52	4.21	2.87	3.17
Sfr/US$	2.43	2.58	3.49	4.03	3.35	3.81

Compared with the related values observed between 1991 and 2001. The predictions were made by using the Gaussian and the Hill model, but using only the data of 1980–1990 for the calibration (out-of-sample).

corresponds to an out-of-sample backtest, and the results of such a test are summarised in Table 6. We did all calculations by using only the data for the years 1980–1990 (see panel B of Table 3 for the related tail indexes), and we assess how well we would have forecast the extreme values of the period 1991–2001. Clearly, the out-of-sample forecasts based on the Hill estimator are not as accurate as the in-sample predictions in Table 4.[7] In the case of the yen/dollar rate, even the Hill estimator fails to capture the size of the extreme returns that occurred in the 1990s, which is not surprising in view of the dramatically changed tail behaviour shown in panel B of Table 3. For the other rates, the Hill estimator still makes more prudent and – generally – more accurate predictions of the future tail behaviour than the Gaussian method, but in the case of the sterling/dollar rate the superiority of the Hill estimator over the Gaussian model in terms of accuracy is no longer so apparent.

These facts give us confidence that the extrapolated values obtained from the Hill estimator will represent a sufficiently conservative estimate of the risk[8], whereas the results indicate that the Gaussian model dangerously underestimates the actual risk. We are not trying here to quantify precisely the extreme movements but rather to capture the essentials of them, so that we can set reasonable limits of exposure.

To conclude this chapter, we turn to the problem of setting limits on open forex positions to restrict the risk of large losses. We first have to decide on the maximum size of the loss we are prepared to

Table 7 Proposed limits for open overnight forex positions according to three different methods (US$ million)

Forex	Method of calculation	Position limits for one daily loss of US$1 m within...				
		5 years	10 years	20 years	30 years	40 years
€/US$	Observed	26	26	–	–	–
	Hill	23	19	16	14	13
	Gaussian	37	35	33	32	32
¥/US$	Observed	28	21	16	–	–
	Hill	25	21	18	16	15
	Gaussian	47	42	40	39	38
£/US$	Observed	31	26	22	–	–
	Hill	29	24	20	18	17
	Gaussian	47	45	43	41	41
Sfr/US$	Observed	31	28	24	–	–
	Hill	28	24	21	19	18
	Gaussian	41	39	37	36	35

incur in a certain period of time. Let us assume that the maximum loss we are ready to risk is US$1 million on any one day and that we do not want to risk losing it more than once every five, 10, 20, 30 and 40 years. Using the numbers given in Table 4, it is now easy to calculate the limits to be set for different forex rates.

In Table 7, we provide the limits for the major forex rates considered in this study, and one sees that if we are using the Gaussian model open positions would be permitted that are about twice as large as would be prudent. We can see from this that risk limit setting according to the Gaussian model may result in unaffordably high losses.

CONCLUSION

Considering the results of our study, we can conclude that daily fluctuations in forex rates are higher than usually assumed, and that the Gaussian model is unable to reflect these extreme fluctuations properly. Luckily, we can quantify this risk by concentrating our attention on the tails of the distribution, provided that sufficient amounts of historical data are available and that we can exclude dramatic regime changes. Thus, it is possible to set realistic limits for trading on the forex market. Quantifying the risks transforms them from a nuisance into an opportunity.

1 For the interested reader, there are more and more review books available on the subject. Here are some: one more oriented towards the theory (Leadbetter, Lindgren and Rootzén (1983)) and two more practically oriented (Adler, Feldman and Taqqu (1998), and Embrechts, Klüppelberg and Mikosch (1997)).

2 The data was obtained from Bloomberg through their Bloomberg Data License (see www.bloomberg.com). Free daily observations of certain forex rates can be obtained, for example, from www.federalreserve.gov/releases/H10/hist/.

3 Actually, the THEOEURO index from Bloomberg.

4 The interested reader can consult the different references given in this chapter.

5 Except for the euro/dollar data, due to lack of a sufficiently long history.

6 Meaning the worst daily movement to be expected within five (10, 20, 30, 40) years.

7 It should, however, be noticed that the setup of the test is extreme in that 10 years of history are used to predict up to 10 years of the future. Moreover, 10 years of historical data are close to the minimum of what is needed to make the Hill estimator significant.

8 Excluding significant regime switches such as the one observed in the yen/dollar data.

This chapter was previously published in *Risk*, February 2003.

REFERENCES

Adler, R., R. Feldman, and M. Taqqu (eds), 1998, "A Practical Guide to Heavy Tails", (Boston: Birkhäuser).

Black, F. and M. Scholes, 1973, "The Pricing of Options and Corporate Liabilities", *Journal of Political Economy* **81**, pp. 637–59.

Dacorogna, M., R. Gençay, U. Müller, R. Olsen, and O. Pictet, 2001, "An Introduction to High Frequency Finance", (SanDiego: Academic Press).

Danielsson, J., L. de Haan, L. Peng, and C. de Vries, 1997, "Using a Bootstrap Method to Choose the Sample Fraction in Tail Index Estimation", Discussion Paper TI97-016/4, Tinbergen Institute, pp. 1–30.

Embrechts, P., C. Klüppelberg, and T. Mikosch, 1997, "Modelling Extremal Events", Applications of Mathematics Stochastic Modelling and Applied Probability 33, (Berlin: Springer).

Embrechts, P., S. Resnick, and G. Samorodnitzky, 1998. "Living on the Edge", *Risk*, January, pp. 96–100.

Hill, B., 1975, "A Simple General Approach to Inference About the Tail of a Distribution", *Annals of Statistics* **3(5)**, pp. 1163–73.

Jorion, P., 1997, "Value at Risk: The New Benchmark for Controlling Market Risk", (Chicago: Irwin Professional).

J. P. Morgan, 1996, "RiskMetrics Technical Document", JP Morgan.

Koedijk, K., M. Schafgans, and C. De Vries, 1990, "The Tail Index of Exchange Rate Returns", *Journal of International Economics* **29**, pp. 93–108.

Leadbetter, M., G. Lindgren, and H. Rootzén, 1983, "Extremes and Related Properties of Random Sequences and Processes", Springer Series in Statistics, (New York, Berlin: Springer-Verlag).

Longin, F., 1996, "The Asymptotic Distribution of Extreme Stock Market Returns", *Journal of Business* **69(3)**, pp. 383–407.

Pictet, O., M. Dacorogna, and U. Müller, 1998, "Hill, Bootstrap and Jackknife Estimators for Heavy Tails", in A Practical Guide to Heavy Tails: Statistical Techniques for Analysing Heavy Tailed Distributions, edited by Murad Taqqu, (Boston: Birkhäuser), pp. 283–310.

Resnick, S., 1987, "Extreme Values, Regular Variation, and Point Processes", (New York: Springer).

16

The Power Law

John Hull

University of Toronto

Risk managers often want levels of confidence as high as 99%, 99.7% or even 99.99% when calculating value-at-risk (VaR). This requires knowledge of the extreme tail of the loss distribution. Trouble is, it's not usually possible to collect enough data to accurately estimate the tail directly. The power law is a way of overcoming this problem.

For many variables, v, it is approximately true that the probability that v is greater than x is given by:

$$\text{Prob}(v > x) = Kx^{-\alpha} \qquad (1)$$

when x is large. Here K and α are constants that depend on the particular variable being considered. This relationship in Equation (1) is known as the power law. It has been found to be true for variables as diverse as the income of individuals, the size of cities and the number of visits to web sites in a day.

Suppose that $\alpha = 3$ and we observe that the probability that $v > 10$ is 0.05. In this case, $K = 50$ and we can estimate the probability that $v > 20$ as 0.00625; the probability that $v > 30$ as 0.0019; and so on.

Equation (1) implies that

$$\ln[\text{Prob}(v > x)] = \ln K - \alpha \ln x$$

If we have a large number of observations on a variable we can do a quick test of whether the power law holds by plotting $\ln(V(x)]$ against $\ln(x)$ where $V(x)$ is the proportion of observations that are

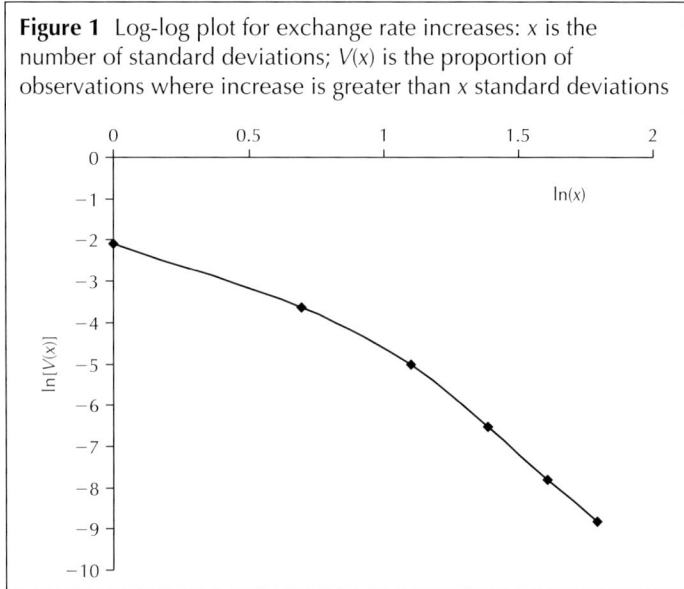

Figure 1 Log-log plot for exchange rate increases: x is the number of standard deviations; $V(x)$ is the proportion of observations where increase is greater than x standard deviations

greater than x. (When the power law holds the relationship should be linear for large x.) Figure 1 shows the result of doing for this daily movements in 12 different exchange rates over a 10-year period. The variable v is chosen as the number of standard deviations by which the exchange rate moves. The log-log plot shows that we have approximate linearity when $x > 3$. The parameter α can be estimated from the slope in Figure 1 as about 5.5.

APPLICATION TO MARKET RISK

Banks are required by regulators to estimate the 10-day 99% VaR for market risk. This is usually assumed to be $\sqrt{10}$ times the 1-day 99% VaR. The most popular way to estimate the 1-day 99% VaR is historical simulation. This involves using historical daily changes in market variables to assess the probability distribution of the change in the value of a portfolio between today and tomorrow. Suppose 500 days of historical data are used. These provide 500 points on the probability distribution of portfolio changes. The 1-day 99% VaR can be estimated as the 5th largest loss. Unfortunately this estimate of the 1 percentile point of the gain/loss distribution has a high standard error. For example, if the estimated 1-day 99% VaR is US$25 million and the gain/loss distribution is approximately normal, it can be shown that a 95% confidence interval for the VaR is likely to be US$21 million to US$29 million or thereabouts.

The problem is that we are relying on a handful of observations to get a handle on the tail of the distribution. Extreme value theory, which provides the theoretic underpinnings of the power law, does not give us an exact answer, but it does improve on the "5th worst case" estimate by smoothing out the tails of the distribution.

Let u be a value of a variable, v, in the right hand tail of a cumulative probability distribution $F(v)$. The distribution has two parameters that have to be estimated from the data, ξ and β. The parameter ξ is the shape parameter and determines the heaviness of the tail of the distribution. The parameter β is a scale parameter.

The first step in calculating the estimate is to choose a value of u. and then estimate ξ and β using maximum likelihood methods. (Usually the 95 percentile point of the empirical distribution works well as a choice for u.) A better estimate of the 1-day 99% VaR is obtained by solving

$$0.01 = \frac{n_u}{n}\left(1 + \xi\frac{\text{VaR} - u}{\beta}\right)^{-1/\xi}$$

so that

$$\text{VaR} = u + \frac{\beta}{\xi}\left[\left(\frac{0.01n}{n_u}\right)^{-\xi} - 1\right]$$

This result naturally follows from Equation (3) in the Theoretical Underpinnings box.

APPLICATION TO OPERATIONAL RISK

The Basel II AMA approach to assessing operational risk requires companies to assess the one-year 99.9% VaR for operational risk. De Fountnouvelle *et al* (2003) using data from vendors find that the power law holds well for the large operational risk losses experienced by banks. This makes the calculation of VaR with high degrees of confidence such as 99.9% possible. Loss data (internal or external) is used to estimate the power law parameters and these are used in turn to estimate the 99.9 percentile of the loss distribution.

An interesting point here is that when loss distributions are aggregated the distribution with the heaviest tails tends to dominate. This means that the loss with the lowest α (highest ξ) defines the extreme tails of the total loss distribution. If all we are interested in is calculating the extreme tail of the total operational risk loss distribution, it may only necessary to consider one or two business line/loss type combinations.

It is difficult to see how the high degrees of confidence that regulators are requiring for operational risk can be accommodated without invoking the power law. Whether regulators – or banks themselves – will accept an argument that one particular type of risk (eg, litigation risk or rogue trader risk) dominates all others in determining the tails of the operational risk loss distribution remains to be seen. In practice there are many hidden benefits in trying to quantify all types of operational risk, including those that are unlikely to have extreme consequences.

CONCLUSIONS

VaR is widely used by regulators for determining bank capital. Although it does have shortcomings (see second article in the series.), it is likely that it will continue to be used by regulators for many years to come. The power law provides an interesting tool for estimating VaR – especially when very high levels of confidence are required.

THEORETICAL UNDERPINNINGS

Extreme value theory provides the theoretical underpinnings of the power law. The key result in extreme value theory was proved by Gnedenko (1943). He showed that the properties of the tails of a wide range of different probability distributions are similar.

Suppose that $F(v)$ is the cumulative probability distribution function for a variable v. Suppose that u is a value of v in the right hand tail of the distribution. The probability that v lies between u and $u + y$ $(y > 0)$ is $F(u + y) - F(u)$. The probability that v is greater than u is $1 - F(u)$. Define $F_u(y)$ as the probability that v lies between u and $u + y$ conditional on $v > u$. This is

$$F_u(y) = \frac{F(u + y) - F(u)}{1 - F(u)}$$

The variable $F_u(y)$ defines the right tail of the probability distribution. It is the cumulative probability distribution for the amount by which v exceeds u given that it does exceed u.

Gnedenko's result is that, for a wide class of distributions, the distribution of $F_u(y)$ converges to a generalised Pareto distribution as the threshold u is increased. The generalised Pareto distribution is

$$G_{\xi,\beta}(y) = 1 - \left(1 + \xi \frac{y}{\beta}\right)^{-1/\xi} \tag{2}$$

The distribution has two parameters that have to be estimated from the data, ξ and β. The parameter ξ is the shape parameter and determines the heaviness of the tail of the distribution. The parameter β is a scale parameter.

The probability that $v > u + y$ conditional that $v > u$ is $1 - G_{\xi,\beta}(y)$. The probability that $v > u$ is $1 - F(u)$. The unconditional probability that $v > x$ is therefore

$$[1 - F(u)][1 - G_{\xi,\beta}(x - u)]$$

If n is the total number of observations, an estimate of $1 - F(u)$, calculated from the empirical data, is n_u/n where n_u is the number of observation greater than u. Using Equation (2) the unconditional probability that $v > x$ is therefore

$$\text{Prob}(v > x) = \frac{n_u}{n}\left(1 + \xi \frac{x - u}{\beta}\right)^{-1/\xi} \tag{3}$$

If we set $u = \beta/\xi$, $\alpha = 1/\xi$, and

$$K = \frac{n_u}{n}\left(\frac{\xi}{\beta}\right)^{-1/\xi}$$

Equation (3) can be seen to be the same as the power law in Equation (1). This establishes the link between the power law and Gnedenko's result.

For most financial data ξ is positive and in the range 0.1–0.4.[1] Equivalently α in Equation (1) is in the range 2.5–10. A more sophisticated way of estimating parameters than the log-log approach in Figure 1 involves the use of maximum likelihood methods in conjunction with Gnedenko's results.

This is an edited extract from John Hull's new book "Risk Management and Financial Institutions" published by Prentice Hall in 2006. John Hull is the Maple Professor of Derivatives and Risk Management at the Joseph L. Rotman School of Management, University of Toronto. www.rotman.utoronto.ca/~hull

1   One of the properties of the distribution in Equation (2) is that the kth moment is infinite for $k \geq 1/\xi$.

This chapter was previously published in *Risk*, March 2007.

REFERENCES

De Fountnouvelle, P., V. DeJesus-Rueff, J. Jordan, and E. Rosengren, 2003, "Capital and Risk: New Evidence on Implications of Large Operational Risk Losses", Federal Reserve Board of Boston, Working Paper, September.

Gnedenko, D. V., 1943, "Sur la distribution limité du terme d'une série aléatoire", *Ann. Math.* **44**, pp. 423–53.

Hull, J. C., 2006, *Risk Management and Financial Institutions*, (Upper Saddle River, NJ: Prentice Hall).

Hull, J. C., 2006, "VAR vs Expected Shortfall", *Risk*, December, pp. 48–9.

17

VaR-x: Fat Tails in Financial Risk Management

Ronald Huisman; Kees G. Koedijk,* Rachel A. J. Pownall

Erasmus University; University of Maastricht

1 INTRODUCTION

The quest for reliable risk management techniques has grown in response to higher volatility and instability on global financial markets, compounded by the enormous growth in trading activity and international exposure. One need only think of the losses made from recent currency and stock market crashes, as well as those resulting from the perilous positions taken, for example, by Barings, Daiwa, Orange County, and Metallgesellschaft. Value-at-risk (VaR) is one such risk management technique developed to improve the management of downside risk. It aims to summarise risk, by estimating the worst expected loss over a chosen time horizon within a given confidence interval. The methodology behind VaR is therefore based on the probabilities associated with large negative returns and hence highlights how financial institutions have had to become more concerned with managing this downside risk. Only through the use of such risk management methods can the exposure towards large negative movements in financial markets be controlled and reduced. However, their benefit rests primarily on the accuracy of the VaR estimates.

*The authors thank Geert Bekaert, Kevin Dowd, Philippe Jorion and Franz Palm for valuable comments. Any errors are the responsibility of the authors.

The VaR estimate is found from the probability distribution of the expected returns. This implies that one needs to make assumptions concerning the actual form of the expected return distribution. This can be done by assuming that the distribution of the expected returns equals the empirical distribution based on past observations or by assuming that the returns are drawn from a specific statistical distribution. The exact form of these analytical distributions is determined by various parameters, estimated using past data, and which have more recently also allowed for the use of conditioning methodologies, such as generalised autoregressive conditionally heteroskedastic (GARCH) processes.

A parametric approach has been the preferred method, since it enables simple conversion to take place (between quantiles and time horizons), and is hence more pragmatic under the framework of the Basel Committee. It also enables conditionality in the data to be easily incorporated into the VaR estimate, making forecasts of VaR more appropriate. The crucial assumption therefore for an accurate estimation of the VaR is that the distribution in the left tail, reflecting the negative returns, is well represented by the specified distribution. Any discrepancy between the parametric distribution and the empirical distribution can result in large errors in the estimation of VaR.

For simplicity and convenience, asset returns are often assumed to be normally or lognormally distributed. However, the return distributions on many assets have been shown to exhibit fatter tails than the normal distribution.[1] This means that the assumption of normality results in an underestimation of the VaR on moving further into the tails. It is the exact nature of this extra mass in the tails of the distribution which is crucial when trying to capture the VaR of an asset. Other fatter-tailed distributions such as Pareto and sum-stable distributions have in the past proved difficult to implement. The normal distribution has therefore been retained as the most convenient proxy for an asset's actual distribution. However, the fatter the tails of the asset return distribution under consideration, the larger the discrepancy with the normal distribution, and the larger the errors made in VaR estimation. These errors become magnified for the million-dollar positions that mutual funds, for example, typically hold.

There is thus a need for simple methodologies to estimate VaR which capture the tail fatness apparent in return distributions. In this chapter, we present such a simple technique. We show that VaR-x estimates, VaR estimates obtained from assuming the Student *t*-distribution as a fit to the empirical distribution, are better able to capture the extra risk involved for distributions exhibiting a higher probability of large negative returns. Since we are looking at downside risk, we are interested in the negative returns associated with the left tail of the distribution. The tail parameter of the Student *t*-distribution, reflected by its number of degrees of freedom, is set equal to the tail index for the left tail, and is a direct measure of the amount of fatness in the tail of the return's distribution. This method offers many advantages over the normal distribution. First, fat tails are captured. Second, focusing only on the left tail means that we do not need to assume distributions are symmetric. The tail fatness may vary between the two tails of the return distribution and hence allows for the possibility for skewness in the distribution. This provides us with a simple and more accurate estimator than would otherwise be obtained from assuming normality.

One attempt to capture the extra probability mass in the tails has been to estimate a GARCH process. The unconditional distribution of a GARCH process does reveal fatter tails; however, it has been shown that the distribution of conditional residuals is still not normal (see Bollerslev (1987)). This results in the VaR still being underestimated at high quantiles for fat-tailed assets. The appealing feature, however, of incorporating conditional volatility is that it allows for a changing distribution over time. Implementing this into a VaR framework means that the VaR estimates are made conditional. This is done in JP Morgan's RiskMetrics, for example, and VaR-x can easily be adjusted to capture conditional volatility.[2]

The plan of the chapter is as follows. VaR and VaR-x are introduced in the following section. The data used and the results are presented in Sections 3 and 4, respectively. Conclusions are then drawn in the final section.

2 VALUE-AT-RISK METHODOLOGY

Exposure to downside risk can be summarised in a single number by an estimate of the VaR. This is formally defined by Jorion (1996) as "the worst expected loss over a target horizon within a given confidence level." Following Jorion, we define W_0 as the initial investment and R as the expected return over the target horizon. W^* is defined as the lowest portfolio value at the given confidence level c, that is, the value of the portfolio should not fall below W^* with probability c. VaR is defined as the dollar loss relative to the expected mean value of the portfolio

$$\text{VaR} = E(W) - W^* \tag{1}$$

Defining R^* as the expected return associated with the portfolio value W^*,

$$W^* = W_0(1 + R^*) \tag{2}$$

gives us the VaR measured as the dollar loss relative to the mean,

$$\text{VaR} = -W_0(R^* - \mu) \tag{3}$$

where μ is the expected return on the portfolio for the target horizon. The crux of being able to provide an accurate VaR estimate is in estimating the cutoff return R^*. In this chapter, we focus on the cutoff return estimated using historical data, and thereby assume that these are representative for the expected return measure.

The statistical methods developed to best estimate these cutoff returns can be divided into two types: parametric and nonparametric. The most obvious nonparametric approach uses the historical distribution itself to compute an empirical estimate of the VaR directly. In the parametric case, one tries to fit the historical distribution by a statistical distribution whose characteristic parameters are derived from the historical data. We shall therefore briefly review the standard ways to estimate VaR before presenting the methodology behind VaR-x. The crucial difference between VaR and VaR-x is that the latter incorporates the tail fatness apparent in financial returns into the VaR estimate, thereby improving the quality of the estimates in a simple and efficient way.

2.1 Methods to estimate the cutoff return and VaR
The cutoff return is defined as the worst possible realisation R^* for a confidence level c, and is found from the following integral for the distribution of expected returns $f(r)$:

$$1 - c = \int_{-\infty}^{R^*} f(r)\mathrm{d}r \tag{4}$$

2.1.1 Empirical VaR

Empirical VaR involves determining the point R^* from a histogram of the empirical distribution based on historical returns. R^* is that point below which are the fraction $1 - c$ of the returns. This number is then plugged into (3) to get the empirical VaR estimate.

The empirical VaR measure has some serious disadvantages to both financial institutions and regulators. In order to obtain accurate estimates a large data sample of the empirical distribution is required. The VaR estimate is therefore subject to the frequency and length of the data sample. A further drawback is the inability to allow for conditionality of the parameters over time. To overcome these flaws, a parametric approach, such as the normal approach, is often adopted. Since the distribution is approximated by a parametric distribution, parameters can be allowed to change over time. Estimation risk on the VaR estimate itself is also reduced, particularly for higher quantiles.[3] Furthermore, the parametric approach has the advantage of not being dependent on the chosen quantile, facilitating the ease with which comparisons between the VaR estimates across various institutions can be made. Parametric conversion, however, will only hold in practice if the parametric approach accurately reflects the distribution at all quantiles in the tail. Indeed, it has been the case that institutions have notoriously chosen confidence levels and time horizons to suit them. The choice of parametric distribution is therefore crucial.

2.1.2 Normal VaR

The simplest parametric approach is to assume that the expected returns are normally distributed with the mean and variance estimated using past data on returns. VaR estimates are then obtained by equating $f(r)$ in (4) to the p.d.f. of the normal distribution. The simplicity of this method also explains its popularity. However, to obtain accurate VaR estimates for higher confidence levels, say more that 95%, the parametric distribution should correctly approximate the distribution in the tails. Since it is commonly known that the distributions of returns on financial assets often exhibit fatter tails than the normal distribution, one could expect a large discrepancy to exist between the tails of the normal distribution and the tails of the actual distribution. Such a discrepancy could lead to serious errors in VaR estimates. These estimates could thus be improved upon by incorporating tail fatness; one such technique that incorporates the fat tails is VaR-x, proposed in the following section.

2.1.3 VaR-x

The evidence that distributions of returns on financial assets have fatter tails than indicated by the normal distribution has meant that the normal approach underestimates the true VaR at high quantiles. It therefore becomes apparent that in order to capture the full risk from fat-tailed assets a parametric distribution that is fatter in the tails should be used. The Student t-distribution, which also nests the normal distribution, is one obvious choice to model $f(r)$ in (4), but its parametrisation has proved tedious and inconsistent in the past.[4]

The Student t-distribution exhibits fatter tails than the normal distribution. The amount of tail fatness is reflected in the number of degrees of freedom. In order to capture tail fatness correctly, one should correctly specify the exact number of degrees of freedom to be used. This has proved to be difficult for exchange rate returns (see Boothe and Glassman (1987), Huisman et al (1998)), but recent advances in extreme value theory makes the issue less complex.

Extreme value theory looks specifically at the distribution of the returns in the tails. Since VaR focuses predominantly on this area in the tail, extreme value theory can bring some valuable insight into improving VaR estimation (see Danielson and de Vries (1997)). The tail fatness that a tail of a distribution exhibits is reflected by the tail index. It measures the speed with which the tail under consideration approaches zero. The fatter the tail, the slower the speed, and the lower the tail index given. A nice feature of the tail index is that it equals the number of moments that exist for a distribution. For example, a tail index estimate equal to 2 reveals that both the first and second moments exist, ie, the mean and the variance, but that higher moments are infinite. All moments exist for the normal distribution, so that its tail index equals infinity by definition. Here also lies the link with the Student t-distribution. The number of its degrees of freedom reflects the number of existing moments, and the tail index can thus be used to set the number of degrees of freedom.[5]

To obtain tail index estimates, we use the estimator presented by Huisman et al (1997). Unlike other tail index estimators, the estimator of Huisman et al is shown to produce almost unbiased estimates

in relatively small samples. This provides us with a superior estimator than previously used, and, as we shall see below, allows us
to obtain robust tail index estimates from a yearly sample of daily
data. Danielson and de Vries (1997) also use extreme value theory
to obtain VaR estimates, but their approach has the drawback that
an extremely large sample of data is required.[6]

Specifying k as the number of tail observations, and ordering
their absolute values as an increasing function of size, we obtain
the tail estimator proposed by Hill (1975). This is denoted below by
γ and is the inverse of the tail index α. Let x_i be the ith increasing
order-statistic, ie, $x_i \geq x_{i-1}$, based on the absolute values of the
observations. The Hill estimator then reads:

$$\gamma(k) = \frac{1}{k} \sum_{j=1}^{k} \ln x_{n-j+1} - \ln x_{n-k} \qquad (5)$$

Following the methodology of Huisman *et al* (1997), we can use a
modified version of the Hill estimator (1997) to correct for the bias
in small samples. The bias of the Hill estimator stems from the fact
that the bias is a function of the sample size. A bias corrected tail
index is therefore obtained by observing the bias of the Hill estimator as the number of tail observations increases up until κ, where κ
is equal to half of the sample size:

$$\gamma(k) = \beta_0 + \beta_1 k + \epsilon(k) \quad (k = 1, \dots, \kappa) \qquad (6)$$

The optimal estimate for the tail index is the intercept β_0. The α estimate is just the inverse of this estimate, and it is this estimate of the
tail index that we shall use in order to parametrise the Student
t-distribution.

The procedure for obtaining the VaR-x estimates is therefore as
follows. First, the tail index referred to by α is estimated using the
Huisman *et al* estimator for the left tail of the empirical return distribution. The focus on the left tail directly reflects the downside risk.
Furthermore, the mean μ and the variance σ^2 of the return distribution are estimated. In the second step, the tail index estimate α is then
used to equate the number of degrees of freedom in the Student
t-distribution. Read the value S^* off the standard Student
t-distribution with α degrees of freedom using appropriate tables

provided in standard textbooks (see Bain and Engelhardt (1987)) or statistical software. This value then needs to be converted, since the standard Student t-distribution with α degrees of freedom has a pre-set mean equal to zero and a variance equal to $\alpha/(\alpha-2)$. The value S^* is then transformed into the real cutoff return $R^* = -\theta S^* + \mu$, where θ is a scale factor given by

$$\theta = \frac{\sigma}{\sqrt{\alpha/(\alpha-2)}} \qquad (7)$$

The value R^* then equals the cutoff return needed to calculate the VaR-x measure for the confidence level c. Plugging the expression for R^* into (3), we obtain the VaR-x estimate for the VaR relative to the mean μ as

$$\text{VaR-x} = W_0\theta S^* \qquad (8)$$

In the following sections, we shall apply all the above techniques to calculate the VaR for US$100 million investments in both US stocks and bonds.

3 DATA

We use data from US stock and bond indices from January 1980 until August 1998, using bi-weekly returns to provide results that can easily be set against the 10-day regulatory framework adopted by the Basel Committee. The use of two different assets exhibiting different tail index alphas enables us to gauge the effect on the VaR estimates from a variation in tail fatness. We use data on the S&P 500 Composite Return Index for the US and the 10-Year Datastream Benchmark US Government Bond Return Index, both obtained from Datastream. The bi-weekly data excludes the crash of October 1987, so that we can estimate the VaR consistent with normal market conditions. Summary statistics are presented using lognormal returns for the sample of stock and bond returns in Table 1.

Over the period, stocks have had an average return of 17.33% per annum, nearly twice the 10.25% return on government bonds. The volatility was however much lower for US government bonds, with the variance around a third of that prevailing on the S&P 500.

Table 1 Summary statistics for stocks and government bond returns. This table contains the statistics on the S&P 500 Composite Return Index and the 10-Year Datastream US Benchmark Government Bond Index for the period January 1980 until August 1998 using 486 bi-weekly total returns. The α estimate is calculated using a modified version of the Hill estimator for the tail indexes and is presented for the left tail

	S&P 500 Composite Return Index	US 10-Year Government Bond Return Index
Annual mean (%)	17.329	10.247
Max return	0.153	0.089
Min return	−0.183	−0.061
Annual st deviation	0.146	0.086
Annual variance	0.021	0.007
Skewness	−0.641	0.503
Kurtosis	9.399	5.163
Gamma left tail	0.233	0.143
Standard error	0.050	0.030
Alpha left tail	4.285	7.009
Observations	118	121

Both assets appear to exhibit significant skewness as well as excess kurtosis. According to the kurtosis statistic, the extra probability mass in the tail areas of the stock returns appears to be high, and, since the distributions appear skewed, the two tails may differ dramatically. For the VaR-x estimates, we hence take any skewness in the tails into account by taking the tail index estimator of the left tail only. The effect on the VaR depends on the exact structure of the distribution of negative returns.

The degree of fat-tailedness is estimated in terms of α, calculated using the estimator developed by Huisman *et al* (1997). From the gamma estimates of the left tail (standard errors given below), the α estimates are 4.29 and 7.01 for the stock and bond returns respectively. For normally distributed returns the α estimate tends to infinity, so we can see that both distributions exhibit a fatter left tail than the normal. Owing to this leptokurtosis, the frequency of large negative returns is greater than that reflected by the normal distribution; hence the greater the downside risk, the fatter the tails, with the equity returns exhibiting more downside risk than the bonds.

4 VALUE-AT-RISK ESTIMATES

Value-at-risk by definition should be highly sensitive to the degree to which the distribution is fat tailed: the fatter tailed the distribution, the higher the VaR for a given confidence level. As we have seen, stocks have more downside risk than bonds, represented by a lower α estimate for the left tail index, and thus have a higher than normal probability of extreme returns. Thus, for higher confidence levels, we would expect an empirical VaR estimate to be larger than that predicted from using the parametric approach assuming normality. The higher the confidence level, and thus the quantile chosen for the VaR estimate, the greater the effect of extreme values in the asset's return distribution. This has the important implication that the existence of a fat-tailed return distribution implies that at high confidence levels the parametric-normal VaR underestimates the exposure to market risk, with the difference likely to become larger for higher confidence levels chosen and fatter tails.

To see by how much the estimates for VaR are affected by the evidence that stocks have a lower α tail index estimate than the bonds, we compute the VaR estimates using the various approaches discussed in Section 2. In Table 2 the VaR is estimated for a US$100 million investment in the two assets, using both the parametric-normal approach (equally weighted moving average method for calculating volatility) and the empirical approach.

We can see how the VaR estimates increase, the higher the confidence level taken. The structure of the difference between the empirical and the parametric-normal VaR estimates is indeed what would be expected for a fat-tailed distribution. For the S&P 500 Composite Return Index, we see that for low probability levels the distribution exhibits a so-called thin waist, since the parametric-normal VaR is larger than the empirical VaR. Moving further into the tails, the VaR estimate assuming normality becomes smaller than the empirical VaR. This means that at low probability levels the parametric-normal VaR overestimates the VaR and then, as we move to higher probability levels, the parametric-normal approach underestimates the VaR.

The magnitude of the error from using the normality assumption is a reflection of the amount of tail fatness, which of course is much more significant for the stock price index. The extent of the

Table 2 Comparison of VaR estimates. The VaR estimates have been calculated for the two asset classes using the empirical approach (historical data)
and both parametric approaches. The normal VaR estimates assume normally
distributed returns, whereas the VaR-x estimates assume a fatter-tailed distribution denoted by the Student *t*-distribution, and use the alpha estimates for the
left tail as given in Table 1. The relative VaR estimates, expressed in millions of
dollars, have been calculated for a position of US$100 million in the particu-
lar asset, and for a range of confidence levels

Confidence level (left tail)	S&P 500 Composite Return Index			US 10-Year Government Bond Return Index		
	Empirical VaR (US$100m)	Normal VaR (US$100m)	Student-*t* VaR-x (US$100m)	Empirical VaR (US$100m)	Normal VaR (US$100m)	Student-*t* VaR-x (US$100m)
95	4.3288	4.7176	4.3563	2.5347	2.7505	2.6812
95.5	4.6174	4.8626	4.5463	2.5986	2.8350	2.7819
96	4.7584	5.0211	4.7613	2.6912	2.9274	2.8942
96.5	4.9716	5.1967	5.0086	2.7648	3.0298	3.0212
97	5.3585	5.3943	5.2993	2.9283	3.1450	3.1678
97.5	5.7897	5.6214	5.6512	3.0463	3.2774	3.3414
98	5.9831	5.8903	6.0950	3.1674	3.4342	3.5546
98.5	6.3505	6.2240	6.6909	3.2729	3.6287	3.8315
99	7.5190	6.6722	7.5825	3.5503	3.8900	4.2273

discrepancy from using the assumption of normality for the
S&P 500 and the Government Bond Index is depicted in Figure 1.

As predicted, the difference is larger for stocks, whose return
distribution exhibits a fatter tail (a lower α estimate), and becomes
much larger for confidence intervals above the 96% level. In the
example, the assumption of normality means that the VaR is underestimated above the 96% level, and greatly underestimated at the
99% level. We therefore conclude that the assumption of normality
appears inappropriate for estimating VaR at high quantiles for a
distribution with an α estimate of around 4.

In Table 2, we indeed see that taking a US$100 million position in
the S&P 500 Composite Return Index generates a relative VaR estimate at the 95% probability level of US$4.72 million, using the
parametric assumption of normality, compared with the US$4.33
million using the empirical distribution. The average bi-weekly
return is US$0.67 million, and the VaR is stated relative to this

Figure 1 Value-at-risk estimates. The graph depicts how much the parametric-normal VaR estimates differ from the empirical VaR estimates for the two assets over a range of confidence levels. The parametric-normal approach assumes normally distributed returns and the empirical approach uses the observed frequency distribution. The difference is the error generated by using the assumption of normally distributed returns and is estimated for a US$100 million position in the particular asset

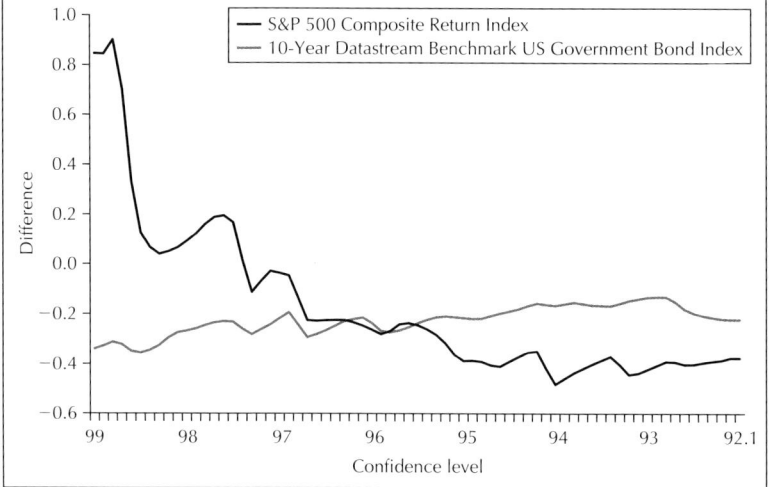

mean. This means that, assuming normally distributed returns, 95% of the time we would not expect to achieve a bi-weekly loss of more than US$4.72 million. However, at the 99% confidence interval, the VaR becomes US$6.67 and US$7.52 million respectively. The large discrepancy of over US$0.75 million between the two approaches shows just how important it is to find as accurate a measure as possible for the VaR. Indeed, since the 99% level is the level required by the Basel Committee, it becomes apparent just how inappropriate the assumption of normality in the tails is.

The VaR-x estimates, which incorporate the fat tails, are also given in Table 2. The α estimates from Table 1 are used to parametrise the Student t-distribution. For the S&P 500 Composite Return Index, the VaR-x estimates provides a much more accurate estimate when compared with the empirical distribution for the whole range of quantiles than the parametric-normal VaR. This is illustrated in Figure 2, where all three estimates for a range of confidence levels are plotted.

Figure 2 VaR-x for the S&P 500 Composite Return Index. The graph depicts how the VaR-x estimates, using the Student-t distribution, compare to the parametric-normal VaR estimates and the empirical VaR estimates for the S&P 500 over a range of confidence levels. The VaR-x uses the modified Hill estimator for the tail index as the parameter in the Student-t distribution, the parametric-normal approach assumes normally distributed returns and the empirical approach uses the observed frequency distribution. The difference is given in million dollars for a position of US$100 million in the particular asset

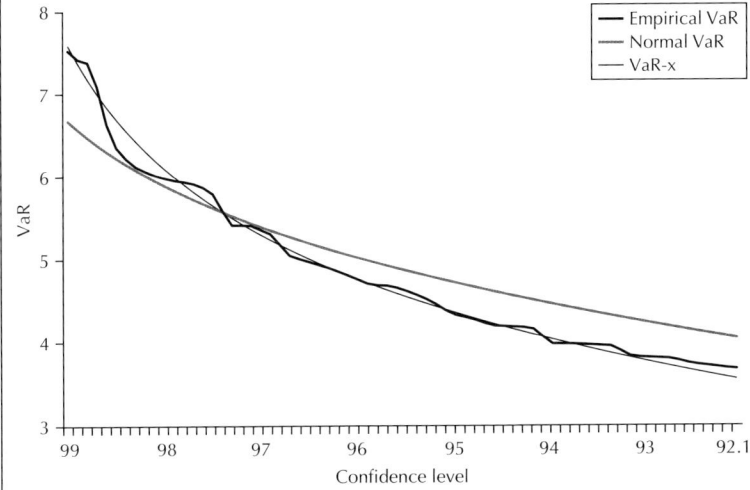

For the US Government Bond Index, the difference between the two parametric approaches is much less (see Figure 3), indicating that an α estimate of around 7 already gives similar results to those under normality.

This approach therefore provides us with an estimator that more accurately reflects the VaR estimates for the whole range of confidence levels, and is thus a more accurate estimate for assessing the downside risk as measured by VaR. We have seen that the estimator performs well for a range of quantiles up to and including the 99% level, and therefore allows for simple parametric conversion to be adhered to. Indeed, time aggregation for various holding periods is merely a simple extension to the framework, so that the estimates provided can easily be converted for different quantiles and time horizons, as required by the regulatory bodies.

Figure 3 VaR-x for the 10-Year US Government Bond Index. The graph depicts how the VaR-x estimates, using the Student-t distribution, compare to the parametric-normal VaR estimates and the empirical VaR estimates for the US Government Bond Index over a range of confidence levels. The VaR-x uses the modified Hill estimator for the tail index as the parameter in the Student-t distribution, the parametric-normal approach assumes normally distributed returns and the empirical approach uses the observed frequency distribution. The difference is given in million dollars for a position of US$100 million in the particular asset

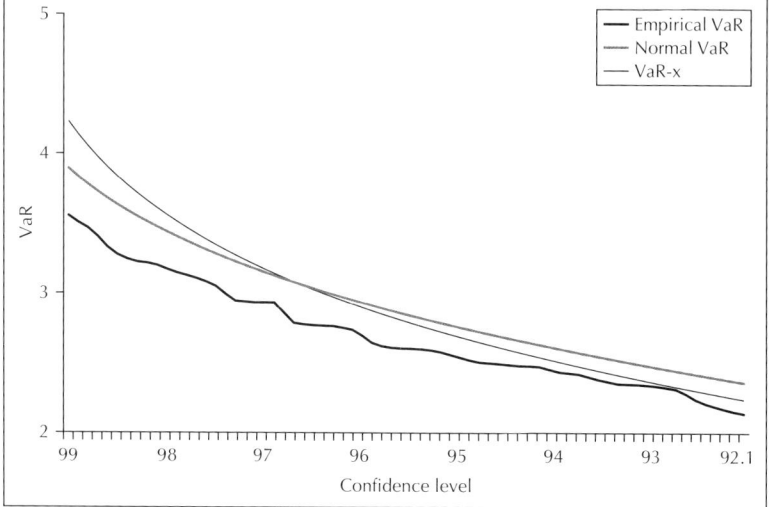

To see how forecasts of the two approaches perform over time, we carry out the following out-of-sample test. We have estimated the rolling 10-day absolute VaR forecasts at the 99% level for the S&P 500 Composite Return Index, using both the parametric-normal and VaR-x methods. These forecasts, using daily returns, are plotted in Figure 4 against the actual rolling bi-weekly returns, of which some appear to look like multiple returns.

From Table 3, we can see that the parametric-normal approach provides VaR forecasts within a 99% confidence interval which are exceeded 1.99% of the time. Since a 99% confidence level requires the actual returns to exceed it only 1% of the time, the VaR-x forecasts have performed much better, with the forecast exceeded only 0.94% of the time. The consistently greater VaR-x forecasts provide evidence of the stability of α, and hence the VaR-x estimates. The

Figure 4 Rolling VaR-x and parametric-normal VaR estimates. The graph shows how the forecasts of the VaR-x estimates, using the Student-*t* distribution, compare to forecasts from using the parametric-normal VaR approach for the S&P 500 Composite Return Index. We have used rolling observations of daily data, over the period January 1994 until August 1998 using 1,216 rolling bi-weekly total returns, to provide forecasts of the value-at-risk at the 99% confidence level. The forecasts are based on yearly samples of daily data, and the α estimate is calculated for the left tail using a modified version of the Hill estimator

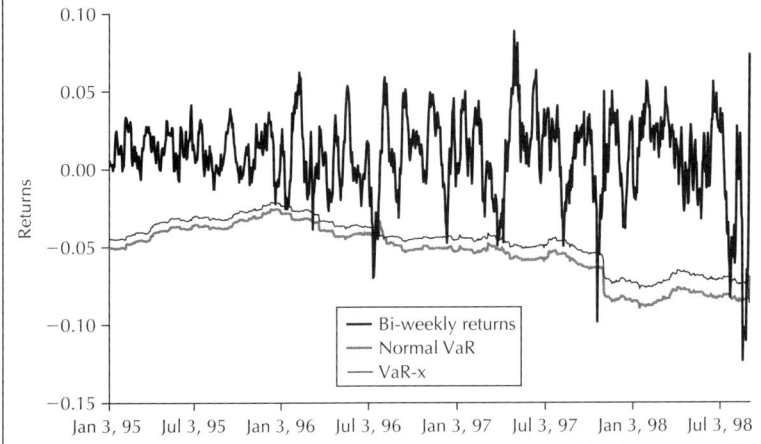

VaR-x method using data on the government bonds showed a slight improvement, yielding 1.15% compared with 1.47% for the parametric-normal approach.

These results clearly show that the VaR-x method provides a more accurate estimate for the VaR than the parametric-normal approach, illustrating the importance of including the tail fatness into the VaR estimate. Indeed, we see that by including a parameter for the distribution's fat-tailedness the estimate assesses the downside risk much more adequately than the assumption of normally distributed returns in the tails. The structure of the VaR-x parametric approach compared to that of the normal provides us with the phenomena of a larger VaR as we move further into the tails. Indeed, as the normal distribution is nested in the Student *t*-distribution, as the α estimates become larger (less fat tailed), the VaR estimates will converge. This therefore provides us with a consistent parametric approach to modelling the additional downside risk

Table 3 Exceedance statistics for rolling bi-weekly returns. This table contains the statistics on the S&P 500 Composite Return Index and the 10-Year Datastream US Benchmark Government Bond Index for the period January 1994 until August 1998 using 1,216 rolling bi-weekly total returns. The forecasts are based on yearly samples of daily data (252 observations), and the α estimate is calculated for the left tail using a modified version of the Hill estimator

	Exceedance of VaR at 99% confidence level		
	Theoretical	Normal VaR	VaR-x
Number of Exceedances			
S&P 500 Composite Return Index:	9.64	19	9
US 10-Year Government Bond Return Index:	9.64	14	11
Percentage of Exceedances			
S&P 500 Composite Return Index: (%)	1.00	1.990	0.942
US 10 Year Government Bond Return Index: (%)	1.00	1.466	1.152

associated with fat-tailed assets, which can easily be extended to allow for further conditionality in the data (see Koedijk and Pownall (1998)).

5 CONCLUSIONS

It is widely known that the distributions of financial asset returns exhibit fatter tails than the normal distribution. This implies that the downside risk of a portfolio containing fat-tailed assets, as measured by VaR, is under-estimated when VaR is estimated with the assumption of normally distributed returns. Furthermore, this suggests that parametric conversion for different confidence levels as adhered to by the regulatory framework of the Basel Committee will provide inaccurate estimates of the VaR. It is no wonder that it has been necessary to "*ad hoc*-ly" multiply the VaR by 3 to provide a larger, more representative, number for the Basel capital requirements. It would be preferable to have a more accurate measure reflecting the true risk from extreme returns, and the avoidance, or reduction at least, of the Basel multiplication factor. In this chapter we present such a measure: VaR-x.

This methodology provides us with a simple approach to finding an accurate estimator for the VaR. The tail fatness apparent in financial returns is incorporated more accurately into the VaR-x estimator by using the Student *t*-distribution as a proxy for the distribution of future returns. We show that for both US stocks and bonds the VaR-x estimates reflect the true downside risk apparent in financial returns much better than those from the standard VaR estimators. The approach is easily extended to include further time-varying parameters, and hence the implications for risk management seem tremendous. Certainly the move towards building portfolios which exploit these departures from normality (see Bekaert *et al* (1998)) will only serve to underline the vital importance of including an additional measure for the downside risk into the risk management techniques of the future.

1   See among others Fama and Roll (1968), Rogalski and Vinso (1978), Boothe and Glassman (1987), Taylor (1986), Jansen and de Vries (1991), Loretan and Phillips (1994), and Huisman *et al* (1997, 1998).

2   See Koedijk and Pownall (1998) for an implementation of a conditional VaR-x approach and comparison of results with RiskMetrics using data on Asian emerging markets.

3   See Jorion (1996) and Kupiec (1995) for a greater insight into the recognition of the estimation error in VaR estimates.

4   Alternative distributions to capture the tail fatness are, for example, the Pareto and sumstable distributions or a mixture of two normal distributions.

5   Huisman *et al* (1998) use this method to fit the unconditional distribution of exchange rate returns.

6   Danielson and de Vries (1997) typically require about 100,000 observations, obtained from high-frequency data.

This chapter was previously published in *The Journal of Risk* **1**(1), Fall 1998.

REFERENCES

Bain, L. J. and M. Engelhardt, 1987, *Introduction to Probability Theory and Mathematical Statistics*, (Boston: Duxbury Press).

Bekaert, G., C. Erb, C. Harvey, and T. Viskanta, 1998, "Distributional Characteristics of Emerging Market Returns and Asset Allocation", *Journal of Portfolio Management*, forthcoming.

Bollerslev, T., 1987, "A Conditionally Heteroskedastic Time Series Model for Speculative Prices and Rates of Return", *Review of Economics and Statistics* **69**, pp. 542–7.

Boothe, P. and D. Glassman, 1987, "The Statistical Distribution of Exchange Rates: Empirical Evidence and Economic Implication", *Journal of International Economics* **22**, pp. 297–320.

Danielsson, J. and C. de Vries, 1997, "Value-at-Risk and Extreme Returns", Working Paper, London School of Economics.

Fama, E. F. and R. Roll, 1968, "Some Properties of Symmetric Stable Distributions", *Journal of the American Statistical Association* **63**, pp. 817–46.

Hendriks, D., 1996, "Evaluation of Value-at-Risk Models Using Historical data", *Federal Reserve Bank of New York Economic Policy Review*, April.

Hill, B., 1975, "A Simple Approach to Inference About the Tail of a Distribution", *Annals of Mathematical Statistics* **3**, pp. 1163–74.

Huisman, R., K. G. Koedijk, C. Kool, and F. Palm, 1997, "Fat Tails in Small Samples", Working Paper, Limburg Institute of Financial Economics, Maastricht University.

Huisman, R., K. G. Koedijk, C. Kool, and F. Palm, 1998, "The Fat-tailedness of FX Returns", Working Paper, Limburg Institute of Financial Economics, Maastricht University.

Jansen, D. and C. de Vries, 1991, "On the Frequency of Large Stock Returns: Putting Booms and Busts into Perspective", *The Review of Economics and Statistics* **73**, pp. 18–24.

Jorion, P., 1996, "Risk: Measuring the Risk in Value at Risk", *Financial Analysts Journal*, November/December.

Jorion, P., 1997, *Value at Risk: The New Benchmark for Controlling Derivatives Risk*, (New York: McGraw-Hill).

Koedijk, K. G. and R. A. Pownall, 1998, "VAR-x: Risk Management in Emerging Markets", Working Paper, Limburg Institute of Financial Economics, Maastricht University.

Kupiec, P. H., 1995, "Techniques for Verifying the Accuracy of Risk Measurement Models", *Journal of Derivatives* **2**, pp. 73–84.

Loretan, M. and P. C. B. Phillips, 1994, "Testing the Covariance Stationarity of Heavy-tailed Time Series: An Overview of the Theory with Applications to Several Financial Data Series", *Journal of Empirical Finance* **1**, pp. 211–48.

Rogalski, R. J. and J. D. Vinso, 1978, "Empirical Properties of Foreign Exchange Rates", *Journal of International Business Studies* **9**, pp. 69–79.

Taylor, S., 1986, *Modeling Financial Time Series*, (New York: JohnWiley and Sons).

18

Value-at-Risk and Market Crashes

Chris Brooks, Gita Persand*

University of Reading

1 INTRODUCTION

The calculation of a securities firm's or bank's value-at-risk (VaR) has become one of the key indicators employed for the assessment of the risk inherent in the firm's trading book. Broadly speaking, value-at-risk is an estimation of the probability of likely losses which could arise from changes in market prices. More precisely, it is defined as the money-loss in a portfolio that is expected to occur over a predetermined horizon and with a predetermined degree of confidence. The roots of VaR's popularity stem from the simplicity of its calculation, its simplicity of interpretation, and from the fact that VaR can be suitably aggregated across an entire firm to produce a single number which broadly encompasses the risk of the positions of the firm as a whole; see Jorion (1996b) or Dowd (1998) for a thorough introduction to value-at-risk.

Broad agreement now exists among both securities firms and regulatory bodies of the usefulness of VaR as a risk measurement tool, but there is far less agreement on the issue of how it should be calculated. For example, value-at-risk can be calculated using the "standard/internal" approach of the Basel Accord, the "building block" approach of the original EC Capital Adequacy Directive (CAD), the "comprehensive approach" of the US SEC, the "pre-commitment

*The authors are grateful to an anonymous referee, to Philippe Jorion, the Editor of this journal and to Simon Burke, for very useful comments on a previous version of this chapter. The usual disclaimer applies.

approach" of the Federal Reserve Board, or by using the "portfolio approach" of the UK's Securities and Futures Authority; see Dimson and Marsh (1995, 1997) for an extensive description of and comparison between these methods. Until recently, securities firms in Europe were not permitted to employ internal risk management models (IRMMs), being bound by CAD-I, which required them to use the building block approach. However, under a revised version of CAD, imaginatively entitled CAD-II, the use of IRMMs for the calculation of capital risk requirements is now permitted in Europe.[1]

Even within the sphere of internal risk management modelling, there are still a wide variety of issues in estimation, which could result in substantial differences in calculated VaRs, that have yet to be resolved. For example, no agreement exists on the appropriate sample size or econometric methodology that should be employed, while various models exist (including, but not limited to, simple averages, exponentially weighted moving averages, GARCH and simulation-based methods). Moreover, there are surprisingly few academic studies that address this important topic. One of the few exceptions is the study by Jackson, Maude and Perraudin (1998), which assesses the empirical performance of various models for VaR using historical returns from the actual portfolio of a large investment bank. They find that nonparametric, simulation-based techniques yield more accurate measures of the tail probabilities than parametric models based on a normal distribution. Alexander and Leigh (1997) offer an analysis of the relative performance of equally weighted, exponentially weighted moving average (EWMA), and GARCH model forecasts of volatility, evaluated using traditional statistical and operational adequacy criteria. The GARCH model is found to be preferable to EWMA in terms of minimising the number of exceedences in a back test, although the simple unweighted average is superior to both.[2] However, Brooks et al (2000) show a potentially serious flaw in the use of standard GARCH models for VaR estimation.

Another aspect of VaR technology that has been the subject of more academic research is that of fat tails in asset return series, that is, the tendency of such series to exhibit higher numbers of extreme movements than would be the case if the data were truly normally distributed. Fat-tailed return distributions will lead the delta-normal model to understate the true VaR (see Jorion (1996a); Huisman, Koedijk and Pownall (1998)). For example, a 5% daily loss is observed to occur approximately once every two years, while if returns were normally distributed, such a change would be expected only once every 1,000 years (Johansen and Sornette (1999)). A number of methods to incorporate the fat tails have been proposed, most importantly the use of extreme value distributions for returns (eg, Embrechts, Resnick and Samorodnitsky (1999)). Eberlein, Keller and Prause (1998) propose a new class of models, known as hyperbolic models, which they argue provide a good fit to the observed fat-tailed unconditional distribution of stock returns data. Hull and White (1998) also tackle the fat-tails problem by offering a model for VaR which allows the researcher to define a class of probability distributions that can be transformed into a multivariate normal.

However, the focus of this chapter is another issue that could have a profound impact on some methods for calculating VaR and which seems as yet to have received little attention in this growing literature. A broad consensus has emerged from various strands of the finance literature that not only are volatilities and correlations time varying, but also that the relationship between them varies in a partially systematic fashion. Specifically, it has been documented that when markets are individually volatile (so that return variances are high), the correlation between the returns of the various different markets increases. For example, Karolyi and Stulz (1996) use 1988–1992 data from American Depository Receipts (ADRs) of Japanese stocks traded on the New York Stock Exchange and a matched sample of US stocks, and find that comovements are high when contemporaneous absolute returns of the national market indices are high. Ang and Bekaert (1999) go further to suggest that equity market correlations increase more in volatile bull than volatile bear markets.

A positive correlation between volatility and correlation potentially presents a large problem for VaR methodologies which rely on them and for investors. If the two are positively related, the benefits of diversification which are implied by a given correlation matrix will be overstated. More fundamentally, the benefits of diversification will run away from portfolios just when investors need them the most. This problem is likely to have the strongest impact on risk measurement systems that are broadly based upon the estimation of volatilities and correlations, such as the JP Morgan (1996) *RiskMetrics* approach. Of course, an increase in correlations will only present a problem for portfolios that are long the component assets.[3]

Chow *et al* (1999) adopt a similar procedure to the one we advocate below by splitting the data into subsamples for "stressful" and "normal" periods, in the context of the determination of mean–variance efficient portfolios. They define outliers to be those observations that fall outside the center of the distribution (those in the outer 25% tails) for a portfolio comprising eight asset classes. Chow *et al* (1999) observe the optimal portfolios to be quite different during stressful and normal conditions. Moreover, they observe that the normal portfolio performs rather poorly during times of extreme market movements and that, equally, the stressful portfolio performs poorly under normal market conditions. Their solution is to estimate separate covariance matrices for the assets under normal and stressful market conditions and to blend them, weighting the normal and stressful covariances according to the investor's degree of risk aversion.

This chapter seeks to extend recent studies on these issues in a number of ways. First, we document further evidence in favor of the conjecture that correlation and volatility are positively related in both bull and bear markets. Second, we investigate the effect of this phenomenon on VaR models which are based upon the volatilities and correlations approach, and compare those effects with an approach based upon full portfolio revaluation at each time step. Finally, we propose methods for allowing volatilities and correlations to be time varying and codependent, one of which is based upon multivariate GARCH models, while the other represents a simple modification to the volatilities and correlations approach. Using out-of-sample tests of model adequacy, our proposed methodologies yield smaller numbers of exceedences of estimated values-at-risk than the traditional volatility/correlation approach. The study is conducted in the context of returns to Southeast Asian stock market indices, an issue of substantial research interest given recent turmoil in these markets, although the results are likely to be applicable to any portfolio of financial assets.

The remainder of the chapter is organised as follows. Section 2 presents a description of the data employed, while the methodologies used for the calculation of values-at-risk are given in Section 3. Section 4 discusses our results, while Section 5 concludes.

2 THE DATA

The analysis undertaken in this chapter is based on daily closing prices of five Southeast Asian stock market indices: the Hang Seng Price Index, Nikkei 225 Stock Average Price Index, Singapore Straits Times Price Index, South Korea SE Composite Price Index and Bangkok Book Club Price Index. The data, obtained from *Primark* Datastream, runs from January 1, 1985 to April 29, 1999, giving a total of 3,737 observations.[4] All subsequent analysis is performed on daily log returns, with the summary statistics being given in Table 1. All five returns series exhibit the standard property of asset return data in that they have "fat-tailed" distributions as indicated by the significant kurtosis coefficients; this characteristic is also shown by the highly significant Jarque–Bera normality test statistics. Bank holidays are not excluded from the analysis, since the markets considered are closed on different days from one another, and hence the removal of bank holiday days from the sample would lead to nonsynchronous observations, which would present a large problem for correlation estimation. Instead, the previous day's trading price is carried forward for a bank holiday, so that the return on the bank holiday day for that market which is closed will be zero. It should be noted that this practice is likely to lead to a modest downward bias in risk estimates.

We also form, and perform subsequent analysis on, an equally weighted portfolio consisting of the five indices listed above. The advantage of diversification is clearly recognised in this case: the variance of the portfolio is less than one-third of the variance of even the most volatile of the individual component series.[5]

The final six rows of Table 1 present the number of observations (and percentage of the total number of observations in parentheses) outside $\pm 1.645\sigma$ and between $\pm 1.645\sigma$ for each series. Although such a criterion would not normally be employed to define a stock market "crash", this represents the definition used in this chapter. Thus both large positive and large negative market movements are considered as "crashes", since they represent large losses for short and long positions, respectively. We conjecture that the results presented in this chapter would be even stronger if we had considered events that were in the first percentile of the return distribution, but we prefer to concentrate analysis on the fifth percentile since it can be estimated considerably more accurately and there are a sufficient

Table 1 Summary statistics

	Hong Kong	Japan	Singapore	Korea	Thailand	Portfolio
Mean	0.00079*	0.00019	0.00039	0.00058	0.00046	0.00048*
Variance	0.00030	0.00018	0.00020	0.00027	0.00030	9.16×10^{-5}
Skewness	−2.263*	0.109*	−1.175*	0.427*	0.175*	−0.609*
Kurtosis	51.674*	10.043*	44.338*	5.478*	9.815*	14.463*
JB test statistic	418,844*	15,706*	306,884*	4,784*	15,014*	32,791*
Number (%)	51	94	53	101	90	131
Extreme "positives" (%)	1.46	2.70	1.52	2.90	2.58	3.76
Number (%)	66	100	58	87	86	143
Extreme "negatives" (%)	1.89	2.87	1.66	2.50	2.47	4.10
Number (%)	3369	3292	3375	3298	3310	3212
Between extremes (%)	96.65	94.43	96.82	94.60	94.95	92.14

Notes: Summary statistics are presented for a sample of daily returns from January 1, 1985 to April 29, 1999, giving a total of 3,737 observations, with extreme observations defined as those lying outside $\pm 1.645\sigma$, where σ is the standard deviation of the whole sample of data; *denotes a statistic which is significant at the 5% level.

number of observations in the tail, according to this definition, to compute all the statistics that we wish. In fact, when an extreme observation is defined as one lying outside $\pm 1.645\sigma$, this constitutes between 1.5% and 4.1% of the total number of observations, depending on the series.

3 CORRELATIONS AND MARKET CRASHES

The simple correlations between the five series using all observations are presented in Panel A of Table 2. The strongest relations seem to be between the Japanese, Singapore and Hong Kong markets, whereas correlations between the Korean market index returns and other markets in Southeast Asia are all less than 10%. Assessing statistical significance is difficult in this instance because of the non-normality of the series, although overlooking this and as a general indicative measure, a simple Fisher test can be calculated. The test suggests that correlations of more than 0.18 are significant at the 5% level, while those of more than 0.21 are significant at the 1% level, for samples of this size. Overall, then, the markets of Southeast Asia seem, as one would expect, to be quite strongly correlated.

In order to gain an insight into the effect of volatility upon the correlations, we split the samples into "positive crashes" (returns in excess of $\pm 1.645\sigma$), "negative crashes" (returns smaller than -1.645σ), and "no crashes" (returns between -1.645σ and $+1.645\sigma$), and the correlations are recomputed. Of course, it is not necessarily the case that in every instance all markets will experience large market movements on the same days, and we can therefore define the extreme movements as being generated by any of the five markets. Thus Panels B to F of Table 2 show the correlations when we normalise, or use that market to define the extreme event days for Japan, Hong Kong, Singapore, Korea and Thailand, respectively. Subpanels (i), (ii) and (iii) present the correlations for the positive crashes, the negative crashes and the sample with extreme movements removed, respectively. The results demonstrate a number of relevant features which suggest that correlation and volatility are correlated. First, whichever country we use to determine where the extreme movements occur, the correlation between the five asset returns series increases substantially. For example, for the Japan normalisation (Panel B), the correlation between Singapore and Hong Kong increases from less than 45% to over 66% for the large

Table 2 Correlation between countries

	Japan	Singapore	Korea	Thailand
Panel A: All observations				
Hong Kong	0.242	0.448	0.054	0.217
Japan	–	0.329	0.048	0.132
Singapore	–	–	0.093	0.296
Korea	–	–	–	0.107
Panel B(i): Japan "positive" crashes				
Hong Kong	0.390	0.661	0.071	0.356
Japan	–	0.499	0.061	0.197
Singapore	–	–	0.142	0.428
Korea	–	–	–	0.128
Panel B(ii): Japan "negative" crashes				
Hong Kong	0.444	0.763	0.249	0.464
Japan	–	0.659	0.268	0.438
Singapore	–	–	0.304	0.577
Korea	–	–	–	0.256
Panel B(iii): Japan "no" crashes				
Hong Kong	0.183	0.359	0.026	0.197
Japan	–	0.191	0.025	0.067
Singapore	–	–	0.062	0.248
Korea	–	–	–	0.094
Panel C(i): Hong Kong "positive" crashes				
Hong Kong	0.472	0.747	0.058	0.237
Japan	–	0.392	0.083	0.253
Singapore	–	–	0.206	0.513
Korea	–	–	–	0.101
Panel C(ii): Hong Kong "negative" crashes				
Hong Kong	0.559	0.789	0.167	0.539
Japan	–	0.593	0.410	0.465
Singapore	–	–	0.297	0.569
Korea	–	–	–	0.329
Panel C(iii): Hong Kong "no" crashes				
Hong Kong	0.186	0.309	0.031	0.163
Japan	–	0.303	0.032	0.100
Singapore	–	–	0.071	0.240
Korea	–	–	–	0.088
Panel D(i): Singapore "positive" crashes				
Hong Kong	0.409	0.750	0.286	0.324
Japan	–	0.504	0.248	0.484
Singapore	–	–	0.365	0.468
Korea	–	–	–	0.222
Panel D(ii): Singapore "negative" crashes				
Hong Kong	0.422	0.796	0.351	0.476
Japan	–	0.773	0.382	0.634
Singapore	–	–	0.420	0.589
Korea	–	–	–	0.264

Table 2 Continued.

	Japan	Singapore	Korea	Thailand
Panel D(iii): Singapore "no" crashes				
Hong Kong	0.191	0.362	0.021	0.154
Japan	–	0.200	0.006	0.040
Singapore	–	–	0.040	0.208
Korea	–	–	–	0.085
Panel E(i): Korea "positive" crashes				
Hong Kong	0.247	0.718	0.076	0.289
Japan	–	0.398	0.064	0.348
Singapore	–	–	0.113	0.469
Korea	–	–	–	0.264
Panel E(ii): Korea "negative" crashes				
Hong Kong	0.604	0.757	0.276	0.357
Japan	–	0.610	0.169	0.395
Singapore	–	–	0.312	0.485
Korea	–	–	–	0.334
Panel E(iii): Korea "no" crashes				
Hong Kong	0.213	0.408	0.029	0.209
Japan	–	0.306	0.030	0.108
Singapore	–	–	0.064	0.278
Korea	–	–	–	0.050
Panel F(i): Thailand "positive" crashes				
Hong Kong	0.351	0.793	0.095	0.451
Japan	–	0.434	0.098	0.341
Singapore	–	–	0.235	0.496
Korea	–	–	–	0.212
Panel F(ii): Thailand "negative" crashes				
Hong Kong	0.359	0.831	0.195	0.534
Japan	–	0.745	0.344	0.439
Singapore	–	–	0.311	0.498
Korea	–	–	–	0.264
Panel F(iii): Thailand "no" crashes				
Hong Kong	0.211	0.430	0.038	0.169
Japan	–	0.237	0.023	0.070
Singapore	–	–	0.060	0.191
Korea	–	–	–	0.083

positive movements and over 76% for the large negative movements. The effect is most noticeable when Thailand is used to determine when the large changes occur; in this case the correlation increases from 22% for all observations to 45% for positive crashes and 53% for negative crashes. The correlation never falls for the crash subsamples compared with the whole series.

Figure 1 The correlation between the returns on the Japanese and Thai equity indices as data from the right-hand tail of the distribution are successively removed

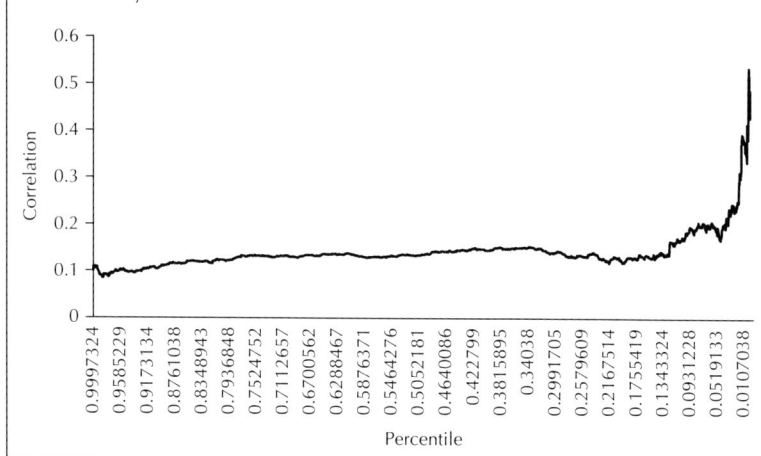

A second interesting and highly intuitive result is that large negative movements lead to greater increases in correlation than large positive movements. For example, when we use Korea to determine the timing of the movements, the correlation between the Hong Kong and Korean market movements is 8% for large positive moves and 28% for large negative moves. This result confirms the predictions of Ang and Bekaert (1999) that correlations are higher during bear than bull runs in equity markets.

A final noteworthy related feature of the results in Table 2 is the degree to which the correlations between the series falls when the extreme observations are removed from the sample. For instance, for all observations, the correlation between movements in the Hong Kong and Singapore markets is 45%, but, when the extreme movements according to the Hong Kong series (Panel C(iii) of Table 2) are removed, this correlation falls to 31%.

To further see how correlations increase as one moves out into the tail of the distribution, consider Figure 1, which plots the correlation between the returns on the Japanese and Thai equity indices as data from the right-hand tail of the distribution are removed one observation at a time, when ordered according to the Japanese equity returns. So, starting from the left of the plot, the correlation is estimated over all of the data. Then, as we move from left to right, the highest remaining return is removed, and the correlation re-estimated over the remaining subsample, until only the last 10 smallest (most negative) returns remain. The correlation estimate remains roughly constant at around 8–15% until approximately the top 88% of the distribution is removed to leave the bottom 12%. Thereafter, the correlation rises to 20% by the fifth percentile, and then increases rapidly, until it reaches over 50% inside the lowest percentile of returns. The upshot is that the correlation has increased by at least fivefold in the lower tail, compared with that in the whole of the distribution.

However, an important recent chapter by Boyer *et al* (1999), argues that the "correlation breakdown", observed in many chapters, could be an entirely spurious statistical artifact resulting from the manner in which researchers split their samples into "stressful periods" and "normal conditions". Specifically, they argue that higher correlations would be expected in the tails of a distribution which has been split via its fractiles than in the center, purely as a result of the fact that the tail deciles are wider and have larger variances, even if the underlying distributions concerned are multivariate normal with constant correlation coefficient. Boyer *et al* (1999, p 15) argue that a valid method of testing for changing correlations should "… begin with a data-coherent model of the data generating process that builds the possibility of structural changes, estimate the model parameters, and only then decide whether the estimated parameters imply changing correlations". This challenge has been taken up by Kim and Finger (2000), who introduce a new test for correlation breakdown which they term the "broken arrow stress test".

Theorem 1 of Boyer *et al* (1999) shows the relationship between the conditional and unconditional correlations for two bivariate normal random variables x and y when conditioning restricts one of the variables. We denote an event restricted to a subset of all observations by A, the unconditional variance by $\text{VaR}(\cdot)$, and the unconditional correlation by ρ. Then the correlation for observations conditional on A, denoted ρ_A, can be written

$$\rho_A = \rho \left(\frac{\rho^2 + (1-\rho)^2 \text{VaR}(x)}{\text{VaR}(x \,|\, x \in A)} \right)^{-1/2} \tag{1}$$

In order to investigate whether the differences in correlations between the central and tail portions of the data shown in Table 2 of this chapter are likely to have resulted from the manner in which the data are split into the tails and the central part, we compute the value of ρ_A from Equation (1) for each pair of series, split so that A represents (separately) the tails and the center of the distribution, and with fixed correlations equal to those given in Panel A of Table 2. The conditional correlation that would be expected for two bivariate normally distributed stationary random variables with these correlations are presented in Table 3. As is evident from the table, in virtually no cases can the manner in which the samples are split be seen as leading to the degree of increase in correlation in the tails that is observed in the actual data. For example, the uncon-ditional correlation between the Japanese and Hong Kong equity returns is 24%, while the observed correlation in the lower tail is 44%, compared with an expected lower tail correlation under a DGP of bivariate normality with fixed correlation of 28%. Thus, the actual correlation observed for the tails (in every single case for the lower tail and in the majority of cases for the upper tail) cannot be explained purely by reference to the way in which the samples were split. Boyer *et al* (1999) also argue that a virtually identical pattern would be observed if the data were distributed as a bivari-ate GARCH with constant contemporaneous correlation, a more realistic data-generating process for stock returns. We would thus conclude from this, as Boyer *et al* (1999) concede in their abstract, that correlation breakdown during stressful periods does still exist, although testing for it can be troublesome.

4 CALCULATING THE VALUE-AT-RISK

The VaR for each individual index was estimated using the simple 5% "delta-normal" approach proposed in the literature,[6] that is,

$$
\begin{aligned}
\text{VaR} = {}&\text{marked position of asset} \\
&\times \text{sensitivity to price move} \\
&\times \text{adverse price move per day}
\end{aligned}
\tag{2}
$$

The sensitivity to price movements is taken to be 1 since we study equities which are linear instruments; the adverse price move per day is equal to 1.645σ, where σ is the estimated standard deviation

Table 3 Correlation between countries expected from bivariate normally distributed data with constant unconditional correlations equal to those given in Panel A of Table 2 to show the effect of sorting

	Japan	Singapore	Korea	Thailand
Panel A(i): Japan "positive" crashes				
Hong Kong	0.279	0.504	0.063	0.251
Japan	–	0.376	0.056	0.153
Singapore	–	–	0.165	0.339
Korea	–	–	–	0.124
Panel A(ii): Japan "negative" crashes				
Hong Kong	0.277	0.502	0.062	0.249
Japan	–	0.374	0.056	0.152
Singapore	–	–	0.164	0.338
Korea	–	–	–	0.124
Panel A(iii): Japan "no" crashes				
Hong Kong	0.177	0.339	0.039	0.158
Japan	–	0.243	0.035	0.095
Singapore	–	–	0.103	0.218
Korea	–	–	–	0.077
Panel B(i): Hong Kong "positive" crashes				
Hong Kong	0.330	0.575	0.076	0.298
Japan	–	0.439	0.067	0.184
Singapore	–	–	0.197	0.399
Korea	–	–	–	0.149
Panel B(ii): Hong Kong "negative" crashes				
Hong Kong	0.332	0.577	0.076	0.299
Japan	–	0.441	0.068	0.184
Singapore	–	–	0.198	0.400
Korea	–	–	–	0.150
Panel B(iii): Hong Kong "no" crashes				
Hong Kong	0.160	0.309	0.035	0.143
Japan	–	0.220	0.031	0.086
Singapore	–	–	0.093	0.197
Korea	–	–	–	0.070
Panel C(i): Singapore "positive" crashes				
Hong Kong	0.414	0.674	0.098	0.375
Japan	–	0.536	0.087	0.236
Singapore	–	–	0.253	0.492
Korea	–	–	–	0.192
Panel C(ii): Singapore "negative" crashes				
Hong Kong	0.439	0.701	0.105	0.399
Japan	–	0.564	0.094	0.253
Singapore	–	–	0.271	0.519
Korea	–	–	–	0.206

Table 3 Continued.

	Japan	Singapore	Korea	Thailand
Panel C(iii): Singapore "no" crashes				
Hong Kong	0.159	0.308	0.035	0.142
Japan	–	0.219	0.031	0.086
Singapore	–	–	0.092	0.196
Korea	–	–	–	0.069
Panel D(i): Korea "positive" crashes				
Hong Kong	0.223	0.418	0.050	0.200
Japan	–	0.305	0.044	0.121
Singapore	–	–	0.131	0.274
Korea	–	–	–	0.098
Panel D(ii): Korea "negative" crashes				
Hong Kong	0.239	0.443	0.053	0.214
Japan	–	0.325	0.047	0.130
Singapore	–	–	0.140	0.292
Korea	–	–	–	0.106
Panel D(iii): Korea "no" crashes				
Hong Kong	0.178	0.342	0.039	0.159
Japan	–	0.245	0.035	0.096
Singapore	–	–	0.103	0.219
Korea	–	–	–	0.078
Panel E(i): Thailand "positive" crashes				
Hong Kong	0.270	0.491	0.061	0.243
Japan	–	0.365	0.054	0.148
Singapore	–	0.159	0.329	–
Korea	–	–	–	0.120
Panel E(ii): Thailand "negative" crashes				
Hong Kong	0.278	0.503	0.063	0.250
Japan	–	0.375	0.056	0.153
Singapore	–	–	0.164	0.339
Korea	–	–	–	0.124
Panel E(iii): Thailand "no" crashes				
Hong Kong	0.165	0.318	0.036	0.147
Japan	–	0.227	0.032	0.089
Singapore	–	–	0.096	0.203
Korea	–	–	–	0.072

of the asset returns over the sample period. The VaRs were estimated using four sample periods: (i) the whole sample period, (ii) the period corresponding to "positive" crashes, (iii) the period corresponding to "negative" crashes and finally (iv) the period with the extreme observations removed altogether. In each case, the standard deviation is computed around the unconditional mean of the whole series (and not around the mean of the subsample).

As well as calculating the VaR for the individual assets, we calculate the VaR of an equally weighted portfolio comprising the five returns series. The historical simulation on the portfolio approach for the estimation of the portfolio's VaR is identical to that above; in other words, we calculate the returns that would accrue to the portfolio and calculate the VaR of this series. On the other hand, the *RiskMetrics* approach makes use of the Markowitz portfolio theory, whereby, for an N-asset portfolio (N = 5 in this study), the value-at-risk can be calculated by using the following formula:

$$VaR_p = \sqrt{\sum_{i=1}^{N} a_i^2 VaR_i^2 + 2\sum_{i=1}^{N} \sum_{j=1,i\neq j}^{N} a_i a_j \rho_{ij} VaR_i VaR_j} \qquad (3)$$

where VaR_p is the VaR of the portfolio, a_i and a_j are the weights given to each of the assets i and j respectively in the portfolio, VaR_i and VaR_j are the values-at-risk of the individual series i and j, and ρ_{ij} is the estimated correlation between the returns of i and j.

The calculated VaR are presented in Table 4 for the four subsamples described above, with extreme market movements defined by Japan in Panel A, by Hong Kong in Panel B, by Singapore in Panel C, by Korea in Panel D and by Thailand in Panel E. The values-at-risk for the portfolio is given in the last two rows of each panel of the table for the historical simulation on the portfolio and *RiskMetrics* approaches, respectively. When calculated using all the observations, the difference between the two is substantial – in fact the historical simulation on the portfolio VaR is almost double that of the volatilities and correlations approach, a result echoed by the big change subsamples. Interestingly, for the subsamples with the crash observations removed, the two approaches give similar answers; indeed the *RiskMetrics* methodology gives slightly larger VaR estimates. The multivariate GARCH model will yield variances and covariances and, therefore, VaR estimates, which will vary over time (both for the in-sample estimation period, and also for the out-of-sample forward testing period). It is therefore not possible to present comparable estimates from the multivariate GARCH model in Table 4, but we note that the in-sample average

Table 4 VaR as a percentage of the marked position

	All obs.	"Positive" crash	"Negative" crash	"No" crash
Panel A: Japan				
Japan	1.553	2.526	2.611	1.542
Hong Kong	2.859	4.334	7.713	2.465
Singapore	2.281	2.834	5.943	1.993
Korea	2.495	3.305	3.664	2.424
Thailand	2.666	4.620	4.735	2.522
HS on portfolio	1.575	2.172	3.089	0.725
Portfolio – *RiskMetrics*	0.811	1.226	1.741	0.730
Panel B: Hong Kong				
Japan	1.553	4.042	2.946	1.462
Hong Kong	2.859	4.009	8.844	1.857
Singapore	2.281	4.800	4.519	1.995
Korea	2.495	4.445	4.995	2.376
Thailand	2.666	5.756	4.522	2.507
HS on portfolio	1.575	2.642	3.095	0.767
Portfolio – *RiskMetrics*	0.811	1.624	2.130	0.782
Panel C: Singapore				
Japan	1.553	3.683	4.538	1.506
Hong Kong	2.859	5.307	9.728	2.296
Singapore	2.281	4.152	6.822	1.484
Korea	2.495	4.087	4.450	2.400
Thailand	2.666	5.908	5.925	2.449
HS on portfolio	1.575	2.790	3.516	0.811
Portfolio – *RiskMetrics*	0.811	1.704	2.534	0.814
Panel D: Korea				
Japan	1.553	2.639	3.526	1.517
Hong Kong	2.859	3.758	4.719	2.755
Singapore	2.281	3.513	3.497	2.195
Korea	2.495	2.289	2.462	1.808
Thailand	2.666	3.867	3.869	2.568
HS on portfolio	1.575	2.166	2.611	0.776
Portfolio – *RiskMetrics*	0.811	1.189	1.621	0.915
Panel E: Thailand				
Japan	1.553	3.396	4.555	1.509
Hong Kong	2.859	4.233	8.899	2.434
Singapore	2.281	3.993	6.360	1.935
Korea	2.495	3.782	3.972	2.433
Thailand	2.666	3.002	3.101	1.787
HS on portfolio	1.575	2.468	3.682	0.698
Portfolio – *RiskMetrics*	0.811	1.416	2.356	0.848

Table 5 VaR as a percentage of the marked position for artificially generated data with given correlations and multivariate normal distributions

	All-observations correlations	All-crashes correlations	No-crash correlations
Japan	1.661	1.665	1.655
Hong Kong	1.618	1.623	1.616
Singapore	1.634	1.654	1.633
Korea	1.631	1.646	1.623
Thailand	1.650	1.654	1.643
HS on portfolio	0.987	1.230	0.932
Portfolio – *RiskMetrics*	0.987	1.230	0.932

VaR is 1.65% of the value of the marked position. This figure is comparable with that obtained from the whole sample estimated using historical simulation on the portfolio (1.58%).

In order to assess further the likely effects of this phenomenon on VaR calculations, we conduct a simple Monte Carlo study, the results of which are presented in Table 5. We use the correlation estimates based separately on the whole sample, for all crashes only (defined by the Japanese market), and with crash observations removed. Sets of standard normal variates (ie, zero mean and unit variance) are generated with these correlations using the Cholesky factorisation (see Jorion (1996b), pp 241–3; JP Morgan (1996)). In this fashion, we have isolated the effect of increased correlation, while keeping the sample sizes for the three sets of artificially generated data, and the volatilities of the individual series, constant and independent of the correlations.

In the first five rows of Table 5, we observe that the sample values-at-risk are, to two decimal places, virtually identical for the whole sample and for the samples with correlations estimated from the "all-crash observations" and "crash observations removed" data. This is entirely expected since we are currently determining the VaR of each series in isolation, which will thus be unaffected by the size of the correlations.

On the other hand, the last two rows of Table 5 present the VaR of the portfolio, estimated using the 3,486 observations on an equally weighted portfolio comprising the returns with correlations estimated as described in the previous paragraph. The VaR for the portfolio with the larger correlations ("all-crash correlations") is, of course, higher than that when the correlations between nonextreme events are used. But the important finding here is that the historical simulations on the portfolio and *RiskMetrics* approaches give exactly the same answer, in contrast to the analysis presented above using the real data. This supports our conjecture that the positive correlation between volatility and correlation is behind the discrepancy between the *RiskMetrics* and historical simulation on the portfolio methods. Our results also demonstrate empirically that the correlation breakdowns observed in Table 2 could not be entirely spurious and due to the splitting of the data into extreme and normal observations, for if this were the case, we may expect the results of the historical simulation on the portfolio and the *RiskMetrics* approach to give identical, or very similar, VaR estimates on the actual data as well.

The discrepancy between the two methods when applied to the real data could arise from empirical distributions that are time varying or nonadditive. It is also not the case that an exact relationship will necessarily hold when we move into the realms of forecasting. For example, a VaR estimate based upon the forecast of the conditional variance of a portfolio, derived from estimation of a univariate GARCH model on that portfolio, could be quite different from a VaR estimate based upon forecasts of the conditional variances of the component assets and the forecasted covariances between them.

The next section proposes two practical methods which could be employed by risk managers for revising the volatilities and correlations approach in order to allow for the comovement of these two quantities, while still allowing the general approach to be retained.

5 SIMULTANEOUS FORECASTING OF CORRELATION AND VOLATILITY

There has been a substantial academic literature on forecasting volatility (see Akgiray (1989); Day and Lewis (1992); Brooks (1998)), which broadly argues that volatility forecasts derived from the prices of traded options are more accurate than, but do not completely encompass, those obtained using econometric models, such as GARCH, or those forecasts calculated using simple averages. Equally, there is a small but rapidly growing parallel literature on the prediction of correlations (eg, Walter and Lopez (1997); Champa and Chang (1998)) using methods based on simple historical averages, exponentially weighted moving average correlation models (proposed, eg, by JP Morgan (1996)), correlations derived from multivariate GARCH models, and implied correlations inferred from the values of traded options.

However, if correlations and volatilities are correlated, then, as has been demonstrated above, it is important that both are forecast together for use in the calculation of VaR. The first method we propose for estimating VaR is based upon a multivariate GARCH model. This study employs the BEKK version of the multivariate GARCH model due to Engle and Kroner (1995). This formulation is a highly parsimonious quadratic form, and its development was motivated by the difficulty in checking or imposing the restriction that the variance–covariance matrix H_t of residuals be positive-definite for general versions of the model, such as the vec specification or the diagonal model of Bollerslev, Engle and Wooldridge (1988). The matrix H_t comprises the conditional variances on the leading diagonal and the conditional covariances elsewhere. The BEKK parametrisation may be expressed as

$$H_t = C_0^T C_0 + A_1^T \varepsilon_{t-1} \varepsilon_{t-1}^T A_1 + B_1^T H_{t-1} B_1 \qquad (4)$$

where C_0, A_1, and B_1 are parameter matrices to be estimated, and ε_{t-1} is a vector of lagged errors. The BEKK parametrisation requires estimation of only 35 free parameters in the conditional variance–covariance structure (compared with 255 in the unrestricted vec model),[7] and guarantees H_t to be positive-definite. The model is estimated for the five series under investigation, and the fitted values for the conditional variances and covariances are noted. The VaR can then be estimated using a generalisation of Equation (3) above, where the conditional correlations are calculated by dividing the conditional covariances with the products of the conditional standard deviations.

It is well known that practitioners have not embraced the employment of GARCH modelling to the extent of their academic counterparts. Much of their disapproval stems from estimation difficulties and, in particular, the huge computational burden of estimating multivariate GARCH models for portfolios with large numbers of assets. The number of parameters increases at such a fast rate with the number of assets that the use of MGARCH quickly becomes infeasible.

A much simpler method of allowing for the correlation between volatility and correlation which can be calculated using a spreadsheet is as follows. First, sort one of the series of returns in ascending order, starting with the most negative returns at the top and ending with the largest positive movements at the bottom. Also arrange all of the other series of returns on the assets in the portfolio in parallel according to that series so that the time index across the series is preserved. Next, split the reordered samples of returns to each individual asset into the extremes (eg, the 10th and 90th percentile, as above[8]) and the central part (eg, the middle 80%) of the distribution. Split each of the extremes into smaller samples, eg, the 1st, 2nd, 3rd, ..., 10th percentile, and the 90th, 91st, ..., 99th percentile of the return distributions.[9] Figure 1 shows that, roughly speaking, it is the outer 10% of the return distribution in each tail where the correlation is markedly different from that of the remainder of the observations.[10] Next, calculate the correlations, the volatilities, and hence the VaR, separately for each of the subsamples. The purpose of this step is to try to capture the relationship between volatility and correlation by estimating these quantities separately for the extremes and the remainder of the data. The VaR for the extreme event subsamples is almost certain to be larger, reflecting the reduction in diversification benefits on those days. Finally, take a weighted average of the VaR estimates, where the weights correspond to the number of observations in that subsample:

$$\text{VaR}_p = \frac{1}{T}\left(\sum_{i=1}^{K^-} T_i \text{VaR}_{p,i} + T_{\text{center}}\text{VaR}_{\text{center}} + \sum_{j=1}^{K^+} T_j \text{VaR}_{p,j}\right) \quad (5)$$

where K^- and K^+ represent the number of subsamples in the left- and right-hand tails, T_i and T_j represent the number of observations in each of these subsamples, and $\text{VaR}_{p,i}$ and $\text{VaR}_{p,j}$ represent the VaR estimates for the portfolio using only the data points corresponding

Table 6 Modified *RiskMetrics* VaR for the equally weighted portfolio as a percentage of the marked position

Data sorted according to:	$K = 14$, $T_{tail} = 25$	$K = 10$, $T_{tail} = 35$	$K = 7$, $T_{tail} = 50$	$K = 2$, $T_{tail} = 175$	$K = 1$, $T_{tail} = 350$
Japan	1.449	1.435	1.434	1.434	1.433
Hong Kong	1.468	1.467	1.465	1.464	1.465
Singapore	1.454	1.446	1.446	1.445	1.443
Korea	1.496	1.487	1.485	1.485	1.485
Thailand	1.472	1.470	1.470	1.470	1.470

Note: K refers to the number of subsamples used in each tail, while T_{tail} refers to the number of observations in each subsample.

to the extremes in that subsample. Each component $VaR_{p,k}$ ($k = i, j$) still employs the 5% one-sided normal critical value.

The results of using such an approach are given in Table 6. We use 14 subsamples of 25 observations for each of the tails plus the remaining sample comprising the central 80% of the ordered observations. We also employ ten subsamples of 35 observations for the tails, seven subsamples of 50 observations, two subsamples of 175 observations, and one subsample of 350 observations, for each tail. Using the notation of Equation (5), we set $K^+ = K^- = K$ and $T_i = T_j = T_{tail}$, with $K = 14$, $T_{tail} = 25$; $K = 10$, $T_{tail} = 35$; $K = 7$, $T_{tail} = 50$; $K = 2$, $T_{tail} = 175$; $K = 1$, $T_{tail} = 350$. It can immediately be seen that, whichever country is used to define the large market movements, a very similar VaR estimate as a percentage of the initial value of the portfolio is obtained – approximately 1.46%. These values are close to the historical simulation on the portfolio figure of 1.57% and far higher than that of the standard *RiskMetrics* approach (0.81%). We can also see that the number of subsamples used in each tail has a minimal impact upon the results; the VaR decreases only very slightly if the number of subsamples in each tail is reduced. The important point, therefore, is to separate the tail portion from the center of the distribution in the VaR calculation.

In order to determine whether the estimated VaR would have been sufficient to cover realised losses for our sample data, we perform back tests (in-sample tests) and forward tests (out-of-sample tests) on the last 250 observations of the in-sample estimation period and a 250 day hold-out sample, respectively. The nominal

Table 7 Backtesting and forward testing of VaR estimated for the equally weighted portfolio

	Long position (%)	Short position (%)
Panel A: Backtesting		
HS on portfolio	5.6	4.4
RiskMetrics	8.8	6.0
Multivariate GARCH(1,1)	4.8	4.4
Modified *RiskMetrics*	5.6	4.4
Panel B: Forward testing		
HS on portfolio	6.4	6.0
RiskMetrics	9.2	6.8
Multivariate GARCH(1,1)	6.0	5.2
Modified *RiskMetrics*	6.4	6.0

Note: Cell entries show the percentage of exceptions in a 250 day in-sample and a 250 day hold-out sample, respectively. The modified *RiskMetrics* model refers 14 subsamples of 25 observations for each tail and a single calculation for the 80% center of the distribution.

coverage rate is 95%, and we do not scale the VaR estimates nor update them on a quarterly basis as the Basel Committee rules require, so that any deviations from the expected coverage rate can be easily discerned. The adequacy of the calculated position risk requirements are given in Panels A and B of Table 7 for back tests and forward tests, respectively. The VaRs are calculated using the historical simulation on the portfolio approach, the standard *RiskMetrics* approach, the multivariate GARCH approach, and the proposed weighted *RiskMetrics* method.

In both back and forward tests, the inadequacy of the standard *RiskMetrics* approach is evident. The VaR from this approach were considerably smaller than those from the historical simulation on the portfolio method, and consequently, the percentage of exceedences is higher than the nominal 5% level. For example, a securities firm with a long position would have expected to exceed the capital risk requirement on 12 or 13 days in the 250 trading day (one year) post-sample validation period, whereas the number of days on which the *RiskMetrics* approach would have implied insufficient coverage is 46. Even with the Basel scaling factor of 3, such a difference could cause a firm to move from the green to the yellow or red zones and place it on the regulators watch list for costly increases in the mutliplier. The performance of the volatilities and correlations method is relatively worse in bear markets (where those with a long position lose) than in bull markets (where those with a short position lose), which again is anticipated since correlations between asset markets have been observed to be stronger in bear than bull markets.

On the other hand, both of the new proposed methods of allowing for correlations to change with volatility lead to numbers of exceedences closer to both the nominal 5% rule and to the historical simulation on the portfolio approach, with slightly fewer than 5% in the back tests and slightly more in the forward tests. In fact, the multivariate GARCH model proves to be the best method for the calculation of VaR when measured in this way, for it produces less than 5% violations in the backtests and only slightly more than the nominal 5% in the out-of-sample tests.

6 CONCLUSIONS

This chapter has investigated whether the volatilities of financial markets are related to the correlations between them, in the context of five Southeast Asian stock market indices. An indication of the existence of such a relationship was found and an important downward bias in VaR estimates, based upon correlations and volatilities resulting from this phenomenon, was highlighted. The historical simulation of the portfolio approach is not affected, since by its very nature, when the markets crash together, the value of the portfolio investing in those markets will fall correspondingly. However, the volatilities and correlations approach to calculating VaR has a number of attractive features, not least of which is that it does not require the portfolio values to be recalculated at each time interval. Two methods for allowing for this anomaly were proposed. The first uses time-varying conditional covariances and conditional standard deviations from a multivariate GARCH model. The second allows the volatilities and correlations methodology to be retained in a slightly modified fashion which involves isolating the extreme observations, calculating their VaR and also the VaR of a subsample with those extremes removed, and taking a weighted average.

Although there is no doubt that many other methods could have been employed, both the methods proposed here were found to mitigate the downward bias and to outperform the standard volatilities and correlations approach. Given the current popularity and widespread usage of VaR and that the employment of internal risk management models for calculating position risk requirements is now permitted in Europe under the Second Capital Adequacy Directive (CAD-II), it is clearly important that more research is conducted with the objective of improving the robustness of VaR models.

1 See Clifford Chance (1998) for a discussion of the implications of CAD-II.

2 Statistical discrepancies in VaR estimation can have serious ramifications. Ju and Pearson (1999), for example, show that traders, who know the possible errors in VaR estimates, can select portfolios which deliberately understate the true VaR relative to the measured VaR.

3 On the other hand, a financial institution can also run into difficulties if it has short positions and correlations unexpectedly fall; see Jorion (1999), who discusses this issue in the context of the failure of Long-Term Capital Management.

4 The first 3,486 observations are used for estimation, while the remainder are used for out-of-sample testing.

5 Throughout, we assume a long position, and it is therefore the left-hand tail of the return distribution that constitutes the losses of interest.

6 Again, we focus on the fifth percentile of the returns distribution by convention and because it can be more accurately determined than the first percentile required by the Basel Committee rules.

7 The BEKK model comprises five parameters for the intercepts in the conditional variance–covariance equations, plus 15 parameters for each of the lagged squared errors and conditional variance–covariance matrices. The vec model, on the other hand, requires many more parameters since separate equations are required for the conditional covariances. For a 5×5 system, 15 equations are thus required, leading to 15 intercept parameters in the conditional variances and covariances, plus 120 parameters for each of the lagged squared errors and conditional variances–covariances.

8 Note that we are estimating a 5% VaR, and not a 10% VaR. Rather, we are using the 10th percentile as a convenient place to split the data into the tail and central parts.

9 In order to capture as much of the variation in correlation as one moves further into the tails, these samples should be as small as possible.

10 Initially, we used only three samples: 10% in each tail and the central 80% of the ordered observations. However, it may prove useful to further split the tails in order to achieve sufficient granularity to capture the dramatic increase in correlation as we reach the first percentile.

This chapter was previously published in *The Journal of Risk* **2**(4), Summer 2000.

REFERENCES

Akgiray, V., 1989, "Conditional Heteroskedasticity in Time Series of Stock Returns: Evidence and Forecasts", *Journal of Business* **62(1)**, pp. 55–80.

Alexander, C. O. and C. T. Leigh, 1997, "On the Covariance Models used in Value-at-Risk Models", *Journal of Derivatives* **4**, pp. 50–62.

Ang, A. and G. Bekaert, 1999, "International Asset Allocation with Time-varying Correlations", NBER Working Paper 7056.

Bollerslev, T., R. F. Engle, and J. M. Wooldridge, 1988, "A Capital Asset Pricing Model with Time-varying Covariances", *Journal of Political Economy* 96, pp. 116–31.

Boyer, B. H., M. S. Gibson, and M. Loretan, 1999, "Pitfalls in Tests for Changes in Correlations", International Finance Discussion Papers No. 597, Board of Governors of the Federal Reserve System.

Brooks, C., 1998, "Forecasting Stock Return Volatility: Does Volume Help?" *Journal of Forecasting* 17, pp. 59–80.

Brooks, C., A. D. Clare, and G. Persand, 2000, "A Word of Caution on Calculating Market-based Capital Risk Requirements", *Journal of Banking and Finance*, forthcoming.

Champa, J. M. and P. H. K. Chang, 1998, "The Forecasting Ability of Correlations Implied in Foreign Exchange Options", *Journal of International Money and Finance* 17, pp. 855–80.

Chow, G., E. Jacquier, M. Kritzman, and K. Lowry, 1999, "Optimal Portfolios in Good Times and Bad", *Financial Analysts Journal* 55, May/June, pp. 65–73.

Clifford, C., 1998, "CAD II Moves Forward", Newsletter: European Financial Markets, London.

Day, T. E. and C. M. Lewis, 1992, "Stock Market Atility and the Information Content of Stock Index Options", *Journal of Econometrics* 52, pp. 267–87.

Dimson, E. and P. Marsh, 1995, "Capital Requirements for Securities Firms", *Journal of Finance* 50(3), pp. 821–51.

Dimson, E. and P. Marsh, 1997, "Stress Tests of Capital Requirements", *Journal of Banking and Finance* 21, pp. 1515–46.

Dowd, K., 1998, *Beyond Value at Risk: The New Science of Risk Management.* (Chichester, UK: Wiley).

Eberlein, E., U. Keller, and K. Prause, 1998, "New Insights into Smile, Mispricing, and Value at Risk: The Hyperbolic Model", *Journal of Business* 71(3), pp. 371–405.

Embrechts, P., S. I. Resnick, and G. Samorodnitsky, 1999, "Extreme Value Theory as a Risk Management Tool", *North American Actuarial Journal* 3(2), pp. 30–41.

Engle, R. F. and K. Kroner, 1995, "Multivariate Simultaneous Generalized ARCH", *Econometric Theory* 11(1), pp. 122–50.

Huisman, R., K. G. Koedijk, and R. A. J. Pownall, 1998, "VAR-x: Fat Tails in Financial Risk Management", *Journal of Risk* 1(1), pp. 47–61.

Hull, J. and A. White, 1998, "Value-at-Risk When Daily Changes in Market Variables are not Normally Distributed", *Journal of Derivatives* 5(3), pp. 9–19.

Jackson, P., D. J. Maude, and W. Perraudin, 1998, "Testing Value-at-Risk Approaches to Capital Adequacy", *Bank of England Quarterly Bulletin* 38(3), pp. 256–66.

Johansen, A. and D. Sornette, 1999, "Critical Crashes", *Risk* 12(1), pp. 91–5.

Jorion, P., 1996a, "Risk²: Measuring the Risk in Value at Risk", *Financial Analysts Journal* 52, November/December, pp. 47–56.

Jorion, P., 1996b, *Value at Risk: The New Benchmark for Controlling Market Risk.* (Chicago: Irwin).

Jorion, P., 1999, "Risk Management Lessons from Long-term Capital Management", Mimeo, Graduate School of Management, University of California at Irvine.

J. P. Morgan, 1996, *RiskMetrics Technical Document*, 4th edn. (New York: JP Morgan).

Ju, X. and N. D. Pearson, 1999, "Using Value at Risk to Control Risk-taking: How Wrong Can You Be?" *Journal of Risk* **1(2)**, pp. 5–36.

Karolyi, G. A. and R. M. Stulz, 1996, "Why Do Markets Move Together? An Investigation of US–Japan Stock Return Comovements", *Journal of Finance* **51(3)**, pp. 951–86.

Kim, J. and C. C. Finger, 2000, "A Stress Test to Incorporate Correlation Breakdown", *Journal of Risk* **2(3)**, pp. 5–19.

Walter, C. and J. Lopez, 1997, "Is Implied Correlation Worth Calculating? Evidence from Foreign Exchange Options", Research Paper 9730, Federal Reserve Bank of New York.

Section 5

Evaluation of Models and Systems (backtests and stress tests)

19

The Relativity of Volatility

Turan Bali; Salih Neftci

Baruch College, CUNY; Graduate School, CUNY, University of Reading

Volatility may have to be measured differently depending on a market practitioner's interest. For an options trader, the important thing is how much the underlying asset price fluctuates in a given time. So, in this case, volatility means the "average" fluctuation of the underlying price measured instantaneously. The standard definition of the second moment of the continuous time price changes provides a convenient measure for such a volatility concept. This is captured by the diffusion parameter in the stochastic differential equation:

$$dS_t = \mu(S_t, t)dt + \sigma(S_t, t)dW_t \tag{1}$$

where S_t is the price of the underlying asset.

An options trader is only indirectly interested in the extreme movements of the underlying price. Some extreme movements may lead to broken hedges or lack of liquidity but, barring these situations, plain vanilla options traders could consider extreme movements as similar to other fluctuations and may be satisfied with a standard definition of volatility as a first approximation. Of course, this changes significantly when it comes to barrier options and other exotics.

On the other hand, for a risk or a portfolio manager, the "small" fluctuations around the mean are meaningless and relatively unimportant. A risk manager has to work with changes in market variables that are beyond a certain minimum or maximum level.

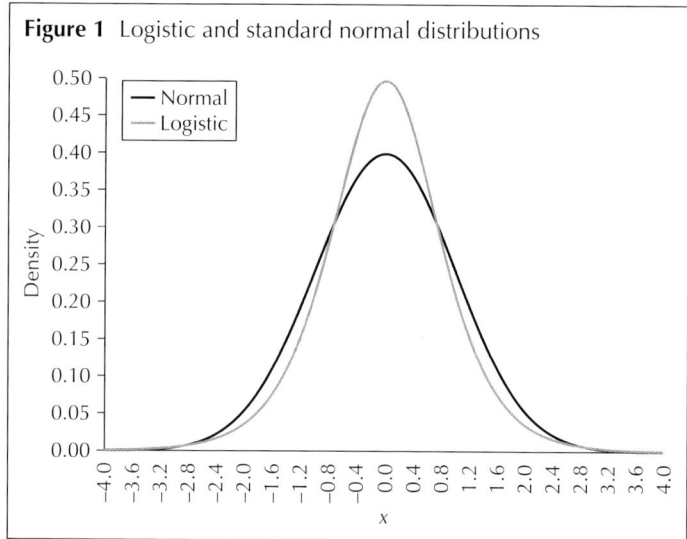

Figure 1 Logistic and standard normal distributions

His objective function is related to the size of the losses in excess of a predetermined level.

This leads to the following. Consider a risk factor (eg, an exchange rate) distributed according to the logistic density shown in Figure 1. This density is given by:

$$f(x) = \frac{2e^{-2x}}{(1 + e^{-2x})^2} \tag{2}$$

and is selected to have a standard deviation that equals 0.90. Note that this volatility is smaller than the volatility of the standard normal density shown in the same figure in black, which has a volatility of one.

Yet, when we look at the intersection points of the two densities we see that the tails of the logistic density are heavier. In fact, if we are interested in the VaR-type measurements, we would mostly be concerned with these probabilities at the tails. And here the logistic density has more probability concentration. In fact, we can easily calculate that this intersection point occurs at $x = \pm 2.9$ and that $P(x \leq -2.9 \mid$ normal density$) = 1.9\%$ and $P(x \leq -2.9 \mid$ logistic density$) = 3.0\%$. That is, the volatility of the underlying series beyond the level ±2.9 is higher in the case of logistic density shown in red in Figure 1, despite the fact that the overall variance is smaller.

Clearly, a risk manager may be more interested in the type of volatility estimation that weighs the extreme movements in the data differently from the classical standard deviation formula:

$$\sigma = \sqrt{\frac{1}{n-1} \sum_{i=1}^{n} (S_i - \bar{S})^2} \tag{3}$$

How can one calculate volatility so that the extremes of the underlying assets or risk factors are weighted differently from the standard case shown in (3). We consider this problem within the setting of interest rate volatility estimation.

Much work has been directed towards modelling and estimating the conditional distribution of interest rates.[1] Yet, despite a bewildering array of models, relatively little is known about the dynamics of short-term interest rate volatility associated with extreme up and down movements in various rates.[2]

We show that the term structure of interest rate volatility displays a clear divergence between historical volatilities calculated in a standard fashion, and those that emanate from extreme interest rate movements only. Our research indicates that when asymptotic extremal theory is used, the estimates of the term structure of historical volatilities are significantly lower than those obtained from the standard formula above. From a trader's point of view, the slope of the volatility structure is also important. When the volatility of the interest rate process is calculated from extremal distributions, the volatility curve exhibits a significantly steeper slope. These divergences have major implications for volatility trading and arbitrage. Also, these term structures yield significantly different volatilities for extreme up and down interest rate movements. Experienced options traders know that one has to differentiate between up-gamma and down-gamma. The use of extremal distributions does exactly this, since it implies a separate estimate for each tail, and hence yields a separate historical volatility estimate that originates from extreme up and down movements.

THE STANDARD, GARCH APPROACH

In continuous time diffusion models, the dynamics of the short rate can be described by the Itô stochastic differential equation:

$$dr_t = \mu(r_t)dt + \sigma(r_t)dW_t \tag{4}$$

where r_t is the instantaneous spot rate, W_t is a standard Brownian motion and $\mu(\cdot)$ and $\sigma(\cdot)$ are the drift and diffusion functions that depend on the short rate and possibly other state variables. μ and σ can be viewed as an (instantaneous) mean and standard deviation of interest rate changes. In discrete time, they are estimated by maximising the log-likelihood function:

$$\ln L((\mu,\sigma); \Delta r_i) = -\frac{n}{2}\ln(2\pi) - \frac{n}{2}\ln\sigma^2 - \frac{1}{2}\sum_{i=1}^{n}\left(\frac{\Delta r_i - \mu}{\sigma}\right)^2 \tag{5}$$

which gives parameter estimates that are unbiased, asymptotically normal and of minimum variance.

Many popular models of the short rate assume that Δr_t is normally or lognormally distributed with a mean-reverting dynamic. However, most empirical work shows that the excess kurtosis values for short-term rates are extremely high and statistically significant, implying that the tails of the distribution of interest rate changes are much thicker than the tails of the normal distribution. In this chapter, the Student-t GARCH model is selected as one of the two benchmark models, and is shown to be a much closer estimate of the volatility modelling via extremal movements.

We let the conditional distribution of $\Delta r_t = r_t - r_{t-1}$ be standardised Student-t with linear mean-reverting drift $\mu_t = \alpha_0 + \alpha_1 r_{t-1}$, GARCH (1,1) variance $\sigma_t^2 = \beta_0 + \beta_1\varepsilon_{t-1}^2 + \beta_2\sigma_{t-1}^2$ and degrees of freedom $v > 2$, ie[3]:

$$r_t - r_{t-1} = \alpha_0 + \alpha_1 r_{t-1} + \varepsilon_t \tag{6}$$

$$\varepsilon_t \big|\Omega_{t-1} \sim f(\mu_t, \sigma_t, v; \varepsilon_t)$$
$$= \Gamma\left(\frac{v+1}{2}\right)\Gamma\left(\frac{v}{2}\right)^{-1}\left[(v-2)\sigma_t^2\right]^{-1/2}\left[1 + \frac{(\Delta r_t - \mu_t)^2}{(v-2)\sigma_t^2}\right]^{-(v+1)/2} \tag{7}$$

$$E(\varepsilon_t^2\big|\Omega_{t-1}) \equiv \sigma_t^2 = \beta_0 + \beta_1\varepsilon_{t-1}^2 + \beta_2\sigma_{t-1}^2 \tag{8}$$

where $\Gamma(\cdot)$ is the gamma function, $\varepsilon_t = \Delta r_t - \mu_t$ is an unexpected shock to r, $f(\mu_t, \sigma_t, v; \varepsilon_t)$ is the conditional density function for ε_t, Ω_{t-1} is the information set available at time $t - 1$ so that $E(\ldots | \Omega_{t-1})$ represents the conditional expectation operator at time $t - 1$, and σ_t^2 is the conditional variance of unexpected interest rate changes. In the GARCH (1,1) model, current volatility is a function of the last period's unexpected news and the last period's volatility.

THE EXTREME VALUE APPROACH

We can also estimate historical volatility using only extreme movements in observed data. This way of looking at volatility may be much closer to the behaviour of a fund manager who is interested in criteria such as maximum draw-down, or to a risk manager's concerns. Options traders who take positions on volatility may also be interested in extreme movements in the volatility of their underlying.

Let $\{X_t\}$ be a stochastic process representing the daily changes in short-term interest rates. We are interested in the behaviour of the maximal and minimal changes in interest rate levels. To find a limiting distribution for the maxima, $X_{\max}$ is transformed such that the limit distribution of the new variable is non-degenerate. The simplest transformation is the standardisation operation. The variate, $X_{\max}$, is transformed using a location parameter, μ_i, and a scale parameter, σ_i, in such a way that:

$$x_i = (X_{\max_i} - \mu_i)/\sigma_i \tag{9}$$

where μ_i and σ_i can be viewed as the mean and volatility of the extremes, respectively. One tries to find the distribution function $F^i(\cdot)$ such that:

$$F(\sigma_i x_i + \mu_i) \to H(x) \tag{10}$$

It is well known that there are three possibilities for the cumulative distribution function $H(x)$ in case the observations are independent identically distributed. These three types can be expressed in the generalised Pareto distribution of the form:

$$H(x) = \begin{cases} 1 - (1 + \phi x)^{-1/\phi} & \phi \neq 0 \\ 1 - \exp(-x) & \phi = 0 \end{cases} \tag{11}$$

where the shape parameter, ϕ, determines the tail behaviour of the distribution. For $\phi = 0$, the tail decreases exponentially. For $\phi < 0$, the distribution is short tailed. For $\phi > 0$, it has a polynomially decreasing tail. This set-up corresponds to the standard parametric case of statistical inference and hence, in principle, can be solved by maximum likelihood methodology. The generalised Pareto distribution presented in Equation (11) yields the following log-likelihood function:

$$\ln L((\mu, \sigma, \phi); X_{max}) = -n \ln \sigma$$
$$- n \left(\frac{1 + \phi}{\phi} \right) \sum_{i=1}^{n} \ln(1 + \phi (X_{max_i} - \mu) / \sigma) \tag{12}$$

Differentiating the log-likelihood function with respect to μ, σ and ϕ yields the first-order conditions of the maximisation problem. Clearly no explicit solution exists for these nonlinear equations, and thus the numerical procedures are needed.

RESULTS

The data sets used in this study are obtained from the Federal Reserve H.15 database and consist of daily observations for the annualised yields on three-, six- and 12-month US Treasury bills.[4] The extremes are defined as those more than two standard deviations away from the sample mean of daily interest rate changes, which corresponds to almost 2% of the right and left tails of the distribution. Panels 1 and 2 of Table 1 report the maximum likelihood estimates of the mean, standard deviation, and degrees of freedom parameters of the Student-t and normal distributions. According to the asymptotic t-statistics given in panel 1, the estimated volatility and shape parameters of the Student-t GARCH model are statistically significant for all Treasury bills. The results in panel 2 indicate that the estimated standard deviation of interest rate changes is highly significant, and the mean of the distribution is almost zero.

Table 1 Maximum likelihood estimates of the student-t GARCH and normal distributions

Interest rates	α_0	α_1	β_0	β_1	β_2	ν	σ
Panel 1: Student-t GARCH model							
3-month T-bill	0.000019 (2.5182)	−0.00045 (−2.4607)	7.15×10^{-10} (4.6316)	0.1013 (16.092)	0.8976 (208.57)	3.8955 (25.010)	0.00081
6-month T-bill	0.000017 (1.7670)	−0.00031 (−1.4541)	3.41×10^{-10} (3.7790)	0.0682 (13.901)	0.9312 (263.67)	3.7600 (24.404)	0.00075
12-month T-bill	0.000005 (0.5571)	−0.00014 (−0.7039)	2.51×10^{-10} (2.6114)	0.0879 (12.483)	0.9116 (311.16)	3.1481 (26.958)	0.00071

Interest rates	μ	σ		μ	σ		μ	σ
Panel 2: Normal distribution with constant mean and variance								
3-month T-bill	0.000003 (0.3588)	0.00099 (569.16)	6-month T-bill	0.000002 (0.2559)	0.00092 (495.86)	12-month T-bill	0.000001 (0.1332)	0.00083 (432.31)

Asymptotic t-statistics are given in parentheses. The last column of panel 1 reports the long-run average standard deviation:

$$\sigma = \sqrt{\beta_0 / (1 - \beta_1 - \beta_2)}$$

Figure 2 Volatility of daily and extreme interest rate changes

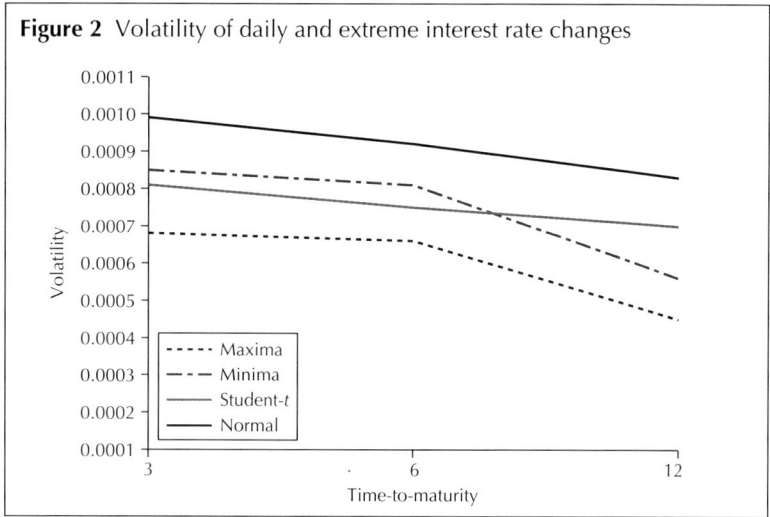

An interesting aspect of the behaviour of short-term interest rates is the shape of the distribution. Normality requires that $1/v$ for the standardised Student-t distribution be equal to zero, and as presented in panel 1 of Table 1, the estimated v is highly significant and equals 3.90, 3.76 and 3.15 for three-, six- and 12-month Treasury bills, respectively. Bollerslev (1987) discusses that when testing against the null hypothesis of conditionally normal errors, ie, $1/v = 0$, $1/v$ is on the boundary of the admissible parameter space, and the usual test statistics will probably be more concentrated towards the origin than a χ_1^2 distribution. Although not presented in the chapter, the maximised log-likelihood values from the normal distribution are much smaller than those from the Student-t distribution. In other words, the likelihood ratio test statistics are substantially greater than the critical value for all Treasury bills, indicating that the distribution of daily interest rate changes is much more leptokurtic than the corresponding normal distribution.

Table 1 shows that the volatility of interest rate changes is overestimated by the standard approach that uses normal distribution. The volatilities of three-, six- and 12-month Treasury bills are in the range of 0.099%, 0.092% and 0.083%, respectively. The corresponding figures for the Student-t GARCH model are about 0.081%, 0.075% and 0.071%. As shown in Figure 2, the term structure of interest

Table 2 Maximum likelihood estimates of the generalised Pareto distribution

	μ	σ	φ	*n*
Local maxima				
3-month T-bill	0.0024	0.00068	0.4926	
	(54.453)	(8.5457)	(4.9796)	287
6-month T-bill	0.0025	0.00066	0.3456	
	(58.546)	(8.3682)	(5.4006)	256
12-month T-bill	0.0022	0.00045	0.4253	
	(68.654)	(8.1662)	(5.7223)	252
Local minima				
3-month T-bill	−0.0027	0.00085	0.2291	
	(−51.441)	(9.4497)	(2.5150)	287
6-month T-bill	−0.0025	0.00081	0.1616	
	(−46.004)	(8.9372)	(2.2521)	256
12-month T-bill	−0.0022	0.00056	0.3293	
	(−60.514)	(8.7737)	(2.8928)	252

This table presents the maximum likelihood estimates of the location (μ), scale (σ) and shape (φ) parameters of the generalised Pareto distribution. Asymptotic *t*-statistics are given in parentheses. The last column reports the number of observations used in generalised Pareto distribution parameter estimation.

rate volatility for the normal distribution plots above the volatility curve for the Student-*t* GARCH model.

Table 2 shows the maximum likelihood parameter estimates of the generalised Pareto distribution, asymptotic *t*-statistics and the number of extremes for the three-, six- and 12-month T-bill rates. According to the asymptotic *t*-statistics given in Table 2, the parameters of the generalised Pareto distribution are statistically significant at the 1% level. The estimated shape parameters (φ) for the local maxima for all data sets are greater than those for the local minima. Since the higher φ, the fatter the distribution of the extremes, the distribution of the maximal changes in T-bill rates is fatter than that of the minimal changes.

The volatility of the extremes measured by the estimated scale parameter, σ, reduces as time-to-maturity rises for both the local maxima and the local minima of interest rate changes. This indicates the downward sloping term structure of interest rate volatility during the extreme movements of the US T-bill market. The estimated volatility of the minimal values turns out to be higher than that of the maximal values. Specifically, the volatility of the minimal changes in three-, six- and 12-month T-bill rates are in the range of 0.085%, 0.081% and 0.056%, respectively. The corresponding figures for the maxima are about 0.068%, 0.066% and 0.045%.

Figure 2 depicts the term structure of short-rate volatility for the extreme and daily changes in T-bill rates. The volatility curve for the minima plots above the volatility curve for the maxima, and the volatility curve for the Student-t distribution lies between the volatility of maxima and minima. The volatility curve for the normal distribution plots above all other curves. The empirical results indicate that the standard approach that uses normal density overestimates the volatility of interest rate changes whereas the same approach that uses the fat-tailed Student-t distribution yields the same volatility estimates as the extreme value approach that uses the generalised Pareto distribution.

CONCLUSIONS

The distribution of extreme observations on interest rates depends on a "volatility" parameter that yields very different estimates for historical volatility. This indicates that the underlying distributions are far from normal, since otherwise the volatility estimates from extremal distributions would be identical to those obtained by assuming normality. The historical volatility obtained via the extremal distributions may thus lead to very different decisions on managing interest rate risk and pricing interest rate sensitive claims.

1   See, for example, Chan *et al* (1992), Ait-Sahalia (1996), Andersen and Lund (1997), Ball and Torous (1999) and Bali (2000), among many others.

2   The recent studies that use extreme value theory to explain the fluctuations in financial markets are performed by Longin (1996), Danielsson and de Vries (1997), McCulloch (1997) and Neftci (2000).

3   It is well known that for $1/\nu \to 0$ the t-distribution approaches a normal distribution, but for $1/\nu > 0$ the t-distribution has fatter tails than the corresponding normal distribution.

4   The three-month Treasury yields extend from January 8, 1954 to December 31, 1999, giving a total of 11,488 daily observations. The data for the six-month Treasury yields covers the period from December 12, 1958 to December 31, 1999, yielding 10,248 daily observations. The data for the 12-month Treasury bill consist of 10,097 daily rates for the period July 17, 1959 to December 31, 1999.

This chapter was previously published in *Risk*, April 2001.

REFERENCES

Ait-Sahalia, Y., 1996, "Nonparametric Pricing of Interest Rate Derivatives", *Econometrica* **64**, pp. 527–60.

Andersen, T. and J. Lund, 1997, "Estimating Continuous-time Stochastic Volatility Models of the Short-term Interest Rate", *Journal of Econometrics* **77**, pp. 343–77.

Bali, T., 2000, "Testing the Empirical Performance of Stochastic Volatility Models of the Short Term Interest Rate", *Journal of Financial and Quantitative Analysis* **35**, pp. 191–215.

Ball, C. and W. Torous, 1999, "The Stochastic Volatility of Short-term Interest Rates: Some International Evidence", *Journal of Finance* **54**, pp. 2339–59.

Bollerslev, T., 1987, "A Conditionally Heteroscedastic Time Series Model for Security Prices and Rates of Return Data", *Review of Economics and Statistics* **59**, pp. 542–7.

Chan, K., G. Karolyi, F. Longstaff, and A. Sanders, 1992, "An Empirical Comparison of Alternative Models of the Short-term Interest Rate", *Journal of Finance* **47**, pp. 1209–27.

Danielsson, J. and C. de Vries, 1997, "Tail Index and Quantile Estimation with Very High Frequency Data", *Journal of Empirical Finance* **4**, pp. 241–57.

Longin, F., 1996, "The Asymptotic Distribution of Extreme Stock Market Returns", *Journal of Business* **69**, pp. 383–408.

McCulloch, J., 1997, "Measuring Tail Tickness to Estimate the Stable Index α: A Critique", *Journal of Business and Economic Statistics* **15**, pp. 74–81.

Neftci, S., 2000, "Extremes, Tail Estimation and Value at Risk Calculations", *Journal of Derivatives*, spring, pp. 23–37.

20

Testing Assumptions

Jeremy Berkowitz[*]

University of California

Research into modelling and forecasting portfolio value-at-risk (VaR) mostly comprises highly parameterised factor models (see Jorion (2001)). To use such VaR models for forecasting, practitioners must take a stand on the distribution of the factors. This is because, unlike with many other areas of applied finance, the output of interest is more than just a point forecast. VaR is an interval forecast, typically a one-sided 95% or 99% interval. Users generally assume that the factors are normally or *t*-distributed or use some variant of historical simulation.[1] It is useful for our purposes to view historical simulation as imposing the empirical distribution – the histogram of observed historical returns.

The choice of whether to impose a parametric distribution or historical simulation can have an important influence on the performance and forecast accuracy of the model. Lopez and Walter (2000) provide evidence that forecasts of portfolio distributions are particularly sensitive to distributional assumptions – indeed, far more so than other design issues that have typically received more attention, such as the method used to calculate covariance matrices. Related Monte Carlo evidence is given in Pritsker (1997) and Berkowitz (2001). Both chapters find significant differences between models that assume normality versus those based on some form of historical simulation.

*The author gratefully acknowledges helpful input from Jim O'Brien and Matt Pritsker.

Further evidence of how contentious the choice of distribution has become can be found in recent reports that practitioners have not converged on a single methodology. A survey by the UK's Financial Services Authority reveals that, in estimating their market risk models, 42% of banks use a variance-covariance approach, 31% use historical simulation and 23% use Monte Carlo methods.

Since historical simulation permits forecasting of VaR without imposing parametric distributional assumptions, why do anything else? In some cases, historical simulation is a reasonable modelling approach. However, implementation of historical simulation can be subject to pitfalls that do not arise under Monte Carlo. Historical simulation, like bootstrapping, involves resampling from historically observed changes in factor prices. Such financial time series invariably display autocorrelation – typically in the mean, as well as in the volatility and possibly in higher moments. Dependence makes resampling with replacement invalid because the resampling procedure fails to preserve the underlying dependence structure.

It is undoubtedly the case that non-stationarity (structural breaks of any kind) can be a problem in financial time series. If so, this can make less recent data irrelevant and invalidate historical simulation.

Monte Carlo simulation bypasses both such problems by allowing the researcher to posit a data-generating process. Rather than try to transform the historical factor changes to make them suitable for resampling, under Monte Carlo methods one simply generates data from an assumed process like GARCH, which has built-in dependence of the kind believed important.

Lastly, in recent work, Pritsker (2001) emphasises that VaR forecasts from historical simulation can be insufficiently responsive to big changes in volatility. This dovetails with Berkowitz and O'Brien (2001), who find that, although historical simulation methods do well, GARCH-based methods do even better.

Despite the significance of these issues, standard statistical methods are not well suited for testing distributional assumptions. The problem is that no model is literally true and thus any VaR model is typically rejected by standard statistical tests. VaR models contain many potentially restrictive modelling assumptions and shortcuts.[2] A simple rejection leaves us with little or no information on the accuracy of the distributional assumption in isolation. Is it the distributional assumption that is inaccurate or have we chosen the wrong set of factors?

In this chapter, we describe a procedure that has power to isolate rejections arising from distributional assumptions. The key is to generate data that is consistent with all aspects of the model other than the distributional assumption. A rejection of the model using this artificial data by construction implies a rejection of the distributional assumptions. We go beyond a simple reject/not reject conclusion and give constructive guidance to researchers as to why a particular model fails (at least in some dimensions).

The rest of the chapter is organised as follows. The following section formalises the notions of factors and distributional assumptions within the context of a risk model. We then present the suggested testing procedures, followed by a discussion of the results of some simulation experiments.

THE BASIC FRAMEWORK

Consider a firm that maintains a risk model that is used to forecast the distribution of possible returns, y_{t+1}, on some portfolio. Denote the distribution of returns, $g(y_{t+1})$. For example, quantile or VaR modelling reduces to estimating a single percentile, say the ninety-ninth, of $g(y_{t+1})$.

Such risk models are composed of two parts. First, the model contains a set of risk factors, such as interest rates and exchange rates. Let x_t be the $k \times 1$ vector of factor returns realised at time t.

The second component of the model is a set of pricing rules, $P(\cdot)$, which predict asset returns as a function of the underlying factors. Typically, this will be a simple linear mapping from the space of factors to assets:

$$\hat{y}_{j,t} = \lambda_j' x_t \tag{1}$$

where $\hat{y}_{j,t}$ is the predicted return of asset j, λ_j is the associated k vector of factor loadings and x_t is a k-vector of factor changes. We might use more complex functions $\hat{y}_{j,t} = p_j(x_t)$ to accommodate assets with nonlinear dependence such as pricing options via Black–Scholes. The predicted portfolio return is then given by:

$$\hat{y}_t = \Sigma_j p_j(x_t) w_j \tag{2}$$

where w_j is the weight of asset j in the portfolio at time t.

In many cases, interest centres on the VaR or distribution of possible portfolio returns. If so, users assume a distribution for the underlying factors $f(x)$. From this distribution, artificial factor price changes are generated and then converted into simulated portfolio returns. For example, factor price changes are commonly assumed to follow a normal or conditionally normal distribution such as GARCH. If we denote a draw from $f(\cdot)$ as $\hat{x}_f^i$, then a simulated value can be written $\hat{y}_{t+1}^i = \Sigma p_j(\hat{x}_f^i)w_j$. This process is repeated many times to build up a set $\{\hat{y}_{t+1}^i, \ldots, \hat{y}_{t+1}^R\}$ where R is a large number chosen by the user. This set of pseudo values is tabulated into an estimate of the distribution.

TESTING THE FACTOR DISTRIBUTIONS

Here we suggest a framework for diagnosing the source of model rejections. The trick is to create a test in which the same pricing model appears in both null and alternative. The alternative hypothesis is different from the null only in the assumptions regarding factor distributions.

Under the null $f(\cdot)$ is some parametric distribution such as the normal. The alternative hypothesis is based on the empirical distribution. If portfolio returns under H_0 are very different than under H_a, we conclude that the parametric assumptions are statistically restrictive.

Write the true but unknown density of portfolio returns as $g[y_t \mid f, p]$ to emphasise that it depends on the factor distributions, $f(\cdot)$, and on the mapping between assets and the factors, $P(\cdot)$. The risk model to be tested is $g[y_t \mid \hat{f}, \hat{p}]$, where $\hat{f}(\cdot)$ is a distributional assumption and $\hat{p}(\cdot)$ is a pricing model. Both the pricing model and the distribution may not be correct.

Suppose the full model is rejected and we would like to see if the distributional assumptions are to blame. If we could study both $g[y_t \mid \hat{f}, \hat{p}]$ and $g[y_t \mid f, \hat{p}]$, we would know that any differences are attributable to $\hat{f}(\cdot)$. In this section, we describe a method of doing precisely that.

To formalise the test, consider the following procedure. Rather than simulated draws from an assumed distribution, use the actual historical factor returns $\{x_1, x_2, \ldots, x_T\}$ in the portfolio pricing model:

$$\hat{y}_{t-i} = \Sigma_j p_j(x_{t-i})w_j \tag{3}$$

for $i = 0, \ldots, T - 1$. Note that the portfolio weights are kept at their time-t values. We can therefore understand the series $\{\hat{y}_1, \ldots, \hat{y}_T\}$ as estimates of what the portfolio returns would have been, had portfolio composition been constant over history.[3] Under stationarity, the distribution of the pseudo-values $\{\hat{y}_1, \ldots, \hat{y}_T\}$ will converge to the distribution of the portfolio $g(y_{t+1})$. It is therefore natural to fit a parametric model to $\{\hat{y}_1, \ldots, \hat{y}_T\}$ as an estimate of $g(y_{t+1})$. For example, we might fit a simple reduced form model such as a conditionally normal GARCH(1,1).

It is equally possible to fit a "non-parametric" model at this point. That is, we could simply form a histogram of the pseudo-values $\{\hat{y}_1, \ldots, \hat{y}_T\}$ or use a non-parametric kernel density estimate of the density function. In either case, $f(x)$ is set to the empirical distribution of x so that, at least asymptotically, we have estimated the distribution $g[y_t \mid f, \hat{p}]$.

Comparing distributions

Given the above machinery, how do we compare the two densities of interest $g[y_t \mid f, \hat{p}]$ and $g[y_t \mid \hat{f}, \hat{p}]$. First define the probability integral transform (PIT) of y_t as $z_t = \int_{-\infty}^{y_t} f(u)du$. Equivalently, we can write $z_t = F(y_t)$ where $F(\cdot)$ is the cumulative density associated with $f(y_t)$.

The utility of the transform stems from the following result. If y_t is a random variable with probability density $f(\cdot)$ then $F(y_t)$ is a random variable that is independently identically distributed uniform(0, 1). This gives us a way of testing a density function. To examine whether $f(\cdot)$ is the density of some data y_t, we simply need to test whether the distribution of $F(y_t)$ is independently identically distributed $U(0, 1)$.

These results have proven particularly useful for risk management. Crnkovic and Drachman (1997) formulate a test of forecast densities on the PIT of portfolio returns. Similar approaches are advocated by Diebold, Gunther and Tay (1998) and Berkowitz (2001). In the present context, however, we would like to test only the distributional assumptions of the underlying risk model. Towards this end, consider the following algorithm:

❏ Use the factor model to calculate the forecasted distribution $g[y_{t+1} \mid \hat{f}, \hat{p}]$.
❏ Generate a series of pseudo-historical data, $y_{t-i}^* = \hat{p}(x_{t-i})$, $i = 0, \ldots, T - 1$. The actual historical realisations of the factor

returns are plugged into the pricing model instead of making any distributional assumptions.

❑ Calculate the PIT $z_{t-i} = \int_{-\infty}^{y_{t-i}} g[u \mid \hat{f}, \hat{p}] du$ for $i = 0, \ldots, T - 1$. The transform of the pseudo-historical data is taken with respect to the full model.

Under the null of correct factor distributions, $z_t \sim$ iid $U(0, 1)$ whether or not the pricing model is accurate. Proposition 1 formalises this statement: if $\hat{f}(\cdot) = f(\cdot)$, then the transformed data $z_t \sim$ iid $U(0, 1)$, regardless of whether the remainder of the risk model is correct. (For proof, see the appendix.)

In this way, we have reduced the distributional assumptions into the statement that a sequence of data should be iid $U(0, 1)$. There are various existing methods for testing this prediction, such as the Kuiper statistic of Crnkovic and Drachman (1997) and Berkowitz's (2001) likelihood ratio statistic.

Note that our procedure also provides an indirect test of the pricing model. To see this, suppose we have rejected the model on the basis of a backtest but we are unable to reject the distributional assumptions. In this case, we conclude that the pricing model is the problem. We are able to state this because we have split the full model into exactly two distinct components.

If, on the other hand, we reject both the full model and the distributional assumptions, we can say nothing directly about the pricing model. The pricing model may or may not be valid. To test it, it is first necessary to have distributional assumptions that match the data. Once that is done and distributional assumptions are no longer rejected, the full model can be recalculated to see if the pricing model is adequate.[4] The suggested testing sequence is shown in Figure 1.

Direct tests of the factor distribution

One could, in principle, directly test the assumed factor distribution. For example, if normality is assumed, one could use a Jarque-Bera test on the empirical distribution of $\hat{f}(\cdot)$. However, there are significant advantages to the proposed likelihood ratio test.

Most importantly, the likelihood ratio testing approach is independent of the assumed distribution $\hat{f}(\cdot)$. If, for example, we assume a t-distribution, the Jarque-Bera test is not appropriate.

Figure 1 Sequential testing procedure

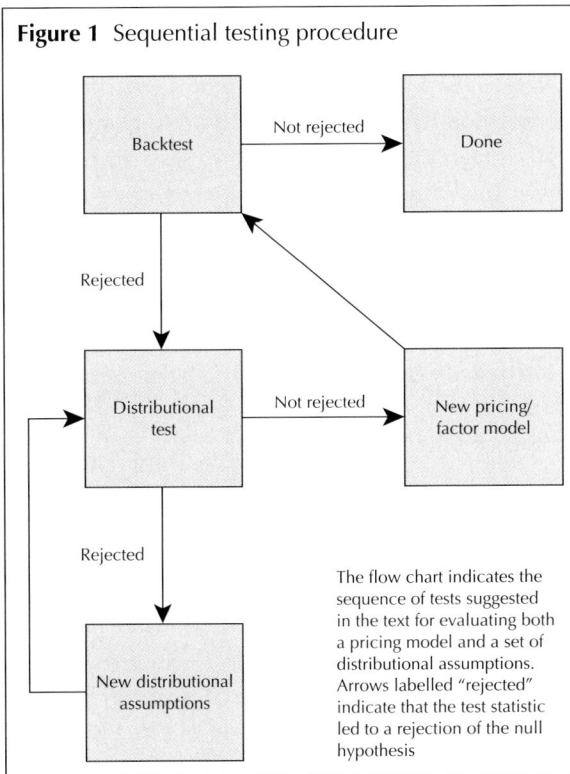

The flow chart indicates the sequence of tests suggested in the text for evaluating both a pricing model and a set of distributional assumptions. Arrows labelled "rejected" indicate that the test statistic led to a rejection of the null hypothesis

Indeed, for most assumptions one would have to resort to moment-based tests that have notoriously bad small sample properties. The proposed likelihood ratio tests are, by virtue of the inverse-normal transformation, always conducted within the normal likelihood framework.

Second, direct tests of the factor distributions do not typically correspond to any economically interpretable criterion. The proposed likelihood ratio test will, in many cases, deliver not just a rejection but a constructive guide as to the cause of the rejection. A rejection because of correlation indicates persistent forecast errors. A rejection because of the wrong mean implies a forecast that is too high (low) on average (see Berkowitz (2001)).

Lastly, risk managers are often exclusively interested in an accurate description of large losses or tail behaviour. They do not want to reject a model that forecasts tail events well because of a failure to match the small day-to-day moves that characterise the interior of the forecast distribution. Berkowitz (2001) shows that the likelihood ratio framework is easily tailored to allow the user to intentionally ignore model failures that are limited to the interior of the distribution by basing the likelihood ratio tests on a censored likelihood. Loosely speaking, the shape of the forecasted tail of the density is compared with the observed tail.

This stakes a middle ground between traditional interval VaR evaluation (counting violations) and the full likelihood ratio approach. Such tests should be more powerful than traditional approaches while still allowing users to ignore model failures that may not be of interest – failures that take place entirely in the interior of the distribution.

MONTE CARLO EXPERIMENTS

Here we investigate the actual behaviour of the suggested procedure for testing distributional assumptions. The risk models are chosen to mimic techniques that are commonly used by risk managers at large financial institutions for constructing interval forecasts.

Data is generated from Heston's (1993) stochastic volatility process:

$$dS(t) = \mu S dt + \sqrt{\sigma_t} S dz_1(t)$$
$$d\sigma(t) = (\alpha - \beta\sigma_t)dt + \eta\sqrt{\sigma_t} dz_2(t)$$

where the drift, μ, is set to 12% and the volatility of volatility, η, is set to 10%. The long-run average of volatility is also 10% with α set to 20% and β set to two. The constant risk-free rate is set to 7% and the process is simulated over a six-month horizon. We consider sample sizes 50, 100, 150, 250 and 500, which may be viewed as corresponding to different observation frequencies, since the time-to-expiry is kept constant. The initial value of the stock is US$40. For each observation, we calculate the true value of a call option, C_t, written on S_t with strike price US$44.

Risk forecasts for the call option are estimated with the BlackScholes model, and the delta and delta-gamma approximations. In addition, we consider two *ad hoc* models that feature modifications designed to capture the stochastic volatility. We take the delta approximation,

$\delta\varepsilon_t + \theta_t$, but instead of drawing ε_t from a lognormal distribution, it is drawn from the (correct) stochastic volatility model. This is akin to the widespread practice of plugging in time-varying estimates of volatility into BlackScholes. The second model is an analogous modification of the delta-gamma approximation.

We subject a portfolio to the statistical test of Crnkovic and Drachman (1997), which is based on the Kuiper statistic, $\max|f(z) - g(z)|$, where $f(z)$ is the observed density of the PIT transformed forecast and $g(z)$ the corresponding theoretical density (uniform$(0, 1)$). If the Kuiper statistic is large, it implies a rejection of the model. We also calculate the Berkowitz (2001) likelihood ratio test in which the PIT-transformed z_t are further transformed from uniform into $N(0, 1)$ variates. The likelihood ratio test rejects the model if these transformed data do not have a mean of zero or a variance of one, as they should in theory.

Table 1 shows the rejection rates of the various models. In all cases, the confidence level of the test is fixed at 0.05. The top of the table reports the Monte Carlo rejection rates when the model is BlackScholes and thus incorrectly assumes lognormality. The first column presents rejection rates for the Kuiper statistic of Crnkovic and Drachman (1997) and the second column the likelihood ratio statistic of Berkowitz (2001). Although there is some variation across columns, the distribution test rejects about 30–40% in samples of 500.

The next two parts of the table show rejection rates if the model is a delta approximation or a delta-gamma approximation, again incorrectly assuming lognormality. There is some variation across tests, but rejection rates are roughly similar at about 30%. This is the case even though the largest sample size we consider is 500.

What about incorrect models with the correct (stochastic volatility) assumption on the factor distribution? The lowest two parts of Table 1 report rejection rates for two such models. The rates should be near 0.05 because, despite the model being wrong, the factor distribution is correct. Indeed, we see from the table that rates are quite close in samples of about 500 observations. Results are roughly comparable whether we look at delta or delta-gamma approximation.

To an extent, Table 1 understates the usefulness of the testing procedure. If we mimic the sequential procedure (Figure 1) and test the distributional assumption conditional on the full model being

Table 1 Backtesting distributional assumptions: stochastic volatility

		Kuiper statistic	LR statistic
Black–Scholes	T = 50	0.063	0.181
	T = 100	0.092	0.197
	T = 150	0.121	0.226
	T = 250	0.184	0.262
	T = 500	0.276	0.358
Delta model (lognormal)	T = 50	0.048	0.052
	T = 100	0.092	0.063
	T = 150	0.132	0.095
	T = 250	0.190	0.156
	T = 500	0.303	0.265
Delta-gamma (lognormal)	T = 50	0.044	0.050
	T = 100	0.089	0.063
	T = 150	0.122	0.083
	T = 250	0.184	0.137
	T = 500	0.294	0.239
Delta model – stochastic volatility	T = 50	0.030	0.025
	T = 100	0.048	0.025
	T = 150	0.049	0.023
	T = 250	0.057	0.024
	T = 500	0.057	0.051
Delta-gamma – stochastic volatility	T = 50	0.027	0.025
	T = 100	0.049	0.025
	T = 150	0.045	0.021
	T = 250	0.062	0.022
	T = 500	0.077	0.024

Note: The table compares the Monte Carlo performance of alternative techniques for validating forecast models over 2,000 simulations. In each simulation, the portfolio of interest comprises call options on an underlying diffusion process. Kuiper denotes the forecast test suggested by Crnkovic and Drachman (1997). LR is the likelihood ratio tests of Berkowitz (2001). The desired size is 5% in all cases.

rejected, power rises substantially. For Table 2, we again generate a total of 2,000 iterations. The distributional test is run only if the full model is rejected. The first column shows the likelihood ratio rejection rates for the various models. The results indicate rejection of the lognormal distribution at a rate as high as 88%, given that we have already rejected the overall BlackScholes forecast.

In the bottom two parts of Table 2, we examine two models that are false but contain the correct factor distribution. In this case, we expect the test to reject the model only about 5% of the time. Suppose, for example, the delta model with stochastic volatility is

Table 2 Sequential testing of distributional assumptions when the factor displays stochastic volatility

	Sample size	Rejection rate
Reject lognormal given	T = 50	0.709
Black–Scholes rejected	T = 100	0.815
	T = 150	0.791
	T = 250	0.870
	T = 500	0.881
Reject stochastic volatility given	T = 50	0.067
lognormal delta rejected	T = 100	0.062
	T = 150	0.053
	T = 250	0.048
	T = 500	0.052
Reject stochastic volatility given	T = 50	0.085
lognormal delta-gamma rejected	T = 100	0.064
	T = 150	0.053
	T = 250	0.060
	T = 500	0.052

Note: The table compares the Monte Carlo rejection rates of the likelihood ratio test described in the text and displayed schematically in Figure 1. A total of 2,000 simulations were generated with the distributional test run only if the full model is rejected. The portfolio of interest is comprised of a call option on an underlying stochastic volatility process for which the Heston (1993) model provides an analytic option price.

rejected, presumably because the delta part is an approximation. Given this rejection, we then test whether the factor distribution is to blame. The table indicates that in samples of 500, we would only reject the model at a rate of 5.2%. Thus, the size properties of the test appear quite good.

DISCUSSION

Given that no risk model is exactly correct, it is not surprising that risk managers and other practitioners have shied away from using formal statistical tests. Such tests, when enough historical data is available, will inevitably deliver a rejection of the full risk model. A more constructive approach is to ask whether a model is acceptably accurate for whatever purpose it is designed. If not, the next step should be to isolate those approximations, shortcuts and assumptions that are most detrimental.

In this chapter, we have taken an initial step in this direction. The aspect of risk modelling that we are interested in isolating is the distributional assumption made about factors. Risk models by their very nature require taking a stand on the factor distributions and yet, as we have emphasised above, no single approach appears to have gained a consensus. It may well be that the best procedure is to test various distributional assumptions against the data and then impose the assumption that fits best. We hope that the tools presented here encourage users to explore this as a way of improving forecasts of portfolio risk.

APPENDIX

Here we present proof of proposition 1. Using the Jacobian of transformation, the distribution of z_t is given by:

$$g_0(y_t^*) \left| \frac{\partial}{\partial z_t} G^{-1} \left[y_t^* \,\middle|\, \hat{f}, \hat{p} \right] \right| \tag{4}$$

where g_0 is the distribution of y_t^* given $\hat{p}$ and the true factor distribution, f.

$$G\left[y_t^* \,\middle|\, \hat{f}, \hat{p} \right] = \int_{-\infty}^{y_t^*} g\left[u \,\middle|\, \hat{f}, \hat{p} \right] du$$

and G^{-1} is its inverse. Because G is monotone, we can simplify this to:

$$g_0(y_t^*) \,/\, \left| \frac{\partial}{\partial z_t} G\left[y_t^* \,\middle|\, \hat{f}, \hat{p} \right] \right|$$

Application of the fundamental theorem of calculus (eg, Courant (1961), p. 111) yields:

$$\frac{g_0(y_t^*)}{g\left[y_t^* \,\middle|\, \hat{f}, \hat{p} \right]}$$

where we have dropped the absolute value sign because $g(\cdot)$ is a density. Now, by definition, $y_t^* = \hat{p}(x_t)$ so that its distribution $g_0(y_t^*) = g_0[y_t^* \,|\, \hat{f}, \hat{p}]$ If $\hat{f}(\cdot) = f(\cdot)$ then $g(\cdot) \circ g_0(\cdot)$, so the quantity (4) simplifies to one. The result follows because the density of a $U(0, 1)$ is identically equal to one.

To establish independence, consider the sequence $\{y_t\}m_{t=1}$. We can write the joint density $g(y_m, \ldots, y_1) = g_m(y_m \,|\, y_{m-1}, \ldots, y_1)g_{m-1}(y_{m-1} \,|\, y_{m-2}, \ldots, y_1)g_1(y_1)$. The joint density of the transformed variables is now given by the multivariate Jacobian of transformation:

$$g_m(y_m)g_{m-1}(y_{m-1}) \cdots g_1(y_1) \left| \frac{1}{\dfrac{\partial G_1}{\partial z_1}} \cdots \frac{1}{\dfrac{\partial G_m}{\partial z_m}} \right|$$

Each of the ratios:

$$g_m(y_m) \, / \, \frac{\partial G_m}{\partial z_m}$$

is the density of a $U(0, 1)$, the product of which yields m-variate $U(0, 1)$. The joint density equals the product of the marginal densities.

1   Within this category there are also models comprised of a mixture of normals such as conditionally normal GARCH models.
2   A well-known problem with capital asset pricing model equity pricing, for example, is that the factor loadings must be estimated and are therefore subject to measurement error.
3   The astute reader will recognise this as a formalisation of a procedure used by practitioners whereby portfolios of hypothetical profit and loss are examined.
4   If the model fails to include all the relevant factors, it will show up as a rejection of the pricing model. It will not show up in a test of the distributional assumptions.

This chapter was previously published in *Risk*, May 2002.

REFERENCES

Berkowitz, J., 2001, "Testing the Accuracy of Density Forecasts in Risk Management", *Journal of Business and Economic Statistics* **19**, pp. 465–74.

Berkowitz, J. and J. O'Brien, 2001, "How Accurate are the Value-at-Risk Models at Commercial Banks?", Forthcoming in Journal of Finance.

Courant, R., 1961, "Differential and Integral Calculus, Volume I", (New York: Interscience Publishers).

Crnkovic, C. and J. Drachman, 1997, "Quality Control", in VAR: Understanding and Applying Value-at-Risk, (London: Risk Publications).

Diebold, F., T. Gunther, and A. Tay, 1998, "Evaluating Density Forecasts", *International Economic Review* **39**, pp. 863–83.

Heston, S., 1993, "A Closed-form Solution for Options with Stochastic Volatility with Applications to Bond and Currency Options", *Review of Financial Studies* **6**, pp. 327–43.

Jorion, P., 2001, "Value-at-Risk: The New Benchmark for Controlling Market Risk", (New York: McGraw Hill).

Lopez, J. and C. Walter, 2000, "Evaluating Covariance Matrix Forecasts in a Value-at-Risk Framework", *Federal Reserve Bank of San Francisco*, paper 2000–21.

Pritsker, M., 1997, "Evaluating Value at Risk Methodologies: Accuracy Versus Computational Time", *Journal of Financial Services Research* **12**, pp. 201–42.

Pritsker, M., 2001, "The Hidden Dangers of Historical Simulation", Working paper, Federal Reserve Board of Governors.

21

Regulatory Evaluation of Value-at-Risk Models

Jose A. Lopez*

Federal Reserve Bank of San Francisco

1 INTRODUCTION

The profits of financial institutions are directly or indirectly tied to the behavior of financial time series, such as interest rates, exchange rates and stock prices. This exposure is commonly referred to as "market risk". Over the past decade, financial institutions have significantly increased their use of econometric models to manage their market risk exposure for a number of reasons, such as their increased trading activities, their increased emphasis on risk-adjusted returns on capital and advances in both the theoretical and empirical finance literature. Given these developments, financial regulators have also begun to focus their attention on the use of such models by regulated institutions.

The main example of such regulatory concern is the 1996 amendment to the Basel Capital Accord, which requires that commercial banks with significant trading activities set aside capital to cover the market risk exposure in their trading accounts. The US bank regulatory agencies adopted this amendment and began enforcing it in 1998.[1] Under the amended capital rules, banks' market risk

*The views expressed here are those of the author and not necessarily those of the Federal Reserve Bank of San Francisco or the Federal Reserve System. I thank Philippe Jorion (the Editor), Peter Christoffersen, Frank Diebold, Darryl Hendricks, Beverly Hirtle, Paul Kupiec, Jim O'Brien and Philip Strahan as well as seminar participants at the 1996 meeting of the Federal Reserve System Committee on Financial Structure and Regulation, the Wharton Financial Institutions Center Conference on Risk Management in Banking and the 1997 Federal Reserve Bank of Chicago Conference on Bank Structure and Competition for their comments.

capital charges can be based on the "value-at-risk" (VaR) estimates generated by their own VaR models. In general, such models forecast the time-varying distributions of portfolio returns, and VaR estimates are forecasts of the maximum portfolio loss that could occur over a given holding period with a specified confidence level; that is, a VaR estimate is a specified lower quantile of a forecasted distribution of portfolio returns.

Given the importance of VaR estimates to banks and now to their regulators, evaluating the accuracy of the models underlying them is a necessary exercise. Three evaluation methods based on hypothesis tests have been proposed to date. In each of these tests, the null hypothesis is that the VaR forecasts in question exhibit a specified property characteristic of accurate VaR forecasts. Specifically, the evaluation method based on the binomial distribution, currently the quantitative standard embodied in the 1996 amendment and extensively discussed by Kupiec (1995), examines whether VaR estimates, on average, provide correct coverage of the lower α percent tails of the forecasted distributions. The interval forecast method proposed by Christoffersen (1998) examines whether VaR estimates exhibit correct coverage at each point in time, and the distribution forecast method proposed by Crnkovic and Drachman (1996) examines whether empirical quantiles derived from a VaR model's distribution forecasts are independent and uniformly distributed. In these tests, if the null hypothesis is rejected, the VaR forecasts do not exhibit the specified property, and the underlying VaR model is said to be "inaccurate". If the null hypothesis is not rejected, then the model can be said to be "acceptably accurate".

However, for these evaluation methods, as with any hypothesis test, a key issue is their power, ie, their ability to reject the null hypothesis when it is incorrect. If a hypothesis test exhibits poor power properties, then the probability of misclassifying an inaccurate VaR model as acceptably accurate will be high. This chapter examines the power of these three tests within the context of a simulation exercise using several data generating processes.

In addition, this chapter proposes an evaluation method based on the probability forecasting framework presented by Lopez (1997). In contrast to those listed above, this method uses standard forecast evaluation techniques and gauges the accuracy of VaR models by how well their probability forecasts minimise a loss function directly relevant to the user. By incorporating regulatory loss functions directly into the evaluation of VaR models, this method provides information on the performance of VaR models with respect to regulatory criteria, as opposed to the statistical criteria implied in the other methods. In this chapter, the probability forecasts of interest are of specified regulatory events, and the loss function used is the quadratic probability score (QPS), whose value ranges over the interval [0, 2]. VaR models with lower QPS values can be said to be more accurate than others.

A drawback of this evaluation method is that the properties of the QPS value for a particular model and specified event cannot be easily determined *a priori*, as opposed to the properties of the three aforementioned test statistics. Thus, this method cannot be used, as the other methods, to statistically test whether a VaR model is "acceptably accurate" or "inaccurate" in an absolute sense. Instead, this method can be used to provide relative comparisons of model accuracy over different time periods and in relation to other VaR models, which should be useful additional information for model users in general and regulators in particular. This method's ability to address the issues of VaR model misclassification and comparative accuracy under different loss functions is also examined within the context of a simulation exercise.

The simulation results indicate that the hypothesis-testing methods can have relatively low power and thus a relatively high chance of misclassifying an inaccurate VaR model as "acceptably accurate". With respect to the probability forecasting method, the simulation results indicate that the QPS values for the accurate VaR models are less than those for the inaccurate models a high percentage of the time. Further analysis, using hypothesis-testing techniques that permit a power comparison across all four evaluation methods, indicates that this method's power is roughly in line with that of the other three methods. Thus, even though the proposed method is only as capable of differentiating between VaR models as the other methods, its ability to directly incorporate regulatory loss functions into model evaluations make it a useful complement to the statistical methods currently used in the regulatory evaluation of VaR models.

The chapter is organised as follows: Section 2 describes both the current regulatory framework for evaluating VaR models and the four evaluation methods examined; Sections 3 and 4 outline the simulation exercise and present the results, respectively; and Section 5 concludes.

2 EVALUATING VAR MODELS

VaR models are characterised by their forecasted distributions of k-period-ahead portfolio returns. To fix notation, let Y_t represent portfolio value at time t in dollar terms, and $y_t = \ln(Y_t)$. The k-period-ahead portfolio return is denoted $\epsilon_{t+k} = y_{t+k} - y_t$. Conditional on the information available at time t, ϵ_{t+k} is a random variable with distribution f_{t+k}; that is, $\epsilon_{t+k} | \Omega_t \sim f_{t+k}$. Thus, VaR model m is characterised by f_{t+k}^m, its forecast of f_{t+k}.

Currently, VaR estimates are the most common type of forecast generated from VaR models. A VaR estimate is a forecast of the maximum portfolio loss that could occur over a given holding period with a specified confidence level. The VaR estimate at time t derived from model m for a k-period-ahead return with α percent confidence, denoted $\text{VaR}_t^m(k, \alpha)$, is the quantile of f_{t+k}^m that corresponds to its lower α percent tail. Thus, $\text{VaR}_t^m(k, \alpha)$ is the solution to

$$\int_{-\infty}^{\text{VaR}_t^m(k,\alpha)} f_{t+k}^m(x)\,dx = \frac{\alpha}{100}$$

or, equivalently, $\text{VaR}_t^m(k, \alpha) = F_{t+k}^{m^{-1}}(\alpha / 100)$, where F_{t+k}^m is the forecasted cumulative distribution function. Note that a VaR estimate is expressed in dollar terms as the difference between the current portfolio value and the portfolio value corresponding to it; that is, $\text{VaR}_t^m(k, \alpha)$ is expressed in dollar terms as $\text{VaR\$}_t^m(k, \alpha) = Y_t(1 - e^{\text{VaR}_t^m(k,\alpha)})$.

Given their role in bank risk management and now in regulatory capital calculations, the evaluation of VaR estimates and the models underlying them is of interest to both banks and their regulators. Note, however, that the regulatory evaluation of such models differs from institutional evaluations in three important ways.[2] First, a regulatory evaluation has the goal of assuring that sufficient capital is available to protect an institution from significant portfolio losses, a goal that may not be shared by an institutional evaluation due to issues of moral hazard. Second, regulators, although potentially privy to the details of an institution's VaR model, generally cannot evaluate every component of the model and its implementation as well as the originating institution can. Third, regulators have the responsibility of constructing evaluations that are comparable across institutions. Thus, although individual banks and regulators may use similar evaluation methods, the regulatory evaluation of VaR models has certain unique characteristics that should be addressed.

In this section, the current regulatory framework for calculating market risk capital charges is described, and four methods for the regulatory evaluation of VaR models are discussed. The first three methods are based on testing the null hypothesis that the VaR forecasts in question exhibit specified properties characteristic of accurate VaR forecasts. The proposed fourth method is instead based on standard forecast evaluation techniques; that is, the relative accuracy of a VaR model is gauged by how well a specified regulatory loss function is minimised by the model's probability forecasts.

2.1 Current regulatory framework

The current risk-based capital rules for the market risk exposure of large, US commercial banks, effective as of 1 January, 1998, are explicitly based on VaR estimates. The capital rules cover all assets in a bank's trading account (ie, assets carried at their current market value) as well as all foreign exchange and commodity positions wherever located. Any bank or bank holding company whose trading activity accounts for more than 10 percent of its total assets or is more than US$1 billion must hold regulatory capital against their market risk exposure.

These capital charges are based on the VaR estimates generated by banks' own VaR models using the standardising parameters of a 10-day holding period ($k = 10$) and 99 percent coverage ($\alpha = 1$). In other words, a bank's market risk capital charge is based on its forecast of the potential portfolio loss that would not be exceeded over the subsequent two week period with one percent probability. The market risk capital that bank m must hold for time $t + 1$, MRC_{t+1}^m, is set as the larger of the dollar value of $\mathrm{VaR}_t^m(10, 1)$ or a multiple of the average of the previous sixty $\mathrm{VaR}_t^m(10, 1)$ estimates in dollar terms; that is,

$$\mathrm{MCR}_{t+1}^m = \max\left[\mathrm{VaR\$}_t^m(10,\ 1);\ S_t^m \times \frac{1}{60} \sum_{i=0}^{59} \mathrm{VaR\$}_{t-i}^m(10,\ 1) \right] + SR_t^m$$

where S_t^m and SR_t^m are a multiplication factor and an additional capital charge for the portfolio's idiosyncratic credit risk, respectively.[3] Note that, under the current framework, $S_t^m \geq 3$.

The S_t^m multiplier is included in the calculation of MRC_{t+1}^m for two reasons. First, as described by Hendricks and Hirtle (1997), it adjusts the specified VaR estimates to what regulators consider to be a minimum capital requirement that reflects their concerns regarding both prudent capital standards and model accuracy.[4] Second, S_t^m is used to explicitly link the accuracy of a bank's VaR model to its capital charge. In the current regulatory framework, S_t^m is set according to the accuracy of model m's VaR estimates for a one-day holding period ($k = 1$) and 99 percent coverage level ($\alpha = 1$), denoted as $VaR_t^m(1, 1)$.

S_t^m is a step function that depends on the number of exceptions – defined as occasions when $\epsilon_{t+1} < VaR_t^m(1, 1)$ – observed over the last 250 trading days. The possible number of exceptions is divided into three zones. Within the green zone of four or fewer exceptions, a VaR model is deemed "acceptably accurate", and S_t^m remains at its minimum value of three. Within the yellow zone of five through nine exceptions, S_t^m increases incrementally with the number of exceptions. Within the red zone of 10 or more exceptions, the VaR model is deemed to be "inaccurate", and S_t^m increases to its maximum value of four. The institution must also explicitly improve its risk management system.[5]

Since capital requirements were completely determined by regulatory mandate prior to the 1996 market risk amendment, this "internal models" approach for setting market risk capital requirements indicates an important change in how regulatory oversight is conducted. Having established the formula for calculating the desired capital charges, bank regulators must now evaluate the accuracy of the VaR models used to set them. In the following section, four methods for evaluating VaR model accuracy are discussed.

2.2 Alternative evaluation methods

In accordance with the current regulatory framework and for the purposes of this chapter, the accuracy of VaR models is assessed with respect to their one-step-ahead forecasts; ie, $k = 1$. Thus, given a set of one-step-ahead VaR forecasts, regulators must determine whether the underlying model is "acceptably accurate". Three hypothesis-testing methods using different types of VaR forecasts are available; specifically, the binomial, interval forecast and distribution forecast methods. Their common premise is to determine whether the VaR forecasts in question exhibit a specified property characteristic of accurate VaR forecasts using hypothesis tests.

However, as noted by Diebold and Lopez (1996), it is unlikely that forecasts from an economic model will be fully optimal and exhibit all the properties of accurate forecasts. Thus, the evaluation of a model's forecasts based on the presence of a specific statistical property will provide only limited information regarding model accuracy. In this chapter, an evaluation method, based on the probability forecasting framework presented by Lopez (1997), is proposed. With this method, the relative accuracy of VaR models is evaluated by how well their probability forecasts minimise a regulatory loss function. Thus, this evaluation method can provide additional information on VaR model accuracy with respect to regulatory criteria, as opposed to the statistical criteria implied in the hypothesis-testing methods.

2.2.1 Evaluation of VaR estimates based on the binomial distribution

Under the current regulatory framework, banks will report their one-day VaR estimates (denoted $\text{VaR}_t^m(k, \alpha)$ or simply $\text{VaR}_t^m(\alpha)$) for $\alpha = 1$ to their regulators, who also observe whether actual portfolio losses exceed these estimates.[6] Under the assumption that the VaR estimates are accurate, such observations can be modelled as draws from an independent binomial random variable with a probability of occurrence equal to one percent or, more generally, a specified α percent. The binomial method that regulators have chosen is based on the number of times that ϵ_{t+1} is less than $\text{VaR}_t^m(\alpha)$ (denoted here as x) in a sample of size T. Accurate VaR estimates should exhibit the property that their unconditional coverage, measured by $\alpha^* = x / T$, equals the desired coverage level α. Thus, the relevant null hypothesis is $\alpha^* = \alpha$, and the appropriate likelihood ratio statistic based on the binomial distribution is

$$\text{LR}_{uc}(\alpha) = 2[\log(\alpha^{*x}(1 - \alpha^*)^{T-x}) - \log(\alpha^x(1 - \alpha)^{T-x})]$$

Note that the $\text{LR}_{uc}(\alpha)$ test of this null hypothesis is uniformly most powerful for a given T and that the statistic has an asymptotic $\chi^2(1)$ distribution. So, if we decide to set the size of the test at five percent, we would reject the null hypothesis if $\text{LR}_{uc}(\alpha) > 3.84$.[7]

However, the finite sample size and power characteristics of this test are of interest here. With respect to size, the finite sample distribution for a specific (α, T) pair may be sufficiently different from the $\chi^2(1)$ distribution that the asymptotic critical values may be inappropriate. For this chapter, the finite-sample distributions for specific (α, T) pairs are determined via simulation and compared to the asymptotic one in order to establish the actual sizes of the tests. As for power, Kupiec (1995) describes how this test generally has a limited ability to distinguish among alternative hypotheses and thus has low power, even in moderately large samples.

2.2.2 Evaluation of VaR interval forecasts

VaR estimates can clearly be viewed as interval forecasts of the lower left-hand tail of f_{t+1} at a specified coverage level α.[8] Interval forecasts can be evaluated conditionally or unconditionally; that is, forecast performance can be examined over the sample period with or without reference to the information available at each point in time. The $\mathrm{LR}_{uc}(\alpha)$ test is obviously an unconditional test since it ignores this type of information. However, in the presence of the higher-moment dynamics often found in financial time series, testing for conditional accuracy is important since interval forecasts ignoring such dynamics may have correct unconditional coverage, but may have incorrect conditional coverage at any given time. As shown in Figure 1, variance dynamics can lead to clustered exceptions that may permit correct unconditional coverage but certainly not correct conditional coverage. Thus, since the $\mathrm{LR}_{uc}(\alpha)$ test does not have power against the alternative hypothesis that the exceptions are clustered in a time-dependent fashion, it is only of limited use in the evaluation of VaR estimates.

The $\mathrm{LR}_{uc}(\alpha)$ test proposed by Christoffersen (1998) is specifically a test of correct conditional coverage. For a given coverage level α, one-step-ahead interval forecasts are formed using model m and are denoted $V_t^m(\alpha) \equiv [-\infty, \mathrm{VaR}_t^m(\alpha)]$. From these forecasts and the observed portfolio returns, the indicator variable $I_{t+1}^m(\alpha)$ is constructed as

$$I_{t+1}^m(\alpha) = \begin{cases} 1 & \text{if } \epsilon_{t+1} \in V_t^m(\alpha) \\ 0 & \text{if } \epsilon_{t+1} \notin V_t^m(\alpha) \end{cases}$$

Accurate VaR interval forecasts should exhibit the property of correct conditional coverage, which implies that the $I_{t+1}^m(\alpha)$ series must

Figure 1 GARCH(1,1)-normal process with one-step-ahead lower five percent conditional and unconditional interval forecasts. This figure graphs a realisation of 500 portfolio returns from a GARCH(1,1)-normal data generating process along with two sets of lower five percent interval forecasts. The variance dynamics are characterised as $h_{t+1} = 0.075 + 0.10\epsilon_t^2 + 0.85h_t$, which imply an unconditional variance of 1.5. The straight line is the unconditional interval forecasts based on the unconditional $N(0,1\frac{1}{2})$ distribution, and the jagged line is the conditional interval forecasts based on the true data generating process. Although both exhibit correct unconditional coverage with 25 exceptions (ie, $\alpha^* = \alpha = 5\%$), only the conditional confidence intervals exhibit correct conditional coverage or, in other words, provide five percent coverage at each point in time

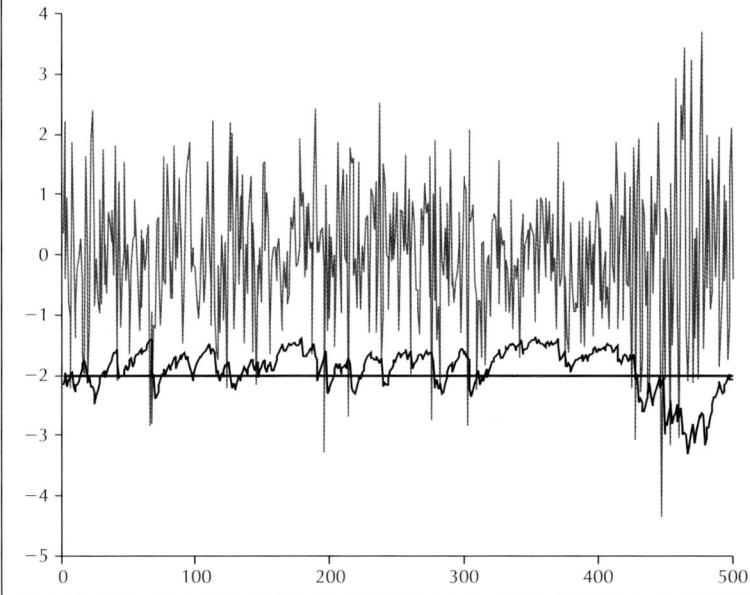

exhibit both correct unconditional coverage and serial independence. The $LR_{cc}(\alpha)$ test of this joint hypothesis is formed by combining tests of each property. The relevant test statistic is $LR_{cc}(\alpha) = LR_{uc}(\alpha) + LR_{ind}(\alpha)$, which is distributed $\chi^2(2)$.

Note that the $LR_{ind}(\alpha)$ statistic is a likelihood ratio statistic of the null hypothesis of serial independence against the alternative of first-order Markov dependence.[9] The likelihood function under this alternative hypothesis is $L_A = (1 - \pi_{01})^{T_{00}} \pi_{01}^{T_{01}} (1 - \pi_{11})^{T_{10}} \pi_{11}^{T_{11}}$, where the T_{ij} notation denotes the number of observations in state j

after having been in state i the period before, $\pi_{01} = T_{01}/(T_{00} + T_{01})$ and $\pi_{11} = T_{11}/(T_{10} + T_{11})$.[10] Under the null hypothesis of independence, $\pi_{11} = I_{11}/(T_{10} + T_{11})$, and the relevant likelihood function is $L_0 = (1 - \pi)^{T_{00}+T_{10}} \pi^{T_{01}+T_{11}}$, where $\pi = (T_{01} + T_{11})/T$. Thus, the relevant test statistic is formed as $\mathrm{LR}_{ind}(\alpha) = 2[\log L_A - \log L_0]$, which is distributed $\chi^2(1)$.

2.2.3 Evaluation of VaR distribution forecasts

Since VaR models are generally characterised by their forecast of f_{t+k}, Crnkovic and Drachman (1996) propose to evaluate such models based on their entire forecasted distributions. The object of interest in this evaluation method is the observed quantile q_{t+1}^m, which is the quantile under f_{t+1}^m in which the observed return ϵ_{t+1} actually falls; that is,

$$q_{t+1}^m(\epsilon_{t+1}) = \int_{-\infty}^{\epsilon_{t+1}} f_{t+1}^m(x)\mathrm{d}x$$

This evaluation method tests whether the observed quantiles derived under a model's distribution forecasts exhibit the properties of observed quantiles from accurate distribution forecasts. Specifically, since the quantiles of random draws from a distribution are uniformly distributed over the unit interval, the observed quantiles should be independent and uniformly distributed.

Crnkovic and Drachman (1996) suggest that these two properties be examined separately and thus propose two separate hypothesis tests.[11] As in the interval forecast method, the independence of the observed quantiles indicates whether the VaR model captures the higher-order dynamics in the return series. To test for this property, the authors suggest the use of the BDS statistic (see Brock *et al* (1991)). However, in this chapter, the focus is on their proposed test of uniform distribution.[12] The test of the uniform distribution of the q_{t+1}^m series is based on the Kupier statistic, which measures the deviation between two cumulative distribution functions.[13] Denoting $D_m(x)$ as the cumulative distribution function of the observed quantiles, the Kupier statistic for the deviation of $D_m(x)$ from the uniform distribution is

$$K_m = \max(D_m(x) - x) + \max(x - D_m(x))$$

where $x \in [0, 1]$. Note that for this chapter, the finite sample distribution of K_m as generated in the following simulation exercise is used.[14] In general, this testing procedure is relatively data-intensive, and the authors note that test results begin to seriously deteriorate with fewer than 500 observations.

2.2.4 Evaluation of VaR probability forecasts

The evaluation method proposed here is based on the probability forecasting framework presented by Lopez (1997). In contrast to the hypothesis-testing methods discussed above, this method is based on standard forecast evaluation tools and gauges the accuracy of VaR models by how well their probability forecasts minimise a regulatory loss function. Thus, by directly incorporating regulatory loss functions into the forecast evaluations, this method provides useful information on the performance of VaR models with respect to regulatory criteria as opposed to the purely statistical criteria implied by the hypothesis-testing methods.

The proposed evaluation method incorporates the interests of the regulators (or, more generally, forecast evaluators) into the forecast evaluation in two ways.[15] First, the event of interest to the regulator must be specified.[16] Thus, instead of focusing exclusively on a fixed quantile of the forecasted distributions or on the entire distributions themselves, this method allows the evaluation of VaR models based upon the regions of the distributions that are of most interest. In this chapter, three types of regulatory events are considered, although many are possible.

The first type of event is whether an observed ϵ_{t+1} lies in the lower tail of its unconditional distribution based on past observations, denoted $\hat{F}$. Specifically, the lower α percent quantile of $\hat{F}$ is determined, and probability forecasts of whether subsequent returns will be less than it are generated. In mathematical terms, the relevant probability forecasts, conditional on the information available at time t, are

$$P_t^m = \Pr\left(\epsilon_{t+1} < CV(\alpha, \hat{F})\right) = \int_{-\infty}^{CV(\alpha, \hat{F})} f_{t+1}^m(x)dx$$

where $CV(\alpha, \hat{F}) = \hat{F}^{-1}(\alpha / 100)$ is the unconditional quantile of interest.

The second type of event is a portfolio loss of a fixed magnitude; that is, regulators may be interested in determining how well a VaR model can forecast a portfolio loss of p percent of y_t over a one-day period. The corresponding probability forecasts generated from model m, conditional on the information available at time t, are

$$P_t^m = \Pr\left[y_{t+1} < \left(1 - \frac{p}{100}\right)y_t\right] = \Pr\left[y_t + \epsilon_{t+1} < \left(1 - \frac{p}{100}\right)y_t\right]$$

$$= \Pr\left[\epsilon_{t+1} < \frac{-p}{100}y_t\right] =$$

The third type of regulatory event corresponds to whether a bank's capital is sufficient to cover portfolio losses (in dollar terms) over a certain time period. Suppose an amount of C dollars is set aside to cover the expected maximum portfolio loss that might occur, relative to Y_τ, over the period $[t + 1, t + T]$ for $\tau \leq t$. Capital C is sufficient to cover losses if $Y_i > Y_\tau - C \ \forall \ i \in [t + 1, t + T]$. To translate this inequality into portfolio returns, the equivalent expression $Y_i > Y_\tau e^{-\gamma(C)}$ is used, which implies that $y_i > y_\tau - \gamma(C)$. A regulator may be interested in a VaR model's ability to forecast, conditional on the information at time t, whether this capital level was not sufficient to cover portfolio losses. The corresponding probability forecast generated from model m is then

$$P_t^m = \Pr(y_{t+1} - y_\tau < -\gamma(C)) = \Pr(y_t + \epsilon_{t+1} - y_\tau < -\gamma(C))$$

$$= \Pr(\epsilon_{t+1} < -\gamma(C) + y_\tau - y_t) = \int_{-\infty}^{-\gamma(C)+y_\tau-y_t} f_{t+1}^m(x)dx$$

Note that this type of event does not depend on how the capital level C is determined; for example, C may be mandated by the regulators or completely determined by the bank. An interesting example of the latter case is the "precommitment" approach in which a bank reports C to the regulator and is penalised if the dollar value of portfolio losses over the following quarter at any time exceeds C; see Kupiec and O'Brien (1995) for further discussion.

The second way of incorporating regulatory interests into this evaluation method is the selection of the loss function used to evaluate the probability forecasts. Regulators should select a loss function that most directly represents their concerns. For example, the quadratic probability score (QPS), developed by Brier (1950), specifically measures the accuracy of probability forecasts over time. The QPS is the analog of mean squared error for probability forecasts and thus implies a quadratic loss function.[17] The QPS for model m over a sample of size T is

$$QPS_m = \frac{1}{T} \sum_{t=1}^{T} 2(P_t^m - R_{t+1})^2$$

where R_{t+1} is an indicator variable that equals one if the specified event occurs and zero otherwise. Note that $QPS_m \in [0, 2]$ and has a negative orientation such that smaller values indicate more accurate forecasts. Thus, since accurate VaR models are expected to generate lower QPS values than inaccurate models, QPS_m values closer to zero should indicate the relative accuracy of the VaR model. The QPS measure is used in this chapter because it reflects the regulator's stated goal of evaluating a bank's VaR model based on the accuracy of its VaR estimates.

A key property of the QPS is that it is a strictly proper scoring rule; that is, forecasters must report their actual probability forecasts to minimise their expected QPS score. To see the importance of this property for the purpose of regulatory oversight, consider the following definition. Let P_t^m be the actual probability forecast generated by a bank's VaR model, and let $S(p_t, j)$ denote a scoring rule that assigns a numerical score to a probability forecast p_t based on whether the event occurs ($j = 1$) or not ($j = 0$). The reporting bank's expected score conditional on its model is

$$E[S(p_t, j)|m] = P_t^m S(p_t, 1) + (1 - P_t^m)S(p_t, 0)$$

The scoring rule S is strictly proper if $E[S(P_t^m, j)|m] < E[S(p_t, j)|m]$ $\forall\, p_t \neq P_t^m$; that is, the expected score can only be minimised by reporting the actual probability forecast generated by the model m. Thus, truthful reporting is explicitly encouraged since the bank receives no benefit from modifying its actual forecasts.[18] This property is obviously important in the case of a regulator evaluating VaR models that it may not directly observe.

An important drawback of the probability forecast evaluation method is that the properties of the QPS value for a particular model and specified event cannot be easily determined *a priori*, as opposed to the three aforementioned test statistics whose distributions are known. Thus, this evaluation method cannot be used, as the other methods, to statistically classify a VaR model as "acceptably accurate" or "inaccurate" in an absolute sense. Instead, it can be used to monitor the relative accuracy of a VaR model over time and in relation to other VaR models, which should be useful information for both model users and regulators. Although there are challenges to making this method operational, regulators may use this information on the relative accuracy of VaR models to complement that of the hypothesis-testing methods.

3 SIMULATION EXERCISE

The following simulation exercise gauges the ability of the four VaR evaluation methods to avoid model misclassification. For the three hypothesis-testing methods, this is a direct analysis of the power of these tests, ie, determining the probability with which the tests reject the specified null hypothesis when in fact it is incorrect. If the power of a test is low, then it is very likely that the corresponding evaluation method will misclassify an inaccurate VaR model as "acceptably accurate". With respect to the probability forecast method, its ability to correctly classify VaR models is gauged by how frequently the QPS value for the true data generating process is smaller than that of the alternative models. Further analysis of the QPS values using hypothesis-testing techniques proposed by Diebold and Mariano (1995) permit a power comparison across the four evaluation methods.

The first step in this simulation exercise is determining what type of portfolio to analyse. VaR models are designed to be used with typically complicated portfolios that contain a variety of financial assets, possibly even derivatives. However, for the purposes of this exercise, the portfolio value in question is simplified to be $y_{t+1} = y_t + \epsilon_{t+1}$, where $\epsilon_{t+1}|\Omega_t \sim f_{t+1}$. This specification of y_{t+1} is representative of linear, deterministic conditional mean specifications. It is only for portfolios with nonlinear components, such as derivative instruments, that this choice presents inference problems; further research along these lines, as by Pritsker (1997) and Berkowitz (1998), is needed.

The simulation exercise is conducted in four distinct, yet interrelated, sections. In the first two sections, the emphasis is on the shape of the f_{t+1} distribution. To examine performance under different distributional assumptions, the simulations are conducted by setting f_{t+1} to the standard normal distribution and a t-distribution with six degrees of freedom, which has fatter tails than the standard normal. The next two sections examine the performance of the evaluation methods in the presence of variance dynamics. Specifically, innovations from a GARCH(1,1)-normal process and a GARCH(1,1)-$t(6)$ process are used.

In each section, the true data generating process (DGP) is one of the seven VaR models examined and is designated as the true model. Traditional power analysis of a hypothesis test is conducted by varying a particular parameter and determining whether the corresponding incorrect null hypothesis is rejected; such changes in parameters generate what are usually known as local alternatives. However, in this analysis, we examine alternative VaR models that are not all nested, but are commonly used in practice. Such models are here considered to be reasonable "local" alternatives, although no definitive metric is used to support this claim. For example, a popular type of VaR model specifies the variance of f_{t+1}^m, denoted h_{t+1}^m, as an exponentially weighted, moving average of squared innovations; that is,

$$h_{t+1}^m(\lambda) = (1 - \lambda)\sum_{i=0}^{\infty} \lambda^i \epsilon_{t-1}^2 = \lambda h_t^m + (1 - \lambda)\epsilon_t^2$$

This VaR model, a version of which is used in the well-known *RiskMetrics* calculations (see JP Morgan 1995), is calibrated here by setting λ equal to 0.97 or 0.99, which imply a high-degree of persistence in variance.[19] A description of the alternative models used in each section of the simulation exercise follows.

For the first section, the true DGP is the standard normal, ie, $\epsilon_{t+1}|\Omega_t \sim N(0,1)$. The six alternative models examined are normal distributions with variances of 0.5, 0.75, 1.25 and 1.5 as well as the two calibrated, exponentially weighted VaR models with normal distributions. For the second section, the true DGP is a $t(6)$ distribution; ie, $\epsilon_{t+1}|\Omega_t \sim t(6)$. The six alternative models are two normal distributions with variances of 1 and 1.5 (the same variance as the true DGP) and the two calibrated models with normal distributions as well as with $t(6)$ distributions.

For the latter two sections, variance dynamics are introduced by using conditional heteroscedasticity of the GARCH form; ie, $h_{t+1} = 0.075 + 0.10\epsilon_t^2 + 0.85h_t$, which has an unconditional variance of 1.5. The only difference between the DGP's in these two sections is the chosen distributional form. For the third section, $\epsilon_{t+1}|\Omega_t \sim N(0, h_{t+1})$, and for the fourth section, $\epsilon_{t+1}|\Omega_t \sim t(h_{t+1}, 6)$. The six alternative models examined in these two sections are the homoscedastic models of the $N(0, 1)$, $N(0, 1.5)$, and $t(6)$ distributions and the heteroscedastic models of the two calibrated models with normal innovations and the GARCH model with the other distributional form.

In all of the sections, the simulation runs are structured identically. The results are based on 1,000 simulation runs. For each run, the simulated y_{t+1} series is generated using the chosen DGP; for example, the standard normal in the first section. After 1,000 initial observations and 2,500 in-sample observations, the seven VaR models are used to generate the specified one-step-ahead VaR forecasts for the next 500 out-of-sample observations. In the current regulatory framework, the evaluation period is set at 250 observations, but 500 observations are used here since the distribution forecast and probability forecast evaluation methods are data-intensive.

The VaR forecasts from the alternative models are then evaluated using the appropriate evaluation methods. For the binomial and interval forecast methods, VaR estimates for coverage levels $\alpha = [1, 5, 10]$ are examined. For the distribution forecast method, the entire forecasted distribution is examined, and for the probability forecast method, the three types of regulatory events previously discussed are examined. Specifically, for the first event, the empirical distribution function $\hat{F}$ is based on the 2,500 in-sample observations, and the desired α percent critical values CV(α, $\hat{F}$) are determined. The probability forecasts of whether the observed returns in the out-of-sample period will be less than CV(α, $\hat{F}$) are generated for $\alpha = [1, 5, 10]$, and in the tables, these simulation results are labeled QPSe1(α). For the second event, a fixed one percent loss of log portfolio value is set as the one-day decline of interest,[20] and probability forecasts of whether the observed returns exceed that percentage loss are generated as

$$P_t^m = \Pr(y_{t+1} < 0.99 y_t) = \Pr(y_t + \epsilon_{t+1} < 0.99 y_t)$$
$$= \Pr(\epsilon_{t+1} < -0.01 y_t)$$

In the tables, these simulation results are labeled QPSe2.

For the third event, $\gamma(C)$ is 10 percent of the last in-sample log portfolio value denoted y_0; ie, $\gamma(C) = 0.1 \times y_0$.[21] The choice of 10 percent is related to certain regulatory reserve requirements. Thus, the probability forecast of interest is

$$P_t^m = \Pr(y_{t+1} - y_0 < -\gamma(C)) = \Pr(y_t + \epsilon_{t+1} - y_0 < -0.1 y_0)$$
$$= \Pr(\epsilon_{t+1} < 0.9 y_0 - y_t)$$

In the tables, these simulation results are labeled QPSe3. Note that, given the nature of this event (ie, whether a stochastic process ever dips below a specified barrier), it is likely the event may never occur in certain simulations. In such cases, the probability forecasts for all the models are extremely small and, to insure efficient computer simulation, are rounded down to zero whenever $P_t^m < 0.0001$. However, this adjustment can lead to QPS values exactly equal to zero, which must be accounted for in the analysis of the results. To do so, such zero-value simulation results are removed from the analysis, and the QPS analysis is based on the smaller number of simulations. The rationale behind examining these adjusted results is that model accuracy cannot be examined well if the event in question does not occur. Overall, the inference drawn from this type of regulatory event will generally be less useful due to the lower frequency of occurrence.

The main object of interest from these simulation results for the probability forecasting method is the frequency with which the QPS value for the true model is less than that for the alternative model. If this frequency is high (say, greater than 75%), then this evaluation method is generally capable of gauging model accuracy and can then be used to monitor the relative performance of VaR models over time and across models. However, since in current practice regulators have only one set of forecasts to work with, it is worthwhile to conduct a power analysis of this method to make it comparable to the other methods. To do so, the differences in QPS values, denoted $d_m = (2/T)\Sigma_{t=1}^{T}(P_t^{\text{true}} - R_{t+1})^2 - (P_t^m - R_{t+1})^2$, are

examined using techniques proposed by Diebold and Mariano
(1995). Specifically, the null hypothesis that $d_m \geq 0$ is tested using
the statistic

$$S = \frac{d_m}{\sqrt{\hat{\sigma}_m^2 / T}} \sim N(0, 1)$$

where $\hat{\sigma}_m^2$ is an estimate of the sample variance that is robust to possible time-dependent heteroscedasticity. (Note that to test this
hypothesis, the differences in QPS values must be covariance stationary, a condition determined empirically for this exercise.)

4 SIMULATION RESULTS

The simulation results are organised below with respect to the four
sections of the exercise. Three general points can be made regarding
the results. First, the power of the hypothesis-testing methods against
the incorrect null hypotheses implied by the alternative VaR models
varies considerably. In some cases, the power of the tests is high
(greater than 75%), but in the majority of the cases examined, the
power is poor (less than 50%) to moderate (between 50% and 75%).
The results indicate that these evaluation methods are thus quite
likely to misclassify inaccurate models as "acceptably accurate".

Second, the probability forecast method seems capable of gauging
the accuracy of alternative VaR models relative to the true DGP. In
pairwise comparisons between the true model and an alternative
model, the QPS value for the true model is lower than that for the
alternative model in the majority of the cases examined. However,
further analysis of this method's power indicates that this performance is not superior to that of the three hypothesis-testing methods
in all cases. Even though the proposed method is only as capable of
differentiating between VaR models as the other methods, its ability
to directly incorporate regulatory loss functions into model evaluations make it a useful complement to the statistical methods currently used in the regulatory evaluation of VaR models.

Third, for the cases in which variance dynamics are introduced,
all four evaluation methods generally seem more sensitive to misspecifications of the distributional form than to misspecifications of
the variance dynamics. That is, the four methods seem more capable of correctly classifying as inaccurate VaR models with correct

Table 1 Finite-sample critical values for $LR_{uc}(\alpha)$, $LR_{cc}(\alpha)$, and K test statistics

	Test rejection size 5%
Asymptotic $\chi^2(1)$	6.635
$LR_{uc}(1)$	4.813
	(7.5%)
$LR_{uc}(5)$	3.888
	(6.3%)
$LR_{uc}(10)$	4.090
	(6.2%)
Asymptotic $\chi^2(2)$	5.992
$LR_{cc}(1)$	4.801
	(1.8%)
$LR_{cc}(5)$	5.773
	(4.7%)
$LR_{cc}(10)$	6.237
	(5.5%)
K	0.0700

The $LR_{uc}(\alpha)$ statistic tests the null hypothesis that the VaR estimates $VaR_t^m(1, \alpha)$ exhibit correct unconditional coverage. The $LR_{cc}(\alpha)$ statistic tests the null hypothesis that the VaR estimates $VaR_t^m(1, \alpha)$ exhibit correct conditional coverage. (Note that α is defined here as one minus the usual confidence level; thus, the commonly used 99% VaR estimates correspond to a = 1.) The finite-sample critical values for the $LR_{uc}(\alpha)$ and $LR_{cc}(\alpha)$ test statistics at the five percent significance level are based on 10,000 simulations of sample size $T = 500$. The percentages in parentheses are the quantiles that correspond to the listed asymptotic critical values under the finite-sample distributions. The K statistic tests the null hypothesis that the empirical quantiles associated with VaR model m are uniformly distributed. The finite-sample critical values for the K test statistic are based on 1,000 simulations of sample size $T = 500$.

variance dynamics and incorrect distributional shape than models with incorrect variance dynamics and correct distributional shape. Thus, these evaluation methods are likely to allow regulators to more readily detect when banks are using inappropriate distributional assumptions in their VaR models. Further simulation work must be conducted to determine the robustness of this result.

As previously mentioned, an important issue in examining the simulation results for the statistical evaluation methods is the finite-sample size of the underlying hypothesis tests. Table 1 presents the finite-sample critical values for the three statistics examined in this chapter. For the two LR tests, the quantiles corresponding to the asymptotic critical values under the finite-sample distribution are also presented. The finite-sample critical values are based on 10,000 simulations of sample size $T = 500$ and the corresponding α. Although discrepancies are present, the differences are small. The finite-sample critical values in Table 1 are used in the power analysis that follows. The critical values for the Kupier statistic are based on 1,000 simulations of sample size $T = 500$. Note that the critical values used with respect to the Diebold–Mariano statistics are the asymptotic normal ones since the finite-sample power properties of a normal distribution for $T = 500$ should be very close to the asymptotic ones.

4.1 Simulation results for the homoscedastic standard normal data generating process

Table 2, Panel A presents the power analysis of the three hypothesis-testing methods for a fixed test size of five percent. For the homoscedastic alternative models in the first four columns, the power results vary considerably. The power of the tests is highest for the $N(0, 0.5)$ and $N(0, 1.5)$ models that are the furthest away in variance from the true $N(0, 1)$ model. However, as this difference is diminished for the $N(0, 0.75)$ and $N(0, 1.25)$ models, the power results drop considerably, although the K test retains moderately high power. For all three tests, asymmetry arises across these alternatives; that is, the tests have relatively more power against the alternatives with lower variances than against those with higher variances. The reason for this seems to be that draws from the true DGP exceed the VaR estimates of the lower variance models more frequently and thus lead to a higher rejection rate of the false null hypothesis. With respect to the calibrated heteroscedastic models in the last two columns, the three tests have no power, due to the fact that, even though heteroscedasticity is introduced, these models and their associated empirical quantiles are quite similar to the true DGP.

Table 2, Panel B contains the five sets of comparative accuracy results for the probability forecast method. Each row presents, for each defined regulatory event, the percentage of simulations for which the true model's QPS value is lower than that of the alternative model. In most cases, these results indicate that the QPS value for the true model is lower a high percentage of the time. Specifically, the homoscedastic alternatives are clearly found to be

Table 2 Simulation results for the homoscedastic standard normal DGP (units: percent)

	Model $N(0, \frac{1}{2})$	$N(0, \frac{3}{4})$	$N(0, 1\frac{1}{4})$	$N(0, 1\frac{1}{2})$	$N\lambda(97)$	$N\lambda(99)$
Panel A. Power of the $LR_{uc}(\alpha)$, $LR_{cc}(\alpha)$ and K Tests against alternative VaR models[a]						
$LR_{uc}(1)$	99.9	54.6	32.3	70.0	3.3	6.5
$LR_{uc}(5)$	99.9	68.3	51.5	94.2	2.7	9.2
$LR_{uc}(10)$	99.9	61.5	47.4	93.1	2.3	7.3
$LR_{cc}(1)$	99.9	56.6	33.2	70.4	4.2	8.0
$LR_{cc}(5)$	99.9	64.3	40.3	89.3	3.2	9.4
$LR_{cc}(10)$	99.8	53.0	36.5	86.5	3.2	6.8
K	100	87.7	60.6	99.3	1.6	2.3
Panel B. Accuracy of VaR models using the probability forecast method[b]						
QPSe1(1)	86.4	76.5	83.1	97.2	78.3	66.1
QPSe1(5)	98.9	84.4	82.5	97.9	80.5	74.3
QPSe1(10)	99.6	89.5	82.9	95.3	81.2	76.6
QPSe2	94.0	78.0	64.1	72.7	67.5	68.6
QPSe3[c]	57.6	48.5	66.4	73.6	60.1	60.2
Panel C. Power of the probability forecast method using the Diebold-Mariano test[a]						
QPSe1(1)	42.8	30.3	52.3	75.0	50.6	39.7
QPSe1(5)	84.2	48.3	51.2	71.1	37.5	34.8
QPSe1(10)	89.1	55.7	34.6	64.6	45.8	35.3
QPSe2	64.6	47.3	38.6	43.9	37.1	31.3
QPSe3[c]	26.1	13.9	44.4	47.5	25.0	23.8

Table 2 contains the simulation results for the homoscedastic standard normal DGP; that is, $\epsilon_{t+1}|\Omega_t \sim N(0, 1)$. The alternative models are normal distributions with variances of 0.5, 0.75, 1.25 and 1.5 (denoted $N(0, \frac{1}{2})$, $N(0, \frac{3}{4})$, $N(0, 1\frac{1}{4})$ and $N(0, 1\frac{1}{2})$, respectively) and normal distributions whose variances are exponentially weighted averages of the squared innovations calibrated using $\lambda = 0.97$ and $\lambda = 0.99$ (denoted $N\lambda(97)$ and $N\lambda(99)$, respectively). The results are based on 1,000 simulations.

Panel A presents the percentage of simulations for which the null hypothesis corresponding to each row is rejected with the test size set at the five percent level. If a test exhibits power against an alternative model, then this percentage should be high. The $LR_{uc}(\alpha)$ rows correspond to the binomial method and examine the null hypothesis that the VaR estimates have correct unconditional coverage at the α percent level. The $LR_{cc}(\alpha)$ rows correspond to the interval forecast method and examine the null hypothesis that the VaR estimates have correct conditional coverage at the α percent level. The K row corresponds to the distribution forecast method and examines the null hypothesis that the observed quantiles are uniformly distributed.

Panel B presents the percentage of simulations for which the QPS value for the true DGP is less than that of the alternative VaR model. If this method is capable of distinguishing between the true DGP and an alternative model, then this percentage should be high. The QPSe1(α) rows correspond to the QPS values for the probability forecasts $P_t^m = \Pr(\epsilon_{t+1} \leq CV(\alpha, \hat{F}))$, where $CV(\alpha, \hat{F})$ is the α percent quantile of the empirical cumulative distribution function $\hat{F}$. The QPSe2 row corresponds to the QPS values for the probability forecasts. The QPSe3 row corresponds to the QPS values for the probability forecasts $P_t^m = \Pr(y_{t+1} < 0.99y_t)$. The QPSe3 row corresponds to the QPS values for the probability forecasts $P_t^m = \Pr(y_{t+1} - y_0 < -\gamma(C))$, where $-\gamma(C)$ is the rate of return that would reduce Y_0 to the selected capital level C.

Panel C presents the percentage of simulations for which the null hypothesis that the QPS value for the true DGP is greater than or equal to that of the alternative model is rejected at the five percent level. If a test exhibits power against an alternative model, then this percentage should be high.
[a]The size of the tests is set at five percent.
[b]Each row represents the percentage of simulations for which the alternative model had a higher QPS value than the true DGP.
[c]The QPSe3 row has removed from it the simulations for which the QPS value of the true DGP for the third event is rounded down to zero; ie, 23.1% of the simulations.

inaccurate with respect to the true model, and the heteroscedastic alternatives only slightly less so. Note that, as expected, the adjusted results for the third event are less sharp than for the other events, mainly due to its lower frequency of occurrence. To conduct a comparable power analysis, Panel C presents the percentage of simulations for which the null hypothesis that $d_m \geq 0$ is correctly rejected at the five percent level. Using this stricter criteria, this method's power is comparable to that of the other three methods. Overall, however, this method does seem to provide information on the relative accuracy of VaR models for this simple DGP.

4.2 Simulation results for the homoscedastic $t(6)$ data generating process

Table 3, Panel A presents the power analysis of the hypothesis-testing methods. Overall, the power results are poor for the two sets of LR tests. In the majority of cases, the alternative models are incorrectly classified as "acceptably accurate" a large percentage of the time. With respect to the homoscedastic models, both LR tests generally exhibit moderate to high power against the N(0, 1) model at low values of α, but poor results for the N(0, 1.5) model, which has the same variance as the true DGP. The results for the K test are basically indistinguishable and moderate across these two models. With respect to the heteroscedastic models in the last four columns, the power of the LR tests against these alternatives is generally low with differences between the sets of normal and $t(6)$ alternatives occurring at high values of α. However, the K test clearly has more power over the models based on the $t(6)$ distribution mainly because the incorrect variance dynamics create conditional $t(6)$ distributions much more different from the true DGP than the conditional normal distributions.

Table 3, Panel B contains the comparative accuracy results for the probability forecast method. Overall, the results indicate that a moderate to high percentage of the simulations have QPS values for the alternative models that are greater than those of the true model. With respect to the homoscedastic models, the QPS values for the N(0, 1) model are more frequently higher than the true model than for the N(0, 1.5) model, which has the same unconditional variance as the true model. With respect to the heteroscedastic models, the two models based on the $t(6)$ distribution are more clearly classified as

Table 3 Simulation results for the homoscedastic $t(6)$ DGP (units: percent)

Model	$N(0, \frac{1}{2})$	$N(0, 1)$	$N\lambda(97)$	$N\lambda(99)$	$t\lambda(97)$	$t\lambda(99)$
Panel A. Power of the $LR_{uc}(\alpha)$, $LR_{cc}(\alpha)$ and K tests against alternative VaR models[a]						
$LR_{uc}(1)$	13.0	86.9	19.6	25.3	21.2	18.1
$LR_{uc}(5)$	11.5	62.1	3.8	3.1	68.1	52.7
$LR_{uc}(10)$	25.7	35.5	13.9	8.0	73.9	60.0
$LR_{cc}(1)$	14.8	89.4	20.7	15.8	26.0	33.1
$LR_{cc}(5)$	6.1	58.2	2.3	3.7	51.0	62.9
$LR_{cc}(10)$	17.3	29.9	8.7	14.0	61.2	70.9
K	69.5	49.8	57.0	64.4	97.6	98.7
Panel B. Accuracy of VaR models using the probability forecast method[b]						
QPSe1(1)	68.1	84.9	79.1	76.6	96.3	91.0
QPSe1(5)	64.5	88.4	90.5	79.0	98.2	95.2
QPSe1(10)	76.6	79.2	90.0	80.9	97.2	94.2
QPSe2	71.7	76.2	79.7	80.4	84.0	84.1
QPSe3[c]	52.3	48.5	55.1	55.9	74.3	73.1
Panel C. Power of the probability forecast method using the Diebold–Mariano test[a]						
QPSe1(1)	26.0	40.6	37.9	30.9	73.2	67.1
QPSe1(5)	19.6	51.4	50.0	39.0	76.1	67.6
QPSe1(10)	41.4	43.1	63.3	42.2	65.3	69.0
QPSe2	30.6	18.0	44.2	39.6	47.1	47.3
QPSe3[c]	32.4	18.2	31.6	25.7	40.4	42.6

Table 3 contains the simulation results for the homoscedastic $t(6)$ DGP; that is, $\epsilon_{t+1}|\Omega_t \sim t(6)$. The alternative models are normal distributions with variances of 0.5 and 1 (denoted $N(0, \frac{1}{2})$ and $N(0, 1)$, respectively); normal distributions whose variances are exponentially weighted averages of the squared innovations calibrated using $\lambda = 0.97$ and $\lambda = 0.99$ (denoted $N\lambda(97)$ and $N\lambda(99)$, respectively); and $t(6)$ distributions with the same calibrated variances (denoted $t\lambda(97)$ and $t\lambda(99)$, respectively). The results are based on 1,000 simulations.
  Panel A presents the percentage of simulations for which the null hypothesis corresponding to each row is rejected with the test size set at the five percent level. If a test exhibits power against an alternative model, then this percentage should be high. The $LR_{uc}(\alpha)$ rows correspond to the binomial method and examine the null hypothesis that the VaR estimates have correct unconditional coverage at the α percent level. The $LR_{cc}(\alpha)$ rows correspond to the interval forecast method and examine the null hypothesis that the VaR estimates have correct conditional coverage at the α percent level. The K row corresponds to the distribution forecast method and examines the null hypothesis that the observed quantiles are uniformly distributed.
  Panel B presents the percentage of simulations for which the QPS value for the true DGP is less than that of the alternative VaR model. If this method is capable of distinguishing between the true DGP and an alternative model, then this percentage should be high. The QPSe1(α) rows correspond to the QPS values for the probability forecasts $P_t^m = \Pr(\epsilon_{t+1} < CV(\alpha, \hat{F}))$, where $CV(\alpha, \hat{F})$ is the α percent quantile of the empirical cumulative distribution function $\hat{F}$. The QPSe2 row corresponds to the QPS values for the probability forecasts $P_t^m = \Pr(y_{t+1} < 0.99y_t)$. The QPSe3 row corresponds to the QPS values for the probability forecasts $P_t^m = \Pr(y_{t+1} - y_0 < -\gamma(C))$, where $-\gamma(C)$ is the rate of return that would reduce Y_0 to the selected capital level C.
  Panel C presents the percentage of simulations for which the null hypothesis that the QPS value for the true DGP is greater than or equal to that of the alternative model is rejected at the five percent level. If a test exhibits power against an alternative model, then this percentage should be high.
[a] The size of the tests is set at five percent.
[b] Each row represents the percentage of simulations for which the alternative model had a higher QPS value than the true DGP.
[c] The QPSe3 row has removed from it the simulations for which the QPS value of the true DGP for the third event is rounded down to zero; ie, 11.8% of the simulations.

inaccurate than the two normal models, as in Panel A. Note that, as expected, the adjusted results for the third event are less sharp than for the other events due to its lower frequency of occurrence, except for calibrated models with the *t*-distribution. The power results presented in Panel C mirror these results and are generally low to moderate, as are those in Panel A.

4.3 Simulation results for the GARCH(1,1)-normal data generating process

As presented in Table 4, Panel A, the power results of the hypothesis-testing methods seem to be closely linked to the differences between distributional assumptions. With respect to the heteroscedastic models, these tests have low power against the calibrated VaR models based on the normal distribution, since these smoothed variances are similar to the GARCH variances of the true DGP. However, the results for the GARCH-*t*(6) model vary greatly according to α. Both LR statistics have high power at low α, while at higher α and for the K statistical tests, the tests have low to moderate power. These results indicate that these tests have little power against alternative models characterised by close approximations of the true variance dynamics but have better power with respect to models with incorrect distributional assumptions, especially further into the tails. With respect to the homoscedastic VaR models, these methods are generally able to differentiate between the $N(0, 1)$ and $t(6)$ models. However, the tests have little power against the $N(0, 1.5)$ model, which matches the true model's unconditional variance.

Overall, the results in Table 4, Panel B indicate that the probability forecast method is generally capable of differentiating between the true and the alternative VaR models. With respect to the homoscedastic models, the loss functions are minimised for the true model a high percentage of the time in all, but the third, regulatory events. For the heteroscedastic models, this method most clearly classifies the GARCH-*t*(6) model as inaccurate, even though it has the exactly correct variance dynamics. The two calibrated normal models are only moderately classified as inaccurate. Note, again, that the adjusted results for the third event are not as clear due to its less frequent occurrence. As before, the power results presented in Panel C are poor to moderate and generally in line

Table 4 Simulation results for the GARCH(1,1)-normal DGP (units: percent)

	Model $N(0, \frac{1}{2})$	$N(0, 1)$	$t(6)$	$N\lambda(97)$	$N\lambda(99)$	GARCH-t
Panel A. Power of the $LR_{uc}(\alpha)$, $LR_{cc}(\alpha)$ and K tests against alternative VaR models[a]						
$LR_{uc}(1)$	22.7	73.9	71.3	4.3	4.8	91.6
$LR_{uc}(5)$	30.7	73.9	72.0	5.4	6.0	81.7
$LR_{uc}(10)$	29.0	65.7	60.3	5.2	5.7	50.0
$LR_{cc}(1)$	29.3	77.2	72.8	6.1	10.9	91.6
$LR_{cc}(5)$	33.5	73.5	71.1	7.2	12.4	72.9
$LR_{cc}(10)$	29.8	63.6	60.6	6.6	11.2	39.0
K	38.6	80.6	67.6	5.5	5.4	50.5
Panel B. accuracy of VaR models using the probability forecast method[b]						
QPSe1(1)	60.7	66.8	79.2	50.1	51.0	93.0
QPSe1(5)	89.0	92.1	86.4	64.0	66.5	88.8
QPSe1(10)	88.9	93.3	89.9	61.6	66.1	77.1
QPSe2	82.7	85.2	85.1	60.4	63.7	64.1
QPSe3[c]	57.3	49.7	60.1	53.1	52.8	73.1
Panel C. Power of the probability forecast method using the Diebold-Mariano test[a]						
QPSe1(1)	32.9	38.4	50.6	33.8	37.1	56.5
QPSe1(5)	60.0	64.5	56.5	46.4	52.7	60.8
QPSe1(10)	65.3	66.0	63.0	53.2	61.5	53.9
QPSe2	50.6	65.9	54.4	35.1	47.4	35.0
QPSe3[c]	24.1	22.7	28.6	23.9	27.3	55.1

Table 4 contains the simulation results for the heteroscedastic GARCH(1,1)-normal DGP; that is, $\epsilon_{t+1}|\Omega_t \sim N(0, h_{t+1})$, where $h_{t+1} = 0.075 + 0.10\epsilon_t^2 + 0.85h_t$. The alternative models are normal distributions with variances of 1.5 and 1 (denoted $N(0, \frac{3}{2})$ and $N(0, 1)$, respectively); a t-distribution with 6 degrees of freedom (denoted $t(6)$); normal distributions whose variances are exponentially weighted averages of the squared innovations calibrated using $\lambda = 0.97$ and $\lambda = 0.99$ (denoted $N\lambda(97)$ and $N\lambda(99)$, respectively); and a GARCH(1,1) process with the same variance dynamics as the DGP and a $t(6)$ distribution (denoted GARCH-t). The results are based on 1,000 simulations.

Panel A presents the percentage of simulations for which the null hypothesis corresponding to each row is rejected with the test size set at the five percent level. If a test exhibits power against an alternative model, then this percentage should be high. The $LR_{uc}(\alpha)$ rows correspond to the binomial method and examine the null hypothesis that the VaR estimates have correct unconditional coverage at the α percent level. The $LR_{cc}(\alpha)$ rows correspond to the interval forecast method and examine the null hypothesis that the VaR estimates have correct conditional coverage at the α percent level. The K row corresponds to the distribution forecast method and examines the null hypothesis that the observed quantiles are uniformly distributed.

Panel B presents the percentage of simulations for which the QPS value for the true DGP is less than that of the alternative VaR model. If this method is capable of distinguishing between the true DGP and an alternative model, then this percentage should be high. The QPSe1(α) rows correspond to the QPS values for the probability forecasts $P_t^m = Pr(\epsilon_{t+1} < CV(\alpha, \hat{F}))$, where $CV(\alpha, \hat{F})$ is the α percent quantile of the empirical cumulative distribution function $\hat{F}$. The QPSe2 row corresponds to the QPS values for the probability forecasts. The QPSe3 row corresponds to the QPS values for the probability forecasts $P_t^m = Pr(y_{t+1} < 0.99y_t)$. The QPSe3 row corresponds to the QPS values for the probability forecasts $P_t^m = Pr(y_{t+1} - y_0 < -\gamma(C))$, where $-\gamma(C)$ is the rate of return that would reduce Y_0 to the selected capital level C.

Panel C presents the percentage of simulations for which the null hypothesis that the QPS value for the true DGP is greater than or equal to that of the alternative model is rejected at the five percent level. If a test exhibits power against an alternative model, then this percentage should be high.
[a]The size of the tests is set at five percent.
[b]Each row represents the percentage of simulations for which the alternative model had a higher QPS value than the true DGP.
[c]The QPSe3 row has removed from it the simulations for which the QPS value of the true DGP for the third event is rounded down to zero; ie, 19% of the simulations.

with the other three methods, although the differences across models are not as marked as in Panel A. These results further indicate that deviations from the true distributional form have a greater impact than misspecification of the variance dynamics.

4.4 Simulation results for the GARCH(1,1)-t(6) data generating process

Table 5, Panel A presents the power analysis of the hypothesis-testing methods. The power results are again linked to the distributional assumptions used, as shown in the columns for the calibrated models. Unlike in Table 4, Panel A where their distributional assumption was correct and low power was exhibited, here the distributional assumption is incorrect and much improved power is exhibited. Thus, the misspecification of the distributional form has a significant impact on the power of these tests. However, the overall power results are still relatively poor for the three heteroscedastic models, with high power only for $LR_{uc}(1)$, where the differences in distributional form are most pronounced. The K test also has low power against these alternative models. With respect to the homoscedastic models in the first three columns, all three tests have high power, ie, misclassification is not likely.

Table 5, Panel B again indicates that the probability forecast method is capable of differentiating between the true and the alternative models. The comparative results for the first regulatory event with $\alpha = 1$ are poor, due to the fact that the empirical $CV(\alpha, \hat{F})$ values were generally so negative as to cause very few observations of the event. The results for the other events are much better. With respect to the homoscedastic alternatives in the first three columns, this method is able to correctly classify the alternative models a very high percentage of the time, indicating that incorrect variance dynamics can also be detected using this evaluation method. With respect to the three heteroscedastic alternatives, the calibrated normal models are found to generate higher QPS values a large percentage of the time, certainly higher than the GARCH-normal model that captures the dynamics correctly. Again, Panel C indicates that the power of this method against these alternative models is roughly comparable to that of the other three methods. Overall, these results indicate that although approximating or exactly capturing the variance dynamics can lead to a reduction in

Table 5 Simulation results for the GARCH(1, 1)-t(6) DGP (units: percent)

	Model $N(0, 1\frac{1}{2})$	$N(0, 1)$	$t(6)$	$N\lambda(97)$	$N\lambda(99)$	GARCH-N
Panel A. Power of the $LR_{uc}(\alpha)$, $LR_{cc}(\alpha)$ and K tests against alternative VaR models[a]						
$LR_{uc}(1)$	60.8	100.0	96.4	85.8	87.1	86.5
$LR_{uc}(5)$	75.5	100.0	96.9	60.3	63.2	62.1
$LR_{uc}(10)$	80.4	100.0	96.0	36.8	38.5	39.3
$LR_{cc}(1)$	87.5	99.8	96.8	35.1	46.1	87.6
$LR_{cc}(5)$	99.5	100.0	96.9	12.8	36.7	58.4
$LR_{cc}(10)$	98.9	100.0	95.9	27.4	56.0	27.4
K	98.7	100.0	98.2	45.4	49.6	50.6
Panel B. Accuracy of VaR models using the probability forecast method[b]						
QPSe1(1)	60.7	49.3	49.3	46.3	46.7	41.7
QPSe1(5)	99.6	91.8	90.8	84.2	84.0	69.9
QPSe1(10)	100.0	98.6	98.2	90.4	90.6	76.4
QPSe2	93.2	96.2	95.6	82.8	83.0	69.9
QPSe3[c]	63.0	66.5	64.1	55.6	55.5	45.7
Panel C. Power of the probability forecast method using the Diebold–Mariano test[a]						
QPSe1(1)	34.9	34.9	33.9	37.5	34.9	62.7
QPSe1(5)	81.1	81.1	52.8	76.6	80.0	26.7
QPSe1(10)	95.0	95.0	62.5	85.7	94.1	5.3
QPSe2	88.8	91.9	47.3	81.7	90.7	9.7
QPSe3[c]	47.5	43.1	50.0	59.3	48.5	42.6

Table 5 contains the simulation results for the heteroscedastic GARCH(1,1)-t(6) DGP; that is, is, $\epsilon_{t+1}|\Omega_t \sim t(h_{t+1}, 6)$, where $h_{t+1} = 0.075 + 0.10\epsilon_t^2 + 0.85h_t$. The alternative models are normal distributions with variances of 1.5 and 1 (denoted $N(0, 1\frac{1}{2})$ and $N(0\ 1)$, respectively); a t-distribution with 6 degrees of freedom (denoted $t(6)$); normal distributions whose variances are exponentially weighted averages of the squared innovations calibrated using $\lambda = 0.97$ and $\lambda = 0.99$ (denoted $N\lambda(97)$ and $N\lambda(99)$, respectively); and a GARCH(1,1) process with the same variance dynamics as the DGP and a normal distribution (denoted GARCH-N). The results are based on 1,000 simulations.

Panel A presents the percentage of simulations for which the null hypothesis corresponding to each row is rejected with the test size set at the five percent level. If a test exhibits power against an alternative model, then this percentage should be high. The $LR_{uc}(\alpha)$ rows correspond to the binomial method and examine the null hypothesis that the VaR estimates have correct unconditional coverage at the α percent level. The $LR_{cc}(\alpha)$ rows correspond to the interval forecast method and examine the null hypothesis that the VaR estimates have correct conditional coverage at the α percent level. The K row corresponds to the distribution forecast method and examines the null hypothesis that the observed quantiles are uniformly distributed.

Panel B presents the percentage of simulations for which the QPS value for the true DGP is less than that of the alternative VaR model. If this method is capable of distinguishing between the true DGP and an alternative model, then this percentage should be high. The QPSe1(α) rows correspond to the QPS values for the probability forecasts $P_t^m = \Pr(\epsilon_{t+1} < CV(\alpha, \hat{F}))$, where $CV(\alpha, \hat{F})$ is the α percent quantile of the empirical cumulative distribution function $\hat{F}$. The QPSe2 row corresponds to the QPS values for the probability forecasts. $P_t^m = \Pr(y_{t+1} < 0.99y_t)$. The QPSe3 row corresponds to the QPS values for the probability forecasts $P_t^m = \Pr(y_{t+1} - y_0 < -\gamma(C))$, where $-\gamma(C)$ is the rate of return that would reduce Y_0 to the selected capital level C.

Panel C presents the percentage of simulations for which the null hypothesis that the QPS value for the true DGP is greater than or equal to that of the alternative model is rejected at the five percent level. If a test exhibits power against an alternative model, then this percentage should be high.
[a]The size of the tests is set at five percent.
[b]Each row represents the percentage of simulations for which the alternative model had a higher QPS value than the true DGP.
[c]The QPSe3 row has removed from it the simulations for which the QPS value of the true DGP for the third event is rounded down to zero; ie, six percent of the simulations.

misclassification, distributional assumptions seem to be the dominant factor in differentiating between VaR models.

5 CONCLUSIONS

Given the increasing importance of VaR models for bank risk management and especially for regulatory capital requirements, evaluating their forecast accuracy has become a necessity. This chapter examines four methods for conducting such evaluations. The evaluation methods proposed to date are based on hypothesis tests; that is, they test the null hypothesis that the VaR forecasts from a model exhibit properties characteristic of accurate VaR forecasts. If these properties are not present, then the null hypothesis of model accuracy can be rejected at the specified significance level. Although such a framework provides insight, it hinges on the tests' statistical power. As discussed by Kupiec (1995) and as shown in the simulation results above, these tests can have low power against many reasonable alternative models and thus can lead to a high degree of model misclassification. Furthermore, for the linear conditional mean portfolios examined, it seems that these evaluation methods are more sensitive to misspecifications of the distributional shape than of the variance dynamics. Further research on portfolio returns with nonlinear conditional means is needed.

An alternative and complementary evaluation method, based on probability forecasts, is proposed and examined here. By relying on standard forecast evaluation techniques, this evaluation method gauges the relative accuracy of VaR models by how well they minimise a loss function tailored to the user's interests; in this case, the interests of bank regulators. The simulation results indicate that this method can generally distinguish between VaR models; that is, the specified QPS score for the true model is found to be lower than that of the alternative models a high percentage of the time. However, further analysis using hypothesis-testing techniques that permit a power comparison across all four methods indicates that its power can be quite low and generally in line with that of the other three methods. Thus, even though the proposed method is only as capable of differentiating between VaR models as the other methods, its ability to directly incorporate regulatory loss functions into model evaluations make it a useful complement to the statistical methods currently used in the regulatory evaluation of VaR models.

APPENDIX

General design of the simulation exercise

The simulation exercise in this chapter is conducted in four distinct, yet interrelated, sections. In each section, the true data generating process (DGP) is one of the VaR models examined and is designated as the true model. For example, in the first section, the true DGP is the standard normal, ie, $\epsilon_{t+1} | \Omega_t \sim N(0, 1)$.

Focusing on the first section, each simulation run for the $\text{LR}_{uc}(1)$ statistic based on the alternative $N(0, \frac{3}{4})$ model is conducted as follows:

❑ simulate $T = 500 \epsilon_{t+1}$ observations from the true standard normal DGP;
❑ generate the corresponding 500 estimates from the $N(0, \frac{3}{4})$ model, ie,

$$\text{VaR}_t^m(1, 1) = -2.326 \times \sqrt{\frac{3}{4}} = -2.0144 \quad \forall \, t$$

❑ let N be the number of times that $\epsilon_{t+1} < \text{VaR}_t^m(1, 1)$ and $\alpha^* = N/500$;
❑ compute the $\text{LR}_{uc}(1)$ statistic corresponding to α^*; and
❑ reject the null hypothesis of model accuracy at the five percent significance level if $\text{LR}_{uc}(1) > 4.813$, the finite-sample critical value from Table 1.

After 1,000 simulation runs, the power of this hypothesis test to correctly classify this alternative model as inaccurate is the percentage of times that the null hypothesis is rejected. As shown in Table 2, for this case, the power is 54.6%. This analysis is conducted on each of the alternative models to determine the first row of Panel A in Table 2. The other rows in Panel A are determined in the same way for their respective null hypotheses, and Panel A for each of the three other tables is determined in this way.

For the probability forecast method, the simulation runs are structured identically, but in this case the QPS values of the true and alternative models are compared. Using the above example, for each simulation run in the first section, the QPS value for the probability forecasts from $N(0, \frac{3}{4})$ model is compared to the value for the true model. As presented in Table 2, Panel B, for this model, the former QPS value for QPSe1(1) is greater than the latter value

765 out of 1,000 times. Table 2, Panel C shows that the differences in these values are statistically different from zero at the five percent significance level using the Diebold–Mariano test 303 out of 1,000 times, and the power of the probability forecasting method in this case is thus 30.3%. This analysis is conducted on each of the alternative models to determine the first row of Panels B and C in Table 2. The other rows in these panels are determined in the same way, and Panels B and C for each of the other three tables are determined in this way.

1 For a thorough discussion of the 1988 Basel Capital Accord and the US implementation of the 1996 market risk amendment, see Wagster (1996) and Federal Register (1996), respectively. For a related discussion on the regulatory capital requirements for securities firms, see Dimsom and Marsh (1995).

2 For a general discussion of the differences between financial institutions and their regulators on the issues of risk measurement and capital allocation, see Estrella (1995).

3 The specific risk capital charge is used to cover possible adverse price changes due to unanticipated, idiosyncratic events, such as an unexpected bond default. Although an important topic, specific risk is not examined here.

4 Stahl (1997) provides a theoretical justification of the use of a regulatory multiplication factor. Using Chebyshev's inequality, he shows that a multiplication factor approximately equal to three can be used to account for the possible misspecification of the distribution underlying VaR estimates for $\alpha = 1$. Thus, S_t^{m} can be viewed as a regulatory adjustment for model error.

5 The 1996 market risk amendment contains a number of other qualitative criteria that banks' risk management systems must meet in order to be considered appropriate for determining market risk capital requirements.

6 Note that these quantities are reported in dollar terms. Further note that VaR estimates do not capture the financial risks introduced by banks' intraday trading. Regulators are aware of such risks, but have generally chosen to monitor them using qualitative methods, such as evaluating the reasonableness of intraday position limits.

7 Note that the size of the test, which in this chapter is set at five percent, is different from the α percent coverage level of the VaR estimates in question.

8 See Chatfield (1993) for a general discussion of interval forecasts. Interval forecast evaluation techniques are also discussed by Granger, White and Kamstra (1989).

9 Although not done in this chapter, higher-order dependence could be specified. Christoffersen (1998) also presents an alternative test of this null hypothesis based on the runs test of David (1947).

10 Note that the formulae relating the π_{ij} variables to the transition counts are maximum likelihood estimates.

11 Note that other authors have recently proposed other tests based on models' empirical quantiles. Diebold, Gunther and Tay (1998) propose the use of CUSUM statistics, and Berkowitz (1998) proposes likelihood ratio statistics based on a simple transformation of these quantiles.

12 Note that the emphasis in this chapter on just the second property will understate the ability of the overall evaluation method to gauge VaR model accuracy since model misclassification by the test for uniform distribution might be correctly indicated by the test for independence.

13 Crnkovic and Drachman (1996) indicate that an advantage of the Kupier statistic is that it is equally sensitive for all values of x, as opposed to the Kolmogorov–Smirnov statistic that is most sensitive around the median. See Press *et al* (1992) for further discussion.

14 The asymptotic distribution of the Kupier statistic is characterised as $\text{Prob}(K > K_m) = G([\sqrt{T} + 0.155 + 0.24 / \sqrt{T}]v_m)$, where $G(\lambda) = 2 \sum_{j=1}^{\infty}(4j^2\lambda^2 - 1)e^{-2j^2\lambda^2}$, $v_m = max|D_m(x) - x|$, T is the sampel size, and $x \in [0, 1]$.

15 Crnkovic and Drachman (1996) note that the Kupier statistic can be tailored to the interests of the forecast evaluator by introducing a user-defined weighting function.

16 The relevance of such probability forecasts to regulators (as well as market participants) is well established. For example, Greenspan (1996b) stated that "[i]f we can obtain reasonable estimates of portfolio loss distributions, [financial] soundness can be defined, for example, as the probability of losses exceeding capital. In other words, soundness can be defined in terms of a quantifiable insolvency probability." For a more general discussion of probability forecasting in a decision theoretic framework, see Granger and Pesaran (1996).

17 Other scoring rules with different implied loss functions are available; see Murphy and Daan (1985).

18 The scoring rule S is proper if $E[S(P_t^m, j)|m] \leq E[S(p_t, j)|m \; \forall \; p_t \neq P_t^m$. Such scoring rules do not encourage the "hedging" of reported probability forecasts, but they also do not guard against it completely.

19 Note that this model is often implemented with a finite lag-order. For example, the infinite sum is frequently truncated at 250 observations, which roughly accounts for 90 percent of the sum of the weights. See Hendricks (1996) for further discussion on the choice of λ and the truncation lag. In this chapter, no such truncation is imposed, but of course, one is implied by the overall sample size of the simulated time series.

20 Note that, in dollar terms, the event of interest is thus whether $Y_{t+1} < Y_t^{0.99}$.

21 Note that this choice of $\gamma(C)$ implies that $C = Y_0(1 - Y_0^{-0.1})$.

This chapter was previously published in *The Journal of Risk* **1**(2), Winter 1998/1999.

REFERENCES

Berkowitz, J., 1998, "Evaluating the Forecasts of Risk Models", Manuscript, Trading Risk Analysis Group, Federal Reserve Board of Governors.

Brier, G. W., 1950, "Verification of Forecasts Expressed in Terms of Probability", *Monthly Weather Review* **75**, pp. 1–3.

Brock, W. A., W. D Dechert, J. A. Scheinkman, and B. LeBaron, 1991, "A Test of Independence Based on the Correlation Dimension", SSRI Working Paper #8702, Department of Economics, University of Wisconsin.

Chatfield, C., 1993, "Calculating Interval Forecasts", *Journal of Business and Economic Statistics* **11**, pp. 121–35.

Christoffersen, P. F., 1998, "Evaluating Interval Forecasts", *International Economic Review* **39**, pp. 841–62.

Crnkovic, C. and J. Drachman, 1996, "Quality Control", *Risk* **9**, pp. 139–43.

David, F. N., 1947, "A Power Function for Tests of Randomness in a Sequence of Alternatives", *Biometrika* **28**, pp. 315–32.

Diebold, F. X., T. A. Gunther, and A. S. Tay, 1998, "Evaluating Density Forecasts with Applications to Financial Risk Management", *International Economic Review* **39**, pp. 863–83.

Diebold, F. X. and R. Mariano, 1995, "Comparing Predictive Accuracy", *Journal of Business and Economic Statistics* **13**, pp. 253–64.

Diebold, F. X. and J. A. Lopez, 1996, "Forecast Evaluation and Combination", in *Handbook of Statistics, Vol. 14: Statistical Methods in Finance* (ed. G. S. Maddala and C. R. Rao), pp. 241–68. (Amsterdam: North-Holland).

Dimson, E. and P. Marsh, 1995, "Capital Requirements for Securities Firms", *Journal of Finance* **50**, pp. 821–51.

Estrella, A., 1995, "A Prolegomenon to Future Capital Requirements", *Federal Reserve Bank of New York Economic Policy Review* **1**, pp. 1–12.

Federal Register, 1996, "Risk-based Capital Standards: Market Risk", Vol. 61, pp. 47357–78.

Granger, C. W. J. and M. H. Pesaran, 1996, "A Decision Theoretic Approach to Forecast Evaluation", Manuscript, Trinity College, Cambridge University.

Granger, C. W. J., H. White, and M. Kamstra, 1989, "Interval Forecasting: An Analysis Based upon ARCH-quantile Estimators", *Journal of Econometrics* **40**, pp. 87–96.

Greenspan, A., 1996a, "Remarks at the Financial Markets Conference of the Federal Reserve Bank of Atlanta", Coral Gables, Florida.

Greenspan, A., 1996b, "Remarks at the Federation of Bankers Associations of Japan", Tokyo, Japan.

Hendricks, D., 1996, "Evaluation of Value-at-Risk Models using Historical Data", *Federal Reserve Bank of New York Economic Policy Review* **2**, pp. 39–69.

Hendricks, D. and B. Hirtle, 1997, "Bank Capital Requirements for Market Risk: The Internal Models Approach", *Federal Reserve Bank of New York Economic Policy Review*, December, pp. 1–12.

J. P., Morgan, 1995, *RiskMetrics Technical Document*, 3rd edn. (New York: JP Morgan).

Kupiec, P., 1995, "Techniques for Verifying the Accuracy of Risk Measurement Models", *Journal of Derivatives* **3**, pp. 73–84.

Kupiec, P. and J. M. O'Brien, 1995, "A Pre-Commitment Approach to Capital Requirements for Market Risk", FEDS Working Paper #95-36, Board of Governors of the Federal Reserve System.

Lopez, J. A., 1997, "Evaluating the Predictive Accuracy of Volatility Models", Research Paper #9524-R, Research and Market Analysis Group, Federal Reserve Bank of New York.

Murphy, A. H. and H. Daan, 1985, "Forecast Evaluation", in *Probability, Statistics and Decision Making in the Atmospheric Sciences* (ed. A. H. Murphy and R. W. Katz). (Boulder, CO: Westview Press).

Press, W. H., S. A, Teukolsky, W. T. Vetterling, and B. P. Flannery, 1992, *Numerical Recipes in C: The Art of Scientific Computing*, 2nd edn. (Cambridge: Cambridge University Press).

Pritsker, M., 1997, "Evaluating Value at Risk Methodologies: Accuracy Versus Computational Time", *Journal of Financial Services Research* **12**, pp. 201–42.

Stahl, G., 1997, "Three Cheers", *Risk* **10**, pp. 67–9.

Wagster, J. D., 1996, "Impact of the 1988 Basle Accord on International Banks", *Journal of Finance* **51**, pp. 1321–46.

22

Backtesting Within the Trading Book

Gerhard Stahl; Carsten S. Wehn; Andreas Zapp*

Federal Financial Supervisory Authority (BaFin); Deutsche Bundesbank;
Federal Financial Supervisory Authority (BaFin)

1 INTRODUCTION AND MOTIVATION

In 1996, the Basel Committee on Banking Supervision made it possible for banks to use internal risk models – better known as value-at-risk (VaR) models – for regulatory purposes by way of the Amendment to the Capital Accord to incorporate market risk (Basel Committee on Banking Supervision 1996a). These VaR models typically provide forecast distributions of changes in a portfolio's market value over a fixed period of time (see Alexander (1999) or Jorion (2001) for a complete overview). Hence, a process that evaluates forecast quality is obviously of crucial importance. The *ex post* analysis of forecasts and associated realisations is called *backtesting*. The Basel chapter on backtesting describes in depth the regulatory requirements for the forecast quality of the trading book as a whole in order to ensure an adequate calculation of regulatory capital cushions (Basel Committee on Banking Supervision 1996b).

A number of authors have considered the forecast evaluation proposed by the regulators. Diebold and Lopez (1996) provided a general overview of methods of probability forecasting. The relevant literature on VaR starts with Kupiec (1995), who pointed out that backtesting based on a binomial test statistic lacks statistical power. Crnkovic and Drachman (1996) proposed the use of the Kuiper statistic, a goodness-of-fit type statistic based on the whole

*All statements made in the present article are the authors' own opinions and should not be cited as being those of either the BaFin or of the Deutsche Bundesbank. The authors are grateful to the referee for many helpful comments and suggestions.

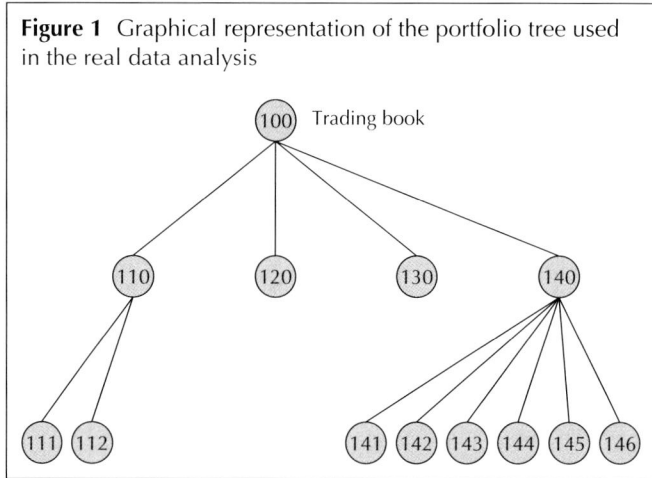

Figure 1 Graphical representation of the portfolio tree used in the real data analysis

forecast distribution. Christoffersen (1998) drew attention to the need to base backtesting on specification tests that focus on the independence property to evaluate forecast quality. Inspired by the ideas of Rosenblatt (1952), Berkowitz (2001) proposed an approach that relies on conditioned forecast distributions. This is very much in the spirit of the chapters contributed by Dawid ((1982), (1986) and (1997); for an overview of his work, which draws on methods applied in the field of meteorology, see Murphy and Winkler (1992)). Finally, Granger and Peseran (2000) used economic decision functions to evaluate forecast distributions. Our own exposition here is closely related to the concepts of Diebold, Gunther and Tay (1998) and Diebold, Hahn and Tay (1999).

This chapter focuses on the application of backtesting methods across the whole portfolio hierarchy (see Figure 1, which makes the notion of a portfolio tree obvious). The nesting feature of a portfolio hierarchy has not so far been covered in the literature on backtesting. Our analysis has a dual purpose: first, it concentrates on the evaluation of the forecast quality of individual portfolios; and second, it offers a tool for analysing the adequacy of aggregation schemes. The former is developed from a toolkit of backtesting techniques, whereas the latter is implemented by applying statistical methods for common distributed random variables and their dependence. Backtesting at sub-portfolio level is of particular importance for the approval processes of banks' internal models to judge, on the one hand, whether the qualitative requirements laid down by the Basel Committee (1996a) are being met – for example, the timeline and complete collection of position data, the adequacy of market data, and so on. On the other hand backtesting is used to evaluate quantitative requirements. Value-at-risk models are large-scale systems. It is therefore important to evaluate the tradeoff imposed by a parsimonious modelling and specification of risk factors. The ideas presented in this chapter are concerned with assessing the adequacy of aggregation schemes that might be erroneous, aggressive or conservative (the latter applies to the data set we use).

The remainder of the chapter is organised as follows. After stating the problem, Section 2 describes the data set used for the analysis, offers some initial insights into the data by means of descriptive statistics and introduces the notation. Section 3 defines the properties of a forecast and how to identify good forecast quality at a particular portfolio level. All the methods we introduce are applied to real-life data. Simultaneous analysis allows us to observe the portfolio tree as a whole. Section 4 presents the main idea of the chapter, namely, backtesting procedures for the aggregation scheme within the portfolio tree. Again, the methods we propose are applied to the data and the respective findings are presented, which in this case are the detection of a conservative aggregation scheme. Section 5 concludes.

2 NOTATION AND DESCRIPTION OF THE DATA SET

2.1 Notation

Let us consider a set of m tradeable assets. Their prices at final time t are unknown in the initial state $t - 1$ and are modeled by a vector of non-negative random variables:

$$\mathbf{P}_t = (P_t^1, \ldots, P_t^m)$$

where P_t^i models the prices of the ith asset. By

$$\mathbf{w}_{t-1} = (w_{t-1}^1, \ldots, w_{t-1}^m) \in \mathbb{R}^m$$

we denote an investor's portfolio, where w_{t-1}^i represents the number of shares of the ith asset. The *gain* of portfolio $\mathbf{w}_{t-1}$ is defined as the scalar product

$$G_t = \mathbf{w}_{t-1}' \Delta \mathbf{P}_t \qquad (1)$$

where $\mathbf{w}'_{t-1}$ denotes the transpose of $\mathbf{w}_{t-1}$ and Δ denotes the difference operator. Using an internal model, a forecast distribution, F_t, for G_t and associated realisations, g_t, are calculated daily. The VaR of level α is defined as

$$V_t = -F_t^{-1}(1 - \alpha)$$

The backtesting, performed according to the Basel Amendment (Basel Committee on Banking Supervision 1996a), is based on a series of forecast–realisation pairs:

$$\{V_t, g_t\}_{t=1}^{T} \qquad (2)$$

where the institute's trading book plays the role of $\mathbf{w}_{t-1}$ in (1).

In this chapter we analyse the forecast quality of a VaR model from a broader perspective by considering the forecast–realisation pairs for all portfolios given in Figure 1 simultaneously. The root node of the tree in Figure 1 is the trading book, and its leaves are sub-portfolios. For example, portfolio 140 consists of the following sum:

$$\mathbf{w}_{t-1}^{140} = \sum_{j=1}^{6} \mathbf{w}_{t-1}^{14j}$$

2.2 The data set

The empirical analysis is based on real data obtained from a German bank and its actual portfolio tree is the one set out in Figure 1. The data comprise 218 forecast–realisation pairs, as in Equation (2), for each node of the tree. The reported level of the VaR figures is 99%, and the observed profit and loss figures, g_t, are realisations of the random variable given by Equation (1). The time series starts on January 2, 2002 and ends on November 1, 2002. During this period the portfolio tree remained unchanged.

The data set is contaminated by errors, which are often caused by operational problems – for example, the risk engines did not run smoothly on some day, with the consequence that V_t was not generated and was substituted by V_{t-1}. The same may be true for g_t, or a portfolio may be flat for some days, ie, $\mathbf{w}_t = 0$ for some t. This type of contamination produces inliers. In that case statistical estimates

Table 1 Summary statistics for the standardised data (V_t, g_t)

(1) Portfolio	(2) Skew	(3) Kurtosis	(4) −(1% quantile of g_t)	(5) Average VaR	(6) Variation of VaR	(7) Average loss exceeding VaR	(8) No. of exceed- ances
100	−0.12	0.92	2.35	3.66	0.19	0.00	0
110	−0.85	5.57	3.66	2.35	0.30	4.31	3
111	−13.54	191.70	0.92	3.42	0.69	14.42	1
112	0.38	21.67	4.07	2.71	1.87	0.00	1
120	−0.16	1.00	2.37	2.73	0.20	2.57	1
130	−1.23	8.06	3.18	2.72	0.32	0.00	0
140	−0.20	6.22	3.95	2.76	0.14	4.06	3
141	0.16	3.54	2.63	1.98	0.26	2.37	5
142	0.45	4.60	2.68	2.10	0.22	4.03	1
143	2.45	20.08	1.83	1.57	0.39	5.10	1
144	−1.00	4.79	4.20	2.04	0.29	3.13	8
145	−0.88	11.85	2.34	3.12	0.10	5.32	2
146	−2.04	30.77	3.08	3.73	0.17	6.36	2

The first column identifies the portfolio as given in Figure 1. For the standardised g_t we give skewness, kurtosis and the 1% quantile multiplied by –1. The next three columns are related to V_t: the average VaR, the coefficient of variation of the VaR time series and the average size of the loss exceeding VaR are shown. Column (8) displays the number of exceedances.

such as the empirical distribution function are obviously misleading because there are too many zeros in the data set. For the empirical analysis we consider a period during which the portfolios were
not sold out and VaR forecasts were not substituted.

Table 1 summarises our data in terms of elementary statistics. To
ensure the anonymity of the bank, the data for Equation (2) were
standardised such that g_t has a mean of zero and a standard deviation of one. This standardisation was performed for every portfolio
individually.

From Table 1 we conclude that the time series g_t is prone to *outliers* if the Gaussian distribution is taken as a yardstick. This is supported by the large values of skewness and kurtosis for portfolios
111, 112, 143, 145 and 146. Whereas portfolio 100 is the trading book
and consists of all the other portfolios, those showing the largest
kurtosis consist of exotic derivatives or structured products (eg, 111,
143 or 146). Portfolio 120, for instance, consists mainly of plain
vanilla interest rate products such as bonds. Compared with 2.33,

the 99% quantile of the standard Gaussian distribution, the 1% quantiles of g_t multiplied by –1 are rather large. This again supports our statement. The presence of outliers suggests the use of robust estimates later on. By and large the estimates of skewness are moderate in size, indicating that the data are approximately symmetric.

Comparing columns (4) and (5), we conclude that the VaR figure for portfolio 100 is a conservative estimate of risk where no VaR exceedances occurred (see the last two columns). A similar picture holds for portfolio 120, though we see one exceedance there. For other portfolios the VaR figures are not necessarily conservative because the quantile of losses is larger than the average VaR. This phenomenon emphasises the importance of analysing the aggregation. Last but not least, the moderate coefficients of variation of VaR show that its volatility is rather low compared with its average value. Again taking the Gaussian distribution as a yardstick, we obtain a value of 2.67 for the average loss exceeding VaR. Hence the figures in the penultimate column indicate heavy tails or outliers.

Another issue revealed by the statistics in Table 1 is the way the nesting and aggregation procedure within the portfolio tree conceals exceedances – see, for example, portfolios 100 or 140, where the losses in one portfolio are obviously compensated by the gains from others. An exception to this rule is portfolio 110. The disappearance of the exceedances at the highest level can also be explained by the conservativeness of the aggregation scheme, as revealed in Section 4.

3 FORECAST QUALITY OF SUB-PORTFOLIOS
3.1 Well-behaved forecasts
In its chapter on backtesting, the Basel Committee on Banking Supervision (1996b) encourages the application of more sophisticated backtesting procedures than those based on the statistic $1_{(-\infty,-V_t]}(G_t)$. In this section we introduce a framework for the implementation of refined backtesting methods. The refinements are twofold. On the one hand we enhance the data set for the evaluation of the forecast of a VaR model by considering the whole vector of forecast–realisation pairs associated with the portfolio tree. On the other hand we apply and adapt the statistical approach defined by Jaschke, Stahl and Stehle (2003) to this hierarchical type of data.

For the evaluation of a forecast model it seems natural to look for transformations, T, such that the time series $T(\theta(F_t), G_t)$ is nearly stationary. In the literature on forecast evaluation the special transformation

$$T(F_t, G_t) = F_t(G_t) \qquad (3)$$

is used as a starting point. A forecast system is considered "good" (Dawid (1984), p. 281) if the values $F_t(G_t)$ are independent and uniformly distributed, ie, $F_t(G_t)$ iid $U[0, 1]$. This corresponds to the concepts "well-calibrated" and "refinement" (= "resolution") used in the literature on weather forecasting (Murphy and Winkler (1987 and 1992)) insofar as the condition $F_t(G_t) \sim U[0, 1]$ essentially means "well-calibrated" and the temporal independence of $F_t(G_t)$ is related to refinement (see Dawid (1986) and Seillier-Moiseiwitsch (1993)). Although Berkowitz and O'Brien (2002) have proposed that banks should report the realised probabilities $F_t(G_t)$ to the supervisory authorities, current rules require only the reporting of G_t and $V_t = -F_t^{-1}(0.01)$. Following Jaschke, Stahl and Stehle (2003), we use the standardised returns defined as

$$R_t := T(V_t, G_t) := z_\alpha \frac{G_t}{V_t} \qquad (4)$$

as the basis of the forecast evaluation in this chapter, where $z_\alpha := \Phi^{-1}(\alpha)$ is the inverse of the distribution function of the standard normal distribution. Thus, for the special case where $G_t \sim \Phi(0, \sigma_t^2)$, with $(z_\alpha \cdot \sigma_t)^2 = V_t^2$, the standardised returns R_t are standard normal distributed. Here, however, we aim to examine these distributional properties and so have to consider the more general case. We call a VaR forecast system *well-behaved* (at portfolio $\pi \in \{100, \dots, 146\}$) if

$$R_t^\pi \overset{\text{iid}}{\sim} \mathcal{L}^\pi \in \mathcal{U}_\epsilon^G \qquad (5)$$

where $\mathcal{U}_\epsilon^G$ is the ϵ-neighborhood of the set of Gaussian distributions with respect to the Kolmogorov distance in the set of probability distributions

$$\mathcal{U}_\epsilon^G := \Big\{ F : \sup_x | F(x) - \Phi(\mu, \sigma^2)(x) | \leq \epsilon, $$
$$ F \text{ is pdf}, \mu \in \mathbb{R}, \sigma^2 \in (0, \infty) \Big\}$$

for some fixed value ϵ. Note that the semi-parametric model – known as Huber's gross error model in the literature of robust statistics:

$$\mathcal{F}_{\epsilon}^{G} := \left\{ F : F = (1 - \epsilon) \, \Phi \left(\mu, \sigma^2 \right) + \epsilon H, \mu \in \mathbb{R}, \sigma^2 \in (0, \infty) \right\}$$

where H is an arbitrary probability distribution – is an important subset of $\mathcal{U}_{\epsilon}^{G}$. For $F \in \mathcal{F}_{\epsilon}^{G}$ the Kolmogorov distance between the distribution F and $\Phi \left(\mu, \sigma^2 \right)$ is

$$d(F, \Phi(\mu, \sigma^2)) \leq \epsilon$$

We use a set of diagnostical tools (see Jaschke, Stahl and Stehle (2003)) to confirm that a portfolio π is well-behaved as defined in Equation (5) with $\epsilon = 0.05$:

❑ *Time plot*: this plot visualises the time series of standardised returns, R_t, given in Equation (4). In the plot bold points indicate the VaR exceedances

$$B_t^{\pi} := \mathbb{1}_{(-\infty, -V_t^{\pi}]}(G_t^{\pi}) = \mathbb{1}_{(-\infty, z_{1-\alpha}]}(R_t^{\pi}) \tag{6}$$

❑ *Calibration plot*: this plot overlays three different plots: first, a traditional P–P plot; second, a needle plot which shows the most recent 20 observations; and third, VaR exceedances, indicated by bullet points at the top of the graphics. The dotted lines correspond to $\epsilon = 0.05$.

❑ *Q–Q plot*: the P–P plot (and the Kolmogorov distance) does not detect *large* deviations from normality as long as they happen with *small* probabilities. A better picture of the fit in the tails is provided by the Q–Q plot of F against normal, which plots $F^{-1}(q)$ against $\Phi^{-1}(\mu, \sigma^2)(q)$ for $q \in (0, 1)$. Additionally, a plot of F against the standard normal distribution (grey points) is shown.

These three diagnostic plots may be produced for each individual portfolio. Two typical outcomes are presented in Figure 2. This shows that portfolio 100, the trading book, is well behaved. This is clearly evident from the Q–Q plot. The needle plot as well as the time plot do not show tremendous dependencies over time. From the Q–Q plot we see that the standardised returns are close to a normal distribution. Note the evident overestimation of risk. This

Figure 2 Time plot, calibration plot and Q–Q plot

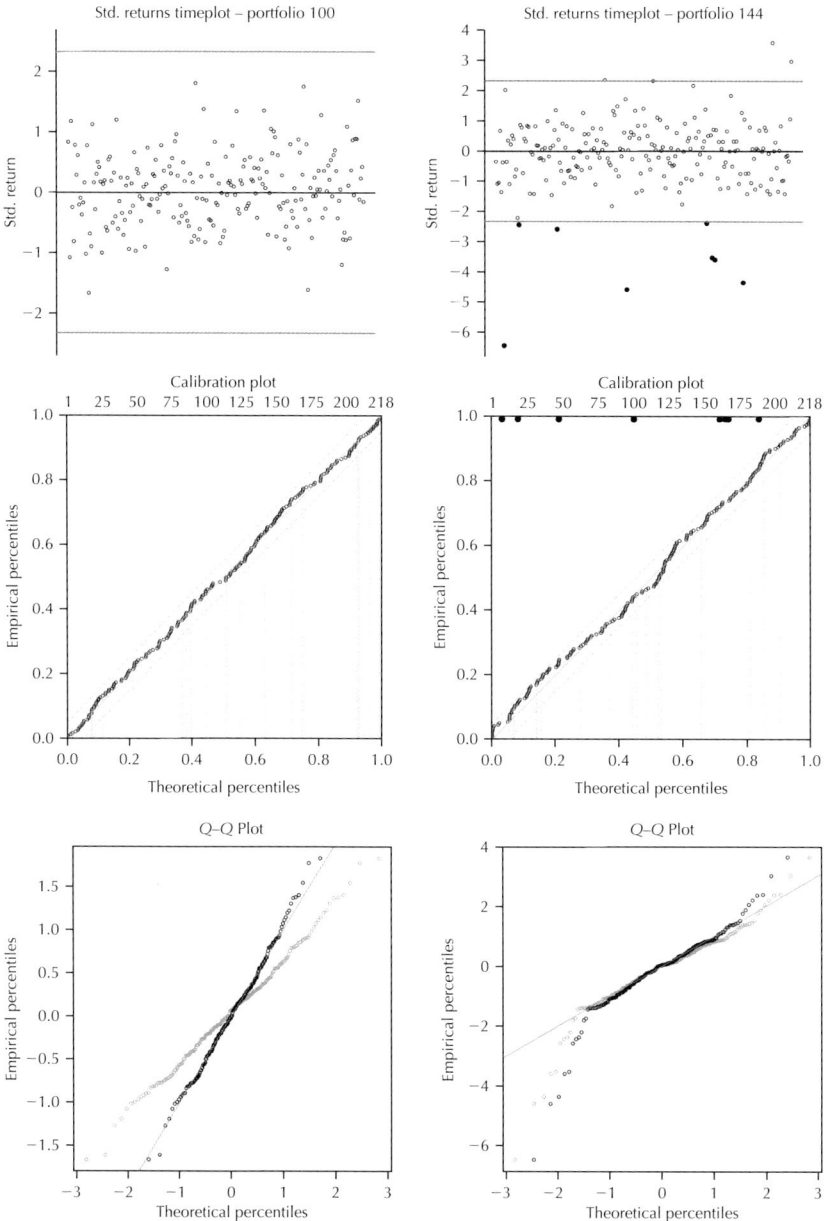

Time plot of the standardised returns, calibration plot (ie, P–P plot, most recent 20 observations and exceedances) and Q–Q plot for portfolios 100 and 144. The Q–Q plot displays the actual distribution of $F_{R_t^\pi}^{-1}$ against $\Phi^{-1}(\mu,\sigma^2)$ (black points) or $\Phi^{-1}(0, 1)$ (grey points), respectively.

Table 2 Standard deviations, σ, of the standardised returns

	Portfolio												
	100	**110**	**111**	**112**	**120**	**130**	**140**	**141**	**142**	**143**	**144**	**145**	**146**
σ	0.61	0.86	0.86	0.40	0.83	0.72	0.77	1.18	0.97	0.95	1.15	0.79	0.59

The standard deviation of standardised returns as defined in Equation (4). Note that a perfect match of the forecast–realisation pairs would yield a σ of 1. Values of σ greater than 1 indicate underestimation of risk, and those less than 1 indicate overestimation of risk.

is concluded from the Q–Q plot and the value of σ reported in Table 2. Turning to portfolio 144, according to our definition the portfolio is still well behaved. The Kolmogorov distance is smaller than 5%. There is a significant number of eight exceedances, indicating that the model will underestimate the risk. This is also in line with the value of σ reported for the portfolio in Table 2.

3.2 Simultaneous analysis

The concept of well-behaved forecast systems compromises distributional aspects and those of dependencies as well. A simultaneous analysis of the distributional properties is provided by a so-called aggregation plot. As mentioned earlier, the analysis of aggregation deserves particular attention. We analyse the distributional shape for each portfolio by plotting the skewness and kurtosis of standardised returns in a scatterplot (Figure 3). To represent the hierarchical structure, the portfolios on the different levels are distinguished by different labels: unfilled circles represent those at the lowest level, solid circles those at the middle level, and the solid triangle represents the trading book. Portfolio 111 is missing from the plot because of its extremely large skewness and kurtosis.

As expected, aggregation defines a smoothing process. There is a co-monotonic relation between the level within the hierarchy and closeness to the Gaussian distribution of the standardised returns. By and large, we conclude from the aggregation plot that the standardised returns are fairly symmetric and prone to outliers. Even if the gains and losses of the different portfolios are neither uncorrelated nor independent, the aggregation plot indicates a convergence towards a standard normal distribution, as would be guaranteed for independent random variables by the central limit theorem.

Figure 3 Aggregation plot

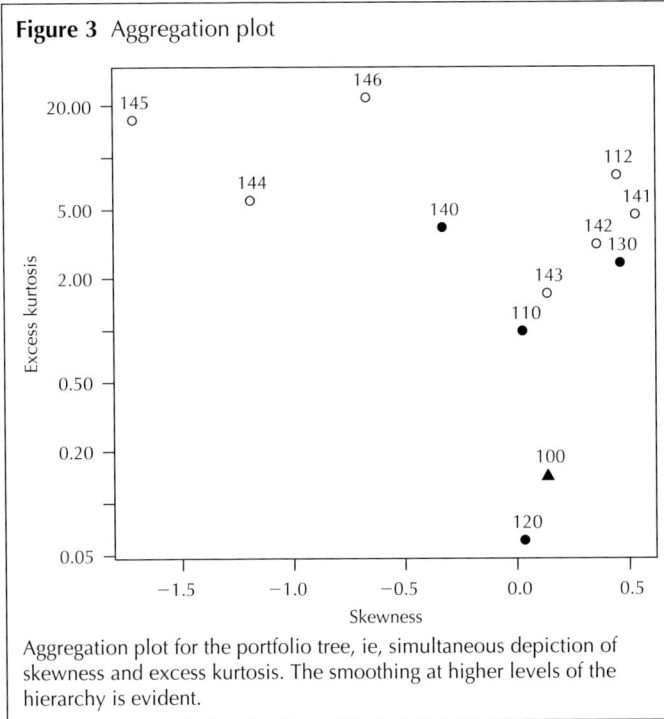

Aggregation plot for the portfolio tree, ie, simultaneous depiction of skewness and excess kurtosis. The smoothing at higher levels of the hierarchy is evident.

As a diagnostic tool to analyse the dependency we use entropy plots. These are plots of time series of vectors where indicator variables for each portfolio are plotted over time. These plots are somewhat similar to contingency tables. The marginal frequencies contain important information either for particular portfolios or about behavior over time. Ideally, the frequencies over time and portfolios should be equally distributed. Hence, deviations from the uniform distribution indicate a non-optimal forecast quality. For that reason we refer to them as entropy plots. Because we consider these plots for different α, we have to assume additionally that $\epsilon = 0$ in Equation (5).

From the nine plots in Figure 4 we conclude that the plots are obviously biased with respect to α. This is seen from the entropy of the marginal distributions and is an artefact arising from the Gaussian assumption. But despite this misspecification the diagnostic still identifies portfolios 112 and 146 as suspicious independently of α. Note that, rather than $\alpha = 0.90$, the first plot is an entropy plot

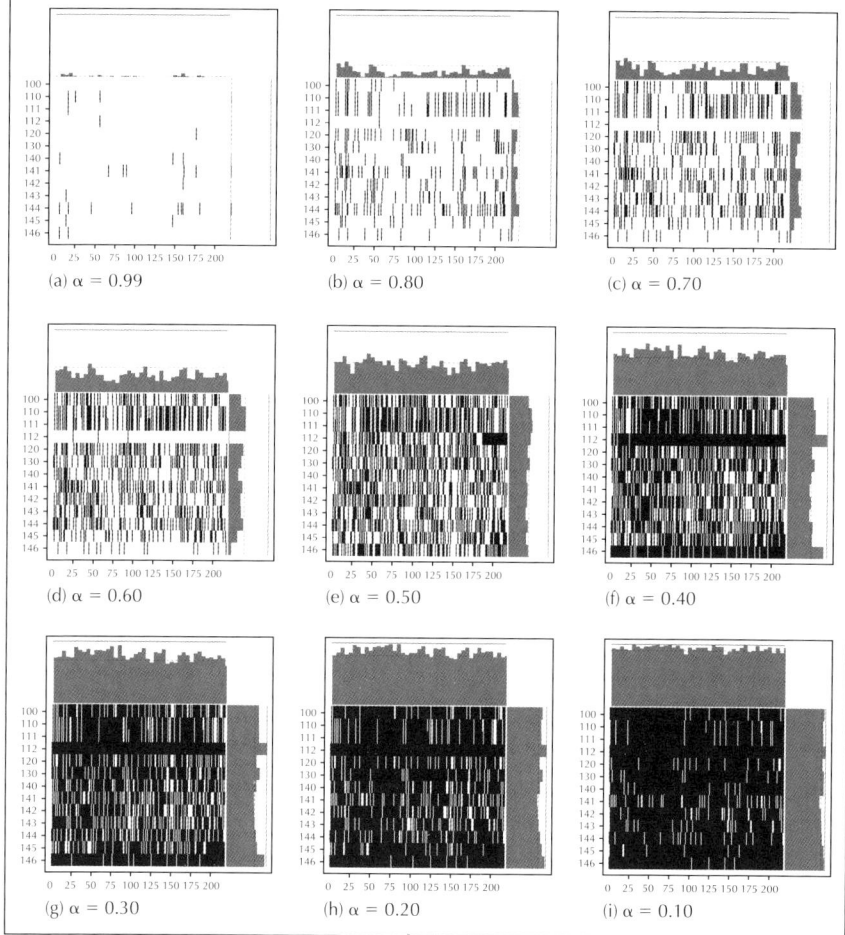

Figure 4 Entropy of the portfolio structure. The graphs simultaneously depict the VaR exceedances for all portfolios and different probability levels, α

with respect to $\alpha = 0.99$, the level corresponding to the VaR figures reported and where the number of exceedances is counted.

4 BACKTESTING THE PORTFOLIO TREE

Up to this point we have considered the forecast quality for every portfolio, π, individually or simultaneously. This section is devoted to a study of the interrelation of sub-portfolios, which are considered as marginal variables of a random vector to be defined later on. In doing so we analyse how the tree structure depicted in Figure 1 ties the marginal variables together for sub-trees. This focus is of particular interest both to practitioners and external auditors because it highlights diversification effects across the portfolio tree.

Let us consider the trading book labeled 100 in Figure 1 as a specific example. Portfolio $\Pi_0 := 100$ together with portfolios $\Pi := \{1i0, i = 1, ..., 4\}$ defines a sub-tree. To compare the distribution of Π_0 with the aggregate of the marginals Π we have to introduce a model for the common distribution of Π. To this end we generalise the approach given by Equation (5). We call Π well-behaved with respect to a Gaussian copula if

$$R_t^{\Pi} := (R_t^{\pi_1}, ..., R_t^{\pi_n}) \quad \text{iid} \quad F^{\Pi} \in \mathcal{C}^{\mathcal{U}} \tag{7}$$

where

$$\mathcal{C}^{\mathcal{U}} := \left\{ \mathbf{F} : F^i \in U_{\epsilon}^G \text{ and } F = C_{\Phi}(F^1, ..., F^n) \right\}$$

C_{Φ} denotes the Gaussian copula (Nelson 1999). Assume for a moment that R^{Π} is multivariate normal distributed. Hence, the sum of squares of the standardised normal distributions is χ^2-distributed with n degrees of freedom. Malevergne and Sornette ((2003), Proposition 1) have demonstrated a completely analogous result in the context of Gaussian copulas with empirical marginals. This allows us to use diagnostic tools (Q–Q and P–P plots) with the χ^2 distribution with n degrees of freedom as a reference distribution to check whether Equation (7) holds for R^{Π}. In contrast to our methods in Section 3, we choose a two-step approach here. In the first step we estimate the copula from one half of the sample. To the other half of the data we apply our diagnostic tools as before.

In Figure 5 we give the results for $\Pi = \{1i0 : i = 1, ..., 4\}$ and $\Pi = \{14i : i = 1, ..., 6\}$. For the portfolios considered, all the graphs in Figure 5 show a satisfactory fit. We supplement the diagnostic analysis with a confirmatory one by bootstrapping a pure significance test (see Malevergne and Sornette (2003) for details of testing the null hypothesis that $R^{\Pi} \in \mathcal{C}^{\mathcal{U}}$ by means of a Kolmogorov–Smirnov type of test). On the basis of the results given in Table 3 the null hypothesis cannot be rejected.

The results justify us in assuming that the common distribution of standardised returns (7) are described by a Gaussian copula as a good approximation. Recall that the gains and losses of an associated

Figure 5 Diagnostic plot for the Gaussian copula hypothesis

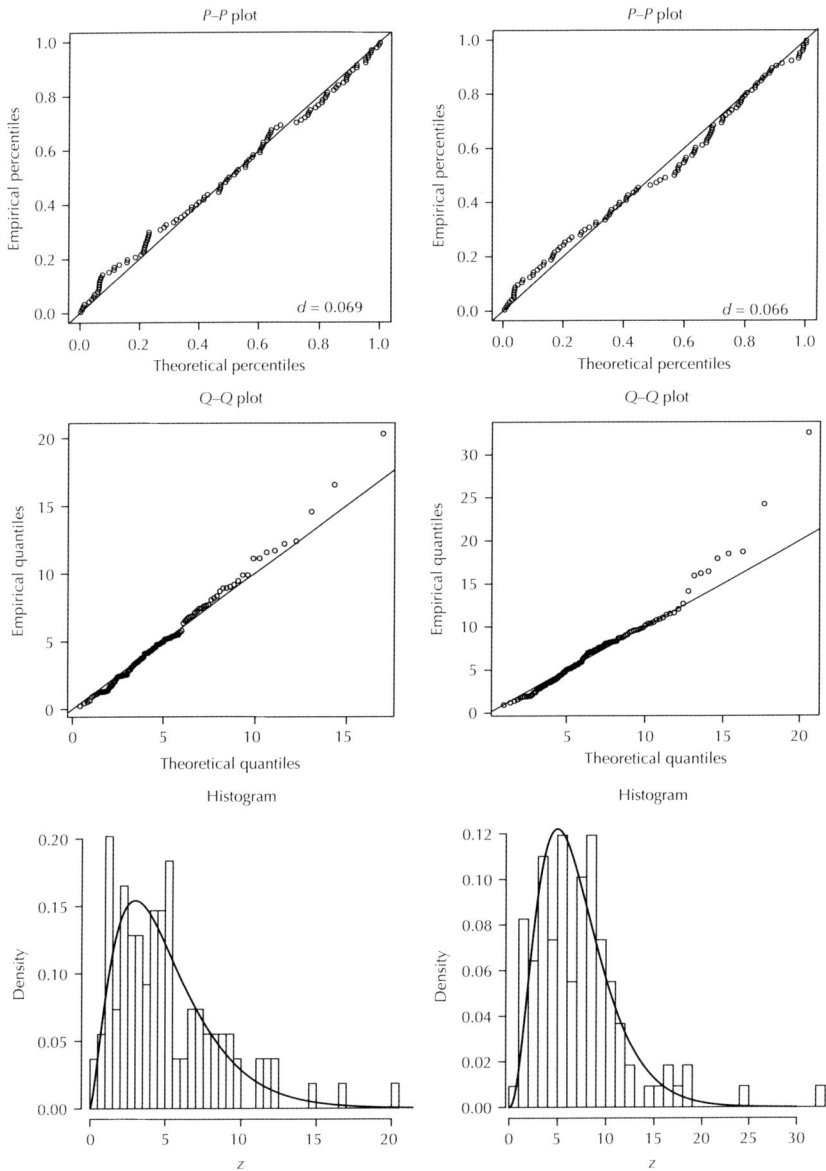

The different graphs analyse the adequacy of the hypothesis of a Gaussian copula for the sub-portfolios of portfolios 100 (left, $\Pi = \{1i0 : i = 1, ..., 4\}$) and 140 (right, $\Pi = \{14i : i = 1, ..., 6\}$).

Table 3 The null hypothesis $R^{\pi} \in C^{U}$ is tested by a Kolmogorov–Smirnov-type statistic. The results show that the Gaussian copula hypothesis for the three sets of leaves cannot be rejected

Portfolio	Observed D	$P(D > d)$
110, 120, 130, 140	$d = 0.069$	0.2964
111, 112	$d = 0.058$	0.5541
141, 142, 143, 144, 145, 146	$d = 0.066$	0.3410

node are just the sum of the gains and losses of the leaves. This motivates an analysis of whether the aggregation is a smoothing feature of the VaR model. The analysis compares the VaR figure of the node variable with that derived by our model across the port-folio tree. Note that – in contrast to G_t, which are the backbone of the backtesting methods – our model refers to standardised variables as in Equation (7). Since V_t is known, it is easy to derive the distribution of G_t from R_t by means of linear transformations. Theorem 2.4.3 of Nelson (1999) justifies the application of these transformations. The convolution of the G_t is determined numerically and the VaR, denoted by V_t^*, is calculated thereby.

Scatterplots of (V_t, V_t^*) are presented in Figure 6. It is evident that the aggregation for portfolio 140 works well, whereas the aggregation

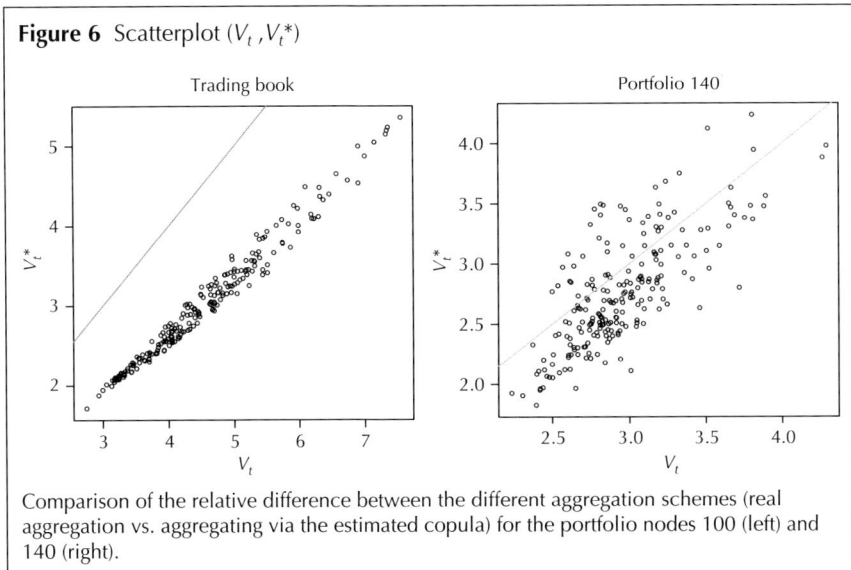

Figure 6 Scatterplot (V_t, V_t^*)

Comparison of the relative difference between the different aggregation schemes (real aggregation vs. aggregating via the estimated copula) for the portfolio nodes 100 (left) and 140 (right).

for the trading book overstates the risk figures. Because the scatter-plot approximates a straight line, the amount of conservativeness is easily calculated. In the case considered it is about 30%. This shows that the method we have introduced identifies sub-trees with different aggregation properties.

5 CONCLUSION

In this chapter we analysed the forecast and aggregation quality of a VaR model across the portfolio tree. With respect to analysing forecast quality, we applied the contamination model-like concept of well-behaved forecast systems at sub-portfolio level and showed that even for these portfolios the VaR model considered here behaves well. Furthermore, a simultaneous analysis allowed us to detect suspect portfolios.

Concerning the quality of aggregation, we investigated two different aspects. First, aggregation is a smoothing process, as the aggregation plot shows. This yields the insight that, the higher the aggregation level, the more the standardised returns converge towards a normal distribution. Second, in terms of precision the suitability of aggregation is evaluated by diagnostics related to a generalised notion of well-behavedness. The method we introduced can be used to check whether an aggregation scheme appears to be adequate or whether it systematically over- or underestimates the risk in a nested portfolio. In that context, and with application to real data provided by a bank, the method revealed a very conservative rule for aggregating portfolio risks while also explaining the low number of VaR exceedances at the top of the portfolio tree.

This chapter was previously published in *The Journal of Risk* **8**(2), Winter 2005/06.

REFERENCES

Alexander, C., 1999, *Risk Management and Analysis, Volume 1: Measuring and Modelling Financial Risk.* (New York: John Wiley & Sons).

Basel Committee on Banking Supervision, 1996a, "Market Risk Amendment", Basel Committee on Banking Supervision.

Basel Committee on Banking Supervision, 1996b, "Supervisory Framework for the Use of 'Backtesting' in Conjunction with the Internal Models Approach to Market Risk Capital Requirements", Basel Committee on Banking Supervision.

Berkowitz, J., 2001, "Testing Density Forecasts with Application to Risk Management", *Journal of Business and Economic Statistics* **19(4)**, pp. 465–74.

Berkowitz, J. and J. O'Brien, 2002, "How Accurate are Value-at-Risk Models at Commercial Banks?" *Journal of Finance* **57**, pp. 1093–112.

Christoffersen, P., 1998, "Evaluating Interval Forecasts", *International Economic Review* **39**, pp. 841–62.

Crnkovic, C. and J. Drachman, 1996, "Quality Control", *Risk* **9(9)**, pp. 138–43.

Dawid, A., 1982, "The Well-calibrated Bayesian", *Journal of the American Statistical Association* **77**, pp. 605–13.

Dawid, A., 1984, "Statistical Theory. The Prequential Approach", *Journal of the Royal Statistical Society*, Series A, **147(2)**, pp. 278–92.

Dawid, A., 1986, "Probability Forecasting", In *Encyclopedia of Statistical Sciences*, pp. 210–18. (New York: John Wiley & Sons).

Dawid, A., 1997, "Predictive Forecasts", In *Encyclopedia of Statistical Sciences*, pp. 464–70. (New York: John Wiley & Sons).

Diebold, F. and J. Lopez, 1996, "Forecast Evaluation and Combination", in G. Maddala and C. Rao (eds), *Statistical Methods in Finance* (*Handbook of Statistics*, Volume 14), pp. 241–68. (Amsterdam: North-Holland).

Diebold, F., T. Gunther, and A. Tay, 1998, "Evaluating Density Forecasts with Applications to Financial Risk Management", *International Economic Review* **39**, pp. 863–83.

Diebold, F., J. Hahn, and A. Tay, 1999, "Multivariate Density Forecast Evaluation and Calibration in Financial Risk Management: High-frequency Returns on Foreign Exchange", *Review of Economics and Statistics* **81**, pp. 661–73.

Granger, C. and M. Peseran, 2000, "A Decision Theoretic Approach to Forecast Evaluation", in C.W. S., L. W. K. and T. H. (eds), *Statistics and Finance: An Interface*, pp. 261–78. (London: Imperial College Press).

Jaschke, S., G. Stahl, and R. Stehle, 2003, "Evaluating VaR Forecasts Under Stress – The German Experience", Working paper 03-32, Center for Financial Studies, Frankfurt.

Jorion, P., 2001, *Value at Risk – The New Benchmark for Managing Financial Risk*, Second edition. (New York: McGraw-Hill).

Kupiec, P., 1995, "Techniques for Verifying the Accuracy of Risk Measurement Models", *Journal of Derivatives* **2**, pp. 73–84.

Malevergne, Y. and D. Sornette, 2003, "Testing the Gaussian Copula Hypothesis for Financial Assets Dependences", *Quantitative Finance* **3(4)**, pp. 231–50.

Murphy, A. and R. Winkler, 1987, "A General Framework for Forecast Verification", *American Meteorological Society* **115**, pp. 1330–8.

Murphy, A. and R. Winkler, 1992, "Diagnostic Verification of Probability Forecasts", *International Journal of Forecasting* **7**, pp. 435–55.

Nelson, R., 1999, *An Introduction to Copulas*. (New York: Springer).

Rosenblatt, M., 1952, "Remarks on a Multivariate Transformation", *Annals of Mathematical Statistics* **23**, pp. 470–2.

Seillier-Moiseiwitsch, F., 1993, "Sequential Probability Forecasts and the Probability Integral Transform", *International Statistical Review* **61(3)**, pp. 395–408.

23

A Review of Backtesting and Backtesting Procedures

Sean D. Campbell*

The Federal Reserve Board

1 THE CURRENT REGULATORY FRAMEWORK

Regulatory guidelines require banks with substantial trading activity to set aside capital to insure against extreme portfolio losses. The size of the set-aside, or market risk capital requirement, is directly related to a measure of portfolio risk. For regulatory purposes, portfolio risk is measured in terms of its "value-at-risk". The value-at-risk (VaR) of a portfolio is defined to be the dollar loss that is expected to be exceeded only $\alpha \times 100\%$ of the time over a fixed time interval. If, for example, a financial institution reports a 1% VaR of US$10,000,000 over a one-day horizon, this means that 1% of the time the institution would be expected to realise a loss in excess of US$10,000,000. In the event that a loss in excess of US$10,000,000 occurs, a 1% VaR "violation" is said to occur. The current regulatory framework requires that financial institutions use their own internal risk models to calculate and report their 1% VaR over a both a one-day, $VaR_t^1(0.01)$, and a 10-day, $VaR_t^{10}(0.01)$, horizon.

Market risk capital requirements are directly linked to both the estimated level of portfolio risk as well as the VaR model's performance on backtests. Specifically, the risk-based capital requirement is set as the larger of either the bank's current assessment of the 1%

*I would like to thank Mike Gibson, Jim O'Brien, Pat Parkinson, Matt Pritsker, Hao Zhou, an anonymous referee and the Editor-in-Chief for useful discussions and comments on an earlier draft. The usual disclaimer applies. The views expressed in this chapter are those of the author but not necessarily those of the Board of Governors of the Federal Reserve System or other members of its staff.

VaR over the next 10 trading days or a multiple of the bank's average reported 1%, 10-day VaR over the previous 60 trading days plus an additional amount that reflects the underlying credit risk of the bank's portfolio. In precise terms the market risk capital is defined as

$$MRC_t = \max\left(VaR_t^{10}(0.01), S_t \frac{1}{60} \sum_{i=0}^{59} VaR_{t-i}^{10}(0.01) \right) + c \qquad (1)$$

where S_t reflects a multiplication factor that is applied to the average of previously reported 1%, 10-day VaR estimates.[1] When a VaR model indicates more risk, the risk-based capital requirement rises. What may be less clear from the above expression is that the risk-based capital requirement also depends on the accuracy of the VaR model.

Importantly, the multiplication factor S_t depends on the number of 1%, one-day VaR violations experienced over the previous 250 trading days. The number of VaR violations is used to classify the model as either "green", "yellow" or "red". Specifically, S_t is determined as follows:

$$S_t = \begin{cases} 3.0 & \text{if } N \leq 4 & \text{green} \\ 3 + 0.2(N - 4) & \text{if } 5 \leq N \leq 9 & \text{yellow} \\ 4.0 & \text{if } 10 < N & \text{red} \end{cases} \qquad (2)$$

where N refers to the number of 1%, one-day VaR violations over the previous 250 trading days. Since the 1%, one-day VaR is expected to be violated 1% of the time, the multiplication factor S_t does not begin to increase until four violations, corresponding to 1.6% of the trading days, have occurred. Thereafter, S_t rises with N until 10 violations occur, corresponding to 2.5% of the trading days, in which case the VaR model is deemed inaccurate, requiring immediate steps to improve its accuracy. This "traffic light" approach to backtesting represents the only assessment of VaR accuracy prescribed in the current regulatory framework.

In what follows, we describe two key statistical properties that can be used to determine whether or not a particular VaR model accurately represents the risks of the underlying portfolio. We then briefly survey various backtesting methods that have been proposed to test the accuracy of a VaR model at a single level, α. The tests, their application and their limitations are discussed. We then discuss a class of backtests that are based on the behavior of a VaR model at multiple α levels, and we propose one such test. Finally, we conduct a small simulation study to examine whether the proposed test improves the chances of detecting an inaccurate VaR model relative to a test based on a single VaR level.

2 THE STATISTICAL APPROACH TO BACKTESTING
2.1 The definition of VaR

Before describing VaR backtests in any detail it is important to have a concrete definition of VaR in mind. Consider the distribution of h-period portfolio profit and loss, $x_{t,t+h}$. In mathematical terms, a portfolio's VaR is defined to be the negative of the α percentile of the portfolio's h-period profit and loss or P&L distribution:

$$\mathrm{VaR}_t^h(\alpha) = -F_h^{-1}(\alpha \mid \Omega_t) \tag{3}$$

where $F(\cdot \mid \Omega_t)$ refers to the quantile function of the h-period P&L distribution, which varies over time as market conditions and the portfolio's composition, as embodied in Ω_t, change. The negative sign is a normalisation that quotes VaR in terms of positive dollar amounts, ie, "losses".

In what follows, I will assume that the frequency with which the VaR and P&L are recorded coincides with the horizon of the VaR and P&L, h, so that the sample consists of non-overlapping observations, $[x_{t+h(i-1),t+hi}, \mathrm{VaR}_{t+h(i-1)}^h(\alpha)]_{i=1}^T$. This is consistent with the setting used to determine the market risk capital multiplication factor in Equation (2), ie, a daily sample of one-day VaR and P&L observations. In some contexts, however, the frequency at which the VaR and P&L are recorded does not match the horizon of the VaR and P&L, resulting in a sample with overlapping observations, $[x_{t,t+h}, \mathrm{VaR}_t^h(\alpha)]_{t=1}^T$. This occurs, for example, when a 10-day VaR and P&L are computed at the daily frequency. The assumption of a sample with non-overlapping observations does much to simplify and facilitate the analysis to follow. In particular, assuming a non-overlapping sample allows one to focus on the key properties of an accurate VaR model that are exploited by many common backtests without having to delve into the complicating issues that arise when there is overlap in the sample. Readers interested in backtests that are appropriate in the presence of overlapping observations may consult Dowd (2006). Finally, for notational convenience, we will consider the case of $h = 1$, ie, daily VaR, and we will omit the h subscript to facilitate the exposition and discussion to follow.

2.2 The statistical framework of VaR backtests

Since the late 1990s a variety of tests have been proposed that can be used to gauge the accuracy of a VaR model. While these tests differ in their details, many of them focus on a particular transformation of the reported VaR and realised P&L. Specifically, consider the event that the loss on a portfolio exceeds its reported VaR, $\text{VAR}_t(\alpha)$. Accordingly, define the "hit" function as follows

$$I_{t+1}(\alpha) = \begin{cases} 1 & \text{if} \quad x_{t,t+1} \leq -\text{VaR}_t(\alpha) \\ 0 & \text{if} \quad x_{t,t+1} > -\text{VaR}_t(\alpha) \end{cases} \tag{4}$$

so that the hit function sequence, eg, (0, 0, 1, 0, 0, …, 1), tallies the history of whether or not a loss in excess of the reported VaR has been realised.

Christoffersen (1998) points out that the problem of determining the accuracy of a VaR model can be reduced to the problem of determining whether the hit sequence, $[I_t(\alpha)]_{t=1}^{t=T}$, satisfies two key properties.

(1) *Unconditional coverage property*: the probability of realising a loss in excess of the reported VaR, $\text{VAR}_t(\alpha)$, must be precisely $\alpha \times 100\%$, or, in terms of the previous notation, $\text{Pr}(I_{t+1}(\alpha) = 1) = \alpha$. If it is the case that losses in excess of the reported VaR are expected to occur more frequently than $\alpha \times 100\%$ of the time, then this would suggest that the reported VaR measure systematically understates the portfolio's risk. The opposite finding that VaR violations are expected to occur too infrequently would, alternatively, signal an overly conservative VaR measure.

(2) *Independence property*: the independence property places a strong restriction on the ways in which VaR violations may occur. Specifically, any two elements of the hit sequence, $(I_{t+j}(\alpha), I_{t+k}(\alpha))$ must be independent of each other. Intuitively, this condition requires that the previous history of VaR violations, $\{\dots, I_{t-1}(\alpha), I_t(\alpha)\}$, must not convey any information about

whether or not an additional VaR violation, $I_{t+1}(\alpha) = 1$, will occur. If, for example, a VaR violation is more likely to occur after a previous VaR violation has occurred, then this implies that the probability that $I_{t+1}(\alpha) = 1$ conditional on the event that $I_t(\alpha) = 1$ exceeds the VaR level, α, indicating that the reported VaR is too small and should be increased.

It is important to recognise that the unconditional coverage and independence properties of the hit sequence are separate and distinct and must both be satisfied by an accurate VaR model. In principle, a particular VaR model could result in a hit sequence that satisfies one property or the other but not both. Only hit sequences that satisfy both properties can be described as evidence of an accurate VaR model.

These two properties of the "hit" sequence, $[I_t(\alpha)]_{t=1}^{t=T}$, are often combined into the single statement

$$I_t(\alpha) \overset{\text{i.i.d.}}{\sim} B(\alpha) \tag{5}$$

which reads that the hit sequence, $I_t(\alpha)$, is identically and independently distributed as a Bernoulli random variable with probability α. These two properties of the hit sequence represent a complete characterisation of an accurate VaR measure at a given level, α.

Ultimately, the main contribution of Christoffersen's (1998) insight is that the problem of determining whether a given VaR measure is accurate can be reduced to examining the unconditional coverage and independence properties of the resulting hit sequence. Accordingly, many of the VaR backtests that have been proposed examine whether the hit sequence satisfies one or both of these properties. We now turn to a discussion of these backtests. First, we discuss tests of the unconditional coverage property, then tests of the independence property, and finally joint tests of both properties.

3 TESTS OF VAR ACCURACY
3.1 Unconditional coverage tests
Some of the earliest proposed VaR backtests focused exclusively on the property of unconditional coverage. These tests are concerned with whether or not the reported VaR is violated more (or less) than

$\alpha \times 100\%$ of the time. Kupiec (1995), for example, proposed a proportion of failures, or POF, test that examines how many times a financial institution's VaR is violated over a given span of time. If the number of violations differs considerably from $\alpha \times 100\%$ of the sample, the accuracy of the underlying risk model is called into question. Using a sample of T observations, Kupiec's (1995) test statistic can be expressed as

$$POF = 2\log\left(\left(\frac{1-\hat{\alpha}}{1-\alpha}\right)^{T-I(\alpha)}\left(\frac{\hat{\alpha}}{\alpha}\right)^{I(\alpha)}\right)$$

$$\hat{\alpha} = \frac{1}{T}I(\alpha)$$

$$I(\alpha) = \sum_{t=1}^{T}I_t(\alpha) \tag{6}$$

and close inspection of the test statistic reveals that if the proportion of VaR violations, $\hat{\alpha} \times 100\%$, is exactly equal to $\alpha \times 100\%$, the POF test takes the value zero, indicating no evidence of any inadequacy in the underlying VaR measure. As the proportion of VaR violations differs from $\alpha \times 100\%$, the POF test statistic grows, indicating mounting evidence that the proposed VaR measure either systematically understates or overstates portfolio risk. In the case of a 1% VaR, if the test is carried out using one year, ie, $T = 255$, of daily data, then a common threshold for determining that a VaR measure is under-reporting the actual 1% VaR is eight violations, or roughly 3% of the sample.[2]

At this point it is useful to draw a connection between tests of unconditional coverage and the current regulatory framework. Recall that the market risk capital multiplier, S_t, is solely determined by the number of times the 1% VaR has been violated in the past 250 trading days. Similarly, the POF test is only a function of the number of VaR violations during the sample period, $\hat{\alpha}$. Accordingly, there is a close connection between movements in the market risk multiplier and the POF test of unconditional coverage. For example, consider the fact that the market risk capital requirement begins to increase after four violations of the 1% VaR have occurred in the previous 250 days. This threshold corresponds to a value of the POF test of 0.76. A realisation of the POF test of this magnitude or larger would be expected to occur roughly 38% of the time in the case that the VaR model under consideration is accurate. At the other extreme, observing 10 VaR violations – in which case the multiplier is set to its maximal value of 4.0 and the underlying VaR model is deemed inaccurate, requiring immediate steps to improve its accuracy – is equivalent to a POF test value of 12.95. Such a large value of the POF test would be expected to occur much less than 1% of the time in the case that the VaR model under consideration is accurate. Accordingly, the market risk capital multiplier can be interpreted in terms of a test of unconditional coverage that mandates a larger market risk capital set-aside as evidence that the VaR model under consideration is inaccurate mounts.

The POF test of unconditional coverage is a well known example of a VaR backtest. There are, however, a variety of statistical tests that could be employed to assess the unconditional coverage property of a given VaR model. One alternative would be to simply base a test directly on the sample average of the number of VaR violations over a given time period, $\hat{\alpha}$. Under the assumption that the VaR under consideration is accurate, a scaled version of $\hat{\alpha}$

$$ z = \frac{\sqrt{T}(\hat{\alpha} - \alpha)}{\sqrt{\alpha(1 - \alpha)}} \tag{7} $$

has an approximately standard normal distribution. Moreover, the exact finite sample distribution of z is known, and so hypothesis tests can be conducted in exactly the same way that hypothesis tests are conducted in the case of the POF statistic.[3]

While tests of unconditional coverage provide a useful benchmark for assessing the accuracy of a given VaR model, these tests are hampered by two shortcomings. The first shortcoming is that these tests are known to have difficulty detecting VaR measures that systematically under-report risk. From a statistical point of view these tests exhibit low power in small samples. Kupiec (1995), for example, reports that the probability of detecting an inaccurate VaR model with the POF test is often in the range of 65%, only slightly better than a coin flip. As a result, the sample sizes needed to detect an inaccurate VaR model with high probability, say higher than 90%, may be considerably larger than the sample sizes used in common practice, eg, one year.

Table 1 Contingency table for Markov independence test

	$I_{t-1} = 0$	$I_{t-1} = 1$	
$I_t = 0$	N_1	N_2	$N_1 + N_2$
$I_t = 1$	N_3	N_4	$N_3 + N_4$
	$N_1 + N_3$	$N_2 + N_4$	N

The table shows the entries needed to compute Christoffersen's Markov test. The rows of the table refer to the value of the hit function in period t, while the columns refer to the value of the hit function in period $t-1$. The total sample size used in constructing the table is N and N_j, $j = 1, 2, 3, 4$, refers to the number of occurrences of each row and column combination.

A second shortcoming of these tests is that they focus exclusively on the unconditional coverage property of an adequate VaR measure and do not examine the extent to which the independence property is satisfied. Accordingly, these tests may fail to detect VaR measures that exhibit correct unconditional coverage but exhibit dependent VaR violations. As a result, they would not be expected to detect a VaR model in which VaR violations occur in runs such that a VaR violation is more likely following a previous violation. A run of unexpected losses may result in even more stress on a financial institution than large unexpected losses that occur somewhat more frequently than expected but are spread out over time. As a result, relying solely on tests of unconditional coverage in backtesting would appear problematic.

3.2 Independence tests

In light of the limited scope of unconditional coverage tests, a variety of tests have been developed which explicitly examine the independence property of the VaR hit series, $I_t(\alpha)$. An early and influential test in this vein is Christoffersen's (1998) Markov test. The Markov test examines whether the likelihood of a VaR violation today depends on whether or not a VaR violation occurred on the previous day. If the VaR measure accurately reflects portfolio risk, then the chance of violating today's VaR should be independent of whether or not yesterday's VaR was violated. The test is carried out by creating a 2×2 contingency table that records VaR violations on adjacent days as in Table 1. If the VaR measure accurately reflects portfolio risk, the proportion of violations that occur after a previous violation, $I_{t-1} = 1$, should be the same as the proportion of violations that occur after a day on which no violation occurred, $I_{t-1} = 0$. In terms of the elements in Table 1 it should be the case that $N_3/(N_1 + N_3) = N_4/(N_2 + N_4)$. If these proportions differ greatly from each other, then this calls the validity of the VaR measure into question.

A more recent independence test that has been suggested by Christoffersen and Pelletier (2004) uses the insight that if VaR violations are completely independent from each other, the amount of time that elapses between VaR violations should be independent of the amount of time that has elapsed since the last violation. In this sense, the time between VaR violations should not exhibit any kind of "duration dependence". The chance that a VaR violation occurs in, say, the next 10 days should not depend on whether the last VaR violation occurred 10 or 100 days ago. Unlike the Markov test, this duration-based test cannot be constructed simply by computing a 2×2 contingency table. Carrying out the test requires estimating a statistical model for the duration of time between VaR violations by the method of maximum likelihood, which must be done using numerical methods. Despite the lack of transparency in the test statistic, Christoffersen and Pelletier (2004) provide some evidence that this test of independence has more power than the Markov test to detect a VaR measure that violates the independence property. They show, for example, that in a setting in which the Markov test identifies an inaccurate VaR measure 28% of the time their duration-based test identifies the inaccurate VaR measure 46% of the time.

While independence tests provide an important source of discriminatory power in detecting inadequate VaR measures, they are subject to one main drawback. Any test of the independence property must fully specify the way in which violations of the independence property are expected to arise. In the case of the Markov test, for example, the independence property may be violated if the chance of violating today's VaR depends on whether or not yesterday's VaR was violated. There are, however, myriad ways in which the independence property might be violated. For example, it might be the case that the likelihood of violating today's VaR depends not on whether yesterday's VaR was violated but on whether the VaR was violated one week ago. If this is the case, Christoffersen's (1998) Markov test will fail to identify the VaR model as inaccurate. In this sense, independence tests are only as useful as the set of departures from independence that they are designed to detect. As a result, the use of independence tests in assessing a VaR model can benefit from a thorough understanding of the circumstances that are most likely to result in a risk model's failure to accurately reflect portfolio risk.

3.3 Joint tests of unconditional coverage and independence

An accurate VaR measure must exhibit both the independence and unconditional coverage property. Accordingly, tests that jointly examine the unconditional coverage and independence properties provide an opportunity to detect VaR measures which are deficient in one way or the other. Both the Markov test of Christoffersen (1998) and the duration test of Christoffersen and Pelletier (2004) can be extended to jointly test for both independence and unconditional coverage. In the case of the Markov test, it is particularly simple to characterise how the joint test examines both properties of the VaR measure.

Recall that the Markov test proceeds by constructing a 2×2 contingency table that records the frequency of VaR violations and non-violations on successive days as in Table 1. The Markov independence test then examines whether the proportion of violations following previous violations is equal to the proportion of violations following previous non-violations. In terms of the notation in Table 1, this is equivalent to examining whether $N_3/(N_1 + N_3) = N_4/(N_2 + N_4)$. If the VaR measure also exhibits the unconditional coverage property, then these proportions should match the total proportion of violations, $(N_3 + N_4)/N$, and this should be identical to α, ie, $N_3/(N_1 + N_3) = N_4/(N_2 + N_4) = (N_3 + N_4)/N = \alpha$. Accordingly, the joint Markov test examines whether there is any difference in the likelihood of a VaR violation following a previous VaR violation or non-violation and simultaneously determines whether each of these proportions is significantly different from α.

The discussion of joint tests so far might seem to suggest that joint tests are universally preferable to tests of either the unconditional coverage property or independence property alone. While joint tests have the property that they will eventually detect a VaR measure which violates either of these properties, this comes at the expense of a reduced ability to detect a VaR measure which only violates one of the two properties. If, for example, a VaR measure exhibits appropriate unconditional coverage but violates the independence property, then an independence test has a greater likelihood of detecting this inaccurate VaR measure than a joint test. The joint test is hampered by the fact that one of the two violations it is designed to detect, namely violations of unconditional coverage, is actually satisfied by the VaR measure. The fact that one of the two properties is satisfied makes it more difficult for the joint test to detect the inadequacy of the VaR measure. As an example, consider a 5% VaR measure which exhibits the unconditional coverage property but not the independence property. Specifically, suppose that a VaR violation occurs 20% of the time after a previous VaR violation but that a VaR violation only occurs 4.2% of the time after a period in which no VaR violation occurs.[4] In a one-year sample of daily observations the joint Markov test detects this inaccurate VaR measure 50% of the time while the independence Markov test detects it 56% of the time. The increased power of detection that comes from choosing a test that focuses on one of the two properties indicates that either unconditional coverage or independence tests alone are preferable to joint tests when prior considerations are informative about the source of the VaR measure's inaccuracy.

4 TESTS BASED ON MULTIPLE VaR LEVELS

All of the backtests discussed so far have focused on determining the adequacy of a VaR measure at a single level, α. In general, however, there is no need to restrict attention to a single VaR level. A VaR measure from an appropriately specified risk model will exhibit the unconditional coverage and independence property at any level α. Crnkovic and Drachman (1996), Diebold, Gunther and Tay (1998) and Berkowitz (2001) have all suggested backtests based on multiple VaR levels. These authors exploit the insight that if portfolio risk is adequately modeled the 1% VaR should be violated 1% of the time, the 5% VaR should be violated 5% of the time, the 10% VaR should be violated 10% of the time and so on. Furthermore, a VaR violation at one level should be independent of a VaR violation at any other level so that, for example, a violation of a portfolio's 5% VaR today should not portend a violation of the portfolio's 1% VaR tomorrow. In short, VaR violations at all levels should be independent of each other.

Crnkovic and Drachman (1996) and Diebold, Gunther and Tay (1998) point out that this insight can be formalised in the following manner. Again, consider $x_{t,t+1}$ to be the realised P&L from time period t to $t + 1$, ie, over one day. Next consider the probability integral transform (PIT), z_{t+1}, that corresponds to the observation $x_{t,t+1}$. In particular, define

$$z_{t+1} = F(x_{t,t+1} \mid \Omega_t) \tag{8}$$

where, $F(\cdot \mid \Omega_t)$ refers to the conditional cumulative density function of the P&L distribution. This transformation takes the observed P&L, $x_{t,t+1}$, and produces a number on the unit interval, $(0, 1)$. It is worth comparing the observed PIT, z_t, to the hit indicator, $I_t(\alpha)$. The reported PIT provides a continuous measure of the magnitude of the realised P&L, while the hit indicator only signals whether a particular threshold was exceeded. In this sense, the set of reported probability integral transforms, $[z_t]_{t=1}^T$, is able to provide more information about the accuracy of the underlying risk model. A probability integral transform series that accurately reflects the actual P&L distribution exhibits two key properties.

(1) *Uniformity*: the series, $[z_t]_{t=1}^T$, should be uniformly distributed over the unit interval $[0, 1]$. This property of z_t is analogous to the statement that the $\alpha \times 100\%$ VaR should be violated $\alpha \times 100\%$ of the time for each and every α and is a direct parallel to the unconditional coverage property of the hit series, $I_t(\alpha)$, in the case of a single VaR measure.

(2) *Independence*: the series, $[z_t]_{t=1}^T$, should be independently distributed. This is analogous to the statement that VaR violations should be independent from each other and that a VaR violation today at, say, the 1% level should not provide any information about whether or not a VaR violation will occur tomorrow at the 1% level. This property of the z_t series directly parallels the independence property that is required of the hit series, $I_t(\alpha)$, in the case of a single VaR measure. It is important to recognise, however, that the independence property that pertains to z_t also has implications for VaR violations at different

levels, α. A violation at the 1% level today, for example, should not provide any information about whether or not a violation will occur tomorrow at the 5%, 10% or any other VaR level.

These two properties are often combined into the single statement

$$z_t \overset{\text{i.i.d.}}{\sim} U(0,1) \tag{9}$$

which reads that the probability integral transform series is identically and independently distributed as a uniform random variable over the unit interval. A variety of statistical tests have been proposed to assess whether a reported probability integral transform series, $[z_t]_{t=1}^T$, accords with the uniformity and independence properties. Just as in the case of assessing the accuracy of a single VaR measure, these tests may be conducted individually or jointly.

The main advantage of these tests over and above tests based on a VaR measure at a single α level is that they, in principle, can provide additional power to detect an inaccurate risk model. By examining the entire range of the probability integral transform these tests can detect violations of the independence or unconditional coverage property across a range of different VaR levels. This increased power to detect an inaccurate risk model, however, comes at some cost. One component of the cost comes in the form of an increased informational burden. In particular, in order to transform $x_{t,t+1}$ to z_{t+1} one must have access to the entire conditional cumulative density function, $F(\cdot|\Omega_t)$. Risk models that assume a particular form of the distribution of portfolio P&L may be reasonable models of extreme outcomes but may not be useful for characterizing the frequency of more moderate outcomes. If the underlying risk model is more focused on characterizing the stochastic behavior of extreme portfolio losses, these models may be misspecified over a P&L range which is not relevant from a risk management perspective. Moreover, tests that employ the entire probability integral transform series, z_t, may signal an inaccurate model due to this source of misspecification.

A second component of the cost relates to a broadening of the definition of portfolio risk. Current regulatory guidelines dictate that portfolio risk be measured in terms of the 1% VaR for the purpose of determining risk-based capital requirements. Statistical tests that examine a variety of different percentiles implicitly broaden the definition of portfolio risk. The extent to which the definition of portfolio risk is broadened, however, may be directly controlled by choosing to examine the uniformity and independence properties of the z series over a particular range of α levels.

4.1 A test based on multiple VaR levels

Traditional tests of unconditional coverage, such as the POF test, examine whether VaR violations at a given level, α, occur more (or less) than $\alpha \times 100\%$ of the time. A natural generalisation of this approach is to examine whether VaR violations over a range of α levels occur more (or less) frequently than expected. An example of one such test is Pearson's Q test for goodness of fit (Q). The Q test is based upon the number of observed violations at a variety of different VaR levels. The use of these tests is not uncommon in applied work. Wallis (2003), for example, uses the Pearson Q test to examine the accuracy of inflation distribution forecasts made by the Bank of England.

The test is constructed as follows.[5] First, partition the unit interval into k different sub-intervals. For example, one could choose the partition [0.00, 0.01], [0.01, 0.05], [0.05, 0.10], [0.10, 1.00], which results in four separate regions or bins on the unit interval. Once a partition is chosen, simply count the number of VaR violations that occur within each bin. The number of VaR violations that occur in the [0.00, 0.01] range, for example, records the number of days on which a loss in excess of the 1% VaR occurred. Likewise, the number of VaR violations that occur in the [0.10, 1.00] range records the number of days on which a loss less extreme than the 10% VaR occurred. With the number of violations that have occurred within each bin in hand, the Q test is computed according to the formula

$$Q = \sum_{i=1}^{k} \frac{(N_{(l_i, u_i)} - N(u_i - l_i))^2}{N(u_i - l_i)} \tag{10}$$

where $N_{(l_i, u_i)}$ refers to the number of VaR violations in the ith bin, k refers to the number of bins and N refers to the total number of days being used to construct the test. Also, l_i and u_i refer to the lower and upper bound of each bin. In the case that the VaR model being tested is accurate, the test is approximately distributed according to the chi-squared distribution with $k - 1$ degrees of freedom, $\chi^2(k - 1)$.

As the equation for Q makes clear, the particular partition of the unit interval that is chosen may be tailored to focus on a particular set of VaR levels of interest. If only percentiles more extreme than the 10th are of interest, for example, one could use the partition [0.00, 0.01], [0.01, 0.05], [0.05, 0.10], [0.10, 1.00]. If only percentiles more extreme than the 5th are of interest, the partition [0.00, 0.01], [0.01, 0.025], [0.025, 0.05], [0.05, 1.00] could be used. In this way the particular partition employed can be used as a means of controlling how broadly risk is defined in terms of the test.

4.2 A small simulation study

In order to have a grasp of the quantitative nature of the tradeoff between increasing power and broadening the scope of the definition of risk, it is useful to consider an example. An experiment is conducted in which daily P&L is simulated over a one-year period from a statistical model. The resulting P&L series is then analysed using three different risk models which are employed by risk managers to varying degrees. Each of the three risk models examined is inaccurate in the sense that none of them accurately models the true underlying P&L distribution. Each model is then used to produce a one-year sample of observed probability integral transforms, $[z_t]_{t=1}^{255}$. The resulting data are then used to compute the Q test and Kupiec's (1995) POF test of unconditional coverage at the 1% level. This process is repeated 1,000 times and the rejection frequency of both the Q test and the POF test is used to assess the increase in statistical power that arises from considering other VaR levels besides the first percentile in the Q test.[6] Also, in addition to these three risk models, we consider the power of the Q test and the POF test in the case that VaR is systematically under-reported. We examine levels of under-reporting that range between 5% and 25%.

The statistical model for portfolio P&L assumes a fixed mean and focuses on time-varying volatility. The model of time-varying risk incorporates three distinct features of volatility that have been widely recognised across a variety of different financial markets. First, the model provides for considerable variation in volatility. Each period volatility changes – and sometimes changes quite rapidly so that a 25% change in volatility over a one-month horizon is not particularly unlikely. Second, movements in volatility are assumed to exhibit a considerable degree of persistence. Much research on financial asset volatility finds that increases and decreases in volatility can be long-lived. Volatility does tend towards a long run mean, but shocks that either increase or reduce volatility often persist for several months. Lastly, the model implies that volatility tends to increase more after large portfolio losses than after large gains. The particular model for volatility employed in the experiment is Nelson's (1991) EGARCH(1, 1) model. This is widely used in empirical studies of financial market volatility, and it also bears a close resemblance to the model employed by Berkowitz and O'Brien (2002) in their empirical study of bank trading revenues and VaR. The model's particular specification takes the form

$$x_{t,t+1} = v_{t,t+1}$$

$$v_{t,t+1} \sim N(0, \sigma_t^2)$$

$$\ln(\sigma_t^2) = 0.02 + 0.94 \ln(\sigma_{t-1}^2) + 0.22 \left| \frac{v_{t-1,t}}{\sigma_{t-1}} \right| - 0.05 \left(\frac{v_{t-1,t}}{\sigma_{t-1}} \right) \quad (11)$$

where the specific model parameters have been chosen to be consistent with the behavior of monthly US stock returns over the period 1927–98. In particular, note that the final term in the volatility specification, $-0.05(v_{t-1,t}/\sigma_{t-1})$, implies that volatility, $\ln(\sigma_t^2)$, rises more after a portfolio loss than a gain.

Three different risk models are used to measure portfolio risk, ranging from naive to more sophisticated. The first and most naive model assumes, correctly, that losses and gains are normally distributed but assumes that the variance is constant. Accordingly, the VaR model uses a simple, recursive estimate of variance, $\hat{\sigma}_t^2 = \sum_{j=1}^{t-1} v_{j,j+1}^2 / (t-1)$. With this variance estimate in hand, the P&L, $v_{t-1,t}$, on any given day can be sorted into its respective bin by computing

$$\left[\hat{\sigma}_{t-1} \Phi^{-1}(l_i), \hat{\sigma}_{t-1} \Phi^{-1}(u_i) \right] \quad (12)$$

for each bin and then assigning the P&L to the bin that brackets $v_{t-1,t}$.[7] Once each P&L realisation has been assigned to one of the k bins both the Q and POF test can be computed.

The second VaR model recognises that volatility changes over time but fails to recognise the particular EGARCH structure of the volatility dynamics. As a result, the model uses an exponentially weighted moving average of past squared P&L to estimate current volatility. The weighted moving average volatility estimate takes the form

$$\sigma^2_{\text{WMA},t} = 0.97\sigma^2_{\text{WMA},t-1} + 0.03v^2_{t-1,t} \tag{13}$$

where the decay factor, 0.97, implies that volatility moves in a rather persistent fashion over time. The exact value of the decay factor was chosen to be consistent with the values that are employed in practice, which often range between 0.94 and 0.97 (Simons (1996)). Again, the P&L on any day can be sorted into its respective bin by computing

$$\left[\sigma_{\text{WMA},t-1}\Phi^{-1}(l_i), \sigma_{\text{WMA},t-1}\Phi^{-1}(u_i)\right]$$

for each bin and then assigning the P&L to the bin which brackets $v_{t-1,t}$.

The third model employs the historical simulation approach. Unlike the previous two models, the historical simulation approach makes no assumptions about the P&L distribution and does not explicitly model volatility. Instead, historical simulation uses the previously observed P&L history and equates the distribution of future P&L with the observed empirical distribution, $\hat{F}$.[8] As is common in the implementation of the historical simulation method, one year of data are first used to construct the empirical distribution function. Each realised P&L is associated with a bin by ranking it among the previous 255 days' trading experience. If, for example, today's loss was the 10th worst loss over the past 255 days, then the loss would be associated with the bin that brackets the fourth percentile ($10/255 = 0.039 \approx 0.04$). More details on historical simulation and its application in risk management can be found in Pritsker (2001).

Aside from these three risk models, we also consider a scenario in which VaR is systematically under-reported. Specifically, the reported VaR is computed by assuming, correctly, that the P&L is normally distributed and also, wrongly, that P&L volatility is equal

Table 2 Power of Pearson's Q test and Kupiec's POF test

Risk model	Q test	POF test
Recursive	33.3	25.5
Weighted moving average	5.00	4.90
Historical simulation	14.8	11.8

The table displays the power of Pearson's Q test and Kupiec's POF test. The column labeled "Q test" reports the proportion of times across 1,000 simulations that the risk model appearing in the corresponding row was determined to be inaccurate by the Q test using a 5% significance level. Likewise, the column labeled "POF test" reports the proportion of times across 1,000 simulations that the risk model appearing in the corresponding row was determined to be inaccurate by the POF test using a 5% significance level.

to a fraction, β, of true volatility. Accordingly, any particular P&L, $v_{t-1, t}$, is sorted into one of the bins

$$\left[(1 - \beta)\sigma_t \Phi^{-1}(l_i), (1 - \beta)\sigma_t \Phi^{-1}(u_i) \right]$$

and varying amounts of under-reporting are considered, ranging from no underreporting, $\beta = 0$, to a level of 25%, $\beta = 0.25$.

It is important to consider how this setting differs from the previous three risk models. In each of the previous three models, VaR is sometimes overstated and sometimes understated depending on whether the estimated P&L volatility is above or below actual volatility. The presence of systematic under-reporting, however, implies that the reported VaR is always below the actual VaR. Accordingly, this scenario may more realistically capture an environment in which a risk model consistently fails to account for a portion of the risk inherent in trading activity.

Tables 2 and 3 display the power of the Q test and the POF test to identify each of the three risk models as well as the systematically under-reported VaR as inaccurate. The power is computed by simulating the statistical P&L model and then computing both the Q and POF test. This process was repeated 1,000 times and the fraction of test statistics that exceed their respective 95% critical value is the estimate of the test's power. In the case of the Q test, the partition [0.00, 0.01], [0.01, 0.05], [0.05, 0.10], [0.10, 1.00] was chosen to focus on percentiles that are associated with relatively rare occurrences.

Table 3 Power of Pearson's Q test and Kupiec's POF test (%)

Backtest	Under-reporting level ($\beta \times 100\%$)				
	5%	**10%**	**15%**	**20%**	**25%**
Pearson's Q	13.5	35.9	63.8	86.0	94.2
Kupiec's POF	6.30	19.4	43.8	69.0	79.7

The table displays the power of Pearson's Q and Kupiec's POF test when the VaR is under-reported by β%, as discussed in the text. Each column refers to a different level of under-reporting ranging from 5% to 25%. Each row reports the fraction of times, across 1,000 simulations, that the associated backtest identified the reported VaR as inaccurate using a 5% significance level.

Table 2 reports the power of the Q and POF test to identify each of the first three risk models – recursive, weighted moving average and historical simulation – as inaccurate. The table suggests that in the case of the recursive risk model, some modest gains in power are attainable by expanding the range of percentiles that are analysed in the backtest. In the case of the recursive model, the Q test identified the recursive model as inaccurate 33.3% of the time, while the POF test only identified the recursive model as inaccurate in 25.5% of all simulations. The power gains are less impressive for VaR models that are less egregiously misspecified. In the case of historical simulation, the Q test only marginally increases power over the POF test from 11.8% to 14.8%. The gain in the case of the weighted moving average model is imperceptible as both tests identify the model as inaccurate in roughly 5% of the simulations. The inability of either test to identify the weighted moving average model as inaccurate is due to the fact that while this model does not perfectly model P&L risk, it provides a very close approximation to the underlying level of volatility. As a result, the power of both tests in a sample size of one year is rather low. These results suggest that the power gains attributable to the Q test may be largest in cases where the degree of misspecification is largest, which is noteworthy since these are precisely the cases in which identifying an inadequate risk model may be most important.

Table 3 displays the power of the Q test and the POF test in the case that VaR is systematically under-reported. The table displays the power results for varying amounts of under-reporting ranging between 5% and 25%. In each case, the Q test exhibits substantially more discriminatory power relative to the POF test. At the 5% level of under-reporting, for instance, the Q test identifies the reported VaR as being inaccurate 13.5% of the time as opposed to only 6.3% of the time in the case of the POF test. Moreover, the difference in power between the Q and POF test tends to increase as the degree of under-reporting increases. In the case of a 25% under-reporting of VaR, the Q test identifies the model as inaccurate 94.2% of the time as opposed to 79.7% of the time in the case of the POF test. These results suggest that while the Q test always enjoys a power advantage over the POF test, the advantages of the Q test may be greatest when the degree of under-reporting is largest.

5 CONCLUSION

Verifying the accuracy of internal risk models used in setting market risk capital requirements requires backtesting. The current regulatory framework uses a "traffic light" approach to backtesting that is related to Kupiec's (1995) POF test. In this chapter, the fundamental properties of an accurate VaR model, independence and unconditional coverage were defined and their relevance from a backtesting perspective was discussed. A variety of extant tests that examine the validity of the independence property, the unconditional coverage property or both properties were reviewed. Also, tests that examine VaR behavior across a range of VaR levels rather than a single level were discussed, and one such test was proposed. The power properties of the proposed test were examined in a small simulation study. The results of the simulation experiment suggest that moderate gains in statistical power relative to the power of a test that only focuses on a single VaR level can be achieved by examining a broader range of VaR levels.

---

1 The constant, c, in Equation (1) is a complicated function that depends on the portfolio's credit risk. Since the focus of this chapter is not on credit risk, we abstract from this component of the capital charge.
2 This is the threshold that is consistent with a type I error rate of 5%.
3 The z statistic is actually the Wald variant of the likelihood ratio statistic proposed by Kupiec (1995). One potential advantage of the Wald test over the likelihood ratio test is that it is well defined in the case that no VaR violations occur. Kupiec's POF test is undefined in this case since the log of zero is undefined. Moreover, the possibility that no violations occur in a period as short as one year is not trivial. Accordingly, it may be advisable to employ an unconditional coverage test which is well defined in this event.

4   These relative frequencies imply that a VaR violation occurs 5% of the time on average.

5   Details concerning the foundations and derivation of this test statistic can be found in DeGroot (1989).

6   We use a significance level of 5% to define the rejection region of both the Q test and the POF test.

7   As usual, $\Phi^{-1}(\cdot)$ refers to the inverse of the standard normal distribution.

8   The empirical CDF, $\hat{F}$, in a sample of T observations is defined as $\hat{F}(c) = (1/T) \times \Sigma_{t=1}^{T} 1(x_t \leq c)$.

This chapter was previously published in *The Journal of Risk* **9**(2), Winter 2006/07.

REFERENCES

Berkowitz, J., 2001, "Testing Density Forecasts with Applications to Risk Management", *Journal of Business and Economic Statistics* **19**, pp. 465–74.

Berkowitz, J. and J. O'Brien, 2002, "How Accurate are the Value-at-Risk Models at Commercial Banks?" *Journal of Finance* **57**, pp. 1093–112.

Christoffersen, P., 1998, "Evaluating Interval Forecasts", *International Economic Review* **39**, pp. 841–62.

Christoffersen, P. and D. Pelletier, 2004, "Backtesting Value-at-Risk: A Duration-based Approach", *Journal of Empirical Finance* **2**, pp. 84–108.

Cassidy, C. and M. Gizycki, 1997, "Measuring Traded Market Risk: Value-at-Risk and Backtesting Techniques", Research discussion paper 9708, Reserve Bank of Australia.

Crnkovic, C. and J. Drachman, 1996, "Quality Control", *Risk* **9**, pp. 139–43.

DeGroot, M., 1989, *Probability and Statistics*. (Reading, MA: Addison-Wesley).

Diebold, F. X., T. Gunther, and A. Tay, 1998, "Evaluating Density Forecasts with Applications to Financial Risk Management", *International Economic Review* **39**, pp. 863–83.

Dowd, K., 2006, "Validating Multiple-period Density Forecasting Models", *Journal of Forecasting*, forthcoming.

Haas, M., 2001, "New Methods in Backtesting", Working paper, Financial Engineering Research Center.

Kerkhoff, J. and B. Melenberg, 2003, "Backtesting for Risk-based Regulatory Capital", Working Paper, Tilburg University.

Kupiec, P., 1995, "Techniques for Verifying the Accuracy of Risk Management Models", *Journal of Derivatives* **3**, pp. 73–84.

Lopez, J. A., 1999a, "Regulatory Evaluation of Value-at-Risk Models", *Journal of Risk* **1**, pp. 37–64.

Lopez, J. A., 1999b, "Methods for Evaluating Value-at-Risk Models", *Federal Reserve Bank of San Francisco Economic Review* **2**, pp. 3–17.

Nelson, D., 1991, "Conditional Heteroskedasticity in Asset Returns: A New Approach", *Econometrica* **59**, pp. 347–70.

Pritsker, M., 1997, "Evaluating Value-at-Risk Methodologies: Accuracy Versus Computational Time", *Journal of Financial Services Research* **12**, pp. 201–41.

Pritsker, M., 2001, "The Hidden Dangers of Historical Simulation", Working paper 2001-27, Board of Governors of the Federal Reserve System.

Simons, K., 1996, "Value at Risk – New Approaches to Risk Management, VAR: Understanding and Applying Value-at-Risk", (London: Risk Publications).

Stahl, G., 1997, "Backtesting Using a Generalisation of the Traffic-light-approach", *Neural Network World* **4**, pp. 565–77.

Sullivan, J., R. Brooks, and Z. Stoumbos, 2003, "Assessing the Accuracy of Value at Risk", Working paper, Rutgers University.

Wallis, K. F., 2003, "Chi-squared Tests of Interval and Density Forecasts, and the Bank of England's Fan Charts", *International Journal of Forecasting* **19(2)**, pp. 165–75.

Index